Fifth Edition

THE WORLD IN THE TWENTIETH CENTURY

From Empires to Nations

DANIEL R. BROWER
University of California-Davis

Prentice Hall

Upper Saddle River, New Jersey 07458

Library of Congress Cataloging-in-Publication Data

Brower, Daniel R.
    The world in the twentieth century: from empires to nations/
Daniel R. Brower. — 5th ed.
      p. cm.
    Includes bibliographical references and index.
    ISBN 0-13-060034-2
    1. History, Modern—20th century. 2. Revolutions—History—20th
century 3. Nationalism—History—20th century. I. Title.
D421.B724 2001
909.82—dc21   2001032738

Editorial Director: Charlyce Jones Owen
Senior Acquisitions Editor: Charles Cavaliere
Associate Editor: Emsal Hasan
Senior Managing Editor: Jan Stephan
Production Liaison: Fran Russello
Project Manager: Jessica Balch, Pine Tree Composition, Inc.
Prepress and Manufacturing Buyer: Tricia Kenny
Art Director: Jayne Conte
Cover Designer: Bruce Kenselaar
Cover Art: Library of Congress (*left & center*); National Archives (*right*)
Director, Image Resource Center: Melinda Lee Reo
Manager, Rights & Permissions: Kay Dellosa
Image Specialist: Beth Boyd
Photo Researcher: Melinda Alexander

This book was set in 10/12 Palatino by Pine Tree Composition, Inc.
and was printed by R. R. Donnelley & Sons, Inc. The cover was printed
by Phoenix Color Corporation.

© 2002, 1999, 1996, 1992, 1988 by Pearson Education, Inc.
Upper Saddle River, New Jersey 07458

Printed in the United States of America

10 9 8 7 6 5 4 3 2 1

ISBN 0-13-060034-2

Pearson Education, Ltd., *London*
Pearson Education Australia Pty. Limited, *Sydney*
Pearson Education Singapore Pte. Ltd.
Pearson Education North Asia Ltd., *Hong Kong*
Pearson Education Canada, Ltd., *Toronto*
Pearson Educación de Mexico, S.A. de C.V.
Pearson Education—Japan, *Tokyo*
Pearson Education Malaysia, Pte. Ltd.
Pearson Education, Upper Saddle River, New Jersey

Contents

Maps

 # Preface

Priding ourselves on shaping history, we function day to day as slaves of the events that inexorably unroll themselves before our eyes, and fear possesses us and hatred follows in its train.

—Jawaharlal Nehru, 1949

When India gained its independence from the British Empire in August 1947, it was a time of triumph and celebration for Nehru. He had led the struggle for freedom, and became India's first prime minister. In India, as in other colonies that achieved independence in the postwar years, liberation appeared to open an era of freedom and hope for the former subject peoples. But independence brought human tragedy as well as triumph. Nehru's confession recalls the anguish, helplessness, and despair that he felt at the ethnic violence and war that followed the departure of the British. It is a timely warning not to exaggerate the achievements or minimize the destruction brought by the post-imperial age.

When mighty empires fall, peoples and their leaders have to undertake extraordinary efforts to create new political foundations for public life, and to forge new bonds of trust to hold together that new political order. These daunting tasks suggest in broadest terms the great scope of renewal that has been attempted in many regions of the world. But they hide a darker side of this transformation, for hostility and fear among peoples produce bitter conflict within new states. Ethnic antagonism has undermined new governments and at times created social chaos; freedom and bloodshed have come hand in hand.

The twentieth century witnessed the collapse of empires and the rise of nation-states throughout the world. That story is the major theme of this textbook. No previous era experienced such dramatic, tumultuous, and tragic changes in the lives of countless millions of people. We no longer share the easy optimism of Westerners before the First World War, who too readily assumed material and spiritual progress to be a logical and inevitable force, almost a natural law. Nehru imagined a far happier time for his country than that brought about by liberation from the British Empire. Those shattered dreams are as much a part of the story of the twentieth century as the achievements of countries such as India. Knowledge of these events can help us to reach a balanced, sober understanding of human relations in our complex world.

Destruction and creation are inseparable parts of the history of the twentieth century. The struggles generated by antagonistic ideals and interests made the world an uneasy, violent place. Perhaps the most appropriate—certainly the most optimistic—image of the century's history is provided by the Greek myth of the phoenix, the bird reborn from the ashes of its own destruction. To discern essential signs of the emerging new era represents the most challenging historical task of any survey of tumultuous eras, particularly a period so close to us. Uncovering the century's defining trends has shaped my choice of thematic focus of the fifth edition of *The World in the Twentieth Century.*

The most visible, and arguably the most profound transformation that the twentieth century brought was the disappearance of empires from the face of the earth, and their replacement everywhere by nation-states (or states seeking a national identity). The textbook's chronological coverage extends back to the late nineteenth century, when old Asian empires and new Western empires dominated vast areas of the world and ruled most of its peoples. It reaches forward beyond the collapse of the Soviet Union, whose domination over peoples and countries in Europe and Asia earned it the title of "last empire." In the final decade of the century, the boundaries of nation-states gave shape to the political map of the entire world. In the same period, the process of increasing global economic integration largely ignored these political boundaries. At the dawn of the twenty-first century, the world appears more complex and dynamic than ever before.

Individual stories and global visions are helpful in understanding the historic events that make up the century's story. Placing these events in their historical context requires identifying the most important issues useful in their interpretation. At the same time, the human dimensions to that story are best grasped by situating it within the lived experience of the people of the time. Individuals found themselves thrust into unexpected, at times tragic prominence as a result of the tumultuous events into which they were drawn. In distinct Highlight and Spotlight sections, the textbook draws the readers' attention in each chapter to a major topical subject, and focuses attention on the life of a single person. Highlight readings discuss topics essential to the broad narrative; Spotlight segments provide biographical sketches of powerless victims as well as powerful actors who participated in historic events.

The single most important characteristic of the twentieth century was the increasing interaction among states and peoples on a global scale. The principal questions I seek to answer follow directly from this premise: What were the significant trends shaping this interaction? How can we explain the emergence of these global trends? What was their impact on the peoples in various parts of the world?

This brief survey cannot possibly explore in detail all the dimensions of this vast and complex set of issues. Three topics have guided my selection of the major trends and events to be addressed, namely, the international history of states, the role of ideology in shaping human aspirations, and the evolution of world economic relations. All three direct attention to related aspects of global interaction.

International history examines the essential factors that have shaped the foreign policies of governments and the relations among sovereign states. These include, first, the political ideals and national interests of states, second, the economic and political influence of states in global affairs, and third, the balance of power among countries. These three factors taken together explain in large measure the evolution of global conflict and cooperation in the twentieth century from the alliance system prior to the First World War to the Cold War conflict between superpowers following the Second World War, and finally to regional peacekeeping after the Cold War. International history offers crucial insight into the reasons for the collapse of empires and the global forces that shaped the new nation-states.

The potent force of *political ideology* emerges from deeply felt convictions of right and wrong, justice and injustice, giving rise to powerful mass movements and guiding the policies of governments. The importance of these aspirations in our time is such that some scholars have suggested calling the twentieth century the age of ideology. Liberalism was the dominant political faith among Western countries in the early century, and it appears in the late century to have won greater support around the world than ever before. Marxism provided for much of the century the broad guidelines for state policy-making and cultural controls in the countries of the communist bloc and in the Third World. Nationalism, of Western origin but without any single intellectual source or text, places the emergence of national communities and the formation of the nation-state at the center of human endeavor. It is undoubtedly the single strongest political bond among peoples in the world today. In studying these ideologies we can appreciate better the motives of important political leaders and the manner in which social discontent has been articulated and expressed in political movements.

Finally, *economic history* stresses the significance of productive resources, of new technology, and of ownership of the means of production. These factors have determined the profound differences separating developed and developing nations and the shifting dispersion across the globe of wealth and poverty. They shaped the economic conditions in which some countries became dependent on others for their very livelihood.

These three realms of inquiry—international, ideological, and economic history—offer points of reference useful in interpreting the forces behind the interaction among peoples. They suggest where and how powerful new historical trends have emerged. In simplest terms, they illuminate the process by which human power in various forms has, for good and ill, reshaped the twentieth-century world.

The story told here adheres to the simple principle that history is a tale of the past revealed over the passage of time. Emphasis upon international, political, and economic trends focuses that tale on the formative influences that shaped the world as we know it. Contemporary opinions and images, in the form of quotes from political leaders and observers, or reproductions of political posters and photographs, point to another important concept, namely, that the proper subject-matter of history is the lived experience of the past. The meaning and purpose that people attributed to those events are as much a part of our history as the events themselves. The tale retold here is one that they first wrote. We may praise or condemn what they did, but first we need to understand what they sought to do.

The judgments that we bring to a past as close as the twentieth century are inescapably influenced by our immediate perception of the world about us. To those who might object that such interpretations commit the sin of "presentism," that is, of distorting the past to make it fit the needs of the present, I would respond that history as we teach and write it is necessarily a dialogue between the present and the past. The voices from the past must answer in their own terms the questions and concerns that appear, from our perspective, historically meaningful.

The writing of the fifth edition of this text has come through years of teaching and innumerable discussions with colleagues who have proven generous with their time and indulgent of my endeavor. The sober understanding of the past that we acquire with the passing of time is a privilege largely denied this text, whose last chapters touch on events that occurred only yesterday on a historical scale. Students in my twentieth-century world history course at the University of California-Davis have lived through the many stages of this work. The yearly renewal of this student audience has constantly challenged my conclusions and incited me to rethink the meaning of the century's events for they will create the history of the twenty-first century.

The text has in its various editions passed through the hands of specialists and experienced users, whose contributions to my work are substantial. In particular, I would like to thank the following scholars for their assistance: Krystyna von Henneberg, Barbara Metcalf, William Hagen, Donald Price, Kay Flavell, Ruth Rosen, and Arnold Bauer. The comments solicited by the publisher from readers have also proved of appreciable help in rethinking my revisions to the text. All are absolved of the sins of omission and commission in the completed text, for which I bear full responsibility. Special thanks in the preparation of the fifth edition go to Julia Kehew for her care and attention to textual matters. This edition is dedicated to Matthew and Michael, with the wish that they, like their parents, may find the world in the twenty-first century a place to say "Fanfare for the Makers!"

Daniel Brower

Twentieth-Century Global Time Chart

	Global Events	*Europe*
1900	World population 1.5 billion (c. 1900)	Paris Exposition (1900) Anglo-French and Anglo-Russian entente (1904, 1907) First Russian revolution (1905)
1910	Outbreak of First World War (1914) U.S. entry into war (1917) Defeat of Central Powers (1918) Founding of Communist International (1919) Paris Peace Conference (1919)	Balkan Wars (1912–1913) German military victories on Eastern Front (1915) Battle at Verdun (1916) Russian revolution (1917) Russian Civil War (1918–1920) German revolution (1918) Collapse of Austro-Hungarian Empire (1918)
1920	Founding of League of Nations (1920) Washington Conference (1921–1922) Dawes plan (1924) Lindbergh solo Atlantic flight (1927) Beginning of global depression (1929)	Fascist regime in Italy (1922) Locarno Pact (1925) Soviet First Five-Year Plan (1928) Stalin dictatorship (1929)
1930	World Depression (1930–1934) End of war debts and reparations payments (1931) Second World War (1939)	Nazi rule in Germany (1933) Spanish Civil War (1936–1939) German reoccupation of Rhineland (1936) Munich Agreement on Czechoslovakia (1938) Stalin's Great Terror (1936–1938) Soviet-German Pact and partition of Poland (1939)
1940	U.S. entry into war (1941) Teheran Conference (1943) Yalta Conference (1945) Bretton Woods Agreement on international trade (1944) End of Second World War (1945) United Nations (1945) Start of Cold War (1947)	German invasion of Western Europe (1940) German–Soviet War (1941) Nazi extermination camps (1942–1945) Stalingrad battle (1942–1943) Normandy landing (1944) German occupation zones (1945) Marshall Plan and Truman Doctrine (1947) Berlin blockade (1948) North Atlantic Treaty (1949) German Federal Republic (West Germany) (1949)

North and South America	Asia	Middle East and Africa
U.S. policy of intervention in Central America (1904)	Boxer Revolt in China (1900) Russo-Japanese War (1904–1905)	Boer War (1899–1902) Discovery of Iranian oil (1901) Young Turk movement in Ottoman Empire (1906)
Opening of Panama Canal (1914) U.S. intervention in Mexican revolution (1914, 1916)	End of Chinese Empire (1911) Gandhi leader of Indian National Congress, Amritsar massacre (1919)	Union of South Africa (1910) Ottoman Empire in First World War (1914) Arab revolt (1916)
Institutional Revolutionary party takes power in Mexico (1920) Stock market crash on Wall Street (1929)	Formation of Chinese Communist Party (1921) Provincial self-rule in India (1921) Chinese Nationalists control China (1928)	French and British mandates in Middle East (1920) Greek-Turkish War (1920–1922) Founding of Republic of Turkey (1923) Egyptian independence (1924) Rule in Arabia by Saudi clan (1925)
Getulio Vargas president of Second Brazilian Republic (1930–1945) Batista in power in Cuba (1933) Beginning of "New Deal" in United States (1933) U.S. "Good Neighbor" policy (1934)	Anti-salt tax movement in India (1930) Japanese invasion of Manchuria (1931) Government of India Act (1935) Sino-Japanese War (1937–1945) Muslim League for Creation of Pakistan (1938)	Palestine Arab revolt (1936–1938) Start of Arabian oil production (1939)
Juan Perón Argentine president (1946–1955) Founding of Organization of American States (1948)	Soviet-Japan Neutrality Pact (1941) Soviet war on Japan (1945) Hiroshima atomic bomb (1945) U.S. occupation of Japan (1945–1951) Partition of Korea (1945) Philippine independence (1946) French war in Indochina (1946–1954) Indian independence and partition (1947) Chinese Communists in power (1949) Indonesian independence (1949)	Formation of Arab League (1945) Independence of state of Israel (1948) First Arab-Israeli War (1948–1949) Nationalist Party in South Africa imposes apartheid (1948)

	Global Events	Europe
1950	Korean War (1950–1953) Hydrogen bombs tested (U.S.: 1952; U.S.S.R.: 1955) Geneva meeting of U.S.–U.S.S.R. (1955) Soviet launching of "Sputnik" satellite (1958) U.S. deployment of ballistic missiles (ICBM) (1958)	U.S. nuclear weapons in Western Europe (1953) Death of Stalin (1953) Krushchev new Soviet leader (1955) Soviet repression of Hungarian revolution (1956) European Economic Community (Common Market) (1958) De Gaulle president of French Fifth Republic (1958)
1960	World population est. 3 billion (c. 1960) Organization of Petroleum Exporting Countries (OPEC) (1960) Cuban missile crisis (1962) Second Vatican Council (1962–1965) Integrated-circuit computers (1964) First communications satellite (1965) Moon landing by American astronauts (1969)	Berlin wall (1961) Brezhnev new Soviet leader (1964) Soviet repression of Czech reform movement (1968)
1970	First manned Soviet space station (1971) Nuclear arms treaty (SALT I) (1972) Oil crisis and global recession (1973) First U.N. International Women's Year (1975) Second nuclear agreement (SALT II) (1979)	British entry into Common Market (1971) Berlin Treaty (1972) End of Franco dictatorship in Spain (1977)
1980	First U.S. space shuttle (1981) World population est. 5 billion (1987) International agreement to protect atmospheric ozone layer (1987) U.S.–U.S.S.R. agreement to destroy intermediate-range missiles (1988)	Solidarity movement in Poland (1980–1982) Gorbachev Soviet leader (1985–1991) Collapse of Communist regimes in Eastern Europe (1989) Free elections in Soviet Union (1989)
1990	U.S.–Soviet arms reduction agreements (1990) United Nations war against Iraq (1991) Global Conference on the Environment (1992) Global Conference on Population (1994) World population 6 billion (1998)	Reunification of Germany (1990) Election of Boris Yeltsin as President of Russia (1991) Fall of Soviet Union (1991) Independence for all national republics of U.S.S.R. (1991) War between Armenia and Azerbaijan (1992–1994) Civil war in Yugoslavia (1991–1995) Treaty on European Union (1994) Peace treaty ending war in Yugoslavia (1996)

North and South America	Asia	Middle East and Africa
U.S. intervention in Guatemala (1954) Castro in power in Cuba (1959)	Chinese conquest of Tibet (1950) Indian Constitution (1951) Partition of Vietnam (1954) Bandung Conference (1955) Beginning of Japanese economic boom (1956) Tibetan revolt (1957–1971) Mao's Great Leap Forward (1958–1960)	Nasser in power (1952) French war in Algeria (1955–1963) Suez crisis (1956) Ghana (Gold Coast) independence (1957) Formation of French Community (1958) Egyptian-Syrian Union (UAR) (1958–1961)
Brasilia new frontier capital of Brazil (1960) Soviet-Cuban cooperation (1960–1990) Cuban Bay of Pigs invasion (1961) Military dictatorship in Brazil (1964) Launch of Operation Amazonia in Brazil (1965)	Sino-Indian War (1962) Death of Nehru (1964) U.S. war in Vietnam (1965–1973) End of Sukarno rule (1966) Chinese Cultural Revolution (1966–1975)	Belgian Congo (Zaire) independence (1960) Imprisonment of Nelson Mandela (1961–1993) Independent Algeria (1963) Creation of Palestine Liberation Organization (1965) Israeli-Arab Six-Day War (1967) Biafra Civil War in Nigeria (1967–1970)
Military dictatorship in Chile (1973) Sandinista regime in Nicaragua (1979)	Indo-Pakistan war and independence of Bangladesh (1971) Death of Mao (1975) Communist conquest of South Vietnam (1975) Market reforms in China (1978) Soviet invasion of Afghanistan (1979)	Israeli-Arab War (1973) Soweto demonstrations in South Africa (1976) Egyptian-Israeli Treaty (1979) Iranian Revolution (1979)
Democratic government in Argentina (1985) End of military dictatorship in Brazil (1985) U.S. invasion of Panama (1989) Democratic government in Chile (1989) Election of anti-Sandinistas in Nicaragua (1989)	Assassination of Indian leader Indira Gandhi (1984) Repression in China of democratic movement (1989) Soviet troops withdraw from Afghanistan (1989) Muslim revolt in Kashmir, India (1989)	Iraq-Iran war (1980–1988) International economic boycott of South Africa (1984) Palestinian uprising in Israeli-occupied lands (1988) Election of de Klerk as South African president (1989)
North American Free Trade Agreement (1994) U.S. intervention in Haiti (1994) Brazil-Argentina-Chile Free Trade Agreement (1995) Mexican financial crisis (1995) End of PRI dictatorship in Mexico (1997)	Economic boom in China (1990–2000) Asian financial crisis (1997) Taliban conquest of Afghanistan (1998)	Iraq invasion of Kuwait (1990) Gulf War (1991) End of apartheid (1993) Peace Agreement between PLO and Israel (1993) Nelson Mandela president of South Africa (1994) Israeli-Jordanian Peace Treaty (1994) Massacre of Tutsi people in Rwanda (1994) War in Zaire (Republic of Congo) (1996–1997)

Part I: The Age of Empires

 CHAPTER ONE

Empires in Flux

THE WORLD IN THE EARLY

TWENTIETH CENTURY

The twentieth century was a turbulent, exciting time. Wars and revolutions created extraordinary turmoil in the lives of many millions of people in lands throughout the world. These conflicts also inspired grandiose projects and lofty expectations for a better, more just life for future generations. Destruction and creation are twin, inseparable themes of the history of that century.

At the beginning of the century, empires ruled over most of the world's population. By the end of the century, nation-states had replaced them everywhere. This process was well underway by the time the First World War began in 1914; it accelerated in the aftermath of that war. The Allied victors of that war were themselves empire-builders, who acquired more overseas colonies as a result of that war. Economic resources lay at the foundations of empire then, as they had for all previous empires. That war seriously weakened the economies of Great Britain and France, greatest of the Western empires. The depression of the 1930s, then the Second World War, fatally weakened their capacity to hold their colonial lands. In those years a new revolutionary state appeared. The Soviet Union's leaders preached the violent overthrow of capitalism and of imperialism.

When war came again in East Asia and in Europe, the United States joined the global confrontation against the Axis. U.S. leaders were, in their own way, opponents of colonial empires, arguing for democratic national self-determination for all peoples. In these circumstances, the age of empires could not survive the triumph of the Soviet Union and the United States in the Second World War.

The legacy of empire-building proved enduring. The borders drawn by the Western imperial map makers around their colonial territories remained those of the new nations. They were a visible relic of imperialism that complicated the task of nation-building. The languages that predominated in the colonies, sometimes English or French, sometimes local languages promoted to the status of a territorial "common tongue," continued in use. In these and in other ways, the age of empires continued to make itself felt to the end of the century.

Some of these vast imperial states began the century on the verge of collapse. The Ottoman and Chinese empires had glorious histories behind them. They had once been centers of civilization and mighty warrior states. By the end of the nineteenth century, both were powerless to prevent new empires from seizing their borderlands. The Spanish Empire, once an enormous collection of colonies extending over much of the Americas and into the eastern Pacific Ocean, had already lost most of its territory in revolutions and wars. Internal political opposition and social unrest were growing in all these states. With inadequate economic resources and feeble political leaders, these ancient empires were doomed soon to disappear.

New empires emerged to take their place. Western empires had, in the nineteenth century, spread far overseas. They employed new "tools of empire" for colonial domination. Their leaders claimed these lands by right of conquest and cultural superiority. Similar arguments came from the leaders of the Japanese Empire, which had reequipped itself with modern industry and armaments to seize its own overseas colonial lands. The French and British empires were the largest, with colonial territories stretching through Africa and much of Asia. By the early twentieth century, they had created the apparatus of imperial control to effectively dominate the many peoples of their empires. They used brutal methods of repression to suppress periodic revolts, which revealed the widespread opposition to their rule. At the same time, they enrolled some of their subject peoples in administrative and military functions. Missionaries carried the word of God, as their churches understood it, to create centers of Christianity in these colonies. Nations at home, these empires called upon nationalist loyalties in their homelands to win popular backing. They also utilized the technological skills and wealth of their homelands' industrial economies to sustain imperial expansion.

Empire "boosters" proudly boasted of their great conquests as proof of the natural superiority of their nation. This arrogance expressed itself as racist attitudes toward the "yellow," "brown," and "black" peoples of their colonies. Prejudice directed against other peoples extended as well to other nations of Europe. Nationalist antagonism worsened the diplomatic rivalries among European states. The First World War had its origins in these conflicts and rivalries among European states. These conflicts were growing more acute in the early years of the new century. The belligerence of Western governments and the deadly armaments produced by the industrial economy threatened the very stability of their empires.

The Chinese Empire was the first to collapse. Its forces suffered humiliating defeats by, first, the Japanese navy, then by a Western military expedition. Its emperor no longer enjoyed the "mandate of heaven" that had been his pledge to protect this once-mighty state. Its disappearance in 1911 seemed at the time the natural fate of an ancient, outdated civilization. Chinese nationalists fought to create in its place a new nation. Similar conflicts erupted in the Ottoman Empire. These internal disputes provoked widespread unrest and violence. Yet their destructive effects proved to be part of the agonizing process, repeated in many other colonial lands, by which the age of empires gave way to the age of nations.

ANCIENT EMPIRES

The tradition of empire-building was as old as human civilizations. It had begun 5,000 years ago with the first warrior-states in the Middle East, and continued into modern times. The simplest definition of *empire* is a state whose peoples are gathered together by a conquering army and that is ruled from a central territory by these conquerors. The mightiest of these conquerors had come from the Eurasian heartland. Nomadic tribes of northern Asia, organized in powerful cavalry forces, periodically invaded China, India, the Middle East, and Europe in search of wealth and power. Their armies left in their wake great swaths of destruction and bloodshed. Once the conquerors had settled in their new lands, they usually adapted their ways to the religious practices and imperial institutions of previous rulers. Arabic and Turkish-speaking tribes, united around their new Muslim religion, had in the Middle Ages conquered an enormous territory stretching from the Mediterranean to India. Their empires were for centuries brilliant centers of civilization, commercial enterprise, and wealth.

European conquerors came last of all to the task of empire-building. They made the oceans their path to conquest. In the sixteenth and seventeenth centuries, they created trading centers along the coasts of Africa and Asia. A few daring explorers and determined Christian missionaries ventured far beyond the coast. In the Western Hemisphere, European conquerors extended their empires far into the interior regions. They brought to the native peoples their own civilization, and their own infectious diseases. Spanish forces destroyed the empires of the Aztecs and the Incas in their search for gold and silver. Their own empire left a deep, painful mark on their conquered peoples. Spanish officials, the Spanish language, and the Catholic missionary settlements were the tangible signs that a distant, alien empire had taken control. Native Americans suffered particularly in the French and British settler colonies of North America. Their lands were taken for farming; they were forced further and further into the interior. The expansion of Western peoples transformed, in places, the very landscape of imperial territories.

The ancient empires of Africa and Asia differed in basic ways from the Western empires of the nineteenth and twentieth centuries. They were governed by a hereditary monarch or emperor, supported by an administration and army made up largely of the conquerors. They ruled over peoples of widely differing customs, languages, and religions. These subject peoples were often allowed to retain their customs and culture, but they were denied access to power and wealth unless they adopted the language and religion of their rulers.

Such imperial regimes had, at times, taken a hand in encouraging commerce and manufacturing. They did so for the sake of the tax revenues generated by this economic activity. Enterprise and exploration did not interest them for their own sake. Land trade across Asia, and European ocean commerce, did continue to bring new manufactured products and agricultural crops to distant lands. In the Middle Ages, silk reached the West from China along routes protected by Asian nomadic empires; these routes also carried the bubonic plague to Europe. Spanish travelers transported new plants such as potatoes and corn from the

Americas to Asia and Europe; they also conveyed deadly diseases to the New World. These empires, therefore, had profoundly influenced human history. By the early twentieth century, the few remaining ancient empires were surviving on past glories and at the pleasure of the empires of Europe and Japan.

The Fall of the Chinese Empire

In the seventeenth century, the last Asian conquerors, the Manchu, had seized control of the Chinese Empire. They founded a new imperial dynasty, the Qing (also written "Ch'ing"). They were proud of their warrior culture and disdainful of the Chinese people. But, like other conquerors before them, the Qing rulers adopted the Chinese system of rule. Mastery of a complex corpus of writings on morality and government remained the essential requirement for entry into the empire's administration. Written more than two thousand years earlier by the philosopher Confucius, these writings suited the needs of the new dynasty well. His philosophy emphasized the overriding need for social harmony and order. At the heart of this system were the Three Bonds of Obedience— subject to ruler, son to father, and wife to husband. State and family were all part of the same system, in which moral obligations, not rights, were the essential guide to behavior.

Unique traditions and religious practices had evolved around this state-sponsored morality. Ancestor worship was widespread, within a set of religious practices known as Taoism. Among eminent families, women remained in seclusion. The mark of their attractiveness (and suitability for arranged marriages) was foot-binding, achieved by gradually breaking a young girl's foot bones to reduce by one-half the size of her feet. The practice gradually spread to the lower classes. Only the peasant women escaped, for their work in the fields required that they be fit to walk. It satisfied Chinese men's taste in female beauty; it also revealed the implacable force of the Confucian bonds of obedience.

The coherence of the Confucian imperial system of rule was the secret to its survival for 2,000 years. New dynasties found that it met their needs to maintain order and guaranteed them an effective, loyal set of administrators to carry out their orders over that vast, populous empire. The Qing followed this tradition. For two centuries, China enjoyed peace and economic well-being. Its economic productivity was in the eighteenth century still the equal to any other region in the world.

The Qing's powers began to decline in the next century. A civil war, known as the Taiping Rebellion, lasted for two decades in mid-century, devastating large parts of the country until the Qing army defeated the rebels. The dynasty has survived, by relying on traditional administrative and military methods of rule. It was the wrong message to have learned, though, when the Qing faced new enemies from abroad.

The new threat to China came from across the seas. With the backing of their governments, Western traders had begun arriving in their sailing ships in increasing numbers in the eighteenth century. Chinese luxury goods, such as silk and porcelain, were much in demand in the West. But traders had a harder time finding goods that interested the Chinese. Opium sold well. The British merchants obtained it easily in India. The Chinese authorities attempted to restrict foreign access to their market and to block the sale of opium. British traders appealed to their government to defend open access to Chinese markets.

In the mid-nineteenth century, Great Britain waged two brief wars against China, winning both. As a result, the island of Hong Kong, on the south coast of China, became a part of the British Empire. British citizens (as well as other Westerners) obtained the right to live in a few Chinese port cities in their own settlements, under their own laws. A small section of Shanghai became a flourishing miniature Western city, with Western-style houses and broad streets where its own police force kept public order. It was also a refuge for political enemies of the dynasty. And the opium trade flourished.

At the end of the century, the Chinese Empire lost another brief war. The victor this time was the Japanese Empire. The Japanese government had decided to create its own overseas empire in East Asia. Its first target was the kingdom of Korea; for centuries Korea's rulers had paid tribute to and acknowledged the suzerainty (in foreign affairs especially) of the Chinese Empire. But China could no longer protect its borderlands. In one decisive battle in 1894, the new Japanese navy destroyed Chinese naval forces. The Chinese government once again had to accept a humiliating defeat. Victory in war gave the Japanese control of Korea (which it soon made a colony) and the island of Formosa. Earlier, the Russian Empire had taken over an enormous territory on the northern edges of China. In the last half of the century, the French Empire gradually extended its conquest over the southern region that it called Indochina. In the early twentieth century, even the Buddhist leaders of the mountainous land of Tibet, on the southwestern borders of China, turned to British protection to escape Chinese rule. China was falling apart.

The crisis propelled frightened Qing leaders into desperate action. They gave support to a secret anti-foreign and patriotic society that in 1899 prepared a popular uprising directed against foreign settlements, traders and missionaries, and even Chinese converts to Christianity. Called by Westerners the Boxer Uprising, its leaders appealed to their followers to "Support the Qing, destroy the foreigners." But the rebel's militia forces were too poorly armed and disorganized to withstand attacks from organized Western troops. A coalition of forces, mainly from Russian, British, and Japanese armies, defeated the Boxers. They had its leaders executed, and they occupied the capital city of Beijing (also written "Peking"), whose foreign settlement had been under siege for weeks. In the process, they burned and looted large parts of the city. Shortly afterwards the Chinese government, in a last-minute, desperate effort to reform the state, set about creating a modern administrative system and a Western-type educational system, and retraining and rearming its armed forces. But it was too late.

The Qing dynasty's most serious opponents came from within the country. Even the generals charged with setting up a modern army had lost faith in its leadership. In coastal cities, a new Chinese middle class, enriched largely by the booming overseas commerce, turned against the traditional Chinese system. They were sympathetic to the aims (if not the methods) of revolutionary nationalists. These rebels organized the Guomindang (Chinese Nationalist Party), under the leadership of Sun Yat-sen, a skilled doctor trained in the new Chinese medical schools. This movement called for the end of the empire and the creation of a democratic republic. In 1911, an ambitious general seized control of the government, taking the infant emperor prisoner. The next year the Nationalist Party proclaimed the creation the Chinese Republic. The Chinese Empire, with no one to defend it, disappeared.

SPOTLIGHT: The Empress Dowager of China

The Empress Dowager (1835–1908) was the last powerful ruler of the oldest empire of the world. She became the "dowager" when in 1861 her husband, the emperor, died. His death placed in her hands the care of their son, the heir to the Chinese throne. She had come to the court as one among the emperor's many wives. It had been her good fortune to give birth to his heir son. In the imperial court, as in all important families of traditional China, a wife became a noteworthy person when she produced a male heir. The Empress Dowager acquired her initial position of influence by giving the empire its future ruler.

Her responsibility for the well-being of the infant after the emperor's death brought her directly into the highest court circles of the imperial dynasty. She took the name of "Empress of the West" (*Cixi* in Chinese). Her political activities began in the following years, when she proved her determination to protect the dynasty and to ensure the survival of the empire. She pursued that goal with determination until her death in 1908. Three years later, the empire collapsed.

Her personal accomplishment is remarkable when set against the forces undermining the empire. Her own imperial court was deeply divided by personal rivalries and by opposing programs for the defense of the Chinese Empire. Her country confronted powerful foreign states, also called empires but organized, equipped, and led very differently from her own. The Russian, English, and Japanese empires had seized Chinese territory and forced her government to grant their citizens special economic and legal privileges in China. Their armies and navies were equipped with deadly modern weapons capable of overwhelming Chinese forces in war. Their emissaries in China were scornful of the Chinese for their lack of scientific knowledge and technical skills, and for their traditional customs. Western diplomats and visitors to Beijing mocked the Empress Dowager as the "dragon lady" (the dragon was the symbol of the empire), believing the rumors that told of her corruption and brutality.

The Empress Dowager herself had little education and had to rely on the advice of court officials in dealing with the crises that confronted her country. She had no confidence in the emperors, first her son, and after his death her nephew. She believed them to be weak and irresolute, and she was right. Her loyalty went entirely to the dynasty and to the Chinese imperial tradition to which it was heir. She was prepared to be ruthless to defend that cause, even though it seemed virtually hopeless. The foreigners moving into her land brought new, alien customs. She distrusted them both because they challenged sacred Chinese ways and because they threatened her dynasty. The backing that she secretly gave in 1900 to the Boxer Rebellion was a measure of her despair at the decay of the Qing dynasty and decline of the empire.

The defeat of the Boxers forced her to renounce her commitment to traditional Chinese imperial rule. For the first time, she received foreign guests. She allowed a Western photographer to take a picture of her dressed in her imperial finery. Most important, she finally accepted the advice of court officials urging fundamental reforms of her empire. But it was too late to save the Chinese Empire from collapse.

The Empress Dowager of China 1903 (*Courtesy of the Freer Gallery of Art, Smithsonian Institution, Washington, D.C.*)

The Decline of the Ottoman Empire

At the western end of the Asian continent and in the same decades, the Ottoman Empire confronted similar threats from Western empires and experienced internal turmoil nearly as great as the Chinese Empire. This ancient empire had existed since warrior tribes from Central Asia had conquered the lands of the Byzantine Empire. These tribes spoke a Turkish language and were ruled by descendants of their first great leader, Osman (deformed in English to "Ottoman"). Ruling from the ancient city of Constantinople (later renamed Istanbul), the Ottoman emperors governed an enormous territory that at its peak stretched from the Hungarian plains in Central Europe to the borders of Persia, and from the northern shores of the Black Sea and the Caucasus mountains to the Atlantic shores of Morocco. In their lands lived peoples of many different cultures, languages, and religions. They them-

selves adopted the Muslim religion, which became the religion of state. The Ottoman ruler's political title was "sultan," to which he later added that of "caliph." This title was taken from medieval Arab Muslim empires and elevated the sultan to the rank of titular leader of Sunni Muslims. The empire tolerated all religious communities, permitting them to preserve their rites and customs at the price of a special tax.

The strength of the empire lay in its fighting forces and in the extensive commerce that passed through its lands. Ottoman armies and navies were the best in the entire Mediterranean basin in the sixteenth century. But by the nineteenth century, their armies suffered defeat after defeat at the hands of modern Western forces. Its economy flourished until Western seaborne trade replaced the caravans that had carried goods from Asia to Europe and Western industrialization turned out products far cheaper than any Ottoman subjects could produce. By

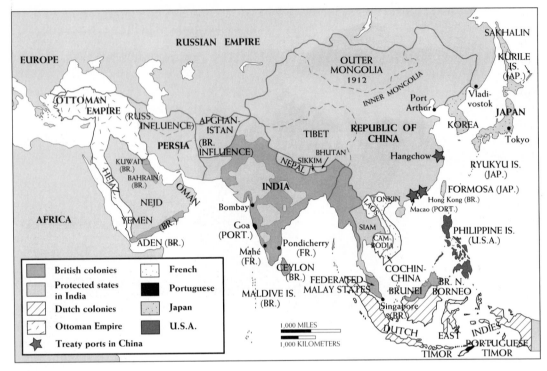

Empires in Asia, 1914

the middle of the nineteenth century, the Ottoman leaders confronted a military and financial crisis.

As in the case of China, conservative forces within the imperial court and among Muslim clerics stood in the way of reform. The Ottoman Empire was tightly bound to traditional Muslim values. These were defended by religious leaders ready to condemn any cultural and social innovations, especially those inspired by Western practices, as violations of Muslim law and customs.

The sultan and his court proved nearly as hostile to fundamental reforms of the state. They lived in isolation from the outside world, assured sumptuous comforts in the great palace of Topkapi in Istanbul. It also housed the sultan's enormous harem, gathered from influential Ottoman families and

allied princely families. This absence of leadership in the face of the mounting crisis placed responsibility for reform on the army. It also opened the way for uprisings and nationalist movements among its minority Christian peoples.

The empire's decline came from military defeats at the hands of Western empires. Its lands in southeastern Europe were a tempting prize for neighboring Christian empires, no longer fearful of Ottoman might. The rulers of the Russian and Austro-Hungarian empires claimed the right to protect Christian subjects of the sultan. They even enlarged their claims to include small areas of Jerusalem, holiest of Ottoman cities, where Christian churches stood on sacred sites. Wars along the borders of the Ottoman Empire had by the late nineteenth century reduced Ottoman territory in Europe to a tiny portion of the Balkan peninsula. In North Africa, the French Empire had conquered Algeria, and the British Empire had made Egypt its protectorate. The British had moved into Egypt to protect the Suez Canal, a vital new link for its imperial commerce and communication. The leaders of the empires of Austria-Hungary and Russia began to lay plans for the Ottoman Empire's destruction.

The European governments were in profound disagreement about whom among them should benefit most from these spoils of war. In 1877–1878, a short conflict between the Ottoman Empire and Russia produced such a crushing defeat of the Ottoman forces that Russia's army almost reached Istanbul before war's end. In reaction, leaders of all the other major European states intervened to prevent the Ottoman state from falling under Russian domination. By then, the sultan's regime was so impoverished and indebted to Western bankers that it had to accept Western control of part of its tax revenues to pay back its debts. The very existence of the Ottoman Empire was by then in doubt.

In this growing crisis, members of the ruling Ottoman elite concluded that radical reform was the only salvation for their state. Army officers claimed that they held the secret for restoring Ottoman might by learning from Western states. They observed that these countries relied upon their national communities to contribute voluntarily to public needs. It seemed clear to them that their own Turkish-speaking community could become the national core of a reformed empire.

Internal opposition to their reform program came from all sides. Islamic religious leaders were bitterly opposed to their program, inspired by secular (that is, nonreligious) ideals. They viewed the empire as the center of Islam, within whose borders Muslim pilgrims could restore their faith and the

Mustapha Kemal (Ataturk) in Traditional Uniform of Ottoman Officer, 1914 (*Hulton-Deutsch Collection/ Corbis*)

purity of their practices at Mecca, holiest of Muslim sites, and at the religious centers in Istanbul. Secular reform appeared to them a greater danger than foreign enemies.

Non-Turkish peoples also resisted the reformers' program. To create a Turkish national community meant favoring Turks, at the expense of the other peoples, whose protected status within the empire had insured them some degree of security. Turkish nationalism threatened to destroy the delicate ethnic balance there. The Armenian community, concentrated within the empire's eastern territory, began to experience persecution from surrounding Turkish (and

Kurdish) Muslims. The nationalist program of Turkish reformers stirred up a nationalist movement among Armenians. Reforming this multi-ethnic, multi-religious empire posed social and religious problems so acute that they could undermine the empire that the reformers hoped to save.

The core of Ottoman reformers, calling themselves Young Turks, came from the officer corps of the Ottoman army. Organized in secret societies, their goal was reform by the Ottoman government. They did not begin with political revolution in mind, but they were prepared to use force to obtain concessions from their sultan, Abdulhamid II. In 1908, they organized mutinies among army units and threatened to attack Istanbul. The sultan capitulated, accepting the Young Turks' demand that he grant the empire a constitution guaranteeing free elections and representative government. The rebels took over the new government, and in the next few years they attempted to institute basic reforms while still keeping the empire intact.

The Young Turks' priority was strengthening the empire. Constitutional rights and the rule of law meant less to them than saving the Ottoman state in the face of recurring insurrections among its subject peoples and new wars with European states. Their leadership lacked popular support; among themselves they could not agree on the vital measures needed to cope with social unrest and political decay. Their survival required outside help.

They turned to the German Empire. Its economy was the most productive in Europe, its army the mightiest, and it was hostile to the Russian Empire. The Ottoman reformers welcomed German financial and technical assistance. With this help, they built new railroads (including one down the Arabian Peninsula to Muslim Holy Places); German military advisers also helped strengthen Ot-

toman armed forces. At the time, these links with Germany suited the reformers' needs, but the consequences ultimately proved fatal to the empire. After European war began in 1914, they succumbed to German pleas to join the Central Powers. The Ottoman Empire in 1914 was a pale shadow of the once-glorious domain of the conquering Turks.

EMPIRES OF THE INDUSTRIAL AGE

As these ancient empires declined, new imperial states emerged to take their place. These modern empires were concentrated in Europe until the United States and Japan joined their ranks at the end of the nineteenth century. Some, such as France, Great Britain, and Russia, had behind them centuries of expansion. Germany and the United States were newcomers to empire-building.

In the late nineteenth century, all these states shared important characteristics unique to the new imperialism. Each was home to a relatively advanced economy that incorporated the technological skills and productive factories of the Industrial Revolution. With industrial resources, empire-builders had the capability to send their armies and officials across vast oceans and great deserts in pursuit of new conquests. In ways never before possible, the most distant areas of the globe were open to imperial exploration, conquest, and economic exploitation. In addition, within these states nationalists supported empires in the name of national glory and a civilizing mission. In national exhibitions, school books, and newspaper stories, the promoters of empire portrayed colonial rule as a part of the great epic story of the progress of humanity. The new colonies, distant from but tightly bound to the homeland ("metropole"), were by the end of the nineteenth century so numerous that we frequently refer to these states as colonial or overseas empires.

⌐ HIGHLIGHT: The New Imperialism ⌐

The entire world became the domain of the new empires. It was also the territory of the "globetrotter," a new term for travelers to distant lands. Readers of the popular novel *Around the World in Eighty Days,* written in 1873 by the French novelist Jules Verne, imagined themselves transported across oceans and continents by boat, train, and horseback alongside the English hero of the story. Phineas Fogg's mad race to circle the globe within eighty days or lose a reckless bet was made easier by the services of a new travel agency, Thomas Cook & Co. His chances were made better, too, because of the technological marvels of the Industrial Revolution. These included rail lines from Europe to Asia and across North America, and steamship lines across the Atlantic and Pacific oceans. Translations of the book appeared in all Western languages, as well as in Japanese. The novel's success was a good indication that an international reading public was prepared to believe that time and distance no longer stood in the way of the ambitious traveler.

For similar reasons, time and distance were also no obstacle to expansionist empires. Clues to the new imperialism emerge within Verne's novel. It hints at an array of technological innovations that accompanied and made possible the triumph of the new empires. These "tools of empire" included new medicine, new arms, and new means of transportation.

The Industrial Revolution made travel far more rapid and reliable than before, thanks largely to the steam engine. Steamships moved rapidly across the seas, passed through mammoth canals to get from one ocean to the next, and sailed up rivers where no large ships had ever dared go. A French engineer, Ferdinand de Lesseps, put his technical and organizational skills to work building the Suez Canal, completed in 1869. It quickly became the crucial transportation link between Europe and Asia. On land, steam locomotives pulled trains through territories where mountains and rivers had once formed virtually impenetrable barriers. Steam engines powered new naval warships that could operate far from their own shores and were capable of carrying imperial forces to new conquests. Messages moved from these lands to the homeland with telegraphic speed, as telegraph wires spread out across continents and under oceans. In 1897, Queen Victoria of Great Britain received a unique gift as part of the celebration of her seventy-fifth birthday: the first telegram sent from London through her Asian colonies and around the world back to London.

Imperial military forces possessed new weapons with a firepower unknown to previous ages. Powerful naval cannons sent shells over several miles; breechloading rifles could be reloaded and fired with a speed unmatched by the old muskets. Most devastating of all, a single, rapid-firing "machine gun" could stop large attacking forces with a hail of bullets. All of these weapons were the product of technological innovation and precision manufacturing possible only with the Industrial Revolution. Imperial fighting forces were often made up of soldiers recruited from colonial populations, trained in the new armaments, and led by officers from the homeland. Though small in numbers, they conquered and held vast territories in Africa and Asia because of their skills in using these instruments of war.

Finally, the chances that travelers, traders, missionaries, and soldiers moving through distant continents could survive deadly diseases were better than ever before thanks to an array of medical discoveries of the late nineteenth century. The most important of these resulted from the so-called "bacteriological revolution." With the help of new equipment such as highly sophisticated microscopes, French and German scientists revealed that bacteria caused many infectious diseases. Before these discoveries revealed the causes of infection, remedies had come, if any were available, through trial and error. Death rates in especially infected areas remained high, since the very nature of the diseases was unknown. The single most devastating illness that hit strangers in sub-Saharan Africa was malaria. By the end of the century, its nature and process of transmission were known; effective cures followed. These medical treatments eased the difficulties of colonial rule for the new empires.

Western medical knowledge and facilities for treatment of these diseases became accessible to the local populations much more slowly. Public health services had only a small place in colonial concerns. Christian missionaries proved often the most effective emissaries of Western medicine. The Scotsman David Livingstone carried basic medicines on his travels through British East Africa. Albert Schweitzer set up an entire clinic in the jungle of French West Africa. These missionaries hoped to spread the word of the Christian religion while ministering to the health of converts and non-Christians among colonial peoples.

Western empires shared an unusual imperial ideology. The yearning to travel, which Jules Verne used as the theme of his novel, was based on more than the desire for adventure. The urge to study and to understand distant lands and peoples accompanied Western moves to construct colonial empires. Explorers traveled to the most remote, inaccessible regions to fill in the remaining blank spots on maps of the world. Both Inner Asia and Africa, the two least-explored areas of the inhabited continents, were thoroughly mapped by the end of the century. Westerners' curiosity extended to the peoples of these lands. The very imperfect science of ethnography attempted to classify societies in terms of habits and customs of the peoples themselves. The impetus for this vast project derived, in part, from the new belief that all humanity shared a common historical evolution. Westerners, of course, had gone furthest on this road. Backward peoples still had a great distance to travel.

This potentially generous objective was accompanied by a profound sense of superiority among the colonizers, including the map makers and ethnographers. They came to these lands with the conviction that their industrial civilization was the supreme achievement of humanity. It followed that the West was superior to peoples not privileged to be a part of this civilization. "Primitive" tribes might hope to learn and adapt to the new way of life; until then, they occupied an inferior position in the hierarchy of humanity. Ancient cultures such as China and India had behind them a rich history worthy of study; still, they appeared in a state of decay. The claim to conquer and rule colonial lands rested in part on the assumption that backward societies had no claim on an independent existence.

Leaders of colonial empires committed their states to raise their colonial peoples from backwardness to civilization. They shared with most citizens of their nations the belief that material and spiritual progress should be shared, at some point, with these peoples. How progress was defined, and how swiftly it should come, was to be the responsibility of imperial leader and colonial officials. Western empires abolished slavery everywhere their rule extended. They introduced, or talked of introducing laws to protect commerce and to encourage the spread of a free market (useful, too, in the sale of the homeland's mass-produced goods)—self-interest was never far from the concerns of empire-builders.

The writer Rudyard Kipling, born in India, became very popular with his tales and poems of empire. He used his writing to urge Westerners to take seriously their responsibility toward colonial peoples. He wrote his most famous imperial message in a 1899 poem, "The White Man's Burden." Its call to serve the needs of "your new-caught sullen peoples" was specifically addressed to the United States, which had just acquired its own small empire. Neither he nor his readers thought to ask these peoples if they wished to be taken in hand.

The desire to aid colonial peoples was interpreted in a somewhat different way by active members of the Protestant and Catholic churches. Missionaries such as David Livingstone wrote extensively to urge his European readers "to help their fellow-men in Africa" by sharing their "social and religious blessings." By the early twentieth century, these missionaries had converted millions in Asia and Africa. Their efforts divided native communities, creating disorder and dissent among peoples previously united in their customs and faith. Conversion opened the way for the new Christians to enter more easily within colonial society. Chinua Achebe, a Nigerian novelist whose own father had renounced his family and ancestral traditions to join a Protestant church, later thought of the arrival of the Christian missionaries and British colonial officials among his people as a time when "things fall apart."

In the late nineteenth century, nationalist passions led political leaders to claim that their own states had to stake claim to more and more territory to prevent rival empires from getting ahead in a competition for land. Success would establish the superiority of their nation; failure, on the contrary, was the mark of decay. The popular theory of Social Darwinism asserted that nations, like animals, competed in a struggle of the "survival of the fittest." Imperialist leaders and their followers feared to be ranked among the unfit.

This attitude drove the Russian Empire far into East Asia. There it encountered another empire equally determined to expand into the same region. The leaders of the Japanese Empire, reformed on a Western model in the previous decades, made sure that their claim to the disputed areas was successful by defeating the Russians in a short war early in the twentieth century. For the first time, Western governments discovered that a non-Western state could put to its own use their tools of empire.

Christianity in Africa: Rural
Church, Northern Rhodesia
(Zambia), approx. 1925
(*Hoover Institution*)

Empires and Industrialism

The economic foundations of the new empires lay in the Industrial Revolution. This profound transformation in the means of production, distribution of goods, and ownership of productive property had begun late in the eighteenth century. By the early twentieth century, it had spread to the outer edges of the Western world and beyond to Japan. It brought to industrialized countries an extraordinary surplus of wealth, concentrated in the hands of successful capitalists, and increasingly controlled by financial and industrial corporations. With that wealth came the power to influence governments. Growing tax revenues fueled imperial expansion and military rearmament. The "tools of empire" depended upon this industrial, technological base.

The Industrial Revolution needed new skills in the areas of engineering, risk-taking, and factory labor. Scientists played an important role in making new discoveries, such as electricity, that were applicable and profitable to industrialists. Inventors and engineers were key in bringing these wonders into the domain of everyday usage. Thomas Edison was a self-taught American inventor and businessman who proved a genius at bringing electricity out of the theoretical, scientific realm into everyday life. Electric lighting transformed public spaces and living conditions among those segments of the population with the means to afford the new products. Engineers worked at making the internal combustion engine a product efficient enough and sufficiently easy to manufacture to permit the mass production of automobiles. Engineering skills brought chemical products, derived from coal and petroleum, into the realm of industrial production and everyday life of consumers. In the industrial age, knowledge was an indispensable tool of economic activity.

These products held out the lure of profits to investors with the financial means and grasp of business skills necessary for the production and sale of new products. The economic system within which they worked is called a market economy, or capitalism. Their success or failure depended on profits or losses from their business, in competition with other business owners also seeking the most productive (hence least expensive) means of operation. They enjoyed the protection of property and contract laws, the backing of governments sympathetic to the work of "capitalists," the unrestricted access to labor, and increasingly the ability to find markets beyond political borders. Successful entrepreneurs built up fortunes, as did corporations whose managers were responsible for bringing yearly profits to stockholders. The system was open to newcomers, provided they had the funds, the skills, and the daring.

The economic freedom of choice that it required was its greatest strength, and its greatest weakness. Capitalism opened the way for greater economic initiative than had been possible in feudal times. But it operated in disregard for the needs of those lacking the social and economic means to protect their well-being. By the late nineteenth century, cycles of prosperity and depression set the course of European and international economic development. When hard times came, they hit most severely the laboring population. Social welfare was not a part of this capitalist system. Workers' grievances became the source of mass movements of protest and the inspiration for the socialist alternative to capitalism. Karl Marx, the great prophet of socialist revolution, concluded his *Manifesto* with the ominous appeal: "Workers of the world, unite! You have nothing to lose but your chains."

The growth of the industrial economy relied on labor in the factories and fields. An abundant and cheap supply of factory workers, drawn from rural areas, from artisan trades destroyed by cheap industrial products, and from the rapidly growing population of Europe, helped keep costs to manufacturers low and prevented workers from making effective demands for improved labor conditions. Workers in factories had to acquire increasingly complex skills or remain among the most poorly paid. With those skills, their power to deal with factory owners did increase, sometimes by conflict through labor stoppages and organized strikes. From the countryside came food to feed the growing urban populations. With the development of international commercial links, food supplies were found far beyond the industrial centers, even beyond the oceans. By the early twentieth century, living conditions for the urban population of the industrializing countries were gradually improving. Yet inequalities of wealth remained enormous. Defenders of the capitalist system claimed that those who prospered had proven their superior capabilities. The argument was another version of the harsh theory of Social Darwinism.

The inequalities between the industrialized Western countries and their colonial peoples in distant continents were as great as those within European societies. The major difference in economic terms was the increasing importance of non-Western lands as the source of natural resources needed for Western industry. The lure of finding great deposits of valuable commodities had drawn explorers and investors to lands outside Europe throughout the nineteenth century. Some of them took a direct hand in promoting imperial expansion by their governments. Cecil Rhodes combined ambitious money-making schemes in the diamond fields of South Africa with grandiose projects of British empire-building in east Africa; "coloring the map red" for Great Britain was his way of describing his goal for the continent. But most capitalists played only a secondary role in empire-building. Their activities became important once the imperial might of their country was well established.

The most important of the international corporations were the oil companies. Their search for petroleum took them to the Dutch colony of the East Indies. There, under the protection of the government of the Netherlands, the Royal Dutch-Shell corporation began in the 1890s to exploit one of the world's major oil fields. The British government for its part took a direct hand in backing another oil corporation, British Petroleum, which had discovered and developed the rich oil fields in southwestern Persia (Iran). Persia remained in the early twentieth century a sovereign, ancient empire, but Great Britain (and the Russian Empire) made sure its government did nothing to harm their interests. Chief among these was unimpeded access to its oil fields. Western imperial expansion brought with it the exploitation of those global resources of importance (and profit) to Western industry.

The New European Empires

Both France and Great Britain had in earlier centuries seized overseas territories, partly for purposes of trade, partly for settlement. The turmoil of the French Revolution led to the loss of most of the lands once held by the French monarchy. Expansion began again in the nineteenth century until the new French Empire was second largest in the world. The greatest was the British Empire, which had kept some territory from the previous era and added much more colonial land in the nineteenth century.

The renewal of French imperial annexations came sporadically throughout the century. This was partly the result of ambitious political leaders seeking the glory of foreign conquest. Their ambition led to France's first new colonial conquest. Across the Mediterranean Sea lay North Africa, whose local princes owed allegiance to the Ottoman sultan. It was a tempting target for the French government, unpopular at home and looking for a cause to stir up patriotic support. In a brief war in 1830, its troops defeated the forces of the local princes in that part of North Africa that the French named Algeria. Later in the century, French forces took the lands of Tunisia and Morocco, to the east and west of Algeria. These Muslim peoples, largely Arabic speaking, passed from the nominal rule of the Ottoman Empire to become subjects of the French Empire.

The empire expanded as a result also of the commitment by the French government to protect French Catholic missionaries and French traders operating in Asian and African lands. Their presence periodically stirred up local protest. National pride and lurid tales of suffering produced by the French popular press increasingly brought French imperial forces to settle these disputes. When they were successful, the result

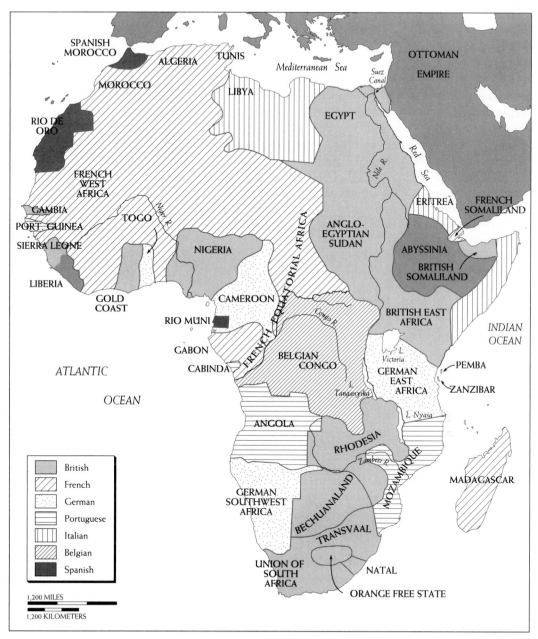

Partition of Africa, 1800–1914. (From Craig, et al., *The Heritage of World Civilizations, 4th ed.*, © 1997. Reprinted with permission of Prentice-Hall, Inc., Upper Saddle River, NJ)

usually was annexation of that region by the empire.

The French had for centuries moved in small numbers through lands in Southeast Asia. There the Chinese Empire exercised a distant and increasingly feeble dominion. When disorders in the 1860s seemed to threaten French lives, French military forces moved into these lands. By the 1890s, the territory that they had seized from the local princes and Chinese forces included a large segment of southeast Asia. The French baptized their colony Indochina. Their pattern of colonial rule, repeated in other colonies as well, included direct administrative and military rule over the peoples of these lands. Catholic missionaries continued to seek and find converts. Colonial officials encouraged assimilation into French culture by establishing a French school system and recruiting native volunteers for French military forces.

Africa became, later in the century, the continent of choice for French expansion. The process was begun in the 1870s by European explorers, moving up the great rivers of west Africa into the interior. After signing treaties (by persuasion or by force) with tribal leaders, they claimed enormous areas of central and west Africa for the French Empire. Without any clear knowledge of either the land or the peoples, the French government accepted these treaties for fear that other European states would seize these areas if it failed to do so. This "scramble for Africa" was driven forward by political ambitions and nationalist passions, pitting the French against the other European imperial states.

Millions of African peoples fell under French rule. New borders divided them (at least on maps) from neighboring tribes whose lands belonged to another imperial power. Their new language of state became French, though only a few translators pos-

sessed the power to communicate between them and their French colonial officials. Their tribal chiefs became the lowest rung of imperial rule. When they rebelled against their new rulers, they faced troops sent from other parts of the empire with modern weapons and prepared to destroy whole villages to "teach the natives a lesson." Imperial rule disrupted African society in profound and permanent ways.

In those same years, the small country of Belgium extended its rule into the Congo basin. The Belgian king had initiated the European "scramble for Africa" by financing exploration of the regions, then by using the explorers' discoveries to claim the territory as the Congo Free State. It was the largest colony in all Africa. Afterwards his officials found in their lands rich mineral resources (especially diamonds and copper), which they began to exploit with the aid of forced labor. This economic benefit made the colony a valuable possession. The Belgian king was pleased, but not some missionaries and humanitarian visitors who denounced the brutality of his officials and traders. Their public campaign against his colonial rule became a human-rights cause in Europe. The king had to pass control of the colony to his government. The international scandal faded, but the Belgian Congo remained, thanks to Joseph Conrad's novel, the "heart of darkness" of European imperialism.

The British Empire expanded through Asia and Africa in much the same sporadic, disorderly way as the French. By the early nineteenth century, British traders and manufacturers had built a vast trading network and had made Great Britain the emporium of the West. They played an important role in pushing the empire forward. The glory of conquest drove the empire onward as well. Ambitious colonial officers stationed in the British coastal trading centers on the Indian subcontinent began in the late eighteenth century to extend their control into the interior. By the 1850s, even the northern plains of India had come under British rule. Control came at a price to the empire. In 1857, resentment at British rule provoked a massive revolt that included troops trained by the British as well as Indian princes who had promised loyalty to British rule. British repression of the rebels took several years and brought brutal punishments.

For the next ninety years, India was a "crown colony." It was the greatest of British possessions, the colony one British statesman called "the jewel in the crown" of his queen. British administrators governed directly in some places and through Indian princes (those who had remained loyal to the empire during the revolt) in others. They set about creating a colony where British law and British education would win over an elite among the native population to collaborate in ruling that vast land. They organized an Indian army, joining Indian soldiers and British officers trained to maintain order in that subcontinent. The Indian army served the empire well. In 1875, the British government proclaimed their queen, Victoria, to be the Empress of India.

To ensure that naval forces could easily reach India and China, British naval authorities built coaling stations along the African, Arabian, and Asian coast. One important consequence of this policy was the British decision in the 1870s to take control of the International Suez Company. Sale of the controlling block of shares seemed to the *khedive* (prince) of Egypt a simple way to pay his debts. The consequences proved momentous. The British government had a vital interest in protecting its influence in Egypt, through whose territory the Suez Canal provided direct maritime access between the Mediterranean Sea and the Indian Ocean. The British government soon afterwards decided that Egypt itself had to come under

imperial control. In 1882, it moved troops into Egypt, though it was legally a province of the Ottoman Empire. It became a British protectorate, where British officers and administrators indirectly exercised political authority in the name of the powerless Egyptian ruler. The British Empire had become the dominant power in the Middle East.

In the rush for lands in sub-Saharan Africa, the British laid plans for territorial annexation to link southern Africa with Egypt in one great north–south band of territory "from the Cape [of Good Hope] to Cairo." That was the vision of Cecil Rhodes, the most dynamic British promoter of African empire. His efforts obtained by treaty and conquest lands in east Africa including Kenya and a territory baptized "Rhodesia" (later Zambia and Zimbabwe). His greatest obstacle was the powerful Zulu kingdom. Its soldiers inflicted in 1879 a major defeat on a small British force that had invaded their land. But a year later the British returned with more troops and defeated the Zulu king, whose land and people became spoils of war for the empire. But "Cape to Cairo" did not become entirely British. The German Empire stepped in ahead of the British to claim in central Africa the kingdoms of Burundi and Rwanda, governed by Tutsi tribes, and the territory that they called German East Africa (later Tanganyika/Tanzania).

The most determined resistance to Rhodes's plans came from the Dutch settlers (called Boers, or Afrikaners) in southern Africa. The small republics of these European colonists, descendants of Protestant settlers from the Low Countries, had been created in the 1830s to free the Boers from British rule (and from laws protecting African peoples whose lands they had seized). Moving north from the Cape to the high plains, they established their farms and

White Settlers in South Africa: Boer Farmer on Way to Town (*Courtesy of the South African Consulate/Hoover Institution*)

practiced their faith in an area between Britain's Cape Colony, at the southern tip of Africa, and Rhodesia. They found in their creed religious justification to treat the Africans as inferiors and to expel the tribes from their land. But they could not so easily get rid of the Europeans who joined the gold rush when in the late-nineteenth century the precious metal was found in their territory. The Boers were determined to keep control of their "new Zion." British imperialists like Cecil Rhodes insisted that this land be incorporated in the British Empire and exploited by British capitalists. The two plans were irreconcilable.

As a result, Great Britain became involved in a major colonial war in sub-Saharan Africa. British administrators and officers in South Africa handled the dispute with the Boers with such arrogance and used their superior military force so provocatively that in 1899 the Boers proclaimed war on the British Empire. The military odds were hopelessly against the Boers. They fought with the determination of religious zealots and the skill of guerrilla soldiers. The conflict did not end until 1902, when the Boer forces finally surrendered. By then even the British government was aware of the destructive folly of that expansionist war.

Soon after, Great Britain set up the Union of South Africa as a self-governing country (similar to Canada and Australia) within the British Empire. They left the Boers free to run their own internal affairs in their territories and to participate in the leadership of the federal Union as well. The Africans themselves played no part in the conflict. They, as well as their land, remained the spoils and the objects of conquest.

Russia, Japan, and War for Empire

On the eastern borderlands of Europe, the Russian Empire combined traits of an ancient empire and of the new overseas empires of Western states. Its autocratic political system, headed by an absolute monarch with the titles of "tsar" and "emperor," was in many ways as ineffective and brutal as that of the Ottoman Empire. Its subject peoples included in its western territories a large Polish population. Three times in the nineteenth century the Poles rebelled against Russian rule in the hope of creating their own nation-state. Each time Russian armies repressed their rebellion. National rights of non-Russian peoples had no place in the authoritarian state of the Russian tsar-emperors. Its domination of these peoples earned it the badge of "the prison of peoples."

Like the European empires, Russia, too, set out in the mid-nineteenth century to seize colonial lands in Asia. Its Cossack soldiers and settlers had long before occupied the northern reaches of Asia inhabited mainly by hunter-gatherer tribes. The empire's enormous Siberian territories possessed abundant natural resources, and its peoples were too few and too weak to resist the Russian advance. Beginning in the 1860s, Russian leaders saw new opportunities for expansion in the oasis lands of Inner Asia ruled by weak Muslim princes. By the 1880s, the borders of the empire reached to Persia, Afghanistan, and China. The British Empire strongly protested the nearby presence of the "Russian bear," but without success. The Russian government built railway lines to bind these distant areas to the imperial center. The most important of these railroads crossed all of Siberia to reach in 1900 the Pacific Ocean north of China and Korea.

The Japanese Empire disputed with Russia control of these east Asia lands. Until the mid-nineteenth century it had remained an isolated island empire. Its rulers, like the Chinese emperor, faced the threat of domination by expansionist Western empires. Western diplomats, backed by naval forces, had in the early 1860s obliged the Japanese government to accept their traders on the same unequal terms as those imposed in China. Confronted with the likelihood that their state, like China, would be humbled by the Western imperial powers, in 1868 a group of young Japanese reformers seized control of their government. They were all nobles from the warrior class ("samurai"), but were convinced that the old feudal system had to be abandoned. They declared their rebellion to be the only means to protect the honor and glory of the empire and their emperor, worshiped as a divine person in the state religion called Shintoism. This so-called Meiji Restoration ("Meiji," meaning "The Great," was the name taken afterwards by the emperor) drew upon the patriotic pride and anti-foreign fervor of the Japanese people. It was a daring effort to make their country as powerful as the Western nations. The reformers' goal was "rich country, strong military." Their project used traditional Japanese institutions to achieve a modern "revolution from above."

Though they claimed to have restored their emperor to power, the new leaders, in fact, ruled in his name. Consciously borrowing Western technology and institutions, they succeeded by the 1890s in laying the foundations of an industrial economy, in forming a well-equipped army and navy, and in forcing Western states to renounce the unequal treaties. To obtain the cooperation of the population, they created the structure of a constitutional, representative government. Its powers were restricted by recognition of the authority of the emperor and his court, and by the informal powers of the leaders of the armed forces. Democracy was a means to mobilize the population, not an end in itself. The "imperial way" united the emperor and the reformed state in an ideology of emperor worship and imperialist expansion.

The reforms were so effective that the government was able to put in motion its plans for colonial conquest. Its goal was to seize neighboring areas on the Asian continent before the Western empires. In 1894–1895, Japan waged a quick, successful war against China to obtain territory and trade concessions in northern China. Their expansion brought protests from the Western empires, whose leaders could not grasp the sudden rise of this "oriental" empire.

The Russian Empire was Japan's major imperial rival. Tempted by the riches of the northern Chinese province of Manchuria, the Russian and Japanese governments each hoped to exploit its economic resources and to enlarge their own sphere of influence at the expense of the feeble Chinese state. The Russian emperor refused to take seriously warnings from the Japanese not to continue expansion into the region. His disdainful attitude toward the "yellow" race blinded him to the reality of Japanese military might. Japan appeared to them an insignificant, inferior player in the global imperial game.

Fearing that Russia was on the verge of seizing all Manchuria, Japanese military forces launched a surprise naval attack on the Russian Pacific fleet in early 1904. Their army then crossed to the mainland to drive the Russian armed forces from north China. By 1905, the Japanese had defeated the Russian navy and had forced the Russian army to retreat far into northern Manchuria. A peace treaty that year recognized the Japanese victory. Although Manchuria remained nominally a part of China, the Japanese army established a sphere of influence in the southern area of the province. Japanese industrialists and workers moved into Manchuria to tap its mineral wealth. Korea became a province of the Japanese Empire. Russian plans for economic and political expansion in the east were blocked.

Japan had emerged as the most powerful state in East Asia. It rivaled Western countries in self-confidence, international might, and expansionist ambitions. Its conquest of Chinese territory stirred a movement of Chinese nationalist protest, directed as much against the feeble Chinese emperor as against the Japanese. Though it was too weak to concern the Japanese yet, it augured trouble in the future for foreign intruders in China. In the early twentieth century, the new empires were beginning to confront political resistance and protest among their colonial peoples. Conflict among the new empires and national movements of protest among colonial peoples were signs that the age of empires would not endure for long.

An Empire for the United States

The expansion of the United States during the nineteenth century was continental in scope. It was a process at times brutal and aggressive. Its settlers and army expelled Native Americans from vast fertile lands, placing them in small "reservations." U.S. forces had waged a brief war against Mexico, taking as the spoils of victory an enormous area stretching from Texas to California. By then U.S. borders extended as far west as the Pacific Ocean. In these terms, the United States was a continental empire.

Soon, it obtained its own small overseas empire. Like the European states, it possessed the tools of empire. Its industrial economy was more productive than any other Western country. It had only a small army and navy, but its weapons of war were as deadly as any other modern military. At the end of the century, its political leaders proclaimed openly their ambition to begin overseas imperial expansion. Theodore Roosevelt, the most forceful of these nationalists, argued that a "really great nation" like the United States had the obligation to use its naval and diplomatic might in international affairs to expand U.S. power and influence. His nationalist ardor in defense of foreign expansion helped give the U.S. an overseas empire. Like the European states, the United States acquired its colonial territory through military conquest and economic expansion.

Almost the entirety of Latin America consisted by then of independent states. A century earlier, the Spanish and Portugese settlers there had successfully rebelled against their European rulers. These states were comparatively weak and impoverished compared to their Yankee neighbor. American investors and bankers bought mines and built railroads and factories there. Latin American peoples depended for their livelihood primarily on agriculture and the export of raw materials. Their governments frequently had to borrow from foreign (usually British) banks to meet the basic needs of state. When they failed to pay these debts, the British government sent naval vessels to their shores to force them to pay. A disillusioned nationalist explained this dilemma by stating that "Latin America is a beggar sitting on top of a mountain of gold." The states there had the appearance, not the substance, of independence.

The process leading to a U.S. empire began on the island of Cuba. It still belonged to the Spanish Empire, whose remaining possessions included a few islands in the Caribbean, and the Philippine archipelago in the Pacific. In the mid-1890s, Cuban nationalists rebelled against Spanish rule. They appealed to the American government for help in winning independence. American nationalist leaders, backed by a newspaper campaign attacking Spanish brutality, took the lead in supporting the Cuban revolutionaries. Newspaper articles attracted readers with stories of Spanish atrocities and with appeals for American intervention on the side of the Cuban nationalists.

In this aggressive atmosphere, an explosion (probably accidental) on the American battleship *Maine,* docked in the harbor of Havana, Cuba, was sufficient pretext for a U.S. declaration of war on Spain. The 1898 war ended quickly after U.S. naval forces near the Philippines defeated the Spanish fleet; at the same time, the U.S. army seized Cuba. The peace treaty signed at the end of that year left these Spanish colonies under U.S. control.

The war for Cuban independence opened the way for U.S. expansion and territorial annexation. Theodore Roosevelt was the most outspoken and eloquent defender for expansionism. He argued that the country's national interest and prestige required that it retain control over the newly freed Spanish colonies. He welcomed what Kipling had called "the white man's burden." Nationalist leaders in Cuba and the Philippines quickly found that their lands had become dependencies of the United States.

The U.S. government claimed (without real evidence) that another European empire would seize the Philippines if its forces left the archipelago. Filipino nationalists had fought alongside American troops against the Spanish forces in the expectation of creating an independent nation-state. When the U.S. troops did not leave, they turned their arms against the U.S. Army. The war lasted several years, ending in U.S. victory. Filipino forces were weak and poorly led, and the peoples of the archipelago were deeply divided by ethnic and religious differences. Like other empire-builders of that era, the U.S. government took its victory as proof that the United States had an imperial mission. The Philippines became a U.S. colony.

Cuba became a part of the U.S. empire, not by annexation, but by becoming a protectorate. The peace treaty ending the war with Spain allowed the Cuban revolutionaries to form their own nation-state. But the U.S. government insisted that the new Cuban leadership grant U.S. authorities the right to intervene in the island's affairs "to protect life, liberty, and individual property." In doing so, they allowed their giant neighbor to the north to intervene in their country's political affairs. By annexation and by treaty, the United States had created its own small empire.

It quickly became the dominant power in the Caribbean region. After Theodore Roosevelt became president in 1901, he actively encouraged the construction of a canal across the Panamanian isthmus. It was a matter of national interests. The fledgling U.S. Navy would, he knew, make good use of the canal to patrol the shores of Latin American countries. U.S. business interests realized as well that U.S. merchant vessels would be able to travel quickly between the Pacific and Atlantic oceans. After negotiations with Colombia collapsed, he helped Panamanian rebels create their own small state. They immediately agreed to cede territory for the construction of the canal, which finally opened in 1914. The Canal Zone, a U.S. possession, was a base for navy and marine forces.

Roosevelt made known to the European powers that the Caribbean was a U.S. sphere of influence, that is, a region in which his government was dominant. The small states there had to accept U.S. supervision of their foreign and domestic policy. That U.S. policy of intervention remained in place for the next quarter-century. If Caribbean and Central American governments failed to pay foreign debts, financial advisers from the north took charge of their treasury. If they could not repress disorders or revolts, gunboats with marines from the Canal Zone arrived to take charge for a time. When, in 1911, civil war threatened Nicaragua, marines assumed the role of police and remained there for twenty years. Roosevelt justified this "gunboat diplomacy" by proclaiming it to be in the spirit of Western empire-building and sanctioned by the moral obligations of "civilized nations." Latin American nationalists disagreed completely. But their countries lay too near the "Yankee giant" to escape U.S. domination.

Only the Mexican people managed to create a truly independent nation-state. It came as a result of a period of violent, revolutionary turmoil. Their revolution began in 1911, when Mexican liberals organized a rebellion to end the long rule of a political dictator. It ended seven years later with the emergence of a nationalist, populist regime which successfully defied U.S. military intervention and overthrew the century-old governing elite of landowners and the military. The Mexican Revolution, in some respects, repeated earlier political struggles for power between authoritarian rulers and liberals demanding representative government and political liberty. But it turned into a social revolution when Mexican workers and landless farmers joined forces against the economic elite of the country. They found leaders adept at articulating their demands for social equality, and at organizing large volunteer armies to fight for their cause.

The revolution turned into a bloody civil war. Rival armies waged major battles in a struggle that cost hundreds of thousands of lives. For a time, Mexico seemed destined to fall apart. Rebel forces under Emiliano Zapata took control of much of the south, while Francisco ("Pancho") Villa's army occupied northern territories. They both confiscated landed estates and proclaimed their determination to fight for a new Mexican nation. They were not socialists, but their action

Revolutionary Warrior: Francisco
(Pancho) Villa (*Clendenon Collection/Hoover Institution*)

spoke to an ideal of social justice. By 1915, the revolution had torn apart the country and left Mexican society prey to roving militia and armies.

The conflict deeply disturbed Mexico's Yankee neighbor. The U.S. president, Woodrow Wilson, supported democratic reform and believed his country had an obligation to support the liberal political movement in Mexico. At the same time, he and American investors sought to protect U.S.-owned companies that had poured funds into Mexican mines, ranching, and oil fields. Social justice in Mexico was not high in the U.S. government's priorities, while constitutional rule was. Wilson became convinced in 1916 that the real threat to Mexican democracy was Villa's army. Villa, for his part, was prepared to fight. His raid on a U.S. border town in Arizona brought the war for a brief moment within the United States.

Villa's aim was a war that he hoped would unite behind his forces all Mexicans who believed in the nationalist cause. Wilson sent the U.S. Army to capture Villa and to end the civil war. Mexicans from all sides immediately condemned this Yankee intervention (but did not join Villa). Even the far-off German Empire, expecting war with the United States that winter, believed Mexico a possible ally and encouraged its ambassador to seek an alliance. This was a misguided act that found no support among Mexican leaders and stirred up a wave of protest in the United States. After a year, the U.S. Army withdrew, having failed to capture Villa and succeeded only in arousing Mexican patriotism.

The revolution ended in 1917 with the triumph of the constitutionalist forces. Mexico emerged from that bloody time with a new nationalist leadership. It gave Mexican peasants much of the land seized from landowners during the civil war. It decreed that the country's vast oil reserves belonged to Mexico, not foreign oil companies. This revolution's social achievements gave a glimpse of the social revolutions of the years to come in other parts of the world. Politics soon came to be dominated by one party (ultimately known as the Institutional Revolutionary Party). The country's independence was real. Mexico, alone among the Latin American countries close to the United States, was able to escape domination by its powerful northern neighbor.

EUROPEAN EMPIRES AND NATIONS

The new empires wielded enormous power over the subject peoples in their colonies. Yet in their European homeland, most of these states recognized the right, usually in some constitutional form, of their own people to participate in a national political community. Most governments respected the fundamental laws guaranteeing their citizens full civil liberties. Empires on the outside, they were nation-states from within.

European Nationalism

Since the revolutions of the eighteenth century, more and more Western states were committed to allowing their peoples, united by a common national identity, to govern themselves. Known usually as liberalism, this set of ideals increasingly recognized that the protection of the individual citizen, through the rule of law and representative government, was the single most important aim of the state. These rights had first emerged in a few countries in the West, and had included only the propertied, male population. But they inherently had no restrictive limits, for "human rights" spoke in universal terms applicable to all humanity.

Nationalism was not so generous. The nation-state was destined for a people sharing a common identity and set of beliefs drawn from their historical experience. This vision hid a profound contradiction. It joined together the state and the people of that state, but left open the question of whether the defining characteristic of that union was the ideals of human rights enjoyed by that people, or the apparent ethnic unity of one people, either ruling themselves or governed by a ruler speaking in their name. These two differing versions of nationalism, one individualistic and the other collectivistic, were present within all Western countries. They reemerged in non-Western countries as nationalism spread in the twentieth century throughout the world.

Nationalism as a form of human rights is usually defined as *civic nationalism*. It first appeared in France during the French Revolution. It asserted that national bonds should be grounded in a shared commitment to the rule of law and to civil and political rights in a democratic nation-state. In other words, it imagined the nation to be open to all ready to share the values defining citizenship (hence the term "civic"). President Lincoln defended this vision when, in his Gettysburg Address in 1863, he proclaimed the United States to be "one nation, conceived in liberty." The people in such a nation-state usually all spoke one language, but it was conceivable for such a nation to be a place of peoples speaking several different languages.

In the nineteenth century, citizens in states such as Great Britain and France appeared to have come closest to achieving this form of nation-state. But even there protesters, also claiming to be nationalists, argued that the "ruling people" speaking the principal language of their country should not grant equal rights and power to peoples of other languages or cultures. In their view, all citizens needed to assimilate into the dominant culture. Their arguments made clear the promise, and the weakness, of civic nationalism. To become truly equitable, the entire population had to agree to join in pluralistic national community, multiethnic and even multiracial. Lincoln's vision of a special American civic nationalism was for a century after the Civil War a tragic failure, since the United States was unable to overcome the racism that excluded blacks from the political community.

Nationalism understood as a community of one people sharing a collective identity based on common ancestry is termed *ethnic nationalism.* Its intellectual roots lay in the glorification by writers in the nineteenth century of the cultural and historical uniqueness of a particular people. This definition of "people" stressed the richness of their folklore, language, and history. The term "ethnic" refers to the special inherited traits of that people. Transformed into a political program, ethnic nationalism stressed the need for each people, within their "native" land, to form their own nation-state. Each people needed their own state to fulfill their true destiny and to defend their needs. Other peoples living in that territory had to accept the rule by the dominant ethnic group. Nineteenth-century writers and political leaders who argued for national unification on these terms assumed special laws should protect the rights of national minorities. In the next century, states where ethnic nationalism denied full civic equality to minority peoples became increasingly numerous.

Popular awareness of national identity had spread widely throughout Europe in the decades before the First World War. Nationalism drew its strength from mass public schooling and generalized literacy, which gave the population access to accounts of the past of a particular nation as transmitted in histories, the press, and literature. Its principal adherents lived in urban centers, where personal contacts and popular culture made shared national identity a lived experience. The sense of shared identity enriched the lives of people by greatly enlarging meaningful human contacts. It was, however, a destructive influence when it increased distrust and even hatred toward other peoples. Nationalism was a new and potent force in human history, creating a new perception of self and the other, of friends and enemies.

In Europe, its revolutionary potential to destroy old states and create new nation–states had become apparent during the nineteenth century. Germany and Italy became nation-states in the 1860s as a result of wars and popular uprisings. In central and eastern Europe, multinational states remained centers of unrest and violent confrontation between governments determined to defend their unity and nationalist movements seeking to break away into separate nation–states. Both the Austro-Hungarian Empire of southeastern Europe and the Russian Empire to the east were home to a multitude of peoples, ruled by Germans and Hungarians in the former empire, by Russians in the latter. Nationalism among their subject peoples was a revolutionary movement.

National loyalties also brought into public view the ill will that had long existed among Christians toward Europe's Jewish population. Millions of Jews living in eastern Europe were the victims of oppression that resulted from laws that deprived them of elementary protection from abuse and from ethnic hatred. Anti-Semitism provoked, in reaction, a movement, led by Theodore Herzl, to found a Jewish national homeland. He called it the Zionist Organization to make clear that the Jewish homeland had to be in Palestine (the Biblical Zion). He argued that only in that land, from which the Jews had been expelled 2,000 years before, would Jews be safe from persecution. In 1900, Palestine was a province of the Ottoman Empire ruled by Muslim Turks and inhabited almost entirely by Arab-speaking Muslims and Christians. Though a few Jewish pioneers had settled in that region before 1914, the Zionist goal of a Jewish national homeland remained still a distant dream.

The Serb nationalist movement in the Balkan region of the Austro-Hungarian Empire demanded the creation, partly out of imperial lands, of a nation-state for all the Serbian-speaking people. Serb nationalist writers and intellectuals believed that all South Slavs (the most numerous people in the Balkans) belonged in one state. These peoples spoke languages that appeared to be linguistically similar despite significant differences of dialect. Serbian nationalists discounted the lack of common language, just as they discounted the importance of the religious barriers that had created separate communities of Catholics (Croats), Muslims (often referred to as Bosnians, since most lived in Bosnia), and Orthodox people (for whom the term "Serb" was commonly used). They argued that since these peoples spoke the same Serbian language, they all shared a national identity and all should lie in one (South Slav, or Yugoslav) state. Most Serb-speaking peoples lived in the Austro-Hungarian Empire. The little Kingdom of Serbia, on the southern borders of the empire, constituted the core around which Serbian nationalists hoped to construct this new nation-state.

This vision could not become reality until the empire itself collapsed. A small group of Serbian nationalists, organized in a secret terrorist society called the Black Hand, believed their cause so urgent that they had to destroy the mighty empire. They hoped that their own deeds would arouse a massive movement of resistance. To achieve that goal, they were prepared to become assassins.

Political terrorism was their chosen means. Like other terrorists then and later, they became assassins to publicize their cause and to inspire less committed supporters to participate in their struggle. Their terrorism was the desperate, destructive gesture of the weak. Black Hand members were convinced that the assassination of leaders of the empire was a righteous act. In 1914, they decided to execute the heir to the Austrian throne. Their action set in motion a conflict that exploded into the First World War. Their deed did lead ultimately to the collapse of the Austrian Empire at the end of the war. The transition from empires to nations brought with it bloodshed and violence.

The Liberal State and Industrial Society

Most Western states recognized in law and practice the liberties that had come to be known as human rights. Great Britain, France, and the United States had evolved over the previous century the institutions of democratic government intended to ensure the protection of these rights. Gradually, more and more states in the Western world followed their example. This process had come at times through reforms granted by hereditary monarchies, who accepted becoming constitutional rulers. At times, it came after revolutions that overthrew monarchs who attempted to preserve their power and to restrict these rights. In 1905, Russian revolutionaries forced their emperor, Nicholas II, to concede some measure of political freedom to his subjects. The struggle for liberty could, like that for nation-states, lead to bitter political conflict. The same situation emerged in colonial lands when these same liberal demands from native subjects met the opposition of their imperial rulers.

The key elements of *liberalism* centered on the rights and powers of the citizen. At its heart was the rule of law, to be embodied in fundamental laws most often contained in a constitution (as in the United States and France). Civil law enforced by the state, in principle, excluded any special legal privilege for citizens on the basis of class, race, or religion. It guaranteed religious toleration. Marriage, family, and property relations came under the jurisdiction of the state's laws, not the laws or customs of a particular religion (a principle usually referred to as *secularism*). The goal was to insure equality before the law of all citizens.

Liberalism promised citizens their civil liberties, including freedom of speech, assembly, and worship. They also enjoyed political rights, principally the right to elect political representatives to whom the powers of government were granted. These powers were limited; legislatures at times chose the executive leadership in the government (Britain's cabinet system), while in other countries citizens voted directly for their leader (the presidential system). Courts could reject illegal acts of the government, and regular elections were intended to prevent political leaders from claiming abusive powers and neglecting the needs of their citizens. Finally, law codes protected individual and corporate property rights in an economy that operated in a free market (capitalism).

The nineteenth-century liberal program hid serious weaknesses. One involved the crucial issue of what part of the population should enjoy the full rights of citizens. Voting rights (suffrage) were a major source of disagreement throughout the nineteenth century. Gradually, universal manhood suffrage laws were adopted, largely as a result of the competition of political parties for voter backing. The issue of women's suffrage stirred up great controversy. Most men still shared the conviction that women, in political affairs, were inferior to men. Conse-

quently, they could aspire only to be second-class citizens. But women's suffrage movements disputed this claim, demanding that the rights called "human" be granted the female half of humanity. They sought "the emancipation of woman as a personality" and labeled their cause *feminism.* The pursuit of liberty, begun in the eighteenth-century revolutions, continued into the twentieth century.

A second failure of the liberal program as practiced in the West in the nineteenth century was its refusal to admit the claim of colonial peoples to the protection of human rights. Most Westerners judged the rule of law and representative government to be unfit for backward peoples. They justified this claim by pointing to what they considered the primitive conditions in their colonies. At best, they offered to these subjects the possibility of attaining some measure of citizenship after a lengthy period of learning, which they assumed required knowledge (and appreciation) of the empire's language and culture. The rulers of the British Empire recognized by the early twentieth century that some of their Asian subjects, especially in India, might one day be fit for local self-rule. But they did not foresee that possibility coming soon. Political paternalism, buttressed by pervasive racism, stood in the path of serious political reform of the colonial regimes of the European empires.

A third serious failing of liberal states was their unwillingness to address the problems of social inequality. The widening of political citizenship came far more easily than the reduction of the great disparities of wealth and property that characterized all industrial societies. Nineteenth-century liberalism did not recognize social welfare to be a human right. Individual citizens had to satisfy their economic needs through their own efforts. That some benefitted while others suffered was judged a sort of law of nature. The working classes formed their own parties to compete in elections, and sought new laws to protect the impoverished and the laboring classes. Some European intellectuals were convinced that the liberal system itself was so flawed that only its profound transformation would bring the working masses social justice and political freedom. The influence of Karl Marx's socialist theories drew upon their rejection of liberalism and capitalism and upon the grievances of Europe's workers.

Despite these flaws, the political ideals of liberalism continued to inspire revolutionary movements in countries outside the Western democracies. The early years of the twentieth century were a period of political unrest in Asia and Latin America. Cuban revolutionaries rebelled in the 1890s against Spanish domination in the name of political liberty as well as national liberation. The Mexican revolution originated in a revolt against a dictator in the name of freedom. It ended with the triumph of the constitutionalist movement whose unifying ideals drew upon liberalism's promise of representative government and protection of individual rights. The Russian liberal movement won mass support in the 1905 revolution by demanding that the tsarist regime renounce absolute rule and grant its subjects the rights of citizens in constitutional democracy. A similar set of demands united the Young Turks in their 1908 revolt against the sultan of the Ottoman Empire. Two years earlier in Persia, the shah was forced by his political opposition to grant the country a liberal constitution. And in far-off China, Sun Yat-sen made the promise of democracy as important as that of nationalist renewal in formulating the program for his new Nationalist Party (Guomindang) following the collapse of the empire in 1911.

None of these liberal revolutions could claim to have fully succeeded in bringing freedom and justice to their people. The promises made were unattainable when leaders fought for power, or when the new regime lost mass support by failing to address social and economic grievances. These regimes had their greatest chance of keeping that support when, as in Mexico, liberals clearly demonstrated their commitment to defend the nation. Nationalism and liberalism together could remake the political map of the world. But opportunities to do so depended on finding the means of satisfying the pressing economic needs of the working masses.

The prosperity of the West in the period before 1914 helps explain the attractiveness of Western liberalism. Social discontent erupted now and then in serious conflicts, but none so great as to threaten democratic rule. And to visitors from non-Western lands, the benefits of industrial society appeared real and closely tied to the liberal program. They were correct, at least, in judging industrialism an economic success.

The Industrial Revolution had, in many ways, brought a remarkable improvement in western peoples' standard of living. Opportunities in the late nineteenth century for individual advancement increased. The extraordinary productivity of the new technology—applied in agriculture as well as industry—and of the factory system provided food and shelter for a European population twice as large in 1900 as in 1800. The greatest hardship—and the areas of massive migration to the Western Hemisphere—was in eastern and southern Europe, where industrialization had just begun. Cities expanded everywhere, their inhabitants enjoying on an average better living conditions than ever before. They attracted migrants from the countryside who sought an escape from rural poverty. Disappointment awaited many new urban dwellers, but still they came. By the first years of the twentieth century, urbanization had created major metropolitan areas throughout the West.

Within these cities, family and class relations experienced dramatic changes. The older business classes were closely tied to industrial production and commerce. At the turn of the century, the fastest growing middle-class occupations were in professional employment, ranging from bank clerk to doctor and lawyer. New terms appeared, such as "white collar," to designate a large array of new jobs that required secondary and advanced education. The poor population had little hope of qualifying, for social barriers and inadequate education still stood in their way. A few unmarried women from the middle classes were able to enter educational institutions to acquire advanced training, but most had to accept positions such as schoolteacher or nurse. Even then, custom dictated that upon marriage a woman must immediately abandon outside work. To be a wife was, in that social sphere, synonymous with being a housewife. In the Victorian Age, power and wealth lay in the hands of middle-class men.

Although fewer workers than ever before suffered constant privation, their labor too often stunted their bodies and shortened their lives. Work depended on economic demand and the needs of private businesses. Depression meant unemployment and hardship. In the early twentieth century, governments did little or nothing to help those unable to work. They still honored the old precept that "God helps those who help themselves."

Profound social and cultural changes were underway among the lower classes in the West. They were beginning to enjoy a share of the benefits of the industrial economy. Adult life expectancy improved, largely as a result of improved diets and hygiene among the laboring classes. Literacy was becoming widespread as a result of universal elementary education. Worker family life was beginning to adjust to new economic conditions. Improved health and food brought longer life expectancy and lower infant mortality. At the same time, birth-control methods became widely available among the middle and working classes. Birth rates were declining throughout the West by the late nineteenth century as families chose to have fewer children than before. The most obvious explanation for this trend was the widespread confidence that most children would survive to adulthood and would thus be able to contribute to the care of elderly parents. The era when three out of four infants died before the age of ten was gone. Small families could share more easily the family's resources while still giving the parents the satisfaction to seeing several children grow to adulthood. This trend, called the "demographic transition" (the decline in an entire society of birth rates), signaled the end of Europe's population explosion of the previous century. The same demographic process, one of the most important means to balance resources and human needs, began to spread to other parts of the world later in the twentieth century.

In these ways, the faith in progress shared by most Westerners reflected tangible improvements in their lives. Marvels of technology were a source of wonder. Motion pictures, the new product of the combination of photographic film and electric light, enchanted viewers with escapist tales of romance, comedy, and adventure. The social conflicts and nationalist passions that divided Western societies hinted at a darker future. *Modernity* is the term by which we refer to both these new social and economic conditions and the cultural attitudes which emerged from the passionate intellectual debates generated by these changes. These trends set a pattern that repeated itself later on other continents. Progress and confrontation were two sides to the history of the twentieth century, a time of greater upheaval than ever in human history.

The Origins of the First World War

Within this new, industrial world, other disturbing signs of conflict had surfaced by the turn of the century. The states of Europe had a long history of war. During the nineteenth century, hostilities had involved few countries and lasted only a short time. By the end of the century this "long peace" was showing serious weaknesses. Nationalism appeared to be aggravating antagonism among European peoples. The Industrial Revolution made possible the construction of new, far more effective instruments of war. And the prosperity of the turn of the century gave governments the funds to engage in massive rearmament programs. When new military conflicts erupted, they were fought in ways that observers knew were revolutionizing warfare. The American Civil War had offered European military observers a good opportunity to grasp the changes underway. Until another great war came, however, most army generals never measured the true scale of bloodshed that warfare could extract from nation-states in arms.

The origins of the European conflict lay in unresolved international issues within Europe itself. Relations among the new empires outside the borders of Europe provoked occasional bitter disputes, but all were settled by negotiation. Imperial claims to territory were not essential to the strategic, diplomatic, or economic needs of the European states. These needs defined what diplomats understood as *interests of state* (or

national interests). The protection of these interests constituted the principal goal of their states' foreign policy.

In the realm of international relations, the independence of these states (their "sovereignty") insured that their leaders were free to decide what these interests were and how they were to be promoted and defended. No international organization restrained their freedom of action; no effective international law set limits on the use of warfare to resolve conflicts. Certain diplomatic conventions did seek to distinguish between combatants, who might kill and be killed, and civilians, theoretically protected from such mayhem on land and on sea. The sovereignty of each state meant that its leaders had the ultimate choice between war and peace.

In those circumstances, European diplomats had come to judge the relative strength or weakness of their countries in terms of the *balance of power*, that is, the relative might of their state and allied states as opposed to that of rival countries. Depending upon their international ambitions, they might be satisfied with a balance sufficient to deter war, or might seek to swing the balance in their favor in order, by intimidation if not actual war, to achieve international gains. None considered war an end in itself. It was the ultimate means that their government or other states might use to attain certain diplomatic objectives.

By the early twentieth century, the major states of Europe had come together in two antagonistic alliances. The choices of allies followed from decisions of national interest made in each state. The new German Empire, created in 1871 in a war against France, chose to join forces with the Austro-Hungarian Empire, which was in need of support against rival states (especially Russia) on its southern and eastern borders. This alliance became known as the Central Powers. French leaders, unwilling to accept the loss of its eastern provinces to Germany in a war fought in 1870, looked for aid to the Russian Empire. Russia, in turn, was prepared to welcome the French alliance to prevent Austria-Hungary and Germany from becoming the dominant powers on the borders of the weak Ottoman Empire, where Russia also sought to extend its influence.

Finally, the British government in the first decades of the century concluded that the principal danger to its imperial interests and strategic defenses was the German Empire's ambitious program of a large navy and imperial expansion in the Middle East. For that reason, it chose to settle its long-standing grievances with its rivals for empire, Russia and France. It quietly began to put together with them the pieces of an informal alliance against Germany. In each case, interests of state dictated the choice of allies. Both major alliances were defensive in intent. Still, they became the basis on both sides for war plans intended in case of hostilities to insure a quick defeat of the rival alliance.

In this tense situation, the event that triggered the war occurred in the city of Sarajevo, capital of the province of Bosnia inhabited by Serb-speaking peoples and ruled by the Austro-Hungarian Empire. The Black Hand terrorists who in late June, 1914, assassinated the Austrian Grand Duke, heir to the throne of the empire, justified their deed as an act for the national liberation of the Serbian peoples. They were citizens of the empire, but their loyalties lay with their nationalist cause and their obedience to their terrorist organization. Confrontation was their objective. In this, they succeeded beyond their wildest dreams.

Slightly over a month later, the states in the European alliances were at war. This dramatic outcome was not the result of any government's plan of conquest. Leaders on both sides struggled to resolve the dispute peaceably, but used the threat of war to make clear their determination to achieve their objectives. A point was reached when generals demanded the power to respond to those threats, taking out of the hands of diplomats the decision for war. In that sense, the outbreak of the war was an accidental event over which statesmen had no control. It represented a cautionary tale for political leaders later in the century (including President Kennedy in the Cuban missile crisis of 1962) seeking to understand how they could avoid unintentionally causing another, even more terrible war.

The first move was the decision by the Austrian government, backed by Germany, to end the independence of the Serbian state. The assassination provided Austria with the pretext in late July to declare war on Serbia. Both Austrian and German leaders expected Russia to protest, but not to risk war over Serbia. They were only partially correct, for to demonstrate its support for Serbia the Russian government ordered the mobilization of its army on the western (German and Austrian) frontier. The Russian action was the second step leading to European conflict. The German generals understood only the military implications of Russian mobilization, which threatened to block their own war plans. They convinced their emperor that war was inevitable unless the Russian government stopped its call-up of troops. But the Russian leaders refused to back down. Claiming that Germany was threatened with invasion, the German emperor declared war on the Russian Empire and France. When German troops marched into neutral Belgium in their drive to encircle the French armies, the British government judged its own national security at risk and joined the conflict on the side of the French. The local Austrian-Serbian war had become a general European war.

Why had peace in Europe come to an end? The debate over the causes of the First

World War began with the first shots and continues to this day. Two general theories have emerged out of the research and interpretations of historians. One places principal responsibility on the conditions that exacerbated international conflict in those years. It points to the aggressive colonial conquests worsening relations among states, to the nationalist hostility dividing peoples of Europe, to the armaments race tempting the best-armed state to prefer war to diplomatic compromise, and to the alliance system creating hostile groups of states. In this perspective, no one state was to blame, for all contributed to the worsening of relations and to the preparations for war. Another, more persuasive theory isolates specifically the expansionist plans of the German Empire and the dangerous German-Austrian decision in 1914 to destroy Serbia. By identifying aggressive policies implemented by German and Austrian leaders, it holds these governments responsible for the chain of events leading to the outbreak of war.

SUMMARY

Before the First World War, the stability and might of empires had rested on the power of their armies, on the cultural and religious traditions that legitimated their authority, and on the economic resources that sustained the enormous apparatus of empire. The fall of the Chinese Empire revealed that ancient empires could not rely on the loyalty of their people in the face of economic hardship and defeat at the hands of foreign states. The success of the Japanese Empire, on the contrary, suggested that the key to survival lay in adapting to a country's needs the political institutions and industrial technology of the Western empires. Japanese leaders had good reason to congratulate themselves on having forced their people to incorporate Western customs and practices.

These new empires had created a new form of imperial rule for their conquered territories. Inventions in science and technology made accessible lands previously beyond their reach. These same tools of empire made possible more intensive economic exploitation of their colonies than ever before, and permitted closer political control over the colonial peoples than earlier. Their railroads and telegraphs facilitated communication and transportation, drawing together colonies and homeland, and binding together colonial territories. The borders that they drew around their colonies became tangible boundaries to the imperial administrators and to the peoples enclosed within them. The names that these Western officials, ethnographers, and geographers gave to these peoples were often arbitrary, and the authority granted local rulers of tribes bore little resemblance to traditional tribal ways. Yet these colonial practices embedded themselves in the life of the colonies just as firmly as the ports, railroads, and telegraphs that the empires constructed.

The fate of these empires rested ultimately on their ability to settle their conflicts without recourse to war. Their failure to resolve the Balkan conflict of 1914 marked, in hindsight, the end of the period of Western imperial triumph. The First World War was the end of a long period of empire-building in Asia and Africa, and of peace within Europe. Though some Marxists argued that the war was the product of the internal weakness and conflicts of the capitalist system, doomed soon to collapse, the immediate origins of the war lay primarily in terrible blunders made by Europe's political leadership. Ultimately, their greatest failure was their inability to understand that war was no longer merely an instrument for achieving national interests. Warfare in the industrial age had become more destructive than ever before. When the new weapons of war were employed by the nation-states of Europe against one another, war destroyed much that had been the pride of European civilization.

DATES WORTH REMEMBERING

1900 World population about 1.5 billion
1900 Boxer Revolt in China
1899–1902 Boer War
1901 Discovery of Iranian Oil
1904 U.S. policy of intervention in Central America
1904–1905 Russo-Japanese War
1905 First Russian Revolution
1906 Young Turk movement in Ottoman Empire
1907 Great Britain in informal alliance with France and Russia
1910 German military aid to Ottoman Empire
1911 Fall of Chinese Empire
1914 Opening of Panama Canal
1914, 1916 U.S. intervention in Mexican revolution
1914 Outbreak of First World War

RECOMMENDED READING

Perspectives on Modern World History

Eric Hobsbawm, *The Age of Extremes: A History of the World, 1914–1991* (1995). A personal, critical view of this century.
*William McNeill, *The Rise of the West: A History of the Human Community* (1963). Despite the title, a history of major civilizations and the importance to their rise of cultural exchange.

Empires and Nations

*Benedict Anderson, *Imagined Communities: Reflections on the Origin and Spread of Nationalism* (revised edition, 1991). Very influential inquiry into the emergence of nationalism, with special attention to the role played by colonialism.
Raymond Betts, *The False Dawn: European Imperialism in the Nineteenth Century* (1875). A brief but succinct interpretation of the new European colonial empires.
Basil Davidson, *Africa in Modern History: The Search for a New Society* (1978). Study of the impact of European empires on Africa.
*David Headrick, *The Tools of Empire: Technology and European Imperialism in the Nineteenth Century* (1981). A perceptive discussion of the role of new inventions in European colonial expansion; also *The Tentacles of Progress: Technology Transfer in the Age of Imperialism, 1850–1940* (1987), carrying the story into the colonies themselves.
Friedrich Katz, *The Life and Times of Pancho Villa* (1998). Saga of one of the leaders of the Mexican Revolution, who went from outlaw to revolutionary to nationalist leader.

Memoirs, Novels, and Visual Aids

*Ivo Andric, *The Bridge on the Drina* (1959). Fascinating fictional history of Bosnia, as experienced by a Muslim–Christian community and its 300-year bridge that brought peoples together until warring states destroyed it in 1914.
*Joseph Conrad, *Almeyer's Folly* (1895). Sardonic view of Europeans in the East Indies, by the Western novelist most intrigued by imperialism.
*Rudyard Kipling, *Kim* (1901). The greatest of English colonial novels and a vivid portrait of British India.

---

*indicates book is available in paperback

CHAPTER TWO

Empires in War and Revolution, 1914–1930

The great test of the new empires came in 1914, when a local conflict on the borders of the Austro-Hungarian Empire unexpectedly began a major war among European states. Soon distant Asian empires and then the United States joined in. At the end of the First World War, several empires in Europe vanished, the victims of war and internal unrest. In the closing years of that war, influential political voices even put in doubt the right of empires to rule colonial peoples—in somewhat timid language by the president of the United States, and in violent terms by the leaders of a new revolutionary state in Russia.

The years that followed the close of the First World War were a period of recovery. Just as no one could have anticipated the extent of destruction wrought by the war, no one could have foreseen the historic changes set in motion by the war. The world was in many respects a different place, and its future appeared radically new to some. Revo-

lutionary visions of social liberation of working masses and of colonial liberation from imperial rule, propounded by the leaders of the new Russian state, echoed throughout the world. The cultural and economic influence of the United States remained a potent heritage of the late war years even after its political leaders retreated from European politics. The war had undermined international economic relations to such an extent that it prepared the way for the severe economic recession that began in the late 1920s. The yearning for a return to prewar conditions was great, especially within Great Britain and France. Their empires emerged from postwar negotiations larger than ever, but their human and material resources proved inadequate for the diplomatic and imperial challenges that lay ahead.

The end of the First World War resolved the question of which states would dominate Europe. Gone were the German, Austrian, and Russian empires. The Western powers were victorious. They set the terms for peace that leaders of the defeated states were forced to accept. The peace plans of the United States appeared for a time to set the terms of that settlement. They had little chance to succeed, however, when in the early 1920s the United States withdrew from active participation in political life in Europe. Its absence from the League of Nations seriously weakened hopes for international peacekeeping. The peace established by the victory of the Allies was built on fragile foundations.

Even before war ended in western Europe, a political revolution had begun within the borders of the Russian Empire. The revolutionary changes undertaken by Lenin and his Communist (Bolshevik) Party destroyed, within a few years, the old Russian social and political order. The old institutions of empire were gone. So, too, were the laws, passed during the revolutionary months of 1917, that had laid the foundations for a liberal democracy and a market economy. The Communists anticipated that their revolution would prepare the way for a socialist society in Russia. In those years, their vision of revolutionary transformation extended as well to the entire world.

Western expectations for a return to prosperity rested on the recovery of their industrial economies after the dislocations of war. Success depended as well on the capacity of the world economy to function again as a free market. But the European war had devoured too much wealth for these wishes to become reality. Disagreement over war reparations from Germany and the repayment of war loans from the United States unsettled economic reconstruction for years after the war. The United States possessed the most prosperous economy of the world. The U.S. government's refusal to lower tariffs seriously hampered free trade and set severe limits on the expansion of European foreign commerce. In the mid-1920s, U.S. private banks and investment institutions financial took a direct hand in European economic recovery. When U.S. investors threw away much of that wealth in the speculative boom and bust of the late 1920s, the United States retreated from the world economy. The absence of the United States from international economic affairs worsened and deepened the global depression of the 1930. The Western world could not return to the comfortable conditions that it had enjoyed before the First World War.

WAR AND PEACE IN EUROPE

The First World War lasted four years. It was fought in Europe on two major fronts almost until the end. The eastern front pitted German and Austrian forces against the armies of the Russian Empire. Russia's collapse in 1917 brought that fighting soon to stop when a new Russian government capitulated. In the west, the fighting continued until the Western Allies had forced Germany to sue for an armistice. The war's terrible damage ensured that, in many ways, Europe was never the same again.

The war's battlefields soon stretched into distant lands. The Ottoman Empire joined the Central Powers to defeat the Russian Empire. It did indirectly succeed, for its blockade on commerce to Russia from the Mediterranean contributed to the internal hardship that led to the Russian Revolution. But it had to share in the 1918 defeat of the Central Powers, and soon vanished from the map of the Middle East. All the peoples of that region had to rebuild their lives within new states. Even East Asia shared in a small way in the fighting when the Japanese Empire joined the Allies, moving troops to seize German territory in China, and later joining Allied forces sent to Russia to defeat the

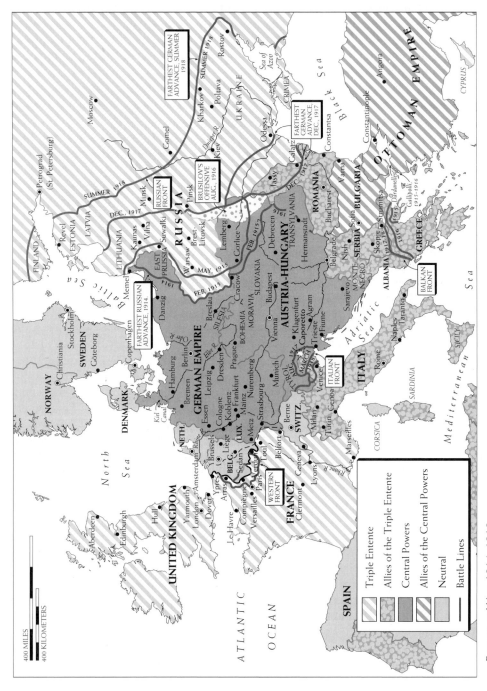

Europe at War, 1914–1918

Communists. That war was international in scope and in its impact. Peacemakers attempted to extend their settlement around the world, creating the League of Nations to stop aggressive wars against member states anywhere. Peace, like the war itself, was a global affair.

The European War

The outcome of the great battles in 1914 on the eastern and western fronts frustrated the prewar military plans for quick victory (see map on facing page). All the military offensives failed to attain their objectives. All the armies remained at the end of these battles with sufficient force to continue fighting. Even the little Serbian army succeeded (for a short time) in holding back the Austrian army's campaign to conquer their small border country. Defensive weapons, especially the mobile, rapid-firing cannon and machine guns, proved the real victors. The most accurate image of war by year's end were the deep trenches, where the combatants sought meager protection from massive artillery bombardments and which, ultimately, became graves for millions of soldiers. The loss of human life was enormous, but military leaders everywhere promised that they would soon achieve victory. In the words of one embittered German officer, the First World War became "the grave of nations."

The likelihood of a long war forced war leaders to alter peacetime social and economic practices. Millions of able-bodied men left for the front, many never to return. The acute labor shortage overrode earlier prejudices against women in the economy. Wartime opportunities and patriotic appeals for their help encouraged women to leave their homes to work on the "home front." For many married women, work in factories could not make up for the loss of their husband's income and increased family needs at a time of worsening living conditions. Governments were forced to enact special powers to impose a wartime economy. They fixed prices, allocated scarce resources to industry, and distributed goods by rationing. Germany confronted the most serious shortages and introduced the most rigorous state economic controls. One German industrialist concluded that wartime state intervention in economic affairs had been "an education in state socialism."

The results proved satisfactory for the armies, much less so for the working classes. Even Russia's armies by 1916 were adequately supplied with the necessities of war. But social conflicts, muted in the early months of the war, returned as the cost of living for the laboring population rose. The price for war production was the decline in the standard of living of the workers. Wage increases lagged behind prices. Farmers preferred to deal in the black market rather than to sell under government regulations. Russia experienced the most serious shortages and, as a consequence, the greatest social unrest. In the winter of 1916–1917, a wave of strikes spread among factory workers in Russian cities. It was sparked partly by food shortages, partly by opposition to the tsarist regime. Female workers, newly recruited to the workforce, took an active part in the movement; they joined in strikes and antiwar demonstrations. In February 1917, women employed in factories in Petrograd (formerly St. Petersburg) went on strike on Women's Day (a new socialist holiday) to demand more food. Their cries of "Give us bread!" attracted the support of other workers. They started the movement that within two weeks overthrew the Russian Empire.

The failure of war plans to bring quick victory transformed the European conflict into a world war. Battles were fought on sea as well as on land. The British navy quickly took control of the high seas and declared a

"The Home Front": Royal Shell Factory, England (*Imperial War Museum/Hoover Institution*)

naval blockade of Germany. German admirals turned to a new arm of naval warfare, the submarine. They counted on this new weapon of war to destroy the British warships and merchant vessels carrying goods to Great Britain and France.

Both the British and the French governments mobilized the manpower and the resources of their empires for the war effort. Great Britain declared all colonies and Dominion lands, where the white settlers had received self-government, to be at war with the Central Powers. Troops from Canada, New Zealand, Australia, and South Africa participated in the battles on the western front and fought in Africa and the Middle East. So, too, did the 1.5 million soldiers of the Indian Army. France mobilized one-half million troops from its African and Asian colonies. These multiethnic forces constituted visible evidence of the importance of the colonies to the war effort.

The demands placed on colonial peoples produced resistance as well as collaboration. Food and industrial production from the empires proved vital to meet war needs, but created serious shortages in the colonies. For the first time, laborers from non-Western lands were needed in the Western economies to replace the men called to arms. Labor conscription was imposed on colonial subjects; their reluctance to serve was in

The Western Front: British Raiding Party, July 1917 (*Imperial War Museum/Hoover Institution*)

places so great it led to open resistance. The war worsened relations between imperial rulers and colonial subjects from Russian Central Asia, where Turkic nomadic tribes fled to China rather than assist the tsarist forces, and to French West Africa, where a revolt among African tribes greeted French efforts to mobilize labor brigades.

Both the Allies and the Central Powers enlarged their military alliances. In the fall of 1914, Germany succeeded in bringing the Ottoman Empire into the war on its side. Ottoman leaders believed the Central Powers would soon win and looked forward to restoring their dominance in the Middle East. Their decision opened a new front in the Middle East against Russia and Great Britain and threatened British control of the Suez Canal. The Allies, in turn, were able in 1915 to obtain the support of Italy, whose

leaders hoped to conquer territory from Austria-Hungary along the Adriatic Sea. That same year, the Japanese government joined the Allies, declaring war on Germany. It immediately seized German-controlled territory in China. It also forced the Chinese government to concede special economic privileges in north China. Japan found in wartime conditions new possibilities to expand its power in East Asia. The world war brought into play for the first time a global balance of power.

Governments undertook secret as well as public propaganda efforts to foment political conflicts in the enemy camp. The German state gave secret financial backing to Russian antiwar revolutionary parties. The Allies for their part aided independence parties among Austria-Hungary's minority nationalities. This propaganda war had its greatest impact on the Ottoman Empire. Exiled Armenian nationalists, backed by Russia, called on Armenians in Ottoman lands to fight the Turks. In retaliation, Ottoman authorities forcibly evacuated 1.5 million Armenians from eastern Turkey. In the course of this violent operation, the Turks were responsible for the death of a half-million or more Armenians. These Armenian massacres set a pattern, repeated many times later in the century, of mass persecution in wartime motivated by ethnic hatred.

The British government turned the hope of national homelands in the Middle East into a weapon to win the backing of minority peoples living in the Ottoman Empire. It supported a national uprising among the Bedouin tribes of Arabia, promising that their victory would lead to an Arab state in the Middle East. The most famous agent in this campaign was the British officer T. E. Lawrence. Bedouin irregular cavalry forces, headed by the Hashemite clan under Hussein Ibn Ali (see Spotlight, pp. 56–58), fought for two years against the Ottomans alongside regular British forces.

At the same time, the British government agreed with Zionist leaders to turn the Palestinian province of the Ottoman Empire into a Jewish homeland. The Balfour Declaration of 1917 made public the British decision to support the Zionists. It promised that, should the Allies win the war, free Jewish immigration to Palestine would become a reality. Encouraging both Arab and Jewish dreams of Middle Eastern lands of their own was an inconsistent policy with potentially explosive consequences. At the time, the British leaders placed victory in war above all other considerations.

The confrontation in Europe between the Central Powers and the Allies remained the key to the outcome of the war. The Central Powers achieved their greatest victories on the eastern front. The Russian Empire lacked competent leadership, and its war resources could not match those of the German Empire. In 1915, German armies pushed Russian forces hundreds of miles into the interior of Russia, causing more than one million Russian casualties. This victory did not force Russia to capitulate, but it did heighten political and social opposition to the regime of Emperor Nicholas II. By the winter of 1917, hostility toward the government's conduct of the war had spread throughout the population of the empire, including even the generals in the army. In March 1917 (February by the calendar then in use in Russia), a wave of strikes protesting shortages quickly turned into political demonstrations under banners calling for the end of the rule of Nicholas II. When he ordered his army to repress the uprising, the Petrograd garrison troops mutinied and joined the demonstrators. Even his own generals chose to support the political revolution rather than to risk civil strife to protect a monarch in whom they had lost all confidence. Nicholas had to abdicate; the empire had fallen.

In this political revolution, the war proved crucial in deciding who would in the end take control of the country. Soldiers in the army and workers from the factories were both disillusioned with the sacrifices demanded by the war. Most political leaders refused a policy of capitulation to Germany. Instead they demanded that the people accept the hardships of war until German forces were driven from Russia. Only the radical socialist party movement under the leadership of Vladimir Lenin was prepared to offer the population "peace, bread, and land." That November, the Bolshevik Party (which changed its name in 1918 to Communist Party) ordered its supporters to seize power by armed insurrection. It was a reckless act, for the party had few adherents and the country was rapidly headed toward economic chaos and civil war. The first action of the new Bolshevik regime was to declare an armistice with the forces of the Central Powers.

In the negotiations, the German military leaders demanded a peace of capitulation. Their terms included the occupation by their armies of all the eastern territory that they had conquered. They also demanded Russian recognition of a new eastern European state, Ukraine. Its peoples had lived under the Russian Empire. Ukrainian nationalists took advantage of the empire's collapse to create their own nation-state, under German protection. Lenin had to accept these terms in March 1918. By then, the Russian army had ceased to exist as a fighting force. The Treaty of Brest-Litovsk reduced the size of the new Russian state to the old northern lands of seventeenth-century Muscovite Russia. It made the German Empire the dominant power in eastern Europe. The Central Powers achieved their greatest triumph in the war. Their negotiators at Brest-Litovsk had allowed the Communists to hold onto power a little longer, but it seemed a worthwhile risk. They expected that victory on the western front would quickly follow.

Allied Victory

Instead of German victory on the western front, the war ended that November with the victory of the Allies and the collapse of the empires of the Central Powers. The reason for this sudden reversal of fortunes was the presence alongside the French and British forces of a new ally, the United States. Without massive American military supplies followed by hundreds of thousands of fresh troops from overseas, the German Empire would probably have won the struggle for mastery in Europe. With them, the tide of battle changed and so, too, did the diplomatic aims of the Allies. For the first time in its history, the United States became an important actor in deciding the outcome of a foreign war and the shape of the peace to follow.

U.S. entry into the war was linked initially with economic ties binding America to the Allies. It was propelled forward by the political objectives pursued by the new U.S president, Woodrow Wilson. Nominated by the Democratic Party on a reform platform in 1912, he held out an optimistic vision of economic opportunity and political freedom. His program won him the presidency that year. When war came to Europe two years later, his emphasis on business interest incited him to protect U.S. foreign trade, crucial for the country's recovery from a recent recession. His democratic ideals gave him the conviction that the United States ought to defend the principles of freedom and rule of law in the world at large. This vision pushed him into the ill-advised intervention in 1916 in the Mexican Revolution. It also explains his decision in 1917 to declare war on the Central Powers.

The outbreak of the First World War ended the isolation of the United States from European affairs. Wilson's first response was to proclaim U.S. neutrality in the conflict. He urged Americans to be "neutral in fact as well as in name, impartial in thought as well as in action." Noninvolvement was difficult to maintain. Still, for three years he managed to keep the United States out of the conflict.

Despite his efforts to defend U.S. neutrality, Wilson faced the reality of the demand for American goods by the Allies. France and Great Britain took full advantage of the U.S. market and placed enormous orders for food, clothing, and munitions. The result was that by 1916, U.S. trade to the Allies had increased four times, and the American economy boomed. Real U.S. neutrality in the war proved impossible to achieve.

The immediate cause of U.S. entry into the war was the German submarine blockade of the British Isles. Commanders of the German navy ordered a total blockade to begin in February 1917. That decision permitted German submarines to attack and sink even vessels of neutral countries. They had made the wildly optimistic promise to the German government that their fleet of 200 submarines could strangle the British economy and force Great Britain to capitulate. They realized that neutral shipping, including U.S. freighters, would be sunk and that this action would be a legitimate reason for a U.S. declaration of war. But they were confident German victory would come long before U.S. forces could reach Europe. It was a fatal blunder.

The German naval blockade was the decisive factor behind Wilson's decision for war. That spring one of every four freighters headed for British ports was sunk by German torpedoes. Among them were U.S. ships. Wilson probably considered the German threat to U.S. security the most important consideration. Still, his convictions, and his need to persuade the American public to support his action, led him to explain the U.S. declaration of war as a moral issue. In April 1917, Wilson asked Congress to declare war on the Central Powers. He condemned German "warfare against mankind," and pledged that the United States was not fighting for "conquest or domination" but rather for "the ultimate peace of the world and for the liberation of its peoples. The world must be made safe for democracy." His speech presented the war in terms of an idealistic plan for political progress and international peace.

Before Wilson could implement his peace plan, the Allies had to defeat the Central Powers. Their first achievement was defeating the German submarine blockade. By late 1917, combined forces of the British and U.S. navies had cut shipping losses in half. When the time came to send U.S. troops to Europe, not one troop ship was sunk. An entire year elapsed, however, before the army was prepared to fight in France. Finally, in the summer of 1918, hundreds of thousands of U.S. infantry began arriving every month on the continent. They formed by that fall a separate armed force of one million troops. Their presence destroyed the last German hope of victory on the western front.

The military collapse of the Central Powers came that summer and fall. Outnumbered and increasingly demoralized, German troops began a steady, uninterrupted retreat across France and Belgium. Small Allied armies in northern Italy and Greece broke through Austrian defenses that fall. At the same time, British and Arab forces in the Middle East advanced through Palestine to the city of Damascus. By late October, the Central Powers ceased to exist as a military alliance. The Austrian armies broke up into units of the various nationalities of the empire, each prepared to protect its own national territory. The empire quickly fell apart, paving the way for the creation of new nation-states of southeastern Europe. Close to victory that spring, in the fall of 1918 the Central Powers were headed toward defeat and revolutionary chaos. In October, the German government asked for an armistice.

The terms of armistice and the plans for peace came principally from the United States. President Wilson's radical plan for a "peace without victors" appealed to an enormous audience in Europe. As important, the economic and military might of the United States forced even those European politicians who were skeptical of Wilson's vision to heed his pronouncements. His principal statement of war aims came in the Fourteen Points, presented in January 1918. Three points were central to Wilson's plan:

national self-determination for all European peoples, democratic governments, and the creation of an international association of states to protect the peace. Wilson placed the prestige and the power of the United States behind liberalism and nationalism.

Victory on Wilson's terms came in early November. On November 11, 1918, the armistice went into effect. The Middle Eastern lands of the Ottoman Empire were in the hands of Arab rebels and Allied armies. The German and Austrian emperors abdicated and their empires collapsed. Nationalist leaders of the Slavic peoples in lands controlled by Germany and Austria-Hungary proclaimed in late October the formation of the nation-states of Poland, Czechoslovakia, and Yugoslavia.

After four years of bloody fighting, the shape of the postwar world to come was much less real than the destruction of the old, prewar life. The casualties of battle, numbering everywhere in the millions, were concentrated among draft-age men. The war resulted in 10 million deaths and another 20 million wounded. No one could anticipate what would be the fate of the territory of the former Russian Empire, where a brutal civil war was already underway between the Communists and their enemies. War and revolution were radically altering the course of human history.

Peacemaking and the League of Nations

President Wilson's goal of a "peace without victors or vanquished" held enormous appeal in a Europe sick of war. His vision for the postwar world called for self-determination for all large ethnic populations. His hope for a just settlement rested on the assumption that peoples, granted national and democratic rights, would never again support militaristic leaders. With the assis-

tance of an international organization that would coordinate the collective resistance to aggression, states would trade freely among themselves and prosper without fear of war. Wilson looked to an end to power politics to ensure real progress for humanity.

But the leaders of the victorious European powers held firmly to the idea of a peace of victors. The defeated states would have to sacrifice territory and wealth to ensure the permanence of the settlement: "To the victors belong the spoils." Great Britain and France looked forward to dividing between themselves the Middle Eastern lands of the Ottoman Empire and Germany's African colonies. Japan had seized German-controlled territory in China. Issues of national self-determination had a secondary place in this peace program. The bitter debates among Western statesmen reflected in large part the profound difference dividing them on the very nature of peace.

The peace negotiations were dominated by the American delegation. Wilson went to Paris determined to "fight for what is right." His influence there was great, for he was at the peak of his popularity in Europe. Behind the scenes, European statesmen knew also that the economic aid from the United States was essential for the first steps of postwar recovery. The American Relief Administration (ARA) brought public and private assistance to the war-ravaged economies of central Europe. It provided food to millions and made available technical assistance to reopen coal mines and railroads. The head of the ARA, Herbert Hoover, ran the operation with a combination of practical engineering efficiency, charitable concern for social hardship, and faith in the ultimate triumph of free enterprise. He argued that his aim was "to prevent Europe from going Bolshevik," but his larger vision looked forward to the restoration of a prosperous Europe and markets for U.S. goods. The popularity of the ARA revealed the importance to Europe of U.S. help in the recovery from war.

The peace provisions proved in the end to be more conciliatory than punitive. They reflected the complexity of the territorial questions and incorporated the conflicting objectives of national self-determination, security against Germany, and collective peacekeeping. Four provisions of the treaties embodied the major features of the compromise reached after months of negotiations. These were (1) a weakened but still united German nation-state; (2) new Polish and Czechoslovak nation-states in Central Europe; (3) German reparations for war damages; and (4) the formation of the League of Nations.

The fate of Germany dominated all other issues. Germany had to cede to France territory on the Rhine it had seized in 1871, and to give up eastern lands to the new Polish state. Still, the new Germany emerged almost as large as the prewar German Empire. The German industrial and agricultural economy was still potentially the most productive in Europe. Its population remained the largest of any European country except Soviet Russia. French acceptance of these provisions came only after the negotiators agreed to limit the size of the German army to 100,000 men and to "demilitarize" the Rhineland region of western Germany, that is, to forbid the German army to occupy the area. Wilson promised that the United States would participate in a defense treaty with France and Great Britain. He made this commitment to satisfy French demands for help in maintaining the new balance of power. In return, the French government collaborated in the formation of the League of Nations. In his eyes, this was the real promise of future peace.

Two new nation-states in eastern Europe received special consideration at the conference. Both Poland and Czechoslovakia bordered on Germany. Both governments claimed territory on their western borders that, though inhabited by Germans, they believed vital for protection against future German expansionist wars. Poland received a "corridor" of territory extending from Polish-inhabited lands to the Baltic coast. The German port city of Danzig, outlet to that sea, became an "international city." Out of the northern provinces of the Austro-Hungarian Empire emerged the state of Czechoslovakia. It grouped in one nation-state separate Slavic peoples (Czechs and Slovaks) granted the right to govern themselves in lands with large minorities of Germans and Hungarians. Czechoslovakia's borders, like those of Poland, represented a compromise between the principles of national self-determination and security. It, too, could survive a new war with Germany only with the military backing of the Western states.

Of all the issues that aroused public debate, reparations for war damages provoked the most controversy in the immediate postwar years. The Allied states all agreed to seek reparations from Germany, a centuries-old practice by which the losers in war had to make financial payment to the victors. In private, they realized European economic recovery and heavy German reparations were incompatible. They sought U.S. financial aid in rebuilding their countries' devastated areas. Their first request was that the American government reduce the size of their war debts, which totaled more than $15 billion. Wilson's refusal to consider making what he called this "gift" forced the Allies to use reparations in place of U.S. aid for reconstruction. From this decision began a long and bitter controversy with Germany. The reparations requirement and the loss of territory in the east appeared to many Germans to be proof that the Versailles Treaty was an unjust, punitive peace. In 1919, German leaders could do nothing to alter the peace settlement. Their country was occupied by Allied troops and was still under naval blockade. Despite their bitter opposition, they had to sign the treaty.

Wilson's plan for an international peacekeeping organization took the form of the League of Nations. He believed the project to be the key to peace. He thought that collaboration among states committed to peaceful relations could replace the balance-of-power system of alliances and armaments. His plan was visionary in its treatment of colonialism, and even more so in its new approach to peacekeeping. Wilson's principle of self-determination appeared to nationalists from colonial lands to signify the end of European colonial rule. It only began that process, however. The Covenant, or binding agreement among League members stipulated that the territories of the German colonies in Africa and the Ottoman Empire's Arab lands were to be administered temporarily by Allied states as "mandated territories." The Allied governments were responsible for preparing these peoples for self-rule, to come sometime in the future. The Covenant said nothing about the colonies of the Allied empires. In these terms, it was a compromise between European colonialism and the new principles defended by Wilson.

The heart of Wilson's plan to end militarism and war was contained in Article Ten of the League Covenant. It declared that each signatory to the document would "respect and preserve against external aggression the territorial integrity and political independence of all members of the League." Governments were to act together to stop aggression by declaring war on the aggressor if necessary. This key provision required that states decide the question of war not only in conformity with their own national interests but also in view of the welfare of other states. It tied the League to the defense of the provisions of the treaties drawn up that year, including the new frontiers and the restrictions on German military power.

Nowhere was Wilson's internationalist idealism more clearly revealed. Article Ten introduced a radical new concept into international relations—the idea of a community of states bound together by a moral commitment to peace and to collective action, regardless of their immediate interests, to protect all independent states against aggression. This vision of a new international order represented to Wilson "the hope of the world." But later in 1919, he failed to win the backing of his own Congress. A large number of U.S. senators were hostile to his concept of international peacekeeping. When Wilson refused any compromise, the Senate rejected the entire Versailles Treaty.

That action represented only one step in the resurgence of isolationism in the United States. Among political leaders, domestic issues became their paramount concern. Business came first for the Republican Party, triumphant in the 1920 elections. International debts had to be paid, even if the debts were incurred in a war that the United States had made its own. International commerce provided a means to promote the sales of American goods abroad. To appease domestic producers, the government enacted in 1922 a protective tariff law to restrict foreign imports, though the restraint on trade made more difficult the repayment by European states of their war debts. In those years, antiforeign pressure among Americans led the government to enact the first restrictive immigration act in American history. The United States applied to international relations the shortsighted precept that private American interests assured the public good.

Foreign alliances had no place in these isolationist policies. The U.S. government never ratified the Versailles Treaty; never joined the League of Nations, and never became a member of a defensive alliance with Great Britain and France to protect them against Germany. With hindsight, it is clear that the withdrawal of the United States from European affairs crippled attempts to rebuild a stable system of international relations. The government's decision to treat war debts and trade relations solely from the perspective of U.S. short-term interests was just as damaging. The United States, having altered profoundly the outcome of the war, left the preservation of the peace to the European states.

Europe's Postwar Revival

The reparations issue proved the source of greatest dispute among European states in the years after 1919. It lay at the heart of the difficulties confronting the West in establishing a new international financial system. Finally, after a long delay, the International Reparations Commission agreed in 1921 on a total of $35 billion. It presented the Germans with a crushing collective mortgage on their financial future.

The German government refused to accept this decision. For two years, the conflict grew until the French military occupied the Ruhr valley, a key industrial region of western Germany. Germans organized a resistance effort, financed by the government and at the cost of hyperinflation that destroyed the value of the German currency and wiped out the savings of middle-class Germans. Both French and German leaders understood that they could not afford the human and economic price exacted by the dispute. Conciliation was the only path to a stable peace. The conflict over reparations involved all European governments, who were determined to avoid another war. It hurt investors and banking interests in Europe and the United States. Their plans for economic expansion and profitable financial investments were disrupted by the political crisis and the uncertainty caused by the Ruhr occupation.

The Republican administration in Washington realized that its war debts would be paid only when German reparations payments flowed regularly to the Allied states. It encouraged U.S. bankers to take part in the formulation of a workable reparations plan. The entire settlement depended, in fact, on the participation of the American financial community, called upon to join in a sort of "dollar diplomacy" in Europe.

Charles Dawes, an American banker, agreed to head a commission to prepare the plan. Presented to a conference in London in 1924, this Dawes plan set up a regular schedule of yearly German payments, starting at $250 million. At the same time, it provided for a massive loan of private funds, mostly from U.S. banks, to assist the German government in making its first payments. In effect, the Dawes plan put in place a cumbersome system for international financial exchange. German reparations flowed primarily to France and to Great Britain. These countries applied the funds to regular payments on their war debts to the United States. American investors continued their profitable short-term loans to Germany, and from there the dollars returned once again in the form of reparations.

Dollars sustained the system. This, in turn, reassured international financial interests. Until 1928, high German interest rates attracted U.S. investment, which by then totaled nearly $3 billion. U.S. loans dwindled after investors in 1928 decided that Wall Street stock market speculation was more rewarding. Then the financial system began to fall apart. While it worked, governments avoided conflict, and U.S. dollars fueled the growth of the international economy.

The second part of the new European agreement on peace put together in the mid-

1920s consisted of a security treaty among all the major European states. In 1925, leaders of the German, British, and French governments met in Locarno, Switzerland, to negotiate a comprehensive diplomatic settlement. The Locarno Treaty was a compromise. European major powers recognized the permanence of the western frontiers of Germany, and Germany accepted the permanent demilitarization of the Rhineland. It left that region bordering on France and Belgium free of its troops (and soon of any foreign troops as well after the occupation forces left). Germany was admitted to the League of Nations. It was an act that symbolized the country's restored status as a major power in Europe.

In those years, the League of Nations still held out the hope that, as Wilson had promised, it could function as a collective force to protect peace. In the absence of the United States, Great Britain and France became the most important participants. Their leaders collaborated in debates of the executive council, where proposals emerged to settle peacefully conflicts among smaller states. As long as no great power was involved, the League appeared capable of preventing war. The World Court, made up of jurists elected by the League, offered its assistance to settle international disputes when the quarreling states accepted outside mediation. A third important component to the new system was the International Labor Organization, whose purpose was to improve working conditions around the world. "Social justice," proclaimed the charter of the organization, was the only sound basis for "the establishment of universal peace."

All three organizations operated on the principle that war was avoidable, that the causes for disputes among states were subject to discussion and compromise, and that statesmen would agree to international cooperation to protect the interests of their nations. The activities of the League represented a new direction in international affairs. Still, it lacked important participants. The consensus among delegates rested on its narrow membership, excluding all colonial peoples and the Soviet Union. Its promises to resist aggression sounded hollow in the absence of the most powerful Western state, the United States. The ideal of the peaceful resolution of international disputes had become a European affair.

Germany's ability to become a liberal democracy was crucial to the success of the postwar system. The founders of the new republic, whose capital was in the city of Weimar, created a constitutional order modeled somewhat on the French system. A majority of German voters indicated throughout the 1920s that they preferred parties committed to democratic rule. Conservative politicians, originally hostile to the Weimar regime, came to accept its existence. Enthusiasm for freedom appeared less noticeable than satisfaction at improved economic conditions of the mid-1920s. It may well be, as one German historian claimed at the time, that "a secret Germany" longed for "its emperors and heroes." If so, the yearning did not disrupt the political stability of those years. In the prosperous years of the late 1920s, political and social hostility was muted and the parliamentary government was able to ensure political stability. Germany appeared a part of the new European system.

COMMUNIST DICTATORSHIP AND THE SOVIET UNION

The Communist Party's seizure of power in Russia in November 1917, abruptly halted the country's slow evolution toward a democratic state and capitalistic economy. Lenin's regime defied Russian patriots and Western Allies alike by signing a separate peace with Germany. Enemies of the Communists united in 1918 to fight the new regime in a bloody civil war. In the course of the three years of fighting, peasants took up arms to seize the property of landlords, workers expelled industrialists from their factories and prosperous urban families from their homes, and nationalist movements fought to create nation-states for peoples previously under Russian imperial rule.

Lenin's Communist Party forged the instruments of power that permitted the new Soviet state to survive. It was the key to the triumph of the revolutionary regime. It imposed a new ideological blueprint on Russia, and later served as a model for revolutionary movements in other countries. It provided the world the first example of an attempt to create a socialist society for humanity. It offered, too, concrete lessons in how a small group of political militants could change the course of history.

Lenin and the Communist Revolution

Lenin and his Communist Party had, in the years before 1917, emerged as a unique radical revolutionary party. They shared with other socialist movements in Europe the belief that the theories of Karl Marx made clear the reasons for the oppression that humanity had endured over the millennia. They drew from his theories the conviction that history would necessarily end with the triumph of a classless society that satisfied the needs and desires of humanity. They differed from other socialists in arguing that only their party possessed the knowledge and organization to lead the revolution of the masses. When the First World War erupted, Lenin went one step further in predicting that the war had brought the entire Western capitalist world to the brink of revolution. To their political enemies, the Communists appeared a dangerous group of fanatics. To their followers in Russia, they seemed a dynamic, disciplined movement capable of leading the country out of its crisis and of creating a just, egalitarian society.

They drew their inspiration directly from Marxism. Three aspects of this socialist ideology were key to their revolutionary hopes. First, Marx's theories convinced them that the ownership of productive property, determining wealth and poverty, indicated who controlled the repressive powers of the state. In nineteenth-century Europe, capitalism gave power to the property owners (the "bourgeoisie"), responsible for the technological wonders and the productivity of the industrial economy. It also created a vast population of workers without property, the "proletariat," who were deprived of the benefits of this economic system and of the political might to alter this system. Second, Marx argued that workers everywhere would come to realize the necessity of overthrowing capitalism. Marxism gave the Communists a global view of capitalism and class conflict.

They accepted Marx's theory of violent historical progress. He affirmed that capitalism, like feudalism before it, was fated to collapse in a violent revolution. In its place, the working masses would move rapidly through a stage of socialist society (with collective control of the means of production) to an egalitarian, communist society guaranteeing everyone a satisfactory life. Wealth would be shared following the simple formula: "From each according to their abilities, to each according to their needs." This conviction that a perfect society can be created on earth is called "utopianism."

Lenin and other Russian Communists like Leon Trotsky were in a hurry to reach this goal. They argued that a "permanent revolution" would carry backward Russia, under their leadership, straight to socialism. To the Communists, this faith justified all the hardships and all the brutality that accompanied their revolutionary crusade to transform Russia.

Their seizure of power in November 1917, came with the support of large numbers of

Russia's lower classes. Key to their victory was the backing of workers and mutinous soldiers who had organized new revolutionary assemblies, called "soviets." Lenin's slogan "All Power to the Soviets" became a call for insurrection. On November 7 (October 25 by the Russian calendar), his forces overthrew the liberal government that had briefly ruled after the fall of the tsarist empire. In its place, they proclaimed the creation of a revolutionary state they called the "Russian Soviet Socialist Republic." John Reed, an American journalist who had traveled to Russia to support their movement, termed that upheaval "ten days that shook the world."

The new regime made bitter enemies within Russia and in the West. Opponents came from all sides. Russian patriots condemned their "sell-out" to the Central Powers. Liberals warned of their ruthless dictatorship. Peasant farmers fought back when the Communists seized their crops to feed workers and their new revolutionary Red Army. Nationalists from the borderlands of the former empire mobilized their meager forces to resist conquest of their peoples by the Communists.

These opponents were aided by Russia's former wartime allies. The Communists had broken all the ties that had bound Russia to the West. Lenin's regime abandoned the wartime alliance to make peace with Germany. It canceled the entire Russian foreign debt, totaling several billion dollars, owed largely to Western states and investors. Its

Lenin Addressing Soldiers of the Red Army, 1919 (*Novosti/Corbis-Bettmann*)

acts of defiance gave meaning to its appeal for "international socialist revolution." Its very existence challenged the international order that the Allies sought to create following victory over Germany.

By mid-1918, Russia was in the grips of a bitter civil war. The Soviet government lost control of large parts of the country, seized by anticommunist "White" forces intent on overthrowing the revolutionary state. Lenin responded by creating the weapons of a revolutionary warfare state. The country's resources had to be mobilized for war to destroy the "counter-revolution." The tsar and his family, state prisoners in the distant Ural mountains, became victims in this cruel war. Lenin ordered their execution to avoid the risk that they might escape to the Whites. Lenin described his state as a "fortress besieged by world capital" and demanded that it become "a single military camp." The Red Army grew to five million men, and a new secret police received the authority to imprison and execute any suspected counter-revolutionaries, class enemies, and enemy agents. To provide the necessary supplies for the army, an economic policy went into effect that included nationalization (i.e., state ownership) of all industry and commerce.

The struggle to win the civil war had a permanent impact on the new regime, for it put in place the basic institutions of communist dictatorship and trained communist militants in the ruthless methods of class war. Government policy making and appointments were under the control of the central leadership in a new party committee, the Politburo. There, Lenin and close advisers such as Leon Trotsky and Joseph Stalin made the decisions that determined the survival of their new state. Their remarkable leadership ability, and the backing of zealous party members, were the key factors in the defeat of the anticommunist forces in the civil war. Allied arms and financial aid could not compensate for the incompetence and disorganization of the Whites. The Reds emerged in 1920 the victors.

The Soviet Union and the World

The end of the Russian civil war left the country in a state of economic collapse. Its population was living in impoverished conditions, epidemic diseases raged among millions of people with little or no medical care, and large cities were emptied after townspeople fled to the countryside in search of food. No one knows how many died in the fighting or as a result of disease and famine. Industrial production fell to one-fourth of prewar levels. At war's end, the country could not continue living in such terrible conditions. Communist dictatorship remained the foundation of their new regime, but economic ruin and social unrest forced them to temporarily renounce their hopes to create a socialist society. In 1921, they had to permit private ownership of land and small business (called the "New Economic Policy") to help with the recovery of the economy. They permitted churches to reopen (temporarily) and allowed limited freedom of the press. They even welcomed foreign industrialists (including the Ford Motor Company) to help rebuild their ruined factories and to train their engineers and workers in modern methods of production. The concessions were distasteful, but they in no way weakened the dictatorship of the Communist Party.

The Communists also had to compromise their internationalist ideals. State-building required that they confront the powerful nationalist loyalties of peoples in their multiethnic country. In the course of the civil war, nationalists in some of these areas had created independent states, often under the protection of the Western powers. Ukraine and Finland had received the support of Germany until 1919; the Baltic republics and the small states in the Caucasus obtained the backing of Great Britain. Fearful of Russia and communist intervention, these eastern European nationalists counted on Western help to insure the independence of their new nation-states. But by 1920, the Allies had withdrawn all their forces from borderlands regions stretching as far east as the Caucasus region. A year later, the Japanese troops pulled out of eastern Siberia. The Soviet government did, in fact, seize those borderlands where they faced little risk of war with the West. The Red Army brought Soviet power on the point of its bayonets to Ukraine, the Caucasus lands, and the Central Asian territories north of Iran and Afghanistan. In the south and the east, the frontiers of the Soviet state resembled those of the Russian Empire.

These ethnically diverse peoples presented the Communists with a serious dilemma. The Marxist revolutionary scenario had assumed that the working masses in a new socialist society were largely factory workers shaped by industrialism and ready to renounce pernicious nationalist passions. Russia and Ukraine had, by 1917, a sizeable working class; nowhere else, however, within the new state had industrialization made a significant impact. In these terms, the Soviet peoples were largely backward. Yet in many areas nationalist movements had still won sizeable support.

In these circumstances, the Soviet leaders had to make concessions to non-Russian nationalism. The various peoples received special recognition in a new federal constitution. Adopted in 1924, it created the Union of Soviet Socialist Republics (U.S.S.R., or Soviet Union). Separate national republics grouped the various major peoples of the country, who received a separate territory with its own Soviet "republican" government. Ultimately they numbered fifteen, including Soviet Ukraine, Soviet Armenia, Soviet Azerbaijan, and Soviet Kazakhstan. Within these lands, minority ethnic groups were also granted small, "autonomous" territories. This bizarre (and in the event irreversible) acknowledgment of ethnic communities created a constitutional order in the Soviet Union based on "native" lands for all its peoples (called "ethno-territorial nationalism"). The Communists assumed that nationalism was a stage in the development of backward peoples. They could reconcile themselves to this compromise in the short term, since their leaders in Moscow made all-important decisions for the entire country. The Soviet Union was a new form of colonial empire.

In other ways, this revolutionary state quickly demonstrated its rejection of "bourgeois" customs and practices. For the Communists, learning was a necessary tool to bring their message to the masses. They organized a campaign to wipe out illiteracy. Secondary and higher-educational institutions were opened to the lower classes through special "worker colleges" to provide rapid remedial training.

The socialist vision of a new era of human achievement following the fall of capitalism included the end of the unequal treatment of women. Communist leaders protested that they were not feminists—true liberation for women could result only from proletarian revolution, according to Marxism. Their new laws did incorporate many ideas from the feminist movement. Marriage became a simple legal procedure and divorce could be obtained on demand. Abortions were legalized. Communist writers extolled the "new Soviet woman," equal in her rights to men and free in her decisions on marriage and the family. In reality, women's place in Russian society changed slowly, particularly among the peasant population. In the cities and among party members, women were able to assert their new rights. The wife of Joseph Stalin, Nadezhda Allilueva, was an emancipated woman with both a family and a career in party work. A scandal among many Westerners, the Soviet feminist reforms later became a model for other countries.

The Communists' attention was directed in those years as much to international as to internal affairs. Their ideological view of global relations blurred the lines between the two, for their vision of revolution recognized no state boundaries. They organized a new international revolutionary organization, the Communist (Third) International, to assist foreign revolutions. They confronted a world which, in their opinion, was dominated by the imperialist Western powers. They expected another war against capitalist states to be as inevitable as the class conflict they foresaw in industrial societies. The Communist International grew rapidly in size as revolutionary Marxists joined from around the world. Its members accepted the leadership of Moscow and on Russian orders reshaped their parties on the Leninist model.

In colonial lands beyond the Soviet borders, the Soviet leaders gave encouragement and support to nationalist movements seeking to end imperial domination. In their view of the conflict with the Western states, this growing resistance to Western colonial rule signaled a new stage in the impending collapse of world capitalism. They sponsored in 1920 a Conference of Oppressed Peoples, held in Baku, a Soviet city on the Caspian Sea between Europe and Asia. It was the first time Asian and African socialists gathered in one place, and the spirit of the meeting was revolutionary. The delegates urged the peoples of colonial lands to rise up against their imperialist rulers. This appeal sought the end of colonial empires. It placed the communist regime firmly on the side of nationalist revolutions in non-Western lands.

The most serious domestic concern among the Communists in those years was the struggle over political leadership. That conflict was linked to the urgent need to find the right policies to bring socialism to their country. Their uncertainty as to the country's future was worsened by the unexpected death of Lenin in early 1924. He had suffered several severe strokes a year earlier, forcing him to abandon policy making to his colleagues on the party's governing committee, the Politburo. In the next three years, Joseph Stalin emerged as Lenin's heir. This revolutionary leader, of Georgian nationality from the region of the Caucasus mountains, was eager to take on this task. His ruthlessness troubled his colleagues. Even Lenin, who had earlier supported him, warned in 1922 that Stalin's personality and methods of rule were "brutal" and destructive. But after his death, Stalin won the other Communists to his side. He promised to correct his errors and won their backing on a program to end quickly the remnants of "capitalism." In 1929, they chose him to be the new leader of the Communist Party. The fate of the Soviet Union rested in his hands.

The economic policies that Lenin had put in place in 1921 proved successful, but their very success created new economic problems. Industry continued to be run by the state, dependent on state subsidies for reconstruction and expansion. The Soviet government formed a State Planning Commission to provide the "scientific guidance" for state economic policy. How was wealth to be channeled toward industrial growth? They knew an industrial economy was the real material base for socialism. But in Russia, the peasant farmers held in their hands the largest share of the productive property of the Russian economy and remained still the vast majority of the population. Communists debated these questions at length, searching for the guidelines by which they could plan their country's economic future. They realized that no help was available from outside and that they, as one of their leaders stated, had on their own to "build socialism in one country." Stalin's task at the end of the 1920s was to resolve this fundamental problem. His choice was to launch a new social revolution.

THE VICTORIOUS EMPIRES IN THE NON-WESTERN WORLD

Wilson and Lenin had, each in his own way, presented peoples beyond the borders of Europe with a vision of liberation from colonial rule. At the same time, the First World War had brought together workers and soldiers from the colonies mobilized by the Western empires in a common cause. It gave them the opportunity to learn of new political ideologies such as socialism and to appreciate their own potential role in ending colonial domination. Everywhere hopes were raised for better economic conditions and for the recognition of national rights. The war and the Russian Revolution marked the beginning of the decline of colonial empires.

Leaders of the Western empires came slowly to the realization that their powers were in decline. One of the fruits of victory that they claimed was overseas territory previously ruled by their defeated enemies. In the short term, the Allies had concrete plans for expanding their control of the non-Western world. They redrew the political map of large parts of the Middle East where the Ottoman Empire had once ruled. Imperial administrators in Western colonial empires grudgingly acknowledged that their "sacred trust," as the British referred to their relations with colonial peoples, included preparing these peoples for self-rule. In Africa, the German colonies passed under Allied "mandate," authorized by the League of Nations.

In the Far East, the victorious states introduced a new formula for international collaboration. There the ideal defended by the

League of Nations for an end to power politics seemed in the 1920s to become reality. Treaties signed in 1920–1921 among several major powers included the renunciation of their spheres of influence in Chinese and Russian lands, and the drastic reduction of their naval armaments in the Pacific Ocean. The treaties seemed to bring Wilson's internationalist ideals to life. They came about through decisions made in Tokyo, Washington, and London regarding peace and political power. The fate of the peace was in Allied hands.

The Allies in the Middle East

The First World War had destroyed the old order in the Middle East. The fighting had given Arab forces a role in the defeat of the Ottoman Empire, and had kindled Arab nationalist hopes. It had also strengthened the influence of Great Britain and France in the area. During the war, Arab tribesmen under the Hashemite clan, headed by Hussein Ibn Ali, had organized—with the assistance of the British—a revolt against Ottoman rule. They had extended their conquest as far north as the city of Damascus, capital of the Syrian province whose borders extended from the eastern shores of the Mediterranean to the province of Iraq.

Hussein and his followers fixed their ambitions on the creation of a large Arab state in the Middle East. It was a vision inspired by the Arab empires of the Middle Ages. But in the twentieth century the Arab-speaking population was divided into many religious and clan groups. Muslims were split into five separate sects (of which the Sunni were the most important); the smaller Christian population was divided as well. These divisions prevented the emergence of a united nationalist movement and permitted the Allied states to divide and rule separate parts of the area.

❋ SPOTLIGHT: Hussein Ibn Ali ❋

The Bedouin tribes of Arabia helped transform the Middle East in the course of the First World War. These Arabic-speaking nomadic peoples had once before emerged as a force for historical change. In the eighth century they had united under the leadership of their prophet, Mohammed, to carry the Muslim faith on the point of their sword in conquering a vast empire. Their leader in the First World War was Hussein Ibn Ali (1854–1931). His family (the Hashemites) traced its ancestry back to Mohammed. In the mid-nineteenth century, it had received from the Ottoman sultan the right to rule the most holy places of Islam, Mecca and Medina, in the area of the Arabian peninsula known as the Hijaz. His was not the only powerful clan in Arabia. Further to the east, Ibn Saud had become sheik (the leader) of a large group of Bedouin tribes. His authority rested on his skill in organizing his followers for successful raids on their neighboring Arabs, bringing them the plunder that was one of the main sources of livelihood of the Bedouin. He also headed a militant Muslim movement, the Wahabis, who claimed that they alone understood the revealed religious truths of Islam. Ibn Saud and Hussein were bitter rivals for power. Hussein proclaimed that his cause was pan-Arabism and the creation of an Arab nation.

In 1908, Hussein received from the Ottoman sultan the eminent (and profitable) post of sharif of Hijaz. He was the protector of Islam's greatest shrines, which were the destination each year of hundreds of thousands of Muslim pilgrims from around the world. Hussein took his religious obligation

seriously. He was also aware of his stature as leader of Arab peoples (most of whom were Muslims). It was a time when a few Arab nationalists had begun organizing secret organizations whose goal was to create a great Arab nation-state in the Middle East. Hussein knew of their subversive activities, for which they risked death at the hands of their Ottoman Turk rulers. Even before the war he revealed to them his desire to support, even to take the lead, in this pan-Arab movement (see Highlight, pp. 62–64). He may well have sympathized with their dream; he also saw in it the chance to become king of the Arabs.

The war between the Allies and the Ottoman Empire gave him the opportunity that he was seeking. The British Empire had responsibility for the war against the Ottoman forces. It had few troops, mostly from its India Army, to send to the Middle East. To generate more support, British agents went to the Bedouin tribes with offers of generous financial backing if they supported the Allies. This was an alluring offer to the poor nomads and provided leaders such as Hussein the means to build up their military forces. The Bedouin nomads were skilled at cavalry attacks, on horseback or camelback, traveling rapidly through the desert to attack their enemies. Hussein's son Faisal was a skilled leader in war. In 1915, Hussein informed the British that he was prepared to champion the cause of "the whole Arab nation" and would lead the Arabs against the Ottoman Turks. He admitted later that the claim was of his own making. But without his leadership the Arabs were lost, he told his British agent privately, since they were "ignorant and disunited." In return, he demanded "the independence of the Arab country." That vast land was to be his kingdom.

His goal appeared for a time to be within his reach. The British government accepted his lofty title of Arab champion. It sent him generous funds, munitions, and a talented agent to collaborate in the Arab revolt. T. E. Lawrence had in the prewar years studied the history of the Arabs and learned their language. The war changed his life as dramatically as that of Hussein. He believed fervently in the Arab national cause, and saw in Hussein and his Bedouin warriors the instrument to forge Arab unity under British (and his own) guidance. After a U.S. war correspondent publicized his exploits in that war, he became known as "Lawrence of Arabia."

In 1916, Hussein launched the Arab Revolt. It took the form of a proclamation promising to "serve Islam and to reclaim the glory of Muslims." The Arab nation could hope for new religious and political influence, as it once had in the great medieval empires. The proclamation made grandiose promises; the reality of the revolt was less awe-inspiring but no less dramatic.

Hussein remained the inspirational leader of the uprising. His son Faisal, aided by T. E. Lawrence, led the military campaign. The two men fought in the first year against forces far larger and better armed than their own. The appeal to Arabs launched by Hussein brought only a smattering of backing. Most Arabs in towns and farming villages distrusted the Bedouin fighters and remained obedient to their Ottoman rulers. The Bedouin had to fight a guerrilla war in the first years, for they were isolated from

the British troops defending the Suez Canal. Hussein's prospects brightened when Faisal and Lawrence, campaigning with the Bedouin cavalry in a Bedouin robe, successfully defeated the Turks along the rail line from Medina to Jerusalem. They joined forces with the British, who by then were moving up the Mediterranean coast. The campaign proceeded slowly until, in late 1917, the combined British–Arab army captured Jerusalem. The city whose holy sites were sacred to Muslims, Christians, and Jews had become a prize of war. In the course of the next year, Arabs and British forces fought their way north until they reached Damascus, capital of Syria and (to Hussein's supporters) of the future Arab state. The Allied victory in November of that year over the Ottoman Empire seemed to promise the achievement of Hussein's dream of his Arab kingdom.

But peacemaking proved for him a terrible disappointment. His son Faisal accompanied Lawrence to the Paris peace negotiations. They already had learned that the British government had in the course of the war promised a homeland in the Palestinian province to the Jews. Great Britain had as well signed with the French government an agreement to partition the lands of the Fertile Crescent. Hussein faced for the first time the realities of great-power politics. The treaties that settled the fate of the territories of the Ottoman Empire came without his participation or agreement. They did not create a single unified state for the Arabs. Instead, several smaller states, "mandated" to the French and British governments and armed forces, emerged in its place. The British created thrones in two of these countries, Iraq and Jordan, for Hussein's sons Faisal and Abdullah. They left Hussein himself with only his original territory of Hijaz, to which he received the title of king. It was a sorry reward. When the British requested that Hussein officially approve the Paris peace treaties, he refused. His fortunes owed nothing to the peacemaking.

Hussein's deception was partly caused by Allied betrayal, partly by the flaws in his own grandiose project. His Arab Revolt had never won the backing even of all the Bedouin tribes of Arabia. Hussein was right in deploring the disunity of the Arabic-speaking peoples of the Middle East. But he deluded himself into believing that his own prestige and authority could overcome these divisions. He refused to accept his petty stature as king of Hijaz. He came to believe that he could capitalize on his religious eminence as ruler of the Muslim Holy Places. When in 1924 the Turkish government abolished the position of caliph, held previously by the sultan, Hussein claimed the title for himself. His effort to become religious leader of the enormous Sunni Muslim community in the Middle East appeared impious to fervent Muslims. It gave Ibn Saud the excuse he needed to launch his Bedouin forces against Hussein.

Hussein could not even win that small war. He fled the Hijaz, leaving Ibn Saud to create the kingdom of Saudi Arabia. His life ended in exile at the court of his son Abdullah in the kingdom of Jordan. Arab unity was a lost cause; so, too, was his dream of becoming king of the Arabs.

Leader of the Arab Revolt: Hussein Ibn Ali (*Imperial War Museum/Hoover Institution*)

During the Allied peace negotiations, the British and French governments laid claim to the area in the Middle East known as the "Fertile Crescent." They had agreed in a secret wartime treaty to partition that part of Ottoman territory extending south from Turkey to the Red Sea and Persian Gulf, and west from the Mediterranean Sea to the borders of Persia. Their claims followed in the tradition of the earlier imperial scramble for colonies. They were not bothered by the wartime promises made by the British government to support the creation of an "Arab nation-state" in that territory. But Wilson's plans for a new world order that included the right of colonial peoples to self-rule stood in the way of their seizure of Ottoman lands.

The Paris peace negotiators reached a compromise by creating the "mandate" system. It was applied to all non-Western lands that had previously been colonies of the defeated Central Powers. In the Middle East, Great Britain and France assumed responsibility in "mandated" territories to provide "advice and assistance" until the peoples there could rule themselves. French and British troops and colonial administrators took, in one form or another, indirect control of these governments. French troops moved into the former Ottoman province of Syria, expelling Hussein's forces from Damascus and setting up the state of Syria and a new country called Lebanon, where most Christians lived. The British controlled the mandated states of Iraq and Transjordan (the area between Iraq and the Jordan River, later called the Kingdom of Jordan). The Arabic-speaking peoples were a majority in all these countries.

Other peoples receive no recognition. The Armenians' dream of a large state in eastern Anatolia, where their medieval kingdom had once flourished, was crushed when the Soviet Union and Turkey agreed to a common frontier. The Kurdish peoples, living in the mountains of the northern Middle East, found themselves a minority group scattered among the new countries. State-building in that region had no solid national basis.

In all these territories Arabs enjoyed a small degree of political autonomy. They chose their political leaders. These governments had to collaborate with the Western empires. Real independence remained a vague promise. Any Arab political protest was immediately repressed. The presence of large oil fields, discovered and exploited first in Persia then in Iraq and Syria, made a sphere of influence in the region a question of vital strategic importance to Western governments. These new states suffered from internal political and social hostility separating rival ethnic and religious groups. No Arab leader enjoyed the support of the masses as Gandhi did in India; no one could

prevent the partition of this region by the Western powers. Rivalries among Arab leaders and Allied states led to the emergence of rival states. This proved the permanent inheritance of postwar peacemaking in the Middle East.

In the territory of Palestine, the peace settlement created a serious conflict among the population. It was divided between Arabs and a growing Jewish community. The 1917 Balfour Declaration had promised a "national home for the Jewish people." The British government honored that pledge, allowing Jews to migrate to that coastal region from which twenty centuries earlier they had been expelled by the Roman Empire. The number of Jewish settlers, most from eastern Europe, rose slowly to 180,000 at the end of the 1920s. In those years, Arabs (Christians and Muslims) totaled 750,000. British leaders set limits on Jewish settlement and assured the Arab population the protection of their political and economic rights. But the Arabs in the region were adamantly opposed to Jewish settlement and refused to cooperate in governing the mandated territory as long as Britain supported this policy.

The key to understanding Arab opposition to the presence of Jewish settlers lies in the ethnic differences separating Arabs and Jews. Ottoman rulers had not practiced religious persecution, treating both Jews and Christians as inferior subjects free to observe their religious customs. They had resisted the Zionist Organization's request to permit large-scale Jewish immigration. The British readiness to open Palestine to Jewish migration altered drastically the ethnic balance there. The postwar influx of Jewish migrants created in the midst of a large Arab population a growing community of settlers of European culture, often well-educated, economically enterprising, and nationalistic. The Jews bought Arab property to set up

400 MILES

400 KILOMETERS

North Sea

Baltic Sea

KARELIA

White Sea

Archangel

Dvina R.

NORWAY
Oslo

SWEDEN
Stockholm

FINLAND

Helsinki

L. Onega

L. Ladoga

Perm

UNITED
KINGDOM

DENMARK

Revel

ESTONIA

Leningrad
(Petrograd
1914-1924)

S O V I E T

Volga R.

Kama R.

Riga
LATVIA

Moscow

U N I O N

Samara

NETH.

Hamburg

Danzig

Kaunas

LITHUANIA

Smolensk

Ural R.

BEL.

GERMANY

Berlin

EAST
PRUSSIA

WHITE
RUSSIA

Saratov

LUX.

Rhine R.

RHINELAND

Weimar

Warsaw

POLAND

Brest-
Litovsk

LORRAINE
FRANCE

ALSACE

Prague

CZECHOSLOVAKIA

GALICIA

Lvov

Kiev

UKRAINE

Tsaritsyn

Volga R.

SWITZ.

Munich

Vienna

AUSTRIA

RUTHENIA

Dniester R.

Astrakhan

Milan

TYROL

Budapest

HUNGARY

TRAN-
SYLVANIA

MOLDAVIA

BESSARABIA

Dnieper R.

Don R.

Rostov

Fiume

BANAT

CROATIA

YUGOSLAVIA

ROMANIA

ITALY

BOSNIA

Belgrade

WALLACHIA

CRIMEA

*Caspian
Sea*

Rome

MONTE-
NEGRO

Bucharest

DOBRUJA

Baku

Adriatic Sea

SERBIA

Sofia

Black Sea

Batum

TRANSCAUCASIA

Tirana

BULGARIA

ALBANIA

TURK.

Istanbul

GREECE

Angora
(Ankara, 1930)

TURKEY
(Republic, 1923)

Tabriz

TUNISIA
(FR.)

SICILY

Mediterranean

MALTA (U.K.)

Smyrna
(Izmir, 1930)

Mosul

IRAN
(PERSIA)

Euphrates R.

Tigris R.

DODECANESE
IS. (IT.)

CRETE

CYPRUS
(U.K.)

Sea

SYRIA
(FR. MAND.)

Baghdad

IRAQ
(BR. MAND.)

PALESTINE
(BR. MAND.)

TRANS-JORDAN
(BR. MAND.)

EGYPT
(BR. INFLUENCE)

*Suez
Canal*

Cairo

SAUDI ARABIA
(1932)

*Persian
Gulf*

Austria-Hungary, 1914

Germany, 1914

Areas lost by Germany in 1919

Areas lost by Bulgaria

Areas lost by Russia

Areas lost by The Ottoman Empire

Europe and the Middle East after the First World War

businesses and to establish their communal farms ("kibbutz"). The Muslims of the area, all Arabic-speaking, remained closely bound to their communal customs; many still kept a pastoral way of life, and were unable to compete economically with the Jews. Religious disputes over access to the Holy Places of Jerusalem brought to a head conflicts whose roots lay in the deep differences separating the two communities.

In the absence of strong Arab leadership in Palestine, the leaders of rival Arab clans all declared publicly their opposition to the creation of a Jewish homeland. With their encouragement, anti-Jewish riots erupted first in 1921 and were repeated on a much larger scale in 1929. The Zionist Organization formed its own armed security forces. Palestine was becoming a land of communal hatred and sporadic ethnic conflict.

The British had no choice but to rule the Palestine mandate themselves. No Arab leaders would collaborate, and the British could not encourage the Jewish minority to assist in rule without provoking Arab violence. A British high commissioner governed with the assistance of imperial military forces. His task became increasingly difficult as Jewish migration accelerated in the early 1930s. The persecution of Jews in Europe forced increasing numbers to abandon their homes. The United States accepted only a relative handful following passage in the 1920s of the restrictive immigration law. Palestine was the Jews' last haven as well as their religious homeland.

This rapid increase in Jewish settlers set off in 1936 the most serious Arab revolt since the war. It lasted until 1938, with Arab guerrilla forces operating in the countryside and Jewish defense forces protecting their settlements from Arab attack. Before the uprising ended, several thousand lives (Arabs and Jews) were lost. By then, British leaders were seriously considering partitioning Palestine into separate Jewish and Arab regions. But

the proposal was unacceptable to Arab leaders. They denied the right of Jews to a Palestinian homeland, demanding that all Palestine be put under Arab rule. The two communities were irreconcilable.

Arab nationalism was strongest in the one state in the area untouched by the Paris peace settlements. At the outbreak of war, Great Britain had severed Egypt's ties to the Ottoman Empire, formally declaring the state a British protectorate. Wartime resistance to British rule encouraged Egyptian political leaders to appeal to the Allied peacemakers in 1919 for independence. When the British refused to allow the Egyptian delegation to leave the country, violent protest broke out in several cities. The nationalists formed their own party and organized a mass campaign against the British in support of Egyptian national independence.

Confronted with this opposition, the British leaders in 1923 proposed independence on the condition that the Egyptian government allow their military forces to remain in the Suez Canal zone. The canal remained as vital as ever to the security of their Asian empire. Still, granting Egypt its independence was a sign of Britain's declining imperial might. The Egyptians agreed to the compromise. Their state remained closely tied to Great Britain, but they were free to govern themselves.

Egypt became a constitutional monarchy, which left in place the Turkish monarch, who possessed very limited influence over policy. Power passed into the hands of the wealthy landowning elite possessing most of the farming lands along the Nile River. They were strongly influenced by Western (especially French) culture. They embodied a future in which progress for Egypt came from Western secular practices, not from the Muslim religion or Egyptian traditional ways. Many Egyptians were troubled by the influx of Western culture. One young nationalist student of the 1930s, Gamal Abdul Nasser, recalled later that "our spirits were still in the thirteenth century" but everywhere "the symptoms of the nineteenth and twentieth centuries infiltrated" Egyptian society.

The way of life of Egypt's Westernized elite provoked an organized movement to defend the practices and laws of the Muslim faith. Such an effort to enforce strict adherence to Islam is called "Muslim fundamentalism." In 1928, religious conservatives formed an organization, the Muslim Brotherhood, to uphold religious authority and Quranic law (the *Shari`a*). Their principal enemies were fellow Egyptians who supported secular education, civil marriage, and women's rights. The Brotherhood's methods of resistance included promoting Muslim religious practices and religious education. It organized mass street demonstrations to protest reforms, and even the assassination of political enemies. The Brotherhood appeared later in the century in other Arab lands where the introduction of Western secular practices and values threatened Islamic ways. After 1923, Egypt was freed from direct British control and became the leading independent Arab state in the Middle East. It could not escape the cultural and social tensions created by the Western international economy and secularization.

▧ HIGHLIGHT: Islam and Modernity ▧

Islam was the second-largest religion in the world at the beginning of the twentieth century. It was the dominant faith in lands stretching from northern Africa to the East Indies. The conquests of European colonial empires brought the peoples of these areas under Western rule. The defeat of the Ottoman Empire in the First World War brought down the last major independent state in the world governed by Muslim rulers. Islam remained a vital force among Muslim peoples. Some of their religious leaders began to work for the renewal of the Islamic faith as the means to isolate Muslims from the corrupting influence of Western culture. Other public leaders believed that the bonds that united the Muslim community formed the basis for new political movements capable of resisting the West by incorporating certain modern institutions and values. Slowly Islam adapted its message and action to meet the challenge of Western domination.

The doctrinal unity of Islam, like Judaism and Christianity, is founded on a sacred text. The Quran (also spelled Koran) is believed by Muslims to be the revelations of God as received by his prophet Mohammed, who lived in the Arabian Peninsula in the eighth century. That divine message defined the essential faith for Muslims, for whom there could be no other God and no other source of religious truth. Wherever they lived and whatever their own culture and language, the Quran, written in Arabic, gave them their religious language and prescribed their basic religious practices. Muslim scholars over the centuries had elaborated religious rules (the Shari`a) governing Muslim everyday life, including family law, marriage, inheritance, and much more. Customs varied from country to country. The requirement that women conceal their faces behind veils in public became increasingly common in many places. In these ways, the Islamic faith made itself a vital presence in the public and private affairs of many millions of Muslims.

The arrival of Western empires served in some ways to give greater scope and vigor to religious activities in the Muslim world. The growth of international and regional trade opened new markets in Asia and Africa. For many centuries, Muslim merchants had worked to make converts to Islam among the unbelievers (infidels) with whom they traded. This missionary work expanded along with commerce in the nineteenth and twentieth centuries, especially in colonial areas of sub-Saharan Africa. Christian missionaries there competed with Muslims, who had the advantage of preaching a faith that stood in opposition to the West.

The expanded sea and rail transportation was a boon also to Muslim pilgrims. Before, pilgrimage to Arabia was a dangerous and arduous trip, causing many deaths among pilgrims. Steamship lines and railroads opened a rapid and much safer route from Muslim lands to the holy places of Islam such as Istanbul, Jerusalem, and especially Mecca. A few Westerners traveled secretly to Mecca, and marveled at the devotion of so many Muslim pilgrims who came together from Asia, Africa, and the Middle East to fulfill the holiest of religious acts.

Despite these common traits, deep divisions had appeared within Islam in the millennium since Mohammed had preached the new faith. Like Christianity, Islam had splintered into religious movements, each claiming to be the only true observers of Mohammed's teaching. The largest of these was the Sunni Muslim community, over whom the sultan of the Ottoman Empire had claimed religious leadership as caliph. The next in size, though much smaller, was the Shi`a Muslim group, centered in Persia (Iran) and Mesopotamia (southern Iraq). Between

the two movements, disagreements led, at times, to violent conflict and religious persecution.

But these disputes mattered less to Muslim leaders in the early twentieth century than the challenge of Western colonialism. In this period, Western beliefs and practices became the source of two widely debated programs for reform among Muslim peoples. One was usually referred to by writers and political leaders as modernism, the other secularism. They identified modernism as the belief that certain characteristics of Western historical development were useful and constructive and had no damaging impact on religious faith. Muslim leaders included science and technology in particular under the label of modern, but some of them extended the list to public schooling in native languages and to knowledge useful in daily life. The most radical reformers even called for constitutional democracy.

The other major issue centered on secularism. This program emphasized the need to substitute civil codes for Muslim customary laws along with the introduction of modernist reforms. It was the most radical set of proposals. Its objective was the creation of a national community in which civil laws, not Islam, governed everyday life. Secularism rejected the claim of the Muslim authorities, guided by religious rules, to exercise legal judgment in the public affairs of the individual and the family (the secular sphere, as opposed to the religious sphere of worship). Marriage, property rights, and inheritance belonged to this secular sphere. Most Muslim religious leaders were vehemently opposed to secularism, since they found in it a deadly threat to the survival of the Muslim community and its spiritual values. They often linked it with materialism, which they understood to be personal gratification through material possessions to the neglect of spiritual duties. The issues raised by modernist and secularist reform programs went to the heart of the crisis confronting Islam.

These discussions emerged in many countries among Muslim scholars and public officials. They were debated most forcefully in the Ottoman Empire in the last decades of its existence. Islam's last independent empire appeared doomed unless drastic reforms of state and society were undertaken; leaders of state and religious authorities were deeply involved in this debate. Conservative religious leaders blamed the decline of the empire on the failure of its peoples and leaders to adhere to Islamic traditions. They called for isolation from Western influence, for the emigration of those Muslims under Western rule into Muslim-ruled lands, and for strict adherence to traditional Muslim practices. But they had no concrete proposals that would keep Western power and culture from intruding in Ottoman society.

The debates over a reform program raised the question of national loyalties within the vast community of Muslim believers. Those religious and political leaders whose program drew primarily on Muslim religious solidarity called their approach pan-Islamism. At heart, they relied on the strength of a revived and renewed Islamic community. They believed that the social responsibilities recognized by the Muslim faithful provided the foundations for new organizations of solidarity and defense of the faith. The Muslim Brotherhood took on these duties, first in Egypt, then in other Middle Eastern lands. They were confident that new, competent leaders would emerge from Islamic schools that taught the political and scientific knowledge of the West but stressed essential religious dogma and defended Muslim law. The

Ottoman sultan supported their cause, hoping that in his role as caliph his powers would expand over this invigorated Muslim community outside his empire.

Other leaders in Muslim lands refused to trust such half-measures of religious reform. They placed their hopes on the emergence of nationalism among their peoples. It had to be based on a shared language and culture. Writers from the Arabic-speaking world called their approach pan-Arabism. From these groups came strong supporters of the secularist program, for they backed reforms modeled closely on what they believed were the essential qualities of Western nation-states. They considered the Western empires to be the greatest obstacle to their ideas, but they were also prepared to cut Arab ties with the Ottoman Empire. For them, Allied victory in the First World War was a step toward realizing their own political goals.

Writers and leaders in areas where the population spoke Turkic languages called their national vision pan-Turkism. Turkic language and culture were the basis for this movement. Islam ceased to be an important guide in their political plans for the future. They believed all Turks should be equals within a national community. The movement emerged first among the Turkish people of the Ottoman Empire. Nationalists there denounced the disdain of the Ottoman elite toward ordinary Turkish people. To them, there could be no inferior subjects with the new Turkish nation. Their ideas spread to army officers in the sultan's army, defeated time and again by Western forces. After the empire's defeat in the First World War, these officers became the spearhead of a new Turkish national army. Their enemies were the Allies, but also the sultan and the Islamic religious authorities. Islam was divided once again, this time by nationalism.

Postwar Colonial Empires in Africa

The Allied peace settlements reached beyond the Middle East into sub-Saharan Africa. The European colonies there had become involved in the war, partly as a result of the acute need of the Western states for African raw materials and manpower, partly because fighting took place there between German and Allied forces. Then and after the war, Western industrial demand for minerals stimulated the expansion of mining, centered in South Africa and the Katanga (Shaba) area of the Belgian Congo. The recruitment of African workers from tribal areas to work in the mines and in other industries was enlarging the African labor force. It created a political problem for white rule in South Africa, where the racism of the Afrikaners (Boers) was shared to a lesser degree with other European migrants. To control these migrants, the South African government augmented its segregation policies to include a "pass" system. It required South African blacks to carry internal passports, severely restricting their right to residence in towns. In that country more than anywhere else in Africa, economic and social development was placing in doubt European domination.

Western colonial rule in Africa altered little in the years following the war. The Allies took control of all German colonies. Under the League's mandate system, they became "trustees" for the peoples there until they judged the population fit for self-rule. In effect, these areas were integrated into the colonial system established by the Western empires in Africa before the war. A handful of Western administrators governed vast territories, relying largely on African tribal leaders to carry out their orders. Both the French and the British encouraged Africans able to obtain Western education to work in their colonial administration. This small, educated elite constituted an important new group in the political life of Africa. Western medicine spread slowly beyond the cities into rural areas, providing assistance against the endemic tropical diseases afflicting the population in those lands.

The bulk of the African population had little contact with Westerners. The spread of cash crops altered the daily lives of farmers, making them more dependent than before on the market for their livelihood. An abiding hostility toward Western-imposed changes colored relations between colonizers and colonized. "They have given us a road we did not need," recalled one African tribal chief in the Belgian Congo, bringing "foreigners and enemies into our midst, making our women unclean, forcing us to a way of life that is not ours, planting crops we do not want, doing slaves' work. [They send] us [Christian] missions to destroy our belief." The presence of the Western colonial states created a clash of cultures that irrevocably altered the way of life of Africans.

The social and psychological stress of colonial rule opened the way to large-scale religious conversion to Christianity and to Islam. Muslim missionaries offered Africans a coherent religious dogma and a strong religious community. The Islamic faith spread rapidly in the postwar years in both East and West Africa, until in the latter region over half the population was Muslim. Christian missions, both Protestant and Catholic, usually worked with the backing of Western administrators. They offered the Africans who came to their centers basic social services, medical care, and schooling, as well as instruction in the Christian faith. Many factors explain the mass conversions to Christianity among Africans in the years after the First World War. Imperial conquest undermined the credibility of the old animistic beliefs and made Christianity the religion of the conqueror. Christianity provided a sort of cultural baggage for those Africans eager to learn and to profit from new economic and political conditions.

Under the pressure of Western colonialism, the old bonds of tribal unity were gradually dissolving. But the cultural and social void was filled very slowly with new institutions and ideologies. Religion itself became a source of dissent The high plains of west Africa became centers of Islam, while the peoples living in the coastal regions were more likely to convert to Christianity. The very process of conversion provoked dissension within the African community. The Nigerian writer Chinua Achebe, whose father had converted to Christianity during British colonial rule, remembered that as a child he and all those in his church community called themselves "'the people of the church'" and referred to all the non-Christians around them as "the heathen or even 'the people of nothing.'" Later in life he condemned this prejudice, but it remained a real source of divisiveness. The drama and tragedy of post-imperial Africa had their roots in the unsettling impact of the West.

New Empires in East Asia

Great power rivalries in East Asia led to a diplomatic settlement as important in its own way as the Paris treaties were for Europe and the Middle East. The end of the war left the Japanese Empire in a more powerful position than ever before. Its navy had the largest fleet in the eastern Pacific; its army was stronger than either the forces of the new Chinese Republic or the Soviet Red Army. At the beginning of the war, it had joined the Allied coalition, though its army and navy had taken no direct role in the European conflict. Those war years were a time of Japanese expansion onto the Asian mainland. Japanese leaders forced the Chinese government during the war to accept a Japanese sphere of influence in north China and Manchuria, subjecting its weakened neighbor to the same humiliating treatment

as the Western states had imposed earlier. Further north, the Allied decision in 1918 to intervene in the Russian civil war gave Japanese military leaders the opportunity to move troops into the far eastern regions of the former Russian Empire.

The initiative for Japanese expansionism lay with the Japanese military. The old feudal traditions glorifying conquest and military valor had reemerged in Japan's modern army. The emperor himself lent his prestige and semi-divine stature to this "imperial way." Expansion was also in the economic interest of industrialists eager to seize new markets and mineral resources. It came at a high price. The Chinese protested Japanese economic privileges. In 1919, Chinese nationalists declared a trade boycott of Japanese goods. Japanese military intervention in Siberia proved costly as well and gave Japan no direct benefits. But expansion continued until it met the strong opposition of the U.S.

U.S. interests in East Asia were the major obstacle to this Japanese sphere of influence in East Asia. American economic and strategic goals there made isolationism an impossibility. U.S. trade flourished in the region, and the Philippines remained a U.S. colony and military base. The U.S. navy was Japan's only serious naval rival in the Pacific, and had expanded its Pacific fleet as part of the U.S. policy to contain Japanese influence in East Asia. Japanese business interests had good reason to appease U.S. concerns. The United States had become an important customer for Japanese goods and was also a vital source of raw materials such as petroleum and iron ore. The economic importance and naval might of the United States brought an end (temporarily) to Japan's expansionist policies.

In a major retreat, the government ordered a halt in 1920 to the army's plans for Asian conquest. It achieved this result by reasserting direct control over the Japanese high command, ending (until the 1930s) the "autonomy of command" claimed by army leaders. In 1921, it accepted the offer of the U.S. government to join an international conference in Washington to discuss East Asian affairs.

The Washington Conference introduced into Asian international relations a model of collective peacekeeping similar to that the U.S. negotiators had taken to Paris in 1919. The Republican administration came to the 1921 conference as eager as Wilson once had been to abandon spheres of influence and power politics. They continued the long-standing policy of the United States to protect China from foreign intervention and to keep its market open to American goods. The other major powers were prepared to accept the U.S. proposals for an end to the diplomacy of power politics in the Far East. Great Britain and France collaborated because they were weakened by the war. Japan's civilian leaders hoped that cooperation with the United States would bring Japan economic prosperity.

When its work was finally completed in 1922, the conference produced a remarkable set of agreements. The most important was the treaty to restrict the total number of warships of each empire. It fixed among the participating states a ratio of the relative number of capital ships they were permitted. Great Britain and the United States were left with the largest navies, followed by Japan, then France and Italy. To meet the treaty restrictions, Great Britain, the United States, and Japan all scrapped a large number of naval vessels—thirty-two for the United States. The British and the Americans promised not to establish any new military bases in the Pacific or to strengthen fortifications in their existing bases at Singapore, and at Corregidor in the Philippines. In exchange, the Japanese military withdrew their troops from Soviet territory. For a few years, the treaties effectively ended power politics in the Far East and stopped the naval armaments race. Like the Locarno Treaty in Europe, the Washington treaties held out the hope of a peaceful era in Asian international relations.

Their success depended, above all, on continued cooperation between Japan and the United States. Misunderstanding over their terms came easily, for these agreements embodied in Japan and the United States very different approaches to global politics. American leaders assumed that a common interest in peace had to be the overriding concern of all states, large or small, and that a treaty, like a contract, was inviolable. At the same time, they had a low opinion in general of "oriental" peoples, whom they expected to follow their own leadership. The isolationist, disdainful attitude of so many Americans toward the outside world led their leaders to seek, and to believe they had achieved, a self-regulating peace in East Asia.

Japanese historical experience gave its people a very different perspective on their country's place in the world. Centuries of isolation, followed by the remarkable revival of Japanese might, bolstered the conviction that their empire was unique and that its national needs and interests were of far greater importance than those of other East Asian lands. The governing elite of Japan interpreted their active role at the Washington Conference and in the League of Nations to be proof of Western recognition of their country's stature as a great power. The civilian government of Japan adopted wholeheartedly the American program of international cooperation. They had to justify their policy to the industrial and military elite, however, by pointing to direct benefits to Japan. The unstated Japanese condition in signing the Washington treaties and withdrawing from the Asian mainland was economic prosperity and the expansion of U.S.–Japanese trade. When prosperity ended and trade declined at the end of the 1920s, so, too, did Japanese compliance with the treaties. The result was the collapse of the security treaties and the renewal of war in East Asia.

THE INTERNATIONAL ECONOMY IN PROSPERITY AND DEPRESSION

Called the Roaring Twenties by exuberant Americans, the ten years following the end of the war gave peoples in the industrial world reason to hope that peace and prosperity had returned. Scientists explored uncharted areas of the natural world; inventors added basic discoveries to the technological marvels of the industrial economy. In that age of exciting discoveries, pessimistic voices warned of darker human forces of destruction. Some writers extolled the glories of violent struggle and national supremacy, carrying into the years of peace the rhetorical violence that had characterized the wartime. The German philosopher Oswald Spengler singled out the postwar "revolutions of stupidity and vulgarity" to prove that Western civilization had, like Roman civilization long before, entered its inevitable final stage of decline. His major work, *The Decline of the West*, was especially successful among fellow Germans, many of whom were deeply pessimistic about the future of their country.

Recovery from War

While these debates reverberated within the world of intellectuals, technological developments produced startling changes in everyday life. The automobile emerged as a vehicle for individual transportation, cheap enough in the United States to be accessible to the middle classes. Architects raised skyscrapers to greater and greater heights; New York, a new center of the world economy, proclaimed its economic prominence by constructing the Empire State Building, the tallest building in the world. Electricity spread through cities and into homes in rural and urban areas. With it came the radio, a new form of communication bringing global events almost instantaneously within reach of individuals. The plane, used extensively first as an instrument of war, became in years of peace a means of rapid transportation across continents and even oceans. Of all the public events of the 1920s, Charles Lindbergh's solo flight in 1927 across the Atlantic aroused the greatest enthusiasm and captured best the popular vision of the future. Acclaimed throughout Europe and America, he appeared the new civilian hero who used the power of technology for the conquest of space, not territory, and whose exploit dissolved national frontiers. In this respect, as in others, the "old" continent looked to the "new" for inspiration.

Economic prosperity was the foundation on which rested real recovery from the material and psychological damage of war. The world economy grew rapidly in the mid-1920s. The bulk of international trade and finance remained concentrated in Western hands. The war had left its traces here, too. Great Britain, drained of much of its international investments, no longer coordinated and stabilized investments and international trade. Japan and the United States enjoyed the highest rate of growth in exports. New York, not London, became the financial capital of the West. The United States, once a debtor nation to European investors, became the major creditor, lending more than $6 billion to foreign countries between 1924 and 1929. Great Britain, by contrast, lent half that amount.

The weakness of European finances and investment led governments there to assume greater responsibility than before for economic growth. They took steps to stimulate commercial exports, disrupted by the needs of war. They raised tariffs to protect their own producers from foreign competition. Only Great Britain returned to free trade and to the gold standard (assuring free purchase and sale of gold) to insure a stable value of the pound sterling. The new states of eastern Europe, which suffered from the decline of international food prices after 1925, raised tariff barriers on industrial imports. Increasingly, trade and financial policies tended to reflect national interests at the expense of the international economic growth. Under these conditions, global recovery from war remained unstable.

In those same years, new economic and social trends were appearing in non-Western countries, colonial and independent. Two key developments emerged then that continued into the post-colonial era. First, these lands were becoming the source of vital minerals and of agricultural produce in the international economy. Second, the gradual diffusion of medical care and improved food supplies had improved living conditions to the point of launching a global population expansion. For the first time, the rate of population growth in Asia and Africa rose above that of Europe. Terrible famines and epidemics, previously the principal natural limits on growth, declined in severity. By 1930, the estimated world population had reached two billion, up from 1.5 billion in 1900. The basic improvements in standard of living suggested by population growth were barely perceptible. Still, they heralded a gradual change in attitudes of peoples, whose fatalism in the face of seemingly unstoppable catastrophes gave way to the hope of better conditions for themselves and their offspring. These trends signaled a profound "revolution of rising expectations."

These non-Western countries were increasingly dependent on the international economy. More and more small farmers were raising cash crops for sale, entering for the first time a regional or even foreign market. In Africa, crops such as cotton and cocoa spread through the countryside, and the good prices on these commodities promised farmers a good income until the late 1920s. At the same time, Western mining corporations were expanding their exploitation of the rich mineral deposits of certain African regions, providing employment for African labor. African miners migrated from great distances to work in the copper mines of the Belgian Congo, in the tin mines of Niger, or in the gold mines of South Africa. Employers welcomed their arrival, since they accepted wages far below those of white workers. Gradually an African working class was beginning to appear around these European-owned enterprises.

In Asian lands an industrial economy, launched by wartime demand, continued to expand in the 1920s. Japan had the most developed economy. Even coastal cities in India showed signs of modernization. In both lands, textile manufacturing had expanded rapidly during the war, and continued to grow in the 1920s.

The principal characteristic—and the greatest weakness—of the Asian and the African economies was their dependence on the export of raw materials. Their markets lay elsewhere, and the prices received for their goods depended on global forces of supply and demand over which they had no control. Until the mid-1920s, prices on these commodities tended to rise. Those good years came to an end when world prices began a long, steady fall. By the end of the 1920s, rubber had lost two-thirds of its value; economies in Latin America and Asia dependent on rubber sales experienced a severe depression. Farmers and laborers whose well-being was tied to producing a single commodity were the first to suffer.

The economic decline of non-Western regions hurt, in turn, international industrial exports and, even before the 1929 financial crisis, pointed to the coming global depression.

The international demand for petroleum products fueled the remarkable expansion of the oil industry. Oil had become a crucial strategic commodity during the war; it became even more important with the economic expansion of the 1920s. Gulf of Mexico oil fields became the foundation of the economic growth of Mexico. The principal international oil corporations—Standard Oil of New Jersey, Royal Dutch-Shell, and British Petroleum—moved into the Middle East, where vast petroleum deposits were being discovered. The oil companies enjoyed excellent profits, only a small fraction of which went in the form of royalties to the governments on whose territory the oil was extracted. Oil from the Middle-Eastern wells found new markets in the industrial West. The low price of crude oil provided a new source of cheap energy for transportation and industry in the Western economies. Mass production of automobiles, led by the Ford Motor Company, sparked new industries in the West and increased global demand for raw materials such as oil and rubber. The boom in road transportation made gasoline a vital commodity. The international economy of 1900 was gradually evolving into an interdependent global economy.

The economic recovery of Europe brought national incomes to prewar levels by 1925. Industrial growth continued at a steady, though slow, pace for three more years in Europe and North America. The United States played a key role in the economic prosperity of those years. It provided the bulk of the investment funds for public and private lenders. It was also the single most important foreign market for European and Japanese manufactured goods.

U.S. political leaders relied on the impersonal operations of the capitalist, free market system to ensure that economic growth continued. They ignored the reckless speculation on the stock market and intervened in economic affairs only to raise tariffs to protect U.S. farmers and manufacturers. Protective tariffs and stock speculation appeared profitable to American investors in the short term. Economists would later conclude that these aspects of U.S. domestic policy seriously damaged stable world economic growth. The United States failed to provide the leadership that Great Britain had once given the global capitalist system. The prosperity of the Roaring Twenties was not built on solid foundations.

The Global Depression

The economic decline that began at the end of the 1920s damaged all the industrial economies of the world as well as the areas supplying food and raw materials to the West. It had the characteristics of earlier recessions, including a severe decline in production and trade, a rapid rise in unemployment, and a drastic fall in the standard of living of the population. Businesses declared bankruptcy; banks were unable to make loans and many were unable to pay their debts to depositors; food prices fell so low that farmers let fields lie fallow though the urban poor went hungry. The recession began in 1929 in the United States and gradually spread throughout the Western world and into East Asia. By the early 1930s, it had become a global economic depression, far worse in its impact and extent than any previous slump. It represented a human tragedy of monumental proportions, creating hardship and suffering, destroying confidence in governments, undermining hope in the future. It led in many countries to a serious political crisis.

The American economy led the way in recession after having launched the prosperity of the 1920s. By early 1929, U.S. industrial production had begun to decline, with the new automobile industry the first to suffer. Declining demand for industrial goods represented an important factor in triggering recession. Added to this condition, however, were other grave problems of American finance and trade that complicated and prolonged the international effects of the recession. Stock values in 1929 reflected speculative dreams, not economic reality. This fact led some major investors to abandon Wall Street in late 1929 for less risky ventures. Their decision, coupled with financial problems in London, burst the speculative bubble and started massive selling. By the winter of 1929, stock prices had declined by one-third, and many speculators who had borrowed heavily were ruined.

When they failed to repay their loans and banks raised their interest rates, investment funds for industry dwindled by almost one half. Factories cut back production even more. The decline in sales of U.S. goods and rising unemployment led to political pressure to keep out foreign goods. In response, in 1930 the U.S. Congress enacted the Smoot-Hawley tariff law. It set tariff barriers 50 percent higher on imports and spread the harmful effects of declining demand to industrial producers in Europe and Japan.

The impact of the American recession on other economies was critical. In the first place, the United States ceased making sizable investments in foreign countries. The financial crisis caused by the Wall Street crash of 1929 penetrated deeply into the world economy. U.S. foreign investments fell two-thirds by 1932. European manufacturers curtailed factory investments. At the beginning of the depression, financial orthodoxy in ruling circles still dictated balanced budgets and high interest rates to attract foreign

money. Both policies were severely criticized later for hindering recovery. The United States, center of world financial dealings since the war, could not provide those funds. The entire system of foreign investments in Europe fell apart as creditors called in their loans.

The long-term effect of the U.S. financial collapse produced a major banking and financial crisis in Europe in 1931. Banks in Germany and Austria defaulted on their own loans; Germany forbade withdrawal of funds to other countries. In Great Britain, the flight of money abroad forced the British government late that year to end its guaranteed exchange of pounds for gold at a fixed value, abandoning its efforts to protect stable international finances. In 1931, Great Britain and France stopped repaying their war debt to the United States. In retaliation, the U.S. Congress prohibited purchase of British and French government securities by U.S. investors. No other country besides the United States had the economic resources to restore world financial stability. U.S. investors had recklessly gambled away their funds, and their government sought primarily to protect American banks and investments.

The second area in which the U.S. recession contributed directly to the global economic decline lay in trade. Instead of opening its market to foreign products falling in price, the U.S. government excluded imports by raising tariffs. Recovery in earlier recessions had come in part because goods at lower prices attracted buyers in foreign countries. The United States did not permit that process to occur. Its prohibitive tariff of 1930 helped reduce foreign imports by almost one-half. Country after country retaliated by raising their tariffs; even Britain abandoned free trade in 1931. In the next two years, world trade declined by one-third. Most countries exporting food and raw materials lost much of their foreign sales by the early 1930s. Japan, dependent on exports to pay for imports of vital raw materials, saw its American market suddenly contract and its total exports decline by 50 percent. The standard of living of its workers fell by one-third. Japan's vulnerability to the international depression encouraged its political leaders to consider East Asia their special market. And the economic decline revived plans by Japanese generals to conquer Asian territory. Economic crisis and war were closely linked.

By 1932, industrial production had declined by one-fourth worldwide and by one-third in Europe. In concrete terms, only three-fourths of the quantity of the manufactured goods once available were still produced. The wealth of the industrial world was shrinking. The economic crisis was particularly acute in the most heavily industrialized countries. Production fell in Germany by 40 percent. As a result, one out of every four German workers was unemployed and many others were surviving on lower pay. The German government, to which employers and workers looked for help, appeared at a loss to devise new remedies to the crisis.

The economic depression undermined the international financial and commercial network of the capitalist economies. States increasingly relied on their own internal markets for recovery. A major international conference gathered in London in 1933 to attempt to put the international trade and finance system back together. European leaders turned to the U.S. government to guarantee a stable dollar, to serve as a source of new investment funds, and to open its economy to increased imports. The new U.S. president, Franklin D. Roosevelt, refused to cooperate. He feared that an international program to promote economic growth would worsen the depression in his own country. The conference was a failure.

International cooperation gave way to short-sighted national interests. The entire process of recovery from war was undermined by the severity of the depression. International collaboration collapsed, political confidence in democracy was shattered, and hopes for peace and prosperity vanished. The harmful effects of the depression were pushing the world toward renewed instability and conflict.

SUMMARY

The 1920s appears, in hindsight, to have been a time of transition toward a new and even more terrible war. The "normalcy" acclaimed by one U.S. president of the 1920s had only a short time to survive. The success of the French and British empires in extending their control into the Middle East could not hide the difficulties both states had in ruling colonies where nationalist movements were beginning to emerge. The new order put together by European statesmen represented a timid effort to find new solutions to the problems of international conflict and economic growth. We may judge these men short-sighted, but we should recognize that their powers were limited, their peoples exhausted by war and fearful of "Bolshevism" as much as of another war.

The world was moving in new directions in the wake of the terrible war. The leaders of the Soviet Union never doubted that their "proletarian revolution" placed them in the forefront of this process, which they proclaimed the path of human progress. By the 1920s, their country had recovered from war and a terrible civil war, and the political institutions of the communist dictatorship were firmly in place. Led by Joseph Stalin, the revolutionary regime was ready to begin the radical social and economic reforms that they believed would bring to life in their land a socialist society. Their vision was utopian, and it inspired communist movements throughout the world.

The international economy was bringing countries in closer contact than before. Farsighted political leaders realized that economic growth could not endure without the creation of a global economy. In the short term, international cooperation was necessary for economic recovery from the war. But that process was fatally weakened by the readiness of states to place the immediate interests of their people ahead of collaboration. The new postwar order hid grave problems. International financial and economic collaboration collapsed when the depression struck the industrial countries.

The United States bore a major share of the responsibility for the failure of the recovery. Its leaders and most Americans refused to acknowledge the new diplomatic and economic role of their country in global affairs. They made the naive assumption that the complex set of international financial and diplomatic arrangements—the League of Nations, the Locarno agreement, the Dawes plan, the Washington treaties—would function by themselves, leaving the United States at peace behind its ocean frontiers. The depression and wars of the 1930s ended these illusions.

DATES WORTH REMEMBERING

1914 Outbreak of First World War
1915 German military victories on Eastern front
1916 Battle at Verdun
1916 Arab Revolt against Ottoman Empire
1917 U.S. entry into war
1918 Defeat of Central Powers
1917 Russian Revolution
1917–1920 Russian Civil War
1918 Collapse of Austro-Hungarian Empire
1920 Founding of League of Nations

1921 Creation of French and British mandated territories in Middle East
1921–1922 Washington Conference on East Asian security
1924 Egyptian independence
1925 Defeat of Hussein Ibn Ali by Ibn Saud clan in Arabia
1925 Locarno Pact
1927 Lindbergh solo Atlantic flight
1929 Beginning of global depression
1936–1938 Palestine Arab revolt

RECOMMENDED READING

War and Peace in the West

*Charles Kindelberger, *The World in Depression: 1929–1939* (1973). Still the best survey of the global origins and impact of the depression.

Edmond Taylor, *The Fall of the Dynasties: The Collapse of the Old Order, 1905–1922* (1963). The history of the fall of the Austrian, German, Russian, and Ottoman empires and the war that destroyed them.

Arthur Walworth, *Wilson and His Peacemakers: American Diplomacy at the Paris Peace Conference* (1986). Generally favorable interpretation of Wilson's role at the Paris peace negotiations.

Communism in Russia

Orlando Figes, *A People's Tragedy: A History of the Russian Revolution* (1997). A careful, thoughtful interpretation, based on recent historical research, of the origins and consequences of the Russian Revolution.

*Sheila Fitzpatrick, *The Russian Revolution, 1917–1932* (3rd edition, 1999). A study linking Lenin's insurrection and Stalin's revolution.

Postwar Empires

Raymond Betts, *Uncertain Dimensions: Western Overseas Empires in the Twentieth Century* (1985). A thematic study of European colonial empires in the twentieth century until their collapse.

Akira Iriye, *After Imperialism: The Search for Order in the Far East* (1965). History of Japan's search for its place in East Asia after World War I.

Efraim & Inari Karsh, *Empires of the Sand: The Struggle for Mastery in the Middle East* (1999). A clear, critical assessment of the historical forces leading to the destruction of the Ottoman Empire and the creation of the modern Middle East.

A. J. H. Latham, *The Depression and the Developing World, 1914–1939* (1981). General study of the origins and impact of 1930s depression on non-Western countries.

Memoirs, Novels, and Visual Aids

*Isak Dinesen, *Out of Africa* (1937). Story of a failed European plantation owner in Kenya (and subject of an excellent film).

*George Orwell, *Burmese Days* (1934). The disillusioned story of the author's years in Burma working in the British colonial service.

*Boris Pasternak, *Doctor Zhivago* (1958). The classic Russian novel of a helpless individual swept along in the tumult of war and revolution (a melodramatic film version is also available).

T. E. Lawrence, *The Seven Pillars of Wisdom* (1926). Lawrence's memoirs and meditations on his life as "Lawrence of Arabia"; his story is also told in vivid color in David Lean's movie "Lawrence of Arabia" (1962).

CHAPTER THREE

Nations versus Empires in Asia

TURKEY, INDIA, CHINA, 1918–1941

In the two decades following the First World War, nationalism brought new life to old civilizations all across Asia. That war proved a critical moment in the history of Turkey, China, and India. Turks were mobilized by their Ottoman sultan on the side of the Central Powers, and suffered a defeat as devastating as that experienced by the Austro-Hungarian and German empires. Indian soldiers fought with the Allies after the British viceroy proclaimed India at war with the Central Powers. The sacrifice made by India encouraged nationalists in the National Congress to demand self-rule for their country. The new Chinese Republic joined the Allies in hopes of gaining international recognition, only to discover that the Japanese Empire was its most dangerous enemy. No battles occurred in India or in East Asia. The peace settlement left intact the prewar colonial possessions there of the Western empires. Still, the end of the war began the decline of these empires and the revival of colonial or semi-colonial regions under the impact of nationalism.

The victory of the Allies fatally undermined the Ottoman Empire. Allies forces occupied Turkish lands. In reaction, officers from the former Ottoman army, led by Kemal Ataturk, founded a nationalist movement to rid the country of foreign troops. Their goal was the creation of a unified Turkish nation-state. To do so, they had to destroy the Ottoman Empire. The authority of the sultan crumbled after he chose, in hopes of preserving his throne, to collaborate with the Allies. Conservative religious leaders tried but failed to arouse Muslims against the nationalists. Modern, secular reforms became the foundation for the new Turkish nation. Within a few years, Turkish leaders had abolished the sultanate, ended the legal supremacy of Islam, and defeated all the foreign invaders. For the first time, the crucible of war forged a new nation-state, the Republic of Turkey.

The First World War had made the peoples in India more deeply involved than ever in the affairs of the British Empire. Indian industrial production grew rapidly to meet imperial needs; the Indian army fought on front lines in Europe and the Middle East. The British recognized that these new conditions required political concessions to Indian nationalism. But their idea of limited self-rule failed to satisfy the major nationalist movement, the Indian National Congress. The remarkable leadership of Mohandas Gandhi turned this small party of intellectuals into a mass movement by identifying liberation from British rule with the needs of the Indian masses. Having begun the process of introducing self-government into India, the British viceroy found himself under increasing pressure from the National Congress to make more and more reforms. But internal divisions within the Congress, especially between Muslims and non-Muslims, threatened to weaken the nationalist movement. While India remained a British colony, by the late 1930s it was headed for complete independence as a free, democratic nation-state. India occupies a central place in the study of Asian nationalism, for it produced one of the most effective reformist independence movements of the twentieth century.

The 1919 peace settlement aroused in China an unprecedented upsurge of nationalist protest. During the war, Japanese troops had occupied German-controlled areas in northern China. Chinese opposition to Japanese occupation was so strong that it produced the first nationalist mass movement in the country's history. The collapse of the Chinese Empire in 1911 had been followed by the disintegration of central rule and civil war. Army generals, called "war-

lords," had in the following years carved out territories where they ruled with their troops like feudal barons. Their presence stood in the way of the efforts after 1919 of the Chinese Nationalist Party to take control of the vast territory of the fallen empire. By the end of the 1920s, the Nationalists appeared close to success. Internal and foreign enemies still stood in the way of their plans to be heirs to the Empire and the founders of the Chinese nation-state.

THE FORGING OF THE TURKISH NATION

The Ottoman Empire could not long survive the defeat in 1918 of the Central Powers. The sultan and his conservative religious and political supporters bore the brunt of blame for defeat. Reformist officers had before the war sought, above all, to mobilize the empire to resist Western domination. These "Young Turks" had put aside their radical political program during the war. Officers such as Kemal Ataturk proved courageous and skillful in holding back Russian offensives in the east and in defeating in 1915 the forces of the British Empire on the Straits between the Mediterranean and Black seas (the Dardanelles campaign). But British and Arab forces had by 1918 pushed their troops out of the Middle East. The empire once again faced defeat by its enemies.

The collapse of the German and Austro-Hungarian empires was the final blow to the Turkish forces. The sultan capitulated. The combined forces of the Allies, which included British, French, and later Greek troops, occupied most coastal regions of the empire. The Young Turks concluded that imperial decay was irreversible; only the overthrow of the Ottoman Empire would permit the national resurgence of the Turkish people. The harsh lessons of war pointed to the need for political revolution.

The Fall of the Ottoman Empire

After the Ottoman Empire surrendered to the Allies in November 1918, much of its territory was occupied by Allied military forces. British troops and their Arab allies controlled the Fertile Crescent, the area from the Tigris and Euphrates rivers to Palestine. Greek troops took control of the islands of the Aegean Sea and the Anatolian coast around the port of Smyrna, where half a million Greeks lived. The straits linking the Black Sea and the Mediterranean, including Istanbul (Constantinople), were under Allied military and naval occupation. The wartime plans for the partition of the empire became the central feature of the peace treaty drawn up in 1919. Presented to the sultan for his approval, it left only central Turkey in a shrunken Ottoman Empire.

The fate of the empire and its sultan mattered less to the Turkish officers of the sultan's army than that of the Turkish people. If implemented, the treaty would have left many Turks under foreign (and Christian) rule, some incorporated in an Armenian state, others in the Greek state. Refusing to bow to Allied terms or the sultan's orders, the officers gathered around a military commander, Mustafa Kemal (later to take the name Kemal Ataturk), to organize a nationalist movement of resistance. Their aim was to create a Turkish nation-state and to form a Turkish army to defend their new state from the threatened partition.

Mustafa Kemal's extraordinary life was the product of the chaos brought by war and the collapse of the Ottoman Empire, and of his own determination to become the leader of the Turkish people. He was born in 1881, the son of poor parents who lived in the Balkan area of the Ottoman Empire. He acquired the surname Ataturk (the father of the Turks) much later, after he had founded the state of Turkey.

His early years were shaped by the institutions and fortunes of the Ottoman Empire. He chose the career of officer in the sultan's army, where his family's poverty mattered less than his remarkable talents. He was a skillful and brave officer. Alongside his career in the military, he (like other officers) became deeply involved in plans for the reform of the declining empire. He was one of the conspirators calling themselves "Young Turks" who, in 1908, forced the sultan to accept a reformed, constitutional monarchy under their leadership. Their first attempt at political leadership failed, though. The sultan had strong allies, including Muslim religious leaders who backed the monarchy. The world war ended temporarily Ataturk's political activity, but the empire's defeat in 1918 renewed his struggle for reform.

Later, he called 1919 "the year of my birth." Ataturk refused the sultan's orders that year to submit to the Allied treaty that partitioned the empire. Instead, he called together representatives of the Turkish people to form a National Assembly. Its task was to create the new state of Turkey. He organized and led a new Turkish army, which fought to expel the foreign invaders and to unify the Turkish people. The sultan and the Muslim authorities ordered his execution, but he had the support of growing numbers of the population. They found in him a dynamic leader whom they came to admire for those mysterious qualities of leadership we call "charisma."

The task of defending the new state was made easier by the weakness of the surrounding states and the unwillingness of the Allies to mount a major offensive against Turkey. In the east, the Turkish army encountered the forces of the newly created Republic of Armenia. It had first emerged amidst the ruins of the Russian Empire on its Caucasian borderland. Its leaders dreamed their own nationalist vision of a state whose borders would extend far into eastern Turkey, where the bulk of the Armenian population had lived for thousands of years. They created their own army, though it was small and poorly armed. For a few years, a few British troops occupied their area. But Great Britain had more pressing concerns than defense of faraway Armenia.

Beyond the Armenian forces were the Soviet Union and its Red Army. The Turkish nationalists did not support communist revolution. In fact, at that time they arrested and executed the leaders of the Turkish Communist Party. Sharing common enemies, however, the two young states overlooked political differences; their leaders preferred cooperation to war. After Soviet troops seized the territory of the Armenia Republic, the two states reached an agreement useful to both. Turkey agreed to the Soviet seizure of eastern Armenia. In exchange, the communist regime provided military aid to the Turkish army.

Despite support in the League of Nations, the Armenians stood no chance to create their own independent state. Ataturk's explanation of their failure was cynical but accurate. The Westerners, such as "poor Wilson," failed to understand that "a frontier which is not defended with bayonets cannot be secured by any other principle." His nationalist revolution had mobilized armed followers ready to die for their homeland, and he was prepared to use them whenever necessary.

Having come to terms with the Soviet state, the Turkish army turned west to attack the occupation forces of Greece. In 1920, Greek leaders had ordered their troops to invade central Anatolia. They believed that their nation should incorporate the territory that 2,000 years before had belonged to the ancient Greek city-states. It was a fantastic, destructive dream. They realized that a Turkish nation-state stood in the way of their vision of Greater Greece. But they underestimated the vitality of Ataturk's nationalist movement. Their decision to take possession of Turkish lands across the Aegean Sea by military conquest proved a political blunder and a tragedy for their people.

In the Greek-Turkish war of 1920–1922, the new Turkish army succeeded in expelling Greek forces from all Asia Minor. The distrust that had long divided Greeks and Turks turned to violent hatred during the war. Of the 1.3 million Greeks living in Anatolia, many died in the course of the fighting. Others abandoned their homes to flee to Greece when the Greek army retreated, fearful of reprisals by the Turkish forces. After the war, the two governments agreed to the repatriation of all remaining Greeks in Turkey, and the departure (in effect, expulsion) of the half a million Turks (including Ataturk's own family) living in Greek territory to settle in Turkey. For the first time, nation-building was accompanied by the flight of millions of refugees to escape rule by another people. Ethnic nationalism was a two-faced cause, presenting on one side an image of strong bonds of trust and solidarity among the people of one nation and on the other the ugly mask of hatred toward other nations.

The Nation-State of Turkey

By 1922, the Turkish army had successfully conquered the entirety of the Anatolian peninsula, the core territory where the Turkish population lived. That year, nationalist leaders formally abolished the position of sultan and with him the remnants of the Ottoman Empire. Their army was a national force, recruited from the Turkish population. Under Kemal Ataturk's leadership, it embodied the national crusade and was the principal instrument to defend that state. He told his people when the sultanate was eliminated that "the Turkish nation has put an end to these usurpers and taken sovereignty into its own hands." The Ottoman Empire had ceased to exist, replaced by the Republic of Turkey.

Two years later, Kemal wiped out the Islamic foundations of the empire. He ended the legal privileges enjoyed by Muslim religious institutions under the sultan. He ordered the abolition of the title of caliphate, the highest post among Sunni Muslims. He stated often that he was a faithful Muslim, but he understood the Islamic faith to be a private affair. He believed the Muslim traditions a relic of the backward past. He was convinced that religion should not dictate the way of life of Turks or the policies and institutions of the new nation-state. He wished Turkey to be a modern state, governed by civil law.

Islamic practices were deeply embedded in the way of life of the Kurdish population of eastern Turkey. This nomadic people, divided by clan loyalties and scattered across the borders of Turkey, Syria, Iraq, and Iran, placed their Muslim spiritual leaders (from the Sufi religious societies) in high regard. By the close of the First World War they had in their midst a few nationalist leaders as well. But it proved far easier to write "Kurdistan" across a map of the northern Middle East than to resist the nationalist revolution of the Turks.

Kurdish leaders traveled to Paris in 1919 in hopes of obtaining from the Allied powers their backing for their own nation-state. They had no allies, however, and little military strength of their own. Their appeal was ignored. They became one of several ethnic minorities within the new Turkish state.

Their leaders, hostile to Turkish rule and to Ataturk's anti-Muslim reforms, launched in 1924 an uprising among their people against the new republic. In retaliation, Kemal sent his army to repress the revolt. At the same time, he ordered the suppression of all Muslim religious societies. No rebellious people or religious group was to stand in the way of his nation-state.

Turkish national unification was complete. In 1925, Kemal Ataturk took the post of president of the republic. He held the position until his death, fifteen years later. In many ways, he embodied the unity of that new country, ruling with an authority so great that he could have become dictator. But he was satisfied to be recognized "father of the Turks."

The Western powers accepted a new peace treaty in 1923, leaving most of Asia Minor, including the straits, within Turkish borders. The Turkish nationalist leaders introduced very ambitious internal reforms, creating a new constitutional order including a parliament and elected president. They ordered that civil law (drawn from Switzerland's civil law code) replace Quranic law in the public affairs of Turkish citizens. Islam remained very influential in the private lives of the Muslim population, but other religions received the right of freedom of worship. The great Christian church in Istanbul, Hagia Sophia, had been a mosque since the fifteenth century, when the Ottoman Turks had conquered Constantinople; Ataturk had it converted in the 1920s into a national museum to commemorate this architectural marvel of Byzantium. Secularism and modernism were the model that the government held up to the people of their new land. Ataturk's army remained the defender of national unity, and the bastion against the revival of Islam in the country. Out of the ruins of the Ottoman Empire emerged a new Turkish state.

National Leader of the Turks: Kemal Ataturk in Modern Military Uniform, c. 1925 (*Hulton-Deutsch Collection/Corbis*)

lands). Literacy for Turks meant fluently using a new set of letters; the Quran now came to them not only in a foreign language, but in an alien alphabet.

The emancipation of women became a major symbol of Ataturk's crusade to modernize his country. The new laws of Turkey ended the legal subordination of women to the head of the family. Schooling and jobs were opened to them. Symbolic of their emancipation was the campaign to end the traditional veiling in public of Turkish women. It was the mark in many Muslim countries of their seclusion from public life. In defying religious custom, Ataturk believed that he was ridding his country of the dead weight of the past.

BRITISH INDIA AND INDIAN NATIONALISM

The history of India placed enormous obstacles in the way of Indian national unity. The Indian nationalist movement emerged after the First World War out of a complex culture, some parts of which it rejected, other parts of which it absorbed and reconfigured to fit the new cause. One of the oldest civilizations in the world, it was composed of a vast and diverse array of peoples, customs, and religious practices. Many different languages were spoken among the 300 million people of the Indian subcontinent, with Hindi and related languages like Bengali dominant in the north and a very different family of languages (such as Tamil) in the south. The British conquest of the subcontinent, completed by the mid-nineteenth century, had left in place hundreds of principalities. Some large, some minute, each governed by its own prince in conformity with its own traditions. Along the coast, merchants and manufacturers produced and traded as capably as any Western entrepreneurs, while elsewhere peasants eked out a

In achieving this goal, the Turks had distanced themselves from the rest of the Middle East. Having once ruled as conquerors, they pulled back into their own land and created new borders that were national and cultural frontiers as well. The single strongest bond among peoples of that region had been Islam. Ataturk sought in every possible way to promote Western, modern practices. Even the alphabet became a subject of reform. The Turkish language had previously been written in the Arabic script, for Arabic was the language of the Quran. The Turkish government ordered that Turkish henceforth be written in the Latin script (used in all Western miserable existence by farming with primitive implements.

Religion and culture emerged in the colonial period as the principal social and cultural bond among the peoples of the subcontinent. Two thousand years before, the Buddha had preached there his message of spiritual salvation through meditation and renunciation of personal pleasures. His sacred shrines in India remained places of pilgrimage from followers in lands such as Tibet and China, but the religion itself had faded from Indian spiritual life. In its place, Hinduism had marked Indian society both by its spiritual values and by the caste system. Later, the Muslim religion had spread widely through Indian society. India's development during the two centuries of British rule accentuated the differences between these two religious communities. Until the end, that conflict remained confined within the colonial borders drawn by the British Empire.

Hinduism and Islam

Hinduism provided the common culture of most inhabitants of the subcontinent. It was an extremely complex religion, with no single sacred book or organization of spiritual leaders. It included the worship of a large number of deities, no one of whom stood out as the principal god. Hinduism emphasized perpetual change, as the wheel of life transported souls through incarnation from one body to the next, as birth was followed by death. Through this cycle of life, souls carried with them the moral consequences of acts of the individuals previously inhabited by these souls. No merit went unrewarded in the end, no sin unpunished. As a result, individuals, in principle, had to accept the life that fate had prepared for them.

A second important aspect of Hinduism was the caste system. It divided the population into hereditary groups according to status and social responsibilities. It translated the moral duty of each Hindu into specific personal obligations and social bonds. The structure included hundreds of separate castes (only some of which might be present in one community), all of which belonged to one of the four major orders of Hindu society. The orders, once actual occupations—priests, warriors, merchants, farmers—had long since become merely social ranks, of which the Brahmins were the highest. The Hindu social hierarchy included one other group: the untouchables, or the "unclean," segregated from all recognized castes and condemned eternally to perform the most degrading, menial tasks. They represented a sizable group, perhaps 15 percent of the population. Taboos governed behavior, including eating, among castes; beef was forbidden to most groups because the cow was sacred. Marriage had to remain within the caste. The customs and taboos governing the caste system had existed for many centuries and were closely bound with the spiritual values of Hinduism.

Before the arrival of Western empires, the most powerful foreign influence had been a new religion, Islam. Carried by merchants and warriors from the Middle East, the Muslim religion had spread through the subcontinent. It embodied a radically different set of spiritual values and social practices. Worship demanded submission by the faithful to one God, Allah; His word was contained in one sacred book, the Quran. The Muslim religion forbade the segregation of the faithful into castes and rejected the lowly status of outcasts or untouchables. It condemned absolutely the worship of any other deity but the one God. Pork, not beef, was forbidden food. In a multitude of practices and habits of daily life, Islam and Hinduism differed.

The populations of the two communities had lived for centuries side by side throughout the subcontinent. The greatest concentration of Muslims lay in the Indus River valley to the west and, in the east, in Bengal. Everywhere, though, village life mingled the two groups, who on a daily basis lived at peace and worked together in the harsh struggle to survive. Yet their communal identities, shaped by religious doctrine and social custom, created invisible but potent barriers. These differences could become the source of dispute, even confrontation. In the late colonial period, "communal violence," that is, attacks by members of one religious community upon members of the other, became increasingly common. Until the mid-twentieth century, no one imagined, however, that the Muslims, a minority among Hindus, would form a separate state to protect their faith and to defend their community.

Out of the contact between the two religions emerged one other important religious community. In northern India, the Sikh religion joined Hindu philosophy with the Muslim worship of one God. Many Sikh men had, during the years of British rule, served in the Indian army, adopting their traditional respect for the warrior to the military code of a modern army. They were concentrated around their holy city of Amritsar, located in the northern province of Punjab, where large Muslim and Hindu populations also lived. For Sikhs, as for Hindus and Muslims, life conducted under a distant British administration in the midst of a multi-religious society was for a century their formative political experience.

British Rule in India

Ruling over this vast population was the British Empire. India was its prize colony. The British monarch was India's emperor. India's colonial borders extended around the entire subcontinent, from Afghanistan in the west to Burma in the east, from the Himalaya mountains in the north to the island of Ceylon in the south. The British found tangible benefits to colonial rule. It provided them with economic profits and manpower for their imperial armies. Its economy was open to British goods. Its soldiers served loyally in African and Asian colonial wars, and in the First World War. Political authority over the colonial subcontinent lay in the hands of the viceroy, appointed by the British monarch (on advice from the cabinet). His powers in India in the early twentieth century were vast, for no parliament or constitution limited his authority. He declared war and set taxes, approved laws and mobilized troops.

In practice, important restrictions tempered the viceroy's absolute authority. Large areas remained under the rule of Indian princes. They had proven their loyalty to Great Britain by supporting the empire; they were rewarded by the assurance of dominion over their territories as long as Britain governed India. They ruled in great splendor, but all had to accept British advisers at their courts. British power over Indian subjects was curtailed as well by the colonial administration's decision, largely for fear of popular protest, to leave in place most of the local laws and customs. British rule imposed an institutional structure and internal economic bonds that left a permanent mark on Indian public life. For one thing, the British organized an Indian Army, staffing it with regular British officers and joining one regular British brigade with two Indian brigades to form integrated regiments. They trained the soldiers in Western military techniques and promoted more and more Indians into the ranks of noncommissioned officers. The army proved its value in both world wars; by the 1940s, Indians had become full officers.

The Indian civil service played an important role in British colonial rule. This body of state administrators slowly expanded in size as the British took on new responsibilities in the areas of public works, public health, and state railroads. Indians had long regarded state service as high-status positions. They took advantage of these opportunities for advancement in the colonial civil service. By 1914, one-fifth of the high civil servants were Indians. A few had even become high court judges, responsible in the English tradition for observing the rule of law. One of these men was a Brahmin named Motilal Nehru, father of the future prime minister of independent India. Gradually the colony acquired a political elite trained in Western methods of administration, ready to move into positions of political responsibility when India won its independence. All through the turbulent years when the Indian nationalist movement issued calls for resistance to British colonial rule, these servants of the British empire remained loyal to the end.

The empire's extensive program of public works in India was a third important legacy of the colonial era. By the early twentieth century, the British network of roads and railroads had become the largest and best internal transportation system of any Asian country. The railroads, at first a military necessity for the movement of troops, facilitated extensive commercial and industrial growth. They served British economic interests, and increasingly were used by Indian traders and workers as the Indian industrial and commercial economy expanded. Irrigation was another key element in British plans for the development of India. The imperial administrators sought crops of benefit to British industry, such as cotton, and food sufficient to alleviate hunger in India. An extensive network of canals opened for cultivation large areas in northern India. It brought water from the complex river system flowing out of the Himalayas to the parched plains of the Punjab province and

elsewhere. By 1940, this irrigation system accounted for one-fifth of India's arable land.

In these and other ways, measures undertaken by imperial administrators to strengthen their own rule opened the country to new economic development. Britain found a vast market for its industrial goods, and as a consequence traditional sectors of the Indian economy suffered. Many small clothing enterprises were ruined by the competition from cheap British cotton products. Gradually Indian entrepreneurs emerged to take advantage of the new industrial technology and the growing market for their goods. During the First World War, the increased demand among the Allies for iron and steel led to the development of the largest metallurgical enterprise in Asia, owned by an Indian family. One small part of Indian society adapted Western capitalist practices; a far larger group became an urban labor force. India gradually began the transition toward an industrial economy.

India's political life evolved rapidly under the British "raj" (the Indian term for rule). Colonial domination provoked strong opposition. At the same time, it trained Indians in English administrative, legal, and political practices. At a distance, the example of the British state exercised a powerful attraction for Indians, both opponents and collaborators in imperial rule. By the twentieth century, India's anti-colonial leaders had put aside the goal of restoring the ancient empire of the Moguls. India's future freedom had to come in the shape of a democratic, multiethnic nation-state. If Indians were to expel the British and they had to do so by learning British skills, acquiring Western knowledge. Upper-caste Indians such as Motilal Nehru earned public esteem even while adopting a Western style of life and making a place for himself in the new Indian administration. Nehru did not reject the goal of Indian independence; on the contrary, for

years he was one of the most outspoken Indians calling for self-rule for his country. For
him, as for his son, liberation came through
the acquisition of Western learning and the
adaptation of British democratic values and
practices to Indian society.

The educational efforts of the British
rulers in India strongly shaped the attitudes
of the Indian social elite. By the First World
War, few educated Indians denied that
Western industrial and scientific achievements had the capacity to transform and
improve the life of the people. The network
of English-language secondary and higher
schools in India provided trained personnel
to staff the civil service, courts, public health
agency, and railroad administration. Grants
were available to a few Indians to study in
England; families also helped their sons
make the trip. Young Mohandas Gandhi
traveled to London to study law in the 1890s
with the aid of his family (though under
the threat of ostracism from outraged relatives). These Indians desired particularly
modern scientific knowledge and professional training. They had to master the
English language, and many were drawn as
well to Western literature. These "England
returned" were usually perfectly bilingual,
fluent in their own language and in English.

The First Steps toward Freedom

The center for Indian nationalist resistance to Great Britain was the Indian National Congress. Formed in 1886, it evolved
after the First World War into a mass political movement seeking a free, democratic
India. In effect, the Congress borrowed from
England the structure and practices of a political party. At first it emphasized collaboration with the British administration to bring
self-rule in India. After 1918, it made its objective the liberation from Great Britain and
national independence.

Although conflicts with the colonial authorities broke out with increasing fre-
quency, the National Congress retained its
respect for English rule of law and democracy. It accepted time and again dialogue
and collaboration in reforms for regional
and then national self-government. The
British, for their part, slowly and often
grudgingly conceded to their colony greater
self-rule and democratic liberties. As Congress pushed for more and more freedom
for the Indian people, the British repeatedly
made compromise proposals leading to
greater responsibilities for elected Indian
leaders. Both the British and Congress, on
the surface bitter enemies, in fact continued
to collaborate in the gradual move toward
Indian independence.

The struggle for independence brought
out the rift in political objectives between influential Muslim participants in National
Congress and the majority of members. In
the early years of the twentieth century, a
group of Muslims created a new organization, the Muslim League. They sought to ensure that the political rights and cultural
values of their minority religious community would not be neglected by the National
Congress, whose members were predominantly Hindu. Representatives of the League
took their place alongside other Indians in
the National Congress. Both Muslim League
and Congress leaders believed that they had
to collaborate in the struggle for self-rule.
But the formation of the League proved to
be the first step toward the political crisis
among Indians that ultimately tore the country apart.

Disagreement over the future of the
colony had deep roots in the differences separating the two religious communities. Until
the late 1930s, the Muslims supporting the
League anticipated that the two great religious groups would coexist, not blend together, in a future independent India. They

feared, with some reason, that a Hindu majority in a democratic state might become the persecutors of the Muslims. When, in the 1920s, the British extended self-rule to its Indian territories, Hindu-Muslim rioting during the electoral contests worsened. A unified Indian nation-state faced serious obstacles arising from the religious and social diversity of its people.

India's participation in the First World War proved the key event in the emergence of the National Congress as a mass political party. The leaders of the National Congress were encouraged in their hope for self-rule by Allied policy statements and by revolutionary events in Russia. They read President Wilson's Fourteen-Point program for peace, which called for recognition of the "interests of the populations" in colonies and for national self-determination. They watched the Communist Revolution in Russia and read Lenin's appeals for the united struggle of proletarian and colonial peoples. War and revolution in Europe were shaking the foundations of Western colonial power.

The British government had itself recognized that Indian mobilization for war required concessions for self-rule. Yet the institutions and habits of imperial domination remained in place. In 1917, the cabinet issued an official declaration promising "the gradual development of self-governing institutions, with a view to the progressive realization of responsible government in India as an integral part of the Empire." But a year later, the British administration in India introduced new repressive laws to combat nationalist agitation. In April 1919, a peaceful meeting of 10,000 Indians in the city of Amritsar ended in bloodshed. Its leaders had defied a British ban on meetings to gather their supporters in protest of these new restrictions. Imperial authorities brought in colonial troops to forcibly disperse the "mob," shoot-

ing into the crowd and killing hundreds of unarmed Indians. The National Congress proclaimed that "all talk of reform is a mockery" and organized a national campaign of protest. It had a new leader to carry the movement to the people—Mohandas Gandhi.

In his early adult years, Gandhi belonged to India's new Westernized class. After legal studies in England, he practiced law in South Africa, where many Indians had emigrated in search of work. There he faced racial prejudice and segregation by the European population and discovered his true vocation, political protest and spiritual reconciliation. Caught between Indian and Western culture, Gandhi set out on a spiritual quest to reconcile Indian religious values and Western individualism. He sympathized deeply with Western socialist demands to improve the lives of the poor and oppressed. At the same time, he remained faithful to the Indian belief in spiritual rejuvenation through meditation and to the principle of nonviolence. Gandhi attached great significance to Christ's message in the Sermon on the Mount that violence be met with love by "turning the other cheek." He studied as well Henry David Thoreau's theory of civil disobedience to resist unjust laws. In this long search, he looked for the common humanitarian message that transcended creed and ideology.

Gradually he put together a unique political creed drawn from these readings, Indian religious values, and his own compassion for the sufferings of his fellow Indians. He demanded of his followers that they willingly and peacefully accept imprisonment from their oppressors rather than obey unjust laws or resort to violence. He relied on an innate sense of justice and what he called the "law of love" among all people to achieve the reforms he demanded. His political crusade in South Africa succeeded in temporarily ending the discriminatory legislation imposed on Indian migrants by the government. He returned to India in 1915 a famous champion of Indian rights.

The crisis that resulted from the Amritsar massacre of 1919 revealed that the National Congress had become a potent nationalist movement. It already possessed an extensive political organization, to which was added Gandhi's inspired leadership and a mass following throughout India. In protest against the massacre and the imperial rule responsible for that outrage, Gandhi organized in 1920 his first movement of noncooperation. He proclaimed that "cooperation in any shape or form with this satanic government is sinful." But when one group of Congress demonstrators attacked a police station, burning it and the police inside, Gandhi called off the campaign. He would not tolerate violence.

His form of mass protest and rejection of collaboration aroused disagreement within the National Congress. Many of its leaders welcomed the British offer to participate in provincial self-rule. The Montford Reforms of 1921 carried out the promises of 1917 for provincial representative government. The British viceroy proclaimed that "the principle of autocracy [i.e., absolute rule by the British state in its colony] has been abandoned." Congress politicians accepted the offer to present candidates for the elections. Gandhi had to adjust his campaign to the electoral interests of the party.

▩ SPOTLIGHT: Mohandas Gandhi ▩

In the long life of Mohandas Gandhi (1869–1948), he never once sought political office or honors. Yet on his death, he was mourned throughout the world as few public figures have ever been. A lawyer by training, he set his goal to help others find justice; "action is my domain," he once said. Yet his greatest achievement proved to be his philosophy of self-purification and humility. He sought nothing for himself, renouncing all material possessions and even sexual pleasure. He lived and died for the sake of his fellow human beings, and first of all for his fellow Indians.

They rewarded his efforts with a veneration that earned him the extraordinary title of "Mahatma" (meaning "great soul"). His action was from the beginning aimed at improving the spiritual life of individuals as well as reforming injustices of the British colonial regime. In his years in South Africa and later in India, his own work included the creation of special communities (called in Hindi "ashram") for close followers committed to a life of moral purification and social reform.

Beginning in the 1920s, his political campaigns against British rule in India mobilized millions of supporters. He expected of them the same readiness to abstain from violence and accept punishment voluntarily (his principle of "satyagraha") that he practiced himself. When some turned to violence and bloodshed, he denounced their action. He publicly condemned the personal and moral shortcomings of fellow Indians with as much zeal as the injustices and oppression of the British colonial regime. His philosophy of moral purification placed stern demands on everyone, and on himself first of all.

His fervent demands for political and social reform at times irritated his collaborators and infuriated his enemies. Despite widespread prejudice against the untouchable class of India, he insisted that these "children of God," as he called them, be given equal treatment alongside even high-caste Brahmins. In 1931, the viceroy invited Gandhi to his palace for negotiations over India's political future. It was recognition from the highest quarters of Gandhi's stature as leader of National Congress. He arrived at the great palace of the viceroy dressed only in a simple tunic and sandals. Winston Churchill, a conservative English politician, was outraged and bitterly protested the presence of "this half-naked rebellious holy man" seated alongside the "representative of the King-Emperor." Even Jawaharlal Nehru, Gandhi's loyal disciple and friend, could not accept Gandhi's program for the "salvation" of India through a return to the traditional way of life stripped of "railways, telegraphs, hospitals, doctors." Gandhi's approach to politics, as well as to personal conduct, was moralistic, not practical.

Gandhi's remarkable personality, combined with the good will that he showed everyone around him, remained to the end the foundation on which his vast popularity rested. When he was in England in 1932 to continue the negotiations for Indian independence, he chose to live in a poor section of London and to visit textile workers whose jobs were threatened by cottons manufactured in India. They, like most English people, welcomed him with respect and admiration. Nehru remained close to him throughout their decades of collaboration, finding in him moral inspiration and personal reassurance. After his death, a grieving Nehru told the Indian people that "a light has gone out of our lives and there is darkness everywhere."

Until the day of his death, Gandhi's message to Indians stressed the need for respect and toleration. Even when Muslims had created their own state, ending his dream of a unified India, he continued to demand equality of treatment for all Indians no matter what their religion. Gandhi's tragedy, like that of his country and other lands whose peoples were deeply divided, was that the hatred of a few could destroy in a short time the good deeds of generations. A fanatical Hindu assassinated Gandhi, blaming him for speaking out for an end to the bloodshed. The assassin preached violence, not reconciliation. His brutal solution to inter-ethnic relations found imitators in many other countries in the decades to come. Gandhi's struggle for peace and tolerance remained a vital cause long after his death.

Nehru and Indian Independence

Provincial self-rule, approved by the British government in 1923, did not weaken the nationalists' determination to obtain freedom for India. In the next decade, the conflict worsened between the National Congress and India's colonial rulers. In 1928, the Congress voted formally for a motion stating "the goal of the Indian people to be complete national independence." This new policy was the work of a talented young party leader, Jawaharlal Nehru. He had joined the National Congress following an

Mohandas Gandhi (*Embassy of India, Washington, D.C.*)

upbringing deeply influenced by British culture. His eminent father provided him with tutors, then with the best English education. Having earned his law degree in London, he returned to India in 1912 prepared to take up a law career modeled on that of his father. An aristocrat by birth and education, he believed deeply in the cause of Indian independence and joined the National Congress. Working for Gandhi gave him, for the first time, an awareness of the social exploitation of "this vast multitude of semi-naked sons and daughters of India."

In the 1920s, he began searching for the solution to social injustice. He looked first to British socialism, then to Marxism-Leninism and the Soviet Union. In 1927, he traveled to the Soviet Union in time for the tenth anniversary celebrations of the 1917 Revolution. Nehru came away with the conviction that the struggle against imperialism had to be joined to the struggle against capitalism. He drew the line at violent revolution, rejecting both the Leninist tactics of armed insurrection and the Stalinist methods of single-party dictatorship. He remained faithful to Gandhi's message of nonviolence and to the goal of a democratic India. He began in the late 1920s a militant campaign for liberation of his country, which he envisioned both democratic and socialist.

Gandhi remained the sole leader capable of organizing this new mass movement. In 1930, he called for a mass campaign against

Nehru's "Semi-Naked Sons of India": Field Workers Winnowing Rice, South India (*Indian National Congress Collection/Hoover Institution*)

the salt tax. It proved the most effective and dramatic protest movement of his entire career. Touching the poor directly and symbolizing British domination, the tax provided the ideal target against which to unite in opposition well-to-do Congress supporters and Indian peasants. Nonpayment of the tax demanded only the will to resist. By the summer of that year, the nonviolent resistance movement had spread throughout the country. Gandhi himself walked halfway across the land to the Indian Ocean to publicize his readiness to use salt taken from the sea in defiance of the law. The Indian army and police arrested demonstrators, including Nehru and Gandhi. The campaign lasted another three years before dying away.

Yet during that time, negotiations continued between the National Congress and the British government. In 1931, Gandhi traveled to London, along with other Indian leaders, to seek Dominion status for his country. The British government had that year created an association of independent former colonies, the Commonwealth, whose members (Dominions) governed themselves yet accepted a common tariff among all associated states, pursued a common foreign policy, and recognized the British monarchy. Only those lands under white rule (Canada, Australia, New Zealand, South Africa) immediately became members.

After several years of hesitation, the British government gave in to most of the National Congress's demands. It issued in 1935 new laws for Indian self-government—the Government of India Act. This statute created the legal structure of Indian political life until independence. It gave India the institutions of a self-governing state, restricted by special powers for the viceroy only in the event of war or internal emergencies. That part of India under the direct rule of the British, eleven provinces in all, received a federal structure somewhat resembling the state of Canada. An Indian central government had its own cabinet, responsible to a federal legislature. The viceroy, representative of the throne, provided the direct link between Great Britain and the Indian government.

The elections in 1937 for an Indian legislature posed a familiar dilemma to Congress leaders: continued struggle against the vestiges of British colonial rule or collaboration in the implementation of self-rule in peaceful elections. Among those members of Congress who argued against compromise were some admirers of the fascist regimes in Europe and others who found in Stalinist Russia inspiration for an Indian revolution. Between these two extremes, Nehru spoke for moderation. After some hesitation, he chose electoral collaboration. He concluded that "we have no choice but to contest the elections." His moderate policy won the support of the National Congress. Nehru proved in that electoral campaign to be Congress's outstanding political leader, campaigning throughout India. His party won a resounding victory in the 1937 elections, gaining control of eight of the eleven provincial governments.

The Muslim League and the Idea of Pakistan

That victory proved ultimately a defeat for the cause of united India. The Muslim League had presented its own electoral candidates on a program of cooperation with Congress. When the provincial cabinets were formed, Congress leaders refused to appoint Muslim League members to ministerial positions in these cabinets. They followed Gandhi's principle that India must not allow religious separatism to weaken their goal of a multireligious, multiethnic Indian nation. The leader of the League, Mohammed Ali Jinnah, declared that "Islam

is in danger," warning that a unified democratic India represented a menace to the Muslim faith and to the very existence of the Muslim community. In place of one India he proposed two states, one of which would be Pakistan.

In 1930, a small group of Muslim intellectuals had first proposed the idea of a separate state for the Muslims of the Indian subcontinent. This totally new concept of a nation based on religious affiliation addressed in its own way the problem of ethnic-religious diversity. The new state (or states) could not possibly gather together all India's Muslims, but only those territories where Muslims constituted a majority of the population. The name that these visionaries gave to their imagined new state, "Pakistan," came from the first letters of the largest of those areas. "P," "A," and "K" referred to lands in the northwest of the subcontinent—Punjab, Afghanistan (not part of the British Empire), and Kashmir. It was an improbable idea and a misguided national project (of the three regions, only one-half of Punjab and a tiny section of Kashmir ultimately became a part of the new state). It made a permanent mark on Indian history.

The campaign for partition was extremely controversial. No clear territorial limits separated the followers of the two religions. The large Muslim community of Bengal shared with Bengali Hindus a culture and language different from the language and culture of the Muslims of the Indus River valley in the west. Many Muslims remained committed to Gandhi's vision of a secular, multiethnic nation-state of all inhabitants of the Indian subcontinent, and some held influential positions in the National Congress. Still, fearing Hindu domination and determined to protect their religious practices and culture from Western secular influence, a growing number of Muslims were drawn to this vision of a distinct Muslim political community. Their search for cultural unity fused with the Muslim League's struggle to defend its political influence alongside and in opposition to the National Congress.

Nationalist dreams produced two very different ideas of India's future. Gandhi would not compromise on the principle of national unity. But his commitment to a civic nationalist creed blinded him to the fears of Muslims that majority rule meant oppression for them. Less moralistic, more ambitious leaders on both sides used religious differences to promote their political aims. Mohammed Ali Jinnah himself was a thoroughly Westernized Indian lawyer who spoke only English. He did not practice the Muslim religion and did not even speak fluent Urdu, the language of most of his Muslim followers. The defense of Muslim political and social needs, not a religious quarrel, explains his support for the cause of Pakistan.

Political interests and nationalist programs are not a sufficient explanation for the rift among Indian nationalists. Communal hostility increasingly split Indian society; democratic political reform appeared only to worsen this ethnic schism. Antagonisms were worst in urban areas such as Calcutta where poverty heightened religious and so-cial antagonism. The growth of violence between the Muslim and Hindu communities made real national unity increasingly an illusory goal. Perhaps there was still time to avoid the tragedy of partition through wise leadership and compromise. But war intervened, and the time never came.

That war began for India, as for Great Britain, in 1939. The Indian viceroy proclaimed India at war with Germany. Congress, while it backed the English cause, refused to be the agent of the British government in a war imposed on India. All Congress cabinets resigned. The Muslim League took their place.

Jinnah proclaimed a Day of Thanksgiving for all Indian Muslims at their deliverance from "Hindu" rule. Muslim deputies became members of provincial cabinets throughout India. The League still looked to the liberation of India from British colonial rule, but not as a unified state. In 1940, the Muslim League agreed on a formal statement called the Lahore Resolution. It demanded the creation of "independent states" for India's Muslim peoples. As the time of independence drew nearer, so too did the likelihood of conflict between India's great religious communities.

☛ HIGHLIGHT: Colonialism and Nationalism ☛

The Western empires lasted but a brief moment compared with the great empires of Rome and China. Still, their legacy proved as influential as that of earlier imperial states. Most important of all was the impulse their presence gave to nationalism among the peoples over whom they ruled. This process unfolded in spite of and against the wishes of imperial rulers. But when their empires collapsed, they left in their ruins the nation-states of the late twentieth century.

Colonialism directly contributed to this momentous change. First, the opposition of subject peoples to imperial rule led them to forge new, national bonds of loyalty around which to unite in resisting Western rule.

Second, non-Westerners searching for an ideological cause to focus and organize an anti-imperialist movement in their land had visible proof in recent Western history of nationalism's power to unite leaders and their people. Third, Western imperial rule forged new colonial territories within whose borders administrators, military forces, economic activities, and education created centers of public life. This experience gave these territories a tangible presence in the daily experience of the peoples living there. Nationalist movements emerging within these lands directed their efforts to overthrowing colonial rule, but left in place the colonial frontiers.

These borders proved tenacious as well because of the distrust among neighboring peoples. The Italian colony of Eritrea, on the shores of the Red Sea, disappeared when the Allies defeated Italy in the Second World War. The large neighboring inland state of Ethiopia absorbed that desert area, claiming that the land had centuries before belonged to the Ethiopian monarchy. But the history that mattered most to the Eritreans, largely Muslim, was their separation from the peoples of Ethiopia, who were mainly Christian and spoke very different languages. After a half-century of federation, in 1993 they voted overwhelmingly to reestablish their independence. Eritrea reappeared on the map of Africa; its borders were those drawn by the Italian Empire.

Everywhere Western overseas colonies forced diverse peoples to live together in a single territory. These colonies extended at times over enormous distances. The island archipelagos of the eastern Pacific were conquered by European states in the sixteenth century. Spanish conquest of the Philippines and Dutch control of the East Indies gave territorial unity to peoples divided both geographically and culturally on islands scattered across hundreds of miles of ocean. Dutch in the East Indies and Spanish in the Philippines became the state language. In each colony, one local language came to predominate among all the dialects and languages spoken there—Tagalog in the Philippines, Malay in the East Indies. Nationalist movements that emerged there in the nineteenth and twentieth centuries set their objective on ending colonial rule, but retained the common local language and the boundaries, both a permanent heritage of the imperial era.

Colonialism had to contend with the internal religious and tribal divisions in existence long before Western conquest. European conquerors moved into lands divided among a multitude of peoples with their own tribal or princely leaders. Administrators drew borders that often disregarded the boundaries separating these peoples. The size of their territories created colonies with many distinct ethnic populations. "Ethnic" is the term we use to refer to a people sharing a collective identity based on their belief in a common ancestry. The African colonies seized by European states in the nineteenth century were the homes of many different peoples. Scholars later counted more than 250 separate ethnic groups in British Nigeria, among whom four were very large. The Fulani and Hausa peoples in the north both practiced the Muslim religion. In the south were the Ibo and Yoruba peoples, among whom Christian missionaries made many converts. A colony such as Nigeria was thus multireligious as well as multiethnic. Frequently, ethnicity and religious allegiance overlapped, reinforcing the differences among these peoples.

European administrators needed the collaboration of colonial peoples in governing their lands. With only a handful of Europeans filling the most important posts, they had to recruit local officials, police, and even military forces. Faced with diverse peoples often hostile toward one another, their solution usually was to recruit their collaborators from one particular group. In Nigeria, the British preferred to select soldiers from the northern Fulani or Hausa peoples. In their small central African colonies of Burundi and Rwanda, the Germans (and after the First World War the Belgians) turned for assistance to the Tutsi people, who had for centuries held power and enjoyed greater wealth than the much more numerous Hutu people living there. Memories of different ancestral roots remained alive, though the two peoples lived close by one another and even intermarried. The two groups were alike also in that most of the population converted to Christianity during the colonial period. Material wealth mattered most in precolonial times, when possession of more cattle might even earn Hutu families the right to call themselves, and be called, Tutsi. Those who lost their possessions might end up labeled Hutu. The two ethnic terms, in other words, were marks of superiority and inferiority.

The Belgian administrators made these differences more tangible by giving preference and power to Tutsi soldiers and administrators, and then by ordering the entire population to acquire identity cards (internal passports) on which everyone had to identify themselves either Hutu or Tutsi. Ethnic groups, there as in other colonial lands, assumed in this process a far greater awareness of (and potentially hostility toward) other peoples than ever before. The ingredients for ethnic conflict were in place.

In these conditions, successful nationalist movements sought to avoid linking their anti-imperialist goals with the objectives of any particular ethnic or religious group. By necessity, they had to establish bonds based on some form of *civic* nationalism, that is, a nationalist ideology promoting shared cultural and political values, not on ethnic or linguistic uniqueness. They retained the borders created by the former colonial rulers, partly for fear of inciting interminable conflicts among peoples and with neighboring states along their frontiers, and partly in the belief that the political future of former colonies had to be multiethnic states. The Nigerian writer Chinua Achebe was ready to "give the [British] devil his due: colonialism in Africa disrupted many things, but it did create big political units where there were small, scattered ones before." In his judgment, Nigeria was a more promising homeland for all the peoples living there than the "hundreds of separate communities" that it replaced.

In the largest of the British colonies, India, the internal divisions were probably greater than in any other European-ruled territory. Nationalists seeking an Indian nation-state for the entire population had to propose a formula based on new principles of unity. These principles and ideas had to offer the population substantial reasons to prefer Indian unity to ethnic or religious separateness. Gandhi and the Indian National Congress confronted a daunting task. Their ultimate failure was a tragedy for India.

The historical past of lands such as Turkey, India, and China became the source of unifying national ideals. In India, Gandhi wrote and spoke of the great historical tradition created by the major religions of his country—Hinduism, Islam, Buddhism. From this tale of spiritual collaboration he drew his inspiration for a doctrine of Indian national solidarity. In China, the political unity and the great civilization that the empire had forged during its 2,000-year existence became points of historical reference to the Nationalist Party of Sun Yat-sen. Its leaders looked to a new Chinese nation, within the borders of the former empire, whose achievements would some day equal those of earlier periods of Chinese greatness. The Chinese Communists had much less sympathy for this tradition, but they too assumed that Chinese political unity was a necessary stage in their revolutionary plans for the Chinese people.

The search for a "useful past" belonging to a particular nation was similar to the efforts earlier by political leaders and intellectuals in Western lands to rewrite the history of their peoples' origins. In some cases the story they told was a generous one, though none came as close as Gandhi to attributing religious humanism to an entire people. Abraham Lincoln sought, in his Gettysburg Address, to make democracy the historical bond of all the peoples of the United States. His speech asked Americans to consider the American Revolution the time when a "new nation [was] conceived in Liberty." This civic nationalism was, in theory, open to all people, no matter what their ethnic or racial origins.

But the new national histories were often written with one ethnic group in mind. Some Western nationalists had shown the way in making history proclaim the superiority of one group of people over others. Ethnic nationalism in colonial and semi-colonial lands looked to the past to give one people a better claim on power and territory than others living in the same land. Ataturk and his fellow Turkish nationalists glorified their people by praising the Osmanli Turkic tribes, invaders from Central Asia who had long before conquered the land he called Turkey. He traced the nation's roots to this conquest. By implication, other peoples in Turkey, such as the Armenians, were inferior members of the new nation-state. These nationalists were convinced that their people were endowed with unique qualities, which had appeared long before and had been passed on from generation to generation. Their goal was the creation of political and cultural symbols around which to unify the population in one national community. These national stories of ethnic groups conveyed a dangerous message, for they easily became justification for racism. History, in this telling, was a story of "blood and belonging." Nationalism was a powerful ideology, both creative and destructive.

One scholar has labeled the ideal of a nation-state an "imagined community." The nation, intended to be the basis of a sovereign state, is so large and so remote from people's everyday lives that it can only be imagined. Yet it still relies on the solidarity of a people believing themselves part of one large community.[1] The political community imagined by nationalists was often a fragile creation, contested by other movements and minority peoples living in the same territory. Colonial empires shaped the borders of lands in which these movements took shape; the fall of these empires put the promise of nationalism to the test in every former colonial land.

---

[1] Benedict Anderson, *Imagined Communities: Reflections on the Origin and Spread of Nationalism* (New York, 1991), pp. 6–7.

THE STRUGGLE FOR THE CONTROL OF CHINA

The Chinese path to national unification began with the overthrow of the Chinese Empire in 1911. It did not end until the communist revolution in 1949. Once an integrated empire and social system, China went through a prolonged period of disorder and struggle. Foreign and civil wars wrought terrible destruction and hardship, adding to the perennial sufferings of the population. Supporters of the Chinese Nationalist Party looked to Western states in laying their plans for a new China, while the Chinese Communist Party conceived of a revolutionary society on the model of the Soviet system. Deeply divided by political ideology, they both distanced themselves from the traditional Confucian order. Bitter enemies, each anticipated that it alone was destined to construct a renewed, unified China. Until the 1940s, the Chinese Nationalist Party appeared the chosen leader.

The Rise of the Nationalist Party

In 1911, the most powerful commander in the imperial army declared his allegiance to a Chinese Republic. The last emperor, still a child, was taken prisoner and the empire fell without resistance. Supporting this rebellion were intellectuals and students educated in Western schools, ready to devote their lives to bringing Western political rights and national unity to their own country.

In the years after the empire's collapse, ambitious Chinese generals in command of sizeable armies seized control of large provinces. One of them took over the entire region of Manchuria, where he governed like a petty prince. These "warlords" depended on their armies and the taxes of their poor subjects to control their territories. They rarely had a reform program, were unwilling or unable to create new political institutions, and fought among themselves in small-scale wars that worsened the suffering of the civilian population. Within ten years of the 1911 revolution, China was a united republic in name only. Central government institutions and functions fell into decay. Foreign states kept their concessions and spheres of influence by dealing directly with these petty military rulers. The rule of the warlords became the major political obstacle to national unification.

Revolutionary parties claimed the right to create that Chinese nation-state. Their organizers were intellectuals educated in "new schools" that taught Western languages and knowledge. Often they had gone abroad, to Japan or to the West, to learn of the modern world. The most influential of these radicals was the veteran revolutionary, Sun Yat-sen. He had abandoned Confucianism, converting to Christianity, and had given up his medical career to organize a secret nationalist movement. His ideals were summed up in a set of Three Principles: (1) nationalism, by which he meant freedom from imperialist domination; (2) democracy, which to him represented Western constitutional government; and (3) socialism, which he understood as an industrial economy and equality of land holdings for the Chinese peasant farmers. He realized that to achieve these goals China required a modern political party. He called his new movement the Nationalist People's Party (in Chinese, *Guomindang*). For him as for other radicals, revolution constituted China's sole path to progress and independence.

Events at the end of the First World War brought his party the mass support it needed to lead the Chinese nationalist movement. The news that the Paris peace negotiators had granted the Japanese Empire territorial rights to northern China set off a wave of protest in Chinese cities, where even business classes joined a boycott of (that is, refusal to purchase) all Japanese goods. Sun Yat-sen and his Nationalist Party took the lead in organizing the boycott. This "May Fourth movement," so named since the news from France reached China on May 4, 1919, gave Sun's party the broad base of support that it needed to challenge the warlords. The Japanese government soon agreed to withdraw its forces from most Chinese territories. The mass backing that Sun Yat-sen had obtained set his party on the path to unify China.

The Nationalists soon found a valuable foreign ally. Their opposition to Japanese expansion and to Western imperialism was shared by the new Soviet Union. The Soviet leaders considered nationalist revolutionary movements in colonial lands to be an important part of their global struggle against Western capitalism. The two groups shared common enemies. Some Chinese radicals found in the revolutionary experiment under way in the Soviet Union a model for their own country. They constituted the core membership of the Chinese Communist Party, created in 1921. Sun Yat-sen did not share their faith in the dictatorship of the proletariat and the inevitable triumph of communism. He did, however, recognize the practical benefits of an alliance with Soviet Russia. For one thing, the Nationalist Party needed a centralized organization like that of the Soviet Communist Party to organize and lead the forces necessary to unify China. For another, he realized that his movement required military aid to defeat the warlords. The Soviet Communists had set up an effective army in their fight for survival during the civil war. They could furnish Nationalist armies with the needed military training for the conquest of China.

In 1923, the Soviet state and the Communist International agreed to provide political and military assistance to the Chinese Nationalist Party. Russian advisers helped to organize a Chinese "party army" and Chinese officers, including Sun's aide Chiang Kai-shek, went to Russia to learn from Red Army officers the skills of modern war. Russian assistance proved very effective, widening the base of support for the Nationalists and strengthening its party organization and army.

In 1926, the Nationalist leadership was ready to undertake its military offensive to defeat the warlords in northern China. From their base in the south, its troops, commanded by Chiang Kai-shek, moved up the coast. Their objective was the imperial city of Beijing. The success of this "Northern Expedition" was probably the greatest triumph of the Nationalists. Warlords surrendered rather than fight their armies. In 1928, the Nationalists captured Beijing. This military victory was of particular benefit to Chiang Kai-shek. He had become leader of the Nationalist party following Sun Yat-sen's death in 1925. His power depended largely on control of the army. It was as much a political as a military instrument of power. For the rest of his life he relied primarily on his armed forces for political as well as military backing. Chiang resembled in this respect the warlords. He did preserve Sun's Nationalist Party and adhered to its program of reform. His military victory conferred on him the mantle of Sun's legitimate heir. He appeared to have achieved Sun's dream of a new China unified under the nationalist leadership.

In those years, Chiang set out to eliminate his principal political rival, the Chinese Communist Party. In 1927, his military forces and police suddenly arrested large numbers of Communists, as well as labor union organizers and other suspected radicals; many of them were soon executed. Urban worker support for the Communists declined as a result of the repression and of their disillusionment at the collapse of the

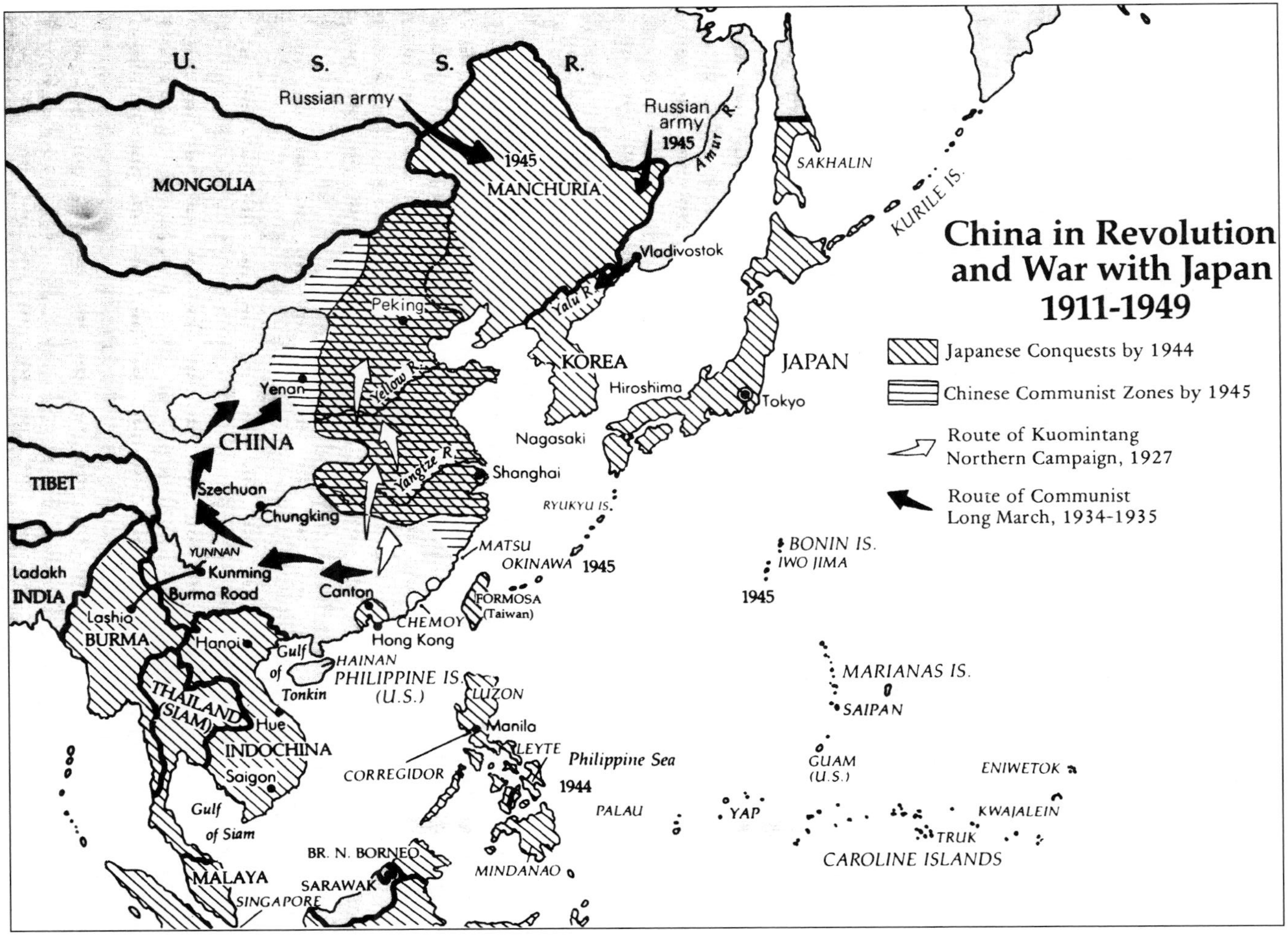
China in Revolution and War with Japan 1911-1949
Japanese Conquests by 1944
Chinese Communist Zones by 1945
Route of Kuomintang Northern Campaign, 1927
Route of Communist Long March, 1934-1935
U. S. S. R.
Russian army
Russian army 1945
1945
Amur R.
MONGOLIA
MANCHURIA
SAKHALIN
KURILE IS.
Vladivostok
Yalu R.
Peking
KOREA
JAPAN
Hiroshima
Tokyo
Nagasaki
Yenan
Yellow R.
CHINA
Yangtze R.
Shanghai
TIBET
Szechuan
Chungking
RYUKYU IS.
MATSU
OKINAWA 1945
BONIN IS.
IWO JIMA
1945
YUNNAN
Kunming
Burma Road
Canton
Ladakh
INDIA
FORMOSA (Taiwan)
Lashio
BURMA
CHEMOY
Hong Kong
Hanoi
Gulf of Tonkin
HAINAN
PHILIPPINE IS. (U.S.)
LUZON
MARIANAS IS.
SAIPAN
THAILAND (SIAM)
Hue
Manila
INDOCHINA
LEYTE
Philippine Sea
1944
CORREGIDOR
Saigon
GUAM (U.S.)
ENIWETOK
PALAU
YAP
KWAJALEIN
Gulf of Siam
TRUK
CAROLINE ISLANDS
BR. N. BORNEO
MINDANAO
MALAYA
SARAWAK
SINGAPORE

China at War, 1911–1949

party in China's cities. In response to Chiang's anticommunist campaign, the Communist International ordered the Chinese Communists to organize a large-scale insurrection, but it failed miserably. The failure that year of Comintern policies in China gave some of the survivors, including Mao Zedong, a bitter lesson in Moscow's inability to understand the Chinese revolutionary struggle.

Mao Zedong and Chinese Communism

This crushing defeat of the urban supporters of the Chinese Communist Party proved the turning point in its history. Its efforts to imitate the Russian Communists' path to revolutionary power had failed miserably. Its entire strategy, even ideology, had to be revised. This became the work of Mao Zedong. He had joined the Communist Party after years of searching for a political blueprint to remake the Chinese state and society. A student at the time of the 1911 revolution, he joined in the struggle against the old order. He spurned his father's wish that he return to help run the family farm, preferring the life of an activist scholar. He wrote then that the "four evil demons of the empire" were "religion, capitalism, autocracy, and the Three Bonds." Moving to Beijing in 1918, he discovered the cause to which he devoted his entire life. Some Chinese intellectuals that year were praising the revolution in Russia as the "victory of the spirit of all humanity." He joined a Marxist study circle to learn of Lenin's theory of revolution. By the time the Chinese Communist Party was founded in 1921, he was a dedicated Marxist-Leninist.

The period in the 1920s of collaboration with the Nationalists gave Mao invaluable experience in revolutionary organization. He devoted his effort to mobilizing Chinese peasants for political action in the campaign against the warlords. He became convinced of the power for revolution in the Chinese tradition of rural rebellion; his experience also taught him how to win the peasants' backing. Most peasants were tenant farmers, subject in those years to exploitation by landlords and tax collectors, and to looting and murder by marauding bands of robbers or soldiers. Their only recourse, as in past centuries, was banditry and mass rebellion. In the years of collaboration with the Nationalists, Mao grasped the idea that China's poor peasants could be mobilized to take up arms against their exploiters and against foreign enemies. Mao had created his own version of communist revolutionary theory and practice.

The destruction in 1927–1928 of the Chinese Communist Party forced Mao to seek refuge among his peasant followers. By 1929, he had carved out a small area in a south China province where he and his peasant guerrilla army were able to construct a "Red Base," the center of his operations. He organized and expanded his territory in spite of repeated "extermination" offensives by Nationalist troops. The survival of his Red Base required an army capable of holding back the Nationalists, and its soldiers had to be recruited among the peasantry. Mao first proved his revolutionary genius in those difficult years. By 1931, his "liberated area" had expanded to include a population of 3 million under the control of a Red Army of 100,000. That year he formally proclaimed it the Chinese Soviet Republic. The proclamation was an act of defiance and a claim to leadership in the Republic of China. He was convinced that the most powerful revolutionary forces of his country were in the countryside, and he was right.

The success of his movement depended on the support of the Chinese peasantry and the organization of military forces capable of sustaining long and arduous guerrilla warfare. Mao's soviet republic gave the poor peasants what they most desired—their own land. Landlords and rich peasants saw most of their property redistributed to the landless farmers. The land and its harvest belonged to individual peasants. They depended upon Mao's soviet republic to retain their farms. They had good reason to support their communist rulers. Many became the recruits in the Red Army on whom the survival of the republic depended.

The army was the military arm of Mao's movement. He and his followers sought to convince the soldiers that their real enemy was "feudalism." This term, in the vocabulary of Chinese Communists, referred to China's oppressive traditions. In fighting the Nationalist forces, his soldiers believed that they were contributing to the historic progress of China. Over the years Mao devised a unique strategy of guerrilla combat, summed up in a simple formula that every soldier learned: "The enemy advances, we retreat; the enemy camps, we harass; the enemy tires, we attack; the enemy retreats, we pursue." Mao had no assurance of ultimate victory save his unshakable faith in the world proletarian movement. He had no protection from his Chinese enemies besides the rifles of his peasant soldiers. In those years of repression of the Chinese Communist Party, the very survival of Mao's soviet republic represented a victory.

China between Nationalists and Communists

In the late 1920s, the Nationalist Party consolidated its leadership of China. For a few years the country enjoyed relatively peaceful times. The Western powers made their peace with Chiang, renouncing the special privileges they had forced upon the Chinese Empire. They were unwilling to maintain strong military forces to protect their territorial concessions. Besides, they knew that the Nationalists did not threaten their interest in trade and investment. The Chinese Republic took over control of tariffs, taxes, and postal services, previously run by Westerners. The foreign concessions disappeared; Chinese law extended throughout the country. The Nationalist leaders could fairly claim to be Sun Yat-sen's true heirs in ending Western domination of their country. They promised an end to old abuses. They banned the cruel practice of footbinding, which was the mark of submission of women to the Chinese patriarchal order.

Despite Sun's promise of constitutional democracy, the Chinese Republic under the Nationalists was an authoritarian state. Under the command of Chiang, its army was the dominant political force in the country. He held semidictatorial powers, calling his regime a "guided democracy" for the young Chinese Republic. His claim to be the head of a unified China was an illusion. Many areas escaped their control; Manchuria remained in the hands of its warlord, only nominally "allied" with the Nationalists. Korea and the southern Manchurian coast were centers of Japanese military forces. Japanese generals were increasingly eager to extend their power into China. They mocked the Nationalist government's efforts to expand its authority, but in private worried that China might once again become powerful. Manchuria was their most tempting target, and in 1931 they chose to seize the moment.

Japanese army officers stationed in the Japanese concession in southern Manchuria claimed (falsely) that Chinese terrorists had attacked Japanese property and military forces. The reality was the reverse. They had decided to seize the province before the Chinese Nationalists could do so. That year, the

Japanese army invaded Manchuria north of the coastal zone it already occupied. Its forces encountered only weak resistance from the troops of the Manchurian warlord. By early 1932, it had conquered the entire province. Japanese occupation authorities turned it into a satellite state, called Manchukuo. In a mockery of "national self-determination," they claimed to give the Manchu people their own state and created a monarchy, placing on the throne the last Qing (Manchu) emperor. He was in fact their puppet ruler.

Chiang made only token gestures of opposition. The Japanese campaign touched a peripheral area, destroying the power of another warlord. He agreed to an armistice, which resembled a capitulation. He knew that his forces could not defeat the Japanese army, and secretly rejoiced at the defeat of the Manchurian warlord. He preferred instead to turn his own troops against his internal enemy.

Chiang's target was the soviet republic controlled by Mao's forces. It was the stronghold of his most dangerous rival for power in China. In the early 1930s, he launched four separate military offensives against the Communists. He turned for help to German military advisers, who taught his troops the methods of encirclement and siege operations. By 1934, his forces had drawn a noose around Mao's troops. They were slowly strangling the soviet area. The Communists' only hope of survival lay in abandoning their soviet republic.

The Long March of Mao's army has become a legend in Chinese history. As such, official accounts of the year-long trek mingle fact and fancy. It started out, in Mao's own words, as a "headlong flight" of about 120,000 soldiers, abandoning their families and possessions and setting out without any clear destination. They were pursued by Nationalist troops seeking their annihilation, through mountainous areas inhabited by people hostile to all Chinese. Taking charge after several months of dissension and debate within the Communist Party leadership, Mao was able to save his movement from destruction.

In that period, he earned the reputation of heroic "helmsman" for the Chinese Communists. They revered him as their courageous warrior carrying the revolutionary torch. Mao selected the Long March's destination, which was to be the northwest province of Shaanxi (old spelling, Shensi). It offered refuge for his forces, since it was the center of another small "liberated area." The choice was a gamble, for it was located at an enormous distance and required that Mao and his followers cross a vast mountainous terrain where few supplies could be found (see map, p. 97). Hunger and disease accompanied the marchers all the way. Those who survived required great moral and physical strength. The legend claims that only 8,000 arrived in late 1935 at their destination of Yanan, a city in Shaanxi. Whatever the actual number of casualties, the Long March proved the revolutionary commitment of Mao and his followers. It forged the leadership that led the party to victory fifteen years later. Mao had saved the core of his movement and found a secure base to continue his struggle.

Recognition of his remarkable achievement came from Moscow. In those years, the Soviet leaders had special need of Mao's help. The Soviet Union had ordered foreign communist parties to mobilize against its enemies, Germany and Japan. In 1935, it sent orders to the Chinese party to organize an anti-Japanese coalition. It was to include Chiang's troops, better equipped than Mao's forces and supported by the West. For Stalin, the strategy promised to divert toward China those Japanese forces which by then had occupied Manchuria as far north as borders of the Soviet Union. Mao supported the new tactics wholeheartedly. He was himself a Chinese patriot, deeply committed to the defeat of China's enemies. In the following years, his party gained the sympathy of many Chinese attracted by its nationalist zeal as much as by its Marxist revolutionary program.

The communist base of operations became north China, in the poor highland region of Shaanxi. Its military forces, numbering in 1936 about 30,000, were strong enough to defeat a new Nationalist encirclement campaign. Almost completely cut off from the outside world, its very existence was a mystery to the West until the American Edgar Snow visited the area and described it in a flattering book called *Red Star over China*. The new soviet republic had to rely solely on the resources of the region. The Soviet Union provided no military or economic assistance. Its leaders still distrusted Mao's "peasant bandits" and preferred dealing with the Nationalist regime. When, in 1937, the Soviet government began delivering military supplies to China, it sent them to Chiang's forces.

Mao could count only on his own military forces and his political movement. In his soviet republic he carried out the strategy of peasant reform and guerrilla war that he had learned earlier. He explained to his followers in 1936 that their "revolutionary war" remained the struggle to destroy imperialism and feudalism in China, embodied in the "counter-revolutionary" regime of the Nationalists. Chiang's forces were very strong, however, and they were weak and small. The Communists' first task therefore consisted of the defeat of the Japanese imperialists; revolution came later.

War against Japan

Mao's alliance with Chiang became reality in 1937. Chiang had resisted joining the coalition until one of his own generals took him prisoner, keeping him hostage until he agreed to the "united front" with the Communists. It was one of the most bizarre and humiliating experiences in Chiang's career. But the alternative was much more unpleasant. His captor might well have shot him, but Mao insisted on methods of "gentle persuasion" until Chiang gave in. The Nationalist leader ended (temporarily) his campaign against Mao's soviet republic, and accepted joint military operations against the Japanese forces. As his reward, his state obtained military supplies from the Soviet Union (more than the United States gave his state in the period before 1941). The Chinese Communists for their part acknowledged their place in the Chinese Republic, renaming their soviet republic the "special regime of the Republic of China" and baptizing the Red Army the "Eighth Route Army." Both sides remained deeply suspicious of the other. Only the distance separating their core territories and the conflict with Japan kept them at peace. The two rivals for power made a fragile partnership; their truce was short-lived.

War with Japan gave them a common enemy. Later in the summer of 1937, full-scale war between Japan and China began. No one yet knows exactly how the military conflict started in an area near Beijing where Japanese troops were stationed. Communist and anti-Japanese Nationalist troops stationed there apparently started small-scale military operations against the Japanese. In retaliation, Japanese generals resolved in a reckless move to crush all the Chinese forces and to make coastal China another "client state" of the Japanese Empire. Major Japanese offensives began that year in the northern and central regions of China. Japanese troops pushed farther and farther into China in an effort to crush Chiang's forces.

The Chinese Republic could not match the military might of Japan. By 1939, the Japanese controlled the principal coastal areas of China, where they set up puppet regimes governed by Chinese collaborators.

Chiang had to retreat far into the interior, placing his capital in the mountainous city of Chongqing (Chungking). He had kept his regime in existence, but only by husbanding his forces and placing strict controls on the offensive operations of his troops. He preferred to hold what territory he could by defensive fighting, avoiding bloody and futile attacks on the Japanese. He feared the Communists nearly as much. Their guerrilla forces proved more successful than his armies in defending Chinese territory and people against the Japanese.

Mao's armies moved into large rural areas of central and northern China behind the Japanese lines. By 1941, their Eighth Route Army totaled 400,000 men and held areas with a combined population of 44 million people. That year the Japanese attempted to wipe out their insurrection. Japanese forces applied to the guerrilla areas the simple, brutal policy of "burn all, kill all, loot all." The Communists suffered severely, their army declining to 300,000, but their war continued. The Japanese occupation forces could not control the areas liberated by the Communists, nor could their armies destroy the Nationalists. Neither Communists nor Nationalists by themselves could expel the enemy from China, however. To end the stalemate, they had to have help from outside.

The only ally capable of providing that assistance was the United States. Since 1937, Soviet Russia had given the Nationalists military aid. When Germany attacked Russia in mid-1941, even those supplies ceased. In 1937, the U.S. government made a diplomatic gesture of support for the Nationalist regime. President Roosevelt praised the "magnificent defense of China." Subsequently, he allowed Chinese purchases of military equipment by disregarding U.S. neutrality laws banning aid to foreign belligerents. The U.S. press publicized Japanese

brutality toward the Chinese, denouncing the massacre in 1938 by Japanese troops of the population of the Chinese city of Nanking. But American isolationism blocked any major U.S. effort to aid China. A growing naval conflict with Germany turned the attention of the United States toward the war in Europe. Until the Japanese regime's expansionist policies took its troops further into East Asia, the Chinese had to fight alone.

SUMMARY

In the two decades following the end of the First World War, nationalist movements in Asian countries began the historic process of moving their peoples from the era of empires to the age of nation-states. The change proceeded then, as later, along paths unique to each country. Different cultural traditions, colonial institutions, and nationalist visions gave the history of these lands their own distinct character. The outcome everywhere was the decline of Western imperial influence.

The Turkish national revolution took the path of rejection of the Ottoman institutions and the Muslim way of life. The struggle included war with Greek invaders, and the repression of internal revolts by minority peoples. Out of this bitter, bloody conflict emerged a Turkish nation-state. It adapted modern secular laws and Western institutions to the needs and character of the Turkish people. Its creation was a national revolution.

The Indian National Congress, after long years of political struggle, won from the British the promise of self-government for the entire subcontinent. The British Empire lacked the resources and the determination to maintain for much longer its hold on India. The leaders of National Congress pressed forward their campaign for independence with zeal, but also with regard to Gandhi's commandments for peaceful methods of struggle. They could not, however, overcome centuries of distrust between the Muslim and Hindu communities. Whether the land would in fact remain united depended on the moderation and realism of the Muslim League and the National Congress. Its fate also rested with the millions of Muslims and Hindus, already in serious conflict.

The rise of the Nationalist party of Chiang Kai-shek brought a superficial appearance of national unity to China and ended finally the most humiliating aspects of Western domination. There, too, the future of the country rested partly on the outcome of an internal conflict, pitting Communists against the Nationalist regime. Their programs for China's resurgence were diametrically opposed. The Nationalists proved less capable than the Communists of implementing ambitious plans to improve the lot of China's impoverished masses. They were powerful enough to contain Mao's revolutionary forces. But they lacked the resources to challenge Japanese expansionism. The greatest threat to China's recovery was the war with the Japanese Empire. The age of empire had not yet come to an end in East Asia.

DATES WORTH REMEMBERING

1919 Gandhi leader of Indian National Congress

1919 Amritsar massacre

1919 Kemal Ataturk leader of Turkish nationalist movement

1920–1922 Greek-Turkish War

1921 Provincial self-rule in India

1921 Creation of Chinese Communist Party

1923 Founding of Republic of Turkey

1925 Abolition of Caliphate by Ataturk

1928 Chinese Nationalists in control of China

1929 National Congress for Indian independence

1930 Anti-salt tax movement in India

1931 Japanese invasion of Manchuria

1935 Government of India Act

1937 Triumph of Indian National Congress in national elections

1938 Muslim League for independent state of Pakistan

1934–35 "Long March" of Chinese Communists

1937–1945 Sino-Japanese War

RECOMMENDED READING

Modern Turkey

Andrew Mango, *Ataturk* (1999). A detailed and massive biography of the founder of Turkey.

Bernard Lewis, *The Emergence of Modern Turkey* (2nd ed., 1968). A comprehensive analysis of the upheaval that produced modern Turkey.

Indian History

Michael Edwardes, *British India, 1772–1947* (1968). A balanced survey of British rule in India.

Judith Brown, *Gandhi: Prisoner of Hope* (1989). The biography of the inspirational spiritual and political leader, with a critical view of his message.

Stanley Wolpert, *A New History of India*, 4th ed., (1993). A broad survey of pre- and post-colonial India, very critical of the British impact on India.

Chinese History

James Sheridan, *China in Disintegration: The Republican Era in Chinese History, 1912–1949* (1975). The story of the failed hopes and plans of the Nationalist party in their years of rise and fall from power.

Jonathan Spence, *The Search for Modern China* (1990). An interpretive history of China, stressing its rich, complex cultural tradition.

Memoirs, Novels, and Visual Aids

Ved Mehta, *The Ledge between the Streams* (1984); *Daddyji* (1979); and *Mamaji* (1975). A vivid multi-volume account of growing up in a Hindu family in northern India divided between its respect for tradition and the attraction of modernity.

Han Suyin, *The Crippled Tree* (1965). The memoirs of a young Chinese girl, later a famous novelist, whose European father and Chinese mother made the conflict between East and West a personal drama.

Gandhi. A somewhat idealized film biography (1982) of the great Indian leader.

The Last Emperor. Film dramatization (1987) of the life of Emperor Pu Yi, who survived war, revolution, and Mao Zedong.

CHAPTER FOUR

The Emergence of Despotic Empires

NAZI GERMANY, THE SOVIET UNION, THE JAPANESE EMPIRE, 1930–1941

Hopes in the 1920s for peace and progress faded in the next decade. Economic prosperity gave way to pervasive world depression. In its wake came bitter political conflicts and violence. Extremist prophets in lands hard hit by the economic decline proposed drastic political solutions to the anguish and hardship of those years. In Germany, their hunger for power and their popular support gave them the chance to put in place a brutal dictatorship. In Japan, a militaristic regime in those years transformed a relatively democratic country into an authoritarian, expansionist state. The aggressive foreign policies of these two despotic states heightened international tensions and pointed the way to a new war. The depression did not produce these changes, but it created the breeding ground for the extremism that afflicted public life in these lands. Despotism,

not democracy, appeared the answer to the crisis of those years.

The model for this brutal political revolution was Italian fascism. It had turned nationalism into a creed of totalitarian dictatorship. The triumph of the Nazi Party in Germany represented the most spectacular victory of fascism. On the other side of the globe, Japanese military leaders took over key positions in government and imposed on the country an ideology of militaristic nationalism so severe that it resembled fascism. A militant ideology set the tone for public life in all three states. It glorified the image of the warrior and military conquest. All three regimes pursued expansionist foreign policies by diplomatic intimidation and war. The empires of Italy, Germany, and Japan destroyed hopes for a new era of peace. For a few years, their conquests seemed to bring the world into a new age of imperialism.

At the other political extreme, the Stalinist state of the Soviet Union announced to the world that its revolutionary deeds and ideology pointed the way to human progress and deliverance from economic hardship. In the years after the 1917 revolution, the Communists had put in place a one-party dictatorship. Stalin took this process one step further, creating a dictatorial regime as despotic as that of Nazi Germany. The message from the Soviet Union affirmed that a new, socialist society had emerged there, freer than any society in the world. The Communists boasted that they had achieved this marvel by means of a "revolution from above." They kept in place a system of elections for Soviet government, but allowed only one candidate to appear for each office. They retained a system of justice with trials and defense lawyers, but these legal officials all followed the orders of the secret police. The peoples of the Soviet Union had to submit to this perverse "democracy," since prison or death awaited anyone who disagreed with the regime.

Soviet foreign policy had to contend with the expansionist threat from Germany and Japan. Stalin, perhaps the most cynical of the political leaders in those years, considered global politics a "jungle" in which only the ruthless could survive. When the opportunity to annex new territories arose at the end of the 1930s, he seized the chance. His state, which ruled over the lands once in the Russian Empire, expanded into western territories whose population had for a few years lived in free nation-states. In this sense, the Soviet Union was a despotic empire in the making.

FASCISM AND NAZI REVOLUTION

The strength of fascist states in the 1930s could be measured by the weakness of the democratic countries. The First World War had damaged all the major countries, but in the West its effects both on the population and on the political leadership were long lasting. By contrast, the spirit of war animated the fascist movements, whose motto was "might makes right." Seeking peace above all, the democratic governments of France and Great Britain proved powerless to resist fascist threats until, too late, they revived defensive alliances like those before the First World War. Fascism seemed the wave of the future.

The Decline of Western Democracies

The lure of fascism in the 1930s arose largely from the profound crisis caused by the depression. The capitalist system's promise to provide people with work and to satisfy their needs had failed miserably. Gradually after 1932 industrial production did begin to rise, but in many countries it remained below the level of prosperity of the late 1920s. The underlying obstacle to global recovery was the lack of free movement of investment funds and consumer and producer goods across borders to stimulate economic growth. The 1920s system had disappeared, replaced by "autarky," a nationalist system of self-reliance and rivalry with competing economies. "Beggar thy neighbor" was the motto of the day. The free market left economic resources and labor idle. Conservative fiscal policies did not offer an adequate solution to the crisis. Critics of conservative policies condemned state inaction and classical economic theory that relied on the "laws" of supply and demand to ensure prosperity. This view appeared in all democratic countries. Franklin Roosevelt, Democratic Party candidate for the U.S. presidency in 1932, rejected the argument of his Republican rival that the economy would improve on its own. "Economic laws are not made by nature," he argued, "they are made by human beings." His conclusion was that, since "men and women are starving," the state had to take action. The crisis in the United States, in his opinion, called above all for political leadership.

A long-term solution to the depression required a fundamental revision of economic thought. The most promising ideas came from a British economist, John Maynard Keynes (see Spotlight, pp. 161–162), who proposed a radical new theory to deal with the crisis. He argued that the free market was inherently unstable. It was incapable of ensuring long-lasting recovery and full employment. By itself, the long-term demand for producer and consumer goods could not rise sufficiently to meet these objectives. Instead, he proposed that governments use their own financial means to invest, spending if necessary during hard times more than they collected in taxes to compensate for the inadequacy of private consumption and investment. His call for government intervention encountered vehement opposition among conservatives, for it violated deeply cherished beliefs in the limits to government powers and in the benefits of the free enterprise system.

Keynes's controversial theories offered a new answer to the crisis. In the United States, Great Britain, and France, leaders improvised policies to improve economic conditions and to meet the needs of their people. In every case, their governments became more active than ever before in helping to alleviate the social hardship caused by the depression. Under strong pressure from their citizens, they expanded the meager aid previously granted the unemployed, the aged, and the sick, and granted new rights to labor unions to protect the interests of the workers. These new policies to assist the needy were called "social welfare." Once considered socialistic by liberals and conservatives alike, they became important not only to protect the welfare of the poor but

also to ensure the democratic consensus on which the political stability of these countries depended.

In the United States, Franklin Roosevelt's victory in the 1932 elections began a period of sweeping social and economic reforms. On becoming president in early 1933, he launched a program for recovery that he called the "New Deal." It started with immediate government action to save the banking system, in a state of collapse at the time, and to revive the economy. His first period of reforms emphasized assistance to producers. It included efforts to save the farmers from foreclosure and businessmen from bankruptcy. Federal regulatory agencies were set up to prevent the abusive action of speculators, judged responsible for the stock market crash of 1929. His major effort to assist the poor at that time was a massive public works campaign. Later in the 1930s, his administration launched the Social Security System. It was enacted to provide pensions for retired people with funding from obligatory contributions by employers and employees. Conservatives called Roosevelt a "socialist" for using federal powers to regulate and limit the powers of business. Roosevelt answered that he was trying to save the capitalist system from collapse. In 1936, the voters showed their support for his policies by giving him an overwhelming victory in the elections that year.

Still, Roosevelt's reforms had only limited success. Recovery from the depression was incomplete, for millions remained unemployed. Even the introduction of government spending measures in 1937, inspired by Keynes's theories, was not sufficient. Only the beginning of intensive armament production in 1940 restored full employment. Domestic measures for economic growth, even in a country as large as the United States, were not sufficient. A new system of global economic expansion was needed, but Roosevelt and his government had no plans for such measures. Political leadership and the majority of the population were as isolationist as ever in those years.

Social and economic reforms in Great Britain and France had similarly meager results. Voters in these countries, as in the United States, remained loyal to democratic parties, refusing to back authoritarian and fascist movements. Improvements in living conditions were slow, and political leadership was increasingly preoccupied by the threat of war. British and French leaders, like their people, desired nothing so much as peace. They collaborated in the policy, known as "appeasement," of conciliating the expansionist fascist states. The great tragedy of that time was that the world was no longer, as Wilson had so optimistically forecast in 1917, "safe for democracy."

The Birth of Fascism

Western democracies had no radical solutions to the crisis. Their very principles of compromise and their guarantee of human rights stood in the way of authoritarian methods of rule. These restraints did not exist for Italian Fascists. The welfare of the people was assured thanks to what they boasted was their "totalitarian" power. The depression heightened the lure of fascist methods. The great appeal of Italian fascism lay in its glorification of national unity and its claim to have ended social discord. The message was attractive to many Italians in the crisis that gripped their country in the years after the end of the First World War.

Fascism was the creation of a skillful political demagogue, Benito Mussolini. He turned political life into an arena of unrestrained violence. He was a former antiwar socialist who had become a fanatical nationalist in the course of the war. Mussolini had served in the Italian army, an experience that marked his personality and his political philosophy. Demobilized after being wounded, he launched a political movement intended to carry the ruthlessness he had learned as a front-line soldier into civilian life. The war provided him, as it did Hitler, schooling for political combat on the national stage.

Joined by other disillusioned war veterans, he preached a message of militaristic renewal of the Italian nation. He called for the expulsion of the "corrupt" politicians from government, the end of labor strikes and agitation, and the defeat of the "subversive, internationalist" Communists and socialists. He scorned the ideal of liberty, preferring "discipline" for the Italian nation. In place of a parliamentary regime, he proposed a strong state purged of all democratic parties under a strong leader. Fascism in its original Italian version was more a set of nationalist slogans and images of masculine valor and violence than a clear doctrine. Mussolini's fertile imagination and talent as a demagogic orator persuaded many Italians that they were a people with a glorious, heroic past, which he projected all the way back to the Roman Empire. He promised to revive that past. In this way, he manipulated ideas of Italian history and ethnic nationalism. Fascism constituted a vague political ideology for nationalist dictatorship, turning the spirit of war into a revolutionary creed.

To defeat his political enemies, Mussolini organized a new type of combat party, the *Fasci di combattimento* (Groups of Combat). From this term came the name of his party. The elite of the movement were the "fighters," a paramilitary group dressed in black shirts with heavy belt buckles useful in street fighting against Communists, labor leaders, and other groups they accused of undermining the strength of the nation. Mussolini glorified war and combat as the true test of a man and of a nation. He cared not at all that his party never won over 15 percent of the vote in free elections. He believed that he and his followers proved their fitness to lead the nation not by popularity but by determination and struggle. In place of a concrete political program, his movement used emotional appeals to national unity, warnings of communist subversion, and attacks on parliamentary incompetence and corruption.

Mussolini turned the internal weakness of the Italian state to his advantage in his plan to seize power. In October 1922, he ordered his fighting squads to "march on Rome" to overthrow the democratically elected government. His action was largely a bluff, for troops and police forces could easily have dispersed his squads. He counted mainly on the reluctance of the authorities to use force, and he was right. Before his squads reached the capital, the king invited him to become prime minister of the Italian cabinet. Mussolini began his rule as the legal head of government.

Within three years, the democratic Italian nation-state had ceased to exist. Political opponents were intimidated by threats of violence, others were attacked, and some were murdered. Soon political parties were banned and the free press closed. Labor unions were placed under the direct control of the state and strikes were outlawed. No social or economic revolution occurred. The new regime was radical only in its destruction of human rights and democratic government.

Italy became a single-party dictatorship, controlled by the Fascist Party and headed by Mussolini. He encouraged the cult of his leadership, and was extolled by his followers as "divine Caesar" and "sublime redeemer in the Roman heavens." Taking the Roman emperors as his model, Mussolini promised Italians that the Fascists would create a new empire as glorious as that of the Romans. For years, these vows remained empty words. The fascist colonial empire consisted simply of an impoverished nomadic population in the desert of Libya. But Mussolini's pompous words and deeds struck a powerful chord in some European countries when depression struck. Fascism remains the best term to describe the extremist, violent nationalist movements that emerged in many countries in Europe after the First World War. In the decades after the Second World War, similar parties appeared in nation-states of the former colonial world. The most destructive of all the fascist movements was the Nazi Party in Germany.

Nazism and Adolf Hitler

The character and political ambitions of Adolf Hitler, the founder of the Nazi Party, bear striking similarities to Benito Mussolini. Both leaders were front-line soldiers in the First World War. Both emerged from war believing that they were chosen leaders for their nation. Both men transformed wartime nationalism into a justification for political revolution. Both extolled the brutality of the warrior as proof of the virility of a nation, and turned that spirit into the inspiration to seize power by force or by intimidation. Both denounced the alleged decadence that democracy and modern life had spread among their people. They blamed toleration of diversity and individualism for these ills. Both scorned human rights, and glorified national solidarity and combat. In mass democracies, they turned the liberties guaranteed citizens into the means to create political dictatorship.

But Nazism was unique among fascist movements in Europe in certain important respects. Most important of all, it made racism a central feature of its nationalist ideology. All fascist parties glorified a particular ethnic nation, appealing to the myth of a glorious ancestry and condemning present-day enemies of their people. None took the idea to such fanatical lengths as did the Nazis. In particular, Nazism turned hatred of the Jews into the central feature of its ideology. At the same time, it elevated the fascist ideal of the warrior to become the driving force behind its plans for Germany's expansion. The restoration of German might in Europe was only the first step to world power. No other fascist movement so thoroughly turned nationalism into a message of conquest. Nazism combined despotic nationalism and racism in a brutal, destructive message of repression and war.

The National Socialist (Nazi) Party was Adolf Hitler's chosen instrument for his movement. He became leader of this tiny ultra-nationalist party shortly after leaving the German army at the end of the First World War. Within a short time, he had surrounded his position with an aura of authority like that Mussolini had created. The concept of "leader" was as important to the Nazi movement as it was to Mussolini's Fascist Party. One of his supporters later proclaimed at a party rally, "Hitler is the People, the People is Hitler!" In concrete terms, the party program became whatever Hitler judged best. He understood the term National Socialist to mean someone "who knows no higher ideal than the welfare of the nation." The Nazi program offered no real promise of social reform. It allied conservative, middle-class values with revolutionary nationalism. But the party and the leader were most important of all. During the 1920s, the movement acquired its unique organization and structure. First, Hitler formed within the party a special paramilitary group, the Stormtroopers (the SA), composed largely of war veterans dressed in a special uniform and prepared for street battle to defend the party against its enemies. Later he added an elite bodyguard dressed in black uniforms called the *Schutzstaffel*

(SS). He demanded of the SS a loyalty greater than that of any soldier in the German army. The SS members had to present documents proving their "racial purity" and had to take a personal oath of loyalty to Hitler, promising to obey him unquestioningly—"the word of Hitler has the force of law."

The depression made the party a mass political movement. It spread its sections throughout the country and built up its membership. By 1932, party membership totaled 800,000, and the SA had enrolled a half-million men. Many were war veterans or people who had found a sense of purpose in the national community of wartime. They became the warriors in the struggle against German democracy, the Jews, and Germany's foreign enemies.

Economic hardship brought millions of German voters to the party. By 1932, the party received the backing of one-third of all German voters. The only other movement that gained votes substantially in those years was the Communist Party, though it never attracted more than 17 percent of the voters. Together the two extremist parties attracted over 50 percent of the total vote. This extraordinary electoral shift revealed a mood of protest among Germans, not only against the ineffectiveness of government policies but also against the entire democratic system so recently adopted.

According to parliamentary rules, the National Socialist Party had earned the right to head the German cabinet in 1932. It had the largest group of deputies in the legislature (Reichstag). Yet it was an avowed enemy of democracy. Hitler had stipulated that his party would agree to support a cabinet only if he himself became its leader (chancellor). The German president, Marshall von Hindenburg, relied on the judgment of his closest advisers, including army generals and conservative aristocrats. Unable to understand the Nazi's ruthless ambition and fanaticism, they thought that they could control Hitler easily. They disregarded the brutality and violence of the Nazi party, seeing in it a mass movement dedicated to nationalism and conservatism. In January 1933, President von Hindenburg yielded to their arguments and appointed Hitler chancellor of the German Republic. Germany had taken a long step toward Nazism.

The Nazi Dictatorship

Taking the law in its own hands, the Nazi Party moved during the winter and spring of 1933 into positions of power. Hitler's armed militia, the SA and SS, intimidated and terrorized Nazi opponents at will. The Berlin building that housed the parliament burned in late February (possibly an event engineered by Nazis). Hitler blamed the Communists and persuaded the president to grant him extraordinary powers "for the protection of the people and the state." He suspended individual liberties, including press and assembly, and obtained parliamentary approval of the Enabling Act. It authorized the cabinet (that is, Hitler) to rule without constitutional restraints. With the passage of the Enabling Act, he was virtual dictator.

During the next several years, the Nazis extended their control over the entire country. In July 1933, the cabinet proclaimed that the Nazi Party "constitutes the only political party in Germany." The country had become a one-party dictatorship. Nazi organizations reached out to all groups of the population, including youth, labor, and professional associations. Even the churches came under state control or made their peace with the Nazis. Individual religious leaders who dared to protest Nazi injustices were arrested and sent to concentration camps. By 1934, the voices publicly opposing Nazism had fallen silent.

The German army still remained beyond Nazi control. Its officer corps retained the traditional solidarity of the old German army. The Nazi movement came to power with its own paramilitary forces, the Stormtroopers. Hitler chose to side with the army against the SA. He promised the generals an expanded army and protection from reform. To end the SA threat, he secretly planned the removal by force of the SA leadership. During the "night of the long knives" in June 1934, SS squads seized and executed over seventy political leaders whom Hitler wanted eliminated. Hitler justified the executions by claiming that he made the law, for he was "responsible for the fate of the German people." By their silence, the army generals condoned this blood purge. They were satisfied to see the radical SA leaders disappear.

That September, Hitler obtained his reward. At the time of the death of President von Hindenburg, he proclaimed himself head of state and commander-in-chief of the Armed Forces. Germany's army was behind him. In a special oath, each soldier and officer in the army swore "unconditional obedience to the Leader of the German State and People, Adolf Hitler," and vowed "as a brave soldier, to stake my life at any time for this oath." Police terror and absolute loyalty to Hitler constituted two central features of the Nazi state.

By then the Nazi regime had created, hidden behind the scenes, a potent instrument of political repression. This was the "SS state," a system of brutal, arbitrary mastery of the country dedicated to absolute, unquestioning service to Hitler. It did not abide by ordinary laws nor were its personnel at all like those of the regular state administration. The Nazi Party embodied the new principles of despotic authority. It orchestrated giant party rallies in the medieval city of Nuremberg to display the awesome might of

Nazism on Display: Hitler Addressing Party Rally, c. 1935 (*National Archives*)

the new regime. It was the source of recruits to the two key groups in the SS state—the SS, expanded in numbers and power after June 1934 to supplant the SA; the secret police, called the "Gestapo," soon incorporated into the SS organization. The powers of the SS extended to the jails for political prisoners and concentration camps for the "reeducation" of "undesirables."

This SS state enjoyed unrestricted power to arrest and to punish. Its only law was the simple command: "The will of the Leader has the force of law." Hitler's dream of a new German nation took the form of a warfare state, led by warriors and supported by

the efforts of the entire population in a new empire, the "Third Reich" (Empire). It would, he proclaimed, last for 1,000 years.

There was no place in this empire for its Jewish population. Nazi hatred of the Jews became the inspiration for a policy of racial segregation and persecution. First in 1933 came the expulsion of Jews from any position in the German administration. Then came sweeping measures of discrimination contained in the Nuremberg Laws of 1935. All Germans with at least two Jewish grandparents lost their German citizenship. Marriages between Germans and Jews became illegal. The goal was the expulsion of

Jews, who had assimilated generations before into German society. In the wake of these laws, municipalities issued edicts forbidding Jew's entry into their cities, posting signs proclaiming themselves "Free of Jews [*Judenrein*]."

By 1938, over 100,000 Jews had emigrated from Germany. They had to surrender everything they owned to obtain the legal right to leave. Among them were outstanding intellectuals such as Albert Einstein. Even more Jews fled after the violent attack on Jews and Jewish property throughout Germany on November 9–10, 1938 ("Crystal Night"), during which all Jewish synagogues were burned. In a country Westerners believed an enlightened, civilized society, blind racism had become law. The foundations for the policy of genocide were in place.

To Germans supporting the new regime, those years before 1939 were good times. They were expected to demonstrate public approval of Nazi policies and to serve the nation in the spirit of Nazism. In return, Hitler promised to put Germans back to work. In its social and economic policies, the Nazi regime proved, as the Italian Fascists had earlier, to be a conservative force. Hitler needed a strong German economy for his rearmament plans. He knew no economic theory; he did believe that people had to be employed, even if the state lacked sufficient tax revenues to pay for work programs. His financial advisers were shocked by his deficit spending, used for public work projects, public housing, and other major building projects. The unemployed were required to enroll in the German Labor Service, which enforced the slogan (also applied to concentration camp inmates) that "Work makes one free."

These government economic policies, plus the rearmament program, spurred economic recovery. A Four-Year Economic Plan introduced in 1936 sought to make Germany economically self-sufficient (and hence better able to wage war). Nazi planners collaborated with and guaranteed profits to Germany's industrialists and financiers. Such economic methods had nothing in common with the command planning introduced in the Soviet Union in the same years. By the middle of the decade, Germans had work and security, and most did not choose to ask for more.

The Expansion of the Nazi Empire

Both expansionist and militarist, Nazi Germany within a few years destroyed the system for European peace put in place after the First World War. Hitler stated in 1937 that "Germany's problem can only be solved by force and this always entails risk." He dreamed of turning his nation into a great world power. His vision of Germany's place in the world was grandiose and pitiless. He had written long before becoming Germany's leader of an extraordinary "battle of the continents" that the German Empire under his command would wage against the United States for "world domination." He had no precise plan of conquest. He had learned in his political career how to take advantage of circumstances and did the same in the pursuit of his goal to make Germany a continental and a world power.

In the three years that followed the Nazi seizure of power, the German government destroyed the peace settlement of the 1920s. In late 1933, it abandoned the League of Nations. Then it ended the Versailles Treaty's restrictions on its military power. In March 1935, Hitler renounced the limits set in the 1919 treaty on the size of the German army. Nazi Germany immediately increased its army to a half-million men. Hitler justified his action by insisting his country deserved "equality of rights" with neighboring states.

Then came the German occupation of the Rhineland in 1936. This frontier area on the northeastern French and eastern Belgian borders had been kept free of German troops. In the 1930s, however, no Allied occupation forces remained there. The only assurance that Germany would honor this restriction on its sovereignty was the Locarno Treaty. Should the German state violate this treaty, the other participants had the right to send their forces back into the Rhineland and, if necessary, to declare war.

Hitler chose to take that risk. His army was still small and his generals warned that German troops would have to retreat immediately if France chose war. He later admitted that "if the French had marched into the Rhineland we would have had to withdraw with our tail between our legs." He dismissed the fears of his generals, however, for he was persuaded that the British and French leaders had lost faith in the peace settlements and that no Allied state had the determination to enforce their provisions. He was right. He possessed an extraordinary talent for picking out the weaknesses in his adversaries. German reoccupation of the Rhineland in March 1936 took place peaceably, to the cheers of the population.

The Spanish civil war revealed the profound differences toward war that separated the Western democracies from the European dictators. In July 1936, a military uprising led by General Francisco Franco attempted to overthrow the Spanish Republic. He and his supporters were enemies of the Popular Front government just elected that year. This reform coalition had laid plans for land reform to aid the poor, and for new laws granting political autonomy to the non-Spanish peoples of the country. In the social turmoil of that year, the Republic's leaders were powerless to prevent some of their followers from attacking property of the Spanish Catholic Church. General Franco's goal

was an authoritarian regime protecting private property, the Church, and the unity of Spain. He was not a fascist, though he accepted help from the Spanish fascist movement, the Phalange. The Popular Front government found its support among liberals and Marxists, workers and peasants. Spain began a bloody civil war.

Many Westerners concluded that the conflict in Spain was part of the European-wide struggle between popular democracy and fascist dictatorship. The civil war became an international cause. Volunteers from the Western democracies helped the Republic's forces. The Spanish conflict had a second international dimension. Mussolini, eager to create an Italian empire in the Mediterranean, immediately sent troops and military equipment to Franco. Hitler also supplied military aid to Franco's rebels. Included in this help were German fighter bombers and pilots, responsible for the brutal bombing of the Basque city of Guernica (the subject of the most famous antiwar painting of the century, by the Spanish artist Pablo Picasso).

The Soviet Union led the international opposition to their intervention. Once German and Italian support for Franco began, the Soviets sent military aid and helped organize international fighting units, the International Brigades, to assist the Republic. Joseph Stalin probably anticipated that Great Britain and France would also intervene in the civil war on the side of the Republic. Instead, the British and French governments, as well as the United States, adopted a nonintervention policy of strict neutrality, refusing arms to either side. The practical result was to deny aid to the Republic. Their objective was to avoid widening the conflict and risking war with the fascist states. This was a matter of greater concern to them than the defense of the Spanish Republic. Appeasement remained their highest priority. In early 1939, the civil war ended with the triumph of

Franco's forces. The Spanish state, like many other European countries in those crisis years, became a dictatorship.

Strengthened by its rearmament, the Nazi regime set out on the dangerous path of territorial expansion beyond its southern and eastern borders. These small states, the successors to the Austro-Hungarian Empire, were weak and easily dominated by neighboring aggressive states. In early 1938, Hitler proclaimed that the Austrian people had to join his Greater Germany. When the Austrian government refused, he sent German troops to seize the country by force. Austria became a province of the new German Empire. The second step came when Germany demanded the annexation of the area in western Czechoslovakia known as the Sudetenland. The proclaimed purpose was the protection of "oppressed" Germans living there. The real objective was to destroy this new state, which was a major obstacle in the path of German eastward expansion. Hitler was ready for war that year. He probably anticipated, though, that the West would once again prefer conciliation.

He threatened, in September 1938, to invade the Czech lands unless his demands were met. In response, Italy proposed a four-power meeting of Germany, Italy, France, and Great Britain in Munich, Germany. The Western states grabbed the olive branch, though both the Soviet Union and Czechoslovakia were excluded from the negotiations. Hitler set the terms. The Munich Treaty that resulted from the conference gave Hitler all he wanted. Great Britain and France forced the Czech government to give up the Sudeten territory to Germany, fatally weakening Czechoslovakia. Their desperate effort to preserve peace in Europe was condemned later as "appeasement," that is, capitulation to aggression.

Neither government was prepared militarily or psychologically for war in defense, as the British prime minister said, of a "far-off place inhabited by people of whom we know little." The treaty itself resulted from years of Western wishful thinking regarding Nazi moderation. It was an illusion to which Western statesmen and citizens clung in the fervent hope that European war would never return. A tragedy for Czechoslovakia, the Munich agreement proved a diplomatic disaster for the Western world.

In 1939, the Nazi leaders took the next steps toward becoming a continental power. That spring, they removed the state of Czechoslovakia from the map of Europe by annexing the western half of the country and creating a puppet government over the eastern half (Slovakia). To the northeast lay Poland, situated between Germany and Soviet Russia and including territory taken from both states. Its "Polish corridor" was a strip of land in western Poland, situated between German territory and leading to the German city of Danzig, made an international city by the 1919 peace treaties. The return of the area to Germany had constituted an objective of German policy ever since the 1920s.

Hitler publicly demanded no more but, as had been the case in Czechoslovakia, his larger goal was domination of Europe. His method of achieving this objective remained force and intimidation. In March 1939, an appeal from President Roosevelt for peaceful compromise evoked from Hitler only ridicule of the distant Americans. Boasting that he, "who twenty-one years ago was an unknown worker and soldier of my people," had "reestablished the historical unity of German living space," he mocked Roosevelt's concern for "the fate of the world." He could easily afford to do so, since isolationism prevented the United States from exercising any real influence in world affairs.

The Soviet Union presented a more serious problem. Hitler had for years treated the

Soviet state as Germany's enemy, yet it possessed the largest army in eastern Europe. That spring, the British government finally abandoned its policy of appeasement and refused any further revision of the Versailles treaty. Instead, it pledged military aid to Poland in the event of war with Germany and began, with the French, to negotiate a military alliance with Soviet Russia. If Stalin decided to join with the Western democracies to protect Poland, he could force Germany into another two-front war.

Reluctantly Hitler chose to negotiate. He presented Stalin with an offer of spoils of war—Polish territory—in exchange for Soviet collaboration in the destruction of Poland. Stalin accepted, and in August 1939 the two states secretly agreed to divide Poland between their two states. The German–Soviet nonaggression pact opened the way for German war on Poland. In September 1939 Hitler's army invaded Poland. Two days later, in a desperate effort to contain German expansion and to save the Versailles settlement, Britain and France declared war on Germany. A new European war had begun.

The immediate cause of the new war, unlike the First World War, was obvious. Nazi militarism and expansionism drove Europe into the conflict. For all their defects, the Versailles treaty had dealt in a fairly equitable manner with the problems of security and national self-determination. From the perspective of 1939, in fact, it was too fair. It had left Germany with the territory, population, and resources sufficient under Nazi leadership to mobilize for war. No one in 1919 had conceived of a German state so fanatical and brutal as the one instituted by the Nazis in 1933.

STALIN'S SOVIET UNION

In the midst of the global depression of the 1930s, the Soviet Union became a powerful industrialized country under the command of a brutal centralized dictatorship. Events unfolded there unlike any other country in the world. In 1929, Stalin had become Lenin's heir and undisputed ruler of the Soviet Union. He was responsible for transforming the country, in conditions of turmoil and hardship. The most important changes consisted of (1) the rapid development of the Soviet industrial economy; (2) the forcible seizure of all farmland, brought together in collectivized, state-controlled farms; and (3) the expansion of the repressive powers of the party and the secret police to perpetuate a system of terror, that is, of arbitrary arrest and punishment unhindered by legal restraints. The transformation of the Soviet Union was so radical that historians have termed that period the "Stalin revolution."

The revolution of 1917 had put in place a communist dictatorship governing a predominantly agricultural country whose land was held and worked by peasant farmers. Stalin created a one-man dictatorship and ended private farming, extending the powers of the state into all areas of the economy and society and developing Soviet industry at an extraordinary pace. He claimed that the social and economic transformation of his country raised Soviet society to the historic stage of socialism. Critics called his regime despotic, and condemned his policies as inhuman.

The Stalin Revolution

The weakness of the Soviet regime in the late 1920s and Stalin's own political ambition were the key factors in his rise to power. In those years, leadership rested in the hands of the members of the Politburo, the governing Communist Party committee that set state policies in that single-party dictatorship. Stalin was only one of the members, and he was also "general secretary" of the party. The communist "vanguard" consisted of a small ruling elite controlling a vast country and fearful of hostile Western states.

Their country was weak and internally divided between a small working class sympathetic to communist aims and peasant farmers determined to keep possession of their land. The Communists had implemented in 1921 what they called the New Economic Policy (NEP) to raise farm production and to restore the country's dilapidated factories and decaying cities. It succeeded partially. It did not provide adequate means to finance the rapid industrial growth necessary to build a strong modern army and create the economy of abundance of which the Communists dreamed. Two considerations, one practical and the other utopian, impelled the party leadership in 1927 to agree on a plan for rapid industrialization. Expensive investments required that the peasantry sacrifice a large part of their income and resources, through taxes and low prices for farm produce, to support industrial growth. The peasants' refusal to cooperate on these terms, apparent in 1928, threw the country into its most serious crisis since the civil war and opened the way for Stalin's rise to power.

The crisis took the form of a serious shortage of agricultural produce, needed for the urban population and for export. The state, which purchased almost all farm production, had lowered the price it paid for major commodities, and many peasant farmers refused to sell their crops. The decline in sales was so severe that in 1928 food rationing appeared in the cities. Soviet agricultural exports, essential to pay for the import of industrial machinery, nearly collapsed. To Western observers accustomed to free markets, the shortages resulted from faults in the market economy. The peasants demanded incentives—good prices, consumer products at cheap prices—that the Communists refused to grant them.

Soviet leaders understood the crisis very differently. Suspicious of peasant "petty

capitalism" and inspired by the brutal methods of the civil war, they blamed prosperous peasants ("kulaks") for seeking to undermine their Soviet state. Stalin was their spokesman. He put in words their fears of peasant opposition and of imperialist attack, warning in the spring of 1928 that "we confront enemies outside the Soviet Union [and] we confront enemies within the Soviet Union." That year he imposed a simple, ruthless solution to the food crisis, ordering police and party officials to take the surplus produce from the peasants, if necessary by force. Moderate leaders were appalled at his brutality. One even accused him of being a new Mongol Genghis Khan, introducing Asiatic despotism in place of proletarian dictatorship.

That year marked the first time Stalin asserted his political leadership. He claimed to be defending the revolution in the spirit of Leninism. The consequences of his action, however, were to launch a new revolution. Most Western historians believe his personal ambition was fixed upon the goal of taking Lenin's place. He turned the crisis of 1928 to his own advantage. We know little of his inner thoughts and motives, for he was a secretive man. His life had been one of escape from poverty and of political combat in the name of proletarian revolution, which he appears to have associated with his own renown. He learned of class conflict and oppression, of the inevitable fall of capitalism, and of the future blessings of socialism, through his study of Marxism. We need not question his faith in these basic ideological precepts, for they gave him the essential conviction in the rightness of his cause and the necessity for conflict. His understanding of Marxism, in other words, fit his combative personality. Lenin was his teacher and leader in that period of learning and fighting. He remained loyal to Lenin through the years of underground agitation and then of war and revolution. All he achieved, including his position as general secretary, he owed to Lenin.

Like the rebellious son, however, in the early 1920s he came to think himself worthy of taking Lenin's place. His political methods were harsh, a fact Lenin discovered too late. Even before Lenin's death in 1924, Stalin began exploiting his key party responsibilities to build up a following among the party cadres who played the key role in choosing new leaders and carrying out policy. They were sympathetic in 1928 to his harsh methods of dealing with the food crisis. With their support, he removed all his rivals from leadership positions in the Politburo. By 1929, he dominated that body and through it the Soviet Union. On his fiftieth birthday late that year, his backers proclaimed that "Stalin is the Lenin of today!"

That year Stalin began what he himself boasted was a "revolution from above." In the Stalinist vocabulary, "revolution" described the transformation of the economy and society at the command of the Communist Party. It took shape through two separate policy decisions. One consisted of the adoption of a Five-Year Plan for industrial production, which was to triple by the early 1930s. The other was the party decision taken late in 1929 to force the 100 million peasants off their private farms and into "collective farms" (referred to usually by the abbreviated Russian term "kolkhoz"), that is, producer cooperatives.

In theory, "collectivization" of farms strengthened socialist cooperation. In reality, it gave the state direct access to agricultural production because state officials dominated the administration of the new farms. These measures marked the end of NEP and of conciliation of the peasantry. Their implementation required that the communist dictatorship expand the repressive powers of the secret police. Ultimately, Stalin's ambition and the vast increase in arbitrary police power came together to turn the Soviet regime into a despotic regime.

Industrialization in the First Five-Year Plan combined revolutionary dreams and the need to increase the state's military might. The production goals of the plan were fixed by the guidelines set out in plans elaborated by the State Planning Commission ("Gosplan"). In a burst of optimism, Stalin ordered the attainment of the plan's objectives by the end of 1932; the slogan was "The Five-Year Plan in four years!" The spirit of Soviet industrialization was warlike; workers had to "storm" ahead and "conquer fortresses" to build socialism. Economists in Gosplan who objected that such extraordinary economic growth would lead to chaos were dismissed or arrested. Under this system of command planning, officials and managers in the state enterprises had to meet production targets set by the Planning Commission or risk being fired or arrested for "wrecking."

These cruel policies met the need to equip a modern army more effectively than they did the goal of creating a socialist society. To Stalin, the former objective was more important. The "tempo" of industrial growth "must not be lowered," he told a meeting of factory managers in 1931. The reason was simple: An advanced "socialist system of economy" would make Russia strong, ending its "backwardness." Stalin warned his audience that the world was still ruled by the "jungle law of capitalism," which he understood to be the simple rule of "beat the weak but be wary of the strong." Speaking more like a Russian ruler than like a Communist, he recited the long list of foreign enemies who had defeated the Russian state in past centuries, from the Mongol Khans in the thirteenth century to the Japanese in the twentieth (omitting the Germans for diplomatic reasons). He demanded that the "socialist homeland" catch up to the capitalist countries in ten years, "or they will crush us." Without realizing where the real danger lay, he anticipated the terrible war that was to come.

The campaign of industrialization proved as chaotic as the skeptics in 1929 had predicted. Russia needed to import foreign machinery and technicians to set up new industries. Among the imports was an entire tractor and truck factory built by the Ford Motor Company. German machinery for steel mills went to the new industrial city of Magnitogorsk in the Ural Mountains. The worldwide depression lowered the price of agricultural commodities and raw materials, major sources of Russia's foreign exchange with which to pay for these imports. The government chose to export more food, though part of the population starved in 1932–1933. Within the country there were not enough railroads, not enough skilled workers, not enough housing, not enough steel and cement for all the new factories. The Five-Year Plan served primarily propaganda needs, cajoling and threatening workers and managers. A priority system similar to wartime decided where the most pressing needs lay and where scarce resources should go.

The most spectacular accomplishments of the industrial plan consisted of giant industrial projects. Accompanied by great publicity, a 1,000-mile railroad, the Turksib, linked the Turkic soviet republics in Central Asia with central Siberia. A mammoth dam on the lower Dnieper River in the southern part of the Ukrainian Soviet Republic generated hydroelectric power to speed the growth of the region's industrial complex. The mountainous region around Kuznetsk, north of Mongolia, became one of the country's major sources of coal. On the parched eastern slopes of the Ural Mountains, a giant iron and steel complex named Magnitogorsk emerged to extract the rich iron ore deposits of the "Magnetic Mountain." To these build-

ing sites went the machinery, foreign experts, and raw materials necessary for rapid construction. Key party leaders personally supervised the work to ensure that the tempo never slackened.

The greatest burden fell on the great numbers of workers brought voluntarily or by force to these construction sites. Members of the Young Communist movement believed the projects to be a socialist crusade. Workers traveled thousands of miles to join in the campaign. One Soviet writer observing them at work asked why they worked so hard in such primitive conditions. Their answer was simple: "We're building socialism. The entire world is looking at us." Alongside them, however, were peasants fleeing the brutal collectivization campaign and misery in the countryside. They worked simply to escape hunger. Hundreds of thousands of forced laborers, mostly peasants arrested for resisting collectivization, served out their sentences on these sites. They lived in tent camps under police guard. The total size of the industrial labor force doubled by the end of the first Five-Year Plan. Workers' living conditions were miserable. Housing was inadequate, and food supplies were so short that rationing remained in effect during the entire period. Like it or not, the Soviet people had to accept great sacrifices in Stalin's industrialization drive.

The Soviet state needed an army of specialists to supervise the work. It inherited from tsarist Russia a small core of well-trained engineers. Their "bourgeois" origins made them suspect in Stalin's Russia. To force them to work for the new regime, the police arrested many of these engineers, whom they accused of sabotage in the pay of capitalist enemies. No evidence was required, for arrest by the secret police was equivalent to conviction. In 1930, two "show trials" in Moscow put on display engineers accused of sham "counter-revolutionary"

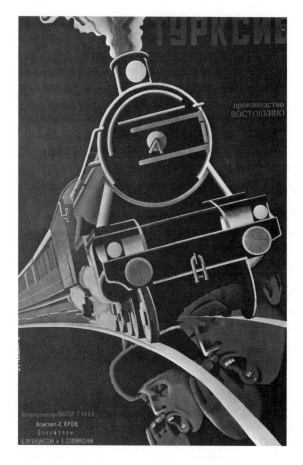

Art in the Service of Stalin's Revolution: Poster for Film "Turksib," 1929 (*Poster Collection/ Hoover Institution*)

activities. All were forced to confess, and then were sent as prison labor to work in the industrial projects. "Justice" had become another tool to manipulate key segments of the population.

The atmosphere in the country resembled that of a besieged fortress, filled with enthusiasm for battle and with fear and suspicion of saboteurs and spies. Part of that battle consisted of the rapid training of "Red specialists," who were Communists from worker backgrounds given technical training on the job. By the end of the first Five-Year Plan, over a half-million people had received promotions to managerial and technical positions through this Soviet "affirma-

tive action" plan. Among them were Nikita Khrushchev and Leonid Brezhnev, future leaders of the Soviet Union. These people owed their careers to the party and to Stalin, becoming the new Stalinist elite of Soviet Russia.

By the end of 1932, industrial production had soared. New industrial plants in Siberia were beginning to turn out great amounts of iron and steel; their total output doubled between 1928 and 1932. Oil production also doubled, while electrical power output increased three times. In the same years, the urban population's standard of living declined by one-third to one-half, for it had a low priority in Stalin's revolution. The urban

The "City of Iron": Magnitogorsk,
c. 1939 (*National Archives*)

housing shortage became so severe that most families had to crowd into single rooms of "communal apartments," forced to share a kitchen and bathroom with all the other tenants. Food remained rationed until 1933. Early in 1934, Stalin proclaimed the First Five-Year Plan a success. The price paid by the population, however, was terribly high.

The peasant farmers suffered worst of all. In November 1929, the party leaders ordered mass collectivization of private farms to begin. Stalin refused any compromise with the "capitalist way" of private farming; the "socialist way" of collective farms had to triumph. The party expected resistance and authorized the use of "administrative measures," that is, of repressive police action, to punish those who resisted. The prime target was the so-called "kulak" group of prosperous farmers. In January 1930, Stalin approved orders for the liquidation in the entire country of 1.2 million peasant households (approximately 6 million individuals). These peasants, the best private farmers in

Russia, were excluded from the new collective farms.

This organized class war represented a monstrous act of retribution against peasant farmers condemned for their presumed hostility toward the communist regime. By early 1932, collectivization was complete in the principal farming areas of the country. At the Seventeenth Party Congress in 1934, Stalin proudly announced the creation of 200,000 producer farm cooperatives. The regime had "eliminated capitalism" among the peasantry.

The price for this social revolution in the countryside was hardship and famine. The enormous state bureaucracy used its power over agriculture to extract the greatest amount of produce at the lowest possible price. It removed incentives from farming at precisely the moment when administrators on the collective farms were struggling to set up "cooperation" in farm work. Peasants had slaughtered nearly half their livestock rather than let it become the property of the collective farms. Draft animals were in terribly short supply, and the state had precious few tractors to replace them. Peasants on the new farms worked halfheartedly. All these factors led by 1932 to a fall in farm production. In late 1932, it was clear that collectivized agriculture was not producing enough both to satisfy the needs of industry and to feed the rural population. Stalin chose to continue state procurements, ordering severe punishments for any officials who failed to deliver the produce.

Although never admitted by the Soviet state, hunger spread through the countryside, leading to famine, epidemics, and the death of untold millions of peasants. Word of the tragedy reached the cities, where even loyal Communists were horrified at the betrayal of their hopes for a better life for all the people. Stalin's young wife, Nadezhda Allilueva, shared those dreams and experienced the disillusionment at the suffering inflicted on the population. That fall, in the midst of the celebrations of the fifteenth anniversary of the Bolshevik Revolution, she had a bitter quarrel with her husband. Afterward, she shot herself in their Kremlin apartment. Her suicide made her another casualty of the Stalin Revolution.

Even Stalin's colleagues in the Politburo concluded that his leadership had led to serious abuses of power. In the spring of 1933, these moderates, including one of his close aides, Sergei Kirov, put in place new policies to end mass terror, to regularize the conditions of the collective farms, and to set reasonable goals of industrial growth in the second Five-Year Plan. They hoped to revive the practice of collective leadership of the pre-1929 years and to curtail Stalin's own authority. The man they supported to lead this effort was Kirov.

But in December 1934, an assassin murdered Kirov in his office. His two personal bodyguards had mysteriously withdrawn just before the event; both men died soon after in mysterious circumstances before they could be interrogated. The Soviet leadership immediately launched a witch-hunt for the supposed "counter-revolutionaries" responsible for assassination. Stalin took the lead. Kirov's death freed Stalin from the party restraints put on his rule. He soon put in action a system of police terror that continued until his death.

Stalinist Terror and Soviet Despotism

The five years that followed produced such an eruption of mass arrests, executions, and public denunciations of supposed traitors that the period has earned the name of "Great Terror." Its bloody methods exceeded by far the Communist Party's brutality in the Civil War. Mass repression had already appeared during the collectivization of the peasantry, and it extended now to all members of the population. Historians are still searching to understand the secret process by which police terror installed itself in Soviet life. The growing power of the secret police facilitated Stalin's task. Soviet leaders admitted long after Stalin's death that the dictator himself, with the aid of agents in the secret police, was responsible for the Kirov murder. They also pointed to the Stalin "cult," that is, the public adulation of the dictator, to explain the ease with which Stalin unleashed police terror. They omitted a third reason, namely, the backing he received from large numbers of Communists whose careers were linked to his. These "Stalin-generation" Communists were collaborators in terror.

The Stalin terror was based on unlimited repressive powers, exercised by the secret police and controlled by Stalin himself. By his personal orders, immediately after Kirov's death the secret police received the power to arrest, judge, and shoot or imprison anyone guilty of "counter-revolutionary activity." Because the police alone were the judge of the existence of this activity, they obtained arbitrary authority to punish at will those whom they considered enemies. To Stalin's suspicious mind, all Soviet officials, party members, and plain citizens who talked or acted in a manner to question his leadership and his policies were traitors. The Kirov assassination was followed by a wave of arrests of anyone remotely connected with opposition to his rule.

Stalin justified his reliance on terror by alleging the existence of a vast network of class enemies and foreign agents operating within Soviet Russia. He argued that "the further we advance toward socialism" the greater will be the "fury of the broken, exploiting classes." Pitiless vigilance and repression alone could deal with these enemies, whom he perceived everywhere. So great was his suspiciousness that historians have suggested he was mentally deranged. Yet his ruthless action revealed the careful, calculating mind of a despot. He turned the secret police into his chosen agents of rule.

Mass repression knew no limits for a few years. The unrestricted power enjoyed by the secret police (known then by the initials of the People's Commissariat of Internal Affairs, NKVD) permitted Stalin to decimate the ranks of party cadres, of the state bureaucracy, of the engineers and managers of nationalized industry, and of intellectuals in literature and the arts. Over half of the Communist Party's high officials vanished in the mass repression. His most dramatic action consisted of the arrest, trial, and execution of almost all the Old Bolsheviks, Lenin's collaborators in the first years of the revolution and frequent opponents of Stalin in that period. Beginning in 1936, they went on trial in three major "show trials," the last of which was held in early 1938. All confessed after

months of interrogation and torture to supposed (and completely fictitious) "crimes against the state." All were convicted and shot, their names removed from party histories, their faces eliminated from group portraits of party officials. Leon Trotsky, whom Stalin had expelled from the Soviet Union in 1929, was tracked down in Mexico by NKVD agents and assassinated. No party leader was left to criticize the dictator.

Stalin and the secret police also singled out for repression the leaders of the national republics that made up the Soviet Union. They claimed that "bourgeois nationalism" had infected the leadership of the non-Russian borderlands; mass arrests hit these regions immediately afterwards. An accusation of lack of loyalty to Stalin and to the Soviet leadership in Moscow was sufficient. Veteran non-Russian party activists, intellectuals, and professionals who had played a vital role in putting in place the multinational system of the Soviet Union disappeared into prison camps or mass graves. The country had become a communist empire governed by Stalinists.

In an action that undermined the efforts to strengthen Russia's military might, the Great Terror extended even to the Red Army. At first Stalin had supported his generals in their effort to turn the army into a professional, highly trained military organization equipped for tank warfare. He appears to have become afraid of their political influence over his foreign policy. No real evidence ever appeared to substantiate the accusation that these officers had plotted against Stalin. Evidence was irrelevant. Even confessions proved unnecessary to convict, for Stalin and the police had judged the officer corps guilty in advance. The terror in the army began in 1937 with the secret trial of five outstanding generals, including the army commander-in-chief, Tukhachevsky. They were convicted and shot as spies for foreign powers. All officers then fell under suspicion, and one-third of the entire officer corps within a year were arrested. Many were executed, and the others sentenced to long terms in prison camps. At a time of growing foreign danger, Stalin gambled his country's security for the sake of his brutal dictatorship.

Out of the terror emerged an enormous secret police empire. It consisted of prisons and a vast network of prison camps extending across the country, especially in the northern and eastern regions of Siberia. Millions of prisoners worked there, a large number dying in inhuman living conditions. In their brutality and hardship, the camps appeared to inmates an extreme form of the police rule that dominated the entire country. The camps constituted a world unto themselves, though, where prison officials reigned as petty despots.

During the Great Terror the secret police became the most powerful political institution in the country. Stalin, probably aware of the potential threat it posed to his dictatorship, had its chief and his followers arrested in 1938, to be shot in their turn as "counter-revolutionaries." He tolerated no potential rivals. The new police chief, Lavrenty Beria, remained at the head of the secret police until Stalin's death thanks to his absolute subservience to the dictator. The terror declined in intensity after 1938, but the system remained in place as long as Stalin lived.

The dictatorship extended into all areas of Soviet cultural life. The encouragement for experimentation and the tolerance for artistic diversity that existed in the 1920s vanished. State-run organizations of writers, artists, musicians, and educators controlled the publication and diffusion of cultural works. Their censorship left little room for individual creativity. Instead, official canons dictated the form and substance of cultural activity. The style of "socialist realism," that

is, of art reflecting the imaginary "reality" of socialist society, was imposed in literature, painting, and cinema. The only new theme was the glorification of Russian nationalism and of Russian military and political leaders from the tsarist past. Tsar Ivan IV (the Terrible) received especially kind treatment, for Stalin viewed very sympathetically his success in eliminating internal enemies and defeating hostile neighboring states. Learning in schools became a dogmatic exercise in memorization stressing simple truths. Among these the most important was the Marxist–Leninist–Stalinist ideology. Teachers were once again, as in tsarist times, the absolute authority in the classroom. Pupils once more dressed in uniforms. Culture was in the service of the Stalinist state.

Judgments on the transformation brought about by the Stalin Revolution aroused bitter controversy. Some observers argued that its greatest achievement was to raise Soviet Russia to the rank of the second-greatest industrial power in the world. The economic statistics prove this claim correct, though they cannot convey the true measure of human hardship endured in that effort. Others emphasize the social revolution achieved by the elimination of private industry, commerce, and farming, pointing to state ownership of the means of production in all areas of the economy as evidence that a new social system had appeared. Communists called it the first "socialist society" in the world; critics called it a command economy ruled by a new class of party bureaucrats.

The most critical judgment stressed the police dictatorship by which Stalin and his supporters controlled the party, the state, and the entire population. In some respects, it resembled Nazi Germany. The two regimes were both labeled "totalitarian" to emphasize the extraordinary powers of the state and its leaders over the population. Stalinism, like Nazism, could not totally dominate society. George Orwell's novel *1984,* based largely on the author's observations of the Soviet regime in the 1940s, provides a nightmarish image of the brutal world of Stalinism.

The Soviet Empire

The new Soviet leadership demanded obedience not only from its own population but also from all communist parties around the world. Stalin had a low opinion of foreign Communists. He valued the Communist International primarily for its service in defending the Soviet Union. He demanded that its member parties help repel the new enemies of the Soviet Union. He ordered the Chinese Communists to organize armed resistance to Japanese forces in northern China to divert Japanese armies away from Soviet territory. These foreign Communists were under orders to assist the "socialist homeland," the Soviet Union.

Stalin followed a simple set of rules to guide Soviet foreign policy in the dangerous world of the 1930s. Judging Western ideals of collective peacekeeping and conciliation a sham, he adopted for his state what he believed to be real Western practice—power politics. He repeated again in 1934 his conviction, first voiced in 1931, that "in our times it is not the custom to respect the weak; only the strong are respected." States used their power, he argued in 1939, to create around their territory "spheres of influence" in which they dominated smaller states for their own protection and profit.

The "jungle law of capitalism," which he had identified in 1931, dictated that, in international relations, might made right. A state's success at this pitiless undertaking brought it more territory, by annexation of bordering states or by an enlarged sphere of domination. By that elementary rule, the Soviet Union had for its own sake to "respect" other

strong states by accepting their spheres of influence. The real threat of war would arise when they disagreed on the borders of those spheres. This simplistic, brutal picture of world relations guided Stalin's conduct of Soviet foreign policy for the rest of his life.

In the 1930s, the Japanese Empire in the East and Nazi Germany in the West threatened the Soviet Union. In each case, Stalin had to prepare for possible war but welcomed agreements that would, even temporarily, avoid conflict and safeguard Soviet security interests. In 1931, Japan had invaded Manchuria; later in the decade, its troops launched several attacks on Red Army forces both in eastern Siberia and in Mongolia (a Soviet satellite state). The Red Army repelled each Japanese attack, inflicting heavy losses on the enemy forces. After the outbreak of war in 1937 between Japan and China, the Soviet government sent large amounts of vital military supplies to China.

The real escape from Asian war came in 1941 when the Japanese government concluded that its most important military objectives lay in the Pacific and southeast Asia, not in northeast Asia. That spring the Japanese foreign minister offered the Soviet government a neutrality treaty. Stalin accepted immediately. He cared not at all where Japanese forces might attack in other areas; he asked only that his country be spared.

Nazi Germany proved in the end the greater danger. Hitler's hatred of "Bolshevism" filled his speeches. Stalin, on the contrary, stated publicly in early 1934 that he did not consider ideological differences between fascism and his state to be a serious obstacle in dealing with the new German regime. "It is not a question of fascism here," he argued. "If the interests of the U.S.S.R. demand good relations with one country or another which is not interested in disturbing the peace [that is, not attacking the Soviet Union], we will adopt this course without hesitation." But Hitler refused the invitation. Stalin had good reason to believe that Germany would move east again, as in the First World War, and that this time its goals would be the seizure of territory and the destruction of his regime.

To protect the Soviet Union from another war with Germany, Stalin attempted to repeat the precedent of the pre-1914 Franco-Russian pact. He agreed in 1935 to a defense treaty with France. It never became the foundation for a Soviet collective security policy, however. At best it offered the possibility that Germany might have to fight first in the west. Soviet aid to the Spanish Republic in 1936 sought to encourage Western resistance to Germany. But the French government clung to its appeasement policy until 1939.

By then, Stalin had returned to his earlier objective of reaching an agreement with Nazi Germany. He seems to have believed that he understood the basic reason for the expansionist policies of Hitler. He judged the Nazi leader a believer, though in an extreme form, in the "jungle law of capitalism." Since the two states dominated eastern Europe, by his reasoning they could avoid war by dividing the region between themselves. He therefore accepted Hitler's offer in the summer of 1939 of a nonaggression pact. It contained secret provisions for the partition of Poland, and for Soviet domination over the small eastern Baltic states. Stalin interpreted the agreement to mean that his state could expand into these territories. Having signed the pact in August 1939, he sent the Red Army to seize eastern Poland, quickly annexed that fall to the Soviet Union. The next year his forces invaded the Baltic states, soon turned into soviet republics. His objectives were territorial control and peace with Germany, if only for a few years. A German war against France and Great Britain did not concern him. Stalin's dictatorship made the Soviet Union an expansionist, despotic empire.

⚙ HIGHLIGHT: Communism and Joseph Stalin ⚙

Communism had its roots in the nineteenth century. Karl Marx's socialist philosophy spelled out a revolutionary program of action based on his theories of the economy, society, and history. It became the inspiration for European socialist parties, which ultimately sought social reforms by working within, not in opposition to, liberal democracies. Marxism also provided the core ideas for revolutionary socialism, whose adherents anticipated that only violent revolution would end capitalism and begin the liberation of the working masses.

In 1917, Vladimir Lenin converted this revolutionary approach to Marxism into a concrete program of insurrection. His theory of the vanguard party, which he argued had to lead the proletarian revolution and take sole control of the state afterwards, became an integral part of the communist ideology. His main achievement was to seize power in Russia.

Stalin's contribution was the wholesale transformation of the country's economy and society. He declared that the radical economic and social changes that he had forced upon the people of his land fulfilled Marx's forecast of the social and economic conditions of equality that the proletarian revolution would achieve. The Soviet Union's socialist society, he claimed, marked the advance of his country to the highest level in human history. (The communist society would appear only when the state itself withered away, no longer needed by people who governed themselves.) Stalin's methods of social revolution, his dictatorial regime, and the principles by which he justified his rule constituted the central features of communism as it was understood by his supporters and enemies alike in the decades that followed. In this way, Stalin made communism his own creation.

His changes to the Leninist ideology consisted of three main points, namely, revolution from above, constant struggle with internal enemies, and the priority of the interests of the socialist homeland. He and his supporters argued that the historical progression forecast by Karl Marx from capitalism to the next stage, the socialist society, had come about in the Soviet Union thanks to the powers of the state itself, controlled and guided by the Communist Party. Marx had never provided a blueprint for progress beyond the proletarian revolution. Marxists had expected that this dramatic social leap forward could come only through collective efforts of the working classes once they were the most numerous group in society. To them, the state was a instrument of political domination; its methods of repression were incompatible with the ideals of a socialist society. Lenin disregarded this warning, claiming that his Communist Party had to step in to lead the small laboring class of Russia. Stalin turned the Marxist formula on its head. Instead of curtailing the powers of the state, his Communist Party vastly enlarged these powers.

This revolutionary state had several tasks. Its major responsibility was to implement the basic economic reforms that assured the "breakthrough" from the capitalist to the socialist society, that is, the society where productive property belonged (in theory) to all the people, not to private interests. Stalin announced in 1934 that his country had at last "cast off its backwardness and ignorance" thanks to the progress—made under state command planning—of its nationalized industry and collectivized agriculture. Critics rejected his claim that this new order constituted a socialist society, but did not deny that he and his followers had created a unique economic system, usually referred to as a "command economy" (see Highlight, pp. 217–219). Communism became the guide by which the Soviet state took in hand the cultural life of the country. It entailed pervasive state controls of all realms of public speech, writing, and belief. Cultural creativity had to conform to the dogmatic proclamations of Stalin and his followers. They were the proper guides to uncovering the principles of truth, beauty, and goodness, all supposedly grounded in Marxist-Leninist ideology. Art and literature glorified the ideal socialist society and the idealized people. Religious faith and practice were repressed and relegated to a superstitious past.

Taken altogether, communism claimed an all-encompassing role in the life of the Soviet Union. As developed in Stalin's years, its powers extended throughout state and society. Its extraordinary scope can be summed up as the "three monopolies": the monopoly of power (the single-party state), the monopoly of property (nationalized industry, collectivized agriculture, state-run commerce), and the monopoly of truth (Marxism-Leninism).

Communism also promised to insure the well-being of the population. Public education, housing, and health care came at almost no cost to the people. What in the West was called social welfare became integral to Soviet socialist society. Though the quality of services was generally low and the peasantry received few benefits, the system remained a key aspect of communism's promise. In exchange, the people had to perform a wide array of social duties. The most important of these was working for the Soviet state economy regardless of personal sacrifice and hardship. The population was required to participate in necessary social activities, volunteering (whether willingly or not) for tasks that in other societies were salaried. Idleness was condemned and unemployment unthinkable in a workers' state. Those who refused to work could be sentenced to prison for the crime of "parasitism."

The second important tenet that Stalin incorporated in the communist ideology was the idea that class enemies remained a constant threat to the socialist society and communist state. Marxist theory had assumed that the fall of capitalism ended class antagonism. Stalin's view, repeated throughout his quarter-century in power, was that the successful construction of a socialist society incited the Soviet Union's enemies to terrorism and subversion. He expected capitalist states to make every effort, including war, to destroy the Soviet Union, since it was the bastion of world communism and the most progressive society in the world. Temporary alliances might ease relations, but the fundamental antagonism between the two systems was inevitable.

For the citizens living in the socialist society, Stalin's most sinister idea was that class enemies and agents of foreign states remained hidden in their midst. These enemies were more dangerous than ever, he believed, for their "desperate methods of struggle are the last resort of the doomed." Enemy agents and wreckers were everywhere, and only the utmost vigilance, denunciation of suspects, and stern police powers could protect the great communist achievements. No evidence was needed once the police arrested a suspected "counter-revolutionary," for their word was final. Their work was so important and their methods so reliable that arrest alone was sufficient indication of a person's guilt. Failure to denounce enemies was suspect, and families and friends of convicted "counter-revolutionaries" were immediately subject to arrest and imprisonment. Even members and leaders of the Communist Party might succumb to evil thoughts and become "enemies of the people."

This paranoid fear of enemies was at the heart of the system of police repression and prison camps that existed throughout Stalin's years in power. A similar reign of terror reappeared in China under Mao Zedung at the time of the so-called Great Cultural Revolution in the late 1960s and early 1970s. It emerged in Cambodia when in the late 1970s the communist Khmer rouge took power and executed hundreds of thousands of their subjects. Each time, the brutal search for supposed enemies reached unbelievable proportions. And each time the terror slowly died away, as had witch-hunts at moments of religious frenzy in the West in earlier centuries. Its disappearance was followed soon by the decline in the faith and solidarity that sustained communism.

The third ingredient in communism that Stalin introduced was the subordination of all foreign communist parties, and later states, to the needs of the socialist homeland, the Soviet Union. Lenin had launched an organization intended to sustain the international communist revolutionary movement. This Communist International became in Stalin's time a weapon for the defense of the Soviet Union, not for the advancement of communist revolution outside his state. His argument was simple: The achievements of the Soviet Union were of such momentous historical importance that no other communist movement could claim equal significance. After communist regimes appeared in Europe and Asia in the years following the Second World War, he forced their leaders to honor this principle. They were expected to serve the interests of the Soviet Union and to obey the orders of the Soviet leaders. Most obeyed; the Yugoslav Communists rebelled, refusing to submit to what they called the "Soviet empire."

Later, the entire communist world split apart when the Chinese communist state under Mao's leadership demanded that the interests of their revolutionary state come first. Like a vast religious movement, communism was splintered by accusations of heresy as rivals charged each other with betraying the true faith. Ultimately, communism vanished from its original homeland, Russia, when the entire system collapsed in the early 1990s. Russians searching to understand their Stalinist past brought from the West the term "totalitarianism." It seemed to capture best the nature of the extraordinary dictatorship that once ruled their land and whose fantastic claims to be the most progressive society in the world masked the reality of a despotic empire. That faith vanished, leaving behind the decrepit relics of an enormous failed experiment in human engineering.

THE JAPANESE EMPIRE

Japan joined the ranks of the despotic empires in the 1930s. It underwent far-reaching political changes in the years that followed the onset of economic depression. From a democratic regime it became militaristic; its foreign policy shifted from international collaboration to expansionism. The conditions leading to militarism had their roots deep in Japan's political and cultural past. The immediate cause of the decline of civilian rule lay in the economic collapse of the early 1930s. The global depression undermined the foundations of Japanese democracy and encouraged plans for Asian war.

Prosperity and Japanese Democracy

In the 1920s, the country appeared set on a path of peace and prosperity. The sweep-

ing political and economic reforms begun in the late nineteenth century had time to become firmly established. In scarcely more than a generation Japan had developed an industrial economy equipped with up-to-date industrial technology and organized to compete on the global market. The formula for success, devised and implemented by an elite group of reformers, emphasized the adaptation to Japanese society of Western skills and capitalist methods. These joined with Japanese commitment to hard work and savings, and with a high rate of government investment, to create a Japanese form of capitalism. Giant corporations permitted a few powerful business leaders to control production in key industrial sectors. They also enjoyed an influential voice in political affairs. Obliged to import vital raw materials—especially petroleum and iron—manufacturers turned their industrial skills to profitable ends, exporting much of their output to foreign lands and thereby paying for further imports.

The First World War had been a boon to Japanese industry. Western exports had dwindled. In their place, Japanese businessmen offered their products to the foreign markets once controlled by European firms. Textile exports doubled and so did the size of the Japanese merchant marine. Foreign earnings poured in so rapidly that Japan ceased being a debtor country. For the first time, its capitalists owned foreign investments of greater value than their own debts to foreign creditors (the United States was the only other country with similar war profits). Japan's gold reserves, still a key measure of national economic well-being, grew to six times the prewar level. The population expanded to over 50 million, and the standard of living, though still far below that of Western societies, gradually improved.

Prosperity strengthened the democratic leadership of the country. Political reforms, copied largely from British and German models, gave Japan the institutions and laws of a Western constitutional regime. In the 1920s, new electoral laws introduced universal manhood suffrage. By then, the influence of the political parties in the Japanese Diet was similar to Western democracies. The majority of the legislators was required to appoint the cabinet, which gave leadership to the state and the country.

Though it resembled a Western cabinet system, the Japanese regime had certain unique characteristics. Behind the scenes, power lay in the hands of a few individuals: party leaders, advisers to the emperor, and military leaders. The key decisions of cabinet appointment came from advisers to the emperor; cabinet ministers only then turned to their political parties for support in the Diet. Successful politicians relied on the financial backing of the giant corporations, whose large campaign contributions made deputies and cabinets careful to heed the wishes of the business elite. The Japanese army and navy command retained control over their own operations and periodically assumed "autonomy of command," allowing them to take military action without approval from the civilian government. These three small groups made up the real political elite of Japan.

The Japanese political system consisted of a delicate balance between elite rule and popular democracy, between business interests and military expansionists. All agreed on the importance of defending national interests and economic markets in East Asia. The emperor was the symbolic leader and, behind the scenes, still an important participant in key policy decisions. He remained the object of religious veneration that the Japanese believed rightfully belonged to the descendant of the sun goddess. Their devotion became a form of obedience when he sanctioned important government policies. In the "empire of the rising sun," power lay in the hands of the small group of civilian and military leaders who served him.

In the 1920s, the balance swung toward party rule and economic interests. Since the 1890s Japan had built up a small overseas empire, extending from Korea and southern Manchuria through occupied areas in China south to Formosa. Its navy possessed bases in the East and South China seas, where it was the dominant naval power. After the First World War, its military forces had moved into eastern Siberia in the midst of the Russian civil war. But a large army and strong navy represented a heavy and unproductive burden on the economy, and foreign conquest aroused the opposition of Japan's most important trading partner, the United States.

In the 1920s, economic interests and strategic concerns prompted Japan's government to halt military expansionism and to cut back expenditures for the military. The

Japanese representatives at the Washington Conference of 1921–1922 decided that the country's interests dictated agreement to limit the Japanese navy to almost one-half the size of either the British or American navies, and to order the withdrawal of Japanese troops from north China and eastern Siberia. In exchange, they obtained Western promises not to fortify new military bases in the Far East, and won international recognition of their state as the major power in East Asia (see Chapter 3). Subsequently, the Japanese cabinet drastically cut the size of the army and reduced the military budget. For the time being, Japanese imperialism was halted.

As long as the world economy expanded, the Japanese government and business leaders could restrain the army. They had solid grounds to argue that peace, not war, best promoted the country's interests in East Asia. Political leaders looked to the needs of the industrial economy and the urban population, ignoring social ills and the farm poor. Their motto might have been borrowed from one American president at the time, who argued that "the business of politics is business." The 1920s were good years for most Japanese, in spite of the terrible Tokyo earthquake of 1923, which killed 130,000 people and caused enormous property damage. Industrial production doubled and exports boomed, with 40 percent going to the giant U.S. market. Another 25 percent went to China, particularly to the relatively prosperous region of Manchuria where Japan established close economic ties and encouraged Japanese migration. The giant corporations expanded their operations to such an extent that they represented probably the largest economic enterprises in the world. One vast enterprise employed almost a million people in Japan and another million overseas and controlled hundreds of individual companies. The urban population grew to include almost half the country's inhabitants, and

the real wages of workers rose by about one-half. In economic terms, Japan enjoyed good times in those years.

Depression and Militarism

The world depression put an end to Japanese prosperity, to civilian rule, and to peaceful foreign relations. The economic and social signs of hard times appeared in all areas of Japanese life. Exports, a key indicator of Japanese economic success, fell to 50 percent of their 1920s level. The U.S. market no longer absorbed an abundance of imports. Then the 1930 U.S. tariff cut the market still further by raising rates on Japanese products by 25 percent. The workers' living conditions worsened. By 1931 their wages had fallen by one-third. Farm incomes declined even more severely as rice prices fell to below production costs and silk prices collapsed. One-half of Japan's rural population worked as landless laborers. Their living conditions, precarious in the best of times, became tragic.

These grim economic trends brought out the old weakness of civilian government and revealed new opposition to democratic rule. The politicians' close ties with business interests discredited their policies when economic decline set in. The small circle of powerful political figures around the emperor was less inclined to back civilian rule. Old class antagonism between rural and urban poor and the wealthy revealed itself in popular support for the army, a traditional escape from poverty.

The traditional glory attached to the exploits of warriors and the attraction of expansionist policies grew once again to provide old answers to the economic crisis. In the same period, patriotic movements closely resembling European fascism appeared in the country to give new meaning to war and imperial conquest. Their followers called for discipline and national unity. They condemned democratic leaders, and even attacked military leaders who counseled foreign restraint. They demanded that the country be led by "men of spirit" who possessed the willpower and ruthlessness to enforce national solidarity and to strengthen Japan's overseas empire. These patriotic societies began a campaign of political assassination, killing political leaders and moderate officers in the army and navy whom they denounced as "traitors" for betraying Japanese honor and renown.

Their nationalist ideology became the inspiration for the militarist leadership of the 1930s. Japanese militarism drew its strength in the 1930s both from traditional sources and from new mass support for authoritarian leadership and imperialism. In those conditions, the political pendulum swung toward military rule. The Japanese invasion of Manchuria in 1931 revealed how influential the Japanese army had become. Crowds welcomed the news of conquest. The government abandoned any effort to limit the military operations. It defended the army's offensive into Manchuria by arguing that Chinese troops were guilty of attacking Japanese forces and pointing out that no war was officially declared.

The League of Nations condemned Japan for aggression and called on its members to enforce sanctions as provided in the League Covenant. The Japanese government's response was to withdraw from the League. The U.S. government was still not a member of the League of Nations. Clinging to its isolationist policies, it refused to collaborate in this League decision. It did refuse to recognize the conquest of Manchuria, which it called a violation of Japan's treaty commitments. The gesture was theatrical and futile, a measure of the weakness of U.S. policy.

Later, the Japanese government renounced the limitations it had accepted at the Washington Conference on the size of its navy. The peace settlement of the 1920s in the Far East collapsed even before that in Europe. In 1933, Manchuria, renamed Manchukuo, became a puppet state within the Japanese Empire.

Militarism gradually took over Japanese political life. Civilian government never completely disappeared, becoming window dressing for imperialist policies. For a few years, political violence remained the tool of ambitious officers and fanatical patriots. Their attacks reached a peak in 1936 when junior officers mobilized over 1,000 troops in an attempt to overthrow the civilian government. The country's military leaders chose to oppose the insurrection, preferring to work through the cabinet and, in their own way, maintaining the appearance of constitutional rule. The rebellion was suppressed and its leaders executed. In 1937, national elections showed that a majority of the voters supported the civilian parties opposed to military rule. The wishes of the people had no influence on the government, however. Power had passed out of the hands of the parties into those of the generals. Civilians continued to run important ministries. In debates on foreign policy they spoke out in favor of peace and compromise. Yet their voices carried less and less influence in policymaking. In late 1941, General Tojo became prime minister, a post he held for the next four years. The military ruled Japan.

This new direction in Japanese policies and leadership was evident by the mid-1930s. The new Japanese regime can best be described as militaristic. The term "militarism" refers to a state in which military leaders are dominant, which pursues a policy of military expansion, and which glorifies a warrior culture. All three traits marked Japanese public life by the late 1930s. This momentous retreat from democratic rule was the work of army generals and naval admirals, backed by Emperor Hirohito, and supported by the great corporations produc-

Japanese Militarism for School Children: Tokyo High School Students at National Spiritual Mobilization Week, c. 1938 (*Hoover Institution*)

ing Japan's war arsenal. The defeat of the 1936 officers' uprising ended attacks by revolutionary officers on civilian government. The spirit of militarism spread through public life in a campaign glorifying discipline, order, and sacrifice for the fatherland.

This militaristic regime differed greatly from the political leadership of the 1920s, yet the changes came slowly and without great fanfare. It did resemble in some respects Italian fascism, yet lacked the essential traits of a charismatic dictator and one-party rule. The Japanese people obeyed their new leaders and responded loyally when called upon to sacrifice their lives and their well-being for the sake of their country and their emperor. Patriotism was a powerful bond among the Japanese. So too was respect for military valor. The two together constituted the cement that held together the population under the new military regime.

Japanese Imperialism

Japan's expansionist foreign policy revived in the 1930s. Its objective was the creation of what Japanese policy-makers called a "pan-Asianist regional order" under Japanese leadership. It included both Japanese economic penetration of China and southeast Asia, and military domination of the entire region, on land and on sea. Japanese leaders emphasized publicly the benefits of their plan for the other countries. They explained later that they sought a "Greater East Asia Co-Prosperity Sphere." Asians, rid of their Western oppressors with Japanese assistance, would aid one another in a vast enterprise of free trade and economic development.

The principal goal was the expansion of Japanese military and economic might. The plan offered the Japanese army and navy a vast territory, never clearly defined, for conquest and glory. It emphasized Japan's strategic interests and, up to a point, the limits to Japan's means to wage war. This program did not seek domination of all Asia and the Pacific. It did risk conflict with the Soviet Union and the United States, both of which were great powers whose security interests were directly threatened by the Japanese plans for an enormous East Asian empire. Most dangerous of all, this policy expanded the powers and encouraged the ambitions of the army and navy until at a certain point their conquests served no purpose save further military victories. The military leaders' ambition for imperial expansion failed to take account of the limits of their country's real power. After ordering them in 1945 to accept surrender, Emperor Hirohito observed that they "had placed too much significance on spirit and were oblivious to science." By then, they had reduced Japan to ruins.

The first step toward Pacific war came in 1937 with the Japanese invasion of China. No decision to conquer Nationalist China was made by the Japanese government. The

The formation of the Japanese Empire

move by field officers to defeat Chinese forces started in motion a process of military mobilization and offensive operations organized and led by army generals. They would accept nothing less than Chinese capitulation. By 1939, they had conquered all the major populated areas of coastal China as far south as the border of Indochina. They created in these areas puppet regimes, administered by Chinese collaborators, resembling their Manchukuo satellite state.

Yet they failed in their principal objective. They could not force Chiang Kai-shek to surrender and dislodge the remnants of his army from their refuge in the interior of China. There Chiang clung to his position of national leader and military commander of China's patriotic forces. The Japanese invasion of China provoked Chinese nationalist resistance among the masses in the occupied areas. Many of them participated in or supported communist guerrilla operations against the Japanese army of occupation. The Japanese military forces retained control of the cities and rail lines but found they could not extend their control over the vast rural population in the countryside. They were caught in an endless war.

Their solution to the dilemma was more war. They were encouraged in this by the German defeat of the Netherlands and France in 1940, and by Great Britain's military weakness. Late that year, Japan joined Germany and Italy in the Tri-Partite Pact, a defensive alliance that strengthened Japan's war party. Western colonies in the Pacific and in southeast Asia became a tempting prize to the militarists. French Indochina, on the southern border of the Chinese Republic, was strategically located, for it provided the one land route for military supplies from the West to reach Chinese Nationalist areas. The Dutch East Indies (later Indonesia), was valuable particularly because of its oil fields. The Indonesian peoples had lived for three centuries under European colonial rule, and some among them were already prepared to support an anti-imperialist, anti-Western revolt. The defeat of France and the Netherlands in 1940 left these colonies defenseless.

Eager for conquest and determined to end China's resistance, Japanese generals in 1940 moved troops to occupy northern Indochina. Their immediate goal was to cut off supplies from that region to Nationalist Chinese forces. The next summer, their forces seized the remainder of Indochina. Militarily the operation proved a simple matter. The French colonial authorities had few troops, and immediately capitulated. Diplomatically, the move proved the greatest mistake the Japanese military made.

The Japanese conquest of all Indochina finally aroused U.S. resistance to Japanese expansion. By then, the balance of power in all East Asia had shifted toward Japan. President Franklin Roosevelt considered military and economic aid to Great Britain in its war with Germany to be the principal U.S. priority. In early 1941, he had moved naval forces from the Pacific to the Atlantic to form the Atlantic fleet. The U.S. Navy had begun a program to expand its fleets, but more ships in the Pacific would not be ready until 1942. U.S. Army units in the Philippines were isolated and weak. Great Britain, desperately fighting German air and naval attacks, had no forces to spare for a Pacific war. At a time of impending conflict with Germany, a war with Japan might force the United States to wage a global war on two remote fronts. Realism suggested U.S. acceptance of Japanese conquests. Stalin did just that in signing a neutrality pact with Japan early in 1941.

But U.S. internationalist policy in East Asia dictated opposition to Japan's flagrant aggression. Only U.S. diplomatic, economic, and (potentially) military power stood in the way of Japanese domination of all eastern and southern Asia and the eastern Pacific areas. Ever since Japan's attack on China, some of Roosevelt's advisers had urged him to place an economic embargo on shipments of vital raw materials to Japan. This was a crucial step because the Japanese economy—and military—depended on these supplies for the war effort. Until 1941, Roosevelt opposed the embargo for fear of Japanese retaliation. There existed good reasons both for appeasement and for resistance to the Japanese.

In 1941, Roosevelt chose the policy of resistance. He believed that the United States was forced to take action by the Japanese conquest of southern Indochina. From there, Japan's troops were in a position to attack Western colonies throughout southeast Asia. That summer, Roosevelt approved a total embargo on all exports to Japan, including petroleum. Dutch authorities in the East Indies ended their oil sales to Japan as well. The U.S. secretary of state declared that his country would not lift the embargo until the Japanese "acts of aggression" had ended. He demanded that Japan withdraw, not only from Indochina but also from China.

The Japanese military rulers had to face the consequences of their reckless expansionist policies. The oil embargo on Japan cut petroleum imports to 10 percent of their previous level. Japanese officials warned that their entire oil reserves would run out within two years unless new foreign supplies were found. The Japanese naval commanders proposed a military solution: invasion of the Dutch East Indies. This step would succeed only if accompanied by the defeat of British and American Pacific forces. Japanese diplomats made one last effort to avoid war. They proposed an agreement with the United States to lift the embargo in exchange for Japanese withdrawal from all Asian areas except north China. But the U.S. government refused to end the embargo without Japanese agreement to withdraw from all of China. Even while these unsuccessful negotiations were under way, the Japanese military were planning their combined naval and land offensive against American, British, and Dutch colonies and bases in the Pacific. On December 7, 1941, their attacks began, bringing world war to East Asia.

⚜ SPOTLIGHT: Admiral Yamamoto ⚜

He became known under the name of Yamamoto, though Isoroku was his real surname. He became famous as the Supreme Commander of the Japanese Navy who conceived the Japanese plan of war on the United States, though he personally believed the war a mistake and victory unlikely. Isoroku Yamamoto (1884–1943) was one of the Japanese Empire's most gifted military leaders during the years when the country's leadership passed from the hands of politicians into those of militarists. Yet he was for years a target for assassination by the patriotic societies, who doubted his zeal to conduct expansionist war. His life offers insight into the reasons for Japan's rise as a great power, and the contradictions and failings that led to Japan's catastrophic defeat in the Second World War.

His family had for many generations belonged to Japan's warrior class (the *samurai*). They had served their great lords well.

When in the late nineteenth century the emperor's advisers decided to create a modern army, Isoroku's father was among the losers. He lost his military standing and the wealth that came with it. Isoroku, the youngest son, had to make his own way in the world. He chose the modern route laid out by the Meiji reformers, attending the new Naval Academy and becoming an officer in the new navy. He had preserved the family tradition of military service. In doing do, he had obtained the education and skills needed to operate the great battleships of a modern navy. Japan's success in its rapid modernization owed much to the collaboration of people such as Yamamoto.

He proved an extraordinarily talented naval officer. He first served his emperor in the Russo-Japanese war, fighting in the great naval battle at Tsushima Straits where the Japanese fleet sank the entire Russian naval squadron. He was seriously wounded and awarded the highest medal for valor. In the following years, he returned to advanced naval staff college. There, part of his training was studying English and learning as much as possible of the American Navy. His superiors already anticipated that their next great rival for power was the United States.

His success as naval commander earned him the respect of one of the great noble families, the Yamamoto. They lacked a male heir, and proposed to adopt him into their family. In Japanese society, such an offer was a great honor. He accepted, taking their family name and immediately marrying an acceptable noblewoman to give his family their heirs for the next generation. He respected and honored his new family, just as he honored his emperor and his "empire of the rising sun." Japan appeared to outsiders a "family-nation." Yamamoto was very much a member of that tight community.

Politics as well as ability determined the next major step in his rise to the top of the Japanese Navy. In the early 1920s, the government chose to collaborate with the Western naval powers in signing the Washington Treaties and agreeing to reduce the size of its navy. Some commanders were bitterly opposed, calling themselves the "fleet faction." Others, the "treaty faction," agreed with the new policy. Yamamoto was among the latter.

His career took a new turn in those years. He traveled to the United States, where he had been appointed naval attaché. He was responsible for observing the innovations in naval armaments and strategy under way in the U.S. Navy. Air power was the source of greatest controversy and debate among American naval strategists. Battleships, with cannons capable of firing shells over many miles, had been the latest word in naval fighting in earlier decades. Now U.S. naval strategists argued that their day had passed. Large ships with flat tops the size of small airfields could carry airplanes far across the seas to attack targets many hundreds of miles away from the naval forces. Yamamoto was persuaded that the aircraft carrier was Japan's naval future.

He returned to Japan convinced of two basic truths about Japan's place in the world. One was that it could never defeat the United States in a prolonged war. He had seen with his own eyes the tremendous economic might on which the U.S. military could rely. The other was that Japan's military influence in the eastern Pacific area would grow only by building aircraft carriers and planes, and by training the pilots and skilled naval personnel capable of giving Japan the most powerful navy in the Pacific Ocean. He successfully argued the case for aircraft carriers in the years that followed.

He even learned to fly, piloting the new "Zero" fighter planes that Japanese engineers had created. But he could not persuade his superiors, the government, or the emperor, that the U.S. was unbeatable.

In the 1930s, his career advanced rapidly. In those years of Japanese military expansion on the Asian mainland, the army won glorious victories while the naval commanders prepared for war with the United States. Yamamoto became admiral in 1930, at the age of forty-six. His task was rebuilding the navy. His emperor had ordered him to join in the preparations for war. His duty, as a patriot and an officer, required him to obey. In private, he continued to warn of the dangers of confronting the United States. But when the European war broke out in 1939 and the Japanese army chose to invade Indochina, he realized that a Pacific war was imminent. His task as Supreme Commander of the Combined Fleets of the Japanese Empire, the post to which he was appointed in 1939, was to devise the means to win that war.

His plan was ingenious. He learned that the U.S. fleet had been concentrated at the naval port of Pearl Harbor in the Hawaiian Islands. The site was many thousands of miles from the Japanese archipelago and Japan's naval bases. Yet he believed that a carrier fleet from the eastern Pacific could, with great care, proceed undetected to within striking distance of the U.S. naval base. From there, its attack planes and torpedo bombers would deal such a destructive blow on the U.S. forces that the United States would have to capitulate within a few months. He did not anticipate that the feeble military forces of the British, at Singapore, or those of the Americans in the Philippines, would offer any real resistance. He nearly succeeded, but that was not good enough.

His plan represented an enormous gamble, and one he would have preferred never to make. When ordered in 1940 to prepare the surprise attack, he explained to a close friend that "to fight the U.S. is like fighting the whole world. But it has been decided and so I will fight to my best. Doubtless I will die on board my flagship and Tokyo will be burnt to the ground." His personal convictions did not matter. Brought up in a society where absolute loyalty to the emperor was expected, he knew no way to resist and, like all Japanese subjects, believed the emperor's decisions to be final. Militarism in its extreme form had no place in his life, yet his career was bound to the brutal expansionist policies that the militarists had imposed on their country. He had, as he understood moral choice, no other way. He died in the war, not on his flagship but on an aircraft shot down in 1943 by U.S. fighter planes. Tokyo was later burned to the ground in a terrible air attack and firestorm in 1945.

SUMMARY

The Western world had undergone great political changes in the ten years since the depression began. Two powerful dictatorships had emerged in Germany and Russia. Their collaboration in the war on Poland signaled a remarkable shift in the European balance of power. These two states, whose ideologies presented diametrically opposed views of humanity's future, strongly resembled one another in their structure and operations.

Admiral Yamamoto, Commander-in-Chief of Japanese Fleet, 1943 (*Stevenson Collection/ Hoover Institution*)

Both concentrated political power in one party dominated by a dictatorial leader, both gave broad authority to a secret police, and both demanded absolute obedience of the population.

Perhaps common forces were at work shaping these two regimes. The cult of violence that both cultivated, each in their own way, provides one link. Stalinism and Nazism glorified violent struggle and the self-styled political warriors who were responsible for the violence. Both Stalin and Hitler mobilized a mass movement to support their own political ambitions. Finally, both turned the institutions and methods of a bureaucratic state and modern technology

into instruments to dominate an entire society. Although both talked of freedom, the word as they used it really meant obedience. Rivals for international power, their totalitarian regimes were deadly enemies of liberal democracy.

The peace settlements laboriously put together by the Western statesmen had vanished by 1939. The European states chose not to enforce these agreements, partly out of reluctance to risk a new war, partly because their countries were weakened by the depression. The war that began that year would not be ended by the European states. The new world war diminished their power and influence so substantially that they lost control of their Asian empires. The war in Asia was as important to the new balance of power as the war in Europe.

The rise of the German and Japanese empires, and the expansion of the Soviet Union, marked a new phase in the era of empires. These lands were ruled by despotic regimes, whose treatment of conquered peoples was far more brutal than that of the Western colonial empires. They pursued the single-minded goal of strengthening their dictatorial regimes and homelands. The Nazis included in this policy the exclusion of Jews from their lands, and ultimately the extermination of the Jewish population. The Stalinist regime physically eliminated by imprisonment or execution supposed class enemies and counter-revolutionaries. Virulent condemnations of Western imperialism occasionally emerged in their public pronouncements. The Japanese claimed to promote the anti-colonial movement of national liberation in Asia. The Stalinist leaders announced that their country's federal system of national republics brought to these peoples real national liberation and was a model for colonial peoples everywhere. But the reality was quite different. These lands all had fallen under the domination of despotic empires.

DATES WORTH REMEMBERING

1922   Fascist regime in Italy
1925   Locarno Pact
1928–1932   Soviet First Five-Year Plan
1929   Stalin dictatorship
1929–1934   World Depression
1931   Japanese invasion of Manchuria
1931   End of war debts and reparations payments
1932   Withdrawal of Japan from League of Nations
1933   Nazi rule in Germany
1933   Withdrawal of Germany from League of Nations
1933   Beginning of "New Deal" in United States
1935   Nazi Nuremberg Laws against Jews
1936–1939   Spanish Civil War
1936   German reoccupation of Rhineland
1937   Japanese invasion of China
1938   Munich Agreement on Czechoslovakia
1936–1938   Stalin's Great Terror
1939   Soviet-German Non-Aggression Pact and partition of Poland
1940–1941   Japanese conquest of Indochina
1941   Soviet-Japanese Neutrality Pact
1941   Japanese attack on British and U.S. forces in Pacific

RECOMMENDED READING

Fascism and Nazism

*William S. Allen, *The Nazi Seizure of Power: The Experience of a Single German Town*, (2nd edition, 1984). Fascinating close-up view of one small town that became a Nazi bastion.

*Walter Laqueur, *Fascism: Past, Present, Future* (1996). A succinct appraisal of the idea and practice of fascism up to the 1990s.

*A. J. P. Taylor, *The Origins of the Second World War* (1985). Provocative diplomatic history of the late 1930s, stressing Hitler's lack of a concrete war plan.

The Stalin Revolution

*Robert Conquest, *Stalin: Breaker of Nations* (1991). The best short biography of the secretive dictator, stressing his political life.

Stephen Kotkin, *Magnetic Mountain: Stalinism as Civilization* (1995). The extraordinary story of one of Stalin's gigantic industrial projects, and in capsule form an excellent glimpse of the agony and enthusiasm of the Stalin Revolution.

The Japanese Empire

W. G. Beasley, *The Rise of Modern Japan* (1990). A brief, perceptive survey of Japan from the Meiji reforms to the present.

Herbert Feis, *The Road to Pearl Harbor: The Coming of the War between the United States and Japan* (1950). A comprehensive study of the growing conflict between the United States and Japan in the 1930s.

Edwin Hoyt, *Yamamoto: The Man Who Planned Pearl Harbor* (1990). A vivid, sympathetic account of the life of Japan's greatest naval commander.

Memoirs and Novels

Lydia Chukovskaia, *Sofia Petrovna* (1991). A deeply moving story of the destructive impact of the terror on one ordinary Soviet woman.

*John Scott, *Behind the Urals: An American Worker in Russia* (1942). Memoirs of a young American who volunteered to work at the new Soviet industrial center of Magnitogorsk.

*Alexander Solzhenitsyn, *A Day in the Life of Ivan Denisovich* (1964). Fictional account of the Stalinist prison camp experience, written by a survivor of the camps and Nobel prize-winning author.

CHAPTER FIVE

The Last World War, 1941–1945

The Second World War was truly global in its scope and impact. It united the peoples of the world in one vast, terrible, human endeavor. Countries from every continent became involved in the conflict. Its fields of battle were scattered across Europe, Africa, and Asia and the islands of the Pacific Ocean; its naval battles extended over (and under) the Atlantic, Pacific, and Indian oceans. Heroism was no longer the sole privilege of soldiers in battle. Resistance movements in countries occupied by the Axis powers (Germany, Italy, and Japan) kept alive visions of a better life to follow liberation. For the first time, armies opened their ranks to women, who were not yet warriors but were no longer merely temporary workers and protectors of the home. New military technology restored mobility to armies, and made aircraft the key element in naval battles and the means to carry the war far behind the front lines. At the end of the war, one single explosive device revealed the capacity of atomic energy to lay waste an entire city. Human ingenuity put fantastic weapons of destruction in the hands of statesmen and their military commanders.

In the first years of the war German and Japanese victories destroyed the old balance of power. The peoples and resources of the conquered territories were at these empires' disposal. Their conquests marked deeply the population within those areas, obliterating old frontiers and overturning established governments. The Nazi New Order in Europe and the Asian empire of Japan differed enormously, but both sought supporters among their conquered peoples. The Nazis recruited fascists and sympathizers in the conquered areas for military service and administration, while the Japanese selected anti-Western nationalists to govern former European colonies. Their success in finding help added a new term to our vocabulary of war, "collaborators"—those who gave assistance to the occupying German and Japanese forces.

United in opposition to the Axis empires was an international coalition of Allied states. Their alliance was the result of Axis aggression; their war aims emerged out of the necessity to crush their enemies. Allied military victories proved, in the end, easier to achieve than political agreement on the postwar peace. By 1944, these victories had made clear that the forces of Great Britain, the Soviet Union, and the United States would soon defeat the German and Japanese empires. The war leaders of these nations—Churchill, Stalin, and Roosevelt—agreed on the short-term objective of complete destruction of the Axis, summed up in the term "unconditional surrender."

Their wartime discussions revealed the great difficulties that they faced in shaping a stable peace. Later, Western critics condemned the failure of British and American leaders to force Stalin, deeply suspicious of his Western allies, to accept the restoration of prewar governments in Europe. But these critics overlooked the limits to Western power and the powerful revolutionary movements that emerged in formerly occupied lands. As the war drew to a close, a new boundary appeared, dividing the lands freed by Soviet troops and those freed by the Western Allies. The peace, like the conflict that preceded it, bore little resemblance to the First World War.

THE EMPIRES OF GERMANY AND JAPAN

The first phase of the European war, from 1939 to 1941, began with rapid German military victories followed by the creation of a German continental empire. Assured of the neutrality of the Soviet Union, German troops easily defeated Polish forces by the end of September 1939. Britain and France had declared war on Germany but were incapable of offensive military operations to save Poland. In the spring of 1940, he directed his military forces against the Western states. In another "lightning war,"

German troops conquered western Europe, defeating France in six weeks.

Great Britain fought on alone, a beleaguered country relying on its navy and air force to hold off a German invasion. Its new prime minister, Winston Churchill, promised a battle to the end, "on the sea, on land, and in the air." The Battle of Britain, waged that fall and winter in the skies over England, left the Royal Air Force the victors and discouraged Hitler's plans for an invasion of the British Isles. Still, Great Britain remained in a desperate situation. Its shipping was being sunk and its navy losing the battle with German submarines. Its maritime communications with its Asian empire were nearly broken. Churchill could hope at best to sustain the war a year or more.

German domination of Europe grew with Italy's entry into the war at Germany's side in 1940. Small states from eastern Europe also joined forces with the Nazis. The third Axis power, Japan, signed a defensive pact late that year with the fascist states. The German conquests in eastern and western Europe made the Nazi state the most powerful military empire in the Western world. Churchill's only hope for victory was the eventual help of the other two great powers in the world, the United States and the Soviet Union.

The United States: Between Neutrality and War

Gradually U.S. isolationism weakened as German power grew. President Franklin Roosevelt had never shared the revulsion felt by many Americans at U.S. involvement in the First World War. He began his political career as a supporter of Wilson's domestic and war policies and had been active in the war effort as secretary of the navy. He shared the belief, first defended in the early 1900s by his elder cousin Theodore

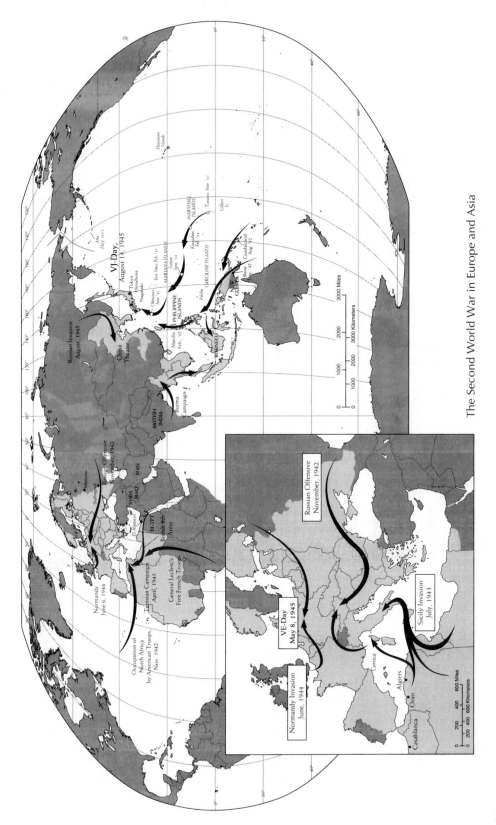

The Second World War in Europe and Asia

Roosevelt, that the United States had to take an active role in world politics. Like Wilson, he considered Great Britain a valuable ally whose defeat in war would constitute a disaster for the United States. He was not as ardent an internationalist as Wilson, however. He appears to have judged collaboration among the leaders of great powers more important to peace than international forums like the League of Nations. A skillful politician and public figure, he learned from the U.S. Congress's defeat of Wilson's peace treaty the necessity to heed the wishes of Congress and the American voters. He continually sought to reconcile attainable with desirable objectives in foreign policy. Until the last years of the 1930s, his attention was directed to domestic reform and the political struggles arising from his New Deal program. Foreign affairs constituted a secondary matter until European conflict once again intruded on American security and economic activity.

The first year of war in Europe forced Roosevelt to confront the consequences of American isolationism. The initial reaction of the U.S. Congress to the outbreak of war in 1939 was to repeat its commitment to the policy of noninvolvement in European conflicts. Earlier in the 1930s, Congress had passed neutrality acts banning the sale of U.S. military supplies to, or the use of U.S. shipping in trade with, any warring countries. Roosevelt had to declare the United States neutral in the 1939 war.

As German conquests multiplied, he began to speak out against isolationism and in support of the British war effort. He feared the strategic threat to U.S. security, especially after German victories in western Europe in 1940. He warned that "if Great Britain goes down, the Axis powers will control the continents and will be in a position to bring enormous military and naval resources against this hemisphere." In 1940, he

ordered peacetime conscription to build up once again the U.S. Army. In early 1941, he created the Atlantic Squadron. It was the first U.S. naval force in the Atlantic since 1918, and was made up largely of ships taken from the Pacific fleet.

Early that year, he obtained the approval of Congress to provide armaments to Great Britain on the Lend-Lease Program. No "lending" at all was involved and payment was never expected; the name, necessary to appease the isolationists, masked a new program of military aid. In the spring of 1941, the U.S. Navy extended its maritime war zone far into the North and South Atlantic. This permitted its vessels to protect from German submarine attacks U.S. ships bound for Britain. That fall, Roosevelt authorized U.S. destroyers to attack and destroy German submarines operating in the Atlantic. The United States was headed toward an undeclared naval war with Germany.

Yet all that time, Roosevelt lacked sufficient political backing for war in defense of Great Britain. His measures directed against Germany were based primarily on considerations of security and power. The American public understood far more readily, however, the rhetoric of internationalism than that of balance of power. His most successful speeches on international affairs discussed the war in Europe in idealistic terms. To win popular support for his policies, Roosevelt spoke out against the threat that Nazism posed to "religion, democracy, and good faith among nations." He pledged U.S. support for a "world founded upon four essential human freedoms": religion, speech, security, and freedom from want. Roosevelt, like Wilson before him, talked of the European conflict in terms that emphasized the defense of democracy and largely omitted issues of U.S. national security. In the summer of 1941, he obtained Churchill's approval for the Atlantic Charter. It committed both nations to "a better future for the world" following the "final destruction of Nazi tyranny." The charter did not constitute a military alliance, however. A majority in Congress still opposed war on Germany. Many Americans considered the growing danger of conflict with Japan to be of greater concern to immediate U.S. interests than the European war. The British had to fight on without the United States.

The German–Soviet War

The Soviet Union became Britain's first important ally. Although it had collaborated with Germany in the 1939 defeat of Poland, the two states were ideological enemies and rivals for power in eastern Europe. Stalin took full advantage of the secret agreements signed in 1939 with Germany (see Chapter 4). Annexing eastern Polish territory and seizing the independent Baltic states were only part of his war preparations through territorial expansion. In the south, he forced the Romanian government to surrender eastern lands. To the north, Soviet forces in the winter of 1939–1940 attacked Finland after its government refused Stalin's demand to give up its eastern territory to his state. Though the Finnish army was tiny by comparison with the Red Army, it fought skillfully to withstand repeated offensives. Its heroic resistance saved Finnish independence, but it had to capitulate after several months' fighting. The peace treaty ceded eastern Finland to the Soviet Union. These military operations enlarged Soviet territory in the western areas where Stalin anticipated war with Germany would come.

At the same time, Stalin sought to appease Nazi Germany. His government signed a trade agreement with Germany providing for Soviet shipments to Germany of vital raw materials, including petroleum, that the German military needed for its war

in the west. The Soviet Union carried out the agreement to the letter; the Nazis never delivered the goods that they had promised. In addition, Soviet border forces in the west were ordered to do nothing to provoke the German army. Stalin believed the German generals to be the principal fomenters of war in the east. The Soviet dictator dismissed as "British provocation" reports in the spring of 1941 from Soviet spies and from Great Britain of a planned German offensive against the Soviet Union. He could not imagine that Hitler, still at war in the west, would attack his country that year. Because his word was law, the Soviet Union was caught unprepared for the greatest military offensive in history.

Hitler did not wait, as Stalin hoped he would, to turn his armies against the Soviet Union. Strategically, Soviet war made no sense, for Germany remained at war with Great Britain and was receiving vast amounts of Soviet raw materials under the trade agreement. Militarily, the Red Army was the largest land army in the world and was backed by a productive industrial economy. None of these concerns swayed Hitler. His fanatical hostility toward communism was as great as that toward the Jews. In the fall of 1940, he ordered that the vast resources of the German Empire and its European allies be mobilized for a "lightning war" against Soviet Russia. It was to be waged along a 2,000-mile front with more than 4 million soldiers spearheaded by 10,000 tanks and supported by 5,000 planes. Plans called for victory in three months. On June 22, 1941, Axis armies invaded the Soviet Union.

The attack initially succeeded beyond the German commanders' greatest hopes. Within two weeks Soviet frontier defenses were crushed and German tank forces had penetrated deep into Soviet territory. Along the way they captured hundreds of thousands of Red Army prisoners. When the scale of the military disaster became clear, in early July Stalin assumed the position of official head of the Soviet government (he previously had held only the position of General Secretary of the Communist Party).

Stalin ordered Soviet soldiers to stand fast against the German offensive. In a radio broadcast (his first), he begged the Soviet people, whom he addressed as "comrades, brothers and sisters, dear friends," to make every sacrifice in what he described as their "Great Patriotic War." Patriotism was the force on which he had to rely to win the support of the peoples of his country. The mechanism of the police state was there to punish those who did not heed his call. Soldiers who shirked their duty and who appeared to have surrendered without good cause were judged traitors. He refused to make any effort to save the life of his eldest son, taken prisoner by the Germans that summer when his fighter plane was shot down. He made no allowances in that war for human weakness, pity, or compassion.

The German offensive continued until late fall. By October, all of western Russia had fallen. Leningrad was besieged, Kiev had been captured, and German troops were nearing Moscow. The Russian losses were enormous, totaling perhaps 2 million casualties, and most Soviet tanks and aircraft were destroyed. Yet the Red Army found new reserves, drawn from the Far East where war with Japan no longer threatened. In addition, bitterly cold winter weather had become the Red Army's ally, slowing the German advance. In December, Soviet troops launched a successful counteroffensive, the first defeat suffered by the Germans in the Second World War. The German "lightning war" had failed, but the front lines were far inside Russian territory.

The spirit of global war possessed Hitler. Although deeply committed militarily on the eastern front and under no diplomatic obligation, he linked the European and Asian wars by declaring war on the United States three days after the Japanese attack on the U.S. naval forces in Pearl Harbor, Hawaii. His action ensured that Roosevelt's hope to join Great Britain in the European war came true. In the west, the war on Great Britain included submarine warfare around the British Isles and frequent bombings of British cities. In North Africa, General Rommel's divisions came to the aid of Italian troops fighting the British in Egypt. In early 1942, Rommel's forces began an offensive intended to seize the Suez Canal and to establish German satellite states in the Middle East.

The eastern front remained the principal European battlefield. Military operations extended along a front from the Arctic Circle southeast to the shores of the Black Sea. The Germans and their allies maintained 1 million troops on that front; the Soviet combat forces, though weakened by the defeats of 1941, numbered more than 2 million and their size was growing. The ferocity of fighting left no room for compassion. Many of the Soviet troops taken prisoner in 1941, left with little or no care by the Germans, died of starvation and cold. The German blockade of Leningrad sought to starve the city into surrendering. That winter it became a frozen wasteland, without food or heat, in which hundreds of thousands of its inhabitants died of starvation and cold.

In a last effort to achieve victory against the Soviet Union, Hitler ordered his generals to prepare in the summer of 1942 an attack from central Russia toward the Caucasus mountains and the Caspian oil fields. South lay the Middle East where he hoped General Rommel would be victorious and would link up with the northern armies. The plan, baptized Operation Blue, exhibited a visionary concept of war so far beyond German capabilities that it bordered on the insane. When it began, German fighting ability, coupled with the weakness of the Red Army, achieved the initial objectives. By September, German units had reached the Caucasus while others had reached the edges of the city of Stalingrad, on the lower Volga River. They had not, however, destroyed the Soviet armies of southern Russia, most of whose troops had retreated beyond the Volga. Victory remained elusive, yet Hitler would settle for no less against his hated enemy. The city of Stalingrad acquired for him symbolic importance. He chose to make its capture, though not originally an important objective, the goal of the offensive. The war of movement became a war of street fighting in a city far to the east of the main German front. The battle of Stalingrad dragged on into the winter.

The German Empire

By the end of 1942, almost the entire European continent had fallen under the domination of Nazi Germany and its allied states. From the shores of the Atlantic Ocean as far east as central Russia, from the Arctic Ocean to the Mediterranean Sea, a German New Order reigned. It relied in part on the collaboration of allied states and of political movements sympathetic to Nazi Germany. Until 1943, Fascist Italy constituted Germany's most important ally, its troops fighting in North Africa, the Balkans, and Russia. In France, a small group of French political leaders collaborated with the Germans, who left them a state in southern France with its capital in Vichy. Most French people in the first years of defeat were resigned to German domination. Similar collaborationist regimes existed in the Netherlands and Norway.

In eastern Europe, some states had allied with Germany as soon as or before the war

began. Romania, Bulgaria, Hungary, and Finland aided the German war effort. In these states conservative nationalists, who were bitter enemies of Soviet Russia, hoped to share in the spoils of a German victory. Fascist parties provided collaborators in the German administration. Volunteers for the SS army divisions from other countries appeared in increasing numbers. National and political hatreds dividing eastern Europeans helped the Germans as well. Ukrainians assisted Germany as police, administrators, and soldiers to fight the Communists, who had inflicted great hardship on them before the war. In Yugoslavia, the Nazis encouraged Croatian nationalists to join them with the promise of an independent Croatia after the war. This collaboration never comprised more than a small minority of these national groups. Opposing them were resistance forces who fought the Germans in forested and mountainous areas, and provided assistance to the Allies. Still, the collaborators served the Germans well in helping to control occupied Europe.

The primary characteristic of the German New Order was exploitation of the conquered lands. All Europe lay at the disposal of the Nazi leaders: French agriculture helped feed German armies and sustain a comfortable standard of living in Germany. The industrial production of occupied Europe augmented German economic resources and supplied military equipment to German armies. The German authorities considered the working population of Europe to be available for their needs. German workers had to serve in the armed forces. In their place, the Nazis deported laborers from other countries to work in miserable conditions on German farms and in factories. From the Ukraine over 1 million men and women were transported to German lands, from Czechoslovakia more than 300,000, from France 1 million—in all, 5 million forced laborers. Germany turned the conquered populations into its subject peoples.

This repressive policy hit the Polish nation and the European Jews with greatest brutality. Poland once again ceased to exist. Much of its western territory was incorporated in Germany and the Polish inhabitants forced to abandon everything to move to the east. The central region became simply the Government-General, an area open to exploitation by German businessmen provided with Polish forced labor. The economic resources of the area went to Germany, leaving, in Goering's words, only the "absolute minimum for the maintenance at a low level of the bare existence of the [Polish] inhabitants."

These racist policies reached their most inhuman level in the extermination of the Jews of Europe. Nazi anti-Semitism constituted a powerful bond among all party members and found supporters among peoples in eastern Europe, where most of Europe's 6 million Jews lived. The Nazis searched for the swiftest way to destroy this hated people. Forced Jewish resettlement in ghettos began in 1940, but Hitler judged unsatisfactory the slow death there by disease and starvation. On the heels of the German troops sweeping through Soviet Russia, special SS death squads spread through the area, executing hundreds of thousands of Jews. Yet these methods too appeared to him insufficient to make Europe "free of Jews."

Hitler's solution was to order the systematic mass extermination of an entire people. In late 1941, he gave his approval to the policy called by Nazi leaders the Final Solution. Its implementation began in 1942. His instrument for this insane policy was at hand—the SS organization, whose members were sworn to absolute obedience to his orders. The entire Jewish population of Europe was to be shipped by train in cattle cars to special camps in Polish territories. These were extermination camps, organized according to the same standards of industrial

efficiency as slaughterhouses for animals. The trains, arriving at the camps usually at night, poured out their loads of men, women, and children. Most of them were immediately herded into special sealed buildings to be killed by poisonous gas, their bodies incinerated in enormous ovens. All that was left were mountains of clothing, gold teeth, hair, and other items taken from the victims. A few prisoners survived for a time to work as forced laborers, only to be killed in their turn.

When reports of the existence of these camps began to reach the West in 1942, they aroused disbelief at first, even among Jews. Allied leaders, in the face of mounting evidence of mass killings, issued public warnings to Germany to shut down the death camps. Their priorities of war took precedence, however, over military efforts to save the Jews. Until late in the war, no Allied bombing raids were directed against the facilities or rail lines of the camps.

The Final Solution remained in operation to the end of the war. What little Jewish resistance broke out proved futile. The 1943 uprising of the remaining inhabitants of the Warsaw ghetto constituted an act of hopeless, heroic desperation. By the end of the war more than 5 million Jews had been exterminated, the victims of insane Nazi racism and the moral cowardice of Germans. Historians still debate the circumstances and causes of this policy of genocide (the extermination of an entire people). It is a phenomenon so complex and terrifying that it defies adequate explanation. Germany's New Order tore apart the old Europe, its peoples and its states. Nothing could return the continent to its previous condition.

The Japanese Empire

The Japanese war leaders pressed forward their war, pushed by the need for the petroleum of the East Indies, and drawn by visions of a great victory in the eastern Pacific. They set in motion on December 7, 1941, their plan of military conquest. It called for a series of surprise attacks by Japanese naval aircraft to destroy the Pacific fleets of Great Britain at Singapore and of the United States at Pearl Harbor, Hawaii. Subsequently, Japanese land forces were to invade the Philippines, the British colonies in Southeast Asian, and the Dutch East Indies. The attack on Pearl Harbor put the bulk of the U.S. Pacific fleet out of action, missing only the three aircraft carriers sailing on maneuvers at the time. That same day, Japanese planes sank two British battleships that were the sole naval protection for the fortress of Singapore. For the next year, the Japanese navy controlled the Pacific Ocean from the Aleutian Islands south to the Coral Sea near Australia.

Naval victories opened the way for the military offensives of the Japanese army. The great British fortress of Singapore fell to a surprise attack in February 1942. The surrender of the garrison eliminated British rule in southeast Asia and left the Japanese with 90,000 prisoners, many of them soldiers from the Indian Army. That spring, Japanese troops completed the conquest of the Dutch East Indies. In May, the last American forces in the Philippines surrendered in the single greatest military defeat ever suffered by the United States. The Japanese military dealt harshly with the captured Western troops, whom they treated as virtual slaves to be deprived of adequate food and employed for forced labor. Japan's forces swiftly conquered Thailand, Malaya, and Burma, where its army prepared to attack British forces in eastern India. In half a year, it had conquered a territory with 140 million people, destroying in the process the Western empires of southeast Asia.

The Japanese government ruled these areas with occupation forces and local political leaders ready to collaborate with the con-

querors. Throughout southeast Asia nationalists administered these occupied lands in place of the vanquished Westerners. The Dutch East Indies became Indonesia, whose administration was led by the Indonesian nationalist leader Sukarno. Burma became a model Japanese satellite, receiving formal independence in 1943. Throughout the Philippines the Japanese found influential political leaders from the land-owning elite ready to collaborate in governing the population. They offered Indian prisoners of war, captured when Singapore fell, the opportunity to join an Indian National Army to fight British imperial forces on the Indian front, promising them that victory would bring independence to India. Thousands of Indian prisoners volunteered, many simply to escape death in the prisoner-of-war camps. Assurances of national liberation and the military triumphs of 1942 won for Japan the collaboration of nationalists from every conquered land.

China remained the major prize, and its Nationalist government the most elusive conquest. The Japanese regime had put in power collaborationist Chinese governments following their conquest of the coastal areas of northern and central China. Former leaders in Chiang's Nationalist Party were figurehead leaders of the central Chinese puppet state, whose capital was located in the one-time Nationalist capital of Nanking. In 1942, further Japanese military triumphs incited several Chinese generals commanding about one-half million troops to abandon the Nationalists and join the Nanking regime. Its army grew in size until it numbered almost 1 million soldiers by the end of the war. It assisted the Japanese in their operations against both Chiang's army and the Chinese Communist guerrillas. In this respect, the war in China constituted another chapter in the civil war that had followed the fall of the empire in 1911.

Japanese plans for their Asian empire extended over this entire conquered area.

China, along with Indonesia, the Philippines, Burma, Thailand, and Indochina were all to participate "through mutual cooperation" in an "order of common prosperity and well-being based on justice." The promise never came true. War occupied first place in the Japanese priorities. The resources of its empire and of the lands ruled by collaborators served the needs of the Japanese military. Indonesian petroleum fueled the Japanese navy and food supplies went to the army and to the Home Islands. This economic exploitation alienated the population and fueled resistance movements that sprang up in every country. Later, trade among the conquered lands dwindled when the American submarine war on Japanese shipping made the sea a battlefield and isolated the various countries from one another. The war against the Allies, not "co-prosperity," was the dominant feature of Japanese occupation policy.

Despite the impressive victories of their armies and navies, the Japanese High Command could not bring the war to a successful end. By mid-1942, the U.S. Pacific fleet had recovered sufficiently to launch its own attacks on Japanese naval forces. In China, Japanese campaigns against communist-held regions did not end the guerrilla war. The Japanese continued their offensives against the Nationalist armies. One-half of their overseas forces were tied down in that war in China. Chiang, still out of reach in his mountain capital of Chongqing far up the Yangtze River, would not surrender. Neither the German military triumphs nor the great conquests of the Japanese gave these states the final victory their leaders had sought.

THE FORMATION OF THE GRAND ALLIANCE

The alliance opposing the Axis states came together at the end of 1941. The German declaration of war against the United States gave Great Britain and the Soviet Union the ally that they needed in the European war. Great Britain and the entire British Empire were at war with Japan as well, but their major effort had to be the defeat of Germany. The "Grand Alliance" was complete.

The Western Allies and the Soviet Union were unlike one another in many respects. They fought on different battlefronts, they pursued separate war aims, and their political systems were the product of opposing ideologies. These differences created barriers to understanding and were the cause of serious disagreements. Gradually, though, through meetings of foreign ministers and international conferences the Allies agreed upon a set of common objectives. These goals set the guidelines for military collaboration and for the postwar reconstruction of Europe and East Asia.

The United States in the Grand Alliance

With U.S. entry into the war, the global conflict found a central focus. Decisions made in Washington were influential in the course of the war in Europe and Asia, and in the elaboration of the diplomatic aims of the Allies. This situation was the result primarily of the global military presence of U.S. forces and of the economic aid provided by the United States to its allies.

The United States soon came to possess the greatest array of modern armaments of any belligerent. By 1943, the U.S. fleets in the two oceans counted the largest number of fighting vessels ever to sail under one flag. The naval construction program, begun by Roosevelt in 1940, produced quick results, replacing the ships sunk at Pearl Harbor even while expanding the Atlantic fleet. Only the United States had access through its naval forces to the shores of every continent and island where the war was being fought. The U.S. Air Force grew in size to surpass that of Great Britain. By 1943, the combined forces of the two states controlled the skies over Germany. In the Pacific, the planes of U.S. aircraft carriers overwhelmed the carrier-based planes of the Japanese and by 1943 sank most of the Japanese carriers. Only on land was the U.S. Army outnumbered by another ally. The Soviet Red Army constituted the largest land army in the world, a fact of crucial importance for the ultimate fate of the states of eastern and central Europe.

Another reason for U.S. wartime leadership lay in its enormous economic resources. After remaining partially unused throughout the depression, factories and farmlands

U.S. Homefront Recruitment Poster: "She's a WOW: Woman Ordnance Worker" (*Poster Collection/Hoover Institution*)

resumed full operation when war production began. The nine million unemployed in 1940 found jobs, and business boomed. The "home front" needed women to return to work; the patriotic poster "Rosie the Riveter" was a vivid appeal for women to enter the labor force, using the nickname of a real California riveter helping to build military transport ships. Mobilized for a two-front war, the U.S. economy equipped its own military forces on land, sea, and air. It also provided great quantities of supplies to its allies. Roosevelt had started a program of military assistance to Great Britain even before the United States entered the war. This Lend-Lease aid began to go to the Soviet Union shortly after the German invasion of Russia.

When the United States became a belligerent, all previous political obstacles to economic aid vanished. The only barriers were the consequence of the war itself. Help reached the Chinese Nationalists by air throughout most of the war, as long as Japan controlled Burma. As a result, China received only a small amount of wartime aid. German submarines and air force blocked direct access to the Soviet Union. Ultimately, the path taken to ship massive aid to Russia passed through Iran, whose territory was occupied jointly by the Soviet Union, Great Britain, and the United States. They build roads and railroads from the Iranian coast to the Soviet border. In 1943, supplies began to pour into Russia, providing $11 billion in aid, principally food, aircraft, and military vehicles. The single greatest recipient of U.S. assistance, though, was Great Britain. Together with the Commonwealth countries, it received $30 billion in Lend-Lease supplies.

The United States and Great Britain had for half a century formed a working diplomatic partnership based on shared interests and objectives. It had become a wartime alliance once already in 1917–1918. Churchill and Roosevelt had begun forging new ties even before Pearl Harbor. The diplomatic objectives of the two governments were not identical. While the U.S. leaders championed the cause of independence for colonial peoples everywhere, including India, Churchill sought to retain as much imperial territory as possible. But his country was terribly weakened by two years of military defeats. In the winter of 1941–1942, the combined U.S.–British Atlantic fleet had to keep supplies flowing to Great Britain. Its convoys could barely cope with the German submarine attacks, which reduced to critically low levels the food and fuel supplies reaching the British Isles.

Both countries depended heavily on the military contribution of their Soviet ally. Throughout the war, Roosevelt was guided in making strategic military decisions by the conviction that he must minimize U.S. war casualties as much as possible. He preferred building up vast armaments before risking major land offensives. The invasion of northern Europe had to wait. Until 1944, only the Red Army prevented total German victory on the European continent. Without an eastern front, the Western Allies would face the bulk of German forces when they finally attempted their European invasion.

The U.S. government believed the alliance with the Soviet Union indispensable also for military victory in East Asia. The Red Army appeared to them the only military force in position to defeat Japan in Manchukuo and north China. In both the European and Asian wars the Soviet Union was an extremely valuable ally.

In the first years the U.S. and British governments could do little to take the enormous burden of fighting off the Red Army. Stalin continually reminded his Western allies of this fact, begging them in 1942 to open a western front to relieve his armies retreating once again before the German offensive. But Roosevelt agreed with Churchill that their military lacked both the naval power and infantry forces capable of staging a successful cross-channel invasion. In 1942, the Soviet Union had to continue fighting alone in Europe.

In that situation, a diplomatic gesture acquired special significance to prove to Stalin that the West valued the Soviet alliance. The United States and Britain promised in early 1943 not to accept any peace terms from Germany except "unconditional surrender." The real meaning of the declaration was that under no circumstances would the two powers negotiate a separate peace with Germany. Obtaining Stalin's agreement to the policy signified to them that Soviet Russia would remain in the war, even without a second front in the west. The Soviet Union was a vital yet mysterious member of the Grand Alliance. Western statesmen realized from the start that the Soviet Union would occupy a dominant position in central Europe when Germany was defeated. The greatest mystery for Westerners surrounded the international objectives pursued by the Soviet Union.

Stalin had in the previous decade conducted Soviet foreign policy on the principle that whatever was in the interest of Soviet territorial security and power had first priority for his country and for world communism. He used the Soviet-German nonaggression pact of 1939 to expand Soviet territory in eastern Europe. He later made known to the Allies his determination to retain those lands after the war. He protected the Soviet Union and its sphere of influence in East Asia by signing the 1941 neutrality treaty with Japan. He abided by the treaty until four years later when Roosevelt promised him substantial rewards for joining the war in East Asia. Revolutionary expansion played no part in these foreign dealings. In appearance the Soviet Union was a revolutionary communist regime, but its policies were those of a great power. In both respects, it constituted a troubling presence in the coalition.

Since the outbreak of war with Germany in mid-1941, Soviet objectives concentrated on the defense of the country. The war had begun with disastrous military defeats and the loss of most of western Russia and the Ukraine. Faced with this crisis the country mobilized for total war. Stalin took direct control of political and military affairs. He followed the actions of his generals closely, and reorganized the nationalized economy for war. His dictatorial powers obliterated the distinction between political and military leadership. They permitted him later to adjust military operations to diplomatic interests of state.

The vast powers of the state and the Communist Party were turned to the war effort. The apparatus of the police state remained in place. Its energies during the war were directed to stiffening the will of the population to fight. Its arbitrary powers of arrest were used against suspected collaborators and traitors as well as against those who dared criticize Stalin. Army deserters were shot. The prison camps remained in place, though their inmates were at times ordered to the front on suicide missions; the few survivors received their freedom. Stalin's demand that the people of his country "must fight to the last drop of blood" became the overriding feature of Soviet life.

The war required the mobilization of all the economic resources of the country. German victories in 1941 had deprived the Soviet Union of some of its most important industrial areas and most productive agricultural regions. The Siberian industrial economy proved its real defense value in that period. The Red Army was still poorly equipped in 1942, but the new armaments it did possess came from the eastern factories. People had to survive on the meager food supplies remaining; many were hungry and in some areas famine set in. Food aid from the United States began to appear in that year, and at times the one meat dish available to civilians came from a can from "Amerika" bearing the unusual name of Spam.

The population responded with extraordinary patriotic fervor, though the sentiment was not universal. People in the western regions seized by the Red Army in 1939 and 1940 welcomed the German invaders. Non-Russian nationalities in the southern Soviet areas provided a sizable number of collaborators for the Germans. Among the Russian population, though, the war against Germany became a national cause. The population of the blockaded city of Leningrad endured inhuman conditions of hunger and cold in a spirit best described as collective heroism. Over a million lives were lost before the Red Army forces forced an end to the Axis siege in early 1944. The Great Patriotic War, as the Russians called the war with Germany, demanded and received widespread support.

The greatest sacrifice came from the front-line soldiers. In the first two years, the Red Army lacked sufficient military equipment and skilled officers to match the powerful German army, since many of the older, experienced Soviet officers had died in the Great Terror. This weakness was particularly apparent in the first summer of fighting. Military defeat and encirclement of whole armies led soldiers to surrender in enormous numbers. This remained the case in 1942 as the German offensive swept through southern Russia to Stalingrad. Soviet generals replaced the missing armaments by demanding suicidal heroism from their soldiers. Front-line infantry could hope at best to survive one month of battle before suffering serious wounds or death. By war's end, Soviet military dead had reached 10 million.

In these desperate circumstances, Soviet authorities ordered Communists in the occupied areas of Europe to organize anti-Nazi guerrilla forces wherever possible. Their feeble military operations were useful to weaken the German war effort in the east. In eastern Europe, and in France and Italy as well, communist resistance groups made effective guerrilla forces. They proved most successful in Yugoslavia. Tito, leader of the Communist Party, built a guerrilla army that gradually took control of the mountainous regions of the country. It received substantial military aid from the Western Allies. Moscow remained for him and his followers their Mecca, and revolution was their ultimate goal.

Soviet military operations began to achieve some measure of success in the battle of Stalingrad. After stubbornly defending a small area of the city on the very banks of the Volga River, in November 1942 a major Red Army counteroffensive encircled the German forces there. Two months later, the remnants of the German army surrendered. The Red Army lost probably half a million men in the battle, but the Germans lost as many. The German army retreated to central Russia. In the summer of 1943, the eastern front still lay deep in Russian territory.

The battle that decided the outcome of the German-Russian war occurred that summer on the plains of central Russia. Hitler attempted one last major offensive. It was the biggest tank battle in the entire Second World War. This time, the Red Army was prepared with equipment, troops, and competent generals. In the end, the Soviet military machine proved mightier than the German army, beaten and in full retreat. By the late fall, the German withdrawal had reached western Russia. Victory was at last becoming a tangible reality for the Soviet leaders.

Allied Cooperation

In those conditions of newfound military strength, Stalin was ready to negotiate a real diplomatic alliance with the Western powers. At the conference of Teheran in the fall of 1943, he finally met with Churchill and Roosevelt. The Western leaders for their part were able to make the firm commitment of a second front in France in the spring of 1944. That conference marked the high point of good relations among the Allies. The three leaders agreed on the basic terms of their Grand Alliance, focusing on three important objectives. First, they repeated their intent to pursue the war against Germany to total victory. Following German surrender, the country would be divided temporarily into occupation zones. Policies of demilitarization, denazification, and reparations payments would be imposed on the German population.

The Western leaders accepted Stalin's demand that the Soviet Union retain its new western lands. Informally, they also agreed that Poland, having lost eastern territory to the Soviet Union, would receive German lands along its western border. They reluctantly accepted Soviet territorial annexation and new Polish frontiers for the sake of the alliance. In doing so, they contributed to the creation of a new postwar Soviet sphere of domination in eastern Europe.

Stalin, for his part, consented to enter the Asian conflict following victory in Europe. Roosevelt, heeding the advice of his military advisers, was convinced that only the aid of the Red Army would end the war against Japan quickly. Stalin's promise of military assistance constituted a major achievement

Leaders of the Great Powers: Stalin and Roosevelt at the Teheran Conference, 1943 (*National Archives*)

for the U.S. president. For its sake, he was prepared to agree to Soviet Union territorial gains and a new sphere of influence in Europe and East Asia.

The great battles of 1944 made the Alliance's power apparent to Allied and Axis states alike. In June, the combined naval and land forces of the Western Allies opened a front on the Normandy coast of France. After weeks of fighting, American armored columns were able to begin a rapid offensive through central France, capturing several hundred thousand German prisoners. In August, Allied forces liberated Paris. But the

hope that Allied armies would be able to penetrate German territory was frustrated by the British offensive's failure that fall to reach the lower Rhine River in the Netherlands. Germany had suffered a major defeat in the west, but the war remained still outside German territory.

In the east, German forces suffered a defeat as overwhelming as the Normandy battle. That summer, Stalin assisted the Allied invasion by ordering a major Soviet offensive along the entire Central Front, located in western Russia. Hitler's instructions to the German Army were to fight without retreat, a hopeless task but one that his general obeyed. The Red Army was able to defeat and to encircle most of the German military forces along the front, approximately 300,000 men. The destruction of the Central Front opened the Soviet path to Poland and to eastern Germany. By August, its advance divisions had reached the outskirts of Warsaw.

The approach of the Red Army triggered an uprising in Warsaw by the underground noncommunist Polish National Army. Its leaders were intent on capturing the city before the Russians reached it, fearing that otherwise they stood no chance of forming the new Polish government. Then the Red Army stopped. For months, it remained east of Warsaw while a German division slowly suppressed the uprising and destroyed the city itself. Only in January 1945 did the Red Army resume its offensive there. Historians still debate whether the Soviet halt was a military necessity or political expediency. It is certain that German annihilation of the Polish National Army forces in Warsaw ended the principal obstacle to Soviet political domination of Poland.

These great military victories triggered the collapse of the Axis alliance. One of the Axis powers had capitulated even earlier. The Allied landing in southern Italy in 1943 had finally roused Italy's generals to join the opposition to the Fascist state and to Mussolini. They and most of the Italian people had no desire to pursue further a hopeless, destructive war. With the help of the Italian king and leading Fascist politicians, they succeeded in removing Mussolini from power in mid-1943 and in signing an armistice with the Allies. Immediately afterward, however, German armored divisions occupied the country and replaced the Italian troops in the front lines. The fighting in Italy, never an important theater in the war, dragged on for another two years. Nazi Germany more than ever provided the real force in the Axis coalition.

By 1944, the German air force could no longer protect the country from continual Allied aerial bombardments. Massive British and American bomber attacks using explosive and incendiary bombs turned some cities to ruins, with the loss of hundreds of thousands of German lives. The "fire storms" caused by these attacks were as destructive as the first atomic bomb explosions. The worst occurred in early 1945, when the city of Dresden was bombed, with losses estimated between 50,000 and 80,000 lives. Despite Nazi fanaticism and the grim determination of German troops, Axis defeat was by then inevitable. But the war continued, for Hitler and his Nazi followers preferred death in battle to defeat.

❦ HIGHLIGHT: War, Peace, and Internationalism ❦

The dream that peace should reign among countries has existed for as long as modern states have waged war. In the nineteenth century, Western writers and political leaders committed to human rights and democracy formulated a new project for insuring peace among nations. Their internationalist theory became the basis of President Woodrow Wilson's peace proposals to end the First World War. The tragic destruction and loss of life brought by that war convinced many Westerners that such a conflict must never again occur. It had to be "the war to end all wars." But for the dream to come true, it had to be based on a new system of international relations. Despite Wilson's failure, President Franklin Roosevelt revived in a modified form this view of a world at peace. It guided him in laying plans for the postwar international order.

Roosevelt's peace proposals drew inspiration from the core arguments of internationalism. With some reservations, he was ready to place the ultimate responsibility for wars on the principles of balance of power and "reason of state" that had governed diplomatic relations since the seventeenth century. To change this system meant altering the very process by which states settled disputes and maintained peaceful relations among themselves.

Those who defended the traditional system called themselves "realists." They claimed that the foreign policy of states had to pay attention to the real power possessed by independent countries, not to the visions of idealistic dreamers. They observed that the process of international relations was often a struggle among sovereign states, since no higher law or binding moral code restrained the behavior of states. A government might hope for good will and cooperation from other states, but it had to be prepared for the possibility that one or several of them would prove a threat to its well-being.

The reasons for war that these realists cited were, first, that some leaders are always tempted to abuse their political power, particularly at the expense of foreign countries. Second, each state has a certain array of special needs and objectives that at times compete with those of other states. These interests of state dictate the guidelines of the foreign policy of any country, which is bound at times to have to confront another country whose interests clash with its own. A government might hope that negotiation and compromise would settle these disputes, but the ultimate defense of its interests, and first of all the defense of its people and territory, had to depend on its ability to defend itself in war. Realists for centuries had argued that individual states had to be the final arbiters of these interests. What they called "reason of state" was the only rational foundation of international relations. They believed that alliances help maintain a stable balance of power, that is, prevent any aggressive state from dominating others. War remained a regrettable but likely eventuality.

Internationalist critics judged this defense of war intolerable and immoral. Long before the First World War had proven the destructiveness of modern war, they had condemned the realists for assuming that states were forever destined to struggle among themselves. They had found inspiration in the liberal democratic ideology, especially its emphasis on human rights, and in economic trends of the nineteenth century that strengthened trade and financial cooperation among states. The First World War reinforced their conviction that they had to succeed in bringing to a halt wars that had become so destructive there could be no real victors or vanquished. Their liberal belief in democracy persuaded them that most human beings were reasonable and capable of understanding the importance of common interests shared by states and peoples. If the right democratic institutions and obstacles to aggression were put in place, wars could be halted. Modern states had brought an end to feudal wars; internationalists proposed to do the same for wars among states.

The nineteenth century had given them special reasons to believe that their project was realizable. The spread of democracy placed power in the hands of masses of voters. They argued that the people had solid grounds to oppose a political leader who plotted military aggression, since their own lives and property would suffer most in the event of war. Internationalists believed that the interests of economic leaders also lay in the preservation of peace, particularly in conditions of a growing international economy. They expected that economic interests and common sense would combine to create an enlightened public opinion throughout Western countries. Generals or dictators, unaccountable to the people, were the likely source of conflict. They had to be restrained, but the means to that end was international cooperation. All peaceable states ought to agree among themselves to insure the security of each state, for by standing together, they would dissuade aggression. They had to be prepared to act collectively, however. Their individual sovereignty (the right to act independently) would at times have to be subordinated to the need for collective action against aggressors. The preservation of peace among nations was certainly worth this sacrifice.

Woodrow Wilson had been the first leader of a great power to make internationalism the core of his foreign policy. When at the close of 1916 he had called on the warring European states to end their fighting, he made clear his vision for the future. A "just and secure peace," he had argued, would end the "organized rivalries" of the balance of power. Most important, it had to recognize the right of peoples to choose their own governments, whose "just powers derive from the consent of the governed." "National self-determination" was the foundation for peaceful governments. Finally, these governments had to be prepared to cooperate in an organized "community of nations" charged with settling international disputes. It was an extraordinary proposal, called for by the catastrophe brought upon the West by the war.

Wilson held up a visionary plan that did not vanish with his political defeat after the war. "Wilsonianism" was the term by which political leaders in the United States often referred to internationalism. Franklin Roosevelt revived its essential elements. He appealed in the name of world peace to the American people to accept the terrible sacrifices of the new war. He promised that its victorious outcome would restore freedom and allow peoples around the world to proceed with the creation of their own nation-states.

The dream of an international concert of states to protect peace survived the disappearance on the eve of that war of the League of Nations. Wilson's vision appeared closer than ever to fulfillment in the reordering of global relations that followed the defeat of the Axis and the decline of Western empires after the Second World War. The United Nations was the League's direct successor, and its membership grew rapidly with the entrance of the new nation-states that replaced the fallen empires. In the last decade of the twentieth century, peacekeeping forces operating under the United Nations flag and at the orders of the Security Council appeared in country after country where civil wars or regional conflicts threatened the lives of the population and the security of the region. Internationalism remained alive and vigorous.

THE DEFEAT OF THE AXIS EMPIRES

In early 1945, the wars in Europe and Asia were drawing rapidly to a close. The future of the occupied European states and Asian colonies depended in large measure on the policies of the victorious Allied powers, working either together or separately. The Grand Alliance promised cooperation both for war and for the peace to follow. More important for Europe than agreements among the Allies was the movement toward central Europe of Soviet and Western armies. Behind them Soviet and Western occupation authorities began reconstruction; the result diverged greatly between eastern and western regions. While new Allied plans were laid for a common future for Europe, a kind of partition of Europe had already begun to emerge. The fate of Asia was decided soon after, when the world entered the era of nuclear warfare. American military might decided that war. China and Korea experienced a process of partition similar to Europe. The war's outcome was in the hands of the Allies.

The United States and the Liberation of Western Europe

Among the Western statesmen, Roosevelt had the greatest influence in laying plans for the rebuilding of postwar Europe. The American political system placed the formulation of foreign policy in his hands alone, though it left to Congress and the voters the decision to allocate the funds needed for foreign ventures. An astute politician who had lived through the hopes and the deceptions of Wilson's internationalist policies, Roosevelt anticipated that U S. wartime influence would not extend into peacetime. The American people, through their elected representatives, would demand an immediate return to peacetime conditions—the demobilization of U.S. troops and an end to foreign aid. The best Roosevelt could achieve

would be a peace that was self-enforcing, that is, one that did not require permanent U.S. military commitments. Wilson's internationalism shaped his vision of the future peace. He held out the promise of national self-determination for lands occupied by the Axis, even if these areas had previously been Western colonies. He looked forward to collaboration among the Great Powers within the framework of a new international peacekeeping organization, to be called the United Nations.

His plans modified Wilsonianism in two ways. For one thing, his advisers and the British government worked for the establishment of an international economy based on free trade and a stable financial system. U.S. leaders hoped to see global economic expansion after the war; this would benefit the wartorn countries and the American economy as well. Meeting in the United States in late 1944, British and American officials reached agreement on U.S. financial support for international trade and financial affairs. The so-called "Bretton-Woods system" promised a reinvigorated global market economy, buttressed by U.S. economic wealth.

Roosevelt looked forward to peacetime collaboration among the Great Powers. Their leadership in world affairs mattered more to him than the institutional projects of the United Nations. They were to take primary responsibility for the introduction or restoration of democratic government in small nation-states, and for collective action to resist aggressive governments. He assumed that American isolationism was dead, and sought to replace it by a foreign policy that would require only limited U.S. involvement in global affairs. In his speech to Congress after his return from the 1943 Teheran Conference, he made clear how much importance he attached to a new postwar spirit of cooperation. "Britain, Russia, China, and the United States and their allies," he declared, "represent more than three quarters of the total population of the earth. As long as these four nations with great military power stick together in determination to keep the peace there will be no possibility of an aggressor nation arising to start another world war."

He referred to their collaboration as the work of "Four Policemen." He insisted that these states be granted special powers in the Security Council of the new United Nations. It required wishful thinking on his part to imagine Nationalist China capable of becoming the "policeman" of East Asia. Only Roosevelt's deep optimism (and the euphoria of wartime cooperation) justified his hope in continued agreement with the Soviet Union. The alliance had to endure, for he saw no other hope for an enduring peace.

As Allied forces moved toward central Europe, the key role of the occupation authorities became evident. France was the most important country liberated by the Normandy invasion. It had lost all real independence during the war. Its economy had been in the service of the German war machine and its people had been subject to German exploitation. As the years of occupation passed, opposition to the Germans grew and underground resistance forces gathered together in the Free French movement. Its leader, General Charles de Gaulle, was a traitor to his army in 1940 when he refused to accept the armistice with Germany and fled to London. His dedication and eloquence in the cause of French freedom soon placed him at the head of the forces resisting

The Economist among the Diplomats: John Maynard Keynes Addressing the Bretton-Woods Conference, 1944 (*UPI/Bettmann*)

the Germans. As liberation drew near even the Communists acknowledged, albeit reluctantly, his leadership.

De Gaulle had great difficulty obtaining the recognition of Roosevelt. The American president believed that "national self-determination" meant the choice of new leadership by free elections, not by self-proclamation. Yet de Gaulle was the major noncommunist political leader in France, and was committed to free democratic government. This agreement on basic political principles, plus the popularity of de Gaulle among the French people and Resistance forces, earned him the diplomatic backing of the Western Allies shortly before the Normandy invasion. In the months that followed he reached agreement with the French Resistance forces on democratic elections to form a new constitutional republic, in what all hoped would be a new France. In a manner consistent with the principle of national self-determination, France recovered its independence.

☥ SPOTLIGHT: John Maynard Keynes ☥

Until the Englishman John Maynard Keynes (1883–1946) revolutionized economic theory, economists devoted themselves to the scholarly study of what was known as the "dismal science." Classical economics had no role to play in public life, and its specialists sought no place there. They referred to their theory as "laissez-faire" [meaning to "let alone"] capitalism, since they believed that the laws governing economics operated, and had to operate, without any outside intervention. Prosperity and depression followed one another in a natural cycle as inevitable as the seasons. When depression hit, bankruptcies and unemployment spread widely. Recovery would again lead to renewed prosperity, businesses would again prosper and the laboring population enjoy better times. But no one could alter the cycle.

Keynes challenged that theory, making economic conditions a central concern for governments. He was a rebel in his chosen career, just as he was a rebel in his personal life. He belonged as a young man to the Bloomsbury circle of bohemian intellectuals in London, who defied Victorian moral conventions for the sake of personal liberty. Among them, Keynes had no need to hide his homosexuality. His brilliance as an economist earned him a place among English negotiators at the Versailles peace settlement in 1919. There he quickly became disillusioned at what he believed to be the injustices of the German treaty. Afterwards, he taught quietly at Cambridge University, marrying a Russian ballerina and now and then speculating (and usually winning) on the stock market.

His real achievement came when he sought to explain the fundamental economic problems caused by the depression of the 1930s. In those grim years he challenged classical economical theory by arguing that the cyclical evolution of capitalist economies did not necessarily (or even ordinarily) lead to full employment and long-term stability. The promise of laissez-faire capitalism to restore prosperity after major declines in economic activity was false. He spelled out his own theory in a book titled *The General Theory of Employment,* published in 1936. It created an uproar among economists, for it proposed that governments had the responsibility to use their financial resources (and the advice of economists like himself) to reform the imperfect capitalist system. His theory quickly attracted political leaders looking desperately for a solution to the social crisis caused by the depression. Like President Roosevelt, Keynes sought to protect the freedom of the market economy and liberal democracy on which it depended. At a time when communism and fascism were attracting supporters everywhere (including students at Cambridge University where he taught), he wished to find a "middle way between the anarchy of laissez-faire and the tyranny of totalitarianism."

The Second World War carried him one step further to consider the entire global economic system. Recovery from depression and war required a new system of international trade and financial cooperation. The United States had to occupy the central position if the postwar world was to avoid the chaotic, destructive protectionism and economic stagnation of the 1930s. The British and U.S. governments welcomed his help. He was, they recognized, a "true genius." At the negotiations in 1944 in Washington (the Bretton Woods conference), he played a key role in bringing agreement on the international institutions to stimulate reconstruction and multilateral trade after the war. That system did not begin full operations until after his death. It grew in importance to become a central feature of the late-twentieth-century global economy. Keynes had helped build that "middle way" on which the Western world depended.

Soviet Triumph in Eastern Europe

While the Western leaders judged national self-determination suitable everywhere in Europe, Stalin accepted it only where it suited Soviet power politics. His objectives and methods of building peace differed fundamentally from Roosevelt's. The fundamental difference lay in the use of state power. While the U.S. government set out to create a new world order that would require the least possible U.S. international intervention, the Soviet leader proceeded to deploy his military power to ensure diplomatic or political domination in the areas around the Soviet Union liberated by the

Red Army. As in the 1930s, Stalin honored the law of power politics to "respect only the strong" and retained his suspicious view of the "capitalist jungle." The war against Germany had temporarily allied capitalist states and the Soviet Union, but in his opinion the fundamental antagonism between the two social systems remained. In Stalin's world view, applied even more ruthlessly in his dealings with fellow Communists, no one could be trusted of their own free will to work for the common good. He recognized only political and military power.

By this logic, he owed the Western Allies a certain esteem. He well understood the reasons for the global preponderance of the

United States, with its undamaged, productive economy, great navies, and enormous air power. The Soviet Union, bled dry and strained to the utmost to support the Red Army, was no match. For that very reason, he assigned first priority to the strengthening of the Soviet international position. During the war his spies in the United States had passed on word of the development of an American nuclear bomb; even before the defeat of Germany, Soviet scientists had begun work on nuclear weapons. And his strained relations with his wartime allies had done nothing to dissuade him from creating a Soviet sphere of domination around his country.

By 1943, he had begun to assemble the political and diplomatic parts to a postwar protective zone on the Soviet western borders. Its fundamental condition was the demand that the small neighboring states renounce their independence in international affairs. The Czech government-in-exile in London realized very quickly that their hope to return to their country depended on satisfying Stalin's requirement. In 1943, it proposed to the Soviet Union diplomatic agreements by which the Czechs accepted postwar Soviet international leadership in exchange for internal self-rule. Stalin agreed to the proposal. When the Red Army liberated Czechoslovakia, it passed control over to this government, which proceeded to reconstruct a parliamentary democracy and coalition government. In 1945, Stalin looked for diplomatic recognition of Soviet power, not communist revolution in Czechoslovakia. He applied this Czech model in his peace treaty with Finland. Realism, not communist ideology, dictated these agreements.

Where communist forces enjoyed substantial power Stalin was prepared to accept their rule on the condition that they too submit to Soviet domination. By 1945, Yugoslavia had come under the control of Tito's guerrilla forces. From their mountain bases, they proceeded to occupy the country following the passage of the Red Army. Implementing their revolutionary plans, they immediately set up, on the Soviet model, a one-party dictatorship and a federal state to govern their multiethnic population. At Soviet insistence they accepted economic agreements providing cheap raw materials from their land for the reconstruction of the Soviet Union.

Events in Poland clearly revealed Soviet aims in eastern Europe to the West. Even before war's end Poland's future aroused controversy among the Allies. A Polish government-in-exile in London claimed the right to reconstruct the Polish nation-state, demolished by the Nazis. The Soviet leaders began negotiations with the London Poles. But in 1943, they broke off talks when Polish officials requested an investigation of reports that Soviet secret police in 1940 had massacred thousands of Polish officers captured in the 1939 war. That the reports were true mattered not at all to Stalin. To him, the Polish request damned their government as disloyal and unreliable, unfit to govern in the Soviet sphere. From that moment, he set about forming another Polish regime out of the remnants of the Polish Communist Party, most of whose leaders his police had executed in the Great Terror. When the Red Army reached Polish territory in 1944, the Soviet occupation authorities immediately began eliminating the remnants of the noncommunist Polish Home Army. At the end of the year they set up a Polish provisional government. Its members were Communists; the London Poles were excluded. The U.S. and British governments protested this mockery of national self-determination in Poland, but to no avail. In that country, Soviet influence extended into the very political life of the nation.

When the Allied leaders met at Yalta in February 1945, they had to discuss the future peace as well as measures to end the war. Agreement on the disposition of German lands, once the Nazis were defeated, posed no problem. Zones of occupation for the four European powers (including France) had emerged from discussions the previous year. Berlin was also to be divided among the Allied forces, though the city itself lay far within the Soviet zone of eastern Germany. Regardless of where troops from east and west met at war's end, these zones set the limits to the area they would subsequently occupy.

The issue of war in East Asia also brought no serious disagreements at the Yalta Conference. In exchange for a Soviet offensive in Manchuria and Korea, Stalin requested Japanese territory (Sakhalin, the Kuril Islands) and concessions in northern Chinese territory (the same as those the Russian Empire had possessed until the Japanese victory in the 1904–1905 war). Roosevelt promised to obtain agreement from Chiang's Nationalist government to these concessions. He had once again become Stalin's collaborator in satisfying the Soviet leader's territorial demands. Even the question of Soviet membership in the United Nations did not create serious problems. Stalin probably concluded that Roosevelt's project, though useless to Soviet interests, posed no real threat. To this extent, the Grand Alliance continued to function effectively.

Its limits were apparent when the Allies discussed the fate of the countries liberated by the Red Army. Roosevelt asked for Soviet acceptance of the principle of national self-determination and democratic elections. Stalin did agree to a Declaration on Liberated Europe promising free elections. But the statement left so many holes for Soviet evasion that, as one of Roosevelt's advisers told him, "you can drive a truck through it."

Soviet domination in Poland, which was the real issue and the principal source of the divergence of Allied views, could not be shaken by diplomatic declarations. Roosevelt asked for no more, however, so important to him was Soviet collaboration in the war against Japan. Historical debate continues on the failure of the United States to ensure a free Poland at the Yalta Conference. Some critics later called its decisions a "sell-out" to the Russians. Yet the imposition of a Soviet-backed communist regime in that country was probably not negotiable. The failure of Stalin to compromise at Yalta on this issue revealed to what extent he was prepared to ignore Western protests to impose a Soviet client state on the Polish people.

He assumed that the Western powers would lay claim to their own spheres. He ordered the Communists in France and Italy to surrender their weapons to the Allied occupation forces. By his understanding of power politics, that area fell in the sphere of the West, and Communists there should bend to Western "bourgeois" democracy. Their future rise to power had to follow the path of social and political struggle, not violent revolution. When Roosevelt talked of a world of peace and great power collaboration, Stalin understood hegemony and spheres of domination. No real meeting of minds or permanent understanding could exist between statesmen of such differing views.

That spring Allied armies proceeded to defeat the remaining German forces. German generals kept the bulk of their troops in the east in an effort to halt the Soviet offensive. By April, Western armies were advancing rapidly through central and northern Germany. Churchill, already foreseeing competition with the Soviet Union over European spheres, urged that Western troops occupy Berlin and Prague. These were politically important cities far within areas designated for Soviet liberation. General Dwight Eisenhower, Supreme Allied Commander, refused to alter his military priorities to make room for political calculations. In April, Roosevelt died. He was replaced by his vice-president, Harry Truman, an inexperienced former senator from the Middle West. The only course of action open to the new president was to follow Roosevelt's guidelines. After Hitler's suicide in early May, German war leaders surrendered to the Allies. The European war ended with Soviet troops in Berlin.

In July, Western troops in eastern Germany pulled back to allow the Soviet army to occupy its occupation zone. Carrying out their part of the agreement, Soviet authorities gave Western forces access to western Berlin. Demilitarization and denazification started, and arrangements for the imposition of reparations began in all areas of the defeated land. The German state had ceased to exist. What took its place depended on the four occupying powers, for the time being cooperating still as Allies.

Victory in East Asia

The war in the Pacific followed a very different course. It continued to be primarily a naval war to the very end. In early 1945, the British finally launched an offensive from India into Japanese-occupied Burma. The Indian Army had continued through the war to fight loyally for the British Empire,

Allied Victory in Europe: Soviet Red Flag atop the Reichstag, Berlin, May 1945 (*Hoover Institution*)

defending India and fighting in the Middle East and Europe. The Indian civil service had performed its duties as expected. Operating from India the supreme commander of Southeast Asia, Lord Mountbatten, prepared for offensives to retake the lost British colonies in southeast Asia. Before his forces could proceed beyond northern Burma, the Red Army invasion of Manchuria and the destruction of Hiroshima and Nagasaki brought the war to a sudden end.

The U.S. naval offensive had begun in 1943. The previous year, U.S. naval forces, in battles in the Coral Sea and west of Hawaii near Midway Island, had defeated Japanese attempts to destroy U.S. military power in the Pacific. Instead, the Japanese fleet suffered serious losses in those naval battles. U.S. carrier-based planes sank most of the enemy aircraft carriers. In that great far-flung naval war, the United States held the decisive advantage from that moment on. By 1943, the U.S. Pacific fleet was superior in number and power to the Japanese naval forces. Gradually, U.S. naval and marine forces moved westward across the Pacific, "island hopping" to establish ports and air-bases closer and closer to Japan. In 1944, they controlled the seas as far west as the Philippine archipelago. That year, army divisions under General Douglas MacArthur's command reconquered that country. MacArthur's next objective was the invasion of Japan itself, where bitter fighting was expected before the Japanese surrendered.

By the end of 1944, the U.S. Air Force controlled the skies over the islands and operated from bases close enough for massive bomber attacks of Japan. Japanese cities lay open to the same "fire storms" that had destroyed German cities. In the spring of 1945, Tokyo was consumed in a raging fire provoked by incendiary bombs, leaving nearly 100,000 people dead. That summer, most Japanese urban centers were in ruins and the

economy of the country was breaking apart. U.S. submarine warfare had effectively destroyed Japanese maritime commerce, depriving Japanese armies and the industrial economy of the Home Islands of vital raw materials. The Japanese war cabinet began in July to consider peace negotiations. Military leaders, backed by Emperor Hirohito, defended war to the death to protect the honor of their country. The civilian cabinet members hoped for continued Soviet neutrality and for Soviet mediation to negotiate a compromise peace with the United States. Japanese leaders were misguided on all counts. Stalin was preparing for Asian war and the United States adhered to its demand for "unconditional surrender."

The U.S. war in the Pacific was in its own way total war. Hatred of the Japanese was high, particularly when stories of Japanese mistreatment of Allied prisoners of war appeared. The refusal of Japanese soldiers to stop fighting in the face of hopeless odds strengthened expectations for prolonged fighting when U.S. troops invaded the Home Islands. At the same time, the Red Army offensive in northern China was intended to capture Japanese armies on the Asian mainland. The U.S. Air Force had already begun its massive bombing raids over Japan. It acquired in the summer of 1945 a new weapon of unimaginable power.

American development of the atomic bomb had first begun out of fear that Nazi Germany would develop the bomb. Germany's defeat in May and the successful testing of the bomb in July 1945 presented the U.S. leaders with new choice. A weapon of unprecedented power was available for use in the war on Japan. Its use was no longer a matter of deterring the enemy, but of destroying an opponent defenseless against air attack and fighting a land war to the death. The U.S. government chose with little hesitation (only some of the scientists advising restraint) to authorize its use by the U.S. Air Force. On August 6, one bomb obliterated the city of Hiroshima, killing over 100,000 people; a second destroyed much of Nagasaki on August 9. The world had entered the age of nuclear war.

The Soviet land war against Japan ended almost as soon as it began. On August 8, the Red Army invaded Manchuria. Stalin had respected to the letter his agreement with Roosevelt at the Yalta Conference to begin war in Asia three months after the hostilities ceased in Europe. Japanese forces were overwhelmed by the Soviet invasion, which swept down Manchuria and into Korea. Despite inevitable defeat, a week elapsed before the Japanese war cabinet accepted surrender. Emperor Hirohito ordered them to capitulate for, in his words, "the unendurable must be endured."

The Soviet offensive and the nuclear bombing had brought that war to an abrupt end. U.S. invasion of the Main Islands proved unnecessary. The debate still continues whether the use of the atomic bomb was needed to avoid that invasion. Historical evidence now suggests that it was. The em-

peror and his advisers, in whose hands lay the choice of war or peace, continued to reiterate their demand that the Japanese people "smash the enemy nations." Their appeals to carry on the war resembled Hitler's refusal to accept defeat. The Japanese population appeared ready to obey. The two atomic bomb attacks, coupled with the Soviet invasion of Korea and Manchuria, forced the emperor to change sides and accept defeat. The concern of American military experts that without use of the bomb the war might endure for months, bringing with it enormous U.S. casualties, was well founded.

The American leaders and people looked upon the atomic bomb as one more weapon of war to achieve victory. The capitulation of the Japanese Empire on August 14, 1945, brought the Second World War to a close. The Allied countries had defeated the mightiest military empires in history, but at a terrible cost.

SUMMARY

The Second World War completed the slow process, begun in the previous war and the

End of the Second World War: Japanese Surrender, August 1945 (*Hoover Institution*)

depression, that ended the era of empires. The defeat of Japan brought down not only its overseas empire, but also the Western overseas empires in east and southeast Asia. Japanese authorities had exploited and mistreated the peoples of their empire, but they destroyed as well the authority of the Western colonial administration that had once ruled these lands. In August 1945, little remained of the Dutch and French empires. The British Empire was weakened and discredited in the eyes of many of its former subjects. The capitulation of the Japanese Empire was complete. Everywhere its troops prepared to leave the conquered lands where they had ruled. A vacuum of power opened up in that enormous area, and no one knew what its future would be.

The destruction produced by Nazi rule in Europe and Allied conquest was appalling. Many millions of people had been reduced to misery, and governments lacked the means to help them. Nearly 50 million civilians and military personnel died in the war. It was one grim measure of the scale of devastation. The United States, which suffered relatively few casualties, emerged the most prosperous and powerful country in the world. The Soviet Union, despite the suffering of its peoples, possessed the military and diplomatic strength of an international power. The war had produced a global division of influence between the two states, each with very different plans for a new global order.

Hopes and dreams of a new world to be built on the ruins of the old emerged out of the passions and hardship of war. These visions were nurtured among the resistance movements. The inmates of the concentration camps and the hordes of refugees and displaced persons could hope for little more than their survival and a new home somewhere. The anti-German, and anti-Japanese guerrilla fighters were moved by the desire to free their nations and also to bring to their countries a better way of life than that they had known before the war. The hope for progress did not die, though in the midst of the war the numbers arrested, tortured, and executed were so great the effort appeared often hopeless. Great expectations for political change and national liberation from colonial rule constituted one heritage of the war. Conflict between the Great Powers was another. At the time, no one realized that they had lived through the last world war of the twentieth century.

DATES WORTH REMEMBERING

1939   Outbreak of Second World War
1940   German invasion of Western Europe
1941   German–Soviet War
1941   U.S. entry into war
1942–1945   Nazi extermination camps
1942–1943   Stalingrad battle
1943   Teheran Conference
1944   Normandy landing
1944   Warsaw uprising
1944   Bretton-Woods Agreement on international trade
1945   German occupation zones
1945   Soviet war on Japan
1945   Hiroshima atomic bomb
1945   Yalta Conference
1945   End of Second World War

RECOMMENDED READING

War in Europe

Lloyd Gardner, *Spheres of Influence: The Great Powers Partition Europe, from Munich to Yalta* (1993). Despite the lurid title, a careful study of European diplomacy from 1938 to 1945.

Charles Hession, *John Maynard Keynes: A Personal Biography of the Man Who Revolutionized Capitalism and the Way We Live* (1984). A respectful life history of the great economist.

Raul Hilberg, *Perpetrators, Victims, Bystanders: The Jewish Catastrophe, 1933–1945* (1992). A thoughtful examination of the human dimensions of the Holocaust, by the outstanding historian of this dreadful event.

John Keegan, *The Second World War* (1989). A succinct military history, magnificently illustrated, of the war in Europe and Asia.

*Voytech Mastney, *Russia's Road to the Cold War: Diplomacy, Warfare, and the Politics of Communism, 1941–45* (1979). The best study of Stalin's wartime foreign policy.

War in Asia

Herbert Bix, *Hirohito and Modern Japan* (2000). A new, very critical story of Emperor Hirohito's responsibility for the Japanese war.

*John Toland, *The Rising Sun: The Decline and Fall of the Japanese Empire, 1936–1945* (1970). A critical history of the Japanese military's effort to conquer and hold an East Asian empire.

Memoirs, Novels, and Visual Aids

*Thomas Keneally, *Schindler's List* (1982). The dramatized history of the ordinary German manufacturer at Auschwitz who became a hero to the Jews (subject of an excellent 1993 movie).

*Primo Levi, *Survival in Auschwitz* (1959); and *Moments of Reprieve* (1986). Memoirs of one prisoner's terrible year at Auschwitz.

Guy Sajer, *The Forgotten Soldier* (1971). The vivid memoirs of an Alsatian volunteer in the German army, who survived the army's great retreat from Russia to the Baltic.

Saving Private Ryan (1999). The best movie version to date of the Normandy Landing and the chaos of the enormous battle that followed.

"The World at War." Outstanding BBC series (in sixteen parts) on the Second World War (available through www.shop.pbs.org).

Part II: The Era of Nations

CHAPTER SIX

Global Conflict and the Decline of Western Empires

THE BEGINNING OF THE COLD WAR, 1945–1950

The Second World War left in its wake the ruins of Western empires. Across much of the world, recovery from war meant rebuilding lives, rethinking human relations, and reconstructing economic and political institutions on new foundations. The human scale of suffering defied imagination, and its impact was felt throughout Europe and East Asia. The political disorder at war's end called for new solutions. Nationalist parties in lands freed from Japanese occupation demanded more forcefully than ever before the end of colonial rule. In some cases, they were able to negotiate independence with their colonial rulers; in other areas, their demands were rejected by imperial authorities. The result was the outbreak of new conflicts, called by their anti-colonial leaders "wars of

national liberation." In those tumultuous years, reform and revolution dominated political life in Europe and Asia.

The vacuum of power left in Europe after the collapse of the Axis states opened the way for the United States and the Soviet Union to take the lead in the reordering European relations. In eastern Europe, reconstruction proceeded in large measure according to the wishes of Soviet authorities and the political goals of communist parties. In western Europe, severe economic shortages and fears of Soviet domination combined to make these countries diplomatically and economically dependent on the United States. Political and human conflicts added to diplomatic insecurity to complicate enormously the peacemaking. Latent fears of a global communist revolutionary conspiracy reemerged in the West, replacing the idealized wartime picture of a loyal Soviet ally. In the Soviet Union, official pronouncements revived the specter of the capitalist–imperialist menace from the Western states. On both sides, the reappearance of this hostile language indicated the breakdown of wartime good relations and reinforced the barriers standing in the way of constructive agreements for postwar peacemaking.

The new conflict between the Soviet Union and the United States produced its own grim vocabulary. The term "Iron Curtain" suggested that an impenetrable wall divided Europe, split apart by communist seizure of power in the states of eastern Europe. The overwhelming military and economic superiority of the United States and the Soviet Union in their respective spheres earned them the label of "superpowers." Soon, the expression "Cold War" captured the ominous character of the hostile relations between the two sides, not actually at war but mobilizing their military and diplomatic forces in anticipation of a new conflict in Europe or East Asia. This global confrontation presented U.S. political leaders, little experienced in power politics and global relations, with complex questions. What was the nature of the conflict? Was the threat communism or was it Soviet power? What areas constituted a vital interest to the United States and where should U.S. support be directed?

The U.S. response to these new circumstances was a peacetime strategy of foreign involvement in the diplomatic and economic reconstruction of Europe and Asia. Baptized "containment," it set the guidelines for U.S. diplomatic and political policies for more than forty years. The Cold War fueled an arms race between the two superpowers. Although the acute phase of hostility ended in the mid-1950s, the failure of postwar peacemaking and the continued U.S.–Soviet rivalry in later decades gave a warlike character to the relations between the superpowers for almost a half-century.

POSTWAR EUROPE

The empires of France and Great Britain survived the war, but their decline had already begun. The real victors in the war, the United States and the Soviet Union, were opposed to colonial empires. They had given encouragement to anti-colonial movements during the war. When they joined in helping create the United Nations, their representatives insisted on full representation for non-Western states. They both repeated, in very different terms, their support for the liberation of the colonies of the Western empires. Their cooperation quickly ended, but the impetus to decolonization remained.

The hopes nurtured during the years of war for rapid peacemaking proved short-lived. They rested on the assumption that the Allies would continue to cooperate once victory was won. The United States under Roosevelt had anticipated that a modified version of internationalism would govern relations among the victors, that is, that they would recognize a common goal in collaborating both to encourage national self-determination in liberated lands and to work within the United Nations to help preserve the peace. The Soviet policy of sphere of influence depended for its full success on Western agreement for communist domination of an area around the Soviet Union so vast it resembled a new Soviet empire. Neither plan was effective. The alliance fell apart, and conflict replaced cooperation.

The Decline of Western Empires

The remaining Western empires lost their colonies one after another in the postwar period. The dramatic change came swiftly in Asia, more slowly in Africa. Pressure for de-colonization came from the colonial peoples, from Soviet and U.S. political leaders, from the United Nations, and from within the imperial states themselves. After centuries of power, the British and French colonial empires disappeared. The long-term consequences altered the very nature of global relations.

The United Nations became, in the years after its formation in 1945, a forum for defenders of national liberation. It came into being through agreement among the Allied states. President Franklin Roosevelt was instrumental in obtaining the cooperation of the Allies for this undertaking. His views on decolonization guaranteed that the Preamble of the U.N.'s Charter recognized formally the "equal rights of nations large and small" and repeated the commitment, made by the League of Nations, to support "self-government or independence" for the man-

dated (now called "trustee") territories. He did, though, insist that the Charter give special powers to the major states. Roosevelt hoped that cooperation among the Allies would insure a long-lasting peace.

Though Roosevelt died before the United Nations came into existence, President Truman carried forward his initiative. Peace-keeping responsibilities belonged to the Security Council. There, Soviet and American delegates, along with the other permanent members, decided upon key U.N. policies. These could also be proposed by the General Assembly, where delegates from all the world's sovereign states had seats. When the British government decided in 1946 it could no longer govern the Middle Eastern area of Palestine (a "mandated" territory), it let the United Nations decide how Palestine should be divided between Jewish and Arab states. Nationalist movements in non-Western lands found a sympathetic audience in the United Nations.

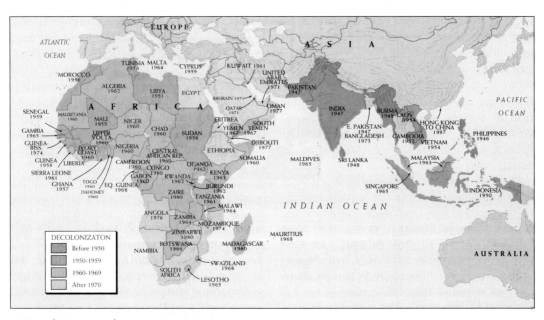

Decolonization of Western Empires since 1945

But the United Nations was vulnerable to antagonism between the Soviet Union and the Western states. The "veto" power given to the Security Council members (enabling any one of them to block U.N. action) opened the way for the U.S.–Soviet rivalry to paralyze the United Nations. Its only effective action to stop aggression came in 1950 when the Security Council, minus its Soviet member who had withdrawn in protest over a Western anti-communist initiative, condemned North Korea for its invasion of South Korea. Soldiers from twenty states fought North Korea under the U.N. flag, with the goal of keeping the Communists out of South Korea. Its intervention placed it squarely on the side of the West in the Cold War.

The recovery from war of the Western states created pressures as well for loosening colonial ties. The participation of the United States government in that reconstruction gave U.S. leaders an influential voice in the foreign policy of these states. The reconstruction of countries that had been liberated by the western Allies lay in the hands of their elected governments. Western postwar policy in Europe rested on the principle of national self-determination, that is, that self-rule and political liberties offered the right path to stable recovery from war. It did not dictate the social and economic reforms that these governments should introduce and assumed that outside powers ought not meddle in their internal affairs. But U.S. foreign aid, especially the Marshall Plan launched in 1947, was a potent means to influence their foreign affairs. The government of the Netherlands discovered this unpleasant fact after it had launched a military campaign in the East Indies to defeat nationalist forces and restore colonial rule there. The United States threatened to cut off all foreign aid to that war-torn country unless the Dutch negotiated a peaceful withdrawal from their most valuable colony. For a few years, the

U.S. leaders made decolonization one of their highest priorities. Seeking to helping create a new world order, they enlarged Wilson's 1919 internationalist program by insisting that colonial peoples should enjoy the "right to national self-determination."

Among the Allied governments, sympathy toward colonial peoples (and reluctance to continue imperial rule) was strong at war's end. Before the war the United States had promised its Philippines colony independence. In Great Britain, the Labor Party won national elections in 1945 on a program that included freeing colonial peoples of the empire. Similar views emerged in France. Defenders of imperial glory and power, such as Britain's elder statesman Winston Churchill, condemned this "betrayal" of empire. In France, the opponents of decolonization were able to call a halt (temporarily) to colonial liberation. Within European countries opinions were deeply divided on the pace and even desirability of freeing colonial peoples.

Both Great Britain and the United States governments intended that independence come to their Asian colonies peacefully, and that the population be given the opportunity to vote on new leaders. In other words, liberation was to come according to Western principles of national self-determination. In Burma, a unified nationalist movement (strengthened by Japan's recognition of Burmese independence in 1942) accepted the offer of the British government to participate in the process. A similar situation existed in the Philippines, where supporters of independence agreed on the terms proposed by the United States.

The British discovered quickly that their withdrawal from colonial areas could bring bitter conflicts. The difficulties arose partly from animosity toward the British imperialists, partly from deep divisions among the population on the future independent state.

Palestine became an arena of irreconcilable disagreement between Jewish settlers, seeking a homeland there, and the Arab population opposed to any Jewish state (see Chapter 10). The British departure in 1948 left in its wake the makings of war between Arab states and the new state of Israel. Similarly, the British negotiators in India could not bring the two major nationalist parties, the National Congress and the Muslim League, to agree on terms for independence (see Chapter 8). Unable to keep the peace, the British forces left their great colony in 1947 in the throes of civil war.

Yet these tragic sequels to negotiated decolonization were hardly more destructive than the colonial wars by European states attempting to hold onto Asian colonies. The Netherlands had governed the East Indies for four centuries; its state-owned oil company, Royal Dutch, had discovered vast petroleum deposits there. The Dutch were not prepared to yield this valuable colonial possession, and sent troops to reoccupy the vast archipelago. Indonesian nationalists organized guerrilla resistance; a colonial war dragged on for three years until the Netherlands accepted the inevitable, granting Indonesia in 1949 its independence.

A similar colonial conflict erupted in the French colony of Indochina, where nationalists and communists had in 1945 renounced all ties to France. Negotiations began with the French government, but in 1946 French military forces, backed by pro-empire politicians in France, set out to destroy the independence movement. That war lasted until 1954, when in its turn the French government acknowledged that it could not win that war of national liberation. Slowly, in conditions of either peaceful negotiation or war, the European colonial empires in Asia gave way to nation-states.

Colonial lands in Africa were much slower to reach the point of massive decolo-

nization (see Chapter 9). Even anti-imperial political parties in Europe, dismissed the possibility that African peoples were prepared for independence. One British colonial official painted a bleak picture of a population scarred by "ignorance and poverty, disease and widespread malnutrition, primitive cultivation and harsh natural conditions, hopelessly inadequate revenues and need for services of every kind." His argument was in many ways justified, but it was also a self-serving claim to continued colonial rule. Without intending it, he revealed how inadequate imperial rule had been to meet the human needs of these colonies.

The European peoples had to turn their principal efforts to recovery from war. The terrible destruction left in the wake of liberation called for ambitious reconstruction, not just of the physical framework of an industrial economy but also of social relations in a more humane society. Hopes and plans looked to a better life for the entire population, and political leaders sought to satisfy these expectations. As a result, labor obtained a greater voice in industrial affairs. Women became active political leaders and new family policies provided state support for child care. The term used to describe the new economic conditions in countries such as Great Britain and France is "mixed economies," referring to the intermingling of nationalized (i.e., state-owned) enterprises and private business. Expensive in the best of times, these reforms exceeded the financial resources of their still impoverished populations. Yet political leaders could not back down. They deeply believed in social justice for their people, whose demand for a "new deal" brought strong pressure for quick action. In those postwar years the governments in western Europe were concerned above all with rebuilding their own countries.

In Great Britain, the close of the war marked the beginning of momentous politi-

Ruins of European War: Budapest, Hungary, 1945 (*Hoover Institution*)

cal and social changes under the leadership of the Labor Party. It called on British voters in 1945 to "face the future" by supporting its plan for democratic socialism. In the national elections that year, it overwhelmed the Conservative Party led by Winston Churchill. It took power at a critical time, for the war had resulted in the death of a million Britishers and had caused tremendous property loss, both to foreign investments and to domestic capital. A year later, it had to ask Washington for a four-billion-dollar loan, most of which paid for food and fuel imports. By the winter of 1946–1947, the British government faced such a serious budgetary crisis that it could no longer pay for both its domestic reforms and its foreign

obligations in India and the Middle East. Decolonization came, in part, out of this near bankruptcy. Social welfare and nationalization of basic industries had highest priority for the Labor government. Domestic interests came first.

Similar reform movements took power in other Western European countries. The need to care for the health, education, and welfare of their populations put a heavy burden on their budgets and required careful planning. Foreign aid from the United States began to arrive by 1948, but it had to be spent with great care. In several countries, the urgent need for guidance in reconstruction led to greater government intervention in economic life than ever before. In France, this took the shape of state forecast planning. It did not seek, as in the Soviet Union, to replace free market forces by state command planning. Instead, its goal was rational use of the scarce resources for optimal economic growth. Railroads had to be rebuilt, and became the property of the French state. Their reconstruction followed the guidelines for modernization and electrification spelled out in the plan. Capitalism and state-run industries operated side by side in this new French "mixed" economy.

This reform movement in western European countries enjoyed the support of the majority of the population. It owed little to the example of Soviet socialism, which before the war had stood out as the only alternative to Western capitalism. After the war, the Soviet command economy and the prestige brought by Soviet victory over Nazi Germany won support from large numbers of Europeans. But Soviet expansionism and the revolutionary communist ideology appeared to most Europeans a new threat as dangerous as that Nazism had once posed. The Cold War was never far from the concerns of Europeans in the postwar years.

These fears were especially great in countries to the south of the Soviet Union. Immediately after the war the Soviet government demanded of Iran and Turkey special territorial concessions—land in northwestern Iran, and in Turkey control over the Straits from the Black Sea to the Mediterranean Sea. Stalin's expansionist ambitions extended to these southern borderlands. Land on the Iranian border would open to the Soviet petroleum industry greater access to the great oil fields of the southern Caspian. Forcing Turkey to give Soviet authorities oversight on ship passage through the strategic sea passage would satisfy a century-old tsarist objective. The leaders of both countries begged for support and aid from the Western Allies against their powerful northern

neighbor. In 1946, Western protests ended Soviet pressure. Soviet interests there were not important enough to risk conflict with the West.

In Greece, the Cold War began with the revolutionary plans of the strong guerrilla movement led by the Greek Communist Party. In 1946, it mobilized its troops, armed and trained in the war against the Germans, in a civil war to seize power from the conservative government. The Greek Communists took inspiration, and received aid from Tito's Yugoslavia. The Greek government asked for military and economic aid first from Great Britain, whose troops had fought there in the war. Then, when the British government concluded in late 1946 that it lacked the means to help, the Greek leaders turned to the United States. In this case, as in China, Stalin had serious doubts about the uprising. On his geopolitical map, both China and Greece belonged within the Western sphere. In early 1947, he privately warned visiting Yugoslavs that the Greek Communists were foolhardy to attack a government that could rely on the help of "the most powerful nation in the world." Revolutionary zealotry was not his approach to postwar global politics. Western observers imagined that Stalin ruled like a tyrant over the foreign communist parties as he did over the Soviet Union. It was a mistaken assumption but found convincing evidence in Stalin's ideological bombast and the communist uprisings in Europe and Asia.

The New Soviet Empire

At the close of the war, the Soviet Union was second only to the United States in military might. It was at the head of an international communist movement more vigorous than ever before. Its victory over Germany gave its leaders enormous influence in lands liberated by the Red Army. The war, though, had weakened terribly the Soviet people and their country. These two contradictory features—Soviet international strength and internal weakness—dictated Soviet international and domestic postwar policy.

Victory created the conditions for Soviet expansion, limited only by the strategic priorities of the Soviet Union and Stalin's recognition of U.S. military might. Recovery from the devastation of war called for massive Soviet investments and brought economic exploitation of the Soviet sphere as well as the continued sacrifices of the Soviet people. His determination to maintain Soviet military and diplomatic power was as great as before.

Postwar Stalinist Propaganda Poster "For Peace, For a People's Democracy," c. 1949 (*National Archives*)

Although Stalin does not seem to have had a master plan for Soviet expansion, he did have certain minimum objectives. These included diplomatic domination in the states along the new Soviet western and eastern frontiers. Soviet policy was expansionist within these limits. Stalin's foreign goals were opportunistic as well, for he was prepared to take advantage of communist revolutionary gains. His policies unsettled the balance of power in Europe and Asia and forced the Western states to reconsider their wartime practice of collaboration.

He remained deeply suspicious of the "capitalist camp." The United States had become, at war's end, the most powerful country among the democratic states. His approach to the West was governed, as in the 1930s, by his conviction that the "law of the jungle" prevailed between those states and the Soviet Union, which he called the leader of the "socialist camp." His country had emerged victorious in the war, and for this reason he had grounds to hope that the capitalist states would acquiesce in his new zone of domination. Still, he relied on the protection that his large land army gave him in East Asia and Europe.

His confidence in Soviet postwar might was undermined by the successful construction and deployment of the atomic bomb in the U.S. war on Japan. Faced with a potential enemy possessing such a devastating weapon, he could not assume that his armies could guarantee control of the new Soviet sphere in Europe and Asia. The lesson he drew from the Hiroshima explosion was a simple one. Gathering the Soviet scientists who had already begun nuclear weapon research, he exclaimed: "Hiroshima has shaken the world. The balance has been destroyed." Their secret instructions were to build a Soviet bomb immediately. The chances for peaceful relations between the former allies were dwindling even at the close of the war.

In the period between 1945 and 1947, Stalin had to take account of the political strength and revolutionary militancy of foreign communist parties. In Yugoslavia, Tito's forces immediately set up a party dictatorship and openly flaunted their admiration for Soviet socialism. Twice they attacked Western military planes flying over their western frontiers; Stalin suggested this was imprudent but said no more. Tito lent active support to the Greek Communist Party in its guerrilla war, despite Stalin's warnings of possible conflict with the West. In the early postwar years, Stalin gave only general guidance to foreign communist parties, some of whose leaders behaved in a far more revolutionary manner than he. Crucial to his cautious action was his knowledge of the devastation war had caused his country, and his determination to protect his country's newly won influence in international affairs.

The war had caused great suffering among the Soviet people. The losses in life were so great no one has ever been able to calculate them accurately. The figure of 26 million civilian and military dead, commonly repeated now, suggests the extent of suffering inflicted on the country. Large areas of western Russia were devastated, the cities reduced to rubble, the countryside stripped of its livestock, the mines flooded. So scarce were food reserves that when the 1946 harvest failed, famine swept the eastern regions. The Soviet government had to request Western food shipments (provided by the United Nations Relief and Recovery Administration) to feed its people.

Recovery required workers for rebuilding. Millions of men never returned from the war or came back disabled and unfit for work. One half of the draft-age men had either died or were seriously wounded in the war. Soviet troops, 11 million strong in 1945, were rapidly demobilized to provide labor for reconstruction. The Red Army declined

to 3 million in 1948, smaller than Western observers believed at the time but still by far the most powerful army in the world. Stalin ended hopes in 1946 for better living conditions for the Soviet population when he proclaimed rapid growth of heavy industry the first priority. Industry was power, and it came before material comfort of the population. Women had to take on the heavy physical work of men, in the cities and in the countryside. Collectivization of all arable land remained the basis of Soviet agriculture, permitting the Soviet state to drain the resources of the collectivized farms (*kolkhoz*). Industrial growth did begin again, but at great cost to the people.

The lands occupied by the Red Army or dominated after the war by the Soviet Union had to provide resources for Soviet economic reconstruction. Before reparations ended East Germany alone furnished approximately $5 billion in agricultural and industrial supplies. Factories in the northern Chinese province of Manchuria, seized in the Soviet war against Japan, were dismantled and shipped back to the Soviet Union before the Soviet troops withdrew in 1946, leaving behind an industrial wasteland. The states within the Soviet sphere had to accept Soviet purchase of their raw materials such as coal at prices far below cost. The Soviet authorities imposed a policy of economic exploitation within their sphere of domination regardless of whether the country was a former enemy, such as East Germany, or a postwar ally, like Poland and Yugoslavia.

Partition of Germany

The acute problems of reconstruction in central Europe brought together the human, political, and diplomatic conflicts that were leading to the partition of postwar Europe. The hatred of other Europeans toward Germany extended beyond Nazism to the Germans themselves. Throughout eastern Europe, the new governments forcibly expelled in 1945–1946 most Germans who had not already fled. The total number of German refugees probably exceeded 10 million; most of them sought refuge in the western zones of Germany. At the same time, the millions of forced laborers taken into Germany during the war sought to return to their homelands or to emigrate to a new country. The Jewish survivors of the extermination camps looked to Palestine, while most Ukrainian and Russian deportees hoped for a new home in the West. These destitute peoples were concentrated in central Europe. Their care fell on the United Nations and the occupying powers, who were also obliged to prevent the inhabitants of the ruined German cities from dying of hunger and cold.

In 1945, the victorious Allies set about destroying the Nazi political and military system before constructing a new Germany. The wartime agreements included the dissolution of the Nazi movement, demilitarization, and an unspecified amount of reparations. The most prominent Nazis were put on trial in Nuremberg in the winter of 1945–1946. Accused of crimes against humanity, all were found guilty by an international tribunal and most were executed.

The first serious East-West disagreement arose over issues of reparations. In their eastern zone of Germany, Soviet authorities claimed the region's agricultural production and mining output for their own desperate needs. Having seen their own palaces and museums destroyed and their contents shipped to Nazi Germany, they proceeded to seize as war booty valuable art collections belonging to German museums and to civilians. They demanded that Western authorities deliver to them large amounts of German industrial equipment as well. In the spring of 1946, the impoverishment of the German economy and growing suspicion of

Soviet policies decided the Western powers to refuse the Soviet authorities any additional goods from their zones. This conflict over the economic spoils of war revealed the importance each side attached to Germany. It was becoming less the enemy and more a front line between East and West. The zones were becoming territorial divisions.

In these circumstances U.S. authorities decided in 1946 to alter their German policy from punishment to reconstruction. This sudden change resulted both from their growing awareness of Soviet power in central Europe and from the economic burden of occupation. The cost of administering the zones grew as German living conditions worsened. A barter economy, in which cigarettes and soap were the most widely accepted medium of exchange, provided the essential items for those Germans with anything at all to trade. Prostitution flourished as desperate German war widows turned to the well-nourished occupation troop. The cost of supplying the Germans in the American zone with minimum food, clothing, and heating—$700 million in 1946—made restoring German economic production an urgent affair for the U.S. government. The British state, faced with near-bankruptcy later that year, agreed to the new objectives.

In early 1947, the British and American occupying authorities united their two zones into one economic unit. Later that year, the French brought their zone in as well. The Western governments put into place a new economic policy for reconstructing that part of Germany under their control, disregarding the vehement objections of Soviet occupation authorities. That year the U.S. government declared that "an orderly and prosperous Europe requires the economic contribution of a stable and productive Germany." One-fourth of the country was excluded from that new policy. Translated into plain language, the new policy of the

Western allies effectively partitioned Germany and marked the end of cooperation with the Soviet Union.

The paths of eastern and western Germany increasingly diverged. In the east, the Soviet authorities created a one-party regime dominated by the so-called "Socialist Unity" Party, run in fact by German Communists. Their treatment of their German subjects was brutal. Their occupying troops, knowing that no punishment would follow, were responsible for the rape of an untold number German women. These women were treated as war booty. Elections continued to be held but the Communists, backed by the Russians, held power in their hands.

Political reform in the western zones looked toward restoring parliamentary democracy. In provincial elections in 1947, voters preferred either the Social Democratic Party, which defended socialist reforms and favored a unified, neutral Germany, or the Christian Democratic Party, which advocated free-enterprise capitalism and reliance on the Western powers to prevent Soviet domination. Political life in eastern and western Germany was increasingly divergent, though in theory the country remained united.

Allied negotiations over Germany's future collapsed in mutual recriminations and accusations. The foreign ministers from the victorious powers met in 1947 to write peace treaties for the Axis countries. They could agree only on a treaty for Italy, never partitioned into occupation zones. Germany represented, for both Soviet Russia and the western powers, a position of strength neither would concede. Failure of German peacemaking was shared by East and West, for neither side originally sought partition. Stalin may have looked forward to a united German state under Soviet influence, but failing in that objective, he resolved to keep hold of his eastern zone. The western Allies sought a united democratic Germany outside Soviet control. When that goal appeared threatened by Soviet domination in eastern Europe, they clung to their zones. Partition came by default, a product of mutual hostility and the very unstable balance of power in central Europe.

From Internationalism to Containment

In the two years following the end of the Second World War, American leaders became increasingly conscious that their wartime expectations for a postwar settlement in Europe were unrealistic. The U.S. policy of collaboration with the Soviets was incapable of yielding satisfactory agreements. The issue causing particular concern among western diplomats was the political reconstruction of eastern European states. They had looked forward to a postwar settlement in which occupation forces would withdraw everywhere to permit democratic elections and the restoration of independent states. But the Soviet sphere of domination in eastern Europe stood in the way of a return to the independent nation-states of the 1920s. The manipulation of democratic elections by eastern European Communists also heightened their concern. Communist parties were undermining rival political movements there to ensure their own political supremacy. Both diplomatically and politically, the fate of eastern Europe lay in Soviet hands.

In 1946, Winston Churchill set out to stir up U.S. public concern about Soviet expansion. He came to the United States that year as the guest of the U.S. president, Harry Truman, to speak out against a return to American isolationism. In his eyes, Soviet political and military might in Europe was so overwhelming that no balance of power was possible without a U.S. commitment to help western European countries. A master of the

English language, he drew a picture for his American audience of a continent cut in two by an "Iron Curtain" erected by communist forces in the east. His appeal for support won widespread backing among a U.S. public hostile toward communism and increasingly fearful of Soviet military strength.

Churchill's aim was U.S. involvement in European affairs to counterbalance the political and diplomatic preponderance of the Soviet Union's armies and allied parties in eastern Europe. He looked for a new balance of power in Europe. Only the United States could help.

Churchill's appeal came at a time when U.S. diplomats in Moscow were proposing a new policy toward the Soviet Union. The most influential spokesman was George Kennan, since 1944 stationed in the Moscow embassy and an outspoken critic of the wartime internationalist policy of conciliation and collaboration with the Soviet state. Kennan proposed a strategy, which he called "containment," to deal with the Soviet Union (see Highlight, pp. 182–184): His assessment of Soviet objectives appeared to fit Soviet postwar diplomacy in places such as Poland and Germany. His proposals coincided with deepening concern among U.S. leaders at the failure of negotiations with the Soviet Union.

In the spring of 1947, President Truman finally turned his back on the internationalist program to implement Kennan's policy of containment. To do so, he needed the approval of Congress and the American people. In those postwar years the public in the United States was immersed in dismantling the economy of war and returning to peacetime living conditions. The economy boomed, and foreign conflicts appeared distant affairs. Isolationism remained a strong presence in the country and in Washington.

To counter this force, Truman made his public appeal for a new global policy in the spirit of internationalism defended by Wilson and Franklin Roosevelt. He spoke out for the defense of political liberty and self-determination for peoples threatened by "aggressive movements that seek to impose upon them totalitarian regimes." He did not explain what strategic interests required the new policy. He empahsized Western internationalist objectives, and not U.S. national security, because of his need to win public and congressional backing for the new policy of containment. Its implementation required an end to isolationism and the readiness by Congress to approve peacetime foreign alliances and massive amounts of foreign aid. The American public remained more attuned to issues of democracy and self-determination for oppressed peoples than to problems of global balance of power. Nothing like Truman's policy of foreign alliances and aid had ever occurred in U.S. history.

In concrete terms, the new policy sought two diplomatic objectives. One was to strengthen particular states which were of strategic importance to the West and in need of outside economic and military assistance. In March 1947, President Truman proposed a program of foreign aid to the Greek and Turkish governments. Greece was in the midst of a civil war in which the Greek Communists were gaining ground. Turkey was threatened by Soviet diplomatic and military pressure. His "Truman Doctrine," intended to protect a Western sphere of influence, took on the appearance of a battle for democracy and against communism, not at all what diplomats such as Kennan sought. It did win public support, and the funds were voted quickly.

The second objective was the economic reconstruction of Europe and Japan. Speaking in mid-1947, Secretary of State George Marshall proposed that the United States, for the first time in its history, offer foreign aid to countries devastated by war. That year, the economic recovery of Western Europe was progressing but at such a high cost it could not continue without outside help. The poor living conditions of the population there contributed significantly to social unrest, an important factor in the electoral strength of communist parties. In 1947, Japan and western Germany looked like important front-line areas along the borders of the Soviet Union's sphere.

The immediate goal of providing aid was economic recovery. The larger aim was to encourage the stabilization of economic conditions in independent states within a global economy. Marshall proposed that the United States provide large sums of financial aid as well as economic supplies to those governments ready to meet certain conditions, chiefly, that they coordinate their use of the U.S. funds and supplies, and make public their financial and economic needs. The Marshall Plan committed the United States to the expansion of the international economy and to the improvement of economic conditions of distant countries without any specific diplomatic rewards or expectation of repayment. The new policies turned the United States away from isolationism and toward involvement in the international affairs of Europe and Asia.

Although the U.S. Congress did not approve the Marshall Plan until mid-1948, the offer received immediate support from all western countries. The Soviet Union and its satellites refused, though not before both the Polish and Czechoslovak governments, under communist leadership, had publicly accepted the U.S. offer. Stalin's orders were outright refusal. The Marshall Plan was not overtly anti-communist; the Truman Doctrine was. Together they altered the very basis of relations with the Soviet Union. They brought the economic resources and potential military might of the United States to bear on areas where the line between Soviet and western spheres of influence remained ill-defined. The rejection of Marshall Plan aid by eastern European states made clear that Europe was split in two.

ⓓ HIGHLIGHT: Containment and Anti-Communism ⓓ

The Soviet Union appeared to many Westerners a mysterious and threatening presence among the victorious powers of the Second World War. Its history had followed a very different path from that of the liberal democracies. Its leaders explained international relations using a language of class conflict completely unfamiliar to the Western public. Winston Churchill had been so puzzled in 1939 by Soviet policies that he called the state "a riddle wrapped in a mystery inside an enigma." Its actions remained equally difficult to understand after the defeat of the Axis powers, when it had become a key player in global politics.

One solution to the riddle pointed to the role of communist ideology in Soviet politics. Communist leaders extolled Marxism–Leninism–Stalinism as the source of truth in history, politics, and human relations. Revolution was, in theory, the only path to progress. Since 1917, enemies of communism in America and elsewhere in the West had warned that the Soviet Union was the homeland of a revolution that, unless resisted, would destroy Western civilization. Their anti-communist persuasion made them fear an inevitable confrontation between the Soviet Union and the West. Preparations were urgent to resist the revolutionary offensive of the Soviet state and its supporters. It was not clear whether that attack would come from Soviet armies or a series of communist political conspiracies and insurrections. Whatever methods the communists used, the threat remained real as long as the Soviet Union existed. The anti-communist theory of Soviet international behavior foresaw inescapable conflict, even war, with the homeland of communism.

Another answer to the mystery of Soviet expansion came from lessons drawn from the history of the rise and fall of empires. In the past, aggressive new states had expanded by conquering and taking control of territories and peoples beyond their borders. Their leaders sought power and wealth through territorial aggrandizement and were prepared to use threats and force to achieve this goal. But these great empires had invariably met obstacles to their aggressive growth. Other states had by diplomatic or military means put up barriers to their rise to power, and their own internal weaknesses had with time forced them to contract and ultimately to fall. From this historical perspective, the Soviet Union had acquired the might and size of a great empire because its leaders were expansionist, like others before them. The communist ideology strengthened their suspicion of other states, but was not the explanation for Soviet territorial expansion. Their foreign policy did constitute a threat to the security and interests of independent neighboring states and to the hope for a stable peace. But a historical approach suggested that the reasonable response, as in

earlier times, was to put together diplomatic and political restraints to contain this new imperial power.

The historical explanation of Soviet aggressiveness was the key idea behind the new U.S. foreign policy of containment. It appeared in the late 1940s at a time when Franklin Roosevelt's policy of international collaboration and conciliation had failed to bring fundamental agreements with the Soviet Union on peace in Europe and Asia. George Kennan, the principal architect of the new policy, argued that the old internationalist approach could not possibly produce satisfactory results. His observations and understanding of what he called "Soviet conduct" convinced him that Soviet leaders were deeply suspicious of the West and fanatically determined to overcome the perils that they believed threatened their rule.

In Kennan's opinion, the origins of their hostility lay in the historical experience of Russia. It had, time and again, confronted aggressive foreign enemies, whom only military might could repulse. He never made clear how the memories of this long past had shaped the suspicious world view of Soviet leaders. At times, he argued that their communist ideology bore a large measure of responsibility for their particular antagonism toward the capitalist states in the West, and that Stalin's own ruthless personality shaped Soviet political life. But his understanding of the Soviet Union drew above all on his conviction that it showed the historical traits of an expansionist empire. It relied on despotic authority within its borders, and was prepared to expand its diplomatic and political influence beyond those borders whenever weaknesses appeared in neighboring states.

Soviet hostility and expansionism stood in the way of a permanent peace settlement. Conciliatory gestures from the West had no chance of moderating the Soviet leader's suspicions. They relied only on their country's military and diplomatic might, not international agreements, to protect Soviet interests. They were unresponsive, in Kennan's words, to the "logic of reason." But his long years of study of Soviet conduct convinced him also that they were not "adventuristic" in seeking to expand the power of their state and were prepared to avoid "unnecessary risks" when they encountered resistance. In other words, they understood the "logic of force." This formula gave Kennan the key to formulating a new long-term U.S. policy less appeasing than Roosevelt's internationalist approach, but less belligerent than the anti-communist agenda.

In the short term, his containment strategy called for resistance to, not conciliation of, the Soviet leaders' efforts to expand their sphere of domination around the borders of the Soviet Union. Kennan had seen firsthand the consequences of appeasement of Nazi Germany in 1938 (he was stationed in Czechoslovakia during the Munich crisis). Containment was his answer to the danger of appeasement. It called for U.S. diplomatic backing and economic aid to certain strong, independent states that were capable of resisting Soviet expansionism. With U.S. support, these countries would become secure allies of the West and centers of regional stability. They included states in western Europe, the Middle East, as well as Japan. The threat from the Soviet Union was not military aggression. Kennan was persuaded that Soviet leaders recognized their military and economic weakness relative to the United States. He urged that diplomatic alliances and economic prosperity become the principal barriers to contain the Soviet Union.

This policy did not promise a quick solution to the conflict with the Soviet Union. International peace, as he understood the term, was a dream that could never be fully achieved. The protection of human rights was an ideal that for him ought not prevent collaboration with authoritarian states vital to containment. Allies ought not be excluded on grounds of their internal politics. Kennan did not believe that U.S. foreign policy had to respond to the communist ideology with an anti-communist crusade. He disagreed with anti-communists about the nature of the Soviet threat, and he disagreed with them as well about the correct U.S. response. His policy was in some respects too realistic. Presidents Wilson and Roosevelt had promised that the U.S. involvement in foreign wars furthered the cause of democracy and national self-determination. In other ways it was too restrained to win complete approval. Some U.S. leaders were sympathetic to the warnings of the anti-communists and favored a vast rearmament program and a system of global military alliances.

Yet his program remained the core of U.S. policy toward the Soviet Union. Despite moment of anti-communist fervor and crises that threatened nuclear war, the U.S. government did not attempt to force a Soviet retreat and resigned itself to the existence of a vast Soviet sphere of domination. It also initiated or accepted negotiated settlements, occurring more and more frequently after Stalin's death. Kennan had foreseen the day when this patience would be rewarded by the internal decline of Soviet power. Forty years after he proposed his policy, that decline began. It culminated a few years later with the complete collapse of the Soviet Union and the end of the Cold War. Containment succeeded beyond his wildest dreams.

THE COLD WAR IN THE WEST

By the winter of 1947–1948, nothing remained of the Grand Alliance. Negotiations had ceased and had been replaced on both sides by public denunciations. The United States launched a massive program of economic aid to Europe, coupled with shipments of armaments to Greece and Turkey. Stalin remade the Soviet sphere of domination into a Soviet empire, where all important policies were decided in Moscow. Actual military conflict did not occur, but the talk was of war between the superpowers. From the perspective of several decades later, clearly Stalin never intended a military offensive against the West. To that extent, Western fears were exaggerated. He did, however, use the international position of strength acquired in the German war to impose the diplomatic and political domination of his state beyond its borders. He thereby contributed most of all to the failure of the peace.

Western fears of Soviet military aggression played a part as well in the growing hostility between East and West. American leaders magnified Soviet military strength beyond its real level and argued that it, plus Soviet communism, was proof of Soviet aggressive intentions. Partly because they needed to win American support, partly because they mistook Soviet power politics for revolutionary communism, their new policy appeared a global struggle against communist expansionism. Out of this climate of hostility and fear emerged military alliances and the arms race.

Soviet Satellites
and Divided Germany

The new U.S. containment policies of 1947 brought a swift reaction from the Soviet Union. Predictably, Stalin pronounced these initiatives to be a threat to his sphere of domination in Europe. He responded by drastically strengthening Soviet control over the states in his sphere and by calling on other communist parties to resist the "aggressive" U.S. initiatives. Late in 1947, Soviet leaders organized a meeting of European communist parties, ostensibly to create a new international organization, the Communist Information Bureau (Cominform). Its real purpose was to make clear Moscow's somber view of the new threat from the West and to mobilize communist parties and governments within and outside the "socialist camp" for action. Reviving the rhetoric of war, Stalin's aide Andrei Zhdanov called for opposition to the Marshall Plan and to the "expansionist and reactionary policy" of the United States. He warned that a new "struggle against the U.S.S.R." had begun. His message was clear: Communists had to rally to the defense of the socialist motherland.

The mobilization of international support for the Soviet Union entailed three new developments. It increased Soviet control over communist parties and governments; it required the elimination from power in the eastern European governments of the remaining noncommunists; it encouraged militant campaigns by communist guerrilla forces to establish their own revolutionary regimes in areas where they had seized control. Czechoslovakia experienced the most dramatic political upheaval as a result of Stalin's new Cold War policy in eastern Europe. In February 1948, the Czech Communist Party forced the democratic parties in the coalition government out of power, destroying parliamentary democracy and forming a single-party dictatorship.

Increased Soviet power within its sphere brought with in a secret campaign to dominate the communist parties in the area. It succeeded everywhere except in Yugoslavia. In that country the Yugoslav leaders understood national independence to be the fundamental condition of their revolution. Tito had protested in 1946 that his state was not part of anyone's "sphere of influence," though he did explain later that of course he did not have the Soviet Union in mind. The Yugoslav Communists were revolutionaries, committed to one-party dictatorship and social revolution. They were also nationalists, unwilling to accept Soviet domination. When, in early 1948, Stalin's agents attempted to replace Tito with a compliant Yugoslav leader, he was powerless against a united Yugoslav party leadership. Failing in his secret maneuvers, he made the conflict public. In the spring of 1948, the Soviet Union withdrew its economic and military advisers from Yugoslavia. It was a warning of Moscow's displeasure.

That summer the Cominform expelled the Yugoslav party from its membership. It accused Tito of confusing Soviet international policy with "the foreign policy of the imperialist powers" and of "boundless ambition, arrogance, and conceit." Its real goal was the overthrow of the Yugoslav leader. Stalin privately boasted that "I will move my little finger and Tito will fall." He did more than that, for the Soviet Union and its satellite states imposed an economic blockade on Yugoslavia. The Yugoslav party rallied around Tito; Stalin's agents found themselves in prison. For the first time, Communists loyal to their own country had defied Stalin and the Soviet Union. It was an unequal conflict that Western observers compared to the Biblical contest between David and Goliath.

Germany was the location of the first open conflict between the United States and the Soviet Union. The dispute originated in the new Allied policy toward the three western German zones. In 1947, their occupation authorities joined the three to make one economic unit. This union was an important step in their efforts to revive the west German economy. It was still suffering from the destruction of war, serious shortages of food

and other vital goods, and an inflation so rampant that the German currency ceased to have real value. No longer were economic policies formulated for all Germany; negotiations with the Russians had broken down. The western Allies' ultimate objective was the creation of a new German state (leaving aside the problem of Berlin). To achieve this, they were prepared to disregard the wartime agreements on Germany. In the spring of 1948 the Western occupying powers announced the introduction in their zones of a new German currency. This was an important step toward an independent West Germany.

West and East had split in the middle of Europe. The West was in the process of rebuilding a new Germany. Even without the eastern German lands this state would have a population of fifty million and an industrial base sufficient to make it a major economic power in Europe. Supported by the United States, it became a front-line region. The Western occupation forces no longer protected the Allies against Germany. Instead, they protected the German areas they controlled against the Soviet Union.

Stalin opposed creating of a unified western Germany as strongly as he objected to an independent Yugoslavia. Once again, he turned economic blockade to get his way. To stop unification required halting the currency reform, and to achieve that goal that he ordered the Berlin blockade. When the new currency first appeared in June 1948, Soviet troops stopped all rail, road, and canal traffic into west Berlin along the three narrow land passages from the western zones. They cut off electric power from the east to 2.5 million inhabitants of west Berlin. The Soviet objective was not to seize all Berlin, which was only a pawn. Stalin's goal was to block the formation of a united western Germany by imposing hunger and cold on west Berliners. They were completely dependent on supplies from the West. Stalin expected that, faced with the suffering of helpless Berliners, the Western powers would abandon their unification plans in exchange for an end to the blockade.

He did not take into account the capabilities of modern air transport, since his state had few of its own. The Western powers kept supplies moving along the air corridors, which the Soviets could not block without an act of war. The airlift worked. At its peak that winter one plane arrived every two minutes in Berlin. The blockade failed, and in May 1949, Soviet officials finally opened the passages to Berlin. Neither side had used military force, for both sought to keep the conflict within political and diplomatic limits. Yet the blockade greatly heightened the Western fears of war. Stalin's clumsy policy had succeeded only in accelerating the unification of the Western zones and the formation of a Western military alliance.

The German Federal Republic came into existence in 1949. German politicians and lawyers wrote the constitution under Allied supervision. It gave West Germany a federal structure under parliamentary rule. In the first national elections of 1949 the Christian Democratic Party obtained the majority of the votes, and selected the Republic's new chancellor (head of the government). He was Konrad Adenauer, a prisoner during the Nazi years and a strong believer in Germany's rightful place within a unified western political and military community.

Gradually the West German state recovered its full sovereign powers. In 1951, Adenauer obtained full control over German foreign policy. He was instrumental in bringing his country within the European Common Market, alongside Germany's age-old enemy, France. In 1955, his state entered the Western military alliance (NATO) and recovered the right to form a German army. A nationalist and conservative, Adenauer did not recognize the legality of the new western borders of Poland, far within old German lands,

nor did he accept the permanent partition of the German lands. In his opinion, West Germany had to speak for the real German nation, since its people were free. His state welcomed East German refugees, and subsidized West Berlin's reconstruction to make it a showplace of prosperity in the middle of gray, drab East Germany.

Western European Recovery

Western Europe underwent a remarkably rapid economic recovery from the war. The Marshall Plan went into effect in mid-1948. By 1952, it had supplied more than $10 billion in financial and economic assistance to European countries, the largest shares going to Great Britain ($3.2 billion), France ($2.7 billion), and West Germany ($1.5 billion). Each government chose the appropriate use of the aid. In Britain, it helped rebuild old industries. In France, it provided the means for modernizing French industry and transportation. The West German government used the funds to lay the foundations of a free-enterprise industrial system (called the "social market economy"), in which the state encouraged capitalists to reinvest their profits and asked workers to accept low wages and long hours. The result was what came to be known as the German economic miracle. By 1952, German production climbed to 50 percent above the prewar level.

By then, Western European economic growth averaged 5 percent a year. This growth came with large imports from the United States and increased trade among the European states. The European and U.S. economies were becoming increasingly interdependent. Gradually they adapted to the new system of international monetary exchange, conducting foreign trade in dollars. The U.S. formula for economic aid to promote political stability and industrial expansion among western European countries proved a resounding success.

The economic recovery of the West benefited from the new institutions for international finance and multilateral trade created during the war. At the 1944 Bretton Woods conference in the United States, representatives from western governments had agreed on guidelines for postwar international trade and financial cooperation among the major industrial states (see Chapter 5). The misery brought by the 1930s depression, when protectionism was rampant and countries found their own resources inadequate for recovery, had taught Western leaders a lesson. They had agreed in 1944 that an international bank, the World Bank of Development, should become a source of long-term loans to nations requiring assistance for economic growth. At the same time, they created a special reserve of funds, held by the International Monetary Fund (IMF), to facilitate trade through short-term loans to states lacking adequate foreign currency to pay for needed imports. Finally, they had laid plans to encourage governments to participate in multilateral trade agreements to lower tariffs and encourage trade on a global scale. This plan ultimately became the General Agreement on Trade and Tariffs (GATT).

All three reforms were intended to meet the need for an institutional basis on which an international free market could function. The goal was economic growth on a global scale. The system's international currency was the dollar, just as its principal banker had to be the United States. Though the Bretton Woods plans were of less help in postwar recovery than U.S. economic aid, they did become a permanent part of the new global economy of following decades.

Containment and Military Alliances

In 1948, the U.S. government moved beyond its containment policies of military and economic aid to consider rebuilding its own military arsenal. Western European leaders encouraged this reversal of postwar U.S. demobilization to overcome, in George Kennan's words, "their own military helplessness" and their "lack of confidence in themselves." Military conscription began again in the United States. In 1949, U.S. international obligations widened with the creation of a collective security pact uniting North American and western Europe states. Called the North Atlantic Treaty Organization (NATO), it obligated each member to assist in the defense of the others against any aggression. In real terms, the presumed enemy was the Soviet Union, and the principal defender of the NATO states was the United States.

Large amounts of U.S. military supplies were already going to the Greek government to help in its civil war against the Communist-led guerrillas. Outnumbered by the regular Greek army and deprived after 1948 of Yugoslav support, the insurgents finally gave up the struggle in 1949. Their leaders and the remnants of their army fled to Soviet satellite countries, taking with them thousands of Greek civilians. Western military and economic aid was probably the decisive factor in preventing that country from becoming a communist dictatorship and Soviet satellite.

Primarily political and diplomatic in 1947, the U.S.-Soviet rivalry focused in the next years increasingly on issues of military balance of power and the development of new nuclear weapons. In the context of the Cold War, scientists became warriors and laboratories the key places where future wars were planned. Neither side envisioned this armaments race to be the means of launching an aggressive war, but each feared the power new weapons would give the other. This logic was as true in the Soviet Union as in the United States.

In 1949, the Soviet Union exploded its first atomic bomb. Soviet scientists had succeeded, far more quickly than anyone in the West anticipated, in carrying out Stalin's orders in 1945 for the development Soviet nuclear weapons. They already had begun research on the hydrogen bomb. The destructive capacity of this weapon exceeded by a thousand times that of the atomic bomb. In those years they set out to develop ballistic missiles as well. These rockets were capable of carrying nuclear weapons in a matter of minutes from Russia to the United States and were a greatly improved substitute for long-distance bombers, of which the Russians had very few. Each new Soviet step heightened pressure in the United States for new armaments in a cycle that appeared endless.

Deeply suspicious of Soviet intentions, the U.S. government undertook an intensive program to expand its armed forces in 1950 (even before the outbreak of the Korean War). Its crucial ingredient was to be an enormous arsenal of nuclear weapons, including the hydrogen bomb. U.S. military leaders ordered aboveground tests of nuclear bombs on Pacific islands, and in the western United States. They turned the tests into experiments in destructive might, positioning entire naval fleets near the Pacific bomb sites and building mock towns for the land tests. They encouraged U.S. citizens to build backyard air raid shelters and to lay in supplies to survive weeks below ground. A third world war became an imaginable event.

Convinced of the aggressive intent of Stalin, the U.S. government believed that national security lay in military superiority over the Soviet Union. In Allied countries near Soviet borders, the United States built air bases for its Strategic Air Command, whose bombers were in position to attack the Soviet Union. By the early 1950s, military preparedness came to dominate U.S. Cold War thinking. Tragically, both Soviet and U.S. leaders could find no other way to ensure their countries' ultimate protection than to apply nuclear power to military use.

U.S. leaders enlarged the containment strategy in those years to include military alliances with countries near the Soviet Union or areas of communist insurgency. They offered the inducement of foreign aid in the form of armaments to strengthen the military forces of allied countries. These global anti-Soviet policies extended through the Middle East and Asia. The United States signed alliances with a number of states individually, including the Philippines and Taiwan. In the 1950s, the U.S. and British governments each organized military alliances in these regions: The South East Asia Treaty Organization (SEATO) included states extending from Pakistan to New Zealand; the Baghdad Pact included Turkey, Iraq, and Iran. The most visible effect of these alliances was the distribution of armaments to dictators and democratic governments alike and the formation of a vast U.S. sphere of influence.

 SPOTLIGHT: Eleni Gatzoyiannis

The tragedy of Eleni Gatzoyiannis (1912–1948) was to find herself on the front lines of the Cold War. She knew that she and her children were caught in the middle of a civil war, but terms like "socialist camp" or the "Truman Doctrine" meant nothing to her. The communist guerrillas occupying the remote mountainous region of northern Greece where she lived believed their real enemy to be the forces of capitalism, not the Greek government troops in the valley below. In such a war, everyone had to join the battle, and those who disobeyed had to be punished. Eleni understood the struggle differently and defied their orders. She did so to save her children but at the price of her life.

The village where she lived was close to the borders of Albania and Yugoslavia. The Greek king and his government were far away in Athens. Politics had no place in the lives of the mountain villagers. Living was very hard there, and the men of the village traveled far away, even to America, to earn enough to support their families. Her husband made his living working in America. He came back often, but never for very long. He was scarcely more than a visitor with gifts and stories about a faraway land. In the first eight years of their marriage, they had five children, four girls and a boy. It was the law of the village that wives and children stay behind. The stern moral code of the mountain people dictated that women care for their children and serve their own parents, keeping together the family while the men were away. Eleni obeyed that code.

When the war came to Greece in 1940, her family helped her stay alive. Her husband could not return and could not even continue sending money since mail from America no longer reached their village. Her father brought the food that kept the family from going hungry. Young men from her village joined the guerrillas fighting the Germans. German army units swept through the area, pursuing the guerrillas and burning the villages suspected of helping them. She was lucky, for her farmhouse survived while many others around it were destroyed. At war's end, she had kept her family intact. Peace returned, and Eleni begged her husband to bring the family to America. He promised to do so, just as soon as he had

saved enough money. In the meantime, she had to stay.

And then the civil war began. In 1945, the communist guerrillas had fled to Yugoslavia to escape the army of the Greek government. Then in 1946, they came back. War, not political campaigns and elections, was to be their path to power. They followed the example of the Yugoslav Communists, who helped train and provided arms to their forces. Their Democratic Army faced a strong Greek army trained and equipped by the British and the Americans. They were not strong enough to move out of the mountains. In 1947, with Stalin's encouragement they organized their own provisional government in what they called their liberated area of northern Greece.

The villagers became the citizens of this tiny, infant state and its unwilling laborers. Children learned in school to salute the portraits of Stalin, and to sing "Onward to the struggle for our precious freedom!" The Communist Party promised the villagers to protect "our friends who work with us," but swore punishment for any who collaborated with the "monarcho-fascist" enemies. The only immediate change to the villagers' well-being was the loss of grain that the new government collected as taxes, and the time they had to give to work brigades organized by the new authorities. Eleni herself was often ordered to work harvesting the grain in the fields that the guerrillas had taken for themselves.

Soon, the Communists ordered young women to serve in their army. Eleni saved her eldest daughter from that service by pouring boiling water on her foot and then burning it with a hot branding iron. The local authorities suspected her of having defied them. There was nothing she could do, without being arrested, to prevent her second daughter from being conscripted. It was harder and harder to protect her children.

Then in the spring of 1948, the Communists decided to transport to Albania and Yugoslavia the children between five and fourteen years old living in the villages in their territory. They called it the "gathering up of children," who they claimed they were protecting from the war. But it was really their way of forcibly enlisting new followers for the long combat to come. Their struggle was not going well. Their leaders refused to admit defeat, though, and anticipated retreating north beyond the Greek borders to find a refuge for themselves and their followers in nearby Communist-controlled countries and to prepare for new war. They knew parents would resist the abduction of their children. Their police had to seize the children by force. Within a few months they had rounded up 25,000 involuntary young refugees.

Eleni refused to let this happen. The front lines of the government forces were just a few miles away, and behind the lines were her parents and brothers. Secretly, she and neighboring women found guides to take a group of twenty women and children down the mountain and through the front lines to the valley and safety. Just before they were to leave, the guerrillas ordered her again to work in the fields. She had to go, for had she tried to join the fugitives the security police would have been alerted and caught them. So in the end she had to abandon her children.

The authorities were furious that so many people had escaped. They had never trusted her, calling her the "Amerikana." They blamed her for conspiring with the enemy and put her on trial. They tortured her to make her confess, and forced neighbors to testify against her at the little show trial in the village organized by the chief of the area. They had decided in advance that she was guilty. She was shot by a firing squad two months after her children had fled.

Stalin's Empire

In eastern Europe, Stalin ruled the small communist countries on the Soviet Union's western borders through his ambassadors and secret police officials. These governments became "satellites," that is, states whose decisions on leadership and key policies were made in Moscow. In the years after 1948, all were miniature replicas of the communist regime in the Soviet Union. Their leaders ruled with the same dictatorial power as Stalin, employing similar repressive police methods. In some countries little "show trials" put on display leading Communists accused of "national deviation" and "Titoism." These mockeries of justice repeated the experience of the Soviet trials of the 1930s. All the accused confessed their guilt, and most were executed.

The Soviet socialist model was applied by force to eastern European societies. Industry and commerce were nationalized. Peasant farmers were forced to sell their produce to the state at low prices. State plans set ambitious targets for industrial growth, achieved at the cost of miserable living conditions for the population. The Stalinist literary style of socialist realism was imposed on writers and artists who had to glorify Soviet socialism and Stalin's "genius." A gray uniformity colored public life, forced into the Stalinist mold.

Of all the eastern European states, only Yugoslavia escaped Stalinist domination.

Escapees from the "Gathering Up of Children": Greek Refugee Children and Mothers, Athens, 1948 (*Christopher Emmett/ Hoover Institution*)

The expulsion of the Yugoslav Communist Party from the Cominform in 1948 was followed by the political and economic isolation of the Yugoslav state. Its trade with all other communist states ceased, and Soviet and all eastern European states broke diplomatic relations. For a year, Tito continued to claim his fidelity to Stalinism and to Soviet socialism. Finally disillusioned, he took apart bit by bit the framework of Stalinism which he had used to guide Yugoslavia's foreign and domestic policies. He joined the leaders of newly independent Asian states in founding the so-called "nonaligned movement" of countries refusing to join either Western or Soviet military alliances. But the Yugoslav one-party dictatorship remained, a remnant of his years of loyalty to Soviet communism.

His country kept its constitutional order as a federation of national republics. Tito maintained peace among the many peoples who lived there by giving each a small degree of political autonomy. The Serbian people were the most numerous and the peoples living in the north of the country (Slovenes and Croats) were the most prosperous. He made sure that all shared the available income and economic resources. His authority and the power of his party made this formula work. A rebel against Stalinism, he even loosened slightly his dictatorial powers in the early 1950s. Among the satellite countries his state alone enjoyed real independence and his people were spared Stalinist terror.

Despite Tito's public defiance of Soviet hegemony, Stalin chose not to invade Yugoslavia. Although Red Army forces surrounded Yugoslavia and made threatening moves, they never attacked. Perhaps Stalin feared prolonged Yugoslav resistance; perhaps he was determined to avoid any risk of war with the United States. In matters of European security the dictator pursued a very cautious policy. Tito's revolt did not disrupt Soviet domination elsewhere along its borders. After 1949, the Soviet Union disposed of nuclear weapons, but it remained militarily inferior to the United States. It possessed only a few long-range bombers and its navy was little more than a coast guard protecting its shores. Whether through prudence or fear, Stalin pursued a foreign policy of domination but not aggression.

The Soviet leader was growing old. In 1949, he celebrated his seventieth birthday, receiving so many gifts from within the Soviet Union and around the world that they filled two entire warehouses. He continued to rule with dictatorial powers, feared by his subordinates within the ruling party committee, the Presidium (formerly called the Politburo). His successor, Khrushchev, remembered later how Stalin could "without warning turn on you with real viciousness." His suspiciousness remained acute. Public denunciations of "Zionists" revealed a worsening of Soviet persecution of Russian Jews, more numerous there than in any other country. These signs of a new wave of terror suddenly ceased in March 1953. That month a cerebral hemorrhage brought Stalin's life to an end. His death closed an extraordinary, terrible period of Russian history and of Soviet communism.

THE COLD WAR IN ASIA

Like Europe, the lands of East Asia became an arena for the Cold War. There, too, Soviet and U.S. troops took up in key areas the role of occupying forces. In other lands liberated from the Japanese, nationalist forces emerged after the war claiming the right to construct new nation-states. The fall of the Japanese Empire and the western colonial empires took place in such conditions of disorder that the peaceful transfer of power was nearly impossible. Though the influence of the Soviet Union and United States was great, they too could not control the course of local wars. But when in the late 1940s their rivalry worsened, it brought the Cold War to East Asia. The Cold War was a global conflict.

New Wars in East Asia

The collapse of the Japanese Empire left vast areas of East Asia without effective rule. The Japanese home islands became a part of the U.S. Pacific zone of occupation. Manchuria was occupied by Soviet forces, and Korea was partitioned between Soviet and American occupation troops. Elsewhere, no political authority could take the place of the Japanese troops. In many areas, guerrilla forces emerged from the countryside, claiming the right to create independent states. Communists had collaborated in the anti-Japanese struggle, and they had their own plans for leadership after the war. The Allied Commander of southeast Asia, headquartered in India, was forced to call on Japanese soldiers in distant parts of his area to serve as police until Allied troops arrived.

In Indochina, French army and naval units returned in strength in 1946. They confronted a strong Communist-led nationalist movement under Ho Chi Minh. He had proclaimed the formation the independent state of Vietnam at the time of the Japanese retreat in 1945. Though his declaration of independence cited passages from the 1775 American Declaration, his objective was socialist as well as national revolution. The French refused to recognize his new state. They set about reconquering their former colony. Ho's forces retreated to the rural and mountainous areas of Indochina. They began a new guerrilla war that, with interruptions, lasted thirty more years.

In China, the Nationalist government claimed sovereign powers in the Republic of China. Chiang Kai-shek, president of the republic and heir to Sun Yat-sen at the head of the Nationalist Party, was more determined than ever to take control of the entire country. He had enjoyed the backing of the United States during the war and had received substantial amounts of military and economic aid. President Roosevelt's plans for postwar East Asia relied on Nationalist China to be a regional center of stability and authority, one of the "four policemen" who were to collaborate in setting up a new world order. It was an illusion. Chiang's forces had failed to win any major battles against the Japanese and remained confined at the close of the war to the mountainous interior. Communist guerrilla forces had conquered large rural areas within the Japanese puppet states on the coast. Their troops were too weak, though, to seize control of major cities.

The U.S. government continued after the war to place its hopes on the Nationalists. President Truman ordered 50,000 marines to the northern coast of China to keep order while U.S. planes and ships transported Nationalist troops into the areas being evacuated by the Japanese. He also made available surplus military supplies worth $1 billion to the Nationalists. In no other war-torn country did the United States become so directly involved in the task of postwar recovery.

The burden of rebuilding China lay in the Nationalists' hands. It proved a task they could not handle. Behind a facade of power, the Nationalist state was weak. Chiang's government was incapable of administering the country in an efficient manner. Nationalist generals in command of newly reoccupied provinces conducted their affairs like the old warlords, interested above all in enhancing their own power. They did little for the people. The inefficient Nationalist state and expensive army proved an obstacle to economic recovery. Exorbitant government spending fueled rapid inflation, which became ruinous in the postwar years. The most serious weakness of the Nationalist regime was its inability to win the confidence of the Chinese people. Corruption and abuse of power discredited its claim to national leadership. Its failure to implement land reform for the peasantry deprived it of support among the masses of the population.

The war had swelled the power and authority of the Communists. Their army had grown to 1 million and their liberated territories held a population numbering 50 million. Mao Zedong and Chiang had been rivals for power in the decade before war began with Japan, and resumed their contest as soon as peace returned. The U.S. government, faithful to the same principle of national self-determination that it followed in Europe, encouraged the two sides to form a coalition government. It was an arduous task. The U.S. Secretary of State, General George Marshall, traveled personally to China to persuade the two leaders to reach agreement.

He had the indirect assistance of Joseph Stalin. The Soviet leader practiced the same power politics in Asia as in Europe. He considered that China belonged to the American sphere of influence. In late 1945, he signed a ten-year treaty of friendship with the Nationalist government. In exchange, he obtained important economic concessions in Manchuria (including control of a seaport). With these spoils in hand, he urged the Chinese Communists to give up their hopes of seizing power by force and to accept instead a political coalition with the Nationalists. He later recalled that, when a Chinese Communist delegation came to Moscow in 1945, "we told them that we considered the development of the uprising in China had no prospect, and that the Chinese comrades

Chinese Communist Leaders (far right, Mao Zedong; far left, Zhou Enlai) with General George Marshall in Yenan, 1945 (*Philip Sprouse Collection/Hoover Institution*)

should join the Chiang government and dissolve their army." The combined pressure of the United States and the Soviet Union brought together the former enemies. In January 1946, the Nationalists and Communists signed a cease-fire and began discussions to form a joint government.

The agreement quickly collapsed. Outside intervention proved incapable of effacing the bitter rivalry between the two contenders for power. The United States could not force Chiang to put aside his deadly hatred of the Communists. The Soviet Union had no means to impose on Mao Zedong the dissolution of his peasant army and the abandonment of his liberated areas. These were twin elements to the policy on which Mao had based his revolutionary hopes ever

since 1928. At the end of 1946, fighting between Nationalist and Communist troops began again over the perennial issue of territorial control. Manchuria was the prize, occupied by Soviet troops until late that year. Their withdrawal began a contest between Nationalists and Communists to take over that once-prosperous region.

In the battle for control of Manchurian cities, the Nationalists had the initial advantage. The Communists, less well equipped and fewer in number, had to retreat to the countryside to resume guerrilla war once again against their old enemy. In late 1946, the United States finally abandoned efforts to bring the two sides together. General Marshall declared impossible an agreement between, in his words, "the dominant reactionary group in the [Nationalist] government and the irreconcilable Communists." By late 1947, Communist Party forces were 2 million strong and had succeeded in cutting off north China from the central regions. Only force of arms would decide the victor.

Communist Victory in China

That conflict was one of the greatest wars of the twentieth century. On one side was the Nationalist state, with over 3 million troops equipped with U.S. military supplies. It appeared the dominant political movement in the country, but its strength was rapidly declining. The weaknesses apparent in 1945 became more serious with each passing year. The army was poorly led and, with the exception of several crack divisions sent to Manchuria, consisted of conscripts who deserted at the first opportunity. The population was increasingly hostile to the Nationalist government, incapable of assuring public order and of preventing the collapse of commerce and industry. When forced to choose, more and more Chinese turned to the Communists.

Their forces were fewer in number in 1948 than the Nationalists, but the balance was beginning to shift in their favor. Social, political, and military factors explain their increasing power. The party leadership under Mao Zedong proved effective and skillful in mobilizing popular support and in forming a military and political organization capable of governing large areas of the country. The Communists had to rely on their own resources, for no aid came from the Soviet Union. They fixed their own political objectives, paying polite attention to Stalin's recommendations but never obeying him blindly.

In 1947, Stalin's militant policy for the international communist movement came at the same time that their civil war with the Nationalists was turning to their advantage. That year they began a social revolution in the rural areas they controlled. Farms of landlords and wealthy peasants were confiscated and the land was redistributed among poor peasants. They ordered the end of hired labor and promised all peasants a modest amount of land. A new revolutionary order was emerging in the Chinese countryside, and support among the masses of the peasantry grew correspondingly. Ten years before, Mao had proclaimed that "political power grows out of the barrel of a gun." That gun was held in the late 1940s by peasants who believed that they were fighting for their own land as well as for a liberated Chinese nation.

The Communist Party cadres enforced these reforms ruthlessly, often brutally. Still, they proved effective administrators capable of maintaining order in the "liberated areas." After decades of war, firm and orderly rule appealed to many Chinese. Another factor behind the growing strength of the Communists was military leadership. The commanders of the People's Liberation Army (PLA) had, after years of guerrilla fighting, learned to lead massive army groups in battles increasingly resembling a regular war. They proved superior to the Nationalist generals. Their soldiers (among whom were increasing numbers of Nationalist deserters) remained disciplined, increasingly confident of victory and convinced of the justice of their cause. The power of the Chinese Communists lay principally in their morale and leadership, not in numbers.

Communist strategy shifted to the conquest of Manchuria in 1948. That spring communist armies blockaded Nationalist garrisons throughout the region. In mid-1948, they began the systematic destruction of the best troops the Nationalists could field, who by then were cut off from the bulk of Chiang's forces in China. By the end of 1948, the Nationalists had lost thirty divisions. Half these forces had deserted or surrendered without fighting. All Manchuria lay under Communist Party rule, and panic was spreading among Nationalist troops elsewhere.

In early 1949, the balance of military forces between the two sides was tilting toward the Communists. The U.S. government had done as much as possible to help the Nationalist government with economic and military aid. President Truman refused to send U.S. troops to fight in place of Chiang's demoralized army. The Communists, unaided by the Soviet Union, obtained most of their arms from American supplies captured from the Nationalists. The U.S. government condemned the military offensive of the Communists, and Stalin may have warned the Chinese comrades to show caution—to no avail. In the Chinese civil war, no outside powers could contain the conflict.

In the winter and spring of 1948–1949, the PLA launched massive military offensives all through north and central China. One Nationalist army, surrounded in the capital city of Beijing, surrendered in January 1949, with the loss of half a million troops. A few months earlier, armies of the Communists, numbering 500,000 soldiers, attacked the main defensive line protecting Nationalist areas in central China. By February 1949 the defenses there were breached and the Nationalist armies routed. Between the spring and fall of 1949, Mao's forces moved south across the Yangtze River and into southern China. That summer entire Nationalist armies, generals as well as troops, deserted to the Communists. By the fall of 1949, no important areas of resistance remained.

In October 1949, the Communist Party leadership proclaimed in Beijing the formation of the Chinese People's Republic. The most populous country in the world, land of the world's oldest civilization, had passed under the communist rule. A successor state had taken power, ending the long period of disorders in China following the fall of the Chinese Empire in 1911. The Communist Party leaders did not consider the war at an end until they captured the island of Formosa (Taiwan), where Chiang and remnants of his Nationalist forces had fled. Their Peoples Liberation Army (PLA) prepared for an amphibious invasion of the island, planned for the summer of 1950. Nothing appeared to stand in its way.

The U.S. government had no clear idea of the intentions of the new Chinese leadership. Seeking to make clear what part of East Asia lay in its security zone, it publicly outlined in 1949 its military forces' "defense perimeter." This strategic area included Japan; it excluded all lands on the Asian continent (including Korea) as well as Formosa. The U.S. Army, in other words, took no responsibility on the Asian mainland to fight communist states. At the same time, new Asian nationalist regimes from South Korea to the Philippines obtained U.S. economic and military aid. Early in 1950, the U.S. government agreed to assist the new noncommunist state of Vietnam, largely a French creation to win the backing of nationalist groups in the war with the Vietnamese communist guerrillas. These anti-communist policies did not appear in late 1949 to exclude recognition of the new People's Republic of China. Secret talks began that winter between Chinese Communist leaders and the United States in preparation for the possible opening of diplomatic relations.

To Mao Zedong, the Chinese Peoples Republic needed first of all to establish good relations with the Soviet Union. He traveled to Moscow in the winter of 1949–1950 on his first trip outside China to begin lengthy and difficult negotiations with Stalin. The Chinese Communists requested a military alliance, economic assistance, and the end to Soviet occupation of Chinese territory. These Soviet-controlled areas included a port and railroad in Manchuria and a large area of

Chinese Central Asia. The Chinese were in effect requesting the end to Soviet imperial domination in East Asia. Chinese and Russians shared a common Marxist-Leninist ideology, and Mao revered the wisdom and achievements of the Soviet party. Though the Chinese desperately needed Soviet help rebuilding their war-torn country, they were determined to obtain Stalin's recognition of their new revolutionary state.

For his part, Stalin persisted in treating China, even though Communist, as a subordinate member of the Soviet sphere of influence. He apparently distrusted the Chinese Communists, whose independent behavior must have reminded him of the Yugoslav Communists. Mao later recalled that "Stalin feared that China might degenerate into another Yugoslavia and that I might become another Tito." Stalin certainly was concerned at the possible weakening of the Soviet sphere of influence in East Asia, which extended from Central Asia through Mongolia to North Korea. Alongside the Chinese leaders in the negotiations were Communist representatives from these lands. The negotiations dragged on for two months.

In the end, Stalin agreed to Mao's request for a military alliance and economic aid. He promised the withdrawal Soviet forces from Manchuria, though in a few years. In exchange, Mao had to recognize the independence (under Soviet protection) of Mongolia and to tolerate the existence of a special autonomous region in Manchuria under a Chinese Communist leader taking orders from Moscow. Between these two enormous states, relations remained "fraternal" in public, and the Chinese honored Stalin's ideological leadership. Yet Communist China did not join the ranks of Soviet satellites.

Divided Korea

The Cold War frontier reached as far east as the country of Korea. In 1945, Soviet invasion forces invaded Korea just as the Japanese Empire capitulated. They withdrew into the northern half of the peninsula, respecting the wartime agreement with the United States calling for partition of Korea between United States and Soviet occupation troops until an Allied peace treaty with Japan restored Korean independence. The desire for national unity was strong among Koreans after a half-century of Japanese rule. The partition became an insurmountable obstacle to unification, however.

The U.S. authorities opened their southern half of Korea to exiled nationalists under the leadership of Syngman Rhee. In 1948, he became head of the Republic of Korea. U.S. forces withdrew from the south. Their military base was Japan, which the U.S. government made into its East Asian strong point in the Cold War. Rhee governed South Korea with dictatorial powers, suppressing the Korean Communist Party and its labor unions and damning the Communists as traitors to the nation. He vowed that national unification would be his doing, warning that his army was prepared to seize by force the northern half of the peninsula. The U.S. government, as opposed there as in China to becoming directly involved in civil war, took seriously the threat of war. To restrain Rhee's nationalist fervor, it provided the South Korean army with only defensive weapons.

Soviet occupation authorities in the north formed a civilian government under the control of the Korean Communist Party. Following the example of the United States, in 1948 it permitted the Communists to create their own state, the Korean Democratic Republic and withdrew its occupation forces. North Korea's leader was Kim Il Sung, a veteran Communist who had learned his revolutionary lessons in Moscow in the 1930s, then had acquired military skills fighting alongside the Chinese Communists in the war against Japan. He admired Mao's revolutionary exploits, especially his defeat of the Nationalists and his unification of all China. Kim hoped to do the same for Korea, for (like Mao and Ho Chi Minh in Vietnam) he was a nationalist as well as revolutionary. But unlike these other Asian Communists, he could not on his own begin a war for Korean unity. His devotion to Stalin was reinforced by the economic and military aid provided his state by the Soviet Union. North Korea was a new Soviet satellite.

Armed by the Soviet Union, his army was ready for war. He still needed Stalin's approval to undertake the conquest of southern Korea. Through the winter and spring of 1949–1950, he bombarded Moscow with telegrams begging for the Great Leader's backing. His army had already fought in the Chinese civil war and was better armed than the South Korean forces. He assured Stalin that military victory would come in two weeks. All Korea would be under the Communists. The moment was right, for though Rhee talked of war against the north, he had not yet sufficient military strength. Unstated but understood by both Kim and Stalin was the argument that what the Chinese Communists had already achieved, Kim's forces should be permitted to do in their turn. Revolution was his goal, and no U.S. troops stood in his way.

SUMMARY

The Cold War could not provide a permanent settlement to the Second World War. Stalin's intent to create a diplomatic and political sphere of domination around the Soviet Union ensured a partition of Europe that followed the approximate line of farthest advance of Soviet armies. His warning after 1946 of the inevitability of war with the capitalist powers kept his country in virtual wartime conditions. Privately he admitted that this war would not come soon. "Respecting the powerful" dictated that he avoid risky actions that might provoke the United States. West Berlin was blockaded, not seized, by his troops; Yugoslavia was isolated, not invaded. The Soviet dictator's limited expansionist aims undermined a stable balance of power in Europe. Peace could not be ensured in these conditions.

The U.S. policy of containment encouraged the formation of politically and economically sound states in strategic areas around this Soviet empire. In these terms it constituted a creative and ultimately successful global strategy. But the U.S. government turned increasingly to military containment, rebuilding its own armaments and supporting regional anti-Soviet military alliances even where the Soviet Union posed no real threat. This revision of the containment policy accelerated the nuclear arms race, and led to the creation of military alliances that gave the U.S. hegemonic influence so great that it seemed to be building its own global empire.

Both the massive destruction of war and international tensions contributed to the emergence of two distinct new global systems in the decade after the war. In the East, one-party regimes imposed command economies on their lands, following the Soviet model of collectivized agriculture and nationalized industry run by a mammoth state and party bureaucracy. In the West, countries were bound together through trade and investment in an international capitalist economy. The United States was the center of this Western system. The dollar was the stable currency of exchange, and U.S. technology provided key tools of modern production. U.S. foreign aid and private investments were vital ingredients for economic growth in foreign lands. The economic crisis of the depression appeared resolved for the time being. The new challenge was to avoid a war between the superpowers, each possessing nuclear weapons whose use would bring civilization to an end.

In the background to the Cold War, new political and social forces were reshaping the world. Both sides proclaimed that the age of colonial empires had past, and expressed opposition to Dutch and French military re-occupation of their Asian colonies. Yet in a real sense the Soviet victory in the Second World War had brought that country an enlarged empire around its borders, where national frontiers were meaningless divisions within a vast territory governed from Moscow. The old age of empires had disappeared in the turmoil of the Second World War. The new world of nations had only begun to take shape.

DATES WORTH REMEMBERING

1945   Formation of United Nations
1945   Partition of Korea
1945   Victory of Labor Party in British elections
1946   Philippine independence
1946–1949   Civil war in China
1946–1949   Greek civil war
1946–1954   French colonial war in Indochina
1946–1949   Dutch colonial war in East Indies
1947   Indian independence and partition
1947   Marshall Plan and Truman Doctrine
1947   Start of Cold War
1948   Communist seizeure of power in Czechoslovakia
1948   Yugoslavia rejection of Soviet domination
1948   Berlin blockade
1949   Chinese Peoples Republic
1949   North Atlantic Treaty
1949   German Federal Republic (West Germany)
1950   Sino-Soviet treaties of aid and alliance
1953   Death of Joseph Stalin

RECOMMENDED READING

The Cold War

*John Lewis Gaddis, *Strategies of Containment: A Critical Appraisal of Postwar American National Security Policy* (1982). A very perceptive study of U.S. containment policy from its origins to the late 1970s; also, *We Now Know: Rethinking Cold War History* (1997), for the author's views on reading secret Soviet documents from the Cold War period.

Anders Stephanson, *Kennan and the Art of Foreign Policy* (1989). An intellectual biography of the diplomat, stressing the cultural forces that shaped his world view.

Daniel Yergin, *The Shattered Peace: The Origins of the Cold War and the National Security State* (1977). A study of the disturbing transformation of U.S. political life under the impact of the Cold War.

Soviet Foreign Policy

David Holloway, *Stalin and the Bomb: The Soviet Union and Atomic Energy, 1939–1956* (1994). The engrossing story of the start of the nuclear weapons race from the Soviet side.

Voytech Mastny, *Cold War and Soviet Insecurity: The Stalin Years.* (1996). A convincing interpretation of Stalin's postwar foreign policy.

Memoirs and Novels

*Milovan Djilas, *Conversations with Stalin* (1958). Unique personal record of three secret meetings between Yugoslav communist leaders and Stalin between 1944 and 1947.

Nicholas Gage, *Eleni* (1983). The story of a Greek mother as told by her son after he had become a correspondent for *The New York Times* and had returned to Greece to reconstruct her life and tragic death in the Greek civil war.

*Czeslaw Milosz, *The Captive Mind* (1953). Enthralling real-life portraits, by an eyewitness (later emigre) Polish poet, of intellectuals who collaborated in the formation of communist Poland.

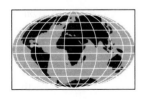

CHAPTER SEVEN

Revolution and Revival in East Asia, 1950–1990

Last of the empires in East Asia, the Japanese Empire lost all its colonial lands in the cataclysm of defeat. Its troops departed from the Asian mainland, abandoning Indonesia, Burma, Indochina, China, and Korea. Disorder sustained by terrible poverty was widespread and claimants in those lands to the title of national leadership were bitterly divided. Left with only their archipelago of main islands, the Japanese people had to remake their lives in the ruins of cities and under American occupation authorities. In many respects East Asia had to be remade.

The countries of the region retained the boundaries drawn by Western imperial powers. The revolutionary armies of the Chinese Communist Party never recovered all the outlying lands that the empire had once ruled, but the new state did keep by negotiation and force of arms the bulk of its territory and population. It was still a multiethnic country, with large Turkic and Tibetan minorities in its western regions. The preponderance of Han-speaking people

gave it greater claim than ever before to be the land of the Chinese nation. Still, its size and diversity left it in appearance like the old empire, whose borders the new communist rulers still hoped to recover. The new China appeared in many ways an empire-nation.

The leadership and character of new states in Korea and in Indochina were shaped by bitter civil wars in which Communists and noncommunists, each backed by a superpower, struggled for control of these lands. The settlement of the Korean conflict left that country partitioned between communist and noncommunist states, like Germany a reminder of the Cold War. In Indochina, on the contrary, the war lasted far longer and had a very different outcome. For three decades civil war and foreign intervention tore apart the former French colony. In the end, the military triumph of the Vietnamese Communist Party made it the ruling force throughout that land, still separated from its neighbors by the borders drawn by the French in the nineteenth century. The existence of these frontiers was one visible sign of the permanent impact of the West on East Asia.

The Soviet Union and the United States were a constant and important presence, both by the influence they exerted and by the opposition they encountered, in the evolution of the East Asian countries. Chinese Communists depended in the early years of their revolution on the Soviet Union for ideological inspiration and military support. When they denounced their Soviet neighbor, the conflict led to a profound alteration in the Asian balance of power. The United States played a key role in the reconstruction of Japan, both as occupying power and as a source of economic aid, until for a time the Japanese economic "miracle" became a model for American industry. To understand the evolution of those states we must pay attention both to internal political forces in each country and to the policies of the two superpowers. Their global ascendancy made post-1945 world history in some measure a product of their actions.

COMMUNIST CHINA

The future of China, the oldest existing civilization in the world, lay in the hands of the Communist Party. The long years of civil war had divided the population and devastated much of the country. Despite the destruction that the Japanese war had produced, it proved indirectly a unifying influence. The Communists' struggle against a hated foreign enemy brought the party the support of Chinese patriots and nationalists. It paved the way for political unification of the country following the military victory of the communist forces. Mao Zedong came to power both as the "Helmsman" of his party and as the heir to an ancient imperial state.

Mao Zedong and the Communist Dictatorship

The Chinese Communist Party undertook after 1949 the monumental task of transforming the Chinese state and society and of remaking the behavior and attitudes of the Chinese people. The enormous influence of Mao Zedong, who was the object by then of a semireligious cult resembling that of Stalin in Soviet Russia, infused Chinese communism in its first decades with unique revolutionary traits. Ever since the 1920s, Mao had placed his hope for revolution in China above all in the peasant masses. He preserved that faith when the time came to overthrow, as he explained in his Marxist vocabulary, the old ways of "feudalism" and to "build socialism." What to skeptics appeared impossible was attainable, he believed, since "the masses of the Chinese people" were, under proper party inspiration and guidance, capable of "miracles." This extraordinary confidence in the Chinese masses remained with him throughout his years in power and inspired grandiose—and ultimately disastrous—experiments in Chinese communism.

The People's Liberation Army (PLA) was an integral part of the communist movement. It had been the spearhead of the party in the seizure of power. Its discipline and dedication set the model for the whole revolutionary vanguard, of which it was, in some respects, the elite. No earlier communist movement had placed such heavy responsibilities on its military organization in the struggle for political power. Mao believed that his understanding of communism offered the country a unified body of revolutionary wisdom. His supporters called it "Maoism." The message incorporated two principal lessons: (1) The revolutionary ideology of Marxism-Leninism had to be adapted to Chinese conditions; and (2) Mao possessed the creative knowledge to discover the Chinese path to the socialist society and to lead the party and the country to this glorious life. His beliefs were utopian; for a quarter-century they marked China's path to the future.

For a few years, the Chinese Communists conceived of their country's immediate future primarily in the form of Soviet communism. During their first years in power they idolized the achievements of the Russian Communists and looked to the Soviet Union for their model of political dictatorship and economic revolution. They considered at that time that the Soviet Union had successfully achieved a socialist society. In doing so, its leaders had uncovered the correct policies which China had to follow on its own road to socialism. Mao declared on his visit to Moscow in the winter of 1949–1950 that Soviet farm collectivization, nationalized industry, and command planning were "models for construction in New China." While the Japanese were in those same years reconstructing their state and economy on the basis of Western democratic and capitalist institutions, China was closely bound to Soviet communism.

China, Stalin, and the Korean War

That alliance became a reality in the Korean War. Soviet, Chinese, and Korean Communists became involved in a conflict that deeply marked the Cold War and changed the course of East Asian history. Throughout the winter of 1949–1950, Kim Il Sung had begged Stalin to approve an invasion of South Korea. Without Stalin's word he could not act. In his telegrams to the Great Leader, his arguments emphasized the strength of his army, capable in his opinion of victory within a few weeks. That spring, Stalin gave his consent. In June 1950, North Korean troops invaded South Korea. Korea, like

China, seemed destined to become another revolutionary triumph for communism.

Stalin's readiness to allow that war came only after he had obtained the support of the Chinese Communists. Mao showed no hesitation in backing his Korean comrades. Moved by a sort of revolutionary conceit, he seems to have believed that his forces could conquer Taiwan that summer, and North Korea could conquer the south, without U.S. military opposition. He too credited North Koreans with armed might to overwhelm their enemies in the south. Even if the United States did reverse its policy of keeping troops off the Asian mainland, Kim Il Sung's assurances of a rapid triumph made it likely no U.S. forces could intervene in Korea in time.

The Korean conflict ceased being a local war two days after the invasion when President Truman declared that his country would defend South Korea. This sudden reversal of U.S. policy was due to two factors. First, the U.S. leaders realized that a communist Korea would extend the ring of Soviet satellites to a short distance of Japan, kingpin of the U.S. Asian defenses. Second, U.S. failure to resist the North Korean offensive would have conveyed a message throughout the world that the policy of containment hid military weakness, reviving memories of the 1930s appeasement policies toward Nazi Germany. Having emphasized the military dimension of containment, the United States had to prove its readiness to resist military expansion backed by the Soviet Union.

The Korean fighting quickly became a full-scale war. North Korean forces routed the South Korean army. This forced the United States immediately to send troops from Japan to stop the offensive. The U.S. government appointed General Douglas MacArthur commander of the forces in Korea. He fought under the United Nations'

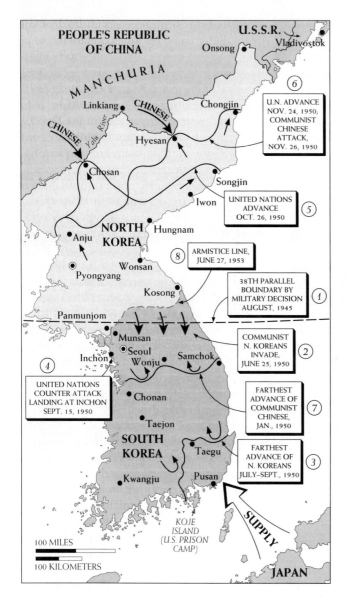

PEOPLE'S REPUBLIC
OF CHINA

MANCHURIA

U.S.S.R.

Onsong

Vladivostok

Linkiang

CHINESE

Chongjin

CHINESE

Yalu River

Hyesan

Chosan

Songjin

⑥ U.N. ADVANCE
NOV. 24, 1950;
COMMUNIST
CHINESE
ATTACK,
NOV. 26, 1950

Iwon

⑤ UNITED NATIONS
ADVANCE
OCT. 26, 1950

NORTH
KOREA

Hungnam

Anju

⑧ ARMISTICE LINE,
JUNE 27, 1953

Wonsan

Pyongyang

Kosong

38TH PARALLEL
BOUNDARY BY
MILITARY DECISION
AUGUST, 1945 ①

Panmunjom

Munsan

Seoul

COMMUNIST
N. KOREANS
INVADE,
JUNE 25, 1950 ②

④ Inchon

Wonju

Samchok

④ UNITED NATIONS
COUNTER ATTACK
LANDING AT INCHON
SEPT. 15, 1950

Chonan

FARTHEST
ADVANCE OF
COMMUNIST ⑦
CHINESE,
JAN., 1950

Taejon

SOUTH
KOREA

Taegu

FARTHEST
ADVANCE OF
N. KOREANS ③
JULY–SEPT., 1950

Kwangju

Pusan

SUPPLY

KOJE
ISLAND
(U.S. PRISON
CAMP)

100 MILES

100 KILOMETERS

JAPAN

Korean War, 1950–1953

flag when the U.N. Security Council (minus the Soviet representative, away protesting the failure of the United Nations to seat communist China) approved the defense of South Korea in a formal motion condemning North Korea's aggression. MacArthur's own vision of the war extended as far as the ulti-mate destruction of communism in the Far East, in China as well as Korea. The U.S. government lent some support to that idea when in July it reversed its decision not to defend Taiwan. U.S. naval forces of the Seventh Fleet sailed into the Straits of Formosa to block Chinese troops preparing to invade

New War in Asia: U.S. Counteroffensive against North Korean Forces, Sept. 1950 (*National Archives*)

the island. Suddenly, the front lines of the Cold War extended around Communist China.

U.S. objectives in the Korean conflict did not become clear until late that fall. General MacArthur's immediate goal was the defense of South Korea. Two months after the invasion, U.N. troops landed in the middle of the peninsula, forcing the North Korean army to flee north to escape encirclement. Supported by President Truman, MacArthur pushed U.N. troops beyond the line of partition into North Korea that September. His forces quickly reached the very borders of China. His goal was complete military victory and the capitulation of North Korea. The U.S. government had already received Chinese warnings of military intervention if U.S. land forces approached Chinese territory. MacArthur dismissed these warnings, believing mistakenly that his armed forces could defeat Chinese troops (and perhaps welcoming the possibility to bring the war into China).

The Chinese leaders carried out their threat. Their reasons for intervening appear mainly strategic. U.S. troops occupying territory on the very borders of their country constituted a serious threat to the stability of their regime. In November, 300,000 Chinese troops attacked the U.N. forces, which were quickly overwhelmed and forced to retreat back into South Korea. There the front soon stabilized in the region of the old border. The war dragged on for almost three years. The United States suffered more than 100,000 casualties and the Chinese nearly one million. China and the United States had become enemies. In 1951, the U.S. government dismissed MacArthur from his position of commander-in-chief. His dreams of military victory were out of touch with the limited objectives of U.S. military strategy. The U.S. government sought only to protect South Korea, refusing to use its nuclear weapons in a war for containment of North Korea.

The Korean War continued for another two years. It was marked by bloody, inconclusive battles that failed to break the stalemate. In the course of the war, North Korean cities were destroyed by intensive U.S. aerial bombardments. Responsible for the outbreak of hostilities, Stalin apparently prevented a compromise settlement. It confirmed his grim view of the inevitability of capitalist war, and forced Communist China to depend on the Soviet alliance and Stalin's leadership. In 1951 the first peace negotiations began, only to stall over minor issues of prisoner repatriation raised by the Communists.

Shortly after his death in 1953 the prisoner issue no longer mattered to the communist negotiators. Both Chinese and Soviet governments were suddenly eager to bring both the Korean and the Indochina wars to an end. They undoubtedly knew of the threat by President Eisenhower's new administration to increase its military effort in Korea. They also may have heard the rumors (spread intentionally by the U.S. government) that it was considering the use of nuclear weapons. The Korean War ended in

1953 in an armistice, but that was sufficient for the Chinese, Soviet, and U.S. negotiators. The leaders of North and South Korea had to accept the decision.

North Korea remained under the rule of Kim Il Sung and the Communist Party. For the next half-century, he adhered to dogmatic Stalinist ideology. Kim became North Korea's Great Leader and the subject of public adulation. He maintained a strict one-party dictatorship, and kept industry and agriculture in a rigid command economy long after it was abandoned in China. The army prospered, sending infiltrators over the demilitarized zone into the south and periodically threatening to resume the crusade for national unification. The Communists forbade any communications with the south. Until the end of the century, Stalinism had a secure home in North Korea.

In the south, Syngman Rhee's authoritarian regime had charge of recovery from war. After his death in 1965, a series of military rulers seized control of the government. They threw the country's meager resources into building an industrial economy. Their statist methods of "guided capitalism" closely resembled the Japanese model. To increase savings (and funds for investment), they imposed stringent controls on consumption, even forbidding Koreans to take their vacations outside the country. By the 1980s, their methods and the people's industriousness succeeded in creating a South Korean "economic miracle." Their troops, assisted by an entire U.S. Army division, were permanently stationed along the demilitarized zone. The division of the globe into rival armed camps was a visible part of the Korean peninsula.

Revolutionary China

The Chinese leaders faced enormous problems implementing their revolutionary plans. They had extensive experience governing comparatively small areas during their years of guerrilla war. Suddenly they found themselves in control of a land larger than the continental United States with a population approaching 600 million. Among these people were many who had fought for or supported the Communists' enemies. Political convictions and self-interest had incited many Chinese to work with the Nationalists, while others had collaborated with the Japanese. China remained an impoverished country, severely damaged by decades of war, whose new leaders dreamed of building a socialist society of abundance and equality. The revolution had a great distance to go, and some of its leaders, especially Mao, were very impatient.

The formation of the structure of a new state came first. The ruling organs of the Chinese People's Republic state copied the Soviet one-party system. When the new constitution went into effect in 1954, it gave the Chinese state a National Assembly, chosen by popular election, whose responsibilities included selection of the president of the Republic and of the Council of Ministers. The new order formally acknowledged the existence of national minorities by creating an "autonomous region" for each people. Tibetans, Turks, Mongols possessed (in theory) the right to their own local government, schools, and culture. Behind this democratic facade lay, as in the Soviet Union, the monopoly of power of the Communist Party. All candidates to elected political positions had the advance approval of party authorities. Only one candidate for any office ever appeared on electoral ballots. Voters merely registered their approval of the party's decisions. Communists appointed in Beijing kept firm control over the autonomous regions, where units of the PLO were ready to repress national unrest. Democracy meant what the leaders of the Chinese Communist

Party believed served best the revolution and enhanced their authority.

The Communist Party itself followed the Leninist principle of centralization of command in the hands of the Central Committee and the Politburo. Mao Zedong was chairman of these powerful committees. He held also the positions of president of the Republic and head of the People's Liberation Army. Taken altogether, these responsibilities confirmed his preeminence over the state and the party. His authority was uncontested in those years. Like Stalin, whose power and eminence Mao admired, he set the guidelines for state and party policy. The fate of China lay in his hands, to the extent that any man could exercise supreme power in so enormous and complex a country. Around the great square in Beijing were hung the portraits of the intellectual giants of revolutionary Marxism, beginning with Marx and Engels, then Lenin and Stalin, and finally Mao. This picture of the "apostolic succession" of world communism elevated Mao to the rank of world leader.

Making a socialist revolution on the ruins of the oldest civilization in the world required the purging of enemies and the elimination of rival ideologies. The Communists' measures for the "repression of the enemy classes" began with a purge of the population conducted by the army, the courts, and the secret police (the National Security Forces). A law against "counter-revolutionaries" in 1951 encouraged mass meetings and public denunciations of anticommunists. No one knows the numbers arrested and sentenced; moderate estimates mention one to three million executions. A vast system of prison camps emerged in remote parts of the country to "reeducate" the prisoners, many of whom spent decades as forced laborers. The "party-state" did not tolerate diversity of religion or political persuasion. It imposed its own ideological mold on the country's intellectual and cultural life.

The social reforms undertaken in those years were directed against the subjugation and "bonds" that had held together imperial Chinese society. The Communists' attack on old China included among their targets the traditional family, which was the bastion of Confucianism and ancestor worship. They championed the principle of the equality of rights of women. Applied to Chinese society, it required the abolition of the old marriage practices, including infant and forced marriage, concubinage, and infanticide. Divorce became legal, as did abortion. The new regime wiped out the practice of foot binding, which had been a symbol of women's subjugation and a relic of that "feudal" past whose destruction was key to the success of the revolution. All these reforms were contained in the family law of 1950. It challenged the customs of centuries.

These reforms could become effective only after massive propaganda campaigns and new edicts drove home the message that the revolution would not spare the family. In those years, the regime promoted birth-control methods to limit the rapid growth of the population. Other new social policies included ruthless campaigns against drug addiction, which was virtually wiped out within a few years, and against illiteracy, which slowly diminished. Political dictatorship and sweeping social reforms brought the power of the new state and of the party into the personal lives of the Chinese population.

The Great Leap Forward

Stalin's death in early 1953 opened a new period in Soviet relations with China. The new Soviet leaders publicly acknowledged China's status as an equal in the "socialist camp." They renounced the special territor-

ial concessions that Stalin had obtained. They expanded their economic aid program, providing China in the following five years with machinery, credits, and technical assistance worth billions of dollars. The next few years were a honeymoon in the relations between the Soviet Union and China.

Following the Soviet example, the Chinese leaders adopted the principal institutions of the Soviet command economy—command planning, collectivization, and rapid industrialization. In 1955, they launched their first Five-Year Plan for economic development. That same year Mao ordered the party to begin a rapid campaign for farm collectivization on the Soviet model. In 1955 the state nationalized the remaining private commercial and industrial enterprises. Imitating Soviet practices, the Chinese leaders strictly limited peasant consumption in order to turn agricultural production to the benefit of the cities and the industrial population.

By 1956, the entire Chinese economy was under state control. Mao expected miracles of socialist development, pointing to the Soviet experience to justify his claim. "The Soviet Union's great historical experience in building socialism inspires our people," he wrote that year, "and gives them full confidence that they can build socialism in their country." Never again did he refer in such glowing terms to Soviet socialism.

In fact, within a year Mao denounced (at first in private, then publicly) the Soviet leaders for failing in their commitment to socialism. It is not clear what happened to bring him to that startling reversal of opinion. He revealed later that he judged the Soviet leaders guilty of permitting the existence in their country of substantial inequalities in salaries and incomes. To him, this amounted to the revival of capitalism and the decay of socialism. He attacked the Soviet bureaucracy, whom he believed guilty of corruption and profiteering. In Marxist terms, he was right on both counts, but later events proved that his own utopian socialism was equally flawed.

The conflict quickly assumed the proportions of a religious schism. In the spirit of a Protestant church reformer challenging the Catholic papacy during the Reformation in sixteenth-century Europe, Mao believed that he, better than any other Communist, understood how to achieve a just, egalitarian socialist society. The conflict between the Soviet Union and China began in the tones of a doctrinal quarrel. United until then by their universal vision and shared ideals, they proceeded to condemn each other as sinful heretics.

In early 1958, Mao set out to prove that the Chinese way to socialism was the correct path. He based his hopes on his conviction that the Chinese masses were capable of such prodigies of work, of such superhuman efforts, and of such radical improvements in their collective institutions that their willpower and his leadership would bring to China in a few years both abundance and social equality. He wrote that the "600 million people of China" were like a "clean sheet of paper" on which "the newest and most beautiful pictures [could] be painted." He asked that they assist him in a "Great Leap Forward."

In concrete terms, his vision required that China abandon the Soviet-type economic policies that it had just adopted a few years before. Economic planning had to end, for it was misguided and harmful. He argued that in a year Chinese workers and peasants could by their own efforts raise economic production by 100 percent, could complete enormous dams and flood control projects, and could transform collective farming into communistic farming. He demanded the creation of "people's communes" in the countryside, relatively few in number and grouping up to 100,000 peasant households, to replace the collective farms. They were to

be organized on egalitarian principles, with no special benefits to good workers and no separate garden plots or private houses. Families would organize their lives collectively, with meals and childcare provided by the commune. Mao wrote just before the campaign got underway that "there is no difficulty in the world" the masses cannot overcome "if only they take their destiny into their own hands." Since mass work was required, more Chinese were needed, and birth control had to end (it did not return until twenty years later when the country's population had grown by another 300 million). The Great Leap Forward revealed Mao's extraordinary revolutionary populism and utopianism.

The reality was disaster. The worst consequences resulted from the radical reorganization of agriculture. Peasant farmers lost the incentive to work, were taken from their farming for great irrigation and flood prevention projects, and spent long hours in political indoctrination meetings. Agricultural production in 1959 and 1960 declined so seriously that famine spread through the Chinese countryside. The full extent of the catastrophe of the early 1960s became public knowledge decades later. Despite severe rationing and the decision in 1961 to import large quantities of grain, millions of Chinese rural inhabitants died (recent estimates suggest more than 40 million) as a result of famine, hunger, and disease. Mao's disastrous experiment in mass mobilization was responsible. These critical conditions permitted Mao's opponents in the party leadership to end the Great Leap Forward. They publicly criticized "guerrilla methods" in governing the country and took control of the government by pushing aside Mao, who complained he was being treated like a "dead ancestor." He was, temporarily, dethroned, but his authority as Great Helmsman of the Chinese revolution ensured his stature in the party. For a few years, he had to suppress his dissatisfaction with the course of his country's development. His vision of egalitarian socialism no longer set policy, and his influence dwindled among the party leadership.

His revolutionary policies hastened the breakup of the Sino-Soviet alliance. Many issues divided China and the Soviet Union in the late 1950s. Disputes over territorial questions and differing policies toward the United States were bound to strain the ties between the two most powerful communist states. In 1960, Mao accused the Soviet Communists of betraying Leninism and selling out the cause of world revolution. In retaliation, the Soviet leaders stopped all Soviet assistance, refusing any further help in Chinese nuclear development and breaking the economic aid agreement. Within a few weeks, all Soviet technicians left and factories being built by the Russians stood abandoned. To Soviet leaders, good relations with neutral Third World countries became as important as their relations with China. At about the same time as their quarrel erupted with China, they agreed to sell arms to India. In the circumstances, it was a hostile act toward China.

India and China had been unable to settle a territorial dispute on their long Himalayan frontier. In 1950, Chinese troops had conquered and annexed the kingdom of Tibet. They later began building a strategic highway into that land from the northwest through mountainous territory claimed by India. Rebellious peoples, Turkic in the west and Tibetan in the southwest, lived in territories at both ends of the projected road. The Chinese government wanted rapid access to these lands in the event of unrest. In fact, in 1957, the Tibetan people did rebel against the Chinese. Tibet had become a Chinese colony. The strategic highway's use in keeping together this new Chinese empire was clear.

The Chinese government was determined to establish its control over the territory claimed by India. By 1960, the quarrel had become a military crisis. The Indian government refused to cede the area needed and began to move its own troops there. Although isolated, the Chinese leaders prepared for war. In 1962, their troops, operating in difficult mountainous areas all along the Indian border, attacked and defeated Indian forces in a brief border war (see Chapter 8). Having occupied the area of the highway, they halted the war. Without any outside support—the Soviet Union remained neutral—the Chinese regime had proven that it was a major power in Asia.

⚜ SPOTLIGHT: The Dalai Lama ⚜

For most of his life, the Dalai Lama (1935–) has been a political refugee. He remains the legitimate leader of the Buddhists of Tibet, though he had to flee the country in 1959 to escape imprisonment by the Chinese Communists who ruled his land. He, like many millions of other political refugees in the twentieth century, became the victim of war and revolution.

As practiced in Tibet, the Buddhist religion had for many centuries formed the core of the life of the population in that remote mountainous kingdom. The Dalai Lama is the name given to the person, chosen while still an infant, who is believed to be the reincarnation (reappearance after death) of the spirit of the Buddha himself. Monks in Tibet's many monasteries preserved the religious teachings of the Buddha. They regarded the Dalai Lama as the source of wisdom and guidance in religions and political affairs. Until the twentieth century, these monasteries were the center of Tibetan life, and the source of law and public order. The Dalai Lama was, in effect, absolute ruler as well as religious leader, a "God-King." For a time, Tibetan leaders had recognized Chinese suzerainty (political authority) over the country. Still, nothing the Chinese Empire did threatened their way of life and religion.

When the Western world (first in the form of British explorers) "discovered" Tibet, they brought with them tools of modern life unknown to Tibetans. Electric power and steam engines suddenly became tangible, and desirable items. The Tibetan rulers had need of a foreign policy, ambassadors, and a postal system. In 1911, the collapse of the Chinese Empire was their chance to proclaim Tibet an independent country.

That calm period ended when the Chinese Communists invaded their land in 1950. As soon as the Chinese Communists had conquered the central regions of China, they moved their troops to the western borderlands, claimed by right of imperial heritage. Tibet, with a tiny army and primitive weapons, was an easy conquest. The Communists claimed to have "liberated" Tibet from the "imperialists." Their conquest and subjugation of the land resembled the policies of a conquering empire. They brought to the Buddhist people of Tibet their own version of modernity. It included war on religion, the end to monastic rule, and the exploitation of the natural resources (including

Dalai Lama (*Photograph courtesy Freda Utley/Stillwell Collection/Hoover Institution*)

uranium) hidden in the remote region. The life of Tibetans was never the same again.

In the first years of Chinese rule, the Dalai Lama (still a young man) tried to conciliate the Communists and to preserve Buddhist practices. He had had little contact with foreigners, but had begun to learn of the world beyond the Himalayas from occasional visitors (and from two German prisoners-of-war who had fled captivity in India). India was Tibet's other powerful neighbor, and a land where respect for the Buddhist religion was widespread. The Dalai Lama could expect moral support from Indians, and even might hope for diplomatic backing from the Indian government. Until the border war erupted between India and China, the Indian leaders discouraged him from challenging the Chinese invaders. He had to become a player in the "great game" of power politics in those crisis years.

Mao's Great Leap Forward brought the full force of the Communists' anti-religious campaign to Tibet. In early 1957, Chinese Communists and PLA soldiers began systematicly destroying Tibetan Buddhism, attacking the monasteries, expelling the monks, destroying religious relics, and tearing down the ancient buildings. The Dalai Lama's deepest religious and political convictions required that he speak out against these vicious measures. They aimed at the "extermination of the religion and culture of the Tibetan race." He risked his own life in condemning the Communists. In 1957, Tibetans joined in a massive revolt against their Chinese rulers. The PLA was there to suppress the rebellion, though it took fourteen years to do so.

The Dalai Lama could no longer remain in his country. In the midst of the violence, he secretly fled across the high mountain passes to India in 1959. There, with more than 100,000 Tibetan refugees, he asked for political asylum. Though the Chinese Communists protested India's "imperialist" intervention in their affairs, the Indian government agreed to their request. The Chinese victory in the Sino-Indian war of 1962 insured that the Dalai Lama's exile would last for a long time.

He and his followers created what they called "Tibet in exile," located in one of the old British hill stations in the Himalayan foothills. He continued to act as the true leader of the Tibetan community, heading a government-in-exile and receiving foreign statesmen. Prime Minister Nehru was the first to visit. His was a discouraging message, for the Indian government would not back the cause of Tibetan independence. Secret messengers kept the Dalai Lama in touch with Tibetans living in Tibet. He devoted his time largely to religious matters, but politics kept intruding in his life. The agonies of the Buddhists during Mao's Great Cultural Revolution brought from him expressions of sympathy and pleas to the Chinese for toleration, all to no avail. Tibetans again revolted against the Chinese, and for several years fought a desperate guerrilla war. But the Chinese were too strong.

In 1974, the Dalai Lama begged his followers to cease armed resistance. He presented to Tibetans a pacifist program of opposition, arguing for nonviolence in defense of the rights and liberties of his people. At first, he called for a neutral Tibet that would take no part in the power politics of Asian states; later he asked only for full autonomy for Tibet within the People's Republic. For his courage and moral strength, the Dalai Lama won the Nobel Peace Prize in 1989. The Chinese leaders paid no attention to his proposals and denounced his "subversive" activities. Exile was to be his fate.

The Cultural Revolution

The years between 1960 and 1966 were a period of temporary calm in China before a new and even more violent revolutionary offensive by Mao and his supporters. The people's communes were disbanded and smaller collective farms reinstalled. The recovery of agriculture required a large investment of state funds, allocated in those years according to pragmatic criteria of need and productivity.

Although powerless to prevent these changes, Mao refused to compromise. He rebuked his colleagues for their "bourgeois" spirit contrary to true communism. He promoted his ideals—and his cult—in a little red book entitled *Quotations from Chairman Mao*. Its distribution was assured by the People's Liberation Army, which printed one billion copies to make sure copies went to the entire Chinese population and to foreign supporters. Its most ardent readers were China's youth, among whom admiration for the Great Helmsman was deep and unquestioning. Mao welcomed their "socialist education" and their support for his ideals.

By the mid-1960s, he became convinced that his revolution was caught in an ongoing conflict between forces of evil—his enemies—and of good—the masses, the army, and the students. He imagined Chinese youth to be uncorrupted by avarice or ambition, and ready for combat against "enemy classes." His immediate objective was to end the "counter-revolutionary restoration" of those he called a new "exploiting bourgeoisie"—well-paid professionals, intellectuals, and party bureaucrats. In a manner recalling Stalin's Great Terror, he prepared to undertake a new class war against his own party and the educated elite of his country.

The decade of turmoil that began in 1966 had no parallel in the history of earlier revolutions. It involved both the Chinese state and society. It undermined party institutions and rule, produced a prolonged upheaval in education, industry, and agriculture, and destroyed the works of traditional Chinese culture. So chaotic were conditions that the full story remains obscure. In 1966, Mao was still the revered leader of his people, able to mobilize supporters among the students, workers, and soldiers to participate in what he referred to as a Cultural Revolution. That year he made clear whom the enemies were, warning that "the bourgeois agents who have infiltrated the party, the government, the army, and all sectors of cultural life constitute a gang of counter-revolutionary revisionists."

Mao's principal weapon in this class war was a mass movement to promote his "Great Proletarian Cultural Revolution." His immediate goal was nothing less than the destruction of the old party leadership and the creation of a new revolutionary regime, consisting of "revolutionary mass organizations" running a country rid of greedy bureaucrats, profit seekers, and egotistical intellectuals. Somehow he managed to win sufficient backing from party leaders to begin a campaign that they must have known threatened their policies and their power. In 1966, he obtained the authority to create and to lead a special committee charged with organizing his Cultural Revolution. This organization started a propaganda campaign in mid-1966 calling on all 700 million Chinese to "destroy the old world." The first recruits for the Cultural Revolution came from the student youth, organized in units called Red Guards. That fall all regular university and high school studies ceased (the interruption lasted nearly ten years). Students had better things to do than learn, for Mao called them to lead his new revolution.

The Red Guards were the revolutionary organization of Chinese youth. Their appearance coincided with Mao's emergence at the head of the Cultural Revolution. That August, he gathered together 1 million Red Guard youths at the Gate of Heavenly Peace in Beijing, appearing before them just as the sun rose in the east. His message was simple: "Destroy the old and construct the new." That fall and winter violence swept the country as these self-proclaimed revolutionaries organized mass demonstrations, attacked alleged counter-revolutionaries, imprisoned party officials, and destroyed old monuments and precious relics of China's past. Centers of resistance emerged when party officials mobilized their own supporters to oppose this children's crusade. Street demonstrations often degenerated into open fighting between rival political factions.

The next ten years were a time of extraordinary turmoil. Serious disorders accompanied the attack on party officials and factory administrations. Rival groups of Red Guards fought for leadership and battled with worker organizations claiming to defend the true Maoist line. Punishment for "class enemies" included public humiliation, exile to the countryside, imprisonment, even death by beating. Cities like Canton and Shanghai experienced so much violence that the conditions there resembled civil war.

Soon units of the People's Liberation Army began to intervene to enforce a minimum of public order in China's cities and towns. In 1967, Mao authorized the army to supervise the economic and political affairs of the provinces. The army commanders did not seek to militarize the Chinese state. Instead, they organized revolutionary committees, grouping representatives of workers, students, and the military in very disorderly and unstable coalitions. They replaced the old regional and city party committees, which were a prime target in the Cultural Revolution. The guiding principle of action of these committees was the "three loyal-

ties": loyalty to the "person, the thought, and the policies" of Mao Zedong. Maoism was the very essence of the Cultural Revolution.

Mao's revolutionary regime proved incapable either of governing the country effectively or of establishing new institutions for socialist revolution. The PLA became by default the backbone of political rule throughout the country. At a party congress held in early 1969, the head of the PLA, Lin Biao, second only to Mao in political power, proclaimed that the Great Cultural Revolution had triumphed. The reality appears to have been endemic disorder and chaos. PLA provincial military commanders held onto meager remnants of political authority in the country. The tasks of industrial construction, training of professionals, and scientific research had all been abandoned in the upheaval. Hundreds of thousands of scientists, specialists, and teachers were forced to seek "reeducation" by performing menial tasks in agricultural communes. China had entered a period of permanent revolution from which it did not finally emerge until after Mao's death in 1976.

In those years, relations with the Soviet Union became so strained that war appeared likely. Mao's supporters treated the Soviet Union as if it had become the principal enemy of China. The Chinese press published maps that claimed for China most of eastern Siberia as part of China (the Chinese Empire had exercised a distant supervision of these lands before the nineteenth century). Pitched battles erupted with Soviet forces on the Manchurian border in 1969; sporadic violence broke out all along the enormous Chinese–Soviet frontier that year and the next. The Soviet government concluded that Mao was as dangerous and aggressive as Hitler had once been. They believed the threat of war with China so serious that they moved large military forces, including nuclear missiles, to their eastern region bordering China. The conflict between the Soviet Union and China became a new cold war.

Gradually other party leaders, appalled by the internal turmoil and foreign danger Mao had created, brought an end to the period of revolutionary zealotry of the Cultural Revolution. Zhou Enlai, the chairman of the council of ministers and the most influential moderate party leader, resumed his role in policy making. The process by which power changed hands again remains unclear. In 1972, the party leaders formally disbanded the Red Guards. Most of its members were sent to work in the countryside, where they could no longer champion Mao's Cultural Revolution. But as long as Mao remained alive, no one challenged his utopian vision of Chinese socialism, and no new reforms appeared to provide a remedy to the havoc that his policies had created.

"To Get Rich Is Glorious"

In the late 1970s, this Maoist revolutionary order fell apart. The key that opened the door to sweeping changes in China's economic system was Mao's death in 1976. He received all the honors due the founding father of the new China. He was elevated to the status of "venerated ancestor" for citizens of the People's Republic. His survivors could do no less, for their power ultimately rested on the revolution that he had launched. Mao's successors had learned by painful experience from their leader's terrible utopian experiments. Abiding poverty for over one-half of the population, who still had barely enough food for survival, was too great a price to pay for socialist egalitarianism. The future development of China, and their own authority, depended on putting China on the road to economic growth.

By 1978, all Maoist supporters had fallen from power. A new party leadership, headed by Deng Xiaoping, was in a position to bring to an end the quarter-century of Mao's destructive revolutionary experiments. That year Deng declared publicly that Maoism was "wrong in its theories, policies, and slogans." After a quarter-century of utopian experiments, communist dreams ceased to have any role in economic policies.

The new leadership sought pragmatic reforms that would give the Chinese population the opportunity and incentive to get to work. Education, science, and technology became a high priority. Command planning was curtailed. Foreigners obtained the right to open their own businesses. Private traders could offer goods of their choosing and at prices that the market could bear.

Deng drew the line at nationalized industry. He was unwilling to abandon the enormous network of state-run factories, which remained a foundation of China's socialist economy and an assurance of worker support. Their guarantee of work, housing, and welfare to their employees and workers created what observers called China's "iron rice bowl." Deng did order that these nationalized enterprises, notoriously inefficient, earn profits on their production. Events proved his hope to be misplaced as the factories continued to lose money, surviving only on state subsidies.

Deng's immediate concern was to give the Chinese rural population the economic incentive to raise food production. China's very survival depended on their efforts. The end of collective farming had the greatest impact on the lives of the Chinese masses, most of whom still lived in the countryside. In 1978, the new leaders revised so thoroughly the regulations that had kept farmland under state supervision that they in effect returned farms to individual ownership. Prices on farm produce were largely freed from state controls, permitting the farmers to make profits from their work. In the years that followed, the government opened private commercial networks to bring to the countryside consumer goods desired by the farmers. These soon included expensive durable items like refrigerators, television sets, and motorcycles imported from Japan. The formula was remarkably successful.

Within a short time, Chinese farmers were able to double the level of the country's farm production. They introduced new, highly productive strains of rice and wheat that had been developed a decade before in the West as part of the "Green Revolution." By the mid-1980s, China had a surplus of food for export. By then, the economy was expanding by the remarkable rate of ten percent each year. At the end of the decade, only one-tenth of the population (still 100 million people) were still living in poverty. Deng Xiaoping himself proclaimed that the motto for the new China was: "To get rich is glorious!"

Chinese socialism survived in the rhetoric of the Communist Party. The party-state was sacred. Its powers grew even greater when in 1980 it dictated a birth-control policy restricting each family to only one child. Penalties for violations were very strict, at times brutal. At the extreme, local officials could force a pregnant woman who had exceeded the limit of children to have an abortion. The leaders could find no alternative to controlling the rapid rise in population, which by then had passed 1 billion.

The Chinese Communist Party possessed all the means of repression of a dictatorship. Its leaders were prepared to wield these brutal methods when their power was challenged by the democracy movement in the late 1980s. The supporters of democratic reforms, drawn largely from China's intellectual elite and student population, asked for representative government and free speech.

They drew their ideas from Western liberal institutions and from the political reforms under way in the Soviet Union (see Chapter 11). The movement grew so powerful that in the spring of 1989 its supporters organized massive demonstrations in Beijing against the party dictatorship. They were backed by many workers, but had no encouragement from the country's rural population. Political liberty remained an affair of China's urban population. Symbolizing their goal was a statue baptized the Goddess of Democracy, which demonstrators constructed in the center of Beijing (Tiananmen Square).

The party leaders refused any compromise with those they considered "counter-revolutionaries." They could not conceive of any weakening of their single-party dictatorship. Their revolution was irreversible, for they still believed, like Stalin and Mao, that history was on their side. In early June 1989, they called in reliable army units to disperse the demonstrators, thousands of whom were killed or injured.

The party leadership insisted that the party alone possessed the wisdom to lead the people to socialism. But no one claimed to know what a real socialist society was or when it would emerge in China. The Chinese government increasingly emphasized its nationalist program for a united China. Chinese migrants moved, with state support, into borderland territories of non-Han peoples in the western regions of Tibet and Sinjiang. Ethnic Chinese nationalism was a threat to these peoples, but movements among them to claim political rights met with immediate repression. The Chinese government demanded that Great Britain cede Hong Kong, Britain's small colony on China's southern coast. The British complied, handing the territory to the Chinese Republic in 1995. The Chinese Communists threatened periodically to invade Taiwan, which had become a prosperous country integrated in the global economy. Claiming to be the legitimate heir to the Chinese Empire gave the communists the stature of champions of the Chinese nation.

The post-Mao leaders redefined their foreign policy goals in those years to place national interests above world revolution. Their invitation to President Nixon to visit Beijing in 1972 signaled the beginning of normal diplomatic relations with the United States. By the end of the century, the United State had become the most important market for China's exports. The Chinese Communists ended their quarrel with the Soviet Union as well, though the two states never returned to the earlier alliance. Maoism was dead, and past wars, though not forgotten, did not get in the way of power politics. In the world of the 1990s China was a major independent power in East Asia.

☯ HIGHLIGHT: Revolution and Command Economies ☯

When independent nation-states spread through Asian lands, many of their leaders turned to the Soviet Union to learn how their countries could build a modern industrial economy. Stalin repeatedly proclaimed that his country was well on its way to the "shining future" of socialism. His prestige was at its peak in the years after the war. He and his supporters had no doubts that Soviet victory in war had come thanks to the socialist system that he and his party had imposed in the 1930s. History, they announced, was on their side. The argument made many converts, not only among Communists but also among nationalists in former colonial lands who repudiated Western capitalism along with Western colonial rule.

The great attraction of the Stalinist reforms lay in their apparent ability to insure rapid economic growth and their features that seemed to meet the ideal of socialism. In other words, they were both a means to industrial development and a socialist end in themselves. The term "command economy" best describes the Stalinist economic system, since the state possessed the powers to control all economic activities—in industry, commerce, and agriculture—and issued the commands that set production, price and wage targets. The goal was to maximize resources for economic development. When the communist regimes in China and Vietnam set out to bring revolution into the lives of their peoples, they recreated the institutions and policies of this command economy. Many nationalist regimes in Asian and African countries also introduced important aspects of this system. During the half-century after the Second World War, the economies of countries throughout the Third World resembled more closely that of the Soviet Union than Western capitalism.

Two characteristics of the command economy were particularly important in its operations. The first was the ownership and supervision by the state of all productive property within that state. The second was the control by the state of all trade with foreign countries. Taken together, these powers brought state administration in the economic affairs of the population to a far greater extent than existed in capitalist countries. Nationalization was an essential step in creating a command economy. In the Soviet Union, as later in Communist China, the government issued decrees soon after the seizure of power dispossessing all the owners of industrial enterprises and commercial businesses. Even agricultural production came under the supervision of the state after collectivization of private farms.

The only private property left in the hands of individuals were their personal possessions and, in the countryside, the houses and surrounding plots of land where the peasants lived (and at times even these were taken away). Private production and sales for profit became illegal. The authorities denounced these vestiges of "capitalist" behavior. Illegal private trading never disappeared from the command economies, since their inefficient distribution system and endemic shortages created a ready market for some goods. But the state declared this private trade the work of criminals, to be punished by imprisonment and, in extreme cases, even death. The command economy of the communist regimes justified the repression of activities that in free market economies brought profit and praise.

All foreign economic operations also fell under the supervision of the state. Governmental agencies were responsible for the purchase of goods and services from foreign countries. Other agencies decided whether and what amounts of goods from its country should be sold abroad. The command economy permitted the state to isolate its people from the outside world more completely than Western countries during the 1930s depression. No international corporation or bank could make decisions that directly helped or hindered its plans for economic growth. The fluctuations of international prices could not block the import of items its leaders judged useful or desirable. At a time when Western economies were moving toward an interdependent global economy, communist regimes kept tight reins on all foreign transactions. They were protected from capitalist interference and were also cut off from the technological innovations of the Western economies. Most important, these controls assured the political leadership enormous power over the economies of their countries.

The socialist economies operated at the command of the state. In countries like the Soviet Union or the People's Republic of China, the state in turn was under the control of the Communist Party. Its political dictatorship extended into all areas of economic activity, in theory governed by the plans created by state planning agencies. The "science" of command planning made fulfillment of the yearly plans the key measure of the success of economic activity. Managers of the state enterprises executed the orders of their ministries, while workers followed the orders of their factory bosses. No labor unions were permitted to hinder production by calling strikes, which were illegal.

The consumers whose living conditions depended upon this tightly controlled economy had to take what goods they could find, at prices fixed not by supply and demand but by state ministries. The socialist society guaranteed jobs to workers and a minimally adequate standard of living for all consumers. Choices were few, but everyone enjoyed a certain measure of security. Leaders like Mao Zedong altered important elements of the system, but never considered abandoning it. Socialism for them was unthinkable without maintaining its essential qualities.

Yet it hid fundamental flaws so serious that by the 1990s, socialism had vanished from almost all the countries where it had existed. These defects included the inability to assimilate effectively and rapidly technological innovations, the disregard for the choices of the population, a very low level of agricultural productivity, complete indifference to the environmental damage caused by economic projects, and incompetence of the officials who ran the system. In effect, the command economic system turned the entire economy of a country into one great corporation, whose board of directors consisted of the political leaders of state, whose employees worked in a vast bureaucratic network of ministries, and whose products enjoyed an absolute monopoly on the market.

Nowhere in the system did there exist any incentive to take risks, such as introducing more productive farming, experimenting with more productive methods of manufacturing, or offering new products for consumers. Beginning in the 1950s, Western economies undertook a vast retooling as electronic, telecommunication, and computer technologies brought revolutionary new methods of production and communication. Nothing comparable happened in the communist countries.

There, state ministries continued to prescribe gigantic economic undertakings that fulfilled the plans but wasted scarce resources. These projects were of little use to consumers, whose most effective means to acquire new products was the black market. They also did grave damage to the environment, for no organizations or laws forced the ministries to take account of environmental costs. But the flaw that ultimately undermined the entire system was the unfitness and corruption of the political and economic leaders. They held in their hands the wealth of their country, but had little interest and no training in how to use that wealth productively.

The all-powerful state bureaucracy was increasingly tempted to profit from its economic power and influence. These officials lived in seclusion in conditions immeasurably more comfortable than any ordinary citizen. Large numbers of officials took bribes in exchange for personal favors, extending even to illegal, black market operations. In the 1950s, one eastern European critic of the command economy called the communist bosses a "new class" who exploited their economies as ruthlessly as nineteenth-century capitalists. They failed to keep the promise of socialism and were incapable of achieving the economic performance of the capitalist countries. In economic terms, the command economy proved ultimately to be bankrupt.

WAR AND REVOLUTION
IN INDOCHINA

On the southern edges of China, the land that the French had named Indochina passed from the French to the Japanese Empire in the early years of the Second World War. In the late nineteenth century, the French had created in the region one colony made of many peoples, among whom the Vietnamese and the Khmer were the two largest ethnic groups (and were bitter enemies). Indochina was also divided by religion, with many Buddhists but also an important Catholic community. Like China, its economy was based primarily on agriculture, with extensive large estates owned by a few wealthy landowners (many of them French) and worked by a poor peasant population. It resembled other colonial lands in the fact that, by the middle of the twentieth century, many of its people were prepared for nationalist revolt against colonial rule.

The French Colonial War

The colonial conflict in Indochina began in earnest at the end of the Second World War. The struggle was centered in the populous coastal region known as Vietnam. It provided the recruits for the Vietnamese Communist Party, whose founder and leader was Ho Chi Minh. He grew up and was educated in Vietnam, but left for Europe while a young man and did not return until 1940. For thirty years, he wandered through Europe and Asia. He spent several years in France, where he discovered the communist ideology and began his career as a revolutionary. He became an agent of Moscow's Communist International, helping the Chinese Communists and then creating in 1929 what he first called the Indochinese Communist Party. From that point on, his cause was independence and communism for Vietnam. He, like Mao Zedong, firmly believed in the inevitability of global proletarian revolution, one chapter in which was the fight against imperialism. He honored the leadership and wisdom of the Russian Communists, but, also like Mao, he and his party were an independent revolutionary party in the world communist movement.

The immediate objective of the Vietnamese Communists was the liberation of all Indochina from foreign rule. That struggle began with the war against Japan. In 1940, Ho organized and took charge of guerrilla war against the Japanese occupation forces. The jungles and mountains of Vietnam were the refuge of the guerrillas, while Japanese troops held onto the cities and coastal region. At war's end, the Japanese commander had, in a gesture of defiance of the Allies before surrendering, proclaimed Vietnam's independence. The withdrawal of his forces permitted the Vietnamese Communists, the principal anti-Japanese resistance force, to assume leadership of the Republic of Viet-

nam. Ho read in the course of the ceremony an independence statement that included passages from the American Declaration of Independence. He had no intention of following the American political path, but was keenly aware at the time of the need to convince the American forces in Asia of his reliability.

Prepared to negotiate with the postwar French government, Ho traveled to Paris in 1946. Had an agreement been reached there, Vietnam would very soon have become a communist state. The French colonial authorities were not impressed by his appeal to democratic principles. While talking of eventual freedom for Indochina, French officials and military commanders there were adamantly opposed to granting power to the Vietnamese Communists. Resolved to restore some form of French colonial authority, in 1946 they attacked the communist-occupied areas in Vietnam and quickly moved their troops into the inland regions of Cambodia (land of the Khmers) and Laos. The Communists and their nationalist allies retreated to the countryside, where they, like their Chinese comrades to the north, resumed guerrilla war.

In its first years solely a French colonial war, the conflict in Indochina entered the Cold War when the U.S. government intervened in 1950 on the side of the French. In the previous years, the war had not gone well for French forces. They had attempted to win the backing of nationalists there by creating in 1949 the independent states of Vietnam, Cambodia, and Laos. They still had to bear the principal burden of the bloody fighting. French generals promised quick victory against the communist guerrillas, but could not end the insurrection. Their army, made up of colonial forces as well as French soldiers, occupied key urban areas, but the countryside lay beyond their control.

In 1950, the U.S. government became actively involved in the Indochina war. It had previously judged the conflict to be a French effort to restore an outdated empire. The Cold War changed that view. By 1950, U.S. leaders had expanded the containment policy to include those colonial areas where communist insurrections were under way. In effect, they incorporated the Indochinese war into the global battle between the Free World and communism.

U.S. leaders believed that Ho's victory in Indochina would constitute a triumph for global communist forces. That was a misguided and ultimately tragic judgment. Its origins lay partly in the growing influence of anti-communist political forces within the United States, outraged at what they considered the "loss" of China. They were so committed to organizing the combat against communism that they paid no attention to the human and material cost that intervention in a colonial region like Indochina would entail. In the background was the pervasive fear of Stalin's expansionism. North Korea's aggression appeared proof of this theory. As a result, the French colonial forces found an ally in the U.S. government.

The United States began to provide France with military and economic aid for the war in Indochina. In return, it demanded of the French that they suppress the communist guerrillas. Not only was the French army unable to do so, but in the attempt it suffered a major military defeat. By 1953, its forces were overextended and weakened by its campaign to wipe out the communist insurrection. It could not protect its mountain fortress of Dienbienphu, encircled that year by the Communists. The surrender of the fort and its 10,000 troops in early 1954 ended the French efforts to retain control of Indochina.

That year a new French government concluded that their forces could not win the war. Their army had suffered 100,000 casualties in a conflict draining the wealth of the French economy for control of a distant country of no vital importance. The glories of colonial dominion in Asia no longer attracted them. Although the French army still occupied much of Indochina, the French government in 1954 agreed to negotiate with the Vietnamese Communists.

At that point the U.S. government expanded even further its involvement in Indochina. It was one of the participants at the Geneva conference that negotiated the end to the war. Representatives from the Communist and noncommunist Vietnamese governments and France were there, as were delegates from China and the Soviet Union. Peace in Indochina was an international affair. The French and American negotiators sought a partitioned Vietnam, limiting the Communists to the northern half of the country where their centers of strength were located.

Ho's delegates found no support, even from the Soviet Union and China, for the formation of a unified Vietnamese communist state. The Russians and Chinese, determined on a quick settlement to the war, promised Ho that he would soon attain his goal of national unification without further fighting. They assured him that his forces, still the only strong, organized political movement in northern and southern coastal areas of the country, would easily win all Vietnam in the elections that the peace negotiators planned to hold in 1956. Communists in other lands had proven adept at manipulating elections, through intimidation and violence, to win the voters to their side; Ho and his followers expected to do the same. National self-determination, the principle guiding this peace settlement, offered the Communists an apparently easy opportunity to take control of all Vietnam. Ho accepted the temporary partition of Vietnam, and in 1954 the French war in Indochina came to an end.

North and South Vietnam

The U.S. government was determined to prevent the Communist Party's seizure of the south. Although U.S. officials warned that South Vietnam had a slim chance to survive, the U.S. brought out of exile a nationalist leader, Ngo Dinh Diem, to become ruler of the new state. U.S. agents from the new international intelligence service, the Central Intelligence Agency (CIA), began to organize the hunt for Communists in the southern half of Vietnam. U.S. military advisers took over the task of forming a new Vietnamese army. U.S. economic and military aid poured into the country.

By 1960, South Vietnam had received more than 1 billion dollars in American assistance. This was vital to the very functioning of its state and economy. The result was the emergence of a U.S. political satellite under client nationalist leaders who could not survive without American aid. In President Kennedy's words, South Vietnam was "our offspring."

That effort at creating a noncommunist Vietnamese state represented an audacious gamble, probably doomed from the start. In a land divided by political rivalries and with no strong institutions or outstanding noncommunist nationalist leader to guarantee the stability of a new political order, state-building was in the best of circumstances a daunting task. Nearly 1 million refugees had fled from communist rule in the north, most of them Catholics fearing Ho's political dictatorship and repression of their religion. Most of the southern Vietnamese were poor peasants, reluctant to support either the Communists or the Diem regime for fear of persecution by the other side. Diem's main interest lay in strengthening his personal power. Like Syngman Rhee in South Korea, he was persuaded that by building an authoritarian regime he could defeat the

communist underground movement (called the Vietcong) in his infant country. With U.S. encouragement, he refused to hold the elections on Vietnam reunification scheduled for 1956. Instead, he built up his police and army, which were used primarily as instruments for internal repression. They proved effective in weakening the Communist Party, many of whose members by 1958 had moved to the north or were in prison.

His goal for South Vietnam was a conservative government protecting landowners and business and subsidized by the United States. A somewhat similar political formula had worked in South Korea at the end of the war there. But he had much less chance of making it work in his country. South Korea's leaders had in their favor their claim to be the rightful national heirs to the long history of a Korean state. Their regime had been independent since 1945. Diem lacked popular support among the Vietnamese and, more importantly, confronted a dynamic revolutionary movement determined to rid the country of what it called the "Western imperialists and their puppets."

After 1954, the North Vietnamese government quickly remade their country into a Soviet-style regime. It formed a single-party state, eliminating all political opposition. With Chinese and Soviet socialism as its model, it forced the peasant farmers into collective farms. In doing so, it disrupted agricultural production and, by its own later admission, permitted the party and police officials to use brutal repressive measures against the rural population. Ho Chi Minh pursued his revolution from above with a fanaticism equal to that of Stalin and Mao.

In 1959, Ho called once again for guerrilla war, this time in South Vietnam against Diem's regime. Communist cadres returned south along the secret "Ho Chi Minh trail" built on Cambodian territory, bringing military supplies and new directives to supporters there. The Communists' first targets were local rural officials, on whose shoulders rested the stability of Diem's rule in the countryside. Political assassination and intimidation spread in areas where the communist underground established new bases of operations.

The weakness of the South Vietnamese state quickly became apparent. Peasants preferred submitting to the communist agents, who protected those who helped them. Diem's officials feared for their lives (2,500 were assassinated in 1960) and retreated into fortified camps. By the end of that year, the communist insurrection had spread widely, and U.S. officials were warning that Diem's state was in serious danger. U.S.-sponsored state-building had not succeeded.

The new insurrection, begun in 1959, gathered strength from the widening circle of South Vietnamese enemies of Diem and the United States, and from the readiness of North Vietnam to commit all its resources to the struggle. Supplies for the guerrillas came partly from captured government material, partly from North Vietnam. Central leadership and party cadres came south to aid and direct the southern Communists. Still a conflict among Vietnamese, the fighting was in 1960 essentially a civil war that the Communists were close to winning.

U.S. Intervention in Vietnam

Then U.S. forces moved in. Opposition to Communist China had become a central feature of U.S. Asian containment policy after the outbreak of war in Korea. U.S. leaders did not consider the fighting in Vietnam to be merely a local conflict. To them, it appeared another step in global communist aggression. If not stopped in Indochina, they feared that other southeast Asian states would fall to communist insurrection "like a row of dominos." The new administration of President

John Kennedy, elected in 1960, judged the South Vietnam civil war to be part of a major struggle in the Cold War to prevent, in the words of one U.S. official, "China's swallowing up southeast Asia." Overly confident in the power of the United States, Kennedy and his advisers anticipated that greater military and economic assistance would assure Diem's victory. Indirect aid seemed the way to avoid direct U.S. military involvement in the war. Very soon, though, it proved insufficient to bring South Vietnam's victory. That failure only led to greater involvement. U.S. leaders were motivated both by the belief that communist conquest of the land would be a serious defeat for the containment policy, and by the conviction that U.S. military might was invincible in a local war. This tragic overconfidence led one U.S. senator later to judge his government guilty of "arrogance of power."

U.S. intervention in the conflict proceeded in two stages. In the first four years (1961–1965), it came in the form of increased military aid to the South Vietnamese army, which was responsible for the actual fighting. This policy brought supplies sufficient to double the army's size by 1963. It was trained by 15,000 U.S. military advisers, not yet combatants but close to it. The political weakness of the South Vietnamese state was far more serious than the problems confronting the Vietnamese army. Increasing numbers of South Vietnamese were opposed to Diem's authoritarian rule. His political ambitions did not match the actual strength of his regime, and he appeared incapable of winning popular support and of reforming his corrupt state.

In 1963, the United States backed a military coup in a desperate attempt to finding leaders capable of building a viable South Vietnamese state. Vietnamese generals, with the tacit approval of U.S. officials, stepped into the internal political struggle. They seized control of the government and assassinated

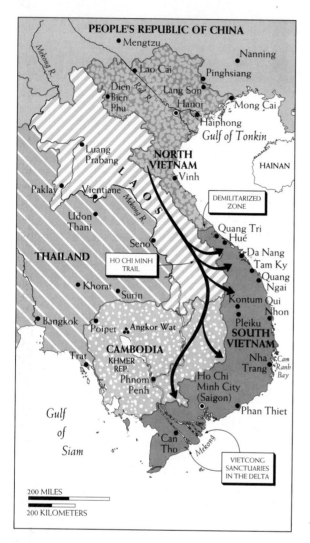

War in Vietnam

Diem (only a few days before President Kennedy's assassination in the United States). The U.S. officials in Vietnam hoped that the generals would restore order, end corruption, and strengthen the Vietnamese forces fighting the Vietcong.

Military rule only increased the internal disorder of the Vietnamese state. Within two years, ten different generals had attempted to rule the country in a self-destructive struggle for political leadership. The most serious consequence was the inability of any of the generals to halt the expansion of communist-controlled areas, which extended over entire provinces by late 1964. Guerrillas had even encircled the capital, Saigon, while Communist Party cadres operated freely in the city. The South Vietnam government had lost its claim to Vietnamese national leadership. Unless the United States itself took drastic action, within a few months the insurrection would succeed.

The prospect of "losing" South Vietnam was unacceptable to the U.S. government. President Kennedy's successor, Lyndon Johnson, was elected in 1964 primarily on a program of extensive domestic social and civil rights reform. Despite his commitment to what he called America's "Great Society," he had to turn his attention to Vietnam. Faced with impending communist victory, he decided that he could not become the "first president to lose a war." His advisers guaranteed quick victory if the United States intervened directly in the conflict. Persuaded by their arguments, Johnson set about organizing direct U.S. military involvement in Vietnam. He expanded enormously the presidential war-making powers. In early 1965, Johnson used those powers to order American combat forces into action in Vietnam. For the second time since the end of the Second World War, the United States entered a land war in Asia. The conflict did not resemble the Korean conflict, however. In guerrilla combat there existed no front lines. The enemy was everywhere, easily confused with the civilians. The only clear separation was that distinguishing Americans and Vietnamese. The Indochina war posed problems the U.S. military had never confronted before.

The formula for victory included two separate military operations. The U.S. objective remained limited, as in the Korean conflict, to the defense of the south. U.S. land forces were responsible, in collaboration with South Vietnamese troops, for the "pacification" of the south, that is, for the suppression of Vietcong guerrilla operations. At the same time, the U.S. military began aerial bombardment of North Vietnam in the expectation that they could force its leaders to end the communist insurrection in the south. The U.S. Air Force began the most intensive bombing campaign in its history.

The bombing failed to bring victory. North Vietnam, an agrarian economy, did not offer targets vital to its economic life, and its people were prepared to endure enormous suffering in that war of national liberation. At no time did the bombardment end the movement of supplies south to the guerrillas or force North Vietnam to seriously consider abandoning the war.

The land war in the south failed as well to achieve its main objective. By 1968, the United States had more than 500,000 troops in South Vietnam, nearly as many as the South Vietnamese Army. Assisting infantry operations, the U.S. Air Force conducted intensive bombing attacks in rural areas of South Vietnam. The immediate result of massive U.S. military involvement was to prevent a Vietcong victory.

The Communist guerrillas lacked the equipment and numbers to defeat the combined U.S.–South Vietnamese forces. They attempted in early 1968 one major offensive to seize urban areas in the south (the Tet offensive), only to suffer a crushing defeat. Their military strength dwindled by one-third, from 300,000 to 200,000, as a result of the bloody battles. North Vietnamese forces assumed the principal role in the fighting. The guerrillas dug hundreds of miles of underground tunnels, some thirty feet below ground, to escape the U.S. bombardments. Many soldiers died, but more took their place.

The diplomatic, political, economic, and human price of U.S. intervention in the Vietnam War grew to the point where it far exceeded the importance of victory to the United States. The most obvious result was heavy casualties among the South Vietnamese, helpless victims caught in the fighting between the two sides. As serious for Vietnam society was social disorder on a monumental scale. This was the result of the destruction of organized village life in many areas, the fall in agricultural production resulting from the bombing and the indiscriminate use of herbicides to defoliate forested regions, and the influx of 4 million refugees to the cities. The human suffering of the Vietnamese appeared out of all proportion to the limited war aims.

The cost to the United States, though it did not compare to Vietnam's hardship, was sufficient to cast grave doubt on the promised rewards of intervention. The total expense of air and ground fighting plus the aid granted the South Vietnamese government raised the price of war to more than $150 billion. Before war's end, the years of fighting left 50,000 U.S. soldiers dead. Within the United States, bitter political conflict arose when predictions of quick victory proved wrong. Many Americans recoiled at the brutality of the war, revealed to them by instant television coverage. The diplomatic price of U.S. intervention proved high as well. The war deflected attention and resources from larger issues of great power relations, such as Soviet-American arms control and the worsening conflicts in the Middle East. The very continuation of the Vietnam War represented a defeat for the United States.

In 1968, the combination of these factors forced the U.S. government to turn again to South Vietnamese armed forces. The new Nixon administration began peace negotiations with the North Vietnamese government. The next year it began the withdrawal of U.S. troops. "Vietnamization" meant passing responsibility for the war to the South Vietnam government, more dependent than ever on U.S. military and economic aid.

The new policy also brought one final effort to end the flow from the north of supplies to the guerrillas. The Ho Chi Minh trail passed through the neighboring neutral state of Cambodia. Years of secret U.S.

bombing had failed to prevent traffic, from bicycles to trucks, from moving along the jungle road. In 1970, American forces invaded Cambodia. The United States became the protector of an anti-communist military government there.

This escalation produced only a widening of conflict. North Vietnamese supplies continued to reach the south, for the jungle lay largely beyond the reach of U.S. infantry. Cambodian insurgents (Khmer Rouge) took over large areas of their country, with the military support of the North Vietnam Communists. The effect of that invasion was to bring Cambodia directly in the war. The Khmer Rouge began their own war of liberation against the United States and its Cambodian allies. Still the U.S. withdrawal from Indochina continued, until by 1972 no combat troops remained in Vietnam or Cambodia.

The disappearance of U.S. forces doomed the South Vietnamese regime. The United States and North Vietnam did negotiate a compromise peace settlement in 1973, but it left the way open for a communist victory. The Vietnamese Communists accepted the existence of the U.S.-backed government in South Vietnam. In exchange, the U.S. negotiators agreed not to demand the withdrawal from the southern territory of all North Vietnamese troops. The continued presence of substantial North Vietnamese forces in South Vietnam gave them the bases from which to launch a new offensive when the right moment arrived.

The South Vietnamese leaders recognized the danger, and refused to sign the treaty. President Nixon overcame their opposition by secretly promising to send in U.S. military forces if North Vietnam did attack. The promise proved worthless, however, after Nixon's resignation from the presidency in 1974. The South Vietnamese leaders were no more successful than before in forming a strong nationalist regime. Nothing the United States did could ensure a strong, noncommunist nation-state in South Vietnam.

In 1975, all Indochina fell to the Communists. That year North Vietnamese troops launched their final offensive. They overwhelmed the southern forces in two months, and along with the army the South Vietnam state collapsed. Soon afterward the Communists joined South Vietnam to their Socialist Republic. At the same time, the Khmer Rouge defeated the U.S.-backed military regime in Cambodia. Their revolution proved as brutal as any previous communist regime. In a three-year period, they imprisoned and executed millions of Cambodians. The belligerence of the Khmer Rouge caused their downfall. In 1978, their troops invaded a border region of Vietnam that they claimed for Cambodia. This action provoked a Vietnamese military offensive, which easily overthrew the Khmer Rouge government. For a few years, the Vietnamese Communist Party ruled all Indochina.

Their dream of bringing all Indochina under communist rule failed in the face of anti-Vietnamese nationalism in Cambodia and the decay of Vietnam's command economy. Civil war in Cambodia continued for years between the new government, controlled by Vietnam, and a coalition of forces hostile to Vietnam. In 1990, Vietnamese forces finally abandoned in their turn that ruinous war. The government of Vietnam accepted to leave the country in the hands of a new Cambodian government.

In Vietnam, the failure of the command economy and the cost of military intervention in Cambodia produced an economic crisis that Vietnam's leaders could not blame on the decades of war. By the 1980s, the standard of living of the country had declined so severely that it ranked as one of the poorest societies in the world. In desperation, hundreds of thousands of Vietnamese fled the country, many by boat, in the hopes of finding refuge in the West. The communist revolution there was in human terms a calamity. The monuments erected in Vietnam and in the United States to the war dead marked the real price of the ruinous struggle for Indochina.

JAPAN'S "ECONOMIC MIRACLE"

In August 1945, the Japanese imperial government surrendered unconditionally to the Allies, accepting American military occupation and the imposition of peace terms decided by the Allies. The defeat was complete, both militarily and psychologically. The Japanese people heard their emperor in his first radio broadcast accept in his name the surrender and the loss of independence, a humiliation "unendurable" and "insufferable" but nonetheless inescapable. For another six years, American occupation authorities governed this defeated empire. Only the position of emperor reminded the people of Japan's vast colonial empire and imperial past. Like Germany, Japan was only a ghost of its former self.

The Reconstruction of Japan

The treatment accorded the two defeated states was not identical, however. Japanese occupation was the responsibility of the United States. Its navy and air force had played the key role in the defeat of the Japanese Empire. American military forces alone occupied the country following the surrender. General Douglas MacArthur, U.S. Army commander-in-chief in the Pacific theater, became the supreme commander for the Allied Powers in Japan. He held absolute power in that country and was accountable only to the U.S. president. The territory he governed remained intact. The Soviet Union requested a separate occupation zone; MacArthur refused, and no Soviet occupation forces reached Japan. An Allied council had nominal authority to oversee MacArthur's work; in fact, it merely approved policies the supreme commander had already decided upon.

Japanese occupation was a U.S., not an Allied, affair. Late in 1945, Stalin complained to the U.S. ambassador in Moscow that the Soviet general on the Allied council in Japan "was treated like a piece of extra furniture," but his protest was halfhearted. He accepted the fact that Japan was in the U.S. sphere of influence.

The fact that the United States exercised such extraordinary control over Japan led to a second important feature of Allied occupation. A central Japanese government carried out the orders of the supreme commander (in Germany no national government existed at any time during the occupation). The symbol of Japan's unity remained the emperor, who despite his purely titular political role continued to be treated as a semi-divine person.

When MacArthur assumed his post of supreme commander in late 1945, Emperor Hirohito made a brief ceremonial call, placing himself at the mercy of the victors. He informed General MacArthur that he wished to assume "sole responsibility for every political and military decision made and action taken by [his] people in the conduct of war" and to be judged for their conduct. Although the U.S. government was determined to punish Japanese war criminals, MacArthur decided not to hold Hirohito responsible. He preferred to obtain the emperor's backing for his occupation policies. His decision spared the Japanese people the humiliation of seeing their emperor tried like a common criminal. Hirohito's responsibility for the conduct of the war was left a state secret. Japan maintained its political unity and its imperial monarch, under American orders.

The country over which MacArthur assumed command was in ruins. Total Japanese casualties numbered 9 million. All major Japanese cities had been destroyed—most by massive U.S. bombing raids, Hiroshima and Nagasaki by single atomic bombs—and millions of civilians were homeless. The merchant marine had lost almost all its ships. Most of the textile factories and coal mines had ceased to function, and food production had fallen by nearly one half its prewar level. To add to the miseries, more than 6 million Japanese who had lived in overseas imperial territories had fled to or were forced to return to Japan.

The destruction went much deeper than life and property. Respect for Japanese military leadership had vanished with the humiliating defeat. American ascendancy over the Japanese state and people undermined national pride and deference to the old elite. The nation-state had lost its guiding code of behavior, leaving many of its people in a state of collective shock.

This psychological response to surrender played an important part, albeit difficult to define, in the success of the American occupation. The most unusual aspect of the adaptation of the Japanese to the conquerors was their readiness to cooperate in the building of the new order imposed by the Americans. It reflected, in the opinion of one Japanese historian, a deep-seated hope that "something [could] be done" despite the terrible destruction, and a widespread conviction that Japan's "path to future greatness lay in absorbing America's technological civilization."[1] The victors, in other words, held the key to recovery.

Reinforcing this attitude was the enormous respect General MacArthur enjoyed

---

[1]Masataka Kosaka, *A History of Postwar Japan* (Tokyo, 1972), p. 35.

Ruins of Asian War: Hiroshima, Dec. 1945 (*James Watkins Collection/Hoover Institution*)

among the Japanese. His imperious manners, disliked by many Americans, embodied in the eyes of the vanquished Japanese the traditional authority of the warrior, displayed with remarkable American informality. Although he traveled daily in an open car to his headquarters, at no time in his six-year reign was he the target of an assassination attempt. The emperor had publicly accepted American rule and demonstrated his willingness to collaborate in the occupation. The Japanese people did the same.

During the years of occupation, U.S. authorities imposed a sweeping set of fundamental political reforms on the country. These included a new constitution, the introduction of universal suffrage, legal protection of women's rights, and the expansion of the entire educational system. More than 200,000 former officers and politicians were to be punished for wartime activities. Many individuals subject to purge vanished temporarily, however, only to reemerge in new positions of authority when the U.S. occupation ended. The purge included the trial and conviction of war criminals. Among the condemned were General Tojo, held guilty of launching the war, and the military commander of the Philippines. Many Japanese, unaware of the brutality of Japanese treatment of defeated peoples, found the principles applied in these trials to be a conqueror's justice. From a global perspective, the trials were a manifestation of Western confidence in an international code of law to govern war.

The new constitution was the principal political reform introduced during the occupation. It drew heavily on the British cabinet system and did not differ substantially from Japanese parliamentary democracy of the 1920s. A popularly elected parliament held sovereign power, choosing the cabinet headed by a prime minister. MacArthur took direct responsibility for the constitutional reform. He presented the Japanese government with the document he expected them to approve. When translated into Japanese, its passages sounded to one Tokyo newspaper commentator "exotically like American English." MacArthur also insisted that it include an introduction stating that "never again shall we be visited with the horrors of war through the action of government." No other constitution in the world made pacifism a political principle. It was another clear indication of the extraordinary circumstances of U.S. military occupation. Despite its exotic aspects, the constitution fitted well the expectations and past democratic practices of Japanese citizens. It became with relative ease the fundamental law of the land.

U.S. economic reforms were intended to restructure Japanese businesses and property holding. They touched agriculture, industry, and labor. The new laws on farming property produced the most important and enduring changes in economic life. They were so extensive that they resembled the initial land reforms in Communist China and earned MacArthur the reputation of a radical. Some American critics called him a "socialist." The American occupation authorities ordered the massive redistribution of farmland. It was taken from absentee landlords who were paid a price so low that their land was, in reality, confiscated. Over one-third of all Japanese arable land was transferred to 5 million farmers, previously tenants without their own land. They be-

came a major conservative political force in the country, supporting the new order that had given them their own farms.

U.S. efforts to encourage small business and labor proved much less successful. The spirit of these reforms resembled Franklin Roosevelt's New Deal reforms of the 1930s. This American version of free enterprise did not take hold among the Japanese business and political elite. An industrial reform broke up several of the giant economic firms, the *zaibatsu*, blamed by Americans for collaborating in the Japanese war effort. The U.S. occupation authorities passed laws intended to "tear down the concentration of economic power" in Japan. They promised that capitalist entrepreneurial initiative would be "redistributed peacefully" among small enterprises. Conditions became more favorable for new business activities. Very large Japanese business firms, however, reemerged within a few years and soon dominated the country's industrial economy.

For a few years, new laws protected and encouraged labor unions for factory workers and state employees. This led to a labor militancy unexpected by the reformers. Workers turned to socialist and communist union organizers and activists. Many unions came under the control of the Communist Party. Continued labor discontent, fed by shortages of basic goods and exploited by communist labor leaders, produced bitter strikes in 1946 and 1947. When the unions called in early 1948 for a nationwide strike, MacArthur used his exceptional powers as Supreme Allied Commander to forbid the strike.

By then the U.S. authorities in Japan had decided that rapid economic recovery was vital to U.S. security interests. Economic stability and social discipline had become their highest priority. They sided with Japanese management and withdrew their support for labor unions. This conservative social policy set the pattern for Japanese capitalism in the decades to come. The U.S. occupation installed in Japan a type of democratic, free enterprise system that promoted political and economic practices closely resembling those in Japan of the 1920s.

The new Japanese political leadership, apparently subservient to the occupation authorities, in fact had an important role to play in the introduction of this new order. Japan had a strong socialist movement, though split into several parties, and the labor unions attracted millions of members on promises of fundamental social improvements. These groups proposed social reforms far more extensive than the measures backed by the U.S. occupation authorities. They had no real opportunity, though, to introduce their reform projects. In the 1947 elections the Socialist Party, with the largest vote, still obtained only 25 percent of the total. It attempted to set up a coalition cabinet. U.S. occupation authorities' hostility to the Socialist Party was decisive in ending this first (and only) left-wing government in Japan's postwar history. They were very suspicious of any socialist reforms. As in Germany, they judged political conservatives best suited to Cold War policies. Political power shifted to the conservatives, organized in the coalition of the Liberal and Democratic parties (soon to become one party). Their leader was Shigeru Yoshida.

Backed by the U.S. authorities, Yoshida became the dominant force in Japanese politics for the following decade. Dissension among the left-wing parties assured the Liberal-Democratic coalition control in parliament and leadership of the cabinet. The goals of the conservatives were to encourage Japanese business interests and to hasten the end of U.S. occupation. Rising Cold War tensions pushed the U.S. authorities to rely increasingly on Yoshida, prime minister after 1948, to assist them in their new containment policies.

In a major policy change (paralleling that in Germany), the U.S. government concluded that Japanese economic recovery was its first priority. The reform of Japanese economic and social institutions became a secondary consideration. MacArthur set out in 1948 to make Japan a "self-supporting nation" capable of resisting Soviet pressure from abroad and radical political agitation from within. In 1949 he used his occupation powers to force the Japanese government to drastically cut its expenses and to reduce the budget deficit to bring down inflation. This fiscal conservatism was essential to the country's economic growth under a free enterprise system.

Yoshida cooperated, for the budget cuts ended social reforms. His collaboration had the strong backing of Japanese business and financial leaders, who were key supporters of his party. He also assisted in the creation of an anticommunist labor union movement and in the purge of Communists from administrative and union jobs. The new industrial unions cooperated with management, who held down wages and increased investments (a formula for recovery applied also in West Germany).

Yoshida's collaboration made him a valuable ally for the United States. It also advanced the political fortunes of his party and the conservative program it supported. By 1950, the entire labor union movement had declined, torn by battles between Communists and noncommunists and weakened by conservative U.S. occupation policies. The primacy of business interests, the weakening of labor, and conservative political rule by Yoshida's Liberal-Democratic cabinet remained the dominant trends of Japanese internal politics in the decades ahead.

The Alliance with the United States

Once the enemy, Japan became a close ally of the United States in the Cold War years. The Korean War turned Japan into a major East Asian base for the U.S. military forces. Its geographical position on the eastern borders of the Soviet Union made it a desirable location for air bases for the U.S. Strategic Air Command, and its ports provided harbors to the U.S. Navy. The basic reforms had gone into effect, and Japanese political leadership was in the hands of conservatives. In 1951, the U.S. military ended their occupation of Japan. That year the peace treaty left Japan in possession of its Main Islands. It lost the Kuril Islands and Sakhalin to the Soviet Union. Taiwan was independent, and Okinawa was occupied by the United States. Japan began reparations payments to the countries conquered during the war, except Communist China.

The Japanese government had to put in place its own foreign policy. Its margin of maneuver was small, for it was caught on the front lines of the Cold War and near the borders of the new People's Republic of China. Some Japanese nationalists hoped to restore Japan to a position of independent East Asian power, protected by its own army and navy and free to set its own course between the superpowers. Anti-militarists and pacifists, on the contrary, urged the neutralization of their country. They argued that Japan should take no part in the Cold War and should refuse the presence of any military forces, either its own or American, on its territory.

Prime Minister Yoshida chose a compromise between these two positions. In the U.S.–Japanese Security Treaty of 1952, he accepted a military alliance with the United States, permitting U.S. military bases in Japan and leaving his country (like West Germany) under the protection of the U.S. "nuclear umbrella." He agreed to comply with U.S. Cold War policies. Among Japanese the most controversial policy was non-recognition of Communist China. For

another twenty years Japan had no official relations with its powerful neighbor. Yoshida refused, however, to give in to repeated requests from the U.S. government that Japan rearm beyond the minimum level of its self-defense forces. In those years his country was a disarmed state, relying on U.S. military protection and free to devote its energies and resources to economic growth.

The U.S. alliance aroused bitter controversy in Japan throughout the 1950s. The Security Treaty set the terms of this uneven union between the mightiest military power in the world, the United States, and its former Asian enemy. Opposition to its terms came principally from the Socialist Party and from a very strong pacifist movement. In 1959, when the treaty was being renegotiated, political opposition and street demonstrations grew so violent that the government was for a time paralyzed. This was the most serious crisis that Japan's parliamentary regime had confronted since the war. In the end, the Japanese public turned against the violent tactics of the opponents to the new treaty. It was ratified virtually by force in parliament that year. In return, the conservative prime minister resigned to quiet protests at his undemocratic handling of the crisis.

Japanese Economic Recovery

Japan's phenomenal economic expansion began ten years after the war. First the country had to pass through a period of painful recovery from wartime destruction and the loss of the empire. In the early postwar years, Japanese businessmen, lacking foreign markets and shipping and uncertain about the future, remained reluctant to begin real reconstruction of the economy. In addition, they feared the consequences of worker unrest and U.S. economic and social reforms.

By the early 1950s, both these issues had been resolved to their satisfaction. The political conservatism of Yoshida and the ruling Democratic-Liberal coalition protected and reassured investors, and labor agitation movement subsided. Beginning in 1950, large U.S. purchases of goods for the troops in Korea gave a strong boost to the Japanese economy. The U.S. government permitted Japanese goods unrestricted entry into the American market. It began a major program of economic aid, the Dodge Plan (comparable to the Marshall Plan for Europe). It encouraged the use of these funds for the modernization of the Japanese economy, and opened access to U.S. technology to Japanese entrepreneurs.

These favorable financial, commercial, and technological conditions laid the foundation for what became known as the Japanese "economic miracle." Per capita national income reached the prewar level in 1956. At about the same time food rationing finally came to an end. Japanese families still had to content themselves with a very modest standard of living. Surplus wealth went primarily into economic expansion. The Japanese people put into savings an average of 20 percent of their income (in the United States, savings averaged only 7 percent in the early 1960s). Industries went heavily into debt, using the savings of the Japanese people to invest in new products, new machinery, and the formation of commercial companies engaged in foreign trade. By the late 1950s, the economy was growing at the extraordinary rate of 10 percent a year; national income doubled every seven years. No Western capitalist country had ever matched that rate of expansion.

Foreign and Japanese observers debated the causes of this remarkable turnaround in the economic fortunes of the country. Some emphasized the superior educational level of the Japanese, highly trained and able to adapt easily to a new industrial era of complex electronic technology. Others underlined the favorable international conditions, including U.S. free trade and technology and the rising demand for products in Asia and the West.

Everyone was agreed that collaboration between government officials and leaders of industry had proven successful in their joint goal to expand Japan's share of the global industrial market. The conservative government committed financial resources, decreed legal protection, and created public agencies for the development of Japanese commerce and industry. The principal instrument of this free-enterprise planning system was the Ministry of International Trade and Industry (MITI). Its officials used their extensive authority over the country's financial and trading activities to oversee Japanese economic development.

Bureaucrats in MITI gathered economic data to forecast international trends in technology and industry. With this information they recommended economic objectives for big business. The government used tariffs to create protectionist hurdles to foreign imports competing with Japanese goods. Businesses producing profitable exports received state subsidies in the form of low-interest loans. This so-called "guided capitalism" cemented the alliance of conservative politicians, state officials, and business leaders. The Japanese respected democratic procedures, but behind the scenes real political power depended on what one Western observer termed Japan's "authoritarian institutions and techniques."

A quarter-century after its crushing defeat, Japan had emerged as one of the most productive, prosperous countries in the world. Its form of capitalism was studied and imitated by other Asian states. In the 1970s, the formula proved remarkably successful in South Korea, Taiwan, and Singapore, which together with Japan were labeled the "Four Dragons" of East Asia. Their economies boomed. With growth rates of nearly 10 percent a year, they doubled their economic wealth every ten years. Many Asian leaders heralded "guided capitalism" as the "Asian way" to economic prosperity.

New industries sprang from the enterprise of Japanese businessmen. They proved remarkably capable at turning Western technology into reliable, inexpensive products. The story of some of these entrepreneurs reveals important characteristics of the Japanese "economic miracle." In the late 1940s, a young Japanese mechanic, Sochiro Honda, began to make motorcycles at a price far below Western imports. By the end of the 1950s his firm was the largest maker of motorcycles in the world, with markets throughout Asia and in the West. He enjoyed even greater success when his factories shifted to automobiles. When electronic inventions in the West opened up a new consumer market for television, a Japanese electronics engineer started a small firm in 1958 with $500 and seven workers to make some of these electronic items. His firm, Sony, became one of the principal world producers of television equipment. Recognition of new opportunities and quality work were important factors assuring the success of Japanese entrepreneurs offering new products for consumers in the expanding global economy.

Individual initiative combined in Japan with the old techniques of giant corporate management and government support. The major enterprises, called by the Japanese "business communities," brought banking, transportation, and sales operations into one firm, with branches extending into Asia and the West. Their employees and workers, grouped in company unions with guaranteed lifetime employment and high wages, were the aristocracy of the labor force. They

were far better off than those workers in small business, where labor was poorly paid and unemployment a constant threat.

Deprived of its overseas empire by defeat in war, the Japanese state made its economic might the foundation on which it built up a regional sphere of influence. The United States remained the major market for Japanese exports. Soon Japanese investors and exporters established important business connections in southeast Asia. Japanese-owned factories appeared throughout the region, assembling products made with inexpensive labor and Japanese technology. With the government's encouragement, Japanese businessmen invested in the new electronic industry. By the 1980s, Japan was a global center of computer manufacturing. Rapid expansion of the country's nuclear-power industry was another key decision of the Japanese government. In an era of Middle Eastern oil crises, it was determined to free the country from dependence on imported petroleum and coal. Until the 1990s, guided capitalism remained Japan's key to economic success.

By then, the U.S.–Japanese alliance had become an unusual, awkward partnership. U.S. diplomatic and military influence remained great, but Japanese financial and technological achievements gave its banks and industrial corporations an important role in the U.S. economy. Each year Japanese exports brought in tens of billions of dollars in foreign earnings. A part of these funds was reinvested in the U.S. financial and real estate markets. Each country depended upon the other. The Japanese economy was earning profits on a par with U.S. businesses. The Japanese population had reached a standard of living equal to that of Americans. Although Emperor Hirohito's death in 1989 briefly revived memories of the war and Japanese military defeat, by then it seemed part of a distant past.

SUMMARY

War and revolution had profoundly altered the history of East Asia. Japan no longer possessed a great empire or was ruled by a militarist regime. Having occupied a vast area of East and southeast Asia, it had to abandon all its conquered territories. Its defeat opened the way to revolution and the emergence of new nation-states in that vast area.

The internal transformation of East Asian lands depended in large measure on forces unique to each country. The victory of the Chinese Communists transformed the political landscape of East Asia. Chinese nationalism fused with communist ideology to sustain a long revolutionary war. Although Mao's vision of utopian socialism brought the country two decades of political and social turmoil, the Communist Party dictatorship was unshakeable. The Chinese Statue of Democracy, erected by supporters of democratic reform on Tiananmen Square in 1989, fell that June when the tanks of the PLA crushed the protest movement. Ten years later, Japan's new Statue of Liberty (copied from the U.S. statue) was a tourist attraction as well as a symbol of Japan's postwar transformation. Japanese national pride suffered terribly in the aftermath of defeat, but the nation's ability to collaborate in the new economic endeavor brought Japan back among the great powers of the world.

Behind the diversity of historical experiences, important similarities are apparent of the recent history of that region. This pattern repeats itself in different ways in other parts of Asia, the Middle East, and Africa. Movements for national independence became powerful political forces. The goal of economic development became an integral part of political action and of popular hopes. In China, unheroic but effective programs for economic growth replaced Mao's utopian campaigns of communist equality. The South Korean economy, guided by authoritarian leaders, managed to join the ranks of the "new industrial nations" by the 1980s. Only North Korea remained trapped in a Stalinist political and economic mold that left its people impoverished and oppressed. The goal everywhere else was to raise production and to improve the people's standard of living and well-being.

East Asia became more, not less, involved in global affairs after the fall of the great empires. The superpowers extended their rivalry into the region, and governments there looked to the West or to the Soviet Union for economic aid and for military support. Global markets lured manufacturers and governments to risk competing on an international scale. National independence and global interdependence constituted two inextricable facets of the postwar history of East Asia.

DATES WORTH REMEMBERING

1946–1954	French war in Indochina
1950	Formation of Vietnam, Cambodia, and Laos
1950–1953	Korean War
1950	Chinese conquest of Tibet
1954	French withdraw from Indochina
1955	Creation of North and South Vietnam
1956	Beginning of Japanese economic boom
1957–1971	Tibetan revolt
1959	Flight of Dalai Lama to India
1959	Communist insurrection in South Vietnam
1958–1960	Mao's Great Leap Forward
1963	United States military aid to South Vietnam
1965	U. S. military intervention in Vietnam
1966–1975	Chinese Cultural Revolution
1973	Withdrawal of U.S. troops from Vietnam
1975	Death of Mao

1975 Communist conquest of South Vietnam and Cambodia
1978 End of collective farms in China
1980 Beginning of Chinese economic boom
1980 Introduction of "one child" policy in China
1989 Communist suppression of democratic movement in China

RECOMMENDED READING

Communist China

John Avedon (1988), *In Exile from the Land of Snows: The Dalai Lama and Tibet since the Chinese Conquest* (1984). A sympathetic history of contemporary Tibet and its leader.

Sergei Goncharov, John Lewis, Xue Litai, *Uncertain Partners: Stalin, Mao, and the Korean War* (1993). The best study to date of the murky origins of the North Korean invasion.

Ross Terrill, *Mao: A Biography* (1999). A critical reassessment of the life of this great revolutionary leader.

Postwar Japan

John Dower, *Embracing Defeat: Japan in the Wake of World War II* (1999). An thoughtful study of Japan's painful renewal following defeat.

Akira Iriyi, *The Cold War in Asia* (1974). An international history of East Asia that integrates Japan into the Cold War conflict.

*Edwin Reischauer, *The Japanese Today: Change and Continuity* (1995). A brief survey of recent Japanese social, cultural, and political history, by one of the senior historians in the field.

War in Indochina

Jean Lacouture, *Ho Chi Minh* (1968). A brief critical biography of the communist leader.

A. J. Langguth, *Our Vietnam: The War 1954–1975* (2000). A thorough examination, by the *N.Y. Times* Vietnam correspondent in the late 1960s, of America's failed experience in state-building and anticommunist war in Vietnam.

Memoirs and Visual Aids

Orville Schell, *To Get Rich is Glorious: China in the Eighties* (1984). The perceptive observations of an old China hand watching with amazement the reemergence of capitalism in China.

Platoon. A brutal film version (1980) of the Vietnam war seen from the perspective of the ordinary U.S. soldier.

Seven Years in Tibet. Film version (2000) of the story of Dalai Lama's friendship with a Westerner, with vivid scenes of Tibetan life.

CHAPTER EIGHT

New Nations in South Asia

Within a few years of the end of the Second World War, the Western empires in South Asia had vanished. The Dutch left their colony in the East Indies, the United States gave full independence to the Philippines, and the British granted freedom to India, Burma, and Malaya. The political transition, coming in some cases after centuries of colonial rule, was abrupt. The move to independence was accompanied in some countries by civil war and ethnic conflict, leaving bitter memories and antagonism among the newly freed peoples. Though the Western states had ruled their colonies by force of arms, they also recruited and trained increasing numbers of their colonial subjects for military and administrative service. The languages in common use within their colonial borders gave ethnically diverse peoples a useful, and relatively noncontroversial means of communication. Their years of rule led to economic investment for the extraction of raw materials needed in Western in-

dustry, and to the construction of railroads and ports for the movement of goods. In these and other ways the centuries of imperial rule left their mark on economic and political life in the new states to follow.

Throughout South Asia the anti-colonial movements that took power made national unity the foundation of their plans for independence. It was a generous vision that held together leaders and supporters as long as the immediate aim was the expulsion of Western colonial rulers. It proved a difficult ideal to incorporate afterwards into the life of the new states. Leaders spoke of a nationalism that would transcend the deep internal social, religious, and cultural divisions within their countries, implying that they sought a nation-state of toleration and freedom for all. But they found that ethnic and religious bonds remained a powerful force among their peoples. Separatist movements often emerged whose goal was to defend the interests and integrity of their own community. Ethnic nationalism threatened the newly won unity of these states. Faced with abiding social disagreements and conflict, leaders often turned to authoritarian rule as a substitute for elusive national unity.

Freedom brought with it a very distinct sense of fundamental differences between the newly independent lands and the rest of the world. The broadest definition of this uniqueness came from the Indian leader Jawaharlal Nehru. Decolonization had, in his opinion, created the collective need for peace among the liberated peoples of the globe. He sought to distance his country from the international conflicts of the Cold War. Many other leaders shared his view and supported a policy of "nonalignment," refusing to ally with either the West or the Soviet bloc. Nehru described their place in the new world order as the "Third World," separate from the democratic "First World" and the communist "Second World."

The differences were not so great that these new nation-states could ignore the more industrialized countries. Their leaders confronted acute problems of poverty and economic backwardness that required outside help and aid. Their efforts to raise living conditions and to stimulate economic growth relied in some cases on the free-enterprise system of the West, in others on the central government controls resembling the command economy that Stalin's Russia had instituted. While often looking to foreign lands for aid and guidance, they adapted and altered these policies and institutions to suit their needs.

THE NEW ISLAND REPUBLICS

The history of the countries of southeast Asia in the quarter-century after the war followed a common pattern. The first years were a period of decolonization, that is, the elimination of political ties to Western states and the first stages of state-building. The new regimes set out to define a new international policy in their relations with East and West, gathering to discuss common problems and policies even when they were deeply divided on the most desirable course to take. Their political development in the following decade shifted toward authoritarian rule, with small groups of leaders controlling elections by means of political followers and clients. Everywhere, economic development was an increasing concern. Poverty remained an abiding presence among both urban and rural masses, while business and bureaucratic elites built up great wealth. Social and ethnic unrest erupted at times in spontaneous uprisings, giving support to guerrilla movements organized by revolutionary parties. State-building constituted a complex, often violent, process.

Philippine Independence

Liberation of the Philippines from Japanese rule came with the return in 1944 of General MacArthur and U.S. forces, two years after their defeat by the Japanese. Before the war, the U.S. government had granted the Philippines self-rule in a political system, copied from the American constitution, with an elected president and legislature. Dominating the political life of the islands were powerful families, whose influence lay in their great wealth and in a patronage system of rule by which they built up a large following of political "clients." Japanese occupation only worsened the hardship of the peasant farmers, forced to pay heavy taxes to their conquerors. A major peasant uprising erupted in 1943. The rebels attacked both the Japanese and the great landowners, many of whom collaborated with the Japanese occupation forces. Rural unrest and ethnic revolts remained an abiding problem in the postwar years.

In 1946, the United States formally granted independence to a new Philippine government. The first elected president had himself worked for a short period with the Japanese. His administration, like the preceding one, made no effort to punish collaborators. The transfer of political power to the Philippine people did not weaken the dominance of landowners and business elites. No revolutionary movement swept in new leaders or offered the peasant population a concrete plan for land reform. Independence came peaceably without upsetting the privileges and comforts of the Philippine upper classes.

Important features of the colonial past marked the country's economic and diplomatic relations with the United States. The new Philippine regime joined the Western bloc in the Cold War, signing a military alliance with the United States that left in place American naval and air bases in the Philippine archipelago. In exchange, it received military and economic aid from the United States. It preserved the laws introduced in its colonial period that protected capitalist economic development.

The country depended for its foreign trade as much as before on the United States. Special trade agreements permitted Philippine goods to enter the United States without tariffs, and few restrictions stood in the way of Philippine families who wished to migrate to America. In return, U.S. investors received special financial incentives to found companies in the new republic. Close ties existed between Philippine traders and industrialists and U.S. bankers and manufacturers. The interests of the Philippine government and middle classes were closely tied to those of the U.S. government and economy. Socialist experiments had no place in the new order.

Social inequality and ethnic diversity continued to divide the Philippine people and to complicate policies for national unity. The wartime peasant uprising on the main island of Luzon continued for years. Initially successful in taking control of large areas of the countryside, the insurgents lost support when the Philippine government finally passed reform laws to give land to tenant farmers. Ramon Magsaysay, the dynamic and popular commander of the army, organized effective resistance to the guerrillas. To induce peasants to abandon the rebellion, Magsaysay offered them ownership of their own land. He proved a charismatic nationalist leader popular with the masses. His formula of reform and reconciliation successfully ended the insurrection by 1951. Philippine voters elected Magsaysay to the post of Philippine president, which he retained until his death in 1957. For a few years, the new Philippine nation-state enjoyed a period of peace, democratic government, and economic growth.

In the next decade, the republic's democratic laws and representative government turned into a facade for elite rule. Real power lay in the hands of a few political bosses. The Philippine leader Benigno Aquino, writing in the late 1960s, lamented that his land was "consecrated to democracy but run by an entrenched plutocracy," and "dedicated to equality but mired in an archaic system of caste."[1] The ambition of a power-hungry politician, Ferdinand Marcos, revealed how fragile was the political compact that kept the Philippines united and at peace.

Elected president in 1965, he used his legal position under the constitution and the peculiar informal network of supporters that political patronage gave him to expand enormously his presidential powers. Muslim groups in the southern Philippines rebelled against the central government and the privileges that Catholics and the Catholic Church enjoyed on their islands. In northern

---

[1] Cited in Stanley Karnow, *In Our Image: America's Empire in the Philippines* (New York, 1989), p. 25.

islands, communist-led guerrilla movements reappeared among the poor peasantry. Marcos justified his authoritarian rule by the need to end political revolt, social disorder, and ethnic conflicts. His brutal methods and corrupt regime only increased the disorder.

Rather than give up office, Marcos proclaimed in 1972 a regime of martial law. With the backing of the army, he arrested his political opponents and ended democratic government. He used his authoritarian powers to amass enormous wealth for his family (some estimates after his fall placed his total wealth at more than one billion dollars) and to bribe and enrich his cronies and his powerful political machine. Power brought enormous benefits to him and to his followers.

His dictatorship failed to resolve any of the major problems confronting his country. His regime was incapable of repressing the communist and Muslim uprisings. It was unable to improve economic conditions in the cities and in the countryside, despite vast amounts of U.S. military and economic aid. By the early 1980s, his measures of political repression had aroused outrage throughout the country. Even the Catholic church joined the call for his removal from power. In 1986, he had to flee the country when army leaders turned against him. By then the political opposition had reached the proportions of a mass movement.

His successor as president was Corazon Aquino, widow of a prominent opponent of the regime (Benigno Aquino) whom Marcos had ordered assassinated in 1983. She promised to restore democratic rule and reunite the country, but the heritage of decades of economic decay and authoritarian rule posed enormous problems. Despite continued unrest among the Muslim populations on the southern islands, the country had preserved its national unity and its democratic government. In 1994, nationalists rejoiced at the closure of the last U.S. naval base, whose buildings Filipino investors

converted into headquarters for start-up computer and Internet companies. The global economy had replaced the Cold War as the Philippine's major link to the outside world.

Sukarno and Indonesia

In the East Indies, years of colonial war between Indonesian nationalists and Dutch forces followed liberation from Japan. Before capitulating in August 1945, the Japanese occupation authorities had allowed nationalist collaborators to proclaim the independence of their country. No Allied troops reached the East Indies until weeks later. In the interval, nationalists created a government for a state that they had earlier baptized "Indonesia." Their leader was Sukarno. For the previous twenty years, he had campaigned against Dutch rule, preaching a semireligious message of Indonesian nationalist revival. His Five Pillars of national liberation—democracy, internationalism, nationalism, social prosperity, and belief in God—were less important, though, than his charismatic hold over the Indonesian peoples. They found inspiration in his promise of Indonesian rebirth following independence.

When in late 1945 Dutch armed forces reached the islands, they ended this first brief moment of independence. The leaders of the Netherlands had desperate need of their vast colony, whose valuable resources, especially petroleum, were vital for the reconstruction of their war-torn homeland. For the next four years, they attempted to reestablish by force of arms their control over the East Indian archipelago. U.S. opposition to their colonial war and the inability of Dutch forces to end the insurrection brought the conflict to an end in 1949.

In 1950, the independent republic of Indonesia reappeared. Its borders were those put in place by the Dutch colonial rulers, and its state language was the Malay dialect that the Dutch had used in ruling their subject peoples there. Its new constitution promised parliamentary democracy to the 80 million people of the vast archipelago, whose islands stretched across 3,000 miles. The peoples were divided by great inequalities of wealth, different cultures and languages, and an age-old distrust of peoples of neighboring islands. Most of the population practiced the Muslim religion. Buddhism continued to exert a strong influence among peoples in the central islands of Java and Bali, and Christian communities had emerged where Catholic and Protestant missionaries had been active. Political parties representing the various peoples feuded among themselves, weakening their authority in a state unified only by its leader and by the nationalist liberation movement.

Sukarno was the national hero and became the first president of the republic. His stature rested not only on constitutional power and his nationalist ideology, but also on his magnetic hold on the Indonesians. Many virtually worshiped him. Sukarno was the guarantor of Indonesian national unity. His state, which still functioned as a parliamentary democracy, was increasingly the scene of bitter political quarrels. Fundamentalist Muslims demanded that the state enforce Islamiç religious practices. Regional rivalries opposed the leaders of the various islands, many of whose peoples were deeply attached to their local culture. The army was the only effective national institution and means to enforce the peace.

Sukarno needed the backing of the army, just as its commanders needed the national legitimacy that he embodied. In the mid-1950s, the alliance between the two became the foundation for authoritarian rule. Like many other leaders of Third World countries, Sukarno was persuaded that the unity and welfare of his new state depended upon his personal leadership. In 1956, he declared to Indonesians that he had dreamed of "burying" the old constitutional order and of giving his people what he called a "Guided Democracy" and a "Guided Economy." His dreams translated into political dictatorship, state planning, and diplomatic nonalignment. In 1957, he took command of the state. Authoritarian rule replaced parliamentary democracy in Indonesia for the next forty years.

The leadership provided by Sukarno relied more on personal inspiration and favoritism than on coherent policy. His government seized all Dutch and other foreign businesses and estates, nationalizing the great oil fields of Royal Dutch-Shell. It lacked the trained personnel to run these state enterprises, however. As a result of this hasty nationalization, the country's economy passed through several years of painful recession. Sukarno accepted the economic assistance of Western and communist governments, since both sides were competing for good relations with his state. To win the backing of the many political factions in his country he offered their leaders positions in the largest cabinet of any country in the world. His one hundred ministers worked largely for their own benefit, and that of their followers. Cronyism wasted enormous sums of money on useless projects in the state-run businesses. Meanwhile, the country went deeper and deeper into debt, and foreign trade declined for lack of funds to pay for imports.

Sukarno's dictatorship brought with it his own personality cult and nationalist ideology. He received the grand titles of "Permanent President" and "Great Leader of the Revolution." Boasting that his country was "living dangerously," Sukarno declared war on "neocolonialism" (shortened to NEKOLIM in his speeches) in all its forms. It was responsible, he claimed, for the economic hardship that his ineffective and corrupt regime had created. He encouraged the Indonesian army to seize islands on the borders

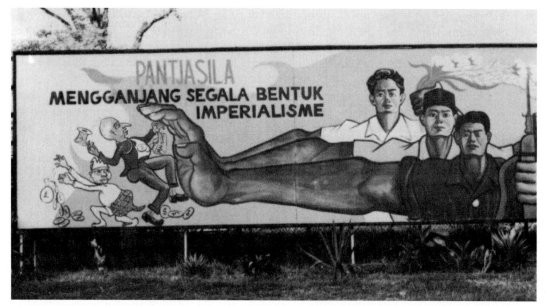

National Heros and Imperialist Devils: Indonesian Government Poster "The Five Pillars [of Indonesian National Liberation] Crush All Forms of Imperialism," c. 1960 (*Howard Jones Collection/Hoover Institution*)

of Indonesia, claiming them for his nation. Unity remained a fragile, contested creation. Sukarno and army kept the island republic together, but the price was the worsening of ethnic hostility to Indonesian rule.

Sukarno's nationalist posters, slogans, and speeches hid serious political weaknesses. He realized that his personal powers were inadequate to maintain national unity. His solution was to search for a mass movement on which he and his regime could rely. He came to believe that the Indonesian Communist Party, the largest political organization in the country, would provide him with that disciplined popular support. He hoped that their backing would bring him the diplomatic and military support of China, for Indonesia was increasingly isolated. His rhetorical sparring with the West and expansionist foreign policy rested on a grandiose (and illusory) vision of Indonesia as a great power in south Asia.

The encouragement he gave the Communists proved to be his downfall. By encouraging them, he became the center of a violent struggle for power. The Indonesian Communist Party and the army were bitter rivals. In 1965, the Communists secretly organized an armed uprising to seize control of the government. They seem to have believed that they had Sukarno's backing (though he was careful not to commit himself openly to their cause). In mid-1965, they set in motion their insurrection by capturing and executing several of Indonesia's top military leaders.

Their uprising failed, and in the upheaval provoked ethnic killing worse than any the East Indies had ever experienced. The surviving generals, led by General Suharto, mobilized their troops and appealed to the population to join in resisting the Communists, "godless enemies" of the nation. Ethnic and social animosity within Indonesia, stirred up by pressures of nation-building, suddenly erupted in violence. It produced a terrible butchering of Communists and their supporters.

Throughout the islands mobs attacked Chinese communities, on the pretext that the Communist Party found supporters and financial support there. Chinese migrants had moved to the East Indies during the centuries of Dutch rule. Many had become prosperous through trading and commerce. In a time of economic hardship, they became an easy target for the discontented, of which there were many in Indonesia in the mid-1960s. The bloodbath was as well the product of suspicion and hostility toward these "outsiders," practicing a different religion, speaking a different language. Ethnic discord and rivalry produced, there as elsewhere among the new nations, the seeds of mass violence. No one knows how many people died in the 1965 massacres. The most conservative estimates range from 200,000 to 300,000 dead. Sukarno, no longer trusted by his generals, lost power to the head of the army, General Suharto, who took over the government.

The new military dictatorship ended Sukarno's attempt at imposing a socialist Guided Economy on the country. They accepted foreign aid from East and West. Indonesia remained a neutral, nonaligned country. For decades, though, it depended on loans and aid from Japan and the United States. General Suharto and the army leaders enforced national unity, holding in check the ethnic unrest and denying the political opposition any public forum. They ended talk of war, sold nationalized enterprises (often to their own cronies), and opened the country to foreign investors (who often had to pay enormous bribes to set up operations). A small group of Indonesian bankers and investors received special favors from Suharto's government. In return, they secretly opened special bank accounts for politically influential individuals, among whom Suharto and his family were the most favored. "Crony capitalism" spread through the islands.

Gradually the Indonesian economy began to grow. By the 1980s, its abundant natural resources had become the cornerstone of an economic boom. Asian timber companies moved into the forested regions of Sumatra and Borneo, removing the valuable hardwood trees, burning the remaining forests, and leaving the land for plantation farming (see Highlight, pp. 390–394). By the 1990s, this Indonesian version of the "Asian way" of capitalism had turned the economy into one of the "newly emerging markets" of Asia.

Orderly Singapore

The fate of the island of Singapore was directly tied to that of the British Empire in southeast Asia. In the British territories of Burma and Malaya, the war years had given nationalist leaders confidence that their colonies were ready for national liberation. The British government offered no opposition to their demand. The British Labor Party, in power after 1945, readily help organize the transfer of power. In return, nationalists there welcomed British troops to repress communist-led uprisings in their lands. In 1948, Burma and Malaya became independent states. The city of Singapore remained a British crown colony. Its economic and strategic importance far outweighed its minute size. It lay on the maritime path to East Asia and possessed the finest naval port in southeast Asia. Its largely Chinese population had been instrumental in making it the commercial and financial capital of the region. It was the exception to anti-colonialism (like Hong Kong), a prosperous remnant of an empire surrounded by independent states.

The British government had no wish, or the means, to maintain an imperial presence in the area. In 1963, it ended its rule over the city, convincing Singapore's leaders to join the Malay Union to form the Federation of Malaysia. This new state was a fragile creation, made up of a multiethnic collection of disparate regions. The Muslim Malay people, largely peasant and lacking the commercial skills of the Chinese, resented the prosperity of Singapore. Their Muslim religious practices and communal organization constituted a vital part of their lives. Many feared that their way of life would suffer if they were ruled by Chinese politicians. The intensity of ethnic antagonism between the two groups led to riots by minority Malay in the city of Singapore and political quarrels within the federal government between the Chinese leaders of Singapore and Malay politicians. Malay leaders, fearing that the ethnic conflict would destroy their young state, decided to expel the city from the federation. In 1965, Singapore was forced to form its own independent state, an island of only 2 million people.

Its isolation proved a blessing. Its leaders were able to create the conditions for an economic boom that rivaled that of Japan. The island-state became a model of authoritarian government and state-supported economic development. In free elections, a majority of its population approved the program of the People's Action Party. Once in power, its leaders introduced a program combining measures for political order and rapid economic growth. They virtually eliminated opposition political parties, independent trade unions, and any separatist ethnic movements among the city's Chinese, Malay, and Indian inhabitants. They severely punished all crimes, with small offenses earning the culprits the punishment of whipping with a birch rod (introduced first by the British). They instructed families to have more children when Singapore's birth rate fell too low.

The head of the People's Action Party and longtime prime minister, Lee Kuan Yew, promised Singapore's citizens an "orderly, organized, sensible, rational society." This authoritarian regime settled down to guide its tiny state on its path to social order and economic wealth. Its unstated bargain with the population was their submission to authoritarianism, which it claimed was rooted in Confucianism, in exchange for rapid economic development. It invited foreign investors to develop oil refining and textile and electronic manufacturing, staffed by the island's industrious, educated work force. It opened the door of the city-state to international banks and welcomed international commercial firms to use its port. On a small scale, it introduced to its island the "guided capitalism" that had succeeded so well in Japan. Not surprisingly, it championed the cause of the special "Asian way" of orderly capitalist countries.

Singapore founded its prosperity on global economic expansion and on its internal political stability. In economic terms, it succeeded beyond its wildest dreams, joining the "Four Dragons" of Asian boom countries. The city's rate of economic growth rose to above 10 percent by the 1970s, remaining at that level for the next twenty years. Soon the population's standard of living was second only to that of Japan among Asian countries. Economic conditions on the island were the envy of surrounding states. Militarily insignificant, its security depended on its vital role in the economic development of South Asia. It, too, was a nonaligned country, seeking good relations with all countries, communist and noncommunist, conducting financial and commercial affairs with whoever had the means to pay. Although it resembled in size a city-state of Renaissance Italy, it contained within its borders all the dynamic economic forces propelling the global boom of the late twentieth century.

☸ HIGHLIGHT: New Nations and Ethnic Strife ☸

The new states that emerged where empires once ruled all presented in one form or another the image of the nation-state. Flags, ceremonies, and heroes (real or mythical) commemorated and celebrated the historical achievements and prestige of a particular national community, united in one state. Leaders claimed that their government embodied special qualities of the people over whom they ruled. This was true in Latin America following the collapse of Spanish and Portuguese empires in the early nineteenth century. It was true in Asia and Africa after the Western empires withdrew from those continents in the decades after 1945. In their early years, these states were weak. Their governments had not, in most cases, had the chance to establish a solid foundation of authority and often were riven by internal rivalries among ambitious individuals and political movements eager for power. The ideology of nationalism promised the new leaders a firm pledge of loyalty from their population. First though, they had to convince the population of their nationalist legitimacy.

This ideology could be a trap for new states if politicians misused it. Its crucial shortcoming was the confusion surrounding the idea of nation itself. The term could refer to all the people within the boundaries of that state, which derived from them a unique civic calling that distinguished it from other nation-states. On the stroke of midnight, August 15, 1947, the Indian prime minister, Nehru, welcomed the freeing of "the soul of a nation" given at that moment its independence. He, like Gandhi, believed freedom and tolerance were by themselves bonds that would maintain the unity of the Indian people and their leaders. Civic ideals constituted a vague moral appeal by contrast with the other bond of nationhood, namely, ethnic loyalty. When this form of nationalism prevailed, the new states confronted serious internal divisions.

All the new states contained within their borders more than one, and often many, separate groups with strong internal, ethnic ties. Ethnic loyalty became especially meaningful in the lives of the population after independence from colonial rule. It offered the people within a particular community the reassurance of a shared collective identity, the social solidarity needed at moments of political unrest, and the bonds of mutual assistance invaluable in hard times.

These bonds of ethnic unity originated in many sources. Language formed one important agent of ethnic identity. Among the population of India were fifteen separate major languages. After Indian independence, leaders of some of these peoples claimed that they should have special political rights as a national community in their "own land." Shared religious practice was another powerful social bond. It was the foundation of the Muslim League's demand for a state of Muslim people to be carved out of the Indian colony. A belief in common ancestry was yet another ethnic link. Leaders of major and even small tribal groups claimed a special place in independent Nigeria because they believed their own people's uniqueness deserved special political rights and privileges. Each time these claims for ethnic recognition appeared, they implied that civic nationalism was less important to some people than their own ethnic identity. That demand, in turn, raised the possibility that the very foundations of the new state were so fragile it could collapse.

The colonial experience, post-colonial politics, and economic hardship all could lead to strife among ethnic groups within one state. The newly freed states often inherited from their colonial past a policy of favored treatment for one particular people. Often the imperial administration had recruited soldiers or subordinate officials to serve their colonial needs. Animosities built up over the colonial decades spilled out in ethnic conflict once independence had lifted imperial control.

This historical experience was only the prelude to the real difficulties created by independence. The new states usually relied in their first years on democratic elections to select state legislators and presidents. Time and again political parties appeared to defend the needs of a particular people. In South Africa, the Inkatha Party spoke for the Zulu people alone, and denied the African National Congress's claim to be the true voice of all African peoples there. Often voters preferred candidates from their own people. Voting on the basis of ethnic loyalty insured that the candidates from the party backed by the largest ethnic group had the best chance of gaining power. Since the winners at times turned political power into an instrument for ethnic favoritism, minority peoples could find themselves outcasts as a result of democratic rule. When the Ibo people of Nigeria believed themselves in this situation in the late 1960s, they rebelled against the central government. The Biafran civil war, which lasted three years, nearly destroyed Nigeria.

The danger of conflict became particularly great when ethnic groups demanded the creation of a separate territory for themselves. Ethnic nationalism rested on the belief in a "native land" that belonged by "right" to a particular people. The assertion was based usually on a people's historical claim of having lived there over many generations. It was even made, though, for lands where a people had not lived for centuries. The Zionist movement affirmed that Palestine was the real homeland for the Jewish people, though the Romans had expelled almost all the Jews from there almost two thousand years before. Nowhere did the inhabitants in a particular area all belong to one ethnic group, nor were all those identifying with that group found in a compact territory. The demand to govern one's "own" land meant necessarily that the other peoples there did not enjoy a comparable right. By its very nature, the claim to a native land created ethnic minorities. If these peoples responded by making a claim to the same land, no peaceful resolution could satisfy both sides. The fifty-year struggle between Palestinian Arabs and Israeli Jews emerged out of that dispute.

The search for a way to reconcile civic and ethnic national loyalties led political leaders to promise legal protection of ethnic differences. In many Third World countries, constitutions spelled out minority rights, the most important of which was usually language rights. Often fundamental laws created a federal political system to divide state powers between the center, whose representatives spoke for all the peoples, and regions where particular ethnic groups obtained their own leadership and local rights. This system became the legal foundation of ethnically diverse countries such as India, Nigeria, and, late in the century, the Russian Federation.

It was a fragile compromise, since in theory it denied to the majority people the right to create a nation-state in its image, and by necessity refused to a minority people the right to their own nation-state. When peaceful compromise failed to satisfy nationalist demands, the result was civil disorder, political repression, and civil war. These conflicts began to appear very early in the post-imperial era in Asia and Africa. They continued to erupt, and with increased intensity, later in the century. One reason was the spreading struggle for a livelihood among impoverished masses in the Third World. The temptation was strong to explain their poverty by blaming other peoples for denying them access to economic benefits. The Chinese minority of Indonesia became a target for other peoples in that republic, especially in times of economic hardship in the 1960s and late 1990s. Another reason was the weakness of central governments, unable to restrain ethnic animosities.

Yet another reason for war emerged out of the drive by minorities to achieve at any cost their own national independence. Many of these revolts were settled by military means. Though the Indian constitution and federal laws guaranteed respect for ethnic rights, the government turned to extralegal powers of repression when violent nationalist movements among the Sikhs, then the Kashmir population, threatened secession and the breakup of India. The Nigerian government triumphed in the Biafran civil war by forcibly bringing the Ibo people under its power again. Only rarely did free elections end in peaceful secession. In 1993, the Eritrean People's Front, after decades of agitation, obtained from the Ethiopian government the possibility to hold an election on independence for the people of the province of Eritrea. Its popular backing was overwhelming, and the new nation-state of Eritrea appeared in Africa. But six years later, it had to fight a major war against Ethiopia to retain its independence.

The decay of multiethnic communist states in eastern Europe produced serious ethnic conflicts. These states, the most important of which were the Soviet Union and Yugoslavia, had contained ethnic hostility among their peoples, but by means that resembled those of the old colonial empires. When they lost power, these animosities quickly reemerged. The worst violence occurred in the Balkan state of Yugoslavia. It had created within its federation separate republics for its peoples, among whom the Croat and Serb peoples were the most numerous. Nationalism among these peoples erupted in civil war when the state collapsed in 1991. Hostility toward minorities was so great that some nationalists were prepared to forcibly expel or murder thousands of innocent civilians living in "their land" who did not belong to their nation. This cruel practice, called "ethnic cleansing," revealed how inhuman ethnic conflict could become.

Verbal protests from outside states and the United Nations could not halt bitter struggles such as the Yugoslav civil war, or the 1994 violence in the African state of Rwanda. The intervention of foreign troops could for a while restrain the mob rioting and killings. At times it seemed that, only when the fighting had created a human wasteland, did exhaustion end the violence. In these places, nationalism had replaced epidemics as the great killer of humanity.

LIBERATION AND PARTITION FOR INDIA

The legacy of the Second World War in India differed from that of other countries in south Asia in one vital respect. Japanese armies had never penetrated deeply into Indian territory. The British viceroy, the Indian civil service, and the Indian army remained the central forces in the united provinces while the six-hundred princes who had accepted British rule continued to govern their principalities. Only those Indian soldiers who had been taken prisoner by the Japanese in 1942 and who had agreed to join the Indian National Army became collaborators against the British. Their welcome as heroes on their return to India in 1945 proved that opposition to the British overrode all other issues confronting Indians in the postwar years.

The Liberation of India and Pakistan

From the beginning of their struggle for independence the National Congress leaders had vowed to preserve the unity that the British had given the subcontinent. They desired national independence and a democratically elected government that respected the rights of the entire population, regardless of religion or social rank. Special consideration to any religious community represented to men such as Gandhi a betrayal of their deepest belief in civic equality within a free Indian nation-state. This vision was challenged by "communalism," that is, by the social antagonism that divided the Muslim and Hindu communities, and by the program of the Muslim League.

The half-century before 1945 had witnessed a rising number of violent incidents and riots pitting Hindus against Muslims. Every province mingled the two communities, though overall Hindus were the large majority. No single territory was exclusively Hindu or Muslim. The population of Calcutta, largest and most industrial of India's cities and the capital of Bengal, was almost equally divided between these two groups. Their very proximity was a cause of friction and political rivalry, since self-rule raised the specter of one community losing power to the other. Individual rights appeared to many Indians less important that communal solidarity. National independence threatened to tear India apart.

The Muslim League preferred the gamble of partition to one unified nation-state. If the new Indian state, ruled democratically, placed government in the hands of the National Congress, the League feared that the new rulers would deprive the minority Muslims of civil and political rights, regardless of the promises of Congress leaders. What to liberal idealists appeared democratic safeguards of individual freedom seemed to the League a threat of minority persecution. Before the war it had demanded special Muslim representation within a new India (see Chapter 3). In the postwar years, it made the achievement of a separate Muslim state of Pakistan its immediate objective. No such state had ever existed. The followers of the Muslim League were prepared after war's end to resort to communal violence to prevent Indian national unification.

Preparing for Indian independence was the first priority for British and Indian leaders. The British Labor government supported freedom for the peoples of the subcontinent as firmly as for the empire's other Asian colonies. Its postwar financial crisis dictated rapid liberation for India, whose rule placed a heavy burden on the impoverished British treasury. Mass demonstrations and violence were a constant threat. The British proposed new elections to select an Indian leadership ready and able to negotiate the terms of independence.

When those elections were held in 1946, National Congress candidates won a majority in nearly all the provinces. Yet the Muslim League received the support of most Muslim voters. Who then spoke for India? Congress and the League both agreed to negotiations with the British, but each on its own terms. Congress refused to recognize the right of the League to represent the Muslim community, fearing that to do so would represent a fatal concession to partition. Mohammed Ali Jinnah, head of the Muslim League, demanded that Muslim representatives be granted an equal voice in negotiations alongside the Congress. In July 1946, he concluded that his party could not become the sole negotiator for India's Muslims by legal means. He called on his Muslim supporters to prove forcefully to the British and to Congress their hold over the Muslim population.

The League's Day of Direct Action in August 1946 was the real turning point in the history of postwar India. Jinnah proclaimed that "the only solution to India's problem is Pakistan," that is, partition of the Indian subcontinent into what he referred to as "Hindustan" and his Muslim state. To make clear that civil war was the alternative, he demanded of Muslims throughout India that they join in "direct action," including strikes, meetings, and demonstrations. He and the other League leaders must have known that rioting would accompany the demonstrations and that communal conflict would inevitably result. He accepted the possibility, saying: "We also have a pistol." The Muslim League's agitation did lead to Muslim-Hindu riots throughout the country. Ethnic hostility and fear deepened as the tragic process of partition began.

Bengal was the scene of the greatest bloodshed. Its capital city was the scene of such violence that observers later called the events of those terrible days the "Great Calcutta Killing." Perhaps 6,000 people died in that city alone, most of them innocent Hin-

dus or Muslims attacked by mobs from both sides. British forces moved into the centers of rioting, gradually restoring order. Gandhi, horrified at the violence, set out on a personal pilgrimage through Muslim as well as Hindu areas of Bengal to restore peace and tolerance by his own personal example and teaching. Although he risked death at the hands of a fanatic, he helped calm the population, but only temporarily.

It was tempting to blame partition on the League. Nehru himself, without any deep religious feeling and cosmopolitan in his political ideology, hated the League and all it embodied. He considered the Muslim religious solidarity that the League cultivated to be "medieval," a dangerous anachronism in a "rapidly changing world of industrialism, science, and nuclear power." He repeated assurances that other religious groups "have nothing to fear from the Hindus." After his visit that August to riot-torn areas of the northern province of Punjab, he expressed despair and "shame" that Indians should have betrayed the "great ideals that [Gandhi] has placed before us." He and the other Congress leaders persisted that year in working for a free and united India. But the country was too deeply and bitterly divided. The Muslim League had inflamed, but not created, that bitterness and hostility. Its fault lay in condoning and leading the mob action. Ultimately, religious and social divisions, not political manipulation by the League, decided the fate of India.

Frustrated and baffled by the impasse in negotiations, the British cabinet in February 1947 proclaimed that Great Britain would pull out of India within a year. It was prepared to leave even if it failed to bring the Indian negotiators to agree on a constitution and the means for the peaceful transfer of power. The statement was a declaration of defeat in the form of an ultimatum. The British government refused to take responsibility any longer for the escalating violence. One British official called the ethnic rioting to be the "natural, if ghastly, process tending in its own way to the solution of the Indian problem." Jinnah had made his point. That spring a new British viceroy, Lord Mountbatten, went to India to make one last effort to achieve a negotiated settlement. He agreed that partition presented the only solution. The Muslim League, he reported, was ready to "resort to arms if Pakistan in some form were not conceded."

The Partition of India

This settlement was impossible without the agreement of the National Congress. It spoke for the majority of India's population. Partition did not have the support of Gandhi, whose entire life and moral preaching had been dedicated to fellowship and toleration. He had pursued national independence because he believed it to be the path to Indian spiritual rebirth. Acceptance of Pakistan meant recognizing communalism and the victory of religious separatism. He considered the partition to be destructive and evil. He did not impede the settlement, however. He allowed Nehru to assume leadership of the National Congress and to take on his shoulders responsibility for Indian independence. That spring Nehru concluded that partition was inevitable. In June 1947, Mountbatten announced to India and the world that the subcontinent would receive independence not as one but as two states.

Partition cut through the fabric of Indian political, economic, and social life. The provinces with a substantial Muslim population would go to Pakistan, the rest to India. The populations of two key provinces, Bengal and Punjab, were divided among religious groups, with Punjab having similar numbers of Muslims and Sikhs, and a smaller group of Hindus. Provincial leaders reluctantly agreed to the partition of their two regions. A British official secretly rewrote the map of India to draw the boundaries separating the two states. The partition left the Indus River valley in the west and part of Bengal in the east in the new Pakistan state, itself divided in two. Three-fourths of the subcontinent's population went into India, under Congress leadership.

The partition required the division of land, communities, economic systems, and the institutions of state administration and army. East Bengal's economy, dependent on the export of jute, lost its principal port and center of industry, Calcutta, which went to India. The vast irrigation system in the province of Punjab was disrupted because the frontier cut across its river and canal systems. The Sikh community there was split in two, with its holy city of Amritsar in India and its capital of Lahore in Pakistan. Millions of Hindus remained in Pakistan, and one-third of all Muslims were still in India. August 15 was set as the day of independence.

Nehru spoke to the Indian people on Independence Day. He exulted in the newly won freedom from empire. "We are a free and sovereign people and we have rid ourselves of the burden of the past." Despite Jinnah's objections, his state kept the name of India. Even with partition, it was the second-most populous country in the world. The removal of the "burden of foreign domination" represented in his eyes a great historic event, part of the liberation of colonial peoples in their move to equality with the Western nations. He had ambitious plans for dealing with the "great economic problems of the masses of the people," including industrial development, redistribution of wealth, irrigation, and hydroelectric projects. First, however, the country had to "put an end to all the internal strife and violence."

In the capital of Pakistan, Jinnah spoke to his people. He prayed that "God Almighty give us strength to make Pakistan truly a great nation among all the nations of the world." He urged that Pakistan Muslims respect the rights of his country's Hindu population. That day the exact boundaries of India and Pakistan were made public, revealing the true dimensions of partition.

Centuries of British rule had created a legacy that helped shape the new states. British administrators had formed the Indian civil service, whose authority extended into the rural districts to the level of village life. British officers had trained an Indian army in Western military skills. After independence, Indian administrative and military personnel immediately began to serve in the new regimes, replacing the departing British officials. English had been the language by which many educated Indians communicated among themselves and acquired direct access to Western learning. It became the first official language in both states.

The constitutional origins of self-government lay in the Government of India Act of 1935. It had created a federal state that allotted separate legislative powers to the provinces. It laid down the principle of legislative control over the executive in a cabinet form of rule, modeled on the British parliamentary system. This constitution provided the basis of government for both Pakistan and India in their first years of existence. The era of British colonial domination also passed on a valuable economic inheritance. The enormous Indian railroad network and the ocean ports, sinews of an industrial economy, became the property of the new states, as did the irrigation system and hydroelectric dams. The formal transfer of power from Great Britain to India and Pakistan occurred remarkably easily, and the new leaders imagined that their populations would heed their calls for peace and accept the partition as the necessary price for their freedom.

Independence and War

Neither the British nor the nationalist leaders understood the intensity of communal fears and antagonism among Muslims, Hindus, and Sikhs. As a result, they failed to anticipate the outpouring of anger and panic provoked by the announcement of the new boundaries on August 15. Westernized leaders such as Nehru and Jinnah had built up a vast following among the masses, yet were separated from them by class and education. They did not heed the warning from Sikh leaders in the Punjab that "our swords shall decide if the Muslims shall rule," or note the rising numbers of Sikh men joining armed bands in anticipation of conflict with Muslims. Only Gandhi sensed the tremendous human tragedy that partition had precipitated.

The two partitioned provinces, Bengal in the east and Punjab in the north, were the regions where greatest violence was likely to occur. Calcutta, capital of Bengal, had been the scene of the worst rioting in 1946. At the urging of Mountbatten and with the backing of the leader of the city's Muslims, Gandhi agreed to go there. He was prepared to place his own life in jeopardy to prevent blood from flowing again in the city. He went to live in the worst slums of the city, proclaiming a fast to death unless the leaders of the religious communities agreed to collaborate in keeping their peoples from rioting. So great was his moral authority that, almost single-handedly, he maintained peace in Bengal that month.

In the Punjab, however, violence erupted immediately. Refugees began to move across the border, becoming easy targets for mobs. Rumors of atrocities on both sides of the boundaries set Hindus and Sikhs against Muslims in Indian Punjab, while in Pakistan Muslim bands attacked Sikhs and Hindus. The 50,000 troops that Mountbatten had at his disposal could do little to stop the rioting. The numbers of refugees swelled to a torrent as terrified families and entire villages set out on foot or in trains to find sanctuary, the Muslims to Pakistan, the Hindus and Sikhs to India. They became victims of roving bands of killers and robbers. The violence spread to the Indian capital of Delhi, where Hindu refugees from Pakistan spread stories of massacre, rape, and looting by Muslims. In retaliation, Hindus attacked the city's large Muslim population. Mountbatten and Nehru, collaborating closely to prevent chaos from engulfing the country, had to call out the army to keep order there.

In the vast countryside, order was restored much more slowly. Perhaps a half-million Indians and Pakistanis died that year as a result of the hardship of flight or of mob violence. By mid-1948, an estimated five million refugees had arrived in India and perhaps an equal number in west Pakistan. Independence brought the worst civil strife in Indian history and left in its wake intense animosity between the peoples of the two countries. Nehru attacked the Muslim League as "fascist" and vowed never to let such religious fanaticism destroy the democratic and nonviolent principles of the Congress movement. Two years later he recalled in a sort of self-confession the anguish of those terrible months, when Indian leaders became "slaves of the events that inexorably unroll[ed] themselves before our eyes" and succumbed to "fear and hatred." He shared with his people the anger aroused by mob violence.

Gandhi himself came to Delhi late in the year to continue his crusade for peace and understanding. His efforts were directed toward the leaders of the two states as well as toward their peoples. He attacked fanaticism no matter who preached intolerance, Hindu or Muslim. He received all who wished to talk with him despite rumors of plots against his life. On January 20, 1948, a Hindu political extremist, outraged at Gandhi's message of peace and conciliation, shot him as he was going to prayer. Gandhi died a martyr's death, another victim of the partition.

In late 1947, the Indian leaders decided to use military force to bring the Himalayan principality of Kashmir into their state. Though the prince of Kashmir was Hindu, the majority of his population was Muslim. Among them were strong supporters of unification with Pakistan. They had begun violent demonstrations to force their prince to agree to unification with new Muslim state. Pakistani troops moved over the border to bring additional pressure on him. But Nehru, whose family was from Kashmir, was determined to keep the mountainous region in his state. That October Indian troops stopped the Muslim invasion and occupied most of the province. Nehru denied that his state was an aggressor nation and claimed that the Pakistani attack represented "aggression of a brutal and unforgivable kind, aggression against the people of Kashmir and against the Indian Union." In fact, both sides were guilty of aggression, turning to their armed forces for control of the vital Himalayan area.

The conflict over Kashmir escalated into open war between Pakistan and India. Pakistani troops attempted to expel the Indian forces from Kashmir. After several months of fighting, both sides agreed to an armistice, with the front lines close to their original location. The war had succeeded only in partitioning Kashmir by force. Their failure to settle this issue left behind a poisonous legacy of Muslim-Hindu hostility in the mountainous province. The final consequence of partition was to turn Pakistan and India into outright enemies. Their conflict endured for the next fifty years, and erupted twice in new wars. Pakistan, the weaker state, sought military alliance and foreign aid from the United States; India accepted military aid from the Soviet Union. In the early 1980s, both states secretly developed nuclear weapons for possible use against their neighbor. The division of Kashmir turned that front-line territory, once so beautiful it was described as "Shangri-la," into a war zone. Partition was a tragedy for the population of the subcontinent and a terrible burden for the two new states.

INDIA AND PAKISTAN IN THE THIRD WORLD

The subcontinent of India was divided into first two, then three large countries whose leaders claimed, in their own terms, to govern nation-states. Complicating state-building was the painful task of healing the wounds caused by the partition of British India between Pakistan and India, then again of west and east Pakistan in 1971. Within India, small but violent nationalist movements among some of its peoples led to civil disorder and military repression. The promise of peace and civic nationalism that the leaders had originally promised proved beyond their ability to fulfill.

Nehru and the New India

A new Indian state took form under Nehru's leadership. In the first violent months, he and the head of the National Congress, V. Patel, ruled virtually as a military government. Yet the Indian government put together the elements of a democratic state. The first step consisted of completing the incorporation of the princely states into Indian provinces. In exchange for generous

allowances, almost all princes renounced their power peacefully. Only the Muslim prince of Hyderabad resisted, until finally Indian troops occupied his land in 1948 to "restore order" in what was officially called a "police action." The removal of the princes from power amounted to a sort of national revolution, achieved almost without force.

The creation of a new administration and army proved relatively painless. Despite Congress's earlier criticism of Indians working for the British civil service and army, the new government accepted willingly their assimilation into the new Indian state. It preferred the stability and efficiency provided by trained administrators and experienced military forces to the dangers of forming a state apparatus from scratch. This personnel proved its worth in those first chaotic months of independence, serving the new state as loyally as the British *raj*.

Enormous responsibility for the shape of the new state rested in Nehru's hands. His political authority was virtually unlimited, for he enjoyed immense popularity as father of his country. His political ideal, as he told an American audience in 1949, was to find "some balance between the centralized authority of the state and the assurance of freedom and opportunity to each individual." National Congress had from the start gathered together diverse groups defending a variety of interests and creeds. The new state had to reconcile these divergent objectives. Nehru valued this diversity, accepting the compromises it forced upon him.

Agreement on basic political goals did unite all factions of the Congress Party. In Asia, only Japan had successfully adapted Western democratic institutions to its public life. It had the advantage of small size, a homogeneous population, and historical unity. Democratic government in India represented in practice an audacious gamble. It appeared to Congress leaders the best

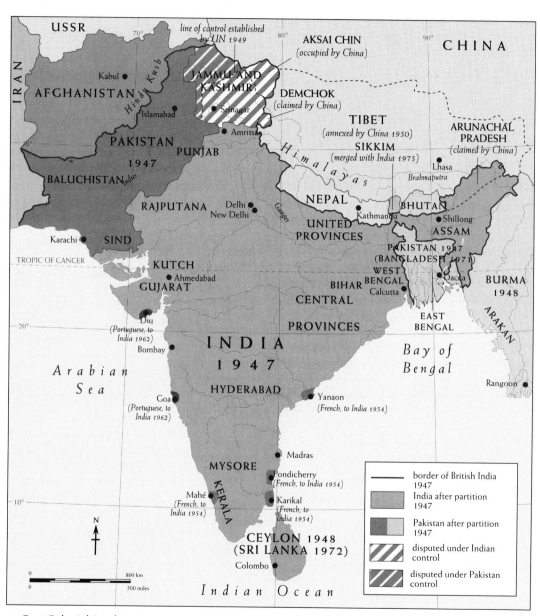

Post-Colonial South Asia

Jawaharlal Nehru (*Embassy of India, Washington D.C.*)

guarantee of toleration and equal rights to all Indians regardless of religion, language, or caste. Political equality of rights was not sufficient for Nehru. He sought as well social reforms to protect and enhance the well-being of the people. These three objectives—democracy, toleration, and socialism—pointed toward the transformation of one of the oldest civilized societies in the world. The task of the Indian leaders was formidable, and the very democratic institutions and diversity that they wished to protect severely restricted their means of action.

The Indian constitution went into effect in 1950. It preserved and extended the federal structure first introduced by the British in 1935. The provincial states and the federal government were all ruled by ministries, de-pendent on majorities in their legislatures to retain power. The position of greatest importance was that of prime minister of the federal cabinet, empowered even to dissolve provincial governments (that is, to violate the principle of federalism) if there existed a threat to the unity of India. Nehru occupied that office until his death. Political and civil liberties were guaranteed to all citizens. Voting was by universal suffrage. The first elections for regular legislative positions took place in 1951. More than 170 million citizens had the right to vote, over half of whom were illiterate. This enormous electorate made India, as Nehru later remarked, the "largest functioning democracy in the world."

Nehru's political stature within India was so great that it might have undermined the very foundations of the free democracy that National Congress defended. Many years earlier he had written for an Indian journal an anonymous portrait of himself, warning that "in this revolutionary epoch Caesarism [i.e., dictatorial rule like that of the Roman general Julius Caesar] is always at the door, and is it not possible that Jawaharlal [Nehru] might fancy himself a Caesar? Therein lies the danger for Jawaharlal and India." He might have added that the danger existed in all the newly independent Asian and African countries. Sukarno of Indonesia did succumb to the temptation of Caesarism. Nehru's restraint was a key ingredient of Indian democracy.

Democratic Socialism in India

The introduction of democratic socialism was an important part of Nehru's program for independent India. His ideal was "a socialist pattern of society which is classless, casteless." His principal concern was the impoverishment of the Indian population. One-half of his people were estimated in

1950 to live in abject poverty, lacking adequate food for an active life. He did not attempt a campaign of expropriation of private property. Peaceful reform and tolerance of diversity forbade that path of reform. Instead, he conceived of an economy divided into public and private sectors, with the state exercising substantial regulatory controls over both. India's established industries remained in private hands, as did its farms and commerce.

For the next forty years, the Indian state played a central role in the country's economic development. It claimed ownership of major industrial projects such as steel mills (built with state funds and foreign aid), of public utilities (gas and electricity), and of new irrigation projects. A National Planning Commission guided the development of India's "mixed economy" (part capitalist, part socialist). Its administrative personnel was responsible for crucial decisions on state investments, agricultural development, transportation, and foreign trade.

The commission employed state funds to guide economic development in a manner best suited (in theory) to improve the living conditions of the people. It relied on a mixture of the Soviet command economy, which Nehru admired, and the collaboration by India's capitalists and peasant farmers. Its most ambitious plan for rural development relied on the voluntary efforts of millions of villagers. The Village Development Program granted state funds to village committees for the construction of wells and schools, for minimum health care, and for other measures essential to fight poverty. Within a few years 150 million Indians shared in the benefits of this program. Indian socialism excluded the use of compulsion and mass mobilization in economic development.

Planning worked well in those first years. India's agricultural production climbed three percent a year, almost twice as fast as population growth. The second Five-Year Plan, though not as successful as the first, did maintain a comparable level of economic expansion. Industrial production, the great hope of that plan, grew six percent annually, a rate that increased to nine percent in the 1960s. A population explosion of almost two percent a year frustrated hopes of freeing India from dependence on industrial imports and insuring adequate food for the country. The country's population soared from 350 million at independence to more than 700 million in the mid-1970s.

Feeding the population became a problem so critical that only Western help saved the country from famine in the mid-1960s. Western agronomists had developed new, high-yield strains of dwarf wheat and rice. They intended their discoveries particularly for poor agrarian lands. These crops were unknown in those areas and required complex farming techniques. Large amounts of chemical fertilizers were needed to sustain substantial harvests year after year. The governments of both India and Pakistan were initially hostile to these exotic crops. India's Minister of Agriculture, faced with a grave population crisis and stubborn opponents, planted his own garden in the capital Delhi with the new wheat to prove its value. His gardening experiment, plus 1,000 "demonstration sites" around the country, proved his point. In 1965, the government distributed the wheat seeds throughout India. Indian grain production soared, and by the mid-1970s, the country was producing harvests sufficient to meet the needs of the growing population. The use of fertilizers spread, produced among other places at a new factory outside the city of Bhopal. Famine in India was averted, at least for a few decades.

The success of the "Indian way" of economic development did not produce miracles, but its results were substantial. Perhaps the best comparison was with China, where famine and economic stagnation followed the Great Leap Forward of the late 1950s. By contrast, India's moderate policies avoided social turmoil and maintained for the first decades a steady rate of economic growth, albeit at a snail's pace.

Improvements also came in health and education. Average life expectancy among Indians doubled between 1950 and 1990, rising from thirty-two to sixty years. It was a phenomenal achievement, resulting from both the relative success of public health and the improvement in the Indian standard of living. Indian efforts to spread education were much less successful. During those same decades literacy spread to only one-half of the population. The key skill opening access to the modern economy remained unobtainable still for hundreds of millions of Indians. The Indian government was determined not to let this handicap get in the way of disseminating its news (and national ideals) among the population. To do so, it set up a national television network, launched a communications satellite, and provided villages with television sets (coming before schools in some cases).

Despite these improvements, poverty remained widespread. In the 1980s, over one-third of the total population was still impoverished. Once hidden in the vast countryside of the subcontinent, the poor became far more visible when, in a desperate search for a livelihood, they moved to urban areas. Places such as Calcutta received in the 1980s a thousand new residents each day. India's cities became focal points of human misery. A wasteland around a new pesticide factory near the city of Bhopal became a shantytown for hundreds of thousands of these poor migrants, until an explosion at the plant spread poisonous gases that killed thousands of the inhabitants in 1984. Urbanization in such conditions was a sign not of economic development but rather of the struggle to survive on the part of hundreds of millions of Indians.

Ethnic Diversity and Secular Democracy

During the same period, the Indian government put into effect laws intended to insure equal rights for all India's peoples, whose pervasive inequality defied their democratic ideals. "Secularism" was the slogan of the National Congress government to promote their program. It was intended to assure the protection of civil law and a common citizenship to the entire population. Social custom, religious laws, and entrenched ways of life stood in the path of these ideals. So, too, did democratic principles of governance. Nehru insisted that progress come in this area "through our own volition, as a result of our own experience," not "through any kind of force or pressure."

The constitution itself abolished the social category of untouchables and declared caste restrictions illegal. It established the principle of social equality for all Indians regardless of religion, caste, or sex. To become effective, however, its principles had to be put in practice, for it confronted the deeply rooted customs of marriage and property ownership, bastions of caste exclusiveness and of the subjugation of women. Caste prejudices continued to divide the population, and intolerance toward untouchables weakened very slowly despite special laws to protect them.

At the heart of the secular project was the commitment of the Indian leaders to keep their state neutral in all religious matters. All official discussions and policies were to avoid even the slightest implication of preference for one religion or another. This concern was most acute in the state's relations with the minority Muslim population. They remained apprehensive at any threat to their religious laws and customs. Though it was not originally intended to do so, secularism turned into a form of defense of Islam. The Muslim community retained its own customary laws governing marriage and divorce. In this domain, the civil laws of the state did not reach all the people.

The majority Hindu population did slowly receive legal protection as individual citizens. In the mid-1950s, the Indian state issued basic laws establishing equality of rights for Hindu women. The Hindu Marriage Act of 1955 and the Hindu Succession Act of 1956 established the legal basis for equality among Hindu Indians. The Succession Act gave women equal rights with men in inheritance and ownership of property. The Marriage Act declared polygamy and bigamy criminal offenses, permitted divorce, and made provision for alimony. Subsequently, marriage dowry was made illegal. In daily life, this equality of condition spread first among upper- and middle-class women in India. They increasingly shared in the new opportunities for education and work.

Among the remainder of the population, social custom and family restraints continued to hold women in lower status. "Purdah" (female seclusion) was still widely practiced among Muslims. The custom of marriage dowries, though illegal, became the source of cruel demands from the husband's family for expensive gifts from the family of the bride. When these were refused, the wife risked beatings, even murder, at the hands of her husband and his relatives. Women's defense groups estimated that in the 1980s between 10,000 and 15,000 women died each year as a result of these dowry murders. Only by comparison with past conditions could one conclude with Nehru that India's secular reforms instituted "equality of status and opportunity" among Indians.

Multireligious and multiethnic, the Indian government held the country together with a mixture of concessions to ethnic communities, appeals to civic nationalism, and military repression of movements that appeared to threaten the unity of the country. Ethnic loyalties, based on religion and culture, constituted a powerful force in a country divided by a multitude of distinct languages and cultures. Leaders of ethnic groups organized campaigns for the redrawing of provincial borders to give their peoples their own territory. Their demands posed the threat of partition if they chose to demand secession from India. Gradually, the government submitted to these pressures. In 1956, several provincial states disappeared, and new provincial territories, each uniting a distinct ethnic group defined by a common language, took their place. This measure opened the door for further agitation among India's peoples, whose bond of unity remained fragile.

Still, Nehru's achievements were substantial, for he focused the attention of Indians on national problems and gave them a sense of national pride. He could not create out of the enormous Indian population one nation in the full sense of the word. Just how important he was to India became apparent after he died in 1964. With only brief interruptions, the National Congress and Indian voters preferred the leadership of his family in the next quarter-century. They first chose his daughter, Indira Gandhi, then his grandson, Rajiv Gandhi, to be prime minister. Their domestic program differed from Nehru's principally in their gradual turn away from those aspects of a command economy that he had introduced. Indian nationalized industry proved to be inefficient and costly, and the "permit state" tied up economic enterprises in complicated and unending requirements for official documentation. The new leadership relied increasingly on Indian capitalists and foreign investors for economic development, new jobs, and technological innovation. Still, Nehru's personal charisma seemed for a time to have become a family heritage, endowing his descendants with the symbolic majesty of national unity.

Ethnic strife was never absent for long from Indian life. In 1989, Kashmir secessionists rebelled against Indian rule. Backed by Pakistan, they demanded for the Muslim population of the province the right to form an independent state. The Indian army was again called upon to enforce Indian unity. Its forces set up a regime of military rule in Kashmir. Occasional border skirmishes with Pakistan troops in the 1990s maintained an unsettled condition resembling low-grade war in the region.

Elsewhere in India, basic political liberties remained a reality for most Indian citizens. The untouchable community was no longer excluded from public life, for they used their voting power to elect their own leaders to provincial government. Parts of the country became centers of the electronics and computer industries, aided by foreign investors such as Microsoft and overseas Indians who had themselves become wealthy entrepreneurs in this "new economy." Despite periodic civil strife between Muslims and Hindus, India retained its national unity and democratic freedoms.

War and Peace in South Asia

Nehru shared with Sukarno and other leaders of the newly independent states their opposition to "neocolonialism," that is, any form of dependence on Western political or economic institutions. He understood decolonization to mean the beginning of a new era of international peace and cooperation. His visionary program confronted two major obstacles. One was the conflict between his country and Pakistan. The second arose from India's serious border dispute with China. The first conflict brought into South Asia military alliances and nuclear weapons. The Chinese dispute proved the undoing of Nehru's idealistic foreign policy.

The Indian government claimed large regions in the sparsely inhabited territories of the Himalayas. Nehru did not attempt to confirm the boundary either by military occupation or by negotiations with the Chinese. Instead, India signed an agreement in 1954, the Sino-Indian Agreement. It recognized Chinese control of Tibet. Nehru chose to deal with the boundary dispute by ignoring it. In the meantime, the Chinese government began building a strategic road through parts of the disputed territory between Tibet and the western province of Xinjiang. How could peace be preserved among the Asian states when they confronted intractable territorial conflicts? Nehru had no solution to that problem.

He slowly worked out his new foreign policy in the years following independence. In spirit, it resembled the National Congress goals for a reformed India. It sought peaceful change through cooperation, with its ultimate goal the equitable distribution of wealth and well-being among all the peoples of the world. Within India, the National Congress had striven to unite groups with varying interests around one common goal, national independence. India acted in world affairs in a similar manner, not allying with any power bloc but proposing its assistance as neutral mediator and unifier among states.

In a speech in 1949, Nehru stated that his country's objectives consisted of the pursuit of peace not by joining any major power or group of powers, but through an independent approach to each controversial or disputed issue. His version of internationalism, reminiscent of Wilson's approach, denied that power politics and balance of power were the basis of foreign relations. His ideals were those of a visionary who dreamed of an era of peace to come with the liberation of subject peoples.

He counted on his prestige as Indian national leader and on the influence of his large state to bring together a group of nations committed to his principles. In the 1954 Sino-Indian treaty, the Chinese Communists supported his Five Principles of international relations: peaceful coexistence, nonaggression, territorial respect, nonintervention, and equality. To them, the principles probably appeared a minor concession to the Indian leader in exchange for recognition of their conquest of Tibet. Nehru came away believing that they had accepted the Five Principles to guide their own policies (including acceptance of Indian border claims).

He defended his policies before a larger audience at Bandung in 1955. This Conference of Non-Aligned States, attended by delegates from countries in Africa, Asia, and Latin America, agreed with his goal that there should be "no domination in the future" by powerful Western countries in former colonial lands. The conference participants were so deeply divided already, however, over the issues raised by the Cold War that they could not agree on Nehru's Five Principles. They merely adopted a vague "Declaration on World Peace and Cooperation."

The Five Principles failed to convince the Chinese government to accept the Indian border proposals. The unresolved border issue and Chinese annexation of Tibet became a source of serious concern by the late 1950s. By then, the Chinese road between Xinjiang and Tibet was nearing completion. It passed through high mountainous regions (14,000 to 15,000 feet) where India had no frontier troops. In 1959, the Indian government welcomed the Dalai Lama when he fled Tibet after Chinese troops had quelled a major Tibetan revolt (see Spotlight, pp. 210–212). In reaction, the Chinese government accused India of "walking in the footsteps of the British imperialists and harboring expansionist ambitions toward Tibet." Chinese and Indian frontier forces moved closer along their long high-mountain border. Nehru acknowledged that China, a "world power or would-be world power," and India confronted a crisis so acute that "for the first time two major powers of Asia face each other on an armed border."

Neither side was prepared to compromise. China was isolated, but its army was well trained and equipped for mountain war. Nehru claimed that justice was on India's side, denouncing China's "unlawful" seizure of Indian territory. He would negotiate with the Chinese on the condition that they concede Indian possession of the disputed frontier regions. The Chinese government refused. Finally, the Indian army began in 1962 to move troops into the remote western areas where the Chinese strategic highway was located. War had become unavoidable. China would not abandon its vital road link, and India chose to back its claim to the frontier region with military force.

The Chinese knew that military superiority was on their side. Indian troops were still few in number and unprepared to fight at high altitude. In late October 1962, Chinese troops attacked along both the eastern and western borders. Everywhere Indian resistance collapsed. Within three weeks, Chinese forces had destroyed Indian frontier defenses and were in a position in the east to invade the Indian lowlands. Nehru accused the Chinese government of violating "all principles which govern normal neighborly relations between sovereign governments" by a "deliberate cold-blooded decision" to invade India. Nonalignment offered no protection at a time of military defeat. Fearing a Chinese invasion of India, Nehru appealed for U.S. naval and air support. The United States agreed, moving ships from the U.S. Pacific fleet into the Bay of Bengal, close to one of the areas of fighting.

Then the Chinese troops withdrew. They had defeated Indian frontier forces and had established control over the territory around the Tibetan road. Their commanders sought no more. In the east, they pulled back behind the original border and proclaimed a cease fire with a twenty-mile neutral zone to separate the opposing sides. The war was over. Although no negotiations followed the end of the fighting, China had settled the border dispute by force of arms. Its army had fought and won a limited war for a specific territorial objective, applying a centuries-old Western principle of using war as a continuation of diplomacy by other means. India was powerless to alter the settlement.

Islam in Pakistan

Pakistan's path after independence diverged dramatically from that of India. The first years revealed the fundamental differences between the two countries. In both states, the colonial political reform of 1935 had provided the first elements of independent political life, creating a federal state and establishing the cabinet system of rule for India. But the Muslim League could not nurture the political conditions needed for democratic government. Its problems were enormous. Its leader, Jinnah, died in 1948. Deep internal social and ethnic differences among Pakistanis thwarted his successors state-building. The Muslim League's backing among the country's population was weak, for it had never succeeded, as National Congress had, in becoming a mass movement.

Only the Muslim religion provided a fragile bond among the population. The constitution proclaimed Pakistan to be an Islamic Republic. It was the first state to lay down the principle that the Quran was the basic law of the land. Many Middle Eastern states with large Muslim populations imitated its example later. A shared Muslim identity was not sufficient, however, to overcome regional and ethnic rivalries. The greatest threat to the unity of the new state was the territorial division of the state into two parts. Its leadership and the state capital were in West Pakistan. The Muslim League government dominated East Pakistan, though the people there were deeply attached to their own Bengali language and culture. After 1954, East Pakistanis rejected the political leadership of the Muslim League, preferring their own parties.

Political leadership proved incompetent and unstable. Prime ministers of Pakistan succeeded one another in rapid succession, six in the first ten years of independence. That instability and the internal conflicts between East and West Pakistan discredited democratic rule. In 1958, parliamentary democracy in Pakistan ceased to exist. The "Caesarism" of which Nehru had warned became a reality in the Muslim state. A general, Ayub Khan, seized power that year and promised to introduce order and to set up "Basic Democracy." The term masked a military dictatorship. He agreed to a military pact with the United States, for the alliance brought his poor country massive U.S. aid—$4 billion between the late 1950s and late 1980s. He accepted the suggestions of American economic advisers to encourage individual enterprise and capitalist development, a strategy that brought economic growth at the price of further deepening the country's social inequalities.

Military rule proved no better able to insure political unity than civilian government. Opposition to rule from West Pakistan grew steadily in East Pakistan. Its leaders protested the government's inadequate aid for their people, who were considered by economists among the most impoverished populations in the world. By the late 1960s, East Pakistan was under military occupation by forces from West Pakistan. Bengali political leaders were placed under arrest.

In 1971, the conflict became open war. That year, Bengalis demonstrated and rioted against Pakistan rule. Repression by the army led millions of Bengalis to flee across the border into Indian Bengal. The Indian government, eager to weaken Pakistan, welcomed the refugees. The conflict escalated quickly. Under pressure from its own Bengal population, the Indian government decided to support the rebellion. When Pakistani forces refused Indian demands to end their military occupation, the Indian army invaded East Pakistan. Once again, India and Pakistan were at war. The fighting ended quickly with Indian victory. The peace settlement required that the Pakistan government withdraw from Muslim Bengal. The rebel leaders proclaimed the independence of their land under the name of Bangladesh.

Pakistan itself remained with less than half the population of the prewar state. Its economy came to depend more than ever on U.S. foreign aid. Poverty and disease were severe among the lower classes, among whom many men migrated overseas in search of work. They remained away, some for years at a time, in Europe and the Middle East. The "remittances" that they sent back to their families came to represent a substantial part of Pakistan foreign earnings. England remained the greatest lure. Migrants settled there in large communities, bringing with them their religious practices and social customs.

The great hopes of the first years of independence faded for many Pakistanis. What was left was the vision of a country uniquely Muslim and the reality of continued internal ethnic quarrels and the threat of war with India. Quranic legal and social regulations became part of the constitutional basis of the state after 1978. Educated Pakistanis who objected to the strict Islamic laws of their country could move to England, for them a place of individual freedom and secular rights. But poverty among a rapidly growing population and social and ethnic strife remained. Backed by the U.S. government, Pakistan provided secret support for the guerrilla uprising in neighboring Afghanistan after Soviet troops invaded in 1979 (see Chapter 11). The only immediate result was to open Pakistan to militant Muslims eager to join the "holy war," embroiling the Pakistan government in factional struggles among the Afghan rebels.

The military rulers were unable to govern their country effectively. Faced with the opposition of political parties and by most of the population, they withdrew from power and permitted democratic government to return to Pakistan in 1988. Ten years later, another general seized power, justifying his action by pointing the religious and ethnic strife tearing his country apart. The Muslim religion remained a dubious symbol of national unity in a land founded on the idea of an Islamic nation.

📖 SPOTLIGHT: Salman Rushdie 📖

Salman Rushdie (1947–   ) grew up in two worlds and turned this experience into the inspiration for his literary work. He was born in Bombay, India. His Muslim father was educated in England, and later in life moved to Pakistan. Rushdie also went to England for his high school and university education. He became fluent in English as well as his native Indian tongue. Though he returned often to Pakistan and India, he chose to live in England and to make a living as a writer.

The decision to remain in the West was closely connected to his desire to become a novelist. The career of writer of fiction had appeared in England two centuries earlier. Creative writers depended for their livelihood upon a vast network of journals, publishers, and critics to maintain creative literature as an honorable occupation, upon a large audience of readers to support new literature, and upon laws protecting writers' freedom of thought and expression. Centuries before, England had developed that vast and complex cultural, economic, and legal network (as had other Western countries). India in the 1960s was just beginning to establish this secular culture. Alongside it flourished another, ancient literary tradition whose writings were passed on from generation to generation, not rewritten or replaced. Novels were not a part of that older civilization.

Rushdie had practical reasons also to choose England. India and Pakistan were lands of many languages. Though English was the language most widely shared among their educated population, it reached only a relatively limited audience. Direct access to an English-speaking public opened to Rushdie the largest readership in the world. England was at the center of this English-language literary world. Rushdie's decision to become an English-language novelist led naturally to the choice of living in England.

His choice had its roots, as well, in his deepest personal convictions. To be a writer meant for him, as for most modern writers, to enjoy the right to express his own ideas and to be protected by laws and courts in that right. The most precious gift to writers in

liberal democracies was freedom of the press. No one, not the state or church or ruling class, enjoyed the power to censor authors. In countries such as India and Pakistan writers were not guaranteed this protection. Bigots, that is, those who refuse to tolerate differing opinions, are found everywhere. But their power to do harm to their enemies, including writers, is far greater where they can claim to defend sacred truth. India was one of those places, as was Iran after its Islamic revolution of 1979. Rushdie was better off in England.

He drew from his experience and knowledge of India and Indians the inspiration for his stories. He found the national independence of India an extraordinary event, but did not believe that everything India's leaders did was wonderful. His novel *Midnight's Children* (1981) was critical of this myth of nationhood as experienced by his novel's very ordinary hero, whose only distinction was to be born at the very instant in 1947 of Indian independence. His second important novel, *The Satanic Verses* (1988) examined the difficult experience of Muslim Indians who migrated to England. In telling his story, he imagined through dreams of the novel's hero, uprooted and losing his faith, that even events in the Quran were just stories written by human beings, not a revelation from God. He was, in these terms, critical of a fundamental religious myth. For this act, he became a hunted man.

Fundamentalist Muslims condemned his book. Some in England publicly burned copies of the novel. The Indian government, fearing Muslim riots, banned the sale of his book in their country. Most serious of all, the religious leaders in the new Islamic Republic of Iran sentenced him to death for the crime of blasphemy, which in the minds of fanatical believers was a sinful act of irrever-

Anti-Rushdie Demonstration, Bangladesh, 1989 (*Reuters/Archive Photos*)

to live in hiding under police protection for a decade. Two translators of his novel (one in Japan, the other in Norway) were murdered. Finally, in 1999, the Iranian government lifted its sentence on the novelist. Rushdie could live a normal life once more.

Rushdie had only remained true to the calling of a writer, as he and the laws of his adopted country understood that term. In the twentieth century, writers from many countries used the power of the pen to attack the abuses committed by dictatorships where human rights were at risk, and to criticize all those in positions of power who brutally exploited the weak. The ability of writers to imagine and share with their readers a universal human condition gave them a special voice in this century's tortured history. One writer, V. S. Naipaul, called their cultural ideals "our universal civilization." It was dedicated in his judgment to "the idea of the individual, the life of the intellect, the idea of perfectibility and achievement."[2] Rushdie belonged to that civilization.

ence toward God. Though he was a British citizen protected by British laws, Iran's government called on "all zealous Muslims" to carry out the sentence. Rushdie was forced

---

[2]V. S. Naipaul, "Our Universal Civilization," *The New York Review of Books,* January 31, 1991, p. 25.

SUMMARY

Did independence bring substantial improvements to the populations of the south Asian countries? The question, which arises also in the recent history of other Third World regions, is controversial and complex. On what grounds does one measure progress in the history of developing nations: national independence, political freedom, economic growth, the lessening of social inequalities, ethnic and religious diversity safeguarded within a nation-state? All of these goals appeared to a greater or lesser extent in the policies of Third World governments and in the public aspirations of the peoples of those lands. None of them was fully achieved in the decades following independence. The disappointment and anger provoked by these failures led to a search for simple explanations.

Neocolonialism provided one easy answer. Sukarno blamed it for Indonesia's economic failures and international weakness in the early 1960s. His search for Western culprits was not, in historical hindsight, convincing. The root of Indonesia's problems under his rule lay in ethnic divisions, poverty, and the incompetence of his government. His fall from power was caused largely by his own short-sighted attempt to impose unity around his charismatic leadership in a one-party state. It opened the way for army generals to use military force to bring order to the vast territories of the state and to impose their own rule.

Colonialism left a complex heritage that the peoples of the former colonies chose to accept or reject in ways that the concept of neocolonialism does not help us to understand. To enhance their power and glory, European conquerors created large colonies out of scattered islands and disparate peoples. The Philippines, Indonesia, and India came into existence as unified lands under colonial rule. Imperial methods of rule did not by themselves create ethnic conflict but did make such antagonism more likely to erupt when the empires collapsed.

Indian nationalists nurtured, sustained, and enriched the idea of the Indian nation during British colonial rule. In Gandhi's hands it became a lofty ideal of human solidarity and moral equality. Responsibility for the tragic collapse of that dream, destroyed in the partition of the subcontinent, rests with the political leaders, imperial and national, and with the deep animosities that divided the Indian masses. There, as in other parts of the world, ethnic antagonism aroused latent fears of outsiders, from within as well as beyond the new state borders. Loyalties were never a simple matter of language, culture, religion, or ancestry. In the case of

Pakistan, its nascent national unity drew primarily on Islamic solidarity. But the state's partition in 1971 revealed that the unique language and cultural traditions of East Pakistan's Bengal people were more powerful bonds than the Muslim faith that they shared with West Pakistan peoples. The new nation-states were fragile creations.

Authoritarianism was a tempting answer to instability. Generals from national armies came at times to believe themselves the saviors of the state, but invariably resorted to brutal methods of dictatorial rule to remain in power. Burma (renamed Myanmar), once a model new nation-state, became in the 1980s and 1990s the worst case of military dictatorship and economic decay in the region. Its generals preferred to seal the country off from the outside world for fear that the free flow of goods and ideas would undermine their regime. National independence and social progress were goals for Asian countries whose means and capabilities could not possibly match their dream.

DATES WORTH REMEMBERING

1946   Philippine independence
1947   Indian independence and partition
1947   Nehru chosen prime minister of India
1947–1948   War between Pakistan and India
1950   Sukarno first president of Indonesian republic
1951   Indian federal constitution
1955   Bandung Conference of Non-Aligned States
1962   Sino-Indian War
1964   Death of Nehru
1965   "Green Revolution" crops accepted by India
1965   Singapore forms independent state
1966   General Suharto becomes ruler of Indonesia
1971   Indo-Pakistan war and independence of Bangladesh

1981	Pakistan aid to Afghan rebels
1982	Sikh rebellion against India
1984	Assassination of Indian leader Indira Gandhi
1989	Kashmir Muslims revolt against India

RECOMMENDED READING

Southeast Asia

*Stanley Karnow, *In Our Image: America's Empire in the Philippines* (1989). A history of the close relations between the United States and the Philippines before and after independence.

C. L. M. Pendus, *The Life and Times of Sukarno* (1974). A critical biography of Indonesia's national hero and deposed ruler.

India and Pakistan

*Larry Collins and Dominique Lapierre, *Freedom at Midnight* (1975). A dramatic history of the personalities and circumstances surrounding liberation of Britain's greatest colony.

Patrick French, *Liberty or Death: India's Journey to Independence and Division* (1997). A balanced historical assessment of India' recent colonial past and the tragedy of partition.

James Harrison, *Salman Rushdie* (1992). A discussion of the writer and his works that covers the bitter controversy surrounding his writings.

Memoirs and Novels

*V. A. Naipaul, *Voyage among the Believers: An Islamic Journey* (1981). A personal voyage of discovery through Asian Muslim countries by a West Indian novelist and essayist.

Salman Rushdie, *Midnight's Children* (1981). A colorful portrait of independent India, as viewed through the eyes of an Indian born at the moment of independence.

*Khrushwant Singh, *Train to Pakistan* (1956). A vivid fictional account of the agony of partition, from the perspective of a Punjab village.

CHAPTER NINE

Africa and Latin America in the Third World

Africa and Latin America were distant continents that confronted a similar dilemma in the last half of the twentieth century. Both areas were largely made up of small states with meager resources to care for the needs of growing populations. The difficulties created by this situation provide an important clue to their history in the decades that followed the end of the Second World War.

By 1945, European empires had maintained effective colonial rule over their African colonies for a half-century or more. Twenty years later, almost all these territories had become sovereign states. The coming of independence was unexpected for both the colonial rulers and their peoples. The sudden move to freedom occurred in large part because small nationalist movements in these areas encountered little or no resistance from their colonial rulers. The governments of Great Britain and France, which held the largest imperial domain in

Africa, had turned their attention to internal affairs after the war. They were primarily concerned with their own economic and social reforms. Africa, in this sense, received freedom by default.

The major tasks confronting Africa's new leaders consisted in constructing stable political regimes and in focusing the skills and resources of their territories on raising the standard of living of their peoples. The nation-state became the chosen political model everywhere. The ideal of national unity informed their political speeches, but the diversity of their populations called for guarantees of political pluralism. Just who would take these tasks in hand remained an issue throughout the vast area. In South Africa, the cruel system of white rule was the white population's answer until international and internal resistance forced its abandonment. By the last decade of the century, very few states had split apart, and no conqueror had seized a neighboring state. But the social and economic conditions of the new African states were dismal.

Often leadership fell into the hands of military rulers. No real political stability resulted, however, as rivals for power struggled among themselves. The consequence was periodic insurrection, and civil war. In the 1990s, outside states providing economic aid put pressure on these dictators to restore some measure of democracy, but the results were disappointing. The decline of Africa was especially apparent in the pervasive economic decay throughout the continent. No easy answer could explain the decline of agriculture and industry. Surveys revealed that the living conditions for much of Africa's population were worse than in the first decade of independence.

In Latin America, political life also involved a struggle for power between political leaders and army officers. There, the conflict had persisted ever since independence from Spain in the nineteenth century, and continued into the late twentieth century. In the decades after 1945, civilian and military governments everywhere used state controls over trade and finances to stimulate economic growth. They set up new social welfare programs for basic improvements in the living conditions of the population. Gradually the standard of living in most regions improved. In a few, such as Brazil and Mexico, economic growth increased so rapidly it seemed in its own way to be a "miracle."

The opposition that military rule provoked in many Latin American countries was so strong that by the late 1980s all these dictators had abandoned power. Unable to govern effectively and confronted by mass political opposition from democratic forces, they yielded power to elected civilian leadership. This political transfer occurred in the same years as governments ended the state economic controls introduced at mid-century. In this move, they followed the trend in Africa and Asia where the system of command economies had failed. The spread of democracy in Latin America was one encouraging sign of the decline of the old system of elite rule. The rise of free market economies offered substantial reason to hope that economic development had become the affair of the population. Only Cuba retained its command economy into the 1990s. Despite the failure of their Soviet-type regime to realize its goals, the Cuban revolutionary leadership refused to abandon their dream of socialism. Free enterprise did not bring social justice, but it appeared more suitable than socialist policies in extending to a large portion of the population the opportunity to construct a satisfactory life on their own terms.

AFRICA'S LIBERATION FROM COLONIALISM

In the late 1950s and 1960s, the African colonies of Western empires won their independence. This sweeping transfer of power took place rapidly. It marked the end of Europe's overseas empires. In the late colonial period, the only independent states in sub-Saharan Africa had been Ethiopia (under Italian control for a few years in the 1930s), Liberia, which was a small state created as a refuge for liberated slaves in the nineteenth century, and South Africa, granted independence within the Commonwealth by the British in 1910. Suddenly almost all the peoples of Africa ceased living under Western imperial rule. Their new leaders spoke proudly of their new African nations, even though many different peoples lived in each state, and promised a better life for their citizens, though these countries were still very poor.

African Nationalism

After the end of the Second World War, the British government began to prepare their African colonies for independence. Even then, its most optimistic goals foresaw a slow process of liberation lasting several decades. But its timetable proved pointless under the pressure for colonial liberation. One British statesman called these forces a "wind of change" sweeping away all the colonial empires. For the first time in African history mass nationalist movements spread across the continent. Faced with this opposition, European states were unwilling for long to use repressive measures to sustain colonial rule.

The emergence of African nationalist movements was a remarkable achievement. The peoples within the European colonies were divided by tribal loyalties, by religion, and by language. The presence of European administrators and soldiers ruling these colonies was the tangible symbol of colonialism; the capital cities that flew the flags of their empires and housed the offices of the key colonial officials became sites of nationalist demonstrations and unrest. The struggle for the overthrow of imperial rule was the common bond uniting African nationalist leaders and their peoples.

The areas where strong movements against white rule first emerged in the 1950s were the British colony of the Gold Coast (later Ghana) in west Africa, and Kenya, located in east Africa. Members of the dominant Kikuyu tribe in Kenya organized a violent struggle against white settlers on their land. They named their organization the Land Freedom Army, but Europeans scornfully called it the Mau Mau. Their nationalist leader, Jomo Kenyatta, united his followers around a program for the end to foreign rule, then land reform. Their greatest weakness, one which was apparent in the nationalist movements of other African colonies as well, was the reluctance of other tribal groups to join the Kikuyu revolt.

The British needed four years to repress the violence. In the process, they mobilized other tribes to join the battle against the rebels and resettled many of their African subjects in fortified villages. They captured Kenyatta, who was sentenced to seven years in prison. The Mau Mau uprising left a total of 13,000 dead among the blacks (both Mau Mau followers and British supporters) and thirty-three whites dead. Kenyatta had succeeded in forcing the British government to grant self-government to the colony.

The first anti-colonial campaign to reach its goal of independence, took place in the Gold Coast (Ghana), located on the Atlantic coast of west Africa. The pattern of political activism, and the difficulties of mobilizing mass support there, reveal important characteristics of African independence movements elsewhere in later years. The Gold Coast nationalist leader was Kwame Nkrumah. He was a dynamic and skillful organizer, who used his Western education to formulate his own nationalist creed of liberation and freedom. He began to gather supporters against British rule in the late 1940s. By then a strong labor union movement had appeared among African workers in the colony's port cities, where cocoa beans, the principal Gold Coast cash crop, were exported to the West. The once-powerful Asanti tribes lived in inland areas where the crop was grown. Those commercial links provided key links between the two ethnic communities; this regional market, suffering from price fluctuations passed on to growers and workers by the international corporations, became one source of grievances against British rule.

In 1949, Nkrumah created his nationalist party, the Convention People's Party, joining together activists from urban and rural populations from as far away as the Muslim north. He promised that freedom would put an end to the hardships of the Gold Coast peoples, and would bring them a new era of progress and opportunity. Using language drawn from the Bible, he told his followers: "Seek ye first the political kingdom and all else will follow." Coupled with these promises he launched a campaign of peaceful disobedience against colonial laws. He drew inspiration for his anti-colonial movement from the example of Gandhi and the Indian National Congress. His party honored those activists whom the British sentenced to prison as the party's "Prison Graduates." By the early 1950s, his movement had won such widespread support that the British government, unwilling to continue its costly and fruitless repression, granted the colony self-rule. A British prisoner at the time, Nkrumah agreed to step into the interim position of the Gold Coast's first prime minister. Both sides preferred to avoid violence by agreeing to political compromise.

Nkrumah's goal was a unified state. In other words, he refused to use ethnic loyalties of any people as the cement for his nationalist cause. But the Asanti tribal leaders feared the rule of the southerners in a centralized government. As a result, the British revised the country's new constitution to create a federal system with separate autonomous territories for the major tribal groups. Nkrumah reluctantly agreed to the new arrangement. He had not abandoned his goal, however, of uniting the country under his rule as soon as independence came in 1957. Ghana became the first African country freed from colonial rule. Nkrumah was its first president and a hero for African nationalists everywhere.

Nationalist leaders such as he could mobilize widespread support against colonialism, but their coalition of forces relied for unity on hostility toward the British enemy. They could not rely on the continued backing of a national community, and did not have in hand a program for state-building satisfactory to all the peoples of the new lands. Decolonization in Africa posed problems of state-building more acute than anywhere else in the colonial world.

In the late 1950s, the British and French governments both chose to end colonial rule in Africa as quickly as possible. International pressures played an influential role in accelerating the African decolonization. The leaders of the newly independent states of Asia made the freeing of African peoples an international crusade. Both the United States and the Soviet Union publicly backed freedom for colonial peoples. The United Nations became a public forum where anti-colonial speakers denounced Europe's outdated imperial system. The weakness of the British and French empires became cruelly apparent in their failure to regain control of the Suez Canal in the 1956 war (see Chapter 10). That event proved decisive in pushing the two governments to grant independence to their African colonial territories. Imperialism was a lost cause.

Independence for Africa

Once an area almost entirely governed by distant European empires, Africa suddenly was transformed into a continent divided into more than forty sovereign states. The process by which liberation came depended, in large measure, on the policies of the imperial states. Great Britain followed the procedure that it had used in Asia of negotiating with nationalist leaders in each colony for the creation of constitutional, democratic government. After the Gold Coast, Nigeria became independent in 1960. There, the leaders of the major tribal groups agreed on a federal government to keep unity among its 35 million people. In 1963, Kenya became an independent state under the leadership of Kenyatta, freed at last from British prison to move immediately to the presidency of the new country. The constitutional order of the new states resembled the British parliamentary democracy. The British considered this Western import best for Africa. Many nationalist leaders thought of it as a temporary measure useful during the transition to independence. Despite the speed of decolonization, the British and African leaders managed to cooperate and to maintain peace among the population during the transfer of power.

French decolonization differed from the British method in one major respect. In 1958, the French government proposed liberation coupled with economic and military advisers and financial aid to all French African colonies. For this purpose, it created an association called the French Community. The alternative offered to Africans was independence outside the community and no French support at all. This policy was the creation of Charles de Gaulle, French wartime hero, who in 1958 once again became president of France. His offer of aid through the French Community was an effort to maintain close ties between France and its former African colonies.

Most African leaders from France's empire accepted membership in the French Community, dismissing charges from opponents that his plan was a form of "neocolonialism." They believed it a helpful measure in holding onto power, for they faced daunting problems of state-building. They hoped as well to obtain substantial French economic assistance, especially to fund expensive industrial investments and to sustain the value of their new currency. Each colony that year voted on joining the Community. In each territory, the voters adhered to the recommendation of their nationalist leaders.

All the former French colonies save one became members of the French Community. They received economic aid, financial advisers and technicians, a monetary union with France, and permanent French garrisons located in strategic locations on call in the event of border conflicts or political unrest. In exchange, they safeguarded French investments in their country. The moderate leaders of these new states were effective opponents of radical revolution. They knew it

to be a danger to themselves as well as to France's economic interests. One African leader concluded later that "General de Gaulle is the greatest African of our time." His opinion revealed how highly he valued political stability, achieved at the cost of very little social reform. The aid that France provided did bring those countries substantial benefits. Among these, political stability in the early years of independence was the most important.

In the largest of all the African colonies, the Belgian Congo (later Zaire), decolonization became a nightmare of civil strife and bloodshed. The area experienced violent anti-Belgian demonstrations for the first time in early 1959. The protests were the work of a small nationalist movement supported largely by urban workers in the capital city, Kinshasa (formerly Stanleyville). This brief moment of political opposition was sufficient for the Belgian government to grant its colony independence immediately. In the previous decades it had made no effort to prepare the colony for self-rule. The nationalists themselves lacked a prominent leader supported by the peoples of that enormous country. Swept along by the "wind of change," in 1960 the Belgians freed their colony in the worst possible circumstances.

The results were tragic for the new state and for its population, both African and European. The colonial institutional structure quickly collapsed. The Congolese army mutinied and turned on the white settlers, who fled the country. Tribal groups fought among themselves. The only political leader with a substantial following, Patrice Lumumba, could not restore order in the army and refused any help from the Belgians. The disorders soon became outright civil war. The southern region of Katanga (later Shaba), which was rich in mineral resources and a center of mining operations owned by Western interests, seceded from the new state and created its own army.

The United Nations agreed to send troops from member states to keep the Congo from complete collapse and anarchy. In the course of the fighting, Lumumba himself was captured and executed by Katanga forces. After a long period of political disorder, a former sergeant of the colonial army, Joseph Mobutu, seized control of the government in 1965. By then the surviving white settlers had fled, the economy of most regions was in ruins, and many thousands of Congolese had died in the fighting and rioting. The Democratic Republic of Congo, renamed Zaire a few years later by Mobutu, had begun its slow decay.

The Triumph of Democracy in South Africa

South Africa, the southernmost country of the African continent, had enjoyed self-rule since 1910. The full rights of citizenship were restricted, however, to the white population. A member of the British Commonwealth, South Africa had a privileged place in international trade because of its valuable natural resources. Like a European democracy, its government passed back and forth between conservative and liberal political parties competing for the majority in the country's parliament. Its constitutional order was watched over by an autonomous judicial system, also modeled on British practices. But it excluded the vast majority of the population from participation in this system, and subjected its African subjects to increasingly severe racial discrimination.

This restrictive democratic system opened the way for the country's Afrikaner people (formerly called Boers, the Dutch-speaking settlers) to insert racial intolerance into the constitutional order of the country. They numbered only 4 million, but their Protestant faith and their war with the British at the beginning of the century had made them a tight-knit community. Their three centuries of life as pioneers and farmers in South Africa had persuaded them that this was their native land. Their religious creed taught them that they were the "chosen people" and that the Africans were an inferior race. Their form of ethnic nationalism was racist at its very core. Their leaders were determined to hold onto this homeland by whatever means were necessary.

The economic wealth of the country, concentrated in gold and diamond mining, was in the hands of the English and other recent immigrants from Europe. Urban commerce was the special domain of Indian migrants, who had traveled there in search of work in the growing cities. Africans, for their part, had taken up labor in the country's vast mining industry. The Second World War had brought prosperity to the business interests of the country, dominated by the Anglo-American Corporation. Its holdings were very extensive; one-half of all the companies in the South African stock exchange were in its possession. Social inequality was not entirely a product of white domination. Most of the Afrikaners were farmers with relatively small plots of land, while some Indians and "Coloreds" (people of mixed ethnic ancestry) had prospered in trade. The poorest segment of the population was made almost entirely of Africans.

The social consequences of economic development constituted a threat to white segregation policies. Laws excluding Africans, Asians, and Coloreds from contact with whites had grown increasingly severe during the first half of the twentieth century. An increasing number of nonwhites were entering the urban economy to meet the needs of commerce and industry. Many of them became supporters of the African National Congress (ANC). This organization emulated the methods and goals of the Indian National Congress. Formed in 1912, its members agitated

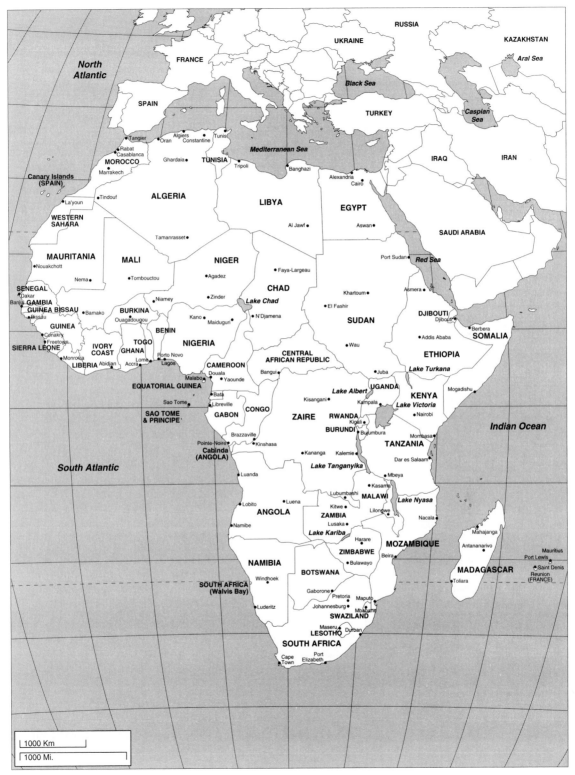

Contemporary Africa

peacefully for democratic freedoms and for an end to segregation in all forms. Its growing influence, and the support it received from liberal whites, presented Afrikaners with a serious threat to their domination.

The Afrikaner people had their own political party, called the Nationalist Party. In the late 1940s, the Nationalist Party triumphed in national elections in which the principal issue was the role in public life to be accorded nonwhites. Its program called for their complete exclusion. It won sufficient backing from the voters to take control of the cabinet. The new Nationalist government proceeded in the next ten years to put in place a policy of racial domination that it called "apartheid." It excluded nonwhites from all political rights, and curtailed their civil liberties. Africans did not even have the right to free choice of residence; they were forced to live in special settlements and permitted into urban areas to work solely as "guests" (the so-called "pass system"). Only the South African court system continued throughout the years of repression to honor (with major exceptions) the British principle of rule of law, even in trials of opponents of apartheid.

The Nationalists denied that the multiethnic, multiracial people of their country could possibly form one nation. Nationalism in their understanding existed only as ethnic loyalty. There was no place for the spirit of civic nationalism in their racist program. Their policies intentionally sought to strengthen the divisions among South Africa's African peoples, whom they referred to as tribes. They were responsible for creating a regime of white supremacy in the very years when the African peoples elsewhere in the continent were obtaining political independence.

The African National Congress was encouraged by the success in the 1950s and 1960s of African nationalist movements to intensify its fight against apartheid. In 1955, it approved a "Freedom Charter," which spelled out clearly its program for a multiethnic, democratic South Africa "belonging to all who live in it." Its Youth League attracted activists impatient with the placid methods of the older members. Young leaders such as Nelson Mandela came forward arguing that the ANC had to fight the increasingly harsh Nationalist racist laws with a new campaign of mass action. Nonviolence remained the basis of their tactics, but the repressive powers of the state were pushing them toward confrontation.

In 1960, the ANC organized large demonstrations against the restrictive pass system applied to Africans. At Sharpsville, an African settlement, South African police fired on the unarmed demonstrators, killing more than sixty. It was a massacre, and like a similar tragedy in India at Amritsar in 1919, it mobilized the ANC to directly confront the regime. More demonstrations followed. In response to massive arrests and brutal imprisonment, the ANC leaders agreed finally to a campaign of violent resistance to accompany its political action. Nonviolence was no longer sufficient. The Nationalists had created a political crisis of their own making.

Their response was to resort to still harsher measures of repression. They outlawed the African National Congress and arrested its leaders on charges of treason. For the next three decades their police hunted down all political opponents. The government pitilessly enforced the pass system and all the laws that maintained white supremacy. It created separate "homelands" for individual African tribes. Africans had no permanent legal residence outside these areas, located in poor regions of the country. The pass laws gave them temporary residence elsewhere in settlements, which became mass ghettos outside the country's major cities. The Nationalists' policies isolated South Africa from the outside world, caused its expulsion from the United Nations, and created a state of emergency in the country.

Resistance came from within and from outside South Africa. The African National Congress retained its mass following (though publicly silenced) and organized itself for survival as an underground organization. Violence within the country erupted frequently as protests were met with repression. In the 1980s, many Western countries joined in an international economic boycott of South Africa. The government found itself in a grave crisis, facing social turmoil and a serious economic recession by the late 1980s. The Nationalist leadership, under a new prime minister, F. W. de Klerk, finally conceded the hopelessness of apartheid. The very survival of South Africa depended upon instituting a new political and social order. The only solution had to be real democracy and racial toleration.

De Klerk's government, formed in 1989, gradually dismantled the laws that had enforced segregation. Many Afrikaners protested, but they had no program of their own to meet the crisis. In a desperate search for a solution to the crisis, the reformers turned to the African National Congress. On 1990, they lifted all the legal restrictions that had denied the ANC the rights of a political party, and freed all its political prisoners.

After a half-century of repression, the Nationalist Party recognized the African National Congress as its equal.

The leaders of the ANC were prepared to cooperate. The Freedom Program had set out the conditions for negotiation. They had never abandoned their belief in the possibility of a peaceful multiethnic land of toleration and freedom. Their claim to speak for all Africans was challenged by a strong political movement among the Zulu people, the largest African tribal group in the country. This Inkatha party, like the Muslim League in India, had no hope of winning in national elections and demanded special recognition to protect the interests of its people. Reluctantly, the ANC agreed to collaborate with Inkatha.

In 1993, negotiations between the Nationalist government, the ANC, and Inkatha produced a new democratic constitution for South Africa. The next year free elections gave the ANC a majority of parliamentary representatives and the right to rule the country. The collaboration of the Nationalists, the ANC, and Inkatha ensured that, despite thirty years of violent confrontation, the transition of power occurred peacefully. This extraordinary, hopeful end to South Africa's political crisis owed much of its success to the remarkable leader of the African National Congress, Nelson Mandela.

❧ SPOTLIGHT: Nelson Mandela ❧

For most of his adult life, Nelson Mandela (1918–) was a political prisoner in South Africa. In 1994, he became president of that state. His decades of imprisonment and sudden rise to power were directly linked to the struggle against and ultimate defeat of the white supremacy regime in that country.

His childhood was spent within one of the African tribal groups living in South Africa. He was born to the ruling family of that tribe. The king sent him to an English-language Methodist secondary school to prepare him to be his heir and successor to the throne. But Mandela chose not to follow in the traditional path. He broke with the religion of his people, joining the Methodist church. After graduation, he left his tribal area to begin a new life in the booming cities of South Africa. He found work in a law office and ultimately earned his law degree.

The racial segregation increasing with every year in his country touched him as much as other Africans and nonwhites who lived there. He chose to make the fight against segregation his calling. When he was twenty-six, he joined the African National Congress, seeking the means to end tribal divisions and unite Africans "as one people." He worked for many years with its Youth League to strengthen popular support for the ANC's program of racial equality and toleration. He was a dynamic, charismatic political organizer and forceful writer. He defended the ANC's program of democracy for all of South Africa's peoples. In his first years in the party, he backed the methods of nonviolent resistance to the racist laws of the Nationalist regime. For that work, he was arrested and accused of treason in 1955. "Because of my conscience," he wrote, "I was made a criminal."

His very life was at risk at the hands of the Nationalist government. The courts finally dismissed the charge of treason. When the Nationalist government in 1960 resorted to violent methods to repress the ANC's campaign against apartheid, Mandela decided that the time had come to abandon nonviolent methods of resistance. South Africa had become, he wrote, a "land ruled by the gun." He saw no choice but to resort to violence, principally attacks on state buildings and key economic installations. This became the special task of his new underground organization, the Spear of the Nation. He became a hunted man, able to speak freely in defense of his cause only during a brief trip to Europe in 1962. When he returned to South Africa, he was arrested, convicted of treason, and sentenced to life imprisonment.

Mandela's long years of prison were a time of moral and physical trial, of isolation and hardship. Yet his commitment to democracy for his country did not weaken, and his political stature grew stronger than

President Nelson Mandela (*Courtesy South African Consulate General, Los Angeles*)

ever. His determination not to give up in the face of the government's repression became an inspiration for ANC followers. In those years, he emerged as the real leader of the ANC. As the international campaign in opposition to apartheid grew stronger, his imprisonment became a measure of the cruelty of the Nationalists' racism. His loyalty to the ANC cause confirmed the inability of their police state to end democratic resistance. In 1980, the Security Council of the United Nations stated that Mandela's release from prison was the first step necessary to permit a "meaningful discussion of the future of the country."

The Nationalists themselves had to concede his prominence as political leader. Mandela had always accepted the principle of peaceful negotiations for the creation of a democratic state granting equal rights to all

its citizens. His release from prison in 1990 came because the Nationalists realized that his active leadership of the ANC was their only real hope to end the country's political and economic crisis. He set the terms of freedom, accepting negotiations only after the government had released all South African political prisoners and had abolished its segregationist policies. In return, he made the peaceful transition of power possible. When the new South African parliament met in 1994 after the country's first free elections, the ANC held the absolute majority. Its representatives elected him to be South Africa's first African president. Mandela had won, as he had always insisted, in a land that belonged to "all who live in it, black and white." Like Nehru in India, he sought to be the leader of a multiethnic nation.

African State-Building and Failed States

During the 1960s the new African states proceeded slowly and painfully along the difficult path of state-building. The experiences of these countries varied greatly, but in the next decade two trends emerged. One was the appearance of authoritarian governments, most frequently under military rule, whose leaders replaced one another in forcible, sometimes bloody struggles for power. The other was economic stagnation and continued impoverishment among the rapidly growing rural and urban population.

Most African leaders quickly abandoned the democratic constitutions adopted at independence. Their peoples had been deprived of the experience in self-rule during the colonial years. After liberation, they

placed the problems of political unification and economic development ahead of the creation of a fair multiparty system of government. Power soon passed into the hands of a political elite, consisting of civilian politicians and ambitious military leaders. One West African politician, whose state was among the best ruled on the continent, explained that "in young countries such as our own, we need a chief who is all-powerful for a certain period of time. If he makes mistakes, we shall replace him later on." He offered his people political stability under strong central rule and believed this the best they could hope for. The experience of other African states suggested that he was right.

In Kenya, Jomo Kenyatta continued in power until his death in 1978. He had no serious political rivals, for his prestige and authority as father of his country was enormous. His political party dominated the government. Violence rarely disrupted public life, though one influential politician from a rival party was found assassinated and his murderers were never captured. Kenya experienced orderly rule and relative prosperity, with white settlers living alongside their former enemies. The army remained small, and the press enjoyed the freedom to report critically on public events. In Kenyatta's lifetime, Kenya represented the best case of independence with a stable government protecting a peaceful society.

Even a few small states proved that liberation from colonialism was a process that both leaders and peoples could successfully manage. The former British colony of Botswana, landlocked and largely desert, had a few advantages that proved decisive. The British had left in place tribal leadership of precolonial times, and independence in 1966 endowed those leaders with new legitimacy as national figures. The desert hid great reserves of diamonds, whose discovery in 1969 and exploitation remained a private business (though with a substantial share of the profits going to the state). Democratic government continued to function effectively. By the 1990s, its funds provided elementary education for all the country's children and adequate health care for a population whose average life expectancy had reached seventy. Along with these benefits, Botswana's citizens enjoyed a standard of living comparable to that of emerging economies in Asia. Key to the country's well-being was effective democracy.

In most new African states, authoritarian regimes brought only instability and misrule. Ambitious politicians sought ever-greater power by manipulating parliaments, extorting state funds for their personal enrichment, and creating mass parties whose only purpose was to serve and to glorify themselves. Little or no political freedom existed, and enemies of the regime ended in jail, or assassinated. Events after independence in Ghana illustrate this trend. Nkrumah had promised an era of great reforms when he took power. He set about reforming the free market system, introducing laws creating a type of command economy. Proclaimed by his party "Man of Destiny" and "Redeemer," he rewrote the constitution to make himself president for life. His greatest ambition was to be recognized leader of all the African nations. He promoted the Organization of African Unity and spent vast sums of money entertaining visiting African heads of state.

His rule proved disastrous for his people. He lacked the skilled personnel and the personal ability to use effectively the resources at his disposal, including large grants of foreign aid. Economic conditions worsened, and the standard of living of the people declined. By 1966, nine years after independence, economic decay and political disorder had undermined his authority. His own military commanders forcibly removed him from power. The army, which was the only national institution with a semblance of legitimacy among the population, became the backbone of dictatorship and army generals took charge of the government. Ghanaians welcomed his departure, destroying the statues and photographs that had glorified his exalted leadership throughout the country.

The usual pattern in many African countries became government by force of arms. During the 1960s, a total of forty successful insurrections took place in the independent African states. They were the work of small groups of leaders and armed followers. Other revolts were attempted but failed. In no African state did a new government come to power in those years in an orderly manner through democratic elections. One African observer sadly concluded: "We will never be at peace again."

In the midst of such political unrest, peoples turned for protection to their tribal leaders. Tribal power frequently determined the winners in the struggle for power; conflict among tribes became a cause of bitter civil war. The bloodiest of these wars was the conflict in Nigeria. It began when northern, Muslim peoples suspected (without substantial reason) that the Ibo people in the south had acquired a commanding role in the government of the Nigerian federation. They were fearful that their own well-being and security would suffer if Ibo people obtained special favors. The rumors were sufficient to set off bloody riots. Ibo settlers were attacked by mobs in areas where they lived among other tribal groups. The federal government appeared incapable of protecting the Ibo, who fled to their homeland.

Ethnic violence led, in a vicious spiral of rumors, riots, and death, to civil war in 1966. An Ibo general convinced his people to secede from Nigeria. He counted on Ibo solidarity, which proved amazingly strong. For three years in the late 1960s the Ibo people fought to establish their own state, called Biafra. Outnumbered and besieged by the Nigerian army, the Ibo abandoned the struggle only after their land was largely devastated and famine had decimated the population. Even then, their leaders refused to admit defeat and demanded that the people fight to the death. The foreign support that they had counted on melted away when the extent of the suffering became known outside Biafra. Nigeria was reunited, but at a terrible price. State-building in these conditions became a desperate effort to preserve, in the face of bitter ethnic rivalry, a country's meager remnants of civil order and political unity.

For the next two decades, authoritarian regimes headed usually by military officers governed most of Africa's new states. Their rule depended on the armed might at their disposal. New leaders appeared usually after the violent overthrow of their predecessors in a turbulent struggle for power. When one strong ruler managed to remain in control for a lengthy period, the country was spared political turmoil. Invariably, though, the price was widespread corruption and persistent violations of civil liberties. At best, these leaders became aware of the urgent economic and social needs of the country. Their authoritarian practices made it fairly easy to end state economic controls and to allow a market economy to take root again. Ghana experienced a remarkable economic recovery in the 1980s after its military rulers abandoned the command economy that Nkrumah had put in place, and opened the way for free trade in farm produce and industrial goods.

At worst, these rulers ravaged the meager level of well-being of their peoples. In the decades after he seized power in 1965, President Mobutu of Zaire (formerly the Democratic Republic of Congo) accumulated enormous personal wealth while gradually dilapidating the meager industry and public services of his vast country. His personal prestige as leader of the largest state in sub-Saharan Africa brought him the support of Western states. Large amounts of foreign aid poured into his country. Most of the funds were wasted, going into his private bank accounts in Europe. He argued in television messages and public speeches that he was the guarantor of national loyalty and solidarity. His message won him the support of those in his country who hoped Zaire's diverse peoples could be united under a just ruler in a multiethnic state. But he failed to satisfy their hopes.

His government nationalized the prosperous mining industry. Instead of reinvesting the profits, he appropriated its income for his own purposes. By the early 1990s, his mismanagement and the growing rebelliousness of his army had produced conditions in Zaire close to anarchy, that is, the absence of any organized system of law and order. The country's administration fell apart for want of funds, the army lacked arms and air transport, road and river transport dwindled, airports ceased operations, and cities lacked police protection, sanitation, or school. The borders of Zaire remained intact, at least on maps of Africa, and its flag still flew among the United Nations flags. In other respects, Zaire ceased to function as a real state by the 1980s. It had become a "failed state," among those places in the world where the essential tasks of a modern state and economy had ceased to exist.

The Cold War penetrated the African region in the decades after decolonization. It came as a result of competition between the Soviet Union and the United States for allies among African states and for access to the valuable natural resources (including uranium) of the continent. The U.S. Central Intelligence Agency (CIA) established close ties with President Mobutu of Zaire, sending him secret military support and financial aid to help sustain his regime even after he proved to be a disastrous ruler. When in the 1970s civil war erupted in the former Portugese colony of Angola, the Cold War rivals took sides in an effort to control the outcome of the conflict. Soviet advisers and Cuban military forces were able (temporarily) to help their Angolan ally to gain the upper hand in that war. That foreign assistance stopped with the end of the Cold War in the late 1980s. The Soviet Union and the United States had become involved for reasons of state interests, not because they had an abiding commitment to the well-being of African peoples. Hardship and civil unrest worsened in these countries.

Effective opposition to dictatorship emerged within African countries from small groups committed to the political and civil liberties promised in their countries' first constitutions. It came as well from Western governments, whose economic aid was increasingly vital to the very survival of some African lands. In 1990, both France and Great Britain announced that their aid would go in the future only to African states that respected their peoples' civil liberties, that permitted voters in democratic elections to select their leaders, and that loosened the state's control over economic life. Many of the military leaders did, in fact, make serious efforts to open political life to parties and permitted elections.

The results were disappointing, however. In Nigeria, the military rulers refused in 1993 to allow the newly elected president to assume office, arguing that they alone could keep the ethnic hostility of the country's peoples from erupting in a new civil war. Another six years passed before free elections finally brought a civilian president to power there, and then in conditions of worsening ethnic conflict. Elsewhere, elections became a moment of struggle among ethnic groups, some of whose political leaders played on the fears of their people to win their votes.

African countries remained deeply divided by religious and ethnic bonds that impeded the formation of strong ties of national loyalty. This "tribalism" appeared to the Nigerian writer Chinua Achebe a form of "discrimination against a citizen because of his place of birth." But his wish for the growth of civic nationalism in his country remained an optimistic vision of the future. Only a few African states had become fully independent and truly unified.

The Slow Decay of African Economies

Closely linked to political decay was the failure of most African countries to achieve economic growth sufficient to sustain an adequate standard of living for most of the people. The population explosion in Africa was greater than in any other part of the world, with growth fluctuating between 2.5 and 3 percent a year in the last decades of the century. Food production fell behind the needs of the people. In some areas, farmers chose or were forced to plant crops for export in place of food crops. Many governments attempted to monopolize farm exports, lowering the purchase price to increase their revenues. In Ghana, the price controls set up by Nkrumah and preserved until the early 1980s by the military rulers brought a fall in cocoa production. Exports fell by almost one-half, in turn cutting back funds available for needed imports.

Political disorders reverberated far into the hinterland of African states. Where civil wars broke out, the rural population had to flee for their lives, abandoning their villages and fields. In other areas, environmental degradation of the land was a visible result of a growing rural population denied adequate state protection. Soil erosion and soil depletion were twin marks of this decay. In countries just south of the Sahara desert, this process led directly to the expansion of the desert ("desertification"). The environmental crisis in its turn contributed to decline in agricultural yields and harvests. These political, demographic, and ecological difficulties produced a critical shortage of food throughout Africa. By the 1970s, the continent was harvesting substantially less food per inhabitant than in the previous decade. The situation worsened in the 1980s. By the end of the decade, overall food production had fallen 20 percent below its 1970 level.

Despite the fact that land had earlier been one of the sources of the continent's wealth, it could no longer adequately feed the population. Malnutrition was a fact of life for half of the continent's population. Economies declined, and families had to migrate to cities within or beyond the borders of their own country in hopes of finding work and food. Fearful of urban disorders, governments continued to keep food prices low to feed its urban masses. They relied in large part on foreign aid programs to supply this inexpensive food. It was all that stood in the way of serious famine.

The agricultural crisis hit even those countries where political leadership had proven effective. In the east African state of Tanzania (formerly Tanganyika), the government under Julius Nyerere put in place an array of welfare programs to improve the level of education, health, and nutrition of the people. Nyerere became president in the first free elections of the former British colony, and remained in that position until resigning twenty-four years later. He was proud of the relative social equality that his policies had achieved. He also remained committed to his dream of collectivized agriculture (rather like the Soviet collective farms). But the results of his farm reform were disastrous. Farmers resisted the state's coercive controls, erosion and soil exhaustion resulted from misguided state agricultural experiments, and food production declined by nearly one-half its precollective farm level.

The promises of economic development could not be kept in conditions of agricultural decay. This factor, more than any other, explains why economic growth in Africa in the decades after independence fell behind the growth of population. The economic statistics tell a tragic tale of stagnation and decline. Until the 1980s, the yearly rate of economic growth (domestic product per person) was less than one percent. The 1980s was a period of actual decline, averaging each year about 1 percent, in percapita wealth in Africa. One observer called that time the "lost decade" in the development of sub-Saharan African lands. For lack of resources, social services fell into decay. Education ceased receiving sufficient funds. Medical care, which had dramatically improved life expectancy and infant care until then, became inadequate in the face of the population explosion and new epidemics. The most devastating of these was the spread of AIDS, carried by war and civil disorder into many African areas. In some countries health experts discovered in the 1990s that one-fifth of the population was infected with the AIDS virus. African migrants, desperate to sustain the well-being of the families, defied immigration laws to seek work in Europe and the United States. The African crisis was a global concern. Aid officials in Western capitals concluded by the early 1990s that they had to cease subsidizing ineffective governments and to put severe conditions on granting economic assistance to African states. The French government curtailed its financial support for the currency used in the French Community of Africa. The resulting decline in the value of the member states' money forced their peoples to pay twice as much as before for imports. Officials from the World Bank, as a condition for loans, requested that African governments end their disastrous intervention in the economy and abolish policies of price and production controls. In its place, they insisted on policies to institute the basic features of a market economy with free enterprise, free prices, and balanced state budgets.

Private investors returned, though cautiously, in search of profitable enterprises. Zambia's great copper mines had once been one of the world's major producers, next only to those of Russia and the United States. Taken over by the government in the optimistic years of national liberation, mismanagement and neglect led to the collapse of production. In the late 1990s, the govern-

ment was forced to sell them to a South African mining company. Years of repairs were needed before the mines could produce as before. Though the presence of these outsiders was often deeply resented, African governments had no choice but to follow their recommendations.

This tragic betrayal of the hopes for independence had many causes. Responsibility lay most directly with incompetent and corrupt rulers, who manipulated state powers in a destructive struggle for the spoils of rule. The sudden withdrawal of the European empires left a vacuum of power, which African peoples had little preparation to fill. They became the victims of their leaders' tragic misuse of political authority. The economic misery with which they struggled and the political insecurity of their lives pushed them to rely on clan and tribal ties and to mistrust leaders from beyond their ethnic group or of a different religion.

The so-called "tribalism" that produced ethnic conflict, flight of refugees, and ugly massacres in country after country in the late 1980s and early 1990s had its roots in the failure of African national leadership. New forms of outside intervention appeared, in the shape of foreign troops sent on U.N. peacekeeping missions, of bankers advising governments on economic policy, and of diplomats suggesting the means of restoring democratic practices. No better alternative appeared capable of helping Africa out of its misery.

LATIN AMERICA IN THE COLD WAR

The end of empire had come for almost all the peoples of Latin America in the early nineteenth century. Nationalist revolution swept the continent. The weak colonial forces of the Portuguese and Spanish empires were quickly defeated. European settlers had led the rebellions, and they became the rulers of the new states. Their understanding of nation was defined by the administrative borders of their former colonies, by the European languages implanted by the empires, and by the population of European descent who had settled the New World. They made no place in their new national communities for the Native American peoples.

These "Indians" made a meager living in the countryside as farmers or farm laborers. The Europeans held in their hands the wealth of countries, in the form of great estates, mines, commerce and industry. In Brazil, many tribes in the Amazon basin remained isolated, some completely unknown, for a century or more. Only the Catholic Church, whose faith had spread among most of the population, had in some measure succeeded in breaching the barrier between the communities. In these terms, Latin America had little in common in the mid-twentieth century with lands in Asia and Africa in the midst of decolonization.

Its history of relations with outside states was unique as well. Its states were diplomatically and militarily weak. In the early twentieth century, the northern regions of Latin America fell within the sphere of influence of the United States. Occasionally, the U.S. government sent military forces or political advisers to small countries in the Caribbean and Gulf of Mexico, and in Central America, to settle civil disorders or political quarrels. Only the strong nationalist state of Mexico escaped U.S. domination after its revolutionary upheaval of the 1910s. President Franklin Roosevelt finally renounced the interventionist policy in the 1930s, promising to practice "good neighbor" relations with Latin American countries. These states remained weak and their peoples largely impoverished.

In the middle of the twentieth century, the United States remained the dominant foreign power. It was the principal source of investments and the major market for Latin America's raw materials, still its major export and principal source of wealth. The U.S. government expected Latin American governments to recognize the importance of its strategic interests. In the Second World War, many Latin American states joined in the alliance against the Axis power. In the Cold War, the United States relied on them to oppose the Soviet Union and the international communist movement. Its diplomatic and economic influence in the region was pervasive, and at times oppressive.

The peoples of Latin America fit well into the category of "Third World" region. Observers coined the term in the 1950s to suggest the social and economic gulf between the underdeveloped and the developed countries, capitalist or communist. Latin American political leaders devised new political and economic projects to end these conditions of underdevelopment. Their hopes centered on new state policies for economic growth. In these terms too the region resembled other Third World countries in Asia and Africa. European and North American corporations continued to control major industries and their banks were an important source of investment funds. Real political and economic independence remained an elusive ideal, but achieving it became the highest priority for many Latin American governments.

Seeking Economic Independence

After the Second World War, a new generation of leaders appeared throughout the region who for the first time took an active role in promoting economic development. The war itself had expanded the global demand for Latin American exports; it also opened markets for its manufactured products. These new opportunities for economic

Contemporary Central and South America

growth offered an escape from dependency of these countries on the United States. Governments there were encouraged to set up programs for subsidies and tariffs to protect domestic manufactured products to replace expensive imports. Latin American economists argued that this "import-substitution strategy" would raise their countries into the ranks of developed economies and improve the living conditions of the population. Political leaders promised as well extensive improvements of the state's social welfare assistance to their peoples. It proved a winning electoral program. But achieving success in both areas proved difficult, at times impossible.

With U.S. backing, the new policies for economic development appeared throughout Latin America in the 1950s. They offered inducements of tax exemptions and cheap labor to international business investors, primarily from North America. U.S. corporations, protected by their state and by Latin American rulers, expanded their ownership of mines, plantations, and industrial enterprises throughout the continent. These investments did not grow as rapidly as expected, however. The disappointing results forced Latin American leaders to continue to rely on their own economic resources to fulfill their promises to the people.

The "import-substitution" plans for development called for active involvement by state agencies in the economic development of their country. Officials, working under government supervision, acquired special authority and resources to bolster domestic industries whose products would replace foreign imports. State funding made subsidies available for the opening of desirable new industries, such as aviation and automobile. State tariffs and other regulations hindered foreign imports that might weaken these infant industries. The success of these plans depended on wise leadership, difficult to achieve in poor countries torn by political rivalries and confronting rapidly growing populations. The lure of increased independence and economic prosperity was all the greater. Conservative in their social policies, many Latin American governments were prepared to experiment with a limited type of a command economy.

The success of these programs depended, as in most Third World countries, on outside financial assistance. Latin American economies looked to Western banks for loans to stimulate industrial growth. Governments also needed loans and foreign aid to pay for basic public services needed to raise people's standard of living. Brief periods of abundant and inexpensive loans were followed, however, by harsh times of international recession and domestic government deficits. Wild inflation resulted from continued financial payments on popular projects. Too often, governments found that as a result of their bad planning and reckless commitments they lacked even the means to repay their foreign debts. Populist political movements defended the social and economic needs of the people, accusing their rivals of collaborating with foreign business interests (a common practice) and demanding increased state welfare policies for the poor (for which funds usually were insufficient). Leaders who refused these demands ran the risk of provoking mass protests. Those who supported the populist program bought popularity at the expense of financial chaos. Political strife, economic dependency, and international weakness kept Latin America in a tenacious grip in mid-century.

Populism in Argentina, Brazil, and Chile

The political and civil liberties promised in the nineteenth-century nationalist revolutions remained 150 years later an ideal frequently ignored in the bitter quarrels among political parties and between civilian government and the military. The 1950s was a time when powerful leaders supported by populist coalitions dominated Latin American politics. Their period in power was often cut short by army insurrections followed by a return to military dictatorship.

In 1946, Juan Perón became president of Argentina. He had promised the voters an end to rule by the country's wealthy elite and a massive program of social welfare. With the strong backing of the country's labor unions, he formed a populist coalition of followers eager to see the country's oligarchy finally dethroned. Argentina was rich in raw materials and agricultural resources. Perón used his presidential powers and political influence to make sure special welfare benefits went to the laboring population. The financial price of his policies was high. When his government had to curtail spending and cut back social programs, labor unrest grew. In desperation, Perón mobilized his supporters in a campaign against the Catholic Church, which he accused of excessive wealth and support for his political enemies. It was a dangerous move in a country with a strongly Catholic population. Argentina's social elite, fearful of Perón's populist program and outraged at his attack on the Church, encouraged ambitious generals to intervene in the political crisis. In 1955, their wish was fulfilled when Argentine military leaders overthrew Perón's regime. Argentina passed rapidly from populist democracy to military dictatorship.

This authoritarian regime remained in power, with brief interruptions, until the 1980s. The generals, claiming to defend the "Western and Christian world," proved to be oppressive and incompetent rulers. Staying in power was their main objective. They were little concerned with finding the means to use the natural abundance that their country possessed to improve the well-being of the people. The country's chances for economic development slipped away and popular discontent grew. In the 1970s, revolutionary groups fought the regime with bombings, kidnapping, and murder. They, too, were unconcerned with immediate economic issues, for violent revolution in Argentina appeared to them to be the country's salvation.

The military dictatorship responded with a ruthless campaign of mass arrests and executions. Tens of thousands of alleged "subversives" simply disappeared, their very names erased from the official records. When they left behind small children, the infants were officially classified as orphans and made available for adoption. Popular discontent with the military dictatorship grew. Their failure in 1982 to win a brief war against Great Britain to seize a few small islands in the South Atlantic doomed their regime. Argentina, once a prosperous land, suffered economically and politically at the hands of these generals.

Like Argentina, Brazil was rich in natural resources but plagued by political instability and a social elite far removed from the poor population in the country's coastal cities and interior jungles. Its history in the postwar decades repeated the same pattern of economic promises and political pitfalls created by ambitious plans for development. Brazilian society posed specially challenging problems, since the country was the largest and most populous of all Latin America. Its coastal regions were centers of modern urban life, while its enormous interior (especially the rain forests of the Amazon basin) remained largely untouched by modern industry and agriculture.

In the 1940s, Getulia Vargas, a dynamic and charismatic political leader, took up the task of stimulating Brazil's economy and improving the livelihood of its people. He mobilized a broad coalition of supporters from the middle and working classes to advance his ambitious program of economic growth and social welfare. He sought above all the expansion of Brazil's industrial economy, using the powers and revenues of the state to subsidize private companies and to create state enterprises in key activities such as oil exploration, armaments manufacturing, and automobile production.

After his death in 1954, his heirs carried forward his vision of a "new Brazil." They made the enormous interior regions, still undeveloped, the object of the greatest colonization drive since the nineteenth-century occupation of the North American Great Plains. The state constructed over 11,000 miles of new roads that penetrated deep into jungle areas where Indians had lived in absolute isolation. The roads brought settlers who carved out of the great rain forest lands for ranching and farming. The Brazilian government spent enormous sums on constructing a new capital, Brasília, in the middle of the wilderness. Intended to be "the capital that [would] unite the whole nation," it was inaugurated in 1960.

The cost of these immense development projects was far beyond the means of the Brazilian government. To pay for them, it had to turn to Western banks, contracting excessive foreign loans whose repayment put a great burden on its budget. As in Argentina, power-hungry generals were the only ones to benefit from the social unrest and political conflict caused by the resulting financial crisis. With the backing of the conservative Brazilian elite, they ended democratic government in 1964, beginning a twenty-year military dictatorship. The prevalence of the military in Latin American political life in the 1960s and 1970s constituted a depressing return to an old form of rule.

The Cold War was a distant event for Latin American countries. Yet the pervasive influence of the United States and the appearance there of revolutionary movements inspired by Chinese and Soviet communism brought this global conflict into the political life of the region. The Cold War made its disruptive effects felt most visibly in the Pacific coast country of Chile. Unexpectedly it found itself the center of ideological and political crisis in the early 1970s.

Once a model of liberal democracy, its political parties were split between radical and conservative forces by bitter ideological issues of social reform. With the backing of workers and peasants, a reform government, led by the socialist Salvador Allende took office in the 1970s. His political strength depended on a coalition of socialist and communist parties. They had agreed on a radical populist program of social and economic reforms, including sweeping nationalization of domestic and foreign-owned industries. Their goals resembled those of socialist governments in Asia and Africa. While looking to Third World reformers, they were tempted by the example of Castro's Cuba to break away from U.S. international leadership (see next section). Theirs was a radical vision of change, and that spirit spread to the countryside where peasants began to seize large estates, and to the factory workers who repeatedly went on strike to demand wage increases. The country was gripped by bitter political and social conflict.

Determined to restore order, Chilean military leaders led by General Pinochet plotted to seize power in 1973. They and their followers were persuaded that the country faced a communist revolution. That fear was shared by the U.S. government, determined to crush any apparent communist threat in Latin America. Its CIA agents began secret operations in Chile that year, organizing opposition to the Allende government. The threat of communist insurgency there was a myth, but one that shaped the U.S. global containment policy in those years. Supported by Chile's middle classes and with the encouragement of the CIA, General Pinochet successfully ended Chile's experiment in socialist government. His army ended Allende's life as well in their siege of his presidential palace. Arrests of supporters of Allende's regime swept across the country; the army and police executed prisoners without trial. For nearly two decades, Chile was ruled by Pinochet's military dictatorship.

Military rule in Chile differed from that in Brazil in one important respect. Capitalism appeared to the Chilean generals to be the path to economic development and social stability. In the decade after the insurrection, they invited American economists to be key advisers in implementing free-market policies to pull the Chilean government out of the economy and to cut back social welfare aid to the poor. All Allende's reforms disappeared, at the price of serious hardship to the working population and in conditions of prolonged recession. The new policies slowly began to produce benefits to the population when the country began rapid economic growth in the early 1980s.

Central America under U.S. Domination

In the 1950s, the U.S. government found its most faithful allies in Central America to be military dictators. It considered the entire region, including the Caribbean islands, to belong to its sphere of influence. The small states there had to adhere closely to the U.S. anti-communist and pro-capitalist policies in their domestic and foreign affairs. The U.S. government took its Central American allies where it could find them.

One of these was the head of Nicaragua, General Anastasio Somoza. He had seized power in his country in the early 1930s, capturing and executing his principal rival, the nationalist leader Augusta Sandino. Somoza's rule earned his family great wealth, insured the landowning elite its comfortable living, and guaranteed the United States a small but loyal ally in the Cold War. Rulers such as Somoza were in effect client politicians in their relations with the United States. They faithfully adhered to its diplomatic guidelines and protected American business interests. In exchange, they obtained economic and military aid from the American government, and an export market in the United States for their raw materials.

Cuban politics in the 1950s duplicated this pattern of rule. The dominant figure was Fulgencio Batista, dictator in the 1930s and then president after he himself introduced a democratic constitution in 1940. Keenly aware of U.S. political and economic interests in Cuba, he bent with the political winds from Washington. In the war years, he heeded the U.S. call for the renewal of democracy. In 1944, he withdrew (temporarily) from politics. The era of democratic government lasted only eight years. In the early 1950s, Batista realized that the United States once again accepted dictators within its Caribbean sphere of influence, on condition that they join in Cold War policies. His appetite for power was as strong as ever. With the support of the Cuban army, he seized control of the government in 1952. Scheduled elections never were held. He banned the Communist Party and ended diplomatic relations with the Soviet Union. The United States asked for no more.

Batista's judgment of U.S. priorities was correct. Like Somoza of Nicaragua, he received generous U.S. military assistance to arm and train his small army. His state followed closely in step with U.S. foreign policy and cooperated with U.S. investors. Cuban nationalists condemned as neocolonialism the commanding role of the United States in the Cuban economy, and accused Batista of subservience to the Yankees. Sugar, the country's major crop sold principally to the United States, epitomized Cuba's continued economic and political dependence on the United States.

Cuba's new period of military dictatorship lasted until 1959. Its economy expanded in those years, for sugar sold well in the United States and foreign tourists flooded in. Impressed by Cuba's flourishing gambling casinos, one American gambler exclaimed: "The future looks fabulous!" Many middle-class Cubans benefitted substantially during these prosperous years. The Cuban standard of living was among the highest of any Latin American country. Economic prosperity was not sufficient to safeguard Batista's rule, however. He proved to be an incompetent and unpopular ruler. His repression of political opposition served only to provoke more resistance. He relied on his army for domination of the Cuban people. He had exaggerated confidence in his military forces, and in U.S. backing. He was wrong on both counts.

The man responsible for the fall of the Cuban dictator was a remarkable revolutionary leader, Fidel Castro. Son of a self-made sugar plantation owner, Castro grew up in comfortable conditions, sheltered from the effects of the depression as a child and given the benefits of education largely reserved for well-to-do Cuban youth. Trained as a lawyer, he entered Cuban politics in the late 1940s on a program of independence from the United States and social reform. In those years, a period in his life Castro later called his "bourgeois thralldom," he was no different from many other aspiring young Cuban politicians. National legislative elections were scheduled to be held in 1952, and he prepared to campaign for office. Batista's military coup ended the campaign. Among

the most bitterly disappointed candidates for office was Fidel Castro. Batista's action transformed him from party politician into a revolutionary leader.

In late 1952 and early 1953, Castro brought together a group of 150 followers, mostly young factory and farm workers, united in support of what they loosely termed the "Revolution." They pledged themselves to the restoration of the 1940 constitution, to "complete and definitive social justice based on economic and industrial advancement," and to liberation from "any links to foreign nations," that is, to the United States. The emphasis on social reform and anti-imperialism constituted the core of Castro's political ideology. It was a romantic mixture of revolutionary fervor, defiance of Yankee domination, and concern for the needs of Cuba's poor. It later became the heart of his revolution. His confidence in his political genius far exceeded his means of action. In mid-1953, he led his small band of followers on a reckless assault on Batista's regime. He was convinced that justice was on his side and that Cubans were prepared to rise up under his leadership. He was wrong and spent two years in Cuban jail as a result.

Castro's determination to combat his country's military dictatorship was undaunted. Immediately after leaving prison in 1955, he fled to Mexico to organize a guerrilla force for a second attempt at overthrowing Batista. Called the July 26th Movement (the date of his first insurrection), its support came from anti-Batista groups prepared to take up arms. A new rebellion was a risky undertaking, since Batista appeared firmly in control of Cuba. In other Third World countries revolutionary guerrilla forces had attempted to seize power from authoritarian regimes, and a few had even succeeded. Nowhere in Latin America did a comparable movement exist, and the United States might prove a serious enemy.

Castro's Revolution

In late 1956, Castro and eighty comrades returned to Cuba on an old boat, the "Granma," to attempt a new uprising against Batista. Within a year he built his guerrilla force into an organized band of 300 fighters supported by an underground political movement in most Cuban cities. He had alongside him his brother Raoul, a member of the Cuban Communist Party who had become his loyal aide and most effective political organizer. With him also was a young Argentine doctor named Ernesto "Che" Guevara, an experienced, long-time revolutionary. They proved dynamic and forceful rebel leaders, and found among the Cuban population many supporters repelled by Batista's brutal methods of rule. The guerrilla movement provided Castro with the instrument to seize power. Those who fought with him there became the leaders of revolutionary Cuba later.

The U.S. government, suspicious of Castro's revolutionary and anti-imperialist program, hoped that Cubans would find another solution to the growing political crisis. In 1958 it ended its military aid program to Batista's regime, clearly a losing cause. It anticipated that a new government would emerge uniting a broad coalition of Cuban parties. But it did not publicly condemn Castro's movement. Its silence helped Castro win the backing of Cubans prepared for the sake of overthrowing Batista to ignore his radical reform ideas. The U.S. policy of nonintervention in the Cuban conflict left to Cubans the choice of political leadership. The consequences proved not at all what President Eisenhower had expected.

In 1958, Batista's power slipped rapidly away. Castro had by then organized a broad coalition of groups under his leadership. That fall, small groups of his Rebel Army operated in all areas of the country. In the cities, an urban guerrilla force, the Civic Resistance, fought police and army units. In December, guerrillas under the command of Che Guevara moved out of the countryside to attack the capital, Havana. Batista's army melted away, and his generals fled for their lives. Batista found no one to defend his discredited regime. On January 1, 1959, he abandoned power and left the country. On his heels came Guevara's Rebel Army. Castro arrived a week later, having traveled across the length of Cuba and received a hero's welcome from hundreds of thousands of Cubans. Castro, at age thirty-two, was leader of his country.

A political revolution began in Cuba that was unlike any that had occurred previously in Latin America. An armed insurrection led by a small rural guerrilla army totaling at most 2,000 fighters had ended the rule of a military dictator. Its political leadership, the July 26th Movement, possessed only the outlines of a reform program and exercised little control over its political allies. In a country of 7 million, Castro's forces were very small. Supporting them were a collection of liberal and socialist organizations and movements. Castro's most valuable ally was the Communist Party, with about 15,000 members and a centralized leadership modeled on the Soviet Communists. It shared Castro's opposition to American domination and brought him the experience organizing mass movements that the July 26th Movement lacked. The coalition of groups that participated in the insurrection shared no common goal. Real unity came from Castro's own leadership. The regime's ruling cadres came from the Rebel Army. This was the case in 1959, and it remained so in the years that followed.

Consolidation of political power was Castro's first objective. His second was radical reform to improve the living conditions of Cuba's lower classes. His third was the withdrawal of Cuba from the U.S. sphere of influence. His aims resembled in many ways those of other Latin American populist movements. The revolution that Cuba experienced bore some resemblance to other revolutions that occurred in Third World countries in the postwar decades. But the consequences in Cuba were unique and unexpected. Within three years after Batista's fall the Cuban economy was run under a system of command economy identical to that of the Soviet Union. The country was governed by a one-party state supported by and dependent on the Soviet Union. Castro's decision to rely on the Soviet Union for economic aid and military protection brought the Cold War to the Caribbean. It led to the most serious international crisis since the end of the Second World War.

From the first year of his revolution, Castro was the central figure in Cuban politics. His program appealed to many Cubans, especially the poor peasant farmers and urban working classes. For them, he was their undisputed national leader. He was determined to maintain political control of the new state. He arrived in Havana in early January of 1959, warning that he would not allow the new leadership to behave "like the many revolutionaries of the past [who] roamed around fighting each other." He quickly made apparent that he understood that task to mean the exclusion from power of any groups that might challenge his own leadership.

Within two months he assumed the formal powers of prime minister. Gradually all the important government positions passed to his colleagues in the July 26th Movement. Free elections were never held. In 1961, Castro formally dissolved the constitution of 1940, claiming it was "already too outdated and old for us." In fact, Castro refused to permit democratic liberties to weaken his political domination of the country.

A Soviet-type centralized dictatorship began to take shape. Castro and those around him intentionally modeled their new regime on the communist one-party states. Leadership of labor unions, once controlled by Batista's supporters, was transferred to Communists. Political opponents were prosecuted by a new security police acting in the name of the "revolution." The state took over control of Cuba's press. Castro called his rule "direct government by the people." Power actually belonged to the former guerrilla leaders.

The conflict between Cuba and the United States began shortly after the revolution. It originated in Castro's early efforts in 1959 to make tangible the ideals, as he understood them, of social equality and economic justice. To aid the urban poor, he ordered housing rents lowered by 50 percent and electric power rates cut by as much. In May, the new regime ordered the expropriation of all landed estates of more than 1,000 acres, including all large sugar plantations owned mainly by foreign companies. Part of the land went to poor and landless farmers, while the largest plantations became collective farms under state control. Nationalization of foreign businesses continued through the rest of the year despite objections from the U.S. government.

The Cuban revolutionaries were determined to liberate their country from domination by the "Yankee imperialists." Castro announced in 1959 that Cuba would adopt a new foreign policy of nonalignment. He condemned U.S. Cold War policies and capitalist exploitation of Cuba's resources. The new Cuban leaders were beginning to search for a way out of the U.S. sphere of influence. But they realized as well that their country depended more than ever before on sugar exports. These sales brought the income essential to finance their expensive reform program. The U.S. government had for decades supported the Cuban economy (and the state) through regular, massive purchases of sugar at a guaranteed price.

Castro presented the U.S. government with an extraordinary demand for economic assistance. It took the form of a request that the United States double its procurement of the commodity and agree to a 20 percent increase in the price. His demand represented a public claim on the wealth of the Yankee imperialists. It was a reckless move, in contradiction with his denunciation of U.S. foreign policy and typical of his revolutionary zeal to transform Cuba. Refusing to believe that the Cuban revolutionaries were beyond control, the Eisenhower administration refused to renegotiate the sugar agreement and demanded that U.S. businesses receive proper compensation from Cuba for their property losses.

Rather than retreat, the Cuban revolutionaries pushed ahead in their search for freedom from the United States. They turned to communist countries for help. In February 1960, the Soviet Union agreed to buy Cuban sugar on a regular basis and to provide Cuba with a major loan to permit Cuban purchase of Soviet machinery, petroleum, and arms. The Soviet leaders viewed the offer as part of their new Third World policy of aid to "bourgeois nationalist" leaders opposed to Western alliances (see Chapter 11). Castro considered the treaty a victory for Cuban nationalism. The Soviet petroleum had to be refined in Cuba, and Castro ordered the U.S.-owned refineries to cooperate. After consulting with Washington, the oil companies refused to handle this "Red oil." In June 1960, Castro seized their property.

His decision proved the breaking point in U.S.–Cuban relations. The U.S. government halted all purchases of Cuban sugar, and later that year declared a complete embargo on trade with Cuba. It had, in effect, begun economic war. Castro responded by seizing all remaining U.S. property in Cuba. He added to this list all the important privately owned industries, banks, and transportation in his country. By the end of 1960, trade and banking, most of industry and transportation, and one-third of the agricultural land belonged to the state.

By then the Cuban leaders had decided to take control of the entire Cuban economy. They viewed the Soviet Union as their model, copying the Soviet command economy system. They introduced laws enforcing command planning, organized collective farming through the countryside, and used state revenues to develop nationalized industry. Their decision was made hastily, and they lacked the skilled personnel and the revenues for this mammoth task. They borrowed heavily from the Soviet Union and welcomed Soviet economic advisers to help in constructing a socialist economy on their island. In doing so, they made their country dependent on the Soviet Union both diplomatically and economically.

The U.S. government had already begun plans to end this pro-Soviet state so close to its shores. President Eisenhower had authorized the Central Intelligence Agency to organize anti-Castro Cubans for a possible invasion. In early 1961, John F. Kennedy, just elected president, publicly warned that Cuba was becoming "Communism's first Caribbean base." His Cold War strategy remained the policy of containment, enlarged by then to include covert measures against states suspected of allying with the Soviet Union. He approved the CIA plan for a U.S.-supported rebel invasion of Cuba. He believed CIA promises that Castro was disliked and that a popular uprising would follow the rebel attack.

Events proved them wrong. The 1,400 Cubans who disembarked from U.S. warships to invade Cuba at the Bay of Pigs in

April, 1961, never got beyond the landing beaches. Cuban police immediately arrested suspected rebel sympathizers, and the new Cuban army quickly defeated the invaders. Victory brought the Cuban revolutionaries greater popularity than ever before. They had defeated forces of the "Yankee imperialists."

Still, their new regime remained terribly weak in the face of their mighty neighbor. They had to anticipate another U.S. invasion, certainly more concerted and massive than the first. That reason alone may have incited Castro to seek a military alliance with the communist states. His understanding of global revolutionary forces had evolved as well. He believed that his country had joined the Third World's crusade against capitalism and imperialism. The enemy in this confrontation was the United States. Castro concluded that his country belonged both in the Third World and in the communist camp. He made this clear in December of 1961, when he announced, "I am a Marxist-Leninist and shall remain a Marxist-Leninist until the day I die." It was an affirmation of faith that contained a direct appeal to the Soviet Union for protection.

The Soviet leaders proposed to him only part of what he sought. He hoped for a Soviet military alliance. Neither the Soviet Union nor the Warsaw Pact (the military alliance of communist states) were ready for this risky move. Instead, in the spring of 1962, the Soviet government offered to place intermediate-range ballistic missiles in Cuba. They were to be installed and controlled by Russians. Castro agreed, believing that his country was obtaining military protection in the fight against world imperialism. The missiles, accompanied by Soviet technical personnel and anti-aircraft units, began to arrive in great secrecy early that fall. Then U.S. military surveillance penetrated the secret. The Cuban missile crisis began (see Chapter 11).

Then the Soviet government agreed to withdraw its military equipment and personnel. It did obtain from President Kennedy a commitment not to launch any future military operations, either with U.S. forces or anti-Cuban groups, to overthrow Castro's regime. The world at large welcomed the compromise agreement, for it avoided nuclear war. Castro did not share in the satisfaction at the settlement. His government received only a U.S. promise of nonintervention. It did not obtain military protection from the Soviet Union. Worst of all, Castro had no voice in the resolution of the crisis. Soviet missiles vanished from Cuba without his approval. From a front-line position in the world struggle against imperialism, his island was reduced to a sideshow.

❧ HIGHLIGHT: The Third World ❧

The term "Third World" appeared in the 1950s to identify a new part of the globe. It was the invention of a journalist who could not have imagined how successful his expression would become. It seemed to him an effective description of the newly independent countries like India and Indonesia whose situation was unlike either the democratic West or the communist East. Its use quickly spread. Leaders of these new nation-states used it to emphasize their prominence in the post-colonial world. Radical politicians and intellectuals went further still by using the expression to identify all those areas of the globe, once colonial or semi-colonial, where revolutions had liberated or would soon completely liberate them from Western, "neocolonial" exploitation. In other words, this term became useful in the ideological debates about the future of the peoples of Asia, Africa, and Latin America after the collapse of Western empires.

Its most meaningful and least controversial message pointed in the decades that followed to the great disparity in economic and social well-being between industrialized and non-industrialized lands. In the post-colonial world, the peoples in many countries were miserably poor, while a few areas enjoyed relative prosperity. At a time when governments in democratic and communist camps (the "First" and "Second" worlds) each argued that their own social and political ideologies were the best guides to human progress, the Third World urged both sides to look to the crying needs of their peoples.

These needs were defined in a variety of ways. Evidence suggested that about one-third to one-half of the peoples in countries of Africa and Asia lived in absolute poverty, that is, lacked sufficient food to meet their basic needs for subsistence. Inadequate medical care for mothers and newborn children meant that one-fourth to one-third of infants in areas of poverty did not live to be one year old. In human terms, conditions of life in these lands truly appeared to belong to another, "Third" world.

Economists built their arguments on the obstacles in these countries standing in the way of economic growth and well-being.

They emphasized the inadequacy of basic facilities for industrialization such as electricity and roads and the lack of technically trained personnel prepared to maintain public services. They stressed the extremely low productivity of agricultural land, on which most of the peoples in Africa, Asia, and Latin American depended for their livelihood. They warned that countries that relied largely on the export of raw materials, true for most Third World economies in the 1960s, lacked funds to pay for needed imports of industrial goods and new technology. They stressed as well the inadequacy of education in most Third World countries, where at most 50 to 60 percent of the population possessed minimal skills of literacy. These figures painted a picture of countries whose population faced a future of misery and disease identical to that of their ancestors. Outside help appeared the only possible way to break this infernal cycle.

That need became a political program in part because of the formation of the Organization of Non-Aligned States. It first met in the city of Bandung, Indonesia, in 1955. India's president Nehru rejected the argument of "some great countries" (referring to the United States and the Soviet Union) that "their quarrels are the world's quarrels and that the world must submit to them." The former colonial lands should not be "aligned" with either side. They had their own needs, the most urgent of which was aid from developed countries, communist or capitalist, for economic development. The United Nations became another forum for political appeals from Third World states. Their numbers grew until they constituted a majority of the membership in the U.N. General Assembly. At their urging, the United Nations launched programs it called

"Decades for Development." The first of these extended through the 1960s. It invited wealthy countries to contribute at least 1 percent of the value of their yearly national income to economic programs for developing areas. Nothing comparable had ever been attempted.

These calls for help incited a large number of governments to begin programs for aid. They did so partly out of humanitarian concerns, partly in response to Cold War competition for allies among the new states. Western governments made the largest contributions in the 1960s. The U.S. program for Latin America, called the Alliance for Progress, brought billions of dollars in aid to that region. It came in large measure in response to the Cuban revolution and Fidel Castro's appeal for revolution in Central and South America. The Soviet Union's aid often went to great construction projects, helping to construct a mammoth dam for the Egyptian government on the Nile river at Aswan. Competition among donors occasionally produced unusual results. India obtained at about the same time three separate steel mills, one built by the United States, one by Great Britain, and one by the Soviet Union.

Economic assistance to the Third World grew rapidly through the 1960s and 1970s. The French government's program of economic assistance was directed especially to its former colonies whose new leaders had chosen to join the French Community. The World Bank made major loans at low interest and for long periods to governments who proposed specific projects, such as road building or the construction of hydroelectric dams. In the 1970s, the oil-producing countries of the Middle East became major donors when rising oil prices increased their revenues. Economic aid in the form of grants or loans to Third World countries became a long-term commitment by international organizations and industrialized states.

The efforts by Third World governments and by foreign aid programs to break the cycle of poverty and economic underdevelopment proved in places a remarkable success, in others a sorry failure. We cannot easily attribute these achievements or disappointments solely to foreign aid, for local and private initiatives played a major role. Economic development and public health programs were at times very effective. One example was the work of Western agronomists, notably Norman Borlaug, to create new, highly productive varieties of wheat, rice, and other crops. The success of their research brought an increase in yields so great that observers called the results a "Green Revolution." India's farmers increased their wheat yield by over 500 percent in the two decades that followed introduction of the new crops in the 1960s, and did so without putting new land under cultivation. Borlaug warned that, unless India's population explosion was halted, these "miracle crops" would provide that country with sufficient food for no more than three decades. But for the time being, famine was held in check.

Other countries experienced remarkable improvements in industry and commerce. The most amazing transformation took place in small countries in East and Southeast Asia. Once poor areas largely devoted to peasant farming, South Korea and Taiwan became by the 1980s important industrial centers selling complex electronic products on the global market. Their growth rates were as high as Japan, whose economic example they seemed to follow. They could no longer fit by any measure the model of Third World countries.

Serious obstacles stood in the way of economic development elsewhere. One was the reluctance of the industrialized countries to sustain massive aid programs, since few ever reached the level of yearly aid at or above 1 percent of their national income. A second was the worsening of the terms of trade between industrialized and non-industrialized countries. Between the 1960s and 1980s, international prices on raw materials fell drastically, sometimes by as much as 50 percent, as poor countries increased production to obtain a greater share of the market. A third barrier emerged when many of the Third World states, having accepted very large loans and grants, were unable to repay these loans. In the 1980s, interest rates on loans rose while prices on exports fell. Third World countries in Africa and Latin America were so deeply in debt to foreign creditors that they could afford only to make interest payments on their loans. In these desperate circumstances, they lacked funds for their own development programs.

A fourth obstacle proved to be the poor political leadership of many Third World states. Governments introduced risky economic reforms (often versions of command economies) that wasted the resources obtained through foreign aid on unproductive programs. Others were attracted to gigantic projects, such as Egypt's Aswan dam, that consumed tremendous funds that might have been used to cope with more pressing needs. Critics argued that simple technological innovations were in the long-run better suited to the population and to the resources of poor countries. "Small is beautiful" was the motto of one economist who favored modest improvements in technology. By the 1980s, it was clear that Third World govern-

ments could not produce miraculous economic development through state policies. Their efforts were better directed to achieving what came to be known as "sustainable" growth that brought steady, small improvements adapted to their economies and resources.

The most serious obstacle emerged from the very success of policies combating diseases in these countries. The campaigns to halt epidemics, eradicate disease-carrying insects, and improve health care quickly raised the life expectancy of the population throughout the Third World. The immediate result was a population explosion in these regions, doubling the world's population between 1950 and 1990 (from 2.5 to 5 billion). This increase ate up the slow rise in farm production and industrial manufacturing. It left countries such as India with scarcely more food per capita in 1990 than in 1950.

"Sustainable Development" at the Grassroots Level: U.N. Sponsored Technology for Cooking (*UN Photo 153352/Kay Muldoon*)

The Third World was changing in shape. Well-to-do, well-educated professional and entrepreneurial classes were making their presence felt within countries such as India. They were nearly as far removed from the poor masses as were the prosperous Westerners. The essential problem of a world deeply divided between wealth and poverty, developed and developing, the well fed and the hungry, endured to the end of the century. The Third World remained a dominating presence in global relations.

DEMOCRACY IN LATIN AMERICA

In the decades that followed the missile crisis, Latin America evolved gradually toward an economically developed region where democratic governments coped, more or less successfully, with the needs of their peoples. Politically ambitious generals attempted for a time to rule many lands, but almost all proved so incompetent that they were forced to withdraw from power. Economic plans for industrial development set in motion a process for development that raised the standard of living of a large part of the population. They curtailed the size of their families and slowed the increase in population. By the early 1990s, the region as a whole no longer belonged alongside sub-Saharan Africa within the Third World.

From Dictatorship to Democracy

In the 1960s, the pressures for social reform and economic development increased dramatically. Three factors help explain the new situation. The Cuban revolution and Castro's stature as revolutionary leader crystallized social opposition to Latin American oligarchies. Castro laid down his guidelines for Third World revolution in early 1962 in his Second Declaration of Havana. He placed Cuba in the forefront of the "upward march of history." Cuba was to be a key player in the forthcoming triumph of socialism, since "the Cuban Revolution shows that revolution is possible, that the people can do

it." He held up the Cuban revolution as the model for revolutionary insurrection and economic development in all Latin countries.

The second reason for expanded efforts at economic growth was the decision of the U.S. government, pushed by fears of revolution, to sponsor economic development and social reform in Latin America. President Kennedy's Alliance for Progress called on the governments in the region to propose development plans. These were assured of U.S. economic and financial assistance, which ultimately totaled $20 billion in the next ten-year period. U.S. advisers strongly encouraged the Latin American leaders to impose heavy taxes on the wealthy to help pay for these programs and to institute land reform to provide farms for the rural poor and landless workers. The U.S. government also increased its military aid, directed specifically at repressing guerrilla movements like the one that led Castro to power.

The Catholic Church began as well to play an influential role in social reform. Pope John XXIII, elected in 1958, had initiated what he called a "reawakening" of the church. The Second Vatican Council, meeting between 1962 and 1965, gave the church's approval to his daring proposals. Many reforms and policies approved there had particular significance for global problems of economic inequality. These addressed the so-called "pastoral" mission of

Catholics to care for the needy and under-privileged. The council looked to the needs of "the whole of humanity," calling on the clergy and the faithful alike to take an active role in social and economic reform to help the poor and oppressed. It welcomed state welfare policies and suggested that the faithful should create special organizations to assist in this enormous task. The Catholic Church was firmly opposed to violent revolution. Its program was meant to be an alternative path to social progress.

The consequences of its call "to all people of goodwill" to work toward peace and social justice had a profound political impact among Catholic faithful, particularly in Latin America. The Catholic Church had for many centuries been an integral part of the daily life of the peoples there. It had exercised a very conservative role, preaching obedience to the state and deference to the social elite. Pope John XXII's "reawakening" changed all that. To implement the decisions made at the Second Vatican Council, all Latin American bishops met in 1968. In the presence of the pope, the delegates laid down the principles of social action by Catholic priests and laity. The goals were those fixed at the Vatican conference—the need for peace based on justice, human betterment through social action, and major social reforms.

The impact of these decisions was long-lasting, though they are not easily measured. Within a few years nearly a million Brazilian Catholics, mainly from the poor laboring classes, had joined religious associations (called "cebs") to undertake local reform measures. In the years of repressive military dictatorship in the 1970s they were the only mass political movement in the country. The effect among Catholic clergy was equally profound. Though upper-class bishops resisted the reform movement, other bishops and priests began to speak out openly

against injustice, at times at the risk of their own lives. While Castro's supporters called for Marxist revolution, the Catholic Church proposed its own ideology of social reform.

The three decades following the Cuban Revolution were a period of political transition to democracy and economic growth in Latin America. Popular demands for better living conditions focused the attention of military and civilian leaders everywhere on the need for economic development. In the 1960s and 1970s, Latin American economies expanded rapidly, in large measure because prices on raw materials were high, and banks were generous in lending funds. Political leadership in most countries lay in the hands of authoritarian military regimes, supported by the traditional, conservative elite. The United States remained a very influential presence, pushing economic development and backing anti-communist foreign policies.

Rule by military dictatorship proved temporary. Their departure was followed by the graduate abandonment of state economic controls. By the late 1980s, all the dictators had vanished. Most were forced to resign as a result of popular opposition to their repressive policies and, often, as a consequence of their inability to cope with a growing financial and economic crisis. Interest rates rose and commodity prices fell in the early 1980s. The old formula of raw materials exports and foreign loans no longer worked. State subsidies dwindled and nationalized industries went deeply into debt. Many Latin American governments were so heavily indebted to foreign banks and international lending agencies that they had to default on payments. Their leaders could no longer count on new loans and had to introduce painful measures of financial and economic austerity. These new policies were beyond the limited competence of the military rulers.

Chile was the exceptional case. General Pinochet's austerity and free-market policies brought substantial economic rewards in those very years. Even there his military regime came under growing popular pressure to return the country to parliamentary democracy. In 1988, he allowed free elections to take place. The choice was between authoritarian rule and democratically chosen leadership. The voters chose democracy and civilian rule. By then the country enjoyed a level of economic well-being remarkable in a region in the throes of serious economic crisis.

The nature of the predicament appeared most clearly in the crisis that faced Brazil in that decade. The military revolt that ended Brazilian democratic rule in 1964 had come in response to the government's extravagant promises of social welfare and the social unrest stirred up by its failure to carry out measures for the redistribution of wealth among the poor. The new military dictators dealt ruthlessly with the revolutionary opposition and cut back on social welfare. Inflation dwindled for a time and foreign debts were paid.

The Brazilian military continued the policy of state-sponsored development. They offered financial subsidies to industrialists and ranchers and poured funds into state enterprises. They expanded the vast program for the development of the Amazon region, still largely a wilderness inhabited by Indians and a few settlers. Their ambitious plans for economic growth came at enormous cost. But they understood little and cared less about the economic and financial risks that their projects created. Their objectives were political. They hoped to increase the independence and international influence of their state. Most important, they hoped to expand the economic opportunities for conservative Brazilian investors and business interests. In opening the Amazon

basin, they anticipated that migrants from Brazil's poorest regions would flood into the area. Social unrest would dwindle, and the country's economy would prosper. Their "Operation Amazonia" was visionary; it was also wildly unrealistic.

Their program did partially achieve its goals. By the mid-1980s, Brazil had developed into one of the major industrial powers in the world. The Amazon basin had attracted an enormous influx of settlers and ranchers. But the program of Amazonian development led to the uncontrolled destruction of large forested areas opened to colonization. The most powerful new settlers were ranchers eager to acquire vast tracts of open land. Small farmers came in their wake, ready to extract as rapidly and cheaply as possible what produce they could grow on land that was quickly depleted. The two groups together burned vast regions of the rainforest. The devastation represented a tragedy for the inhabitants of the Amazon basin, particularly the Indians, but also those whose livelihood depended on the forest, such as rubber tappers. Equally as serious was the fact that the disappearance of the rainforest threatened an ecological disaster to a unique and vital environment. By the mid-1980s the fires had grown so great that the smoke at times shrouded the entire Amazon region. An international campaign to protect the rainforest began.

The price—financial, ecological, and social—that the country had to pay proved so high that the Brazilian generals ultimately were compelled to abandon power. They had authorized reckless state spending during their twenty years of rule. The state went into debt to cover these expenses. The result was a disastrously high rate of inflation and financial instability. Brazil had accumulated an international debt of nearly $100 billion by the mid-1980s, higher than any other Third World country. It could not meet its

debts and its harsh measures of fiscal restraint only heightened popular opposition.
The poor population benefited little from
the country's growth. The Catholic Church
began to speak out publicly in support of the
needs of the poor and backed protest movements in defense of the Vatican Council's reform program. Other political movements
also were increasingly active. In these circumstances, the military government decided in 1985 to withdraw from politics. It
allowed free elections to take place.

A new democratically elected government took over power in Brazil, but in extremely difficult circumstances. Gradually, it
set about dealing with the state's financial
crisis and the economy's inadequate performance. Its solution was to allow a free market to reappear. Within a few years it
abandoned the policies of state-sponsored
development, gradually opening the country to foreign imports and privatizing (selling to private investors) Brazil's nationalized
industry. It promised to curtail destruction
of the rainforest, and in 1992 sponsored the
first United Nations Conference on Environment and Development. Social inequalities
and political instability still remained a part
of Brazilian life, but the crisis appeared at an
end.

Mexico, like other Latin American states,
moved toward political democracy and a
free-market economy. The authoritarian
one-party regime of the Institutional Revolutionary Party (PRI) had been in existence
since the 1920s. It had brought stability to
the country following the revolutionary turmoil of the early century. The price was the
loss of political freedom. One Mexican critic
called its regime the "perfect dictatorship."
In appearance, it respected political and civil
liberties, since it had an elected president
and parliament. In reality, each president
came only with the approval of PRI, which
"suppressed methodically by whatever

Burning Season in the Amazon Basin: Picture,
Taken from U.S. Space Shuttle Discovery, of
Smoke Cover and Plumes Produced by Fires
Burning in the Amazon Forest, Sept. 1988
(*NASA*)

means any criticism that threatened its hold
on power." Newspapers received secret subsidies, and in return published the "news"
supplied by the authorities. On the surface,
the state appeared stable and the country
calm.

Beneath the surface, the PRI dictatorship,
like that in the Soviet Union, was falling into
decay. Corruption spread as powerful gangs
smuggling drugs into the United States
bribed police and party bosses. Bankers and
industrialists found that they could obtain
special treatment with gifts to powerful

officials. The nationalist fervor that had animated the post-revolution generation of Mexican leaders faded, leaving behind a regime devoted primarily to keeping its monopoly on political power.

The Mexican government had followed the same path as other Latin American countries in making the state a key player in the economic life of the country. A state-owned company managed the country's enormous oil fields. The government allocated generous subsidies to important industries and used tariffs and other measures to hinder foreign competition. The government's attempt at economic independence could not meet the needs of Mexico's rapidly growing population (nearly 90 million by the 1980s). Illegal and legal migration to the United States increased dramatically as Mexicans departed in search of a better life. In the 1960s and 1970s, foreign sales of petroleum bolstered the state budget and induced foreign bankers to make large loans. The recession in the 1980s ended those good times, leaving the Mexican economy in crisis and the state unable to repay its foreign loans.

Among the PRI leaders were some who, like Soviet reform leaders of the late 1980s, concluded that the welfare of the country required radical political and economic reforms. They decided that a free-market economy and the expansion of international trade offered the best hope for Mexican economic recovery. The success of their daring program depended on improved trade and economic ties with the United States. In 1994, the Mexican government agreed to join the North American Free Trade Agreement (NAFTA) with Canada and the United States. The reformers realized the next year how important these ties were when wealthy Mexicans and foreign investors suddenly "dumped" (sold) Mexican currency on the international market. The peso, which had already begun a slow decline,

plummeted in value. The Mexican government's salvation from the ensuing financial crisis came from a massive U.S. government loan. It saved the Mexican state from defaulting on all its foreign debts (see Chapter 12). Mexico was entering a new era of cooperation with its former enemy to the north.

Opposition to the reform program came from PRI officials who had enriched themselves by their easy access to public wealth. The reformers came to the conclusion that they had to open Mexico's political system to free elections if they were to succeed in their program of economic recovery. They anticipated that the entrenched PRI leaders would lose power when voters had a chance to vote for opposition candidates. It was a painful, at times violent process. With the strong encouragement of the U.S. government, the Mexican leadership coupled free-market reforms with the restoration of democratic rights. PRI reform leaders formally renounced the party's monopoly of political power. In 1997, for the first time in nearly a century opposition parties won a majority of the seats to the Mexican parliament. Three years later, the winner of the presidential elections of 2000 was an opposition leader, Vincente Fox. PRI had given up its "perfect dictatorship" in what amounted to a peaceful revolution. By the late 1990s, democratic government and a free-market economy had taken hold in almost all Latin American countries.

Cuba, Central America, and the Yankees

Though Cuba remained under U.S. economic embargo after the 1962 missile crisis, the Cuban regime no longer faced the threat of a U.S. military invasion. Castro was free to pursue his socialist reforms. His path was erratic and the results in the next decades disappointing. His country regularly received large amounts of Soviet foreign aid, including petroleum and wheat vital to the Cuban economy. Soviet yearly assistance totaled nearly $5 billion in the 1980s. The Soviet military assisted Castro's army with arms and advisers. Castro was able to send armed forces to aid Marxist regimes in Africa, first to Angola in 1975 then to Ethiopia in 1978. These military adventures were his greatest international success, reassuring him that communist Cuba was still part of the "upward march of history."

The social and economic impact of Castro's reforms brought the people some benefits, but left many dissatisfied. Their living conditions improved in the 1970s, and the country did not experience the extremes of wealth and poverty of societies such as Brazil. Women in Cuba enjoyed greater opportunities and rights than women in most other Latin American countries. A revealing sign of the social revolution in Cuba was the fall in the birth rate, lowest in all of Latin America. Women's liberation was not the whole explanation, however, for most women had to work to support their families in an economy plagued by shortages of consumer goods.

The lure of life in the "capitalist" United States remained great. Many families had relatives who had fled the country after Castro's revolution. Large numbers lived in nearby areas such as Florida; Miami became a "Little Havana" for its Cuban residents. When given the opportunity in 1979 to emigrate to the United States, hundreds of thousands of Cubans departed. Small groups continued illegally to flee in small boats, many of which sank in the stormy seas between Cuba and Florida. But Castro remained convinced of the virtues of Marxist-Leninist socialism, even after the collapse of communist regimes in Eastern Europe and the fall of the Soviet Union in the early 1990s. A billboard slogan appeared in Cuba reading "Socialism or Death!"

In Central America, Catholics, reformers, and revolutionaries joined in opposition to the entrenched social and political elites. Each group chose a different path of opposition. Following the 1968 conference of Latin American bishops, the Catholic clergy took the lead in denouncing military rule and economic injustice. When conditions worsened some even spoke out in favor of insurrection as the only means left to attain freedom and justice. El Salvador's military, fighting revolutionary Marxists in the countryside, turned against these reformist clergy. In 1981 officers assassinated the country's archbishop, Oscar Romero, to silence their critics. In the face of political conservatism and military repression, there was little place for real social reform.

Cuban socialism provided a model for the revolutionary regime that emerged in Nicaragua in the 1980s. The Somoza dictatorship there faced in the late 1970s opposition from a coalition of resistance groups, radical and liberal, calling themselves the Sandinistas (Sandino, a political reformer, had been assassinated by Somoza). The Church joined forces with Marxist revolutionaries in 1979 to organize a popular insurrection that ended the Somoza rule. The radicals in the coalition refused to share power. Much like Castro in 1959, they set out to create socialist institutions similar to those in Cuba. Their small country was incapable of meeting their Marxist expectations, and they faced the bitter opposition of the conservative U.S. government. The United States gave military supplies and training to an anti-Sandinista guerrilla force called the "Contras," and declared an economic embargo of the country. The revolution aroused widespread opposition from the population, whose living conditions rapidly worsened.

Confronted by a grave economic crisis and social unrest, in 1989 the Sandinistas allowed the people to choose their future leaders in free elections. A majority of the voters preferred the democratic opposition, and the Sandinistas left the government. Their socialist experiment was over, leaving an impoverished population as evidence that their reform program was not the key to social justice or prosperity.

Despite some signs of economic growth, at the end of the 1980s most countries of Central America and the Caribbean remained lands of political instability and economic poverty. The precariousness of their governments opened the way for political extremists and dictators whose actions only worsened economic conditions. Close to the United States, these lands remained subject to U.S. military intervention when American leaders judged their internal or foreign policies unacceptable to U.S. interests.

Twice in the 1980s, U.S. military forces occupied countries in the region. In 1983, they forcibly expelled from the island of Grenada Marxist radicals trying to introduce a revolutionary regime there. In 1989, they removed from power Manuel Noriega, the military dictator of Panama. He was involved in international drug smuggling, and had recklessly proclaimed his intention to seize the Panama Canal, still U.S. territory. Close to the United States, these small states remained within the U.S. sphere of influence. In the same years, increasing numbers of migrants from these lands left their homes to settle in the United States. Some were refugees from political oppression, but most sought work and better conditions of life. These small countries remained a part of the Third World on the very borders of the United States.

SUMMARY

When the term Third World appeared in the 1950s, the areas of the globe it described seemed far removed from the West. The readiness of European states to grant independence to their African colonies arose in large part because their leaders and most of their population were prepared, even eager, to distance themselves from lands once regarded as a legitimate part of their empires. The fall of these empires created new states separated from and far removed from Europe's immediate concerns. The nationalist leaders of the African states were eager for independence and the freedom to set the future of their countries. The new postcolonial age in the Third World seemed an era of promise beyond the conflicts of the Cold War. The liberation of South Africa from white rule held the hope that there too a better life was open to all the people. In Latin America, nationalism was winning more converts to the idea that real independence from the Western powers was at last attainable. New leaders everywhere agreed that the path to this goal was economic development.

The obstacles proved to be far more serious than expected. The problems encountered in Africa and Latin America varied from country to country. The most common was incompetent leadership, often from military dictators far more interested in personal power and wealth than in the welfare of their people. Obstacles also arose from a lack of resources and skills, leaving ambitious economic projects to fall into decay. There was no quick route to prosperity and well-being. The promise of Soviet leaders that their form of socialism was both just and productive proved hollow. The Cuban experience revealed that a small, agrarian country remained as dependent on outside powers when it was part of the communist world as when it was within the Western international economy. The experiments in state control over economic development that emerged in Africa and Latin America did initially contribute to short periods of prosperity. Their shortcomings were passed on to the next generation, confronted with social conflict and economic hardship. In the end, the Western system of free-market production and distribution proved to be less wasteful and disruptive. Its idea of social justice was confined within a system where productivity and enterprise received the highest rewards.

In Latin America, economic growth finally yielded results that were impressive and long lasting. One measure of the impact of a rising standard of living was the dramatic fall in the birth rate in countries such as Brazil between the 1960s and 1990s. More and more families were persuaded that their own resources were sufficient for their old age, and that the survival of every one of their newborn children was, if not certain, at least probable. Their lives no longer depended on a desperate daily struggle for food and their future appeared secure. The continued high birth rates in many countries of Africa revealed, on the contrary, how unsuccessful the efforts there had been to cope with poverty. In most areas of Africa local economies were in serious decline. These grave problems brought in outsiders to take a hand in economic reforms there. Western intervention came again to parts of Africa where failed states and decaying economies, worsened poverty. Increasing numbers of migrants left these areas to search for work in distant urban centers. Some traveled on to cities in the Western world. The Third World was by the 1990s more than ever a part of an interdependent world.

DATES WORTH REMEMBERING

Africa

1948   Nationalist Party in South Africa begins apartheid
1955   African National Congress approved "Freedom Charter"
1957   Independence for Ghana (Gold Coast)

1958   French Community for former African colonies
1960   Independence for Nigeria
1960   Independence for Belgian Congo (Zaire)
1960–1963   Civil war in Zaire
1961–1990   Imprisonment of Nelson Mandela
1965   Joseph Mobutu leader of Zaire
1967–1970   Biafra civil war in Nigeria
1993   End of apartheid in South Africa
1994   Nelson Mandela president of South Africa

Latin America

1930–1945   Getulio Vargas president of Second Brazilian Republic
1934   U.S. "Good Neighbor" policy
1946–1955   Juan Peron Argentine president
1955   Beginning of Brazilian plan to develop Amazon rainforest frontier
1959   Castro's revolution in Cuba
1960   Brasilia made new capital of Brazil
1961   Cuban Bay of Pigs invasion
1962   Cuban missile crisis
1962–1965   Second Vatican Council
1964   Military dictatorship in Brazil
1973   Military dictatorship in Chile
1985   Democratic government in Argentina
1985   End of military dictatorship in Brazil
1989   Democratic government in Chile
1992   First United Nations Conference on Environment and Development
1994   North American Free Trade Agreement

RECOMMENDED READING

The Third World

Nigel Harris, *The End of the Third World: Newly Industrializing Countries and the Decline of an Ideology* (1986). An inquiry into the economic success of East Asian lands and its lessons for "Third Worldism."

Akie Hoogvelt, *The Third World in Global Develop- ment* (1982). A historical view of the difficulties of economic development in the Third World.

Independent Africa

Mary Benson, *Nelson Mandela: The Man and the Movement* (1986). A sympathetic biography and portrait of Mandela that relies in part on prison interviews.

Karl Maier. *This House Has Fallen: Midnight in Nigeria* (2000). A perceptive, grim picture of Nigeria's descent into a failed state.

Martin Meredith, *The First Dance of Freedom: Black Africa in the Postwar Era* (1985). A balanced as- sessment of the successes and failures of African states since independence.

Postwar Latin America

*Thomas Skidmore and Peter Smith, *Modern Latin America*, 5th ed. (2001). A brief survey of the history of Latin America with separate treat- ment of major countries.

Tad Szulc, *Fidel: A Critical Portrait* (1986). A de- tailed and critical biography of Castro as a per- sonality and political leader.

Memoirs and Novels

*Chinua Achebe, *Anthills of the Savannah* (1985). A story of lost hopes by a Nigerian novelist whose stories chronicle Nigeria's modern his- tory.

Nelson Mandela, *Long Walk to Freedom: The Auto- biography of Nelson Mandela* (1995). The moving personal reflections on a life that led the au- thor from prison to presidency of South Africa.

*Alan Paton, *Cry, the Beloved Country* (1948). The powerful novel, by one of the country's finest writers, of South Africa's descent into racism.

CHAPTER TEN

Nations at War
in the Middle East

The history of the Middle East after 1945 is dominated by wars, revolutions, and civil strife. More than any other region in the world, it became an arena of political conflict and war. No one state dominated the territories once ruled by the Ottoman Empire. Its collapse after the First World War marked the first step in the remaking of the Middle East.

In the following years, Western governments took charge, in one manner or another, of drawing the borders of the successor states. The lands of Egypt and Iran were already well defined, with frontiers historically established and governments nominally independent. Elsewhere the borders and even the names of states existed only as remnants of Ottoman provinces (such as Syria and Palestine). The territorial outline of these areas became the basis on which the Western powers laid out the frontiers of the new states after the First World War. In that multiethnic, multireligious area, each country gathered peoples of diverse languages, cultures, and clan loyalties within its bor-

ders. Later observers called them "states without nations, nations without states."

Sectarian religious quarrels (principally between the Sunni and Shiite Muslims) and rivalries among ethnic groups presented serious obstacles to political unity. Conservative monarchs (like the rulers of Iran and Saudi Arabia) relied on traditional fidelity to their throne, but their legitimacy was threatened by new ideologies, and by social unrest. The vision of a great Arab nation offered one alternative ideology. Arab intellectuals drew their inspiration for this grandiose national community from the medieval Arab empires that had ruled the entire area. After 1945, Arab political leaders frequently called for the creation of a pan-Arab nation. Often, though, such appeals to Arab nationalism were based on the claim by one particular Arab ruler that his leadership was the only basis for Arab unity.

The most enduring method of state-building proved to be the establishment of authoritarian regimes. By the 1960s, military dictators had taken power in most Middle

Eastern countries. They justified their rule by promoting social reform and, often, by claiming to be defenders of the Muslim faith practiced by most of their peoples. Poverty and deep devotion to Islam combined to make an Islamic form of nationalism a powerful magnet to attract popular support. Still, disunity and the struggle for power among conservative monarchs, Muslim fundamentalists, and ambitious generals sustained conditions of disorder and instability in the political life of these lands.

The violent history of the region was also due to factors outside the Arab community. The Jewish settlers living among of Arab-speaking peoples in Palestine achieved the Zionist dream of a Jewish nation-state shortly after the Second World War. The inflexible opposition of Arab states to the very existence of Israel led to four separate wars between Israel and its Arab neighbors. Pan-Arab nationalism came to mean resistance to Western imperialism and also to Zionism, by which Arab leaders referred to the state of Israel. In later decades, Palestinians entered into the struggle against the Jewish state in an effort to forge their own nation-state. Nationalism was at the heart of the Middle East's turmoil in the last half of the century.

The recent history of the Middle East is also a story of oil. Its oil fields, concentrated in the area around the Persian Gulf, contained greater petroleum reserves of higher quality than petroleum found anywhere else in the world. The dependence of the industrial countries on this vital resource brought the pressures of the Cold War to bear on the oil-rich countries. The Soviet Union and the United States kept close watch on the unstable political leadership there. They both intervened in the political life of these states, and used their global might to protect allied states. The oil-producing countries nationalized their petroleum industry to get direct access to oil revenues, and created an inter-national cartel to set levels of production and prices for this increasingly valuable commodity. The fabulous wealth to be drawn from oil production became in turn the cause of war when Iraq attempted to conquer oil-rich areas on its borders. Internal and international conflict remained the central feature of the postwar history of the Middle East.

WAR AND REVOLUTION IN THE MIDDLE EAST

The Middle East was the birthplace of three major religions—Judaism, Christianity, and Islam. For many millions of people, Jerusalem was the most holy place in the world. It remained a center of pilgrimage and worship for the faithful of all three religions in the twentieth century. It was also the capital of Palestine, which was the area in which Zionists were determined to create a Jewish national homeland. Their eagerness to achieve this goal brought them into conflict with the British rulers of the mandate of Palestine, then, after the withdrawal of the British, with the neighboring Arab states and the Arabic-speaking peoples of Palestine. The new nation-state of Israel extended its borders across a landscape where for centuries Muslim and Christian religious communities had dwelled under foreign rule and worshiped at their own holy sites. National and religious differences combined to make this one small region of the Middle East a cauldron of ethnic conflict and war.

The Struggle for Palestine

The end of the Second World War immediately brought out the long-standing antagonism between Arabs and Jews in the British mandate of Palestine (see Chapter 2). By war's end the other mandated territories—Lebanon and Syria, Iraq and Jordan—had received their independence under constitutional monarchs (in the latter two) or elected parliamentary governments. No political movement or leader enjoyed comparable authority in Palestine, where 600,000 Jewish settlers lived among 1.2 million Arabs. Each community sought political self-rule to the exclusion of the other. Arab opposition to British occupation and Jewish migration had erupted in a prolonged and bloody Arab revolt in the late 1930s. When British forces finally suppressed the insurrection, the British government had laid plans for the partition of the territory. While the Zionist movement had welcomed the prospect of a Jewish nation-state, even reduced in size, Arab leaders were united in opposition and vowed to resist any grant of territory to the Jews. The prewar deadlock in negotiations for Palestinian independence had raised, as in India, the prospect of civil war. The leaders of each community were resolved to control a territory that the other group considered its own.

The Second World War deepened the conflict over Palestine. It brought independence to Arab countries, united in their opposition to a Jewish state in Palestine. In those same years, the horrors of the Holocaust united Jewish peoples as never before in support of the creation of their own nation-state. The Zionist commitment to that cause became a crusade. The war temporarily ended all discussion of future Palestinian self-government, Jewish migration, and partition. The British made the preservation of order in Palestine their sole objective, virtually ending Jewish immigration. Yet those were the very years when Jewish persecution in Europe rendered the establishment of a Jewish homeland in Palestine a matter of life and death.

During the war, the British government hardened its political domination of the region. Fighting remained at a distance, but the Axis powers made themselves felt nonetheless. In Palestine, the Muslim religious leader, the grand mufti of Jerusalem, had publicly announced his support of Nazi Germany and had fled to Berlin. He made radio broadcasts to the Middle East calling for Arab revolt against the British. In Egypt and in Iraq, some nationalists appeared ready to welcome Rommel's German divisions when his offensive reached the borders of Egypt in 1942. The vital importance of the Suez Canal and of the region's petroleum gave the British government reason enough to use its forces to repress any signs of possible Arab collaboration with Germany. In Iraq and Egypt, they forcibly installed political leaders sympathetic to the Allies. Palestinian Jews for their part welcomed the opportunity to join in the war against Nazi Germany, sending 30,000 men to serve in the British Army. They later became the core of the Israeli Army.

The Palestinian crisis erupted immediately following the war. The British government, caught between Palestinian Arabs and Jews and intent on keeping good relations with the Arab states, refused to open the country to more immigrants. Jewish refugees scattered across Europe looked to Palestine for a new home and were helped on the way by the Zionist organization. Desperate migrants sailed from Europe to the Holy Land in decrepit old boats such as the *Exodus*. Some ships sank before reaching their destination. Others were captured by the British, who placed the passengers in internment camps in Cyprus, prisoners again.

The Zionist movement acquired a valuable ally in 1945 when the U.S. government publicly supported their demand for renewed Jewish immigration to Palestine. American political leaders were sympathetic to the cause of a Jewish state, and were under strong pressure from American Jewish organizations to assist in the creation of a Jewish homeland. President Truman's announcement of the new U.S. policy brought the full weight of American international influence to bear on Britain's Palestine problem. It made the crisis an international affair.

The profound disagreement on political objectives and the ethnic strife among the peoples in Palestine made peaceful negotiations impossible. Palestinian Arab leaders all agreed that their land had to become one independent nation-state under the rule of the Arab majority. The Zionists demanded special territorial protection for their people, who they feared would suffer persecution in an Arab-dominated state. Palestinian Jews began in 1945 a forceful resistance movement to force London to heed their demands for immigration and self-rule. Small terrorist organizations even launched attacks against British troops and colonial officials.

Unable to transfer power peacefully to a Palestinian state, the British government turned to outside help. In early 1947, the British government declared that it was placing the fate of its Palestine mandate in the hands of the United Nations. It had abandoned the hopeless effort to bring the two sides together and had resolved, as in India, to withdraw quickly. The U.N. had to determine whether Palestine should become one state or two. The United States played the key role in mobilizing the votes needed for approval of the creation of two states, one for the Arabs and the other for the Jews. Even the Soviet Union and its allies backed the plan, hoping in this way to prove their opposition to "British imperialism." In November of that year, a majority in the U.N. General Assembly voted in favor of the partition of Palestine, to be divided into Arab and Jewish states. As in India, the existence of two deeply antagonistic communities, each intent on defending its own national rights, had produced new borders around areas to become, somehow, nation-states. They had each opted for an ethno-territorial

nationalist formula, and the U.N.'s decision had used it to approve two tiny states.

This solution was unacceptable to the surrounding Arab countries. Opposition to a Jewish state had become a key test of loyalty to the cause of pan-Arab nationalism and to the Palestinian people. An additional factor behind their decision to intervene in Palestine was the competition among Arab leaders for political influence in the Middle East and for control of the Palestinian territory. The king of Jordan hoped to annex lands west of the Jordan River and feared expansionist Syrian plans for a Greater Syria encompassing all the land from Iraq to the Mediterranean. The Iraqi and Egyptian monarchs were rivals for leadership of the Arab countries. On only one point did they all agree—the Middle East had to remain Arab. This objective brought them together in 1945 in a regional organization called the Arab League. They proclaimed its purpose to be "coordinating policies" and "strengthening relations" among its members (Syria, Lebanon, Jordan, Iraq, Saudi Arabia, and Egypt). Its immediate objective was to prevent the formation of a Jewish state in Palestine.

Egypt was the founder and leader of the League. It was the largest and most powerful Arab state. Its population had grown rapidly, rising from 10 million in the early century to 16 million. The standard of living of the urban and rural masses probably had stagnated in those years, creating the conditions for serious social unrest. Conditions of social unrest and political corruption strengthened the role of the Muslim Brotherhood among the Egyptian masses. Its membership after the war rose to over 1 million, and it (with considerable exaggeration) claimed to have a half-million Egyptians in its paramilitary force, the Phalanx. No political party possessed such mass support. It alone offered material help and spiritual guidance to the country's lower classes. Its Muslim fundamentalist program made the Islamic faith its guide to social reform, and the grounds for its unyielding resistance to a Jewish homeland in Palestine.

In the winter of 1947–1948, Palestine was a land torn by civil war. Jewish and Palestinian military units fought each other for control of villages and towns as the British forces gradually withdrew to the coast. The Palestinians received arms from the Arab League, while the Jews had to take their weapons where they could find them. The day after the last British troops left Palestine in May 1948, Jewish leaders formally established the state of Israel. They had achieved their goal, but enemies on every border endangered their new state. Egypt, Iraq, Syria, and Jordan immediately declared war on Israel and ordered their armies to destroy the new state. The first Arab-Israeli war had begun.

Egypt took the lead. The Egyptian army marched off to fight its first war while volunteers from the Muslim Brotherhood's paramilitary forces joined the Palestinian Arabs. King Farouk ignored the warnings of his generals that his army was poorly prepared and equipped for war. He believed that Arab forces would quickly annihilate the outnumbered and ill-armed Jewish army. He, and most Arab leaders, underestimated the ability of the Jews to resist.

Surrounded on three sides by enemies, the Jewish forces fought for the survival of their new state and for their community. The Palestinians did not share the same nationalist fervor. Many Arabs, fearing for their lives and their religion under Jewish rule, fled the Jewish-controlled areas. Only a few Arab forces could match the fighting skill of the Jews. The Jordanian Arab Legion, led by English officers, seized part of the area on the right (western) bank of the Jordan River and the old city of Jerusalem. The ancient

Jewish neighborhood was for months surrounded and under siege before Israeli troops had to withdraw outside the walls of the old city.

The other Arab forces fared poorly. Among the Egyptian officers, some, like Captain Gamal Nasser, fought bravely. Most officers in the army did not share his commitment to the war. The army was badly led, and badly supplied by the Egyptian government. The Egyptian attack on southern Palestine collapsed, and was followed by retreat from the entire Negev Desert. Lacking any coordinated strategy, the Arab forces conducted separate campaigns and could not prevent the Jews from seizing an area even larger than that granted by the U.N. partition plan.

The failure of the Egyptian offensive was the key to ending the war. In February 1949, the United Nations obtained agreement from all sides to an armistice. Israeli forces occupied the coastal region of Palestine, part of the Jordan River valley, and the Negev Desert to the shores of the Red Sea. Jerusalem was divided. The armistice line confirmed the partition of Palestine, which was split between Israel and Jordan. The old city of Jerusalem and much the Jordan River valley stayed in the hands of the Jordanian forces. The armistice confirmed the victory of Israel, a small, oddly shaped state surrounded by enemies. The flight during the war of most Palestinian Arab inhabitants from Jewish controlled areas made Jewish settlers the majority of Israel's population. Palestinians found at war's end that they had no state of their own.

The new Israeli government began the process of constructing a Jewish nation-state. The new state was a parliamentary democracy. It welcomed Jews from any country and made Hebrew, the Biblical tongue not spoken for two millennia, the official language. It bore some resemblance to

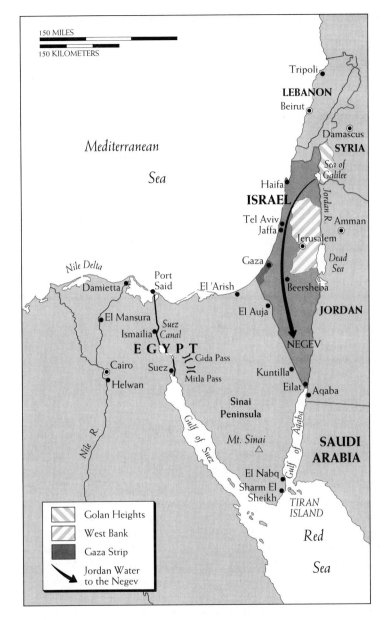

150 MILES

150 KILOMETERS

Mediterranean

Sea

Tripoli

LEBANON

Beirut

Damascus

SYRIA

Sea of Galilee

Haifa

ISRAEL

Jordan R.

Tel Aviv

Jaffa

Amman

Jerusalem

Gaza

Dead Sea

Nile Delta

Port Said

El 'Arish

Beersheba

Damietta

El Mansura

Suez Canal

El Auja

JORDAN

Ismailia

E G Y P T

Gida Pass

Cairo

Suez

Mitla Pass

Kuntilla

NEGEV

Helwan

Eilat

Aqaba

Sinai Peninsula

Gulf of Suez

Nile R.

Mt. Sinai

△

Gulf of Aqaba

SAUDI ARABIA

El Nabq

Sharm El Sheikh

TIRAN ISLAND

Red

Sea

Golan Heights

West Bank

Gaza Strip

Jordan Water to the Negev

Israel and Its Neighbors

a theocracy, that is, a state whose inhabitants were inspired by a religious faith. Yet at the same time it was a modern nation-state whose laws protected political freedom and individual opportunity. It introduced social reforms inspired by the socialist movements of Europe. It supported the creation, begun earlier by the first Jewish settlers, of collective farms, called "kibbutz." Members of these cooperatives shared the revenues from their crops as they struggled to make the desert fertile.

Though Israel guaranteed freedom of religion to its Christian and Muslim minorities, to many Arabs it was the object of abiding hatred. It had broken apart Palestine. Its legal and social order embodied Western secular values rejected by Muslim fundamentalists. Surrounded by enemies, the Israelis had to arm their nation in anticipation of another war.

The defeat of the Arab League's forces was a public humiliation for the Arab countries. A constant reminder of the defeat was the presence of 750,000 Palestinian refugees, scattered throughout the Middle East but concentrated in refugee camps in Egyptian territory. The Palestinians received little help from the Arab states. A few were able to find a new home for themselves in other parts of the Middle East. Most remained in miserable refugee camps under U.N. care, hoping for the day when Israel would no longer exist and they could return to their homeland. In all respects, the Israeli victory was a disaster for the Egyptian monarchy, unable to unite Arab forces and to organize and lead its army. The months of war proved a bitter lesson for Egyptian army officers. They returned to Egypt convinced that the corrupt political leadership of their country had betrayed them, the Egyptian nation, and the Arab cause.

❦ SPOTLIGHT: Golda Meir ❦

Golda Meir (1898–1978) devoted her life to the creation of a Jewish homeland in Palestine. Her family fled the Russian Empire when she was nine years old. By then she had experienced firsthand anti-Semitic hatred, widespread among the population where her family had lived. She had also begun to learn of a new movement called Zionism dedicated to the creation of a Jewish homeland in Palestine. Though she grew up in the United States, she decided when she was twenty years old to make that cause her own. The decision changed the course of her life.

The lifelong service that she rendered to Zionism drew upon her remarkable personal qualities and her commitment to the goal of a Jewish homeland. With her husband, she moved to Palestine in the 1920s. "The Jews must have a land of their own again," she wrote, "and I must help to build it by living and working there." She became a pioneer on a Jewish farm (a "kibbutz") reclaiming desert land. The pioneers laid claim to a Palestinian homeland, in the midst of Arab-speaking Christians and Muslims, by making the land prosper once again. In her words, "only self-labor could make it possible for the Jews to earn a moral right, as well as a historical right," to that land.

Like the other Jewish migrants, she firmly believed that their claim to Palestine was morally and historically justified. The harsh life that she led for the next decades had as its goal the acquisition of a territory belonging to the Jewish people. That land was the birthplace of the Jewish religion, but she did not wish to make it a religious state. The Jews formed a community like other peoples who desired their own nation-state. She believed in toleration for all religions, hoping that the Arabs would "live with us in peace and equality as citizens of a Jewish homeland."

Her dream inevitably meant that those Arabs would have to become a minority nationality in a state of the Jews. Many Muslim Arabs rejected the idea that infidels should govern them and their holy places in Palestine. Their religious convictions excluded the possibility of the Jewish secular state for which Zionists such as Golda Meir struggled. Conflict between Arabs and Jews was unavoidable.

Her own personal life became consumed by her work for the Zionist cause. She admitted later that she had too little time for her marriage and children. She left her family for long trips to Europe and America to encourage Jewish immigration and to raise funds for Jewish settlements, then for the state of Israel. But her greatest contribution lay in political leadership. Along with a handful of other Zionists, she came to embody for many Jews the selfless dedication that had made the incredible dream of Israel come true. When she arrived in 1948 in Moscow to serve as first Israeli ambassador to the Soviet Union, crowds of Jews celebrated outside the Israeli embassy at the risk of arrest and imprisonment.

She also possessed the talents of a far-sighted political leader. The Zionist move-

Prime Minister Golda Meir Reviewing Israeli Soldiers, 1969 (*UPI/Bettmann*)

ment had always regarded women as equal to men in its work, though bias against women in politics remained strong among some Israelis. Her government believed in and needed her abilities. In 1949, it offered her the position of Minister of Labor. She proceeded to lay the foundations of the social welfare policies of Israel. Her greatest challenge was to create a shared loyalty among the "flood of Jews from opposite ends of the earth who spoke different languages and who were ignorant of each other's traditions and customs." They were, she remembered, "the most satisfying and the happiest years of my life."

In a real sense, Israel absorbed her remaining years. She moved from her Labor post to become Minister of Foreign Affairs in 1956. Thirteen years later she reluctantly agreed to become the prime minister of her country. Why, she asked, should a "seventy-year-old grandmother head a twenty-year-old state?" The answer was that no one else could. Her commitment to a Jewish homeland had carried her as a young woman to Palestine. Her sense of duty to that land elevated her ultimately to the most powerful political position in her country. It was a career that few men could match.

Revolution in Egypt

The Egyptian monarchy was increasingly unpopular in the years after the war. Free elections in 1950 (the last multiparty elections until 1984) revealed to what extent parliamentary politics had become the affair of a small political elite. Few voters bothered to cast their ballots. The state was weakened still more by King Farouk's ambition to control the government. The new cabinet mobilized popular support for an anti-British campaign to oblige the British to withdraw their troops from the Suez zone. These forces had stayed on by agreement with the Egyptian government after independence 1924. The British refused to negotiate, and the movement grew increasingly violent. In early 1952, riots broke out in Cairo protesting the British presence along the Suez Canal. The king dismissed the cabinet, took over the government, and called in the army to repress the rioting. In doing so, he sealed his own fate.

Egypt's revolutionary officers chose that moment of political chaos to move into ac-

tion. The leader of this secret opposition was Gamal Nasser. As a student before the Second World War, he had been active in the nationalist movement. For him, as for nationalists in other poor countries, the nation symbolized a new, just community in which "the weak and the humiliated Egyptian people [could] rise up again and live as free and independent men." The son of poor parents, he chose the career of an army officer. It was for him the means to improve his own life, and to advance the cause of Egyptian nationalism. In the first years, army life brought him no glory and little opportunity. It did form the bonds uniting Nasser and other officers, including Anwar Sadat (his successor as ruler of Egypt), who later set about remaking Egypt. His real political career began after the Palestinian war. He and his colleagues realized, as he wrote later, that "our battle was taking place in Cairo. We knew that we had to liberate our country first, in order to be able to fight." Believing themselves betrayed by the monarch and the parliamentary regime, they resolved to restore Egyptian power and influence on their own. Their military conspiracy pointed to a political revolution in Egypt.

The officers, under Nasser's leadership, organized a secret group calling itself the Free Officers. Founded in 1949, it grew to about 1,000 members. When in the summer of 1952 King Farouk ordered the army into Cairo to end the rioting, its members set in motion their plans for a military "coup," that is, the overthrow of the monarchy by military force. They secretly took over command of the armed forces with the help of General Naguib, a senior officer who shared their opposition to the monarchy. Army units surrounded the royal palace and forced the king to abdicate. On leaving the country Farouk warned the victorious insurgents: "Your task will be difficult. It isn't easy, you know, to govern Egypt."

The process of remaking the Egyptian nation-state had only just begun. Few Egyptians regretted the departure of the Turkish king. Several contenders for power aspired to govern the republic. Liberal political parties hoped to preserve constitutional government, as well as the interests of the financiers and landowners who supported them. The followers of the Muslim Brotherhood looked to an Islamic republic to bolster the Muslim religion and to wipe out the social and moral decay that they believed to be caused by Westernization.

The officers were not prepared to tolerate political diversity and dissent. Nasser later referred sarcastically to the "dispersed followers and contrasted remnants, chaos, dissensions, surrender, and idleness" that they encountered in the months after overthrowing the monarchy. It is unlikely that they ever seriously considered sharing the responsibilities and powers of rule. Their response to political rivalries was to eliminate their rivals and to end parliamentary rule. They dissolved parliament and the cabinet,

replacing them with a Revolutionary Command Council (RCC). It consisted of the leaders in the Free Officers conspiracy, under the chairmanship of Gamal Nasser. The council abolished the constitution and in early 1953 disbanded all political parties. Lacking a mass following, the liberal parties disappeared from public life. The small Communist Party became the target of outright repression and its leaders were thrown in jail. Nasser proclaimed that "the Communists are agents who believe neither in the liberty of their land nor in their nation but only do the bidding of outsiders." To the officers, Egyptian nationalism was the ideological inspiration for the resurgence of their country.

The Muslim Brotherhood presented the Revolutionary Command Council with its most dangerous rival. The military leaders opposed the Brotherhood for two reasons. They did not share the Brotherhood's goal of Islamic revolution. They were Westernized officers, for whom the Quran fixed religious belief and practices, not state policy. In addition, the Brotherhood challenged their own political power. In January 1954, Muslim leaders began mass street demonstrations aimed at forcing the council to implement their plans for an Islamic revolution. The ruling officers seized the opportunity to arrest the Brotherhood leadership and to ban the organization. As in previous periods of repression, the Brotherhood went underground. In October 1954, one of its members attempted to assassinate Nasser. The police asserted—though without real proof—that the Brotherhood was plotting to overthrow the new regime. Police repression worsened, and prisons filled with political prisoners. The revolutionary officers had defeated all their rivals for power.

Their new regime immediately incorporated the objectives of pan-Arab nationalism into their foreign policy. They reiterated their determination to prepare for a new war with Israel. At the same time, they took steps to strengthen the national liberation movements underway in North Africa. This was the last area where Arabs lived under Western colonial rule. Arab nationalists from Tunisia, Morocco, and Algeria, still part of the French Empire, found refuge in Cairo after 1953. There they found refuge from French colonial forces and received financial assistance from the new government. Their leadership and popular unrest forced the reluctant French government to grant independence to Morocco and Tunisia in 1956.

Algerian nationalists faced determined opposition, however, from France. French forces had conquered Algeria over a century before and opened the country to colonists from southern Europe, all of whom received French citizenship. This settler colony had a special place in the French Empire. The one million European settlers of French culture and citizenship were deeply hostile to the Arabs and to the idea Algerian independence. The French government refused negotiations with the Algerian National Liberation Front, whose headquarters were in Cairo. In 1954, the Algerian nationalists called for an insurrection against the French. The French government sent in hundreds of thousands of troops, some just withdrawn from Indochina, to defeat the Arab nationalist revolt and to protect the European settlers.

This new French colonial war lasted until 1962. By then it had consumed thousands of lives and kindled terrorist movements on the part of both Europeans and Arabs. The French government, faced with an apparently endless guerrilla war, decided to grant Algeria its independence. More than one million Algerian Europeans and Arabs who had collaborated with the French fled to France. The last colonial war had ended. Western empires had disappeared from the Middle East.

NATIONALISM IN THE MIDDLE EAST

The new Egyptian regime's seizure of the Suez Canal marked in a spectacular manner the collapse of European power in the Middle East. The impact of the growing global economy, fueled increasingly by petroleum, lured Western private companies into the region. Access to petroleum brought great profits to oil corporations, and was of vital strategic interest to all developed economies. Governments of the Middle Eastern lands possessing large oil reserves were themselves eager to obtain revenues from oil sales in this global market. The age of nations took shape in the same years as the new states entered the interdependent global economy.

Nasser and the New Egypt

The military leaders of Egypt had vague plans for social reform and leadership of the Arab countries. They had overthrown Egypt's monarchy claiming that they alone could transform the country into a modern nation. They knew that their experiment was risky. Their country was poor, and their hopes to expand the power of the state and to improve the living conditions of the Egyptian population depended on new revenues. Still, they were convinced that they were the rightful national leaders, the "vanguard," as Nasser wrote in 1953, whose "mission had not ended."

They disagreed among themselves on basic issues of government. Some officers preferred to introduce a constitutional democracy, giving power back to the political parties. Nasser was determined to keep the military in charge of the country. In early 1954, the dispute ended with his victory. Proclaiming that their revolution was threatened by a return to the corrupt practices of the monarchy, he placed his followers in positions of control throughout the Egyptian government. The country's military regime consolidated its hold on the state, and Nasser emerged as the principal leader.

He set about creating a new sort of authoritarian state. In place of political parties, he and his fellow officers created their own mass party. Called at first the Liberation Rally, it changed names frequently in the decades to come. They stipulated that it alone enjoyed the right to propose candidates for election. They imposed censorship on radio and the press and deprived labor unions of the right to strike. In 1956, they introduced a new constitution that created a National Assembly, but it enjoyed no real legislative power. A secret police operated beyond the rule of law to pursue the enemies of the military rulers. A cabinet replaced the Revolutionary Command Council, but it consisted of the same officers who had led the country since 1952. Nasser held the title of president of the Republic. In fact, he was a benevolent military dictator committed to national revolution.

Nasser's most ambitious project was the damming of the waters of the Nile behind a new, giant dam at Aswan. It was to be a structure so huge it would dwarf the pyramids (and the new lake it created would drown precious relics of Egypt's pharonic past). Plans for its use foresaw both abundant water for irrigation (the arable land of Egypt was to increase by one-third) and hydroelectric power in a greater quantity than all the electricity then available. A great source of pride to Nasser, it embodied his hope for social betterment and his grandiose vision of a national revolution in Egypt. He called it Egypt's "pyramid for the living." Paying for the dam presented serious difficulties, however. The Egyptian state lacked the necessary financial means. Like India, it could not initiate important economic projects without outside help.

The most dramatic result of the military revolution was Egypt's defiance of the West.

Following the example of Nehru of India, he adopted a policy of nonalignment for his country. He refused to join the Baghdad military pact with Turkey, Iran, and Iraq. He called the treaty (in terms that echoed Nehru's judgment of SEATO) a "modern version of a protectorate" and condemned its members for collaborating with "Western imperialism." His refusal seriously undermined his state's chances of substantial aid from the United States.

Egypt's conflict with Israel gave a warlike character to Nasser's new foreign policy. Egypt remained formally in a state of war with the Jewish state, and it forbad any shipping bound for Israel to pass through the Suez Canal. Yet the Egyptian army was still badly equipped and needed to import modern weapons. These could be paid for only by foreign loans. The United States hesitated, concerned that aid might fuel a new Arab-Israeli war. The Soviet Union was ready to help. The new post-Stalin leaders were prepared to support reformist governments in the Middle East and in Asia that were not members of Western alliances. Their offers of arms and financial credits presented the Egyptian regime with a tempting source of assistance.

In late 1955, Nasser accepted the offer. He announced that the Egyptian government had signed an agreement with the Soviet Union to obtain a long-term loan, to be repaid in cotton and rice exports. The funds would allow Egypt to buy from communist countries fighter planes, tanks, arms, and naval vessels. He was acclaimed by nationalists throughout the Middle East for his action. He called the arms deal a policy of "positive neutrality." But Cold War passions among Western leaders magnified out of all proportion the implications of both his aid to Arab rebels in French North Africa and his arms agreement. He appeared a dangerous revolutionary and potential communist ally.

The price of his arms deal with the communist countries became apparent in mid-1956. He had begun negotiations in 1955 with the World Bank, which was largely financed by the U.S. government, for a major loan to begin construction of the High Dam at Aswan. He staked the prestige of his regime and of his own leadership on the mammoth project. Negotiations dragged on until July 1956. Suddenly the United States announced its refusal to participate in the projected loan. Great Britain soon made the same decision. Their message was clear: Nasser's cooperation with communist states had cost his state Western financial assistance for the Aswan Dam. The decision represented a public humiliation of the Egyptian leader, and a serious diplomatic blunder by the United States.

The Suez Canal and the 1956 War

In 1956, the Suez Canal was still an economic enterprise run and owned by Westerners, a remnant of the age of Western imperialism. It was also a valuable piece of property bringing substantial income to its owners. The last British troops withdrew from the Suez zone early that year. The Suez Canal was a tempting prize to Egyptian nationalists such as Nasser. He was attracted both by the revenues that it would bring and by the prestige that its seizure would bring to his regime. In July 1956, he declared to an enormous crowd of Egyptians gathered in Cairo that his government had taken possession of the Canal. "Our pride, our determination, and our faith," he cried, had been challenged by the West. Nationalization of the canal proved that "this nation will not accept humiliation and degradation." If the "imperialists" did not approve of his action, they could "choke in their own rage." His defiance of the West brought him and his country into direct confrontation with European states. It was a move enthusiastically applauded by his people.

The Egyptian seizure of the Suez Canal incited the British and French governments to make one final effort to reassert their imperial power in the eastern Mediterranean. They viewed nationalization as a threat to their security. The canal remained a vital pathway for strategic goods, especially petroleum, to Western Europe. They were deeply suspicious of Nasser's nationalist policies. Strategic and ideological reasons incited the two states to launch a reckless, ill-conceived invasion of the canal zone. They found a ready ally in the Israeli government. Israel's economy suffered from the Egyptian blockade of its shipping through the canal, and its leaders feared another Egyptian invasion. The three states attacked Egypt in late October 1956. Israeli tank units raced across the Sinai desert to the canal, while a British and French naval force and paratroopers seized the Suez ports and the entire canal zone. Militarily the operation was a complete success. Politically it failed. Nasser became a national hero for the Egyptian people. Diplomatically the invasion proved a disaster.

Opposition came from all sides. Almost the entire membership of the United Nations condemned the attack. The Soviet Union offered Nasser more military aid and warned Britain and France of its readiness to take "all measures" to protect Egypt. The U.S. government condemned the invasion, for it was outraged by military action and intent on keeping good relations with Third World countries. It made its opposition painfully real by reducing economic aid to Great Britain and France. It also refused to protect the British currency, which was losing value rapidly as panicky Britishers bought up dollars. Lacking U.S. support, the British and French were isolated and unable to continue the war. Faced with global diplomatic protests and a major financial crisis, the British convinced the French and Israelis to withdraw from the canal zone. President Eisenhower had used U.S. economic power and diplomatic influence to defeat their intervention.

The Suez crisis was Nasser's greatest triumph. He had defied the European powers and won. In the Middle East his action revived the popularity of pan-Arab nationalism. To Egyptians he became their undisputed national leader. His forces' only achievement in the war had been to block the canal with sunken ships, closing it to navigation for another year. A serious economic recession swept Europe as a result of the sudden petroleum shortage. In the peace settlement, Nasser accepted a U.N. proposal for the stationing of an international peacekeeping force in Egypt. Its task was to patrol the Egyptian-Israeli frontier to prevent Arab terrorist attacks on Israel and to block a new Israeli invasion. The outcome of the Suez crisis gave Nasser the illusion of great power. His action earned him, for a few years, the standing of leader among Arab states and among nonaligned countries of the Third World.

Egypt and Arab Nationalism

The Suez war gave a sudden impetus to state control of the Egyptian economy. Nasser welcomed the development, calling it "Arab socialism." He implied that these reforms set a model for all Arab lands. Until 1956 the Egyptian economy had functioned along free-market lines, allowing private ownership of banking, industry, and agriculture and welcoming foreign investment. The war brought the state new economic powers. The government suddenly became, without any long-range plan, owner of the Suez Canal Company and responsible for the operations of the canal. During the war Egypt

took possession of foreign-owned and operated enterprises in any way connected with France and Great Britain. These included many banks, insurance companies, and industrial enterprises. The nationalized holdings gave the government an important role in the small Egyptian industrial economy.

The Suez crisis expanded the Free Officers' goal of "social justice" into a larger vision of socialism. It took a form somewhat like the Soviet command economy. The government turned to economic planning to provide the economic guidelines needed by the state to operate the nationalized businesses. It created in early 1957 a National Planning Committee and later that year approved a Five-Year Plan for economic development. Foreign aid came from the Soviet Union for construction of the Aswan Dam. The United States shipped food supplies to help feed Egypt's growing population. Nasser declared that the goal of the Egyptian revolution was "a cooperative, democratic, socialist society." Like India, Egypt became a mixed economy. Small commerce and farming stayed in private hands, while major enterprises were state owned.

For a few years, the Egyptian people benefitted substantially from the reforms. Throughout the 1960s, the economy grew steadily, though its growth slowed from 6 percent in the first years to 2 percent after the disastrous 1967 war. But economic development could not cope for long with the population explosion resulting from an annual increase of 1 million people. The state subsidized the sale of cheap food to Egypt's urban masses to avoid social unrest, for the city had become a place of welfare as well as work. Imported agricultural produce, provided in large measure by foreign aid, became the sole protection against famine.

The Aswan Dam was Nasser's great project for the transformation of Egypt. It was completed in 1970, forever ending the yearly

Pyramid for the People:
The Aswan Dam under
Construction (*Hulton-
Deutsch Collection/Corbis*)

flooding of the lower Nile region. The reservoir, named Lake Nasser, stretched more than 300 miles upstream, impounding water used to generate hydroelectric power (10 billion kilowatt hours per year) and to irrigate agricultural land (one-third more than before). Periodic great floods no longer devastate the Nile basin, and years of low rainfall in the Nile headwaters no longer meant drought for Egypt's farmers.

The dam was a technological marvel and the pride of Egyptians. The ecological price was high, for the irrigation water carried disease through the canals and left deposits of salt on the land, no longer cleansed by flooding. The Aswan Dam illustrated vividly the vision and limits of Nasser's socialism. Its planners could take pride in Egyptian economic growth, but in achieving this goal they permanently destroyed the balance between people and nature that had existed before.

Egypt in the years after the Suez war became the center of pan-Arab nationalism and supported socialist movements in other Middle Eastern countries. From Cairo, the Voice of Arabs Radio defended the cause of Arab unity and called for opposition to imperialism, feudalism (typified by Saudi Arabia), and Zionism (Israel). Nasser revived the vision of a great pan-Arab state to unite all "progressive" Arab lands, that is, states not ruled by conservative monarchs.

He initiated a concrete step toward the pan-Arab dream when in 1958 he signed a treaty of union with the government of Syria. The Syrian government joined in proclaiming its faith in a pan-Arab state and backed Egyptian leadership, but its leaders had more practical reasons for joining Egypt. They needed Egyptian protection in the face of serious internal religious and political unrest and the threat of war with Iraq. What appeared to be a sign of pan-

Arab nationalism was for them an affair of state.

This United Arab Republic (U.A.R.) became an extension of the Egyptian state. Nasser was its president and Egyptian officers assumed important posts in Syria. The U.A.R. proved a disappointment, though, to its Syrian supporters. The breaking point came in 1961 when Egypt imposed its socialist policies on the Syrian economy. Discontent with the U.A.R. brought the Syrian army and business community together. In September 1961, the army seized power and repudiated the agreement with Egypt. At first Nasser considered sending Egyptian troops to invade Syria, then abandoned the idea. He blamed the failure of his political union on capitalist and imperialist enemies. Pan-Arab nationalism proved weaker than the needs and interests of political leaders of the various countries.

In that divided region, the conflict with Israel posed the most serious threat of war. Nasser was the first among Arab leaders in proclaiming his opposition to the state of Israel. Time and again he spoke out for "liquidating the Israeli aggression on a part of the Palestine land." His deeds in the ten years following the Suez war were not, however, warlike. He accepted until the mid-1960s the U.N. peacekeeping force along the Egyptian-Israeli frontier. Purely symbolic, its presence on the Egyptian side of the border absolved Egypt of the responsibility to undertake a dangerous new war. It was an undertaking that the country could not afford and that Nasser's military could not win.

Petroleum and the Middle East

The political revolution in Egypt came just as the Middle East became the principal source of petroleum for the global economy. This was an economic revolution, bringing enormous revenues to a few Arab states and elevating questions of revolution and war in the Middle East to issues of vital strategic interest to major states around the world. The loss of access to the oil in that area posed the threat of economic collapse to developed countries. The 1956–1957 recession in Europe had shown how devastating the interruption of oil shipments from the region could be. The Middle East acquired an international importance that overshadowed the political ambitions of leaders such as Nasser.

The boom in Middle Eastern oil production was the result of the discovery there of vast petroleum reserves. Geologists had detected major oil deposits first in the territory of Persia (Iran) early in the century. Oil fields equally vast were found elsewhere in the region bordering the Persian Gulf, and up the river valleys of the Tigris and Euphrates on the territory of Iraq. By the 1960s, these discoveries revealed that two-thirds of the world's known oil reserves lay in that region. The deserts of impoverished countries like Saudi Arabia hid some of the highest quality petroleum in the world. The people of the tiny principality of Kuwait had previously had to rely mainly on pearl fishing for their livelihood. They soon became immensely wealthy after their ruler in 1946 turned the spigot to pump petroleum from his oil wells to ships in the gulf.

The global market for petroleum became a reality in mid-century. In the Second World War, the mobility of Allied forces depended on ready access to oil. U.S. leaders realized that their country would in the future be forced to rely increasingly on foreign oil as domestic demand grew and American oil fields dried up. The Middle East's oil-producing countries, especially Saudi Arabia, attracted particular attention. President Truman informed the Saudi king after the war that "no threat to your kingdom could occur which would not be a matter of immediate concern to the United States." Strategic interest in Iranian oil led the Western states to intervene secretly in the a major political conflict that erupted in Iran in the early 1950s. They supported the shah (the head of state) in his fight against his enemies, who appeared hostile to the West. National interests brought Western involvement in Middle Eastern politics whatever the wishes of regional leaders.

Until the 1950s, the international oil corporations operated without having to consider the interests of the Middle Eastern countries where their refineries and oil wells were located. Even a strong ally of the West such as the shah of Iran resented the power that they enjoyed over oil production and prices. The rulers of the oil-producing states received royalties based on the profits of these corporations from production. These companies defined their goals principally in terms of price stability and profits.

Sensitive to Western governments' need for oil, they also protected their own corporate interests. When need arose, they limited production and agreed on wholesale prices to avoid ruinous price wars. The postwar discovery of new oil fields continually put their efforts in jeopardy. An economic recession in the West in the late 1950s reduced demand so seriously that they agreed among themselves to lower prices below $2 a barrel to promote sales. In doing so, they aroused the resentment of the Middle Eastern oil-producing states, including Iran and Saudi Arabia.

The rulers of these two countries shared common interests both in preserving their monarchies against internal political revolutions, and in establishing state control over their petroleum industry. They had begun expensive programs of economic development, paid for by the income from their oil royalties. These suddenly declined when the international oil companies cut prices on crude oil. The monarchs of the two states

hoped that by acting together they could force the oil corporations to heed their financial needs.

In 1960, they obtained the agreement of all the major oil-producing states (except the United States and Mexico) to form a new international association, the Organization of Petroleum Exporting Countries (OPEC). The immediate objective was to stabilize oil prices and to coordinate petroleum policies to protect "our interests, individually and collectively." Behind this modest aim lay the audacious goal of fixing levels of oil production and prices. An international oil cartel was born.

While their organization had little immediate impact on oil production, the tremendous increase in Western demand for oil in the 1960s improved their economic situation substantially. By then, petroleum use had risen so rapidly that it provided over half the West's energy supplies. Industrial economies could not function without it. In the late 1960s, oil prices began a slow increase, rising to more than $3 a barrel. Revenues going to the states of Iran and Saudi Arabia reached nearly $1 billion. Although their policies were conservative, the monarchs of these two states had lent their political weight to a radical shift in the global economic balance of power. In the world of international finance and economics, these revenues and the possession of great petroleum reserves gave the OPEC countries new power and influence.

WAR, PEACE, AND ISLAM

War and civil strife in the Middle East erupted several times in the last third of the twentieth century. Each conflict sent its reverberations echoing around the world, at times because Cold War competion intruded, at other times because the global economy had to confront serious oil shortages. A revolution in Iran made Islam a powerful political force after Muslim religious leaders seized control of the government. Their goals were a return to the principles of the Quran. Religious issues became deeply embedded in the Israeli-Arab confrontation. Committed Muslims and Jews reshaped the territorial dispute into a crusade of one religion against another. Calmer judgment among Israeli and Palestine leaders counseled compromise to permit the two peoples to live at peace with one another. The mid-1990s agreement on Palestinian self-rule offered hope for peace, but it faced strong opposition on both sides. War against Israel no longer dominated Middle Eastern politics, but the Palestinian problem remained unresolved.

The Six-Day War

The conflict between the Arab countries and Israel remained in the 1960s the greatest threat of war in the Middle East. Leaders of the Arab states refused to accept the presence of the Jewish state in their midst. In the 1960s, the Palestinian refugees themselves organized their own resistance movement to take back the territory they considered their homeland. They were scattered throughout the Middle East, but their major refugee camps were located in Egypt and Jordan. There they gradually formed new social organizations to help rebuild their lives. In the early years, they received financial aid from Arab leaders who sympathized with their cause. But the Palestinians themselves had to overcome internal quarrels before Arab states would pay real attention to their demands.

In 1964, several Palestinian movements agreed to form a unified coalition that they called the Palestine Liberation Organization (PLO). The founders of the PLO set their goal to be "Palestinian self-determination following the liberation of our country," that is, the destruction of the state of Israel. Arab League backing was still half-hearted. Other issues appeared more pressing to most League members. They hoped to exercise some moderating control over the Palestinians. No Arab leader dared call for a peace settlement, though, since to do so would require recognizing the state of Israel. The king of Jordan maintained secret contacts with his Israeli neighbor, but feared assassination if he openly negotiated with Israel. Arab supporters of the PLO were hostile toward the very existence of a Jewish state in Arab land and hoped to avenge the defeats of 1948 and 1956. As a result of PLO efforts, Arab leaders increasingly talked of a new war on Israel.

The talk led to action in 1966, when new leaders of Syria in the socialist Ba'ath party called for a "revolutionary war" to defeat Israel and to "liberate Palestine." The Syrian regime followed Nasser's example in promising their people a special Arab form of socialism. They condemned conservative Arab monarchs like the king of Saudi Arabia who adhered closely to tribal ways and traditional Muslim practices. Leaders of other Arab states suspected the Syrians of wishing to spread the political influence of their own state in the area of the Fertile Crescent, from Lebanon to the Persian Gulf. These internal divisions were hidden behind public statements in support of the Palestinian cause.

As Nasser had done a decade earlier, the Syrian government turned to the Soviet Union for military and economic aid. The Soviet leaders were eager to enlarge their network of allied states to include Syria. They praised the Ba'ath Party's socialist policies, which they viewed as a politically progressive step and a promising sign of solidarity with Soviet interests. Nasser's Egypt had shown the way for Soviet Third World ties in the Middle East. In 1966, Syria became

Moscow's second ally there. Soviet aid went to the Syrian government. It secretly went as well to the PLO, some of whose soldiers traveled to eastern Europe to receive training from Soviet agents. PLO guerrilla fighters were encouraged by the Syrians to launch raids from their territory on Israeli settlements. The Middle East was becoming an arena of Cold War conflict between supporters of the Soviet Union and of the United States.

U.S. leaders recognized that the strategic interests of the Western alliance required good relations with oil-rich countries, especially Saudi Arabia and Iran. The West's dependence on oil from Arab lands demanded no less. Yet the U.S. government was sympathetic to the Israeli national cause. It embodied the hope of Jewish peoples for a haven from persecution. This tiny state respected human rights better than any other regime in the Middle East. Israel functioned as a democratic state, guaranteeing civil liberties to their 2.5 million Jews and 300,000 Arabs. It protected the religious practices of the Muslims and Christians. Its Arab citizens remained a suspect people, excluded from full political participation in public affairs. They enjoyed fewer rights than the Jews but were protected under the constitution from persecution. No other state there could claim to do as much for its minorities.

The Israeli leaders relied for the defense of their country primarily on their own military forces. The U.S. commitment to Israel took the form of a public promise to protect the "right to exist" of the state of Israel. It was a message directed to Arab countries. The U.S. government had defined its goal in the Middle East to be peace and political stability. Its promises to Arab oil countries and to Israel created a dilemma, for strategic interests collided with its readiness to defend Israel. As the likelihood of war with Syria grew, Israeli generals laid their own plans

for war. Fearing a concerted offensive by the surrounding Arab countries, they conceived the desperate strategy of striking first. Secretly, they prepared to launch an attack on Egypt, Jordan, and Syria in turn, attacking each country separately in the hope of ultimately defeating all.

The PLO campaign against Israel remained the immediate grounds for war. Israeli generals decided to destroy the bases in Jordan and Syria from which PLO guerrillas were penetrating their country. Raids on these camps provoked a public outcry in Arab countries. The Syrian government demanded that Egypt immediately prepare to join the fight against Israel. The danger of a new Arab-Israeli conflict was growing. Nasser could not refuse his support, for he had spoken out too long and too fervently for the "liquidation of Israeli aggression." Of what use was Egyptian talk of Arab solidarity, the Syrian leaders asked publicly, if Egypt kept the U.N. peacekeeping forces between its army and Israel?

In 1967, Nasser abandoned his cautious policy. In May of that year, he ordered the U.N. forces to leave Egypt. At the same moment, he closed the Gulf of Aqaba, on Egypt's eastern border, to shipping bound for Israel from the Indian Ocean. In the tense atmosphere of that spring, these steps signaled preparation for war against Israel. No evidence suggests that he had in fact ordered the Egyptian military to make ready for an invasion. The most likely explanation for his reckless action was his ambition to be leader of "progressive" Arab countries. It was a role he could not sustain except by placing Egypt at the forefront of the impending war against Israel. Nasser's action constituted the fatal step in the outbreak of another Middle Eastern war.

Fearing concerted Arab attack, the Israeli government approved the risky plans of its military for a preventive war on its Arab neighbors. Two decades after the first Arab-Israeli conflict, the same enemies met once again in June 1967. The Arab states proved as poorly prepared as before, and the Israeli army and air force functioned with extraordinary skill and deadly precision. Their "Six-Day" War was a resounding triumph for Israel. It turned into a military disaster for Egypt. That state was Israel's principal enemy, since it possessed the largest Arab armed force. In the first hours of war, Israeli planes destroyed the entire Egyptian air force. In the next three days, Israel's armored columns occupied the whole Sinai peninsula to the Suez Canal. Its army then attacked and defeated Jordanian forces on the west bank of the Jordan River and in the city of Jerusalem. Finally, it forced Syrian troops out of the mountainous border area known as the Golan Heights. It achieved these victories in six days. The defeated Arab states accepted a U.N. truce, leaving Israeli troops in possession of all the territory occupied during the war.

Egypt, Palestine, and Peace with Israel

That war proved a turning point in the recent history of the Middle East. It made clear to Arabs and Jews alike the rewards that Israeli political unity and military skill had brought. In the words of an Arab historian, Arabs understood that "a small state had displayed their historical inadequacy, had seized massive chunks of land, and had devastated the armies whose weapons and machismo had been displayed with great pride."[1] Victory in the Six-Day War brought the Jewish state all Palestine, the ancestral lands of the Jews. Conquest of the Gaza Strip

on the Mediterranean Sea and of Jordanian Jerusalem and the West Bank territory gave Israel rule more than 1 million Palestinians, some in refugee camps but most living in their own communities. To whom should the land of Palestine belong? The question became an urgent political and religious issue for the Israeli government, for the Israeli people, and for the Palestinian Arab population.

In the next two decades, the Israeli answer in policy and everyday practice was that the occupied territories would be integrated into the life of their state. Disregarding the United Nation's resolutions calling for withdrawal from these lands, conservative Israeli leaders offered incentives and protection for new Jewish settlements in the West Bank area. These settlers took possession by the late 1980s of nearly one-third of the entire land, and most of the precious water rights. Palestinians had to make room for the settlers, paying for the defeat in loss of their water and their land. They found work as laborers in Israeli enterprises, often traveling regularly across the "green line" that still separated Israel from the occupied lands.

Politically that line was very real. Palestinians in these areas remained a disenfranchised people, ruled by the Israeli state and under military occupation. In the opinion of one Israeli observer, Israel's 3 million Jews exercised by choice or by necessity in the mid-1980s a sort of "majority tyranny" over the 2.5 million Palestinian Arabs. To him, the process of economic integration of the peoples of Israel-Palestine appeared irreversible, yet political unification seemed unattainable.[2] The secular, national goal of Zionists for a homeland became entangled with religious aspirations of fundamentalist

---

[1]Fouad Ajami, *The Arab Predicament: Arab Political Thought and Practice since 1967* (New York, 1981), p. 12.

[2]Menon Benvenisti, *Conflicts and Contradictions* (New York, 1986), p. 184.

Jewish groups for resettlement of all the ancient territory of the Jewish tribes. Israeli leaders clung to their vision of an enlarged Jewish land and the Palestine Liberation Organization (PLO) continued to demand an Arab state in all Palestine.

For two decades after the war, the PLO attempted to achieve this goal by force of arms. It created military camps for its militia forces. Its troops seized the southern part of Lebanon in the early 1970s after being expelled from Jordan. The PLO clashed with Lebanon's government over the seizure of the southern region. In 1975, a civil war began that tore the tiny country apart. Both Syrian and Israeli armed forces intervened in the fighting, each seizing strategic territory along their borders. Lacking a strong military and unified political leadership, the Lebanese state disintegrated into a collection of warring private armies defending the territory of their Christian and Muslim communities. The PLO's militia failed to advance the struggle against Israel, however. They were incapable even of defending PLO camps from Israeli army attack.

In those same years, the PLO undertook a campaign of international terrorism to pursue "war by other means" on Israel. The PLO launched terrorist attacks on targets associated, even remotely, with Israel. It began the campaign in 1969 with the hijacking and destruction of three airplanes belonging to U.S. airlines. Even Israeli Olympic athletes became their victims when terrorists attacked the Munich Olympic Village in 1972. Many innocent lives were lost in that struggle. A secret war went on for years between the Israeli secret service and international terrorist organizations supporting the PLO. Terrorism proved as unsuccessful in weakening Israel as the PLO's military operations against Israel.

The most effective form of Palestinian political protest against Israel proved to be the mass uprising (called in Arabic the "Intifada") in Israel's occupied lands. It began in late 1987, when thousands of Palestinians in towns and refugee camps spontaneously joined mass demonstrations against Israeli troops. Their only arms were stones, against which Israeli occupation authorities deployed their military and police forces. They had no plan of action, for the PLO had no part in organizing the Intifada. It surprised its leaders (in exile) as much as it did the Israeli government. At the start, the leadership for the demonstrations came from within the Palestinian community. The Intifada extended to strikes and economic boycotts against Israeli enterprises. The Israeli military discovered that force could disperse the demonstrators—with many wounded and some killed—but could not stop the uprising. This first Intifada continued sporadically until the early 1990s. The demonstrations were the first sign of substantial national unity among Palestinians and made clear their refusal to accept the integration of the occupied territories into Israel.

In Egypt, the defeat of 1967 set the Egyptian government on a new course in foreign and domestic policy. Nasser himself died in 1971. His successor, Anwar Sadat, was also a former member of the Free Officers of 1952. He rejected Nasser's policy of state socialism for Egypt and launched a modernist program that was Western in orientation (including laws to protect the rights of Egyptian women). He also did not believe that Nasser's efforts to make Egypt leader of the struggle against Israel was in the country's interests. Sadat did seek to recover from Israel the Egyptian territory beyond the Suez Canal lost in the Six-Day War. He was determined, once this goal was achieved, to remove his state from the interminable conflict draining the resources of his country.

His daring project supposed first of all that he restore Egyptian international stand-

Confronting the Palestinian Uprising: Israeli Troops in Bethlehem, 1988 (*United Nations Relief and Works Agency*)

ing after its crushing defeat in the 1967 war. He had the backing for another war from the other Arab states, including Saudi Arabia. The Saudi king's influence rested on his country's role as exporter of oil. Demand for petroleum in the early 1970s had risen so rapidly that it had become a product in short supply. Oil-producing countries had by then won from the petroleum companies the legal right to control their oil production. They were in a new position of power. With Saudi backing, Sadat decided to risk another war with Israel.

In late 1973, his armies launched a surprise attack across the Suez Canal (the Yom Kippur War). The initial fighting went in their favor. Israeli forces retreated from the canal. Both the United States and the Soviet Union intervened to back their respective allies, and the war turned into a major international crisis. The Soviet Union sent arms to Egypt. The United States rushed military aid to Israel. When the Israeli army succeeded in turn in pushing Egyptian forces back beyond the canal and Soviet leaders threatened to intervene militarily, the U.S. government declared a "stage 3" nuclear alert, readying its forces for possible nuclear war. To support Egypt, the Arab oil-producing countries declared an embargo (that is, a ban) on oil shipments to the United States, and curtailed oil production. The price of petroleum shot up to $14 per barrel, oil rationing began in the United States, and an international recession set in as a result of the oil shortages. The nuclear confrontation combined with the oil embargo put enormous pressure on both sides to negotiate a settlement. A truce ended the war, leaving Egyptian forces in control of a strip of territory on the eastern side of the Suez Canal. Sadat now was in a strong position to negotiate with Israel.

He proceeded in the next years to implement the second stage in his new policy. He turned to Israel with an offer of peace, breaking ranks with the other Arab states, and abruptly ended Egypt's alliance with the Soviet Union. He appealed to the U.S. government to become Egypt's ally and principal source of economic and military aid. He was successful in both endeavors. Egypt and Israel signed a peace treaty in 1979. Egypt, first of any Arab state, formally recognized the existence of the state of Israel. The Israeli government, in turn, restored all Egyptian lands seized in 1967. The U.S. government began shipping military equipment to Egypt and increased its shipments of food, needed to feed the impoverished Egyptian masses. It was more deeply involved than ever in the Middle East, providing aid to both Israel and Egypt.

The danger of a new Arab-Israeli war dwindled, but Sadat's daring moves cost him his life. He had formally recognized that the Jewish state belonged within the Middle Eastern polity. Muslim fundamentalist groups condemned his policies of peace with Israel and his social reforms (including greater rights for women). He was assassinated in 1981 by a group of Egyptian army officers and soldiers, members of a secret terrorist group. This brutal action, motivated by their conviction that their leader had joined the enemies of Islam, was a sign of the rising importance of Muslim fundamentalism in Middle Eastern life.

Despite continued terrorist violence, the Egyptian government stayed faithful to Sadat's political course. It directed its efforts to helping an impoverished population that had grown to 55 million by 1990. It ended the severe restrictions on free enterprise, promoting Egyptian economic development by a combination of state aid and private employment. Egypt became a land of relative freedom among repressive Arab states. Its most serious enemy remained the Muslim Brotherhood. Its supporters began a campaign of terrorism in the 1980s, directed against Egyptian intellectuals such as the Nobel Prize–winning novelist Naguib Mafouz, accused of the sin of modernism (abandonment of Islam), against the Coptic Christian church, and even against foreign tourists. Muslim fundamentalism was a powerful force in Egypt, sustained by religious fanaticism and widespread poverty that the state appeared incapable of ending.

For fifteen years, Sadat's peace initiative remained without sequel. The PLO refused the offer of autonomy for the occupied territories included in the 1978 peace agreement. Its followers clung to their hope of taking back all of Palestine. The leaders of Syria and Iraq competed in their warlike threats against Israel. Israel remained in a state of war with its other neighboring Arab states.

Conditions changed dramatically in the early 1990s. The changes were partly the result of new Israeli political leadership that took power in 1993. The ongoing Palestinian Intifada made clear that the occupied territories could not remain under Israeli rule. For the first time, the Israeli government declared its readiness to negotiate a compromise settlement with the PLO. Prospects for peace improved also because of the decline in power of the radical, anti-Israeli Arab states. Iraq had become the leader of these states in the 1980s. But its defeat in the Gulf War (see next section) brought an end to its regional might and ended the hopes of the PLO for Iraqi backing for a new war against Israel. Palestinian radicals had lost their last patron.

The PLO leader, Yasir Arafat, took a step as daring in its own way as Sadat's peace initiative two decades before. In 1993, he agreed to recognize the state of Israel and discuss a peace accord with the new Israeli government. Arafat was prepared to admit publicly that endless bloodshed could not bring to life their dream of a Palestinian state, and that Israel had itself to be party to the creation of a country for the Palestinians. That year the PLO and Israel reached a peace agreement (the Oslo Agreement). It opened the way for a Palestinian state, to be created in slow stages out of the occupied territories, and recognized officially the state of Israel. The PLO ordered a stop to terrorist attacks, and brought to an end (temporarily) the Palestinian uprising. The next year, the king of Jordan signed a peace treaty with Israel. The period of Arab-Israeli wars had finally come to an end, almost five decades after the creation of the state of Israel.

For a few years, Arafat's authority was sufficient to keep anti-Israeli Arabs from street violence and terrorism. The Palestine-Israel agreement promised Palestinian self-rule in the occupied territories (Gaza, the west bank of the Jordan River). Just what territory (and what part of Jerusalem) should go to the "Palestine Authority" remained to be negotiated. The Israeli government had somehow to curtail the expansionist plans of Jewish settlers whose communities were located in the midst of the lands to go under Palestinian rule. These issues were complex and aroused passionate resistance from extremists on both sides. They still had not been resolved in 2000, when once again Arab militants took to the streets to attack Israeli troops and settlers in the occupied territories. This time they used rifles and machine guns, and the Israeli army resorted to attacks with helicopter gunships and tanks. By the end of the year, four hundred people, most of them Palestinians, died in this second Intifada. Peace in Palestine was not yet a certainty.

The Oil Wars of Iraq

By the 1980s, almost all Middle Eastern states had fallen under the control of authoritarian regimes. Only Jordan and Saudi Arabia retained their monarchs. None of the states functioned as democracies with free elections and with guarantees of civil liberties for their people. The principal reason for this trend toward authoritarian rule lay in the existence of antagonistic social, ethnic, and religious communities in each land. No general agreement on majority rule and minority rights was possible where each community feared the others. A second reason lay in the political ambitions of military and political leaders. They competed in a brutal struggle for power. Though the victors claimed to speak for their nation, for all Arabs, or for Islam, they were mainly interested in enjoying the prestige and the privileges of power.

Iraq was a dictatorship and an expansionist power during the last decades of the century. Its territory centered around the river valleys of the Tigris and Euphrates. The country, once called Mesopotamia, was settled by a diverse population that contained most of the major ethnic and religious groups of the Middle East. These included Sunni and Shi'a Muslims, and small communities of Christians. The country's Muslims were mostly Arabic-speaking, but the northern, mountainous area was inhabited by a large population of Kurdish people, with its own language and culture. Independence from the British mandate in 1940 began the state's slow, tortuous evolution toward authoritarian rule, culminating in the rise to power of Saddam Hussein.

He had begun his political career in the Ba'ath (Renewal) political party. Its policies borrowed heavily from Nasser's socialist, secularist, and pan-Arab program. Inspired by the example of the Egyptian ruler, this party sought to make Iraq a secular state under nationalist rule adhering to Arab socialist policies. It seized control of the country in 1968, overthrowing a military dictator (who had overthrown the Iraqi monarchy). In the next few years, Saddam Hussein manipulated his powers as head of the police to eliminate all his political rivals. Once firmly in control of the government, he set about implementing a reform program that he claimed was inspired by the socialist achievements of the Soviet Union. His methods of rule did somewhat resemble those of Stalin. He had become dictator by eliminating his rivals for power, who were arrested and sentenced to death for alleged treason and conspiracy. He became "President, Leader, Struggler"—his official titles—by "climbing over the bodies of his enemies," as Russians had said of Stalin. By 1979, he was the unchallenged dictator, using the Ba'ath Party, and the police, as instruments of dictatorship.

On close examination, his methods of rule bore a strong likeness to European fascism. The socialism that he professed served as an ideological bond to help hold together the peoples of his divided country. Iraq was a "state without a nation," that is, it lacked one predominant ethnic population. In place of that unity he substituted authoritarian rule. Nationalism became the preferred ideology and propaganda tool in that system. Like fascist leaders of Europe earlier, he used it to claim to speak for and rule over the Iraqi population. Minority peoples who resisted, such as the Kurds in northern Iraq, were brutally repressed. His weapons of war, including the largest army in the Middle East and an arsenal of chemical war devices, were used first of all to eliminate internal opposition. He began a secret program to develop nuclear weapons, which came to an abrupt halt first when Israeli warplanes destroyed Iraq's nuclear reactor in 1981. It finally ceased after his defeat in the 1990–1991 Gulf War. Like Hitler, he turned the human and economic resources of country to military conquest.

His first target was Iran. Its rich oil fields lay on the borders of Iraq. In 1980, it was in the throes of its Islamic revolution (see next section). Its Muslim leaders called for the overthrow of Saddam Hussein's "godless" regime. That year, he ordered his armies to invade Iran in order, he claimed to end this subversive Iranian propaganda. His principal objective was seizure of the Iranian oil fields near the Persian Gulf, which he expected to conquer without difficulty. But Iran's leaders mobilized their people in a "holy war" against the invaders and forced Iraqi forces out of their territory. Iraq deployed all its weaponry, including chemical weapons, to hold back the Iranian forces. Saddam Hussein obtained outside financial and military assistance from neighboring states fearful of Iranian Muslim zealotry. Even the United States sold military equipment to Iraq on the time-tried principle that "the enemy of my enemy is my friend."

The Iraq-Iran war dragged on for eight years until the two states, exhausted by war, declared an armistice. The armies withdrew to the original borders. Saddam's dream of glorious victory left his country with half a million war casualties and $80 billion in foreign debt. Only by the wildest stretch of the imagination could anyone believe that the 1988 cease-fire was an Iraqi victory. He held in public to this fantastic tale though, and no one in Iraq dared to openly dispute his fantasy.

To bolster that claim, Saddam had built an enormous Victory Arch in the center of his capital city, Baghdad. It consisted of two giant crossed swords, planted in the ground and held by huge bronze fists modeled after Saddam's own hand. Around the base of the fists were gathered 5,000 helmets of Iranian soldiers captured during the eight years of war. In his speeches, Saddam compared his rule with that of ancient Mesopotamian kings, at other times with Saladin (a medieval Arab sultan and victor over the Christian crusaders), or simply with Nasser of Egypt.

The reality was that he had squandered Iraq's resources on a futile war of aggression that left his state deeply in debt to other Arab states. Among these was the tiny principality of Kuwait, located on the very borders of Iraq. Its tremendous oil reserves (judged fourth-largest in the world) were tempting booty, and it was defenseless against his large army. Saddam decided for the second time to wage war for petroleum. If victorious, his state would dominate the Middle East.

His troops crossed the borders of Kuwait in the summer of 1990. He expected no effective international opposition to Iraqi seizure of the tiny, neighboring state. The Soviet government, on which his state had once depended for most of its arms, was in the midst of a serious political crisis caused by Gorbachev's reforms. Its advisers in Iraq had lost all influence over his foreign policies. The United States had failed several times in previous years to use its military force effectively in the Middle East. It was unable to free its embassy hostages in Iran in a military operation in 1980, and it had proven incapable of ending the civil war in Lebanon in the early 1980s. International peacekeeping appeared to him an unlikely occurrence. Iraqi troops met almost no resistance from the tiny Kuwait army, and Saddam Hussein

immediately declared Kuwait to be a province of Iraq.

Instead of easy victory, with a few weeks Saddam confronted the largest military coalition since the Second World War fighting under the flag of the United Nations. Iraq's conquest of Kuwait revealed to leaders around the world two important realities about global relations after the Cold War. The first was the simple fact that, without outside protection, any small state was vulnerable to an aggressive neighbor. The United Nations guaranteed in principle the inviolability of states' borders, but only concerted action of its powerful members could make that promise effective.

Equally important was the fact that the globe's economic growth depended upon a steady supply of Middle East oil. Its price decided prosperity or recession in distant lands. Iraqi seizure of Kuwait's oil fields would permit Saddam to dominate the world market. Middle Eastern states around Iraq such as Turkey, Syria, Egypt, and Saudi Arabia, previously divided, discovered in Iraq a common enemy who threatened them all. Governments in areas as distant as Japan and Argentina realized that they shared a common interest in demonstrating their commitment to the protection of states without strong military forces. The leaders of the Soviet Union and the United States, once bitter enemies, found in opposition to the Iraqi invasion a common cause to unite them.

The head of the coalition was the United States. Its government had for forty years argued that the strategic interest to the United States required access to oil from the Middle East. It had publicly extended its protection to Saudi Arabia and to Israel. Saddam Hussein's sudden victory put in question the security of both lands. His forces could easily move beyond Kuwait into Saudi lands. His support for anti-Israeli groups, notably the PLO, raised the specter of another Arab-

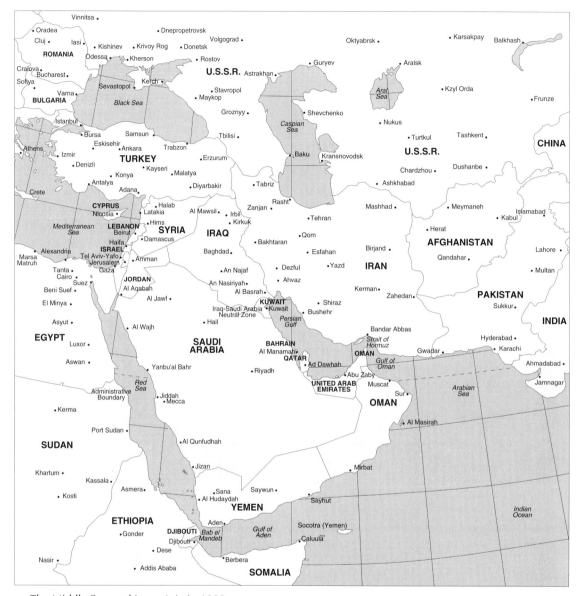

The Middle East and Inner Asia in 1990

Israeli war. When the U.S. government turned to the United Nations for action against Iraq, its members almost unanimously condemned the invasion. The Security Council called for the freeing of Kuwait. This declaration became the basis for the coalition of states, soon numbering over thirty, that gathered around the United States. While proposing negotiations, the coalition prepared for war.

The strategy for defeating Iraq proceeded through two stages. First, an international economic blockade cut off trade to and from Iraq. It was incomplete, though, since the neighboring states of Iran and Jordan did not support the coalition and allowed goods to Iraq to cross their borders. Saddam Hussein refused to take seriously the demand for withdrawal. To end this stalemate, the coalition began military operations. It launched a massive aerial bombardment of Iraq, destroying Iraq's air force. This was followed by a sudden ground offensive in February, 1991, led by American, British, and French armored divisions employing new electronic weapons against the Iraqi army. Cut off in Kuwait, these forces surrendered virtually without resistance after large numbers died in the fighting. Hussein surrendered, agreeing to withdraw all his forces from Kuwait. Before doing so, his agents exploded all the country's 800

oil wells. Enormous oil fires fouled the atmosphere of the region for nearly a year before being completely extinguished.

The war was over, but the coalition's victory was not complete. The principal goal of freeing Kuwait was achieved. But Saddam remained in power. The U.N. invading force stopped before reaching the capital Baghdad. Arab members of the coalition preferred limited victory to the collapse of Iraq, and U.S. military leaders were eager to keep casualties low among their troops. The United Nations did take severe measures to limit Saddam Hussein's powers. The Iraqi government had to dismantle its nuclear weapons and destroy its stock of chemical and biological weapons. It had to allow U.N. inspectors access to their entire country to ensure compliance with these demands.

Fires in the Desert: Kuwait Oil Fields, 1991 (*Reuters/Archive Photos*)

The U.N.'s most unprecedented action was the creation of a protected zone in northern Iraq for that country's Kurdish minority. Of the total 20 million Kurds living scattered across the northern Middle East, more than 3 million lived in Iraq. Their periodic uprisings aimed at freeing themselves from Iraqi rule had ended each time in defeat and the destruction of many Kurdish villages. Kurdish guerrilla forces joined in the 1991 war, risking death at the hands of Saddam's army for themselves, and for their people. To prevent another ethnic massacre, the U.N. demanded that the Iraqi government withdraw its forces from the Kurdish territory. The Kurds were to govern their own area. Allied fighter planes flew regular patrol missions over northern Iraq to keep Iraqi warplanes and troops out of this region. Never before had the United Nations used its powers to divide up the territory of a state that threatened the lives of an ethnic minority. Kurdish leaders posted on the borders of their Iraqi territory a sign reading "Kurdistan."

An unstable peace returned to the Middle East. Saddam's attempt to dominate the region had collapsed. To ensure that he would not be tempted again to send his military into another war, U.S. naval forces remained near the Persian Gulf, and a small number of U.S. air and ground units were stationed in Saudi Arabia. The economic blockade of Iraq continued, though it was increasingly ineffective. Petroleum from Iraq's enormous oil fields reappeared in small quantities on the world market as allowed by the U.N. for purchases of civilian goods. Iraq still possessed the world's third-greatest reserves of petroleum, a natural resource indispensable to the global economy. Saddam's regime relied on that reality in its hopes for future political power. Humbled in the eyes of the world, Saddam remained dictator ruling over an impoverished people forced to live among the ruins of wars for which he bore the responsibility.

Iran and the Islamic Republic

Iran's encounter with modernity, in the shape of a reforming ruler and the wealth brought by petroleum, brought a very different response than that in Iraq. Like other Middle Eastern lands, Iran's population was made up of peoples of different languages and cultures. Almost all were followers of the Shi`a branch of the Muslim religion. In the middle of the twentieth century, its monarch claimed the title of "shah," that is, emperor, but the land had long since lost all ties with the great Persian emperors of antiquity. After the Second Wold War, Iran's ruler, Reza Shah Pahlevi, chose to cooperate with the Western powers. He continued the policy of granting the monopoly on Iran's oil production to the corporation British Petroleum. He placed his country firmly on the side of the West in the Cold War years.

A nationalist alternative to the shah's pro-Western policies briefly emerged in Iran in the years after the Second World War. A coalition of political groups called the National Front, headed by a dynamic political leader, Dr. Mohammed Mossadeq, promised political and economic independence from the West. Iran's religious leaders proclaimed their backing for the movement, which they hoped would protect their "Islamic nation" from the West and modernism. Mossadeq's program included nationalization of British Petroleum's oil properties and neutrality for Iran in the conflict between East and West. With strong backing from voters among Iran's lower classes, Mossadeq's coalition won parliamentary elections in 1951. He became prime minister of Iran. One of his first acts was to order the nationalization of the country's oil wells and refineries. The worsening political struggle within Iran led

Mossadeq to denounce the rule of the shah. Violent demonstrations in support of his government forced the shah to flee the country. Without any coherent plan, Mossadeq had set in motion forces leading the country toward political revolution.

This Iranian affair, which began as a dispute over nationalization of the country's petroleum industry, appeared to the U.S. government a Cold War conflict. In 1953, the Eisenhower administration extended the policy of containment to include opposition to anti-Western regimes in strategic areas around the Soviet Union. The presence of Communists in Mossadeq's political coalition was proof to the U.S. government that his government was a pawn of the Soviet Union. The U.S. Central Intelligence Agency sent covert aid to the shah's supporters in the country. Mossadeq was unable to hold together his National Front coalition. Popular demonstrations against Mossadeq and opposition to his rule by army leaders, secretly encouraged and financed by U.S. agents, forced the prime minister to resign in mid-1953. This U.S.-backed political revolt placed the shah back on his throne. His dependence on the West was greater than ever.

To cope with the country's political and social unrest, the shah laid out three new policies. The first was to bolster his political power. He purged his state of all dissidents and expanded his police force to repress opposition, even when it came from Muslim clerics. He tolerated parliamentary politics but remained the power behind the government. Not a dictator in the full sense of the word, his rule remained authoritarian.

His second objective was to restore cooperation with the Western states. He brought Iran into the Middle Eastern military alliance, the Baghdad Pact, alongside Great Britain, Turkey, and Iraq. He signaled his desire for good relations with the United States by signing a separate defense treaty with the United States. In return, the U.S. government provided his state with large amounts of economic and military aid, more than went to any other state outside the NATO alliance. U.S. advisers helped train his military forces and provided assistance in bolstering his new police force. In global power politics, the shah aligned Iran on the side of the West.

His third objective consisted in the modernization of Iran's society and economy. He called his plan a "White Revolution," combining political order (symbolized by the monarchical color white) and social reform. His objective, he explained was to make Iran the equal to "the most developed countries in the world." With funds from the sale of oil, his government invested heavily in modern industry and urban services. Seizing the extensive land holdings of Muslim religious societies, it redistributed land to peasant farmers.

In social and cultural matters, the shah's goal was a secular society. He looked to the example of Kemal Ataturk's reforms in Turkey as the model for his own modernist program. Islam was to be excluded from public affairs and restricted to the private sphere of worship and morality. Civil law, not Quranic law, set marriage and property relations. The shah ordered an end Muslim traditional practices, such as veiling of women, and challenged the prominence of Islam in Iranian culture. In his opinion, Iranian history began long before Islam reached the country in the eighth century.

Challenging the Muslim religious leaders placed the shah in opposition to clerics such as the Ayatollah Khomeini. Their overriding concern remained the defense of the "Islamic nation." Khomeini, the most forceful of these religious figures, championed a fundamentalist program of strict adherence to Islamic practices and laws. His deepest convictions, like those of the Muslim Brotherhood in

Egypt, turned him against modernism and secularism. For speaking out against the shah's reforms, Khomeini was expelled from Iran in 1963.

The obstacles in the way of the shah's ambitious plans were great. He confronted serious opposition to his regime from groups demanding political liberty—mostly students and educated professionals—and from religious leaders and their followers, principally the poor urban classes. To achieve his economic goals he exhausted his state's revenues. His income from petroleum sales proved inadequate for his grandiose projects. Social unrest worsened as a result of wild inflation and hardship caused by rapid economic growth.

The core of opposition to his regime came from the Muslim clerics. He had given the vote to women, made civil law the foundation of marriage, family, and inheritance, and stripped the Muslim religious institutions of their vast land holdings. His reforms placed Iran on the same path to modernization that Ataturk had chosen for Turkey. For this, the Muslim leaders judged him unfit to rule. In the mid-1970s they organized their supporters to bring down his "godless" rule. Forces opposing the shah grew rapidly. The Muslim clerics proved remarkably effective revolutionaries. In a few years, they brought together a broad coalition of anti-shah groups. In 1979, they orchestrated a mass revolution that ended the shah's reign. Demonstrators took control of the streets of the cities, and workers went on strike, paralyzing production in the oil industry. The army was overwhelmed by this revolutionary upsurge. Its troops mutinied, refusing to shoot the demonstrator. Lacking popular support and the means to repress the uprising, the shah was forced to flee his country.

The victor was Ayatollah Khomeini. He was the inspirational leader of the revolutionaries, and became the principal architect of the theocratic Islamic state that came into existence in 1980. His strict reading of the Quran inspired his radical reform program. He was convinced that by following its precepts, he could create an Iranian Islamic Republic. Its religious purity, in his utopian view, would rival that of Mohammed's original state. Symbolic of the renewal of Islamic practices was his order that women must once again hide behind traditional veils in conformity with Muslim traditions.

This Islamic Republic looked toward the restoration of Muslim law and faith throughout the Muslim world. Its religious leaders held the reins of power in the Iranian government and in the courts, and commanded a vigilante militia charged with punishing Iranians who failed to obey Muslim practices. They denounced the corrupting influence of wealth and the pursuit of individual pleasure. They called on Muslims everywhere to return to the strict guidelines of the Quran and of Muslim law. Their message found supporters among Sunni as well Shi`a Muslims in the years following the revolution. They became a major force behind the upsurge throughout the Muslim world of Muslim fundamentalism in the 1980s. They condemned rulers whose secular reforms weakened Muslim rules and practices. They promised reforms inspired by the Quran's social concern to alleviate the misery of urban masses. Their vision was of a renewed and united community ("umma") of Muslim faithful. The followers in the Muslim world of Iran's clerics called themselves "Islamists," but observers preferred to call them "Muslim fundamentalists" to suggest that many other Muslims did not share their views.

The leaders of the Islamic Republic of Iran spread their militant program by word and deed. Public figures in any sphere, cultural, social or political, were targets of their religious wrath. Ayatollah Khomeini ordered the execution of Salman Rushdie for his novel, *The Satanic Verses*, judged sacrilegious and blasphemous to the Muslim faith (see Spotlight, pp. 262–264). The Iranian government gave its support, including generous subsidies, to terrorist movements in lands where they believed the Muslim faith was threatened. They called on Iraqi Muslims to overthrow Saddam Hussein and urged Iranian troops to destroy Saddam's forces. But their "holy war" was a failure. The Ayatollah's Muslim fundamentalism found few Iraqi sympathizers, and fewer still ready to risk their lives for his religious cause. Gradually in the 1990s, Iran's Islamic Republic weakened its rigorous Quranic laws imposed on the population. But Muslim clerics, still the power behind the state, clung to their dream of a theocratic land leading the entire Muslim world toward the righteous life.

Their message found a sympathetic hearing in many Muslim countries. The Muslim Brotherhood had for decades called for a similar struggle in Egypt against secularism and modernism. Supporters were especially numerous in Muslim lands where governments proved incapable of coping with the impoverishment of the masses. By the early 1990s, several other governments in the Middle East, northern Africa, and Asia had made Muslim law the legal foundation of their states. This rise of fundamentalism was a disturbing trend to those who believed that religious toleration and civil liberties offered the best guarantee of individual integrity. The fundamentalists' defense of their religious faith and practices brought with it the persecution of religious minorities and the rejection of civil liberties protecting individual citizens no matter what their faith. The Iranian revolution revealed that Western liberal ideals and secular reforms had aroused a deep and determined opposition rooted in religious values and practices.

▣ HIGHLIGHT: Social Change and Women's Rights ▣

In the last half of the twentieth century, profound social changes in all major regions of the world altered the status and role of women. In part, these changes responded to international campaigns to grant women greater control over their lives through equality of legal rights. This movement is often labeled feminism, and remains in many countries a subject of great controversy. The United Nations lent its support by designating 1975 International Women's Year (since repeated in 1980 and 1985), and by declaring the years 1975–1985 to be the Decade for Women. International conferences on women's rights drew participants from throughout the world. They were one indication that the issue of women's rights had become a global concern.

A second global trend enhancing the social role of women emerged out of the growing public anxiety over population growth. The social and economic hardship created by the population explosion of the late-twentieth century forced governments, even those hostile to women's rights, to improve women's options in limiting birth rates. This perspective emerged most clearly at the International Conference on Population and

Second World Conference for U.N. Decade for Women, Copenhagen 1980 (*United Nations Photo by Per Jacobsen*)

Development, held in 1994. The principal issue there was the formulation of policies to promote voluntary measures by families to limit family size. The delegates recognized that women had to be granted greater autonomy as individuals in achieving this goal. Their options had to reach beyond the issue of birth control to access to improved living conditions, including education and work. Large numbers of children constituted the essential assurance of family survival when disease and hunger were a constant threat in underdeveloped countries. Families would have increased confidence in and the incentive to restrict family size to two or three children when social improvements touched the lives of women and men.

This recognition of the importance of social and economic processes was rooted in an understanding of profound historical trends with a direct impact on women's roles and family life. These changes have had as important a role in enhancing greater women's control over their lives as international public campaigns and political reforms. Access to education and to employment promised improved relations between men and women, a greater voice to women in obtaining political rights, and a diminished burden on women of motherhood and family bonds. At the heart of this change has been massive urbanization, which has reshaped the social environment of hundreds of millions of people. By the late twentieth century one half of Europe's population lived in urban areas. In the Third World, the move occurred more slowly. The proportion of townspeople there rose from about 5 percent at the end of the First World War to almost 25 percent in 1980. Though this was a time of rapid population growth, urbanization was a consequence above all of the migration of enormous numbers of rural inhabitants to urban areas.

Literacy for Women: Adult Reading Classes in Yemen Arab Republic, 1983 (*U.N. Photo 153539/ John Isaac*)

Families adjusting to this new environment found themselves in unfamiliar conditions. Work for most people came in the form of wage labor. Contact in cities between people with different ways of life, languages, and religious values produced a clash of cultural values. In this same period the governments of new nation-states implemented laws on women's rights and family relations that weakened or outlawed traditional family customs. Western societies had undergone these changes a half-century or more earlier and were the center of the feminist movement in the mid-twentieth century.

In these conditions of economic, cultural, and political upheaval, new opportunities and old constraints were thrust upon women and families throughout the world.

Until recent decades, women's place was separate and unequal in most societies within a patriarchal system. A summary portrait of their condition, though oversimplified, helps to appreciate the dramatic changes in the last half of the twentieth century. In most traditional societies women's roles left them in an inferior position throughout their lives. As infants, they were less desired than boys, and could, in times of extreme hardship, become the victims of infant neglect (infanticide) when parents had to curtail family size. As children, their education was limited or nonexistent, for they had to help with domestic work until marriage, which came at an early age.

Women's sole concern as adults was childbearing and care of the household under the authority of their husbands. The husband controlled family property and was responsible for ensuring the proper protection, even seclusion, of women. Only poverty created a kind of equality of labor, forcing women in peasant families to work in the fields alongside their husbands. Although conditions varied widely from one society to another, this pattern prevailed to some extent in all complex civilizations. The profound global changes of the last half of the twentieth century, among which urbanization was the most influential, gradually undermined this paternalistic way of life.

Driven by economic need, by rising expectations of a better standard of living, and by the desire of women for their own income, husbands were increasingly prepared to allow their wives the freedom of outside work. Small-scale village businesses were accessible, with some financial assistance, to enterprising women even in very poor countries. Another important factor behind the enhanced role of women in the family was the aspiration for better living conditions. In Brazil, it appeared the dominant motivation in bringing large numbers of women into the labor force (probably over one-third of adult women by the 1980s) and in lowering family size (down from an average of four to two children between the 1960s and 1980s). The actual improvement in living standards over those years may not have been substantial. Economic conditions worsened as a result of the global recession of the early 1980s. The case of Brazil, as that of other countries at a similar stage in their development, suggests how important new social aspirations and economic expectations were in lowering family size and in bringing more and more women into the workforce.

In many parts of the Third World, women's access to wage labor was severely restricted. Where women's education was deficient, their economic opportunities were meager. As schooling expanded, the chances to find better paying jobs increased. In China, a major literacy program raised women's literary rates along with men's to well more than 60 percent. They entered the urban workforce in very large numbers in those same years. The Indian case suggest that the reverse was also true. The low level of public education there left two-thirds of the women illiterate. Their lack of basic formal education gave them little hope employment other than the most unskilled, worst-paying jobs.

This working population, unorganized and prepared to accept work at low pay, proved advantageous both to small businesses and to multinational corporations. The latter's total work force in developing countries grew in the 1970s to between 3 and 4 million. Women predominated in garment and assembly-line work for these companies. Dependent on a distant employer and earning low pay, unskilled female labor constituted a new proletariat. In most countries only a small group of educated women were able to enter high-paying, skilled positions. Male prejudice and lack of sufficient education posed major hurdles to improving their economic status. Still, women's wages earnings and activity away from home constituted a major shift away from the traditional paternalistic family pattern.

The issue of women's rights within the family became the subject of political debate in most new nations soon after independence. In India the government's campaign for family equality among Hindus was reinforced by a feminist movement championing compliance with the new standards. The law on child marriage raised the average age of marriage for women to seventeen. This was a substantial improvement over practices at the turn of the twentieth century (Gandhi's wife had been twelve, and he fourteen, when they married). This change contributed as well to India's slowly falling birth rate. Some feminist programs drew inspiration from Western reform movements. The Soviet Union served as the model for gender as well as class equality in communist countries. In 1949, the Chinese Communists confronted a deeply rooted paternalistic way of life, including child marriage and exclusive male right of divorce. Shortly after taking power they introduced reforms intended to eliminate men's social privileges and to integrate women into their new social order.

Most countries with a large Muslim population did not adopt such radical reforms. Fearing communal conflict, the Indian government made no effort to enforce equality of sexes on Muslim families. It left unchallenged among its Muslim population the shari`a (Muslim customary law), which granted men exceptionally broad prerogatives in family and property affairs. Turkey was the only large Muslim state were Islamic law was replaced completely by family laws drawn from Western civil law codes; Iran's laws on women's rights disappeared after its Islamic Revolution. The process of adapta-

tion to urban life often left wives more closely bound than before to the household. The obligation to care for the children fell directly into their hands, since they lacked the help of extended families in the new surroundings. Husbands took advantage of higher incomes to enforce on their wives customs of subordination associated with the upper-classes. This reverse trend was apparent in south Asia, where seclusion of wives had been practiced for centuries among the wealthy. It spread among the new middle-classes in the late-twentieth century. The demands of legal reform and the desire for higher income created pressures for greater equality, but were thwarted still by customary male authority and traditional restraints on women.

The result of these antagonistic forces produced in some lands personal tragedy and political controversy. In India, the social constraints on young women to marry at a relatively young age remained overwhelming. Laws against marriage dowries proved ineffective. The custom, originally a luxury for wealthy families, became a source of bitter conflict when it spread to middle class families. The husband's family, eager to enrich their estate, demanded exorbitant payment from the bride. When the bride's parents refused or were unable to make further payments, she unwittingly became the offender in the eyes of her in-laws. They punished her, and on occasion murdered her to begin a search for another suitable bride. Rarely punished or publicly acknowledged until the late 1970s, these tragic dowry murders numbered by official estimate close to 15,000 each year. In a country where legal reforms had in theory laid the foundations for equality between the sexes, these tragic acts of violence were a cruel reminder of the limited powers of the state faced with deep prejudice and new economic pressures.

Full rights protecting participation by women in democratic countries promoted but did not guarantee ready access to public responsibilities. Women's suffrage itself was important, for it challenged men's control over lawmaking and in particular over policies that touched the affairs of women and the family. The new state of Israel made equality of rights for women in politics, education, the family and the work place and fundamental element in their social order. The first woman to head a government anywhere in the Middle East was Golda Meir, the prime minister of Israel from 1967 to 1973. Even in certain Muslim countries such as Egypt and Pakistan women rose to influential positions in government.

Islam gave no clear definition of the role of women in political life. Political leaders in some Muslim countries campaigned for secular reforms, including voting rights for women. The shah of Iran made the enfranchisement of women an integral part of the reforms that he called his "White Revolution." That policy aroused bitter opposition from the country's Muslim clerics. When they became the leaders of Iran's Islamic Republic in 1980, they immediately terminated the shah's modest reforms for women.

The Islamic Republic reimposed the traditional restrictions on public activities of women and reestablished the Muslim laws governing the family. It abolished the secular family code protecting married women and lowered the legal age of marriage for women. One fervent supporter of this regime, asked to explain what the establishment of the Islamic Republic meant to him, responded: "Getting women back into the veil, getting them off television."[3] Even religious fanaticism could not stop for long the trends pushing toward women's rights in Iranian society. Iranian women protested the severe restrictions of their access to jobs and marriage. The country's population explosion created critical economic and social problems. As a result, the regime had to raise the legal age of marriage and to encourage women to practice birth control. Gradually the government accepted, in the spirit of Islamic law, the resumption of women's public activities and the restoration of voting rights.

By the closing decade of the twentieth century, global trends clearly pointed to the increased control by women over both personal and public aspects of their life. These changes followed no single model. Muslim reforms followed a pattern strongly shaped by religious custom. But the combination of international campaigns and basic social trends in work, education, and family life put in place an array of women's rights and opportunities in society so profoundly different from traditional practices that they could be called a revolution.

---

[3]V. S. Naipaul, *Voyage among the Believers: An Islamic Journey* (New York, 1981), p. 28.

SUMMARY

The political life of the Middle East appeared in the years after decolonization to be an ongoing struggle between civil strife and authoritarian leadership. Only Israel and, to a lesser extent, Egypt enjoyed a consensus among their populations on national unity and political participation. Palestinians living in Israel were excluded from full citizenship by the Israeli government. Most Middle Eastern lands were deeply divided by generations-old animosity among religious and ethnic communities. The fervor with which many peoples clung to communal bonds arose from their distrust of repressive political leaders. These rulers talked of national unity but governed by favoring their own political followers, ethnic community, and clan. Ethnic loyalties were so pervasive that observers called the trend a new form of "tribalism," that is, exclusive ethnic solidarity.

State-building was a mockery in times of civil war among these warring groups. In the case of Lebanon the conflict tore the country apart for an entire decade. Authoritarian rule by military dictators kept divided lands together by force. It also produced corrupt regimes incapable of healing ethnic distrust or of pushing for economic development to alleviate the poverty of their populations. Sales of petroleum on the international market sustained the incomes of those countries, such as Iraq and Iran, fortunate enough to possess large oil reserves. Other countries experienced prolonged economic decline.

The continued importance of religious issues marked the Middle East more than any other part of the postwar world. In Muslim lands and in Israel, fundamentalist movements sustained public concern for religious purity in thought and action and fought secularist and feminist reforms. Misery and the insecurity of everyday life among the impoverished masses led many Muslims to seek support and reassurance in their faith. They were encouraged to do so by religious leaders dreaming of a renewal of spiritual values. The struggle to sustain that faith in the midst of technological wonders and images of Western modernity was at the root of crises in private lives and public affairs throughout the Middle East.

DATES WORTH REMEMBERING

1939	Start of Saudi Arabian oil production
1945	Formation of Arab League
1948	Independence of Israel
1948–1949	First Arab-Israeli War
1952	Nasser in power
1955–1963	French war in Algeria
1956	Suez crisis
1960	Creation of Organization of Petroleum Exporting Countries (OPEC)
1963	Independence for Algeria
1965	Creation of Palestine Liberation Organization
1967	Israeli-Arab Six-Day War
1967	Golda Meir named prime minister of Israel
1973	Israeli-Arab War
1975–1981	Civil war in Lebanon
1979	Egyptian-Israeli Treaty
1979	Iranian Islamic Revolution
1980	World population estimated 5 billion
1980–1988	Iraq-Iran war
1988	Palestinian uprising in Israeli-occupied lands
1990	Iraq invasion of Kuwait
1991	Gulf war
1993	Oslo peace agreement between PLO and Israel
1994	Israeli-Jordanian Peace Treaty
1994	U.N. Conference on Population and Development

RECOMMENDED READING

Postwar Middle East

Samir Khalil, *Republic of Fear: The Inside Story of Saddam's Iraq* (1992). A history of the rise of Saddam Hussein by an Iraqi refugee.

*Bernard Lewis, *History: Remembered, Recovered, Invented* (1975). A study of the recent creation of nationalist myths in Iran and Israel.

*Daniel Yergin, *The Prize: The Epic Quest for Oil, Money, and Power* (1991). A very thoughtful interpretation of the role of oil in the history of the West and the Middle East.

Israel and Its Wars

Michael Cohen, *Palestine and the Great Powers, 1945–48* (1982). A balanced evaluation of the role of the Great Powers in the partition of Palestine and the formation of Israel.

*Larry Collins and Dominique Lapierre, *O Jerusalem!* (1980). A dramatic account of the struggle for Israeli independence.

Charles Smith, *Palestine and the Arab-Israeli Conflict* (1988). A clearly presented history of the wars between the Arab states and Israel.

Postwar Iran

Roy Mottahedeh, *The Mantle of the Prophet: Religion and Politics in Iran* (1985). A thoughtful inquiry into the influential role of the Muslim clerics in Iran in the twentieth century and the rise of the Islamic Republic.

Amin Saikal, *The Rise and Fall of the Shah* (1980). A critical account of the policies and goals of Reza Shah Pahlevi.

Social Change and Women's Rights

Nikki Keddie and Beth Baron, eds., *Women in Middle Eastern History: Shifting Boundaries in Sex and Gender* (1991). Articles on a range of topics on women's roles in Middle Eastern countries.

Elizabeth Bumiller, *May You Be the Mother of a Hundred Sons: A Journey among the Women of India* (1990). The observations of a Western visitor on the condition of women in India.

Memoirs and Novels

*Thomas Friedman, *From Beirut to Jerusalem* (1989). Gripping memoirs by a *New York Times* correspondent in the Middle East during the 1980s.

*Naguib Mahfouz, *Midaq Ally* (1966). An intimate glimpse of Cairo families at the end of the Second World War, written by the Egyptian Nobel Prize author (and target of Muslim fundamentalist attacks).

Golda Meir, *My Life* (1975). The personal memoirs of an extraordinary life from Russian ghetto to head of the state of Israel.

CHAPTER ELEVEN

The Cold War and the Fall of the Soviet Empire, 1953–1991

The Cold War dominated global relations in the decades that followed Stalin's death. The Soviet leadership was determined to keep in place the essential institutions of Stalinism, held up by what appeared to be an invincible dictatorship. The competition between the superpowers spread beyond Europe and East Asia to other parts of the world. Its effects were felt even in Cuba, where the Cuban missile crisis brought the world to within a few hours of nuclear war. The dictator's disappearance did make possible an easing of Soviet–U.S. tensions. The two governments signed important treaties to limit armaments development and to stabilize East–West relations in Germany. Both sides realized that nuclear war would be a global catastrophe. Despite repeated Cold War disputes, these decades turned out the period of the "longest peace" in the twentieth century.

The reconstruction of Europe outside the communist countries was an uncertain and contested undertaking in the early postwar years. The future was unknown. The promise of democratic socialism held the greatest attraction for the war-weary peoples. Functioning democratic institutions and public consensus on liberal political goals gradually became a part of daily life. The process, despite its complexity, proceeded remarkably well. By the 1960s, recovery was complete. Twenty years later, the major debates of public life dealt with the shortcomings of the postwar reforms and with the integration of Europe's nation-states into the European Union.

While western nations improved the quality of life for their people with amazing speed, the entire communist system in the east endured with little change until the late 1980s. Then it suddenly collapsed. The fall of communism occurred with extraordinary swiftness. Weaknesses within the Soviet Union, hidden for decades from outside view, forced the leaders there to undertake risky reforms. The blind faith of some Soviet political and military leaders in the Stalinist system incited them to attempt to overthrow the reform government. They failed miserably, and their defeat discredited the old system so thoroughly that the Soviet Union fell apart. The Cold War disappeared along with the Stalinists and their state, leaving in its wake tens of thousands of useless but lethal nuclear weapons.

In eastern Europe, popular opposition to communism proved so massive that the entire satellite system vanished within a few months in 1989. The crucial first step came when the reformist leaders in the Soviet Union made known their disillusionment with the Stalinist system, still in place in the satellite countries. The profound desire among peoples in these countries to be freed from Soviet domination and communist rule quickly assumed the proportions of a popular uprising. The collapse of these regimes was revolutionary in its speed, and the scope of reform was breathtaking. New leaders introduced a democratic and capitalist order. The process bore little resemblance to earlier revolutions, for it occurred almost without violence. In a sense, it represented a return to the past, for the new central Europe resembled the nation-states put in place in 1919 by the Paris peace negotiators.

The Stalinist period left bitter memories of hardship and a legacy of political repression and destruction of natural resources. The term "totalitarianism" became popular there to condemn that hated past. Lenin, Stalin, and their followers had proclaimed that their communist system was a model for humanity. The liberal reformers wanted the world of the 1990s to know that communism was a bankrupt social experiment and a human tragedy.

EUROPEAN NATIONS AND EUROPEAN UNION

The peoples of western Europe had, first of any region of the world, acquired a strong awareness of national identity. Their nation–states and nationalist ideology became, for good and ill, a model for other peoples in the twentieth century. Both the promise and the defects of nationalism had entered the fabric of European life. The solidarity that emerged within these national communities created enduring bonds of loyalty. The terrible world wars that had pitted nation against nation left no doubt how destructive nationalist fanaticism could be. These nations had created vast colonial empires, which to many Europeans had embodied the superiority of their civilization (and to some, on the contrary, demonstrated the arrogance of Western racism).

The end of the Second World War proved the turning point in their histories. They abandoned their empires to focus their energies on their countries' reconstruction and renewal. Their leaders agreed to cooperate in supranational institutions for the sake of economic development and, most important, to create indissoluble ties among the previously warring states. Europe's governments sacrificed the principle of the absolute independence of their nation-states to overcome nationalist enmity. Their European Union was the outstanding achievement of a new, post-colonial and post-nationalist age.

European Recovery and Welfare States

The destruction of western Europe had appeared so serious and its consequences so threatening to the political stability of the West that the United States government had promised massive economic assistance for reconstruction in 1947 (see Chapter 6). The Marshall Plan was an extraordinary event, not only in the foreign relations of the United States, but in the relations of the European states among themselves and with their former wartime ally.

European governments had agreed to collaborate in making crucial decisions about how vast sums of aid were to be spent. The U.S. government set strict conditions on granting European states billions of dollars of aid (ultimately more than $13 billion). Most controversial was its requirement that all participating governments make public their economic needs and their financial condition. A European-wide committee, called the Commission on European Economic Cooperation (CEEC), united representatives of all the western European countries in administering the Marshall Plan aid. It decided on the priorities in recommending where U.S. aid was to go. European integration was a alluring dream in those years. The Marshall Plan's approach to unification came with an immediate payoff.

The aid proved effective beyond the highest hopes of its planners. By 1952, industrial production in western Europe, even in West Germany, had surpassed the prewar level. The ruins of war gradually disappeared, and food rationing finally came to an end. The future direction of Europe's economy was clearly marked out as well. The postwar international economy possessed effective mechanisms for trade and financial transactions. The Bretton-Woods system (see Chapter 6) had created a set of institutions to insure that countries within the global free market could count on international assistance to keep trade flowing and to encourage them to work to lower trade barriers. The dollar became the principal currency of international exchange, backed by the strength of the U.S. economy.

The collaboration between the United States and western Europe insured that these liberated countries would restore their market economies. European governments became more deeply involved in economic affairs, principally through nationalization of private companies and state forecast planning for economic development. But their powers never extended to the elimination of the market economy. Its key criterion of success was productivity (the efficient use of resources as measured by output and price), and that measure remained a fundamental reality in the economic reconstruction and development of Europe. Ultimately, the failure of nationalized industries to meet that test caused European governments to sell off completely or reduce drastically their nationalized enterprises in the 1980s.

European consumers found more and more goods available as production increased and wages rose. Employment remained at a very high level during the three decades after the war, and personal income increased rapidly along with the standard of living. By the 1960s, leisure became a reality in long weekends and yearly four-week paid vacations. Families traveled to inexpensive vacation resorts such as those created by the new "Club Mediterranee" company. The automobile became a purchase accessible to a majority of the population. The first "dream" car was a Cadillac, but later the German Mercedes-Benz cars claimed that honor. By the 1970s, living conditions in western Europe had improved so dramatically that they approached those in the United States, whose prosperity had been the envy earlier of all Europe. The hardships of depression and of wartime destruction became distant memories.

Two decades after war's end, the era of European empires had passed as well. The process was slow, marked by moments of resistance yet always followed by more negotiation for colonial independence. British negotiations with colonial leaders to prepare for independence began almost immediately after the war. The other European empires gradually abandoned in their turn all their overseas colonies. The Netherlands withdrew from the East Indies, Belgium abandoned its Congo colony, and France pulled out of Africa. The process came at times in the midst of colonial war. The bloodiest of these was France's Algerian war. It was the last attempt to preserve one small part of the French Empire. France's army generals were so committed to this cause that they became key players in organizing a revolt against their government when they learned of negotiations with the Algerian rebels in 1958. Their rebellion ended the short life of the Fourth Republic, created in 1945, and brought to power Charles de Gaulle.

Wartime leader of the French struggle against Germany, de Gaulle returned to power on condition the French parliament write a new constitution for a presidential regime (somewhat like the U.S. system). Once this Fifth Republic began to function, he turned to the Algerian war. He was convinced that this colonial conflict undermined French unity and international prestige, both crucial to his plans for a new France. He envisioned his country the leader in Europe and Africa, where his government launched in 1958 the plans for a "French Community" among newly freed French colonies. Since his army could not defeat the Algerian rebels, he agreed to their demand for independence. Despite terrorist attacks by settlers and attempted revolts by forces within the French army, de Gaulle carried out his project to end French rule in Algeria in 1963.

Decolonization of the once-mighty European overseas empires continued for another decade. The Portugese Empire, the first European overseas empire in the fifteenth century, was the last to disappear. Ruled by a dictator, General Salazar, until 1975, it had sent troops to suppress nationalist rebellions in its African colonies of Angola and Mozambique, and its East Indies colony of East Timor. But when a democratic government took over from Salazar in the mid-1970s, one of its first acts was to free these lands. By then, the only reminder in Europe of that imperial age was the presence of migrants from their former colonies. They left their homes in search of better jobs in Europe with, as their most important entry card, a knowledge of the languages of their former colonial rulers.

The social and economic reforms introduced in the postwar years succeeded remarkably well in overcoming divisions and in uniting the peoples of western Europe. The details of the reforms varied substantially from country to country, but at their heart lay the goal of guaranteeing to all the people a substantial measure of social welfare and security. Postwar socialist movements promised that state ownership would ensure employment and good wages. They, and other reform movements, came to believe deeply in the responsibility of the state to contribute to their people's basic social needs. These including medical care, education, and decent housing. They proposed to pay for these expensive programs by high taxes on the well-to-do and on private enterprises. Extremes of wealth and poverty among the population appeared to them a social injustice. In this sense, all hoped to promote some type of "social democracy" among their people.

These reforms became imbedded in European life. From Italy to Sweden, from Great Britain to West Germany, social welfare and direct state involvement in crucial economic activities guided in one form or another the policies of all governments, whether conservative or liberal. By the 1980s, the most important political issues in western countries focused on correcting shortcomings in the welfare state. No one seriously proposed abolishing the entire system and returning to conditions of the early century.

Weaknesses in the socialist system did lead to calls for remedies. These problems included a high rate of inflation fueled by labor union pressure for yearly wage increases, inefficient nationalized enterprises that required state subsidies to remain in operation, and serious budget deficits (which contributed to inflation) and high taxes caused by the growing cost of paying for extensive welfare programs. The solutions adopted in European countries varied widely, but in every case they entailed restrictions of the scope of state support for social services and the sale (privatization) of state-owned enterprises to private owners. The poor and laboring populations lost some of their benefits, but even sizeable numbers of workers voted for parties that proposed reducing the responsibilities of the welfare state. The "father-state," as the Germans called it, no longer appeared the sole or supreme guarantor of the country's welfare.

The most severe cutbacks to the welfare system to nationalization occurred in Great Britain. There the Labor Party's postwar reforms had gone furthest toward curtailing the market economy and extending generous financial assistance to working people. In 1979, the Conservative Party under the leadership of Margaret Thatcher decisively defeated the Labor Party in elections whose major issue was the welfare state. Thatcher's program constituted a comprehensive rejection of state management of economic affairs and a wholesale reduction of welfare programs. What came to be known as "Thatcherism" entailed the privatization of almost all nationalized enterprises, the reduction by one-half of state payments for various social welfare programs, and the lowering of taxes. Thatcher's principal goal was a productive economy. Welfare was a secondary consideration.

In these terms, the program was a success. By the early 1990s, the economy was booming, inflation ended, unemployment drastically reduced, and the standard of living rose. But even the "Iron Lady" could not eliminate the welfare programs entirely. When she suggested ending free public health care, the popular opposition was so great she had to abandon her plans. The postwar vision of a safety net insuring the basic needs of the population had become a permanent part of the people's expectations in all democratic nations.

The United States joined in the move toward comprehensive welfare programs and greater state supervision of economic affairs in the 1960s. The election in 1960 of John F. Kennedy to the U.S. presidency began a period of extensive social and political reforms, carried on by Lyndon Johnson after Kennedy's assassination in 1963. This "Great Society," the name Johnson gave his 1964 platform, included new laws to protect the civil and political rights of all citizens. The goal was an end the century-long segregation and oppression of blacks. Reforms also brought new welfare policies for a "war on poverty," in spirit and in intent resembling the social welfare measures introduced in Europe after the Second World War. No private enterprises were nationalized. Still, the government's yearly budgets, and controls over banking and interest rates exercised by a federal agency (the Federal Reserve Board) guided the country's economy in a manner inspired by the ideas of John Maynard Keynes. Later, conservative political leaders, echoing arguments in Europe, questioned the high rate of taxes and expensive social welfare programs. In the United States, as in Great Britain, a majority of the voters in the 1980s appeared more concerned with the success of a productive market economy than with state promises of social justice and less economic inequality.

Divided Germany and European Union

The division of Germany was the last great unresolved problem left by the war. The decision of the Western Allies to proceed with the reconstruction of their zones of West Germany had confirmed the partition of Germany between communist and noncommunist regions. It set the western part on a path of recovery that ultimately integrated Germany into a united European Union. German voters in this Federal Republic of Germany voted in the two decades after independence for the conservative Christian Democratic Party, under the leadership of Konrad Adenauer. His priorities lay in erasing the poverty in which Germans lived at war's end through intensive reconstruction of the country's industrial economy. His formula for recovery proved successful.

By the 1960s, the country's industrial economy was the most prosperous of Europe. Its population, swollen by the influx of more than 10 million refugees from eastern Europe, was still not able to meet the economy's need for workers. Migrants arrived to fill these jobs from poor lands in southern Europe, especially Yugoslavia, and from Turkey. Like migrants to Europe's other prosperous countries, they lived as second-class citizens. They enjoyed economic and social benefits, including access to the welfare system, but were excluded from active political participation (in Germany, they were denied the right to citizenship). Countries like West Germany were becoming multiethnic and multireligious, for their prosperity was bringing Third World peoples within their borders.

Adenauer refused to accept the division of Germany between the communist east (the German Democratic Republic) and the democratic west. He remained committed to the reunification of his country. This could come only with the collapse of the communist dictatorship in East Germany. West Germany's democratic regime and its flourishing economy diverged increasingly from the drab conditions in the east. West Berlin, built up as a beacon of prosperity under continued Allied military occupation, turned into a magnet drawing easterners. Young East Germans took advantage of the open border between East and West Berlin to migrate to West Germany. There they were welcomed as refugees and helped to create new lives in the Federal Republic. By 1960, their migration had become a flood as hundreds of thousands of refugees abandoned the communist state to make a new life in the West.

The Adenauer government had no way of ending the partition, however. It was a helpless observer in 1961 when the East German government, backed by Soviet tanks, constructed a wall around West Berlin. The refugee flow was cut off, except for the handful of daring individuals who attempted to break through the barrier. Most were shot down by communist border guards. West German television broadcasts kept alive enticing images in the east of western prosperity and the hope among viewers that their lives might somehow, sometime, change for the better.

In 1969, a new West German government decided to recognize the partition. It was headed by the Social Democratic Party, which had once been a strong defender of Marxist socialism. German prosperity and its electoral weakness forced it to renounce this program. Its new program emphasized expanded social welfare policies, and improved relations with the communist countries. The Social Democratic government put this "eastern policy" in motion immediately. It produced treaties with East Germany and, as important to Soviet leaders, West German acceptance of the postwar frontiers of Poland. Through a number of separate agreements a kind of informal peace treaty emerged, confirming the division of the German nation into two states. The former Allies regarded the partition of Germany and Berlin as a permanent part of the new European international system. They foresaw no alternative for peaceful relations between East and West.

Even the three countries on the southern fringes of the continent ruled for decades by dictators joined the democratic states in the 1970s. Greece, Spain, and Portugal all reverted, after lengthy periods of military rule, to constitutional democracies. Political upheavals in each land brought about the abrupt transition. All three were countries where many people and clandestine political movements had kept faith in human rights through the years of repression. They found in western Europe's successful democratic experience the justification for their liberal faith. In material terms, too, democratic government appeared to assure the people substantial benefits. This was evident to Greek, Spanish, and Portuguese migrants who went in increasing numbers seeking work in the booming northern economies.

In Spain, the political transition occurred with remarkable speed. In 1975, General Franco, dictator since his victory in 1939 in the Spanish Civil War (see Chapter 4), died and was replaced at his request by the heir to the Spanish monarchy. King Juan Carlos had no desire to preserve the dictatorship. He immediately ordered elections to prepare a new constitution. In 1977, he ceded his executive power to the newly elected government. Spain became a constitutional, parliamentary monarchy. Despite protest from a handful of Franco's supporters, the new regime established effective rule in the country within a few years. Dictatorship vanished everywhere in Europe save in the eastern communist lands.

In those years of recovery and renewal, Europe's leaders agreed to begin the process of European unification. To do so, they had to curtail the scope of national sovereignty on which their nation-states had been founded. One hundred years earlier the region had been the heartland of nationalism.

The agonies of two wars had revealed just how destructive were the hatred and intolerance incited by extreme nationalism. Europeans searching for a stable peace realized that bonds had to be forged among nation-states and that a federation of European states might undo the damage that ethnic and nationalist conflict had caused. Political unification confronted the deeply felt sense of national loyalty shared by European peoples. Most serious, many western Europeans harbored an abiding hatred for Germans from the war years.

The experience of collaborating in the distribution of Marshall Plan aid demonstrated that economic cooperation was feasible. The first serious proposal for unification came from the French leader Jean Monnet. A former banker, he made his mark in postwar France as the head of the state's economic planning commission. He grasped the simple truth that a unified Europe could be reached only by stages. He concluded that economic unification was the first practical step in that direction. He proposed in 1950 the formation of a "common market" for iron, steel, and coal. It required that European states agree to abolish all tariffs among themselves on trade in those products. They would create a supranational commission, that is, a governing body whose policies no member state could veto, to coordinate production and wage plans among the enterprises in these key economic sectors.

The European Coal and Steel Community (ECSC) became a reality in 1952. Six states in Western Europe, Italy, West Germany, France, and the Benelux countries—Belgium, the Netherlands, and Luxembourg—signed the treaty creating the ECSC. This unprecedented agreement emerged out of discussions among the political leaders of Italy, Germany, France, all of whom belonged to Christian Democratic parties. Their commitment to a Christian concept of peace and human goodness gave them a set of values for reconciliation among nations and, in particular, the reintegration of Germany within Europe. The specific agreement that they reached was a practical, not an ideological undertaking. It sought new ways to speed the recovery of their economies. The Labor government of Great Britain refused to join, clinging to the dream of British "splendid isolation" and suspicious of the important role that business interests would play in the Community. Although political unification remained a distant dream, the Coal and Steel Community was a historic event in the relations among European nations. It was a first step toward integrating Germany into an association of Western nation-states.

In the next years, its success was measured by pragmatic decisions of the ECSC commission to implement the treaty. Tariffs on coal and steel shipments among the member states quickly disappeared. Managers of nationalized and private mines and factories accepted, sometimes very reluctantly, its orders for production. It even closed unproductive mines, which was an unpopular move but which promised the unemployed miners long-term retraining benefits. The ECSC had proven that economic integration was possible.

Then Jean Monnet initiated the next step toward the economic union of western Europe. He proposed that a "common market" unite the member states in free trade for all industrial, commercial, and agricultural transactions. Agreement once more came quickly. In the mid-1950s, the six governments in the Coal and Steel Community, led by France and West Germany, accepted his plan for a European Economic Community (EEC). It was to begin in 1958. The process toward a "common market" was complex, for it entailed the dismantling of tariffs on trade among these states and the formation

of one unified economic market. It represented a momentous step toward Monnet's dream of a politically united Europe.

The barriers on commerce declined dramatically and far more quickly than the treaty signers had expected. By the mid-1960s, western Europe had begun a new era of economic collaboration. The Common Market operated on the basis of market competition, whether conducted by private or state-owned enterprises, by small farmers or agribusiness. All the political parties (except the communists) in western Europe agreed on the desirability of economic unification. Most looked forward to political integration, though no one could say when a "United States of Europe" might appear. That shared vision of the future ensured that the participating states renounced the sovereign powers in the area of trade. The Common Market was truly supranational.

The prosperity of the EEC countries guaranteed that its influence would grow. The U.S. government acknowledged its new role in the global economy. In 1963, it signed with the EEC a comprehensive treaty lowering tariffs. Freer trade between Europe and America benefited businesses on both continents. It also reinforced the economic and financial ties among the western democratic nations. The economic integration of Europe grew with the gradual addition of new members. In the 1970s and 1980s, six new states were admitted to the EEC, including Spain, Denmark, Greece, Turkey, Great Britain, and Ireland. By the late 1980s, the total population of the EEC countries reached 300 million. At the time, it was the single most populous free-trade region in the world.

The dream among Europeans of political unification led to renewed efforts to strengthen ties in the early 1990s. A new treaty of unification, put into effect in 1994, renamed the group of states the European

Union. Its most ambitious objective was the creation of a single currency for the entire region. To achieve this, governments had to lower inflation rates and balance their budgets, possible only if they curtailed expenditures on social welfare. This new Europe did not attempt to eliminate social inequality, though it did redistribute financial resources from wealthier to poorer member states. The vision of a politically united Europe remained unfulfilled. Institutions for political collaboration were in place, including an elected European parliament, but they possessed no sovereign powers. Still, the momentum toward integration was irreversible.

Not all European Union countries agreed immediately to the monetary union. Great Britain, clinging still to shreds of its traditional "splendid isolation," refused to join, as did other smaller states. Pushed by German leaders, the major continental states proceeded to meet all the conditions for a common currency. For them, financial unity was worth abandoning their own currencies and coordinating fiscal policies. On January 1, 1999, a single European Union currency, called the "euro," went into use.

The borders of this new Europe stopped at the Iron Curtain. The Cold War's division of the continent menaced European recovery, keeping alive fears of another world war in which Europe would be at the center. In an effort to establish principles for a stable peace between East and West, western states invited representatives of the communist lands to Helsinki, Finland, in 1975. The negotiators from the East were eager for agreement on the permanence of the new borders of European states, especially those of the Soviet Union and Poland. The western diplomats hoped in exchange for acknowledgment from the communist countries that human rights (civil and political liberties) constituted the only stable and just basis for government. The communist regimes had

never recognized individual freedom to be a necessary or desirable objective. But for the sake of assurance of permanent state borders, they allowed this cornerstone of democracy to be included in the final Helsinki Agreement. The signers agreed to renounce the "threat or use of force" to settle international disputes, and committed their states to respect "fundamental freedoms, including the freedom of thought, conscience, religion, and belief." It seemed at the time an illusory promise that the eastern governments would disregard.

In the next decade, the human rights provisions remained a dead letter in the Soviet-dominated countries. But when the communist regimes vanished at the end of the 1980s, the Agreement laid out the basic conditions on which eastern Europe could be reintegrated politically into the rest of the Continent. What the last Soviet leader, Mikhail Gorbachev, called the "common house of Europe" had found a new, firm basis for a peaceful future.

THE SOVIET UNION AND THE COLD WAR

The Cold War began in the late 1940s. It ended less forty years later. Its origins lay in the expansion in the years after the Second World War of the Soviet Union into central Europe and northern Asia, and in western fears of Stalinism. It disappeared when the communist regimes of Europe and the Soviet Union collapsed. Its focal point had been the city of Berlin, divided into Soviet and western zones of occupation. It combined power politics and profound ideological differences. This potent combination made compromise and agreement extremely difficult. It posed the gravest threat to civilization in the history of modern states.

The nuclear arms race between the Soviet Union and the United States kept alive the likelihood of nuclear war on a global scale. Each side came to recognize the terrible consequences that use of these weapons would have on their peoples, yet continued to perfect ever more deadly weapons in the expectation that failure to do so would jeopardize its security. The Soviet and western troops stationed in their separate zones of Berlin were hostages to the war plans devised by each superpower to prepare for an unthinkable nuclear war.

The Soviet Empire

Stalin's death in 1953 ended his brutal rule, but not the communist dictatorship that he had put in place in the Soviet Union and the states of eastern Europe. His heirs, a handful of men in the Communist Party's Politburo (then called the Presidium), reverted to the pattern of collective party leadership that Lenin had created. They vied for leadership of the country until, in 1955, Nikita Khrushchev managed to take control of the party and state.

For the next decade, Soviet foreign and domestic policies were shaped by the policies and institutions in place since the 1920s, and by the personality and aims of the new Soviet leader. Born in a poor peasant family, Khrushchev rose through the ranks of the Communist Party in Stalin's years to become a member of the leadership group around the dictator. He, like his colleagues in the Presidium, never doubted the fundamental truths of Marxism-Leninism—the historical superiority of their command economy and egalitarian social system, the inevitable collapse of capitalism and the global triumph of Soviet socialism, and the necessity for communist dictatorship. Their attitudes and methods of rule were formed in the harsh world of Stalinist Russia during years of revolution and war. This political culture nurtured in them a suspicious, antagonistic

view of the West. It sustained their dogmatic conviction that they knew what was best for the Soviet people and for the "socialist camp" of satellite countries.

They broke with the Stalin system on one point. The entire party leadership understood that they had to end Stalin's terrorist methods of rule. The enormous power of the secret police threatened their own political dominance and violated the Leninist system of single-party rule. They proceeded to remove from office and to execute for "crimes against the people" the head of the secret police, Lavrenty Beria. The laws authorizing terror were abolished, and thousands of Stalin's victims were released from jail or prison camp. This quiet "destalinization" did not proceed fast enough for Khrushchev. In early 1956, he publicly denounced Stalin's crimes and the "cult of the personality" that had surrounded the dictator with an aura of superiority. Soviet citizens opposed to all forms of Stalinism took heart when they heard of his speech. Peoples in eastern Europe looked forward to an end of the Stalinist sphere of domination over their lands.

In fact, the Soviet leaders had not entirely abandoned repressive measures when needed to protect their system. They kept the secret police, now called the Committee of State Security, or KGB, to suppress political dissent and religious practices. They still authorized the state censorship committee to enforce the monopoly on truth of Marxism–Leninism. They were determined to keep intact the "socialist camp," by force if necessary.

Khrushchev himself remained in power only as long as the collective party leadership was in fundamental agreement with his policies. He undertook a series of economic and social reforms to raise the poor living conditions of the Soviet people. He even promised them in 1961 that they would live in conditions of abundance within a few years. His vision of "communism in our generation" took the shape of a grandiose welfare state, offering its inhabitants free housing, schooling, transportation, and health care. To him, a communist society (the highest stage of history, according to Marx) meant a egalitarian, satisfactory level of collective consumption. The Western consumer society of private cars, stereos, blue jeans, and rock-and-roll music embodied the evils of corrupt capitalism.

His colleagues were not prepared to let him undermine the privileges that they enjoyed or the stability of their one-party dictatorship. Khrushchev came to see that his reforms were obstructed by "bureaucratism." He blamed bureaucrats in the state and even in his own party for the corruption spreading through the country and the state's disregard for the needs of the people. He dreamed of reviving the revolutionary zealotry of Lenin's years. In a real sense he was the last communist dreamer of the Soviet regime.

He failed in his efforts to end the abuses of bureaucratism. He could not understand that bureaucratic institutions constituted the essential mechanism by which the party retained its monopolies of political power, of property, and expression. Critics called this system the "USSR Inc." Even his own colleagues in the Presidium finally turned against him, voting in 1964 to send him into "early retirement." They undid many of his reforms and ended public denunciations of Stalin's crimes. Dogmatic in their ideological views and fearful of reform, they kept tight control over the population, the vast state-run economy, and the Soviet empire. The Stalinist system remained in place for another twenty years until, too late, another party reformer attempted to remedy its grave defects.

In those years, the Soviet leadership's confidence in this system was bolstered by its popularity in other parts of the world. Khrushchev and his successors looked upon the Third World as an arena where capitalism and socialism contended for dominance. Their Marxist-Leninist faith promised that their side would win. In the short term they were prepared (as Stalin had not been) to provide economic assistance to non-communist regimes in Asia, Africa, and Latin America that were sympathetic to their socialist ideals. They did require that these countries be "non-aligned" in the Cold War conflict. Their new global policy sought to swing the world's balance of power in their favor. Power politics became more than ever a part of the Cold War.

In Latin America, Fidel Castro found a warm welcome when he appealed in late 1959 to Moscow to help his new government construct socialism in Cuba. In Africa, socialist-led regimes in Angola in the west, and Ethiopia in the east, obtained in the 1970s not only Soviet aid but the military assistance from Cuban armed forces in defeating their internal enemies (who themselves received help from the U.S. and its allies). When, in 1977, a group of Afghan Communists seized power in their country, Soviet economic assistance came immediately. The balance of power was in those years as much a concern of Soviet as of U.S. leaders. Soviet intermediate-range missiles reached Cuba in 1962, primarily because Khrushchev judged Soviet strategic interests benefitted. The arms race occupied an important place in this new Soviet world policy.

Confrontation with Soviet Enemies

Khrushchev and his successors were resolved to keep the communist regimes of eastern Europe in power, even in the face of widespread popular discontent. They recognized the urgency of ending the terrorist system of rule and the policies of economic exploitation that Stalin had put in place there. They altered the terms of trade between the Soviet Union and the satellite countries to allow improvements in the people's miserable living conditions. They made concessions to the deep-seated longing of these peoples (as well as Soviet peoples) to develop the cultural and historical traditions of their nations. But they were prepared to use military force to prevent these countries from freeing themselves from Soviet domination.

In 1956, Soviet leaders acted quickly and forcefully to quell a Hungarian revolution. Late that year Hungarian reformers, supported by the entire population, announced their intent to end the dictatorship and break their ties with the Soviet Union. Illegal demonstrations by Hungarian students and workers to protest political and economic oppression quickly turned into a mass uprising against Stalinism. The army joined the protesters and reform Communists took over the government. Destruction of a giant forty-foot statue of Stalin in the middle of the capital Budapest revealed the depths of hatred toward the Soviet dictator and his satellite system. The uprising was successful in bringing to power an independent government. It introduced reforms to restore civil and political liberties, and declared their intention to make Hungary a free, neutral state.

Its plans clashed with Soviet insistence on military control in eastern Europe and on the preservation of communist dictatorship. Khrushchev did not permit desertion from the "socialist camp." A week after the uprising began, Soviet troops invaded the country. They crushed the rebellion and put in power Communists loyal to the Soviet Union. Hungarians lost their hope for national independence.

Europe's most dangerous and visible border separated the communist from the non-communist countries. That line ran through the middle of Germany. To the east, 15 million Germans in the German Democratic Republic were under communist rule. The discontent of East Germans at their political and economic plight was evident in the flight of thousands of refugees to West Germany each year. The drain on the economy of the Soviet satellite was so damaging that Soviet leaders had to take forceful action or see the East German population literally slip away. Their ultimate objective was the withdrawal of the western powers from West Berlin, which would fall under East German control. But the West refused to make any concessions.

Risking an international crisis and possibly war, Khrushchev ordered in 1961 that the open border around West Berlin be transformed into an impenetrable physical barrier. Suddenly that August, East German workers protected by Soviet troops encircled West Berlin with concrete walls topped by barbed wire and guarded by East German border troops. The "Iron Curtain" had closed the last small opening between east and west. The U.S. government preferred not to challenge the Soviet action for fear of provoking a military confrontation. Europe remained divided between Soviet and Western military alliances, between communist and democratic states. The Berlin Wall became, to many Europeans, the symbol of the failure of postwar peacemaking.

In the two decades that followed, Soviet leaders sent off their armed forces twice more to countries where popular resistance threatened the power of communist governments. In Czechoslovakia, the Communist Party was in 1968 powerless on its own to stem a popular movement, led by labor unions, intellectuals, and reform Communists, opposed to the Soviet-style dictatorship and command economy. Czech reformers hoped for Soviet acceptance of their reforms. They promised continued allegiance to the Soviet military alliance. But the Soviet leaders feared that their eastern European empire was a risk if communism disappeared there. In August of that year, their military forces occupied the country and forced upon the Czechs a compliant government of Moscow's own choosing.

Shortly afterward, the Soviet leader, Leonid Brezhnev, defended in principle what Red Army troops had already made evident in practice. His "Brezhnev Doctrine" asserted the right of the Soviet Union to intervene in the affairs of any allied state in the "socialist camp" in need of assistance to maintain communist rule. In 1979, he applied the doctrine once again when he ordered Soviet troops into Afghanistan to keep in power the communist regime. Afghan Communists, in control of the government for only two years, had already antagonized the peoples of that Inner Asian land by their radical reforms. The population was deeply attached to tribal ways and Muslim traditions. Nearly 100,000 Soviet troops went to fight the Afghan rebels. These "mujahaddin" in turn found vital help from neighboring Pakistan and received valuable military assistance from the United States. Once a remote Asian borderland, Afghanistan was transformed a war zone in the Cold War.

The weakness of communist satellite governments was most apparent in Poland. Opposition to the Polish Communist Party came from intellectuals, workers, and the powerful Catholic Church. Polish national unity had emerged out of the centuries of foreign domination. The twentieth century had witnessed Poland's disappearance yet again at the hands of Nazi occupation forces. The state reemerged after the Soviet Red Army swept through the country, only to fall immediately under communist rule. Catholicism remained the core of Polish nationalism. Its influence grew when, in 1978,

a Polish priest became Pope John Paul II. Polish resistance to communism grew even stronger.

In 1980, underground resistance came into the open when Polish workers throughout the country joined a general strike to protest their lack of freedom and harsh living conditions. The Pope publicly applauded their massive, peaceful rebellion. They created a nationwide free labor movement, called Solidarity. The Polish Communist Party lost all authority. Solidarity commanded the respect of the people. The Soviet Union's leaders relied on the threat of military intervention to force Polish submission. They found allies in Polish generals, who were fearful of a Soviet invasion and prepared to use their troops to end that brief moment of political freedom. General Jaruzelski, in command of the army, declared martial law, outlawed Solidarity, arrested many of its supporters, and turned Poland into a military dictatorship.

Soviet control of the eastern European states remained intact until the late 1980s. Moscow's orders were executed by obedient leaders, whose rule rested in last resort on the menace of Soviet repression. Eastern Europe appeared firmly under control on the borderlands of the Soviet empire.

The Cold War and the Arms Race

The combination of Soviet domination of the satellite countries and Stalinist dictatorship had aroused among Western governments and their peoples a deep apprehension of Soviet expansionism (see Chapter 6). The U.S. policy of containment had expanded to include military alliances around the world by the early 1950s. The most important was the North Atlantic Treaty Organization (NATO), uniting North America and western Europe. Containment policy included as well the development of armaments so devastating that Soviet leaders would never consider launching an offensive war against the West. U.S. military forces possessed by the mid-1950s both atomic and hydrogen bombs. Technological advances gave them ever more effective and expensive means of destroying the Soviet Union.

By the end of the 1950s the U.S. armed forces commanders had put in operation their key strategic weapons. Their "triad" of armaments was the fundamental military element of the U.S. policy of containment. They possessed the means to launch nuclear weapons on Soviet targets from supersonic bombers stationed on airfields around the globe, from nuclear-powered submarines equipped with ballistic missiles that patrolled the Soviet coastlines, and from land-based intercontinental ballistic missiles in the United States capable of striking any region of the Soviet Union. Seeking to maintain military superiority over their enemy, their strategy was a spur to the escalating arms race.

After Stalin's death, Soviet leaders continued his expansion of Soviet nuclear armaments. They soon came to realize that these weapons were so devastating that they could not conceivably win a war. Still, they were convinced that their country's security and influence in the world depended upon rivaling the military might of the United States. Khrushchev announced in 1956 that, contrary to Stalin's grim forecast, war with the capitalist states was not inevitable. His (relative) optimism was based on the claim that Soviet military advances held the aggressive Western states in check.

It was a claim to strength that included a recognition of the terrible consequences of modern war. The previous year Soviet scientists had exploded their first hydrogen bomb. In 1957, they launched into space the first satellite, which they called "Sputnik"

(little traveler). The exploit dramatically confirmed Soviet technological skill. It also demonstrated that their military scientists had developed long-range ballistic missiles (rockets capable of carrying nuclear weapons). In the mid-1960s, the Soviet military forces expanded still further to include for the first time a multiocean navy. It included nuclear submarines capable of launching ballistic missiles on distant targets. The United States and the Soviet Union by then possessed the capacity to destroy the other country many times over.

Soviet and U.S. leaders each in their own way understood that the nuclear arms race had no winners, only losers. The cost of their weapons buildup was terribly high, especially for the Soviet economy. The U.S. spent 5 percent of its yearly national income on defense expenditures, while the Soviet economy, less than half as wealthy as the United States, had to commit 20 to 25 percent of its output to its military program. Secret cities in the Soviet Union were entirely devoted to weapons development. This financial burden, and the realization that the arms rivalry worsened relations and heightened the risk of war, gradually made leaders on both sides look to some means of finding limits to the arms race.

Before that happened, however, they confronted for a few critical days the likelihood of nuclear war. The Cuban missile crisis of 1962 had its roots in Castro's revolution and U. S. opposition to Cuban communism (see Chapter 10). Castro's pleas to Soviet leaders for military protection brought help, though not in the shape of a military alliance. In the spring of 1962, Khrushchev proposed stationing a complete Soviet missile division on Cuban soil. It would be so close to the United States that its intermediate-range ballistic missils could strike any part of the United States. The reasons for his reckless offer are still not clear. His own commander

The Arms Race on Parade: November 7th Celebration in Red Square, Moscow, c. 1965 (*Patty Ratliff Collection/Hoover Institution*)

of rocket forces opposed the action. The most likely explanation is that he anticipated from this move an enormous boost to Soviet global power and influence. He did not, however, allow the Cubans to control the nuclear weapons on their soil. This foreign initiative was strictly a Soviet undertaking.

When the U.S. government discovered the missile installations in Cuba that fall, it demanded their immediate withdrawal. President Kennedy and his advisers all agreed (as did the U.S. allies in Europe) that this Soviet move would represent a devastating diplomatic and political defeat for the West. The Cold War had its own peculiar

logic of victory and defeat, measured by the relative diplomatic and military power of each side. Kennedy's advisers disagreed on the proper response. Decisive action was vital, and some U.S. military and political leaders argued that it had to begin with the invasion of Cuba. If the Soviet forces responded with nuclear weapons, or Soviet troops invaded West Berlin in retaliation, war was a certainty. Kennedy put off the invasion, preferring to use a naval blockade of Cuba to stop further Soviet ships reaching Cuba while leaving the opportunity for negotiation open for a few days. His caution was rewarded.

End of the Cuban Missile Crisis: U.S. Destroyer Inspecting Soviet Freighter Carrying Soviet Missiles Back to USSR, November 10, 1962 (*UPI/Corbis-Bettmann*)

With only a day left before the U.S. invasion of Cuba was to begin, Khrushchev accepted the compromise solution proposed by the United States. He withdrew his missiles from Cuba in exchange for a public commitment by the U.S. president not to authorize an invasion of the island. As important to the compromise was Kennedy's secret agreement to withdraw U.S. intermediate-range ballistic missiles from Turkey. Both leaders spoke in private of their overriding resolve to avoid nuclear war. In the language of the time, nuclear "deterrence" pushed both sides to settle the conflict peacefully.

That dangerous encounter demonstrated the urgency to find some common grounds for negotiations to rein in the nuclear arms race. The nuclear arsenals of both superpowers were in the service of their foreign policies, which they defined in terms of both national interests and political ideals. The achievement of international arms controls required that each side put aside their ideological differences to confront directly essential strategic issues. President Nixon's security adviser (later secretary of state) Henry Kissinger made this clear when in 1969 he argued "we have no permanent enemies. We will judge other countries, including communist countries, on the basis of their actions and not on the basis of their domestic ideology."

The readiness of both sides to view their conflicts around the world more from the perspective of interests and less in ideological terms made possible negotiations to separate arms issues from Cold War rivalries. In this perspective, global competition did not require the endless development of ever more powerful weapons of war. These understandings came after each side accepted the logical, but dismaying idea that nuclear weapons were of use solely to deter the other side from beginning, or threatening to begin, a war.

In conditions of mutual suspicion and competition, this elementary truth was the only possible basis for agreement. The two superpowers acknowledged that each state needed sufficient offensive nuclear weapons to "deter" an attack, that is, to be able to defend itself by destroying the aggressor. Each side could guarantee its acceptance of the policy of deterrence by not building defensive nuclear weapons. In the conditions of the Cold War, this became the fundamental definition of peace, appropriately labeled by one American leader "MAD" (Mutually Assured Destruction). It was the key to the success of the first major Soviet-American nuclear arms treaty.

The first Strategic Arms Limitation Treaty (SALT I) was signed in 1972. In it, the Soviet and American governments agreed not to develop or deploy defensive (anti-ballistic missile) systems. Those defensive missiles that they had begun to install had to be destroyed. Inspection of each side's fulfillment of the treaty was insured by the use of U.S. and Soviet military surveillance satellites, constantly stationed over the other country. The agreement ended one part of the nuclear arms race. Deterrence became the cornerstone of peaceful relations between the Soviet Union and the United States.

The treaty remained incomplete, however. It failed to restrict the development of new offensive nuclear weapons. Scientists on both sides were, in the peculiar language of the arms race, constantly "modernizing" their country's nuclear arsenals. Their work

in itself helped to sustain the arms race. To slow this dangerous process, Soviet and U.S. negotiators finally signed in 1979 another arms treaty (SALT II). It limited the numbers of certain offensive weapons, principally intercontinental ballistic missiles and submarine-launched missiles. The arms race had not stopped, but the leaders of the superpowers had at least been able to place certain limits on their nuclear arsenals. In doing so they recognized that their awesome military power could at best maintain between their two states what one American official called "an enduring strategic stalemate."

Good relations between the Soviet Union and the United States remained dangerously vulnerable to local conflicts, new armaments, and political rivalries. The new U.S. president, Ronald Reagan, launched in 1981 an armaments program more extensive (and vastly more expensive) than the programs begun in the early 1950s. The United States introduced a deadly new generation of missiles that could strike a target a few yards square at a distance of hundreds of miles. It deployed another missile that used a secret global positioning radar system that hugged the curvature of the terrain, avoiding Soviet radar defenses. In a search for the ultimate defense, President Reagan authorized a program to create a supposedly impenetrable shield in outer space over the United States. It was to be made of defensive space weapons including giant laser beams, against incoming (Soviet) ballistic missiles. The United States poured billions of dollars into the so-called "Star Wars" program. Reagan's armaments initiative threatened to undermine SALT I, and led the Soviet government in turn to accelerate its missile weapons development. The arms race was a tragic reminder of the superpowers' failure to bring peace to the postwar world.

⚜ HIGHLIGHT: The Cold War in Outer Space ⚜

The dream of exploring space first inspired novelists and visionary scientists. At the time when explorers were completing the mapping of the last unknown regions of the world, the French novelist Jules Verne laid out in his 1865 story *From the Earth to the Moon* a fantastic tale of human space travel and exploration of the moon. One hundred years later, this dream was reality. It was the product of the competition between the Soviet Union and the United States for military might and global prestige. The Cold War penetrated even outer space.

It reached that far initially when rockets became a reliable means to transport nuclear weapons to any point in the globe. Military rockets had first appeared in the German arsenal during the last months of the Second World War. The threat that this weapon posed at the time was not great, since the German research into nuclear weapons had led nowhere and Allied armies were rapidly advancing on Germany. The U.S. and the Soviet governments were both aware of the enormous military potential of this German technology.

U.S. Army forces, the first to reach the German rocket center, seized all the German V-2 rockets. The German space scientists had fled, but soon surrendered to U.S. authorities. Brought back to the United States, this live "war booty" became the founders of the new U.S. rocket program. Extremely expensive, it proceeded slowly for the next ten years. Air Force visionaries were more interested in experimenting with manned flights by rocket-powered aircraft (the "X" series) capable of attaining speeds that would carry them into space, and ultimately would permit them to orbit the earth.

Soviet rocket developments in the late 1950s altered the U.S. space program's pace and direction. The Soviet military had an urgent need for missiles to carry their nuclear weapons, since they lacked adequate long-range bombers like those in the U.S. Strategic Air Command. Stalin himself had given the Soviet program highest priority at war's end. He had personally ordered the release of the country's outstanding rocket engineer, Sergei Korolev, from the prison laboratory where he had been serving a twenty-five-year sentence for alleged "counter-revolutionary activities." Working in absolute secrecy, Korolev proved one of the most inventive and successful scientists working for the Soviet military. His achievements were comparable only to the physicist Andrei Sakharov, who was responsible for developing the Soviet hydrogen bomb. By the mid-1950s, Korolev and his research team had tested long-range liquid-fuel rockets capable of carrying a cargo into space. If that cargo were a nuclear weapon, it could attain any region in the United States in the space of an hour. The intercontinental ballistic missile was a devastatingly effective new weapon of war.

It appeared to Nikita Khrushchev a dramatic means to demonstrate the great accomplishments of the Soviet socialist system to the whole world. At his orders, the first public demonstration of Korolev's rockets came in the form of a small metal ball, containing a tiny radio. In the fall of 1957, Korolev used his new rocket to launch into orbit around the earth the very first artificial satellite, named "Sputnik." It attracted enormous attention, all to the benefit of the Soviet Union. It marked the real beginning of the Space Age. It also set the Cold War on a whole new direction.

The U.S. military program for missiles had also developed powerful rockets. It still had nothing that could rival Korolev's inventions. Accused in 1957 by members of Congress and the press of "losing the Cold War in space," the U.S. government immediately set out on a crash program to launch its own space satellites. The first, hasty efforts produced the predictable fiascos. Observers baptized the failed U.S. launchings later that year "Kaputniks." Urgency grew as Soviet rockets successfully carried still heavier payloads into space. The "Chief Designer," as Korolev was known in the West (his name remained secret until after his death), seemed capable of miracles. If his rockets were so effective, then they could even carry a human cargo into space orbit. The fact that the United States did put reliable rockets into operation and in 1958 placed in orbit satellites that made notable scientific discoveries only accelerated the momentum of the "Space Race."

That race had four dimensions. In the early years, the most visible public achievements came from the determination of both Soviet and American political leaders to accomplish space exploits to enhance the global standing of their political systems. Alongside this propaganda aspect was the very important, and largely secret, military use of space. Soon after, governments and industrial enterprises found in communications and navigational satellites an invaluable, and economically profitable use of space in the electronics age. The pursuit of

scientific knowledge was also an important part of space developments. It produced an enormous array of new discoveries made by manned space stations and voyages, and by unmanned probes of outer space.

The public and political expectations generated by the first satellite launchings quickly focused on the possibilities of placing a human cargo in orbit. Beyond that was the enticing prospect of sending that cargo to the moon and back. The Soviet "Chief Designer" flaunted the competence of his rocket team when a space capsule containing the first "cosmonaut," Yuri Gagarin, circled the earth in early 1961. Within a year, several other Soviet cosmonauts, including a woman, had proven the capacity of humans to survive the rigors of brief space travel.

At an early moment in this series of Soviet victories, the U.S. president, John Kennedy, concluded that the United States could no longer be "second best" in space. He promised that the United States would "land a man on the moon" by the end of the decade. The new National Air and Space Administration (NASA) found itself suddenly with a yearly budget of several billions of dollars to carry out this plan. It faced a public and government demanding that it produce immediate results. The first U.S. "astronaut," Alan Shepard, was launched into space late in 1961. His capsule returned immediately to earth, rising beyond the earth's atmosphere and then rapidly descending like a human cannonball. NASA had an enormous and complex task before it.

Its success in the moon project represented an extraordinary engineering achievement. The secret Soviet program to land a cosmonaut on the moon was a failure. Korolev died in 1965, and his research team was unable to create the reliable rocket and

Winners of the Race to the Moon: U.S. Astronaut and U.S. Flag, Moon, 1969 (*NASA*)

guidance systems necessary for the daring space voyage. In those years, U.S. space engineers designed a giant rocket (the Saturn), thirty-six stories high. It had sufficient capacity to send a space ship with three astronauts into orbit around the moon, plus a landing craft. The first moon landing took place in 1969. The "first steps for mankind," announced by Neil Armstrong when he set foot on the moon, brought the United States its greatest space triumph. His companion Edwin Aldrin followed him out of the craft to plant a U.S. flag in the moon's soil. NASA won the race to the moon.

That achievement was the high point of manned space probes. The United States in those years confronted serious domestic and international problems, and the government had made major financial commitments to expand social welfare programs for the American people. The disillusionment that some Americans felt at the space program appeared on a placard, held by a demonstrator in front of the White House in Washington, which read "You Promised Us Food, but You Gave Us the Moon." Funds to NASA dwindled, and the final lunar landing occurred in 1972.

The military use of space proceeded with great speed. The possibilities for surveillance of earth from space created the alluring prospect of uncovering military secrets, such as rocket installations, weapons, and troop movements, without complex spy projects or risky high-altitude flights. The U.S. military's previous efforts at air reconnaissance of the Soviet Union from jet planes had provoked a serious international incident. A Soviet ground-to-air missile had in 1959 shot down a U-2 spy plane flying 10 miles above Russia. The Soviet government put the U.S. pilot on public trial after he parachuted to earth and was taken captive. His confession broadcast one of the secrets of the Cold War to the entire world.

Satellites performed far more effectively than any pilot. They were placed in orbits passing repeatedly over enormous areas of the globe. Cameras grew increasingly sophisticated, making even objects ten feet square clearly visible on the photos sent back to earth. Both the Soviet and United States military had by the late 1960s achieved marvels of technological perfection in their spy satellites. The nuclear arms limitation treaties (SALT I and SALT II) were trustworthy documents because each side possessed all the photographic evidence needed to confirm any violations, not because they believed the other's promises to respect its provisions. Ironically, the space race produced the means for more effective peacemaking between the superpowers than could ever have been imagined when the Cold War began.

Still, military leaders continued to look upon space as an arena of war. Ballistic missiles acquired extraordinary accuracy by the 1980s. The technology and engineering skills necessary for building ballistic missiles became sufficiently easy to master so that other governments whose military acquired nuclear weapons had their own rockets for use in the event of a possible nuclear war. Space appeared to some U.S. scientists and to President Ronald Reagan the place for the ultimate defense against ballistic missile attacks. The "Star Wars" program wasted enormous funds in the vain expectation that satellites equipped with powerful laser beams could destroy all in-coming missiles before they ever reached the United States. The plan was expensive and unrealistic. An impenetrable space shield covering the United States proved unattainable, since precision space targeting on such a vast scale was impossible to achieve. Research on the program continued in the 1990s, but on a very reduced scale.

The Soviet Sputnik satellite had transmitted signals from a tiny radio solely to let everyone on earth know that it was flying overhead. The lesson was not lost on governments and businesses involved in communications. Suddenly possibilities opened up for instantaneous radio and television signals to reach the remotest parts of the earth. Microwave signals, containing words, numbers, music, or voices, could travel out to satellites in fixed position relative to the earth (approximately 22,000 miles high) and return to waiting receivers ("satellite dishes") so small and inexpensive by the 1980s that consumers could afford them. Industries that relied on the new electronics technology viewed space as a new frontier for economic expansion and profits.

Global television networks appeared, such as the American CNN and the British Star networks, that broadcast commercial programs around the world 24 hours a day. People in countries where state censorship severely restricted television programming, such as China, began buying their own satellite dishes to watch uncensored entertainment and news. Businesses engaged in international financial transactions were able to communicate with branches and conduct their affairs instantaneously throughout the world. Satellite communication made the earth a much smaller place.

Governments, especially in the Third World, that relied on radio and television to spread among their peoples their message of national loyalty and solidarity understood as well the benefit of satellites. By the 1980s, the Indian and Indonesian states possessed their own communication satellites that per-

At Home in Space: Soviet Orbital Station Saliut-7, 1985 (*Hoover Institution*)

mitted the state-run radio and television networks to transmit their programs throughout their vast countries. The U.S. Global Positioning System (GPS) used navigation satellites to give exact longitude and latitude positions to ground stations. Used at first solely for the military, it soon served the needs of shipping companies and sailors seeking reliable information on the position of their boats. Using a small electronic navigation device. GPS became an essential piece of equipment for navigators, whether on giant supertankers and small sailboats. Useful knowledge, financial investments, and national propaganda all moved through these satellites. By the 1990s, they numbered about 500 (with the debris of another 1000 still in space). What appeared shooting stars in the night skies were often their reflected light.

Scientific discoveries accumulated as a sidelight to the propaganda and military exploits. After the frantic space race that ended with the moon landings, the scientific programs of both states became more prominent and received more attention. In many ways they were linked still to Cold War competition. Scientists obtained financing in part for the potential military benefits that might emerge from their research. The Soviet government directed its resources toward the creation of a permanent space station, where their cosmonauts discovered the possibilities and limits of human life in outer space. These Soviet space stations first appeared in the early 1970s. They expanded in size and complexity in the next decades. They were maintained constantly even through the period when the Soviet Union ceased to exist and the Soviet space center in Central Asia suddenly became the property of a newly independent country (Kazakhstan). Cosmonauts remained on board for

seven and eight months at a time. Space for them became a temporary home.

The U.S. scientific space efforts moved in two directions. Its space probes increasingly relied on unmanned satellites filled with equipment that automatically recorded scientific observations. This information brought to light geophysical conditions not only on earth, revealed through space photographs, but also on the moon and planets of the solar system. Satellites reached Mars and Venus in the early 1960s, and ten years later they circled Jupiter. The first U.S. satellite to touch the soil of another planet was the Mars landing of 1975. The most ambitious astronomic experiment was the launching in 1990 of the Hubble Space Telescope. It was a giant precision instrument capable of viewing and photographing distant galaxies with a clarity many times greater than the best earth-bound telescope. It revealed no military secrets, and only later, after serious technical problems were corrected, did it prove its capacity to uncover hidden secrets of the universe. Its achievements belonged strictly to a world beyond the Cold War.

Space shuttles were the second new area of U.S. space developments. The old Air Force dream of a plane capable of going into orbit and returning to land on earth was partially realized when NASA launched the first Challenger shuttle in 1981. These spacecraft were sent up "piggyback" on enormous rockets and kept in space for several days before returning to land like an airplane. The shuttles became orbiting laboratories in which astronauts carried out missions to test materials, to take photographs of earth, to repair other satellites.

Each launching and landing of U.S. space shuttles attracted a large audience. Space continued to hold some of the mysterious attraction that Jules Verne's novel had created among its readers. The success of the missions became the guarantee of NASA's continued funding. When in 1986 one of the shuttles exploded shortly after launching, killing the astronauts on board, NASA was blamed for haste.

After the fall of the Soviet Union, NASA joined in the new international era by collaborating with the Russian space agency. U.S. space shuttles linked up with Russian space stations. In 2000, the International Space Station became the first multi-state endeavor to sustain permanently human activity in space. Construction of the station itself drew on Russian experience. U.S. space shuttles brought the equipment for the Station and provided regular transportation from and back to earth for astronauts and cosmonauts. The Space Station embodied a post-Cold War view of space exploration. The urgency that the Cold War had given to space exploration declined, yet the public interest in and scientific rewards from space probes remained. Viewed from space, the earth appeared a colorful, but very finite and tiny object floating in an incredibly vast universe. The ultimate moral lesson from space exploration was humility.

The Decline and Fall of the Soviet Empire

By the 1980s, the Stalinist system of the Soviet Union was incapable of maintaining the country's role of superpower. The elderly Stalinist leaders clung to the illusion of global might, partly out of dogmatic conviction, partly out of ignorance of the decay of their empire and of their own state and society. A few among them realized the extent of the crisis. By then a group of younger Communists were even beginning to put forward daring plans for reform. But as long as the Stalinists remained in power, nothing could be done.

The Stalinists lost their control of the Soviet government and the Soviet Communist Party in 1985. The generation of Communists old enough to remember and to revere the Stalin revolution of the 1930s was disappearing. Their successors could not continue to hide the country's economic crisis and spreading political corruption. The system inherited from Stalin had failed in key areas to meet the needs of the country. It was too inflexible to adopt the technological innovations revolutionizing Western industry, its bureaucratic command system nurtured incompetence and inefficiency, its rigid, centralized controls ignored the needs and wishes of consumers, and its military forces absorbed nearly one-fourth of the country's yearly national income, and even then could not match the electronic wizardry of U.S. weapons.

Living conditions worsened and the economy virtually ceased growing. Only the export of raw materials, especially oil and natural gas, permitted major investments to continue. An illegal black-market economy offered scarce goods to those people with the means to pay its high prices. In exchange for special favors, corrupt officials protected the illegal operations by halting efforts to enforce the laws against these "speculators." People referred to this alliance of black-marketeers and communist officials as the Soviet "Mafia." Russian economists likened their country's economic condition to that of a state in the Third World.

The single-party communist dictatorship, in theory responsible for the economic well-being of the Soviet Union, was critically weakened by corruption and special privileges. The party bureaucrats held power virtually for life, and many turned their positions into a source of personal wealth. They lived far better than the average Soviet citizen thanks to bribes and influence peddling. It was in their interest to ignore both the real needs of the population and the damage to the environment caused by their economic plans. Claiming to have put their Leninist talents in the service of socialism, these party officials were trapped in their own delusions of power. The entire country suffered as a result. With some variations, a similar political and economic crisis existed in all the communist countries.

A few high party officials, aided by the head of the secret police (KGB), had attempted a few modest reforms even before the last Stalinist leader died in 1985. Their earlier failures made them even more determined to build a reform movement within the new leadership. Their alliance was crucial when the time came to select a new General Secretary of the Communist Party of the Soviet Union. As in the past, the highest Communist Party committee (Politburo) was the body empowered to make the choice. Under pressure from reformers, its members elected in 1985 their youngest colleague, Mikhail Gorbachev, to the position of General Secretary. They realized that reforms were necessary, and expected that the result would be an improved socialist system and revived Soviet empire. Their single-party dictatorship would, they imagined, remain the core of the Soviet system and the pillar of world socialism. They were wrong on both counts.

Gorbachev proved an extraordinarily skillful party leader and a dynamic reformer. He quickly became aware that corrupt and incompetent party officials were deeply entrenched throughout the Communist Party apparatus. They relied on censorship and secrecy to protect their power and privileges. In 1986, they attempted to cover up the terrible accident at the Chernobyl nuclear power complex in Ukraine. Within a few days, detectors of radioactive fallout located across northern Europe relayed the news of an enormous explosion and atmospheric radioactive fallout that proved 10 times greater than the Hiroshima nuclear explosion. Gorbachev was outraged at his officials' arrogance and disregard for human safety. He resolved on the daring move to open up public debate in all the public media (termed "glasnost" in Russian). No longer could they hide behind a curtain of secrecy.

Censorship disappeared. For the first time since the 1917 revolution, access to information became a public right. Television, radio, and the press enjoyed the right to criticize the old order. Old-time Stalinists were outraged, but Gorbachev proved a master of the instruments of power and a daring architect of a new Soviet regime.

He sought political allies wherever he could find them. He released all political prisoners from jail. He authorized religious toleration, allowing churches, synagogues, and mosques to open, permitting religious texts to be published, and joining with Christian leaders in 1987 to celebrate the 1,000th anniversary of the conversion of Russia to Orthodox Christianity. His most radical measure was the call in 1988 for free elections to the Supreme Soviet (the national parliament). For the first time since 1917, voters were given the opportunity to choose among several candidates for one position. With some hesitation, reform Communists ran for office against conservative Communists.

Gorbachev gambled that the voters would reject the Stalinist party officials, and he was right. The elections, held in 1989, revealed that Russians in key urban areas of the country had turned against their old party bosses. As Gorbachev had hoped, the communist old guard lost to reform candidates, and suffered public humiliation in the process. The dictatorship of the vanguard party, instituted by Lenin in 1917, was beginning to give way to democracy in some Soviet republics.

Gorbachev's reform policies opened the way to the collapse of the communist regimes in eastern Europe. He had recognized that the crisis of his country was so grave that renewal could occur only with the collaboration of Western states and investors. Freedom for the peoples of the Soviet satellite countries was the fundamental condition to lasting good relations with the West. To achieve that he was prepared to abandon the Soviet empire in Europe and Asia. He publicly renounced the Brezhnev Doctrine of intervention in defense of communist regimes threatened by internal opposition. To prove his resolve to stand by the new policy, he ordered the withdrawal of all Soviet troops from Afghanistan; the last troops returned to the Soviet Union in 1989. He secretly informed the communist leaders in eastern Europe that Soviet forces no longer stood behind their feeble regimes. In doing so, he gave the peoples of eastern Europe the freedom to choose their own political systems. He realized that these east Europeans would insist on what his minister of foreign affairs termed "the liquidation of those imposed, alien, and totalitarian regimes." No one anticipated the speed with which the communist governments disappeared.

The Polish Communist Party was the first to lose power. The years of Polish military dictatorship after 1981 had forced the Solidarity labor movement to exist as an illegal, underground organization. But its hold on the population, like that of the Catholic Church, remained an insurmountable barrier to restoration of communist rule. The crisis of the Polish command economy remained unresolved. General Jaruzelski was aware of their inability to deal with these problems in the face of general hostility of the population. After Gorbachev initiated his policy of political pluralism in 1988, the Polish leader ordered that free parliamentary elections be held in Poland in 1989. He did so in the certain knowledge that Solidarity would win. What neither he nor the Polish Communists anticipated was that opponents of the Communists would win every single elected seat in parliament. They accepted the results, though, and that summer Poland was governed for the first time since 1939 by a freely chosen, noncommunist government. It began the painful process of dismantling the command economy. The new Poland was to be a democratic nation–state with a free market economy.

Sweeping reforms came rapidly also in Hungary and Czechoslovakia. In both countries they ended with the formation of democratic governments committed to a free-market economy. The Czechoslovak Stalinist leadership, imposed by Soviet troops in 1968, had refused any reforms since then. In late 1989, popular demonstrations led by students quickly assumed massive proportions throughout the country. The police were overwhelmed and the state paralyzed. Without the backing of Soviet troops, Czech communist leaders had to resign.

The leading political opponent of the regime was the playwright Vaclav Havel, who had spent years in prison for his outspoken defense of freedom. At popular demand, he became president of the new Czech democracy. At the end of that year, he thanked the young people for their "love of freedom and civic courage" in fighting the old regime. He promised to help build a new country "with economic prosperity and also social justice, a humane republic that serves the people." His appeal for understanding, toleration, and forgiveness sought to revive national pride and respect for other peoples in a Europe of free nation-states.

The bonds of national loyalty and solidarity were so strong in East Germany (the German Democratic Republic) that they undermined the very foundations of the communist state. The people's hostility to the regime was augmented by their resentment at being denied the freedom and prosperity enjoyed by the Germans living in the Federal Republic to the west. Though the postwar partition of the country had been accepted by the West, it was not acceptable to them. The Berlin Wall was the most visible and repugnant sign of the Communists' refusal to allow their subjects any personal liberty. West German television had for years broadcast its programs to East Germans, spreading vivid images of the West's way of life. The appeal was overwhelming. In the summer of 1989, Germans from the East began to flee to the West by the thousands through Hungary, whose government permitted them to escape to West Germany. That fall the flight had reached the proportions of a mass exodus. Demonstrations began in East German cities against the regime, with banners proclaiming that "We Are the People!"

The collapse of German communism began with the regime's desperate decision to grant complete freedom of travel to East Germans. On the night of November 9, the gates through the Berlin Wall were opened to all. The city became the center of an enormous celebration by East and West Berliners. Some of them climbed the wall itself to celebrate. So great was the attraction to East Germans of the way of life and institutions of West Germany that the German Democratic Republic quickly disintegrated. Free elections in 1990 brought to power the parties that promised the quickest possible unifica-

tion with the Federal Republic. In mid-1990, the West German financial system incorporated the eastern territory. In October, the country was united, and plans began to make Berlin once again the capital of a united Germany.

The restoration of national independence, political democracy, and capitalism in eastern Europe in 1989–1990 was a direct consequence of the reform policies of the new leadership in the Soviet Union. Without their refusal to intervene, communist regimes would have clung to power. But the real initiators of the move to liberal democracy were the populations of those countries. By means of demonstrations and strikes, and under the guidance of oppositional groups, they moved quickly to take control of their countries' governments. Only in Romania did the communist regime fight back, capitulating after a week of street battles. Elsewhere the transition of power occurred remarkably peacefully. Disagreements on the future of the countries appeared as soon as freedom was achieved. Still, agreement was unanimous everywhere that communism had to be removed completely.

The End of the Cold War

In his first years of power, Gorbachev did not grasp the gravity of the economic crisis. He lost precious time before finally accepting the advice of economists to abandon the command economy. His slogan of radical reform (the Russian term was "perestroika") came to mean the introduction of a limited free market in all sectors of the Soviet economy. The structural and social obstacles to such changes were far greater than those he encountered in introducing political and civil liberties. The public had for decades enjoyed state subsidies on essential consumer items, priced far below cost. They continued to rely on these state goods to meet their basic needs. Managers and workers had become accustomed to inefficient methods of work. A popular Russian judgment of this system was the simple comment: "They pretend to pay us, and we pretend to work." The country's industrial and agricultural equipment was obsolete, and the state lacked the resources for the massive investments needed for reconversion and technical modernization. All these problems were the result of wasteful and shortsighted state economic management and the price of the Stalinist leaders' determination to make their country a global superpower.

The economic difficulties worsened the tense relations between the non-Russian nationalities and the Soviet state. Lenin's attempt to create a "community of socialist nations" in the Soviet federal system had failed. Newly elected reform leaders in some national republics publicly likened the Soviet Union to the nineteenth-century tsarist empire, whose regime also kept its peoples under authoritarian rule. The Soviet Union was, in historical terms, the last empire. Decolonization had swept away all European empires except that of the Soviet Communists. The eastern European states had shown the way out of the empire. Soviet republics quickly followed their example.

By 1990, almost all of the fifteen national republics that made up the union had officially proclaimed their "sovereignty" (a formal action with no immediate legal consequences). Even the Russian Republic, largest of all, took this step of protest against the Soviet constitution and Communist Party rule. Nationalism, long forced underground by Soviet repression, suddenly became a powerful movement among Soviet peoples. National bonds of loyalty were far more influential than Soviet patriotism or the Marxist–Leninist ideology.

In the western soviet republics, free elections became the path to independence. The Polish example of national liberation in 1989 inspired nationalists in bordering Soviet regions to attempt the same. Nationalist parties in the Baltic area (Lithuanian, Latvian, and Estonian Socialist Republics) swept regional elections in 1990. Their leaders immediately called for an end to the unlawful annexation of their countries by the Soviet Union. They made public the secret Hitler–Stalin agreement of 1939 to partition eastern Europe. Their goal was secession from the Soviet Union. The country was beginning to fall apart.

In this growing crisis, influential old guard Communists in Moscow demanded that Gorbachev use the Red Army and secret police to quell the nationalist unrest. He resisted, fearing the end of his reform campaign and a new era of hostile relations with the West. In desperation, Stalinist leaders in the party, the army, and secret police organized in August 1991 a conspiracy to overthrow Gorbachev and reinstate the old dictatorship and Soviet order. They were Gorbachev's one-time colleagues whom he had trusted and relied upon to obey his orders. He never suspected them of betrayal. Their attempted uprising proved an abject failure, however.

Mass opposition to the conspiracy revealed that millions of people in Russia had repudiated communism and welcomed democratic reforms. Their leader was a dynamic anticommunist reformer, Boris Yeltsin. He had once belonged to the Communist Party, but in 1988 had resigned in disgust at its corruption and conservatism. He had joined the democratic movement. He set out to take the lead of the reform movement in the Russian Soviet Republic. In the spring of 1991, he campaigned in the first popular election ever for president of the Russian Soviet Republic. His program was democracy, a free-market economy, and Russian nationalism. His electoral victory was overwhelm-

Hero of Russian Democracy: Boris Yeltsin, Moscow, August 1991
(*Hoover Institution*)

ing. With this popular backing, he led the resistance to the Stalinist conspiracy that August. Arguing with Red Army generals that he was the legitimately chosen leader of Russia, he won the army to his side. Hundreds of thousands of Russians took over the streets of the major cities to stand in the way of the forces of the conspirators. The Stalinists backed down, leaving the Communist Party discredited and the Soviet Union in disarray.

Yeltsin and Russian nationalism were triumphant. He outlawed the Communist Party, and moved ahead with his own reform program for Russia. He had already accepted the Baltic republic's secession from the union. Gorbachev's defeat of the August conspiracy and Yeltsin's triumph established Russia as independent in all but legal terms. That fall, Ukrainians voted for independence. Gorbachev and the Soviet government were powerless to stop the disintegra-

tion of the federation. Quickly the leaders of the other fourteen republics of the Soviet Union followed suit, declaring their republics' independence late in 1991. Communism was gone, and so was the Soviet Union.

The disappearance of communist regimes and the collapse of the Soviet Union brought the Cold War to an end. In the late 1940s, George Kennan had foreseen the day when the Soviet empire would decline and negotiations would resolve the basic security issues dividing the United States and the Soviet Union. That time came forty years later. The Warsaw Pact of the Soviet bloc vanished. Its member countries all sought to join the Western military alliance (NATO). Among the countries asking in the 1990s to join the European Union were all the eastern European states freed from Soviet domination. The U.S. leaders signed new arms agreements with Gorbachev, then with Rus-

Europe, 1992

sia's president, Yeltsin. These treaties provided for the actual reduction of nuclear armaments. Intermediate-range and short-range missiles were to be completely destroyed, and intercontinental missiles drastically reduced in numbers. Armies saw their numbers cut throughout the former communist countries and in the West. Defense in-

dustries suddenly lost their booming market for weapons.

The dream of turning "swords into ploughshares" was only partially realized. Nuclear weapons remained in the possession of other states around the world besides Russia and the United States. China, India, and Pakistan all had such weapons, as did

France and Great Britain, and Israel. Still, the terrible threat of nuclear war ceased to dominate global relations. Europe was no longer divided in two. The U.S. government extended economic aid to Russia. Russian athletes in search of high pay joined Western professional sports teams, and Russian students appeared in Western business schools. The walls had fallen.

❧ SPOTLIGHT: Mikhail Gorbachev ❧

The political career of Mikhail Gorbachev (1931–) was from beginning to end that of a Communist. He began his life in a rural family living on a Soviet collective farm. Though some of his relatives had been imprisoned during the 1930s collectivization drive, he chose to collaborate with the Stalinist system. Public education all the way to the university was free to talented youth such as Gorbachev. Opportunities for personal advancement were abundant to those prepared to work in the Soviet state and Communist Party. He took advantage of these possibilities to leave his farming family far behind and, ultimately, to become the head of the Soviet Union.

His skills quickly became apparent to Stalinist leaders. He belonged to the post-Stalin generation, for whom the dictator was only a picture on the wall of their schools. His political career began at the time when the Soviet Union was in its best years of economic development, social betterment, and international triumphs. He passed all the necessary examinations in Marxist-Leninist ideology required of students. He was an active member of the Young Communist (Komsomol) organization. But he, like many of his generation, paid little attention to grand theories of socialism and party rituals. He focused on immediate problems of political rule and economic production. He married another graduate of Moscow University, a young woman majoring in the resurrected discipline of sociology. Authorities had allowed this field of knowledge to reappear in their country to explore the real conditions of the Soviet peoples. Their daily lives and problems were for the first time a concern to Soviet leaders. Gorbachev himself shared that interest. These practical approaches to the problems of the Soviet socialist system marked his entire career.

His advance through the party was swift. His powerful patrons valued his intelligence, his honesty, and his ability to get important political tasks successfully accomplished. In the late 1970s, he was chosen by the Soviet leadership to become a member of the highest party organ, the Politburo. His patron was the head of the secret police, where knowledge of corruption within the party and of economic weakness in the country was of increasing concern. This backing was crucial when, after the death of the last influential Stalinist leader in 1985, the Politburo finally looked for a reform leader.

Gorbachev proved in the next years that he had his own reform agenda, and that Stalinists and conservatives were not going to thwart his plans. He believed that, though corrupt Communists had risen to many positions of influence, he could mobilize reform party members under his guidance to rejuvenate the party and the entire Soviet system. He expected that this revived Communist Party would be capable, with the right leaders, of functioning effectively in a pluralistic (that is, multiparty) state without censorship and with free elections. He did expect that the command economy would vanish, but still believed that a modified form of Soviet socialism would emerge to the benefit of, and with the support, of the entire Soviet population.

He did not realize until it was too late that the peoples of the Soviet Union, when given the chance, preferred their own national leaders to a centrally controlled party dictatorship. Gorbachev's Soviet patriotism was so deep that it blinded him to the nationalism that filled his country. Even after

he returned to Moscow when the 1991 conspiracy against him had collapsed, he still believed that he, the President of the Soviet Union, would remain in power. In reality, the Russian President, Yeltsin, had defeated the Stalinist conspirators. Gorbachev had become irrelevant to the decisions on the fate of his country. That December, Gorbachev moved out of his Kremlin office and Yeltsin moved in. On that same day the red flag with the hammer and sickle of the Soviet Union disappeared from the flagpole over the Kremlin. It was immediately replaced by the old Russian flag, marking the birth of the Russian Federation. Gorbachev's political life ended when the Soviet Union ceased to exist.

SUMMARY

The Cold War had divided Europe and the world into two antagonistic alliances and competing political and social systems. In the first decades, the future of European lands appeared to depend on outside forces. The United States and the Soviet Union, great victors in the war, had the decisive hand in postwar global relations. The European border between their allies was baptized the Iron Curtain. Berlin itself brought together these opposing forces in one tiny spot on Europe's map, where pessimistic observers forecast the Third World War would begin. West German leaders welcomed with some reluctance the "nuclear umbrella" extended over their country by U.S. troops stationed there. It was preferable to being defenseless in the face of the forces of East Germany and the Soviet Union. West Berlin was defended and reconstructed to be a Western beacon and a refuge.

Peoples in the communist countries had no choice but to submit to Soviet domination. If they had been allowed to express their preference, they would immediately have claimed their national independence and made the West, not the Soviet Union, their source of cultural, political, and social values. In these terms, there could be no moral equivalence in the Cold War between East and West, or between Soviet and U.S. foreign policies. The tenacity of Cold War tensions rested on that fundamental reality.

The pressures that brought down the communist system came in part from this abiding hostility of the peoples of the east toward communism. But theirs was, in Vaclav Havel's term, only the "power of the powerless" to refuse to collaborate. The real force that ended the Soviet Union and Soviet domination in eastern Europe lay within the Soviet Union itself, and most especially in the expectations and plans of the new reform leadership. No popular protest forced Gorbachev to launch his radical plans. The political elite enjoyed the fruits of their privileges and powers within the land. But the incapacity of that system to sustain an effective economy, a great-power military force, or a dynamic leadership appeared so grave that Gorbachev and his supporters were prepared to take great risks to remake it. They could not overcome the nationalist loyalties of the peoples of their vast empire. That factor, more than any other, crushed their hopes for reform and destroyed the Soviet Union.

At the end of the twentieth century, nationalism in Europe was not what it had been one hundred years before. In many respects, western Europe set the model for reform in the former communist countries. Liberal democracy set the pattern for European political life. Economic activity lay increasingly in the hands of private interests. European governments had chosen to return most of their nationalized industries to private ownership, keeping only indirect controls over finances and production. Most of the countries freed from communist rule sought membership in the European Union to obtain access to markets and investments. No ideological program dominated the lives of the population of Europe or promised an end to social inequality. People directed their energies to making a better life for themselves, though they confronted in parts of Europe severe unemployment and social unrest.

The Soviet Union, the last colonial empire, had vanished. Europe's map was again divided into independent nation–states. Ethnic and national antagonism resurfaced in many parts of Europe when national liberation permitted popular wishes to be heard in eastern Europe, and when migrants appeared throughout Europe from Third World countries. But the age of nationalist wars and communist revolutions was a thing of the past. The success and popularity in the east of the European Union suggested that Europeans from east and west were prepared to look ahead to a post-national era.

DATES WORTH REMEMBERING

1952   European Coal and Steel Community formed
1952   United States tests hydrogen bombs
1955   Russia tests hydrogen bombs
1955   Khrushchev new Soviet leader
1956   Soviet repression of Hungarian revolution
1958   Soviet launching of "Sputnik" satellite
1958   European Economic Community (Common Market)
1961   Berlin wall built
1962   Cuban missile crisis
1969   Moon landing by American astronauts
1972   Nuclear arms treaty (SALT I)
1975   First Soviet space station
1975   Helsinki Agreement
1977   Parliamentary constitutional monarchy in Spain
1979   Soviet invasion of Afghanistan
1980–1982   Solidarity movement in Poland
1985–1991   Gorbachev Soviet leader
1989   Soviet troops withdraw from Afghanistan
1989   Collapse of Communist regimes in Eastern Europe
1989   Free elections in Soviet Union
1990   Reunification of Germany
1991   Election of Boris Yeltsin as President of Russia
1991   Fall of Soviet Union
1994   Treaty on European Union

RECOMMENDED READING

The Recovery of Western Europe

Denis Kavanagh, *Thatcherism and British Politics: The End of Consensus?* (2nd ed., 1990). A balanced examination of the personalities and politics behind the assault of the British welfare state.

Derek Unwin, *The Community of Europe: A History of European Integration since 1945* (1994). A careful study of the process leading from the Coal and Steel Community to the European Union. Also, *Western Europe since 1945* (3rd edition, 1981). A balanced survey of the remarkable postwar recovery of Europe.

The Soviet Union and the Cold War

Aleksandr Fursenko & Timothy Naftali, *"One Hell of a Gamble": Khrushchev, Castro, and Kennedy, 1958–1964* (1997). A revealing history of the Cuban Missile Crisis using newly opened Soviet archival materials.

*Alex Nove, *An Economic History of the USSR* (3rd edition, 1992). The best account of the rise and fall of the Soviet command economy.

Jonathan Steele, *Eternal Russia: Yeltsin, Gorbachev and the Mirage of Democracy* (1994). The best analysis, and eyewitness account, of the fall of the Soviet Union and rise of Russia, by an English journalist stationed in Moscow in those years.

*Gail Stokes, *The Walls Came Tumbling Down: The Collapse of Communism in Eastern Europe* (1994). The dramatic story of the sudden disappearance of communist regime in the late 1980s.

William Walter, *Space Age* (1992). A beautifully illustrated history of space exploration, focusing on the civilian aspects.

*Tom Wolfe, *The Right Stuff* (1979). An ironic view of the space frenzy that possessed the United States when it confronted the first Soviet space exploits.

Memoirs and Novels

*Robert Kennedy, *The Thirteen Days* (1968). Memoirs of one of the key participants in the Cuban missile crisis; also, film version (2001) with the same title.

Jack Matlock, *Autopsy on an Empire: The American Ambassador's Account of the Collapse of the Soviet Union* (1995). An American's inside view of the politics of the Gorbachev years.

CHAPTER TWELVE

Local Wars, Global Economy

THE WORLD IN THE LATE TWENTIETH CENTURY

Colonial empires had vanished from the world by the 1990s. The term "overseas" referred to distant nation-states, not to territories where an imperial state governed subject peoples. The emergence of hundreds of new nation-states in the place of the fallen empires was the most spectacular and enduring global political upheaval brought by the twentieth century.

New economic bonds replaced the old ties that empires had maintained. The term "global economy" referred both to the spread of industrial and technological innovations to countries around the world and to the growing interdependence of the economies of all the regions of the globe. All new nation-states possessed sovereign rights and flew their national flags as member states at the United Nations headquarters in New York. Their economies depended, though, on international economic relations whose centers were usually far beyond their borders. Pressure came from industrialized countries to open less developed regions to the global economy. Currency speculators paid no heed to the economic needs of the new state in their search for rewarding short-term investments. Prosperity or recession was a global process which smaller countries were powerless to influence.

The most prosperous regions included not only North America and Western Europe, but also countries around the eastern shores of the Pacific Ocean. Japan had become the first newly industrialized state in the area, followed by nations as small as Singapore and as large as China. Their increasingly important place in the global economy gave their leaders a voice in international affairs that bore little relation to the size of their national armies or military alliances. The process of national liberation from empires had divided the political map of the world into hundreds of nation-states. But the regional and global economic relations that they were drawn into were redrawing that map regardless of claims to national independence and outbursts of nationalist rivalry.

This economy operated more or less on the basis of a free market. The old trade and regulatory barriers put up during the depression by governments in capitalist lands had disappeared. The collapse of the command economies of the communist countries ended their isolation from the outside world. Their new leaders welcomed foreign investors and their new, privately owned industrial enterprises struggled to compete on the international market. On a global scale, the big economic forces were the multinational corporations, with branches, factories and sales throughout the world, and major banks and financial institutions whose investments and speculative operations moved trillions of dollars around the world in a single day. Profit set the measure of success or failure, even when the consequences were economic hardship in distant areas.

International preoccupations of the late twentieth century shifted gradually from political revolution and superpower conflict to social and economic issues. The new global concerns focused on complex questions of financial and trade ties among developed nations, the economic impact of the new electronics industry, the environmental crisis, and continuing impoverishment in areas of the Third World. Few people shared any longer the naive faith of pre-1914 Westerners in the wonders of industry and technology and in the inevitability of human progress. The consumption of energy through the burning of fossil fuels, key to the entire Industrial Revolution, had created such atmospheric pollution that it was altering the world's climate. In the closing decades of the century, the process called "globalization"

brought a vast increase in the movement of goods (such as petroleum), services (like finance and banking), peoples (especially labor migration), and air pollution, in a booming market economy linking all the major regions of the world.

The end of the Cold War closed the era of major wars and revolutions that had begun with the First World War. Many parts of the world still suffered from conflicts that erupted within a state's borders or among states within one region. Poverty, ethnic hatred, and political rivalries all in one way or another contributed to the outbreak of violence. Increasingly, countries where civil war became acute found that regional alliances or the intervention of nearby strong states was the only effective means to bring some degree of peace to their people. Where no such forces appeared, these wars endured, often until economies had decayed, cities lay in ruins, and large numbers of the population had become homeless refugees. These wars contributed to the spread of conditions so anarchic that the countries became failed states where the most essential services for their people's security and livelihood were lacking. International nongovernmental humanitarian organizations came to these dangerous regions to offer health care and food to stop hunger and disease. Their efforts, however meager, were often all that stood in the way of famine and epidemics.

In these conditions, the United Nations became more active than ever before. It was freed at last from the quarrels of the Cold War. Its Security Council received urgent pleas time and again to intervene in local and civil wars for which no easy solution existed. The 1990 seizure of the tiny state of Kuwait by the dictator of Iraq began the brief Gulf War. It ended with the triumph of a coalition of United Nations forces led by the United States and aided by, among others, the reform leaders of the Soviet Union. Hopes for a "new world order" rested on the promise of the United Nations to protect states, small and large, from aggression. Woodrow Wilson had come to Paris in 1919 to plead for such a daring innovation. The dream reappeared at the end of the century.

THE EMERGENCE OF THE GLOBAL ECONOMY

The international economy that had emerged among the Western countries in the early twentieth century gradually expanded across the globe into Asian, Latin American, and African lands. With the opening of the communist countries, it incorporated these areas as well. The United States lost its economic hegemony of mid-century after the rapid economic recovery of Europe and the emergence of new industrial regions, especially in East Asia. The political boundaries of nation-states were of less importance than regional economic groupings, usually gathered around one particularly productive, wealthy country. Japan played that role in East Asia. Germany was similarly influential in central and eastern Europe.

Within these very productive economies, major corporations accumulated enormous wealth. The economic resources of companies such as Sony in Japan, Royal Dutch-Shell in the Netherlands, or Microsoft in the United States, overshadowed in wealth the total national income of many countries. The skyscrapers of cities as distant as Tokyo, Singapore, London, and New York were headquarters to most of the multinational corporations. They were the visible sign that these places counted among the world-class cities in the new global economy.

Players in the Global Economy

The United States played a crucial role in laying the foundation for the rapid global expansion of economic production and trade in the postwar decades. The U.S. government financed international institutions for trade and lending (see Chapter 6) to spur recovery from the war. The enormous wealth of the U.S. economy made it the motor behind global economic growth. It was the principal trading partner for countries in Europe and Asia. Soon after the war the dollar became the principal international currency. It had a stable, fixed value. Until 1971, the U.S. government guaranteed one ounce of gold for $30, using the gold standard to sustain the dollar's stable value. U.S. foreign aid to European and Asian states accelerated economic growth. Japan and West Germany, once enemies of the United States, quickly became prosperous and productive centers of their regions and kept close economic ties with the United States.

Trading and investment were, as in the past, particularly vigorous between Europe and the United States. The new prosperity of Europe attracted major U.S. companies, such as General Motors and International Business Machines (IBM). Termed "multinational" because of their vast financial resources invested throughout the world, these firms set up new factories and opened new markets for their goods. Total U.S. investments in Europe jumped from $2 billion in 1950 to $60 billion in the mid-1970s, making western Europe the single most important target in the world for U.S. investors. U.S. banks set up branches in Europe to service these international financial operations. European banks and corporations utilized the U.S. dollar for their trade and financial exchanges. Europe held dollars in such quantities that their holdings earned the name of "Eurodollars."

The U.S. currency gradually lost its place as the sole money of exchange for the global economy. U.S. dollars were flowing across the Atlantic to pay for an increasing amount of imported goods. In the late 1960s, inflation in the United States began to reduce the dollar's value. At one ounce of gold for $30, the price of the dollar was too cheap. International investors and financial speculators turned increasingly to the stable, more valuable currencies of Germany and Japan. This international financial market revealed that it had a will of its own when in those years bankers and financiers abandoned their dollar holdings to buy other currencies. The shift to Japanese yen and German marks was so great that the U.S. government and central bank could no longer hold the dollar at its fixed, low value. In 1971, the U.S. government had to abandon the gold standard. It allowed the value of the dollar to fluctuate according to market demand. Soon $300 were needed to buy one ounce of gold.

For the rest of the century, no currency possessed a stable, international value. Even the U.S. dollar was subject to serious fluctuations. It remained the least risky currency, though. In countries suffering in the 1990s from high inflation, such as Russia, consumers and producers alike preferred to make their transactions in dollars (preferably in $100 bills). Certain small South American states, unable to control inflation in their own currencies, adopted the dollar as the legal medium of exchange.

Monetary instability in the late century stimulated such global currency speculation that at times it created international financial crises. In 1997 and 1998, international investors, fearful of losing money on risky loans in east and south Asian economies, suddenly withdrew their loans and "dumped" their monetary holdings in these currencies. Their massive, panicky selling caused a severe regional recession. The crisis was soon over, but the lesson was clear. The world's financial markets, where trillions of dollars were traded every day, held enormous power over the fate of peoples and countries in the 1990s.

The global economic expansion of the late century was evolving toward greater compe-

tition in foreign trade among Asian and Western countries. It also drew increasingly on technological innovation. The electronics and computer industries became the most dynamic centers of development by the 1970s. Their managers set up production in developed and developing countries, wherever costs were lowest and profits highest. American producers were forced to compete for foreign markets in a world where they no longer held the monopoly of productivity and enterprise. Financial power and technological innovation spread to Europe and East Asia. The enormous appetite in the West for petroleum poured billions of dollars into the oil-producing countries. These fundamental new conditions of global interdependence made a return to the economic isolationism of depression years unthinkable.

Beginning in the 1960s, countries of east and southeast Asia emerged as new centers of economic power and productivity. Their greatest markets were in foreign lands, and the global economy was their lifeline. Western Europe and North America had been the forces behind the growth of world trade and production until then. Alongside these areas appeared first Japan, then the countries called the "Four Dragons" (South Korea, Hong Kong, Taiwan, Singapore), and finally the most populous country in the world, China.

The simplest measure of their remarkable boom in the late twentieth century was their rate of economic growth. Each of these East Asian lands managed to reach an annual growth rate of close to 10 percent. Japan attained this extraordinary level of growth in three decades from the 1950s, the "Four Dragons" in the 1970s and 1980s, and China beginning in the late 1980s. No other region in the world had generated such rapid economic growth. In real terms, these economies were able at that rate to double their annual income every ten years. The economy of China, with a population of over 1 billion, was in the early 1990s producing each year (in total value) as much as Japan.

By that time, many regions of coastal China were more closely bound to other Pacific rim economies than to the poor interior areas of their country. The economic reforms launched by Deng Xiaoping in 1978 gradually opened the country to new private businesses. The reform Communists had firm control of the government by the mid-1990s. They welcomed foreign investors, who poured billions of dollars into the country. Their economy acquired direct access to the wealth of Hong Kong, financial center of East Asia, when Great Britain returned the tiny territory to China in 1997. Years before, wealthy Hong Kong business interests had become the major investors in the People's Republic. The products of these new enterprises found markets in the global economy, especially in the United States. The U.S. had turned into the major trading partner of China. The Chinese state still owned most of the country's major industrial enterprises. The Communists were reluctant to sell them, knowing that private owners would drastically cut back their bloated labor force and create millions of unemployed workers.

The biggest problems faced by the Chinese economy were products of rapid growth, not obsolete factories. Millions of rural migrants left their villages to seek jobs in the coastal cities' booming economy. An increasing number joined the flood of illegal migrants bound for Europe and the United States, going deeply into debt to smuggling gangs and risking death on the long trip in sealed trucks and ship containers. Those who stayed in China's cities found air and water contamination there as bad as the worst polluted urban areas in the world. Groundwater was in increasingly short supply in northern China as a result of wasteful industrial and agricultural use and popula-

tion growth. Without severe restrictions on water usage, the Chinese Academy of Science warned that by the early twenty-first century large areas of the country would face severe, prolonged drought.

Rising demand for energy to power the booming economy persuaded the Chinese government to begin construction in 1995 on the Yangtze River of the single largest hydroelectric dam in the world. Its reservoir was so vast that 5 million people had to be displaced and millions of acres of productive land were lost. The communist government gambled that it could find work for the country's enormous population by pursuing economic modernization no matter what the cost.

The economic fortunes of Russia, the other one-time great socialist society, remained bleak through most of the 1990s. While the Chinese manner of ending the command economy released dynamic and productive forces, the Russian conversion to a market economy led to a serious economic depression. The breakup of the Soviet Union (see Chapter 11) threw up barriers to trade among the newly independent republics, which once had been tightly bound together by Soviet planning and investment. The sudden end of the Cold War brought to a virtual standstill the mammoth Russian defense industry. It lost its lucrative state purchaser and lacked any experience in selling its sophisticated weapons on the international market. The most serious obstacle to Russian economic recovery was the dearth of people who knew how to make a capitalist economy function. Managers of the old state-owned industries had never learned about productivity and efficiency. Chairmen of the state-controlled collective farms had never worried about meeting the needs and tastes of Russian consumers.

The resulting economic depression lowered the country's industrial production by one-half by 1995. The people's standard of living dropped and public services deteriorated. Factories stopped paying wages and other benefits. Millions of urban Russians were forced to acquire plots of farm land to grow their own food. Around the country's major cities appeared vast open-air markets where people scrambled to sell whatever goods came to hand to earn a petty income. It seemed in some areas that Russians had reverted to a barter, or even natural economy.

A few investors, who often were closely allied with political leaders, profited greatly by the purchase of formerly nationalized enterprises, especially those controlling valuable natural resources such as oil and aluminum. One observer called the rapid, chaotic sale of state enterprises "the sale of the century." Critics of the semi-legal or illegal methods of these investors called it "gangster capitalism." These "new Russians," and a new middle class that emerged around them, were still a very small minority of the population.

The chaotic conditions extended to Russia's new democratic political institutions. Local government fell apart for lack of taxes, which most citizens and companies paid rarely or not at all. Police failed to control the growing number of criminal gangs, baptized the "Russian Mafia," and estimated to number about 500 in the mid-1990s. These gangsters prospered by extorting contributions from frightened businessmen, who risked execution if they failed to pay. Soon they branched out into international drug smuggling and prostitution rackets.

The federal government proceeded slowly to put into place the legal framework for the rule of law and for a market economy. Until the late 1990s, the parliament was a bastion of nationalists lamenting the decline of their homeland and of former Communist Party bosses chosen by rural electors. A powerful "agroindustrial" lobby defended the obsolete collective and state farms. The clearest indication of their hostility to a free market was the parliament's refusal until 2000 to approve laws permitting the purchase and sale of collective farm land.

Boris Yeltsin's election in 1996 to his second term as president of the Russian Federation was the most encouraging political development in those years. Voters had the choice between Yeltsin, promising to build a new, free Russian nation and a candidate from the revived Communist Party, whose members clung to Soviet socialist ideals and to the memory of Lenin and Stalin. Two-thirds of the electorate went to the polls, and a majority chose Yeltsin. His quarrels with the parliament and declining health produced a political stalemate in the following years, but his commitment to democratic reform remained strong.

In 1998, he attended the reburial in St. Petersburg's most historic cathedral of the remains of the last tsar, Nicholas II, and his family alongside the tombs of Russia's previous emperors. Organized by the Orthodox Church, it was an act of homage to victims of Soviet terror. For Yeltsin, it was a moment to beg his countrymen to put behind them "a century of bloodshed" and join together in constructing a country of liberty and toleration. His ultimate, dramatic gesture was to suddenly resign his office on New Year's Day, 2000. After an election campaign freer than any in the country's short history as a democracy, a large majority of electors voted for Yeltsin's heir apparent, Vladimir Putin.

Russia's democratic reforms had produced a somewhat authoritarian presidential regime, not a Western parliamentary democracy. It respected and, with some success, enforced the political and civil liberties that the reformers had introduced in the years of the Soviet Union's decline and fall. The Russian army inherited most of the armaments of the Soviet Union's armed forces. They provided the Russian government with the weapons of a superpower. Yet the land was burdened with an obsolete economy, extensive environmental pollution, and a disillusioned population forced to cope with bleak living conditions. A grim sign of the social crisis that still gripped the country was the abrupt decline of Russia's population. The rate of childbirth fell sharply, health care was a shambles, and Russians were emigrating in large numbers to the West. At the end of the century, the construction of a new Russia was only beginning.

In the entire world, only the economy of North Korea remained frozen in the socialist legacy of Stalin's revolution. The country's communist leadership clung to all the institutions that they had copied from Soviet Stalinism in the late 1940s. The result by the 1990s was impoverishment and periodic famine for the population. The collective farm system was incapable of providing adequate food. Nationalized industry barely functioned, with only armaments factories receiving substantial state subsidies to keep operating at full capacity. No foreign investors, except a few South Korean banks and the South Korean state, were prepared to risk their funds in that bankrupt economy. No foreign buyers could be persuaded to purchase its obsolete products. Only donations of food from foreign states kept the country from massive famine. The Stalinist leadership paraded their well-armed troops through the central square of the capital to impress foreign dignitaries. But behind this facade of power the country was a pathetic relic of the Soviet experiment in state socialism.

The New Industrial Revolution

Many of the twentieth century's major scientific discoveries found technological applications by the late century. The subject of modern science is too vast to be discussed here, but two topics are particularly relevant to economic and social changes of recent decades. Fundamental research in astronomy and physics had yielded comprehensive theories on the origins and physical properties of the universe. Space in immediate proximity to the earth became an arena for the development of rocketry and missiles (see Highlight, pp. 362–368). These inventions resulted directly from the nuclear arms race but also became the means for global communications and space exploration. The U.S.-manned moon landings had less influence on the global economy and new nations than the technology for instantaneous worldwide transmission of information.

In another sphere of major scientific discoveries, the biological sciences yielded insight into the very nature of life and the operations of the human mind. Understanding of the chemistry and structure of genes revealed vital information on the processes of heredity. At the same time, it made possible the manipulation of genetic material to develop medicines to cure an increasingly large number of diseases. Good health and a relatively long life became a tangible goal for an increasing proportion of the population in most countries.

The appearance of computers and telecommunications brought the countries of the world into instant contact. Through the instantaneous transmission and analysis of information from almost all parts of the globe, this new electronics industry dissolved borders and opened potential access to a vast pool of knowledge. But political and cultural barriers remained in place. Shared knowledge was restricted, imperfect, and too often misunderstood. This modern technology, like the tools of empire of the early century, was only as effective as its operators could make it. They used it primarily for the sake of the global economy.

Electronics and telecommunications did not exist as important industries until the 1950s. They began to expand at a rapid rate in direct response to new discoveries.

Technological innovations in this area combined the sophistication of rocketry and earth satellites, the extraordinary power of the computer to analyze information, telecommunications equipment for instantaneous transmission of data around the world, and the television screen. The scientific and technological work that went into these inventions was complex and expensive. It was concentrated principally in the United States and Japan, where private companies and public institutions funded extensive research. Much of the new equipment served the needs of businesses, which brought it to other countries in their trading and investment operations. In many respects, these new sectors set in motion the new industrial revolution.

Television had the greatest direct impact on popular culture in developed and developing lands. It provided the channel of communication to enlarge people's awareness of social and political conditions through images as well as the spoken word. Invented before the war, it did not spread widely among Western countries until the 1950s. Almost immediately it began to appear in the newly independent nations of the Third World.

Broadcast companies, privately owned and operated in the United States, came under state control in most countries. The cost of television production required state financing. More important, the choice and interpretation of information to be made publicly available have always been a source of power. When used to promote a political cause such as nationalism and reinforced by visual images, messages communicated by television proved the most potent tool of propaganda ever invented. Television, the most influential form of communication, quickly came to play a central role in plans for nation-building in Third World countries. A means everywhere of education and

entertainment, television represented potentially a revolutionary means of overcoming the barriers of misunderstanding and prejudice dividing peoples. At the same time, it constituted a potent force for national unification and political indoctrination.

New inventions made possible linking peoples of all countries in a network of television transmission to form what one observer termed a "global village." Communications satellites, relaying signals from one continent to another or between distant regions of one country, first went into service in 1965. Ten years later, they were in place over the Atlantic, Pacific, and Indian Oceans. Large countries such as the United States, the Soviet Union, India, and Indonesia operated their own domestic satellites. India in 1980 had fewer than 5 television sets for every 1,000 people (in the United States the proportion was 650 per 1,000). Still, the government concluded that a national television network constituted a vital part of its program to make its citizens aware of themselves as members of one Indian nation. In the early 1980s it launched its own communications satellite, which made possible one integrated national network of radio and television transmission.

Small, inexpensive satellite dishes afforded access to these programs for viewers even in countries that censored news and television programs. The booming economy of the People's Republic of China gave millions of Chinese families the means to purchase satellite dishes to view international television. The Chinese Communists objected bitterly to this "poisonous foreign cultural invasion," issuing in 1993 a law outlawing private ownership of satellite dishes. Similarly, Iran's Islamic Republic ordered Iranians to scrap their satellite dishes, used there to bypass the stultifying propaganda and heavy-handed censorship of the Muslim clerics. Both laws proved a failure. Even dictatorial regimes could not overcome the popular desire for a television window onto the outside world.

This transnational communication emphasized entertainment above all. Sports competition was especially popular. An estimated 2 billion viewers watched the 1998 World Soccer Cup matches. The principal source of foreign programs was the U.S. television industry, whose sales abroad of comedy and drama series (such as *Dallas* and *NYPD Blue*) gave viewers their most vivid pictures of life in America. National television networks attempted with their own programming to stem the flood of films, songs, sports competition, celebrities, and dress fads generated by international (largely U.S.) television entertainment. They created their own "soap operas," adapting the hugely successful American formula of T.V. serials dramatizing everyday life to their own social and cultural conditions. Yet the global popularity of the basketball player Michael Jordan and international markets for Hollywood's entertainment industry gave strong evidence of the alluring power of Western television. The last empires of the late century were media empires.

The new tools of international communication served principally business and political needs. Telecommunications became the principal application of satellite transmission, for it linked far-flung branches of multinational corporations with central offices, foreign personnel with their governments, and military units with command centers. Private industry found these tools highly valuable. Mining companies were able to conduct from space global geological surveys for deposits of valuable minerals. Access to this information remained tightly controlled, either by corporations or by states. The new communications technology, beyond the means of most Third World countries, revealed as clearly as the disparity in wealth the gap separating the developed and developing countries.

Energy in the Global Economy

Economic growth and the hope of improved living conditions for the population came increasingly to depend on the availability of energy. New forms of transportation, industrial production, lighting, and communication required ready access to energy sources. The global demand for energy expanded after the Second World War at an extremely high rate until the late 1970s, when it was four times greater than in 1950. Industrial regions had the highest consumption levels, but they rose rapidly as well in developing areas of Latin America and in the newly industrialized countries of Asia. That period witnessed a fundamental shift in the energy sources. Coal, principal fuel for the Industrial Revolution, was rapidly displaced by oil. By the 1960s, the West obtained over half its total energy from petroleum, fueling power plants, automobiles, airplanes, and industries.

Access to oil became vital to the well-being of the global economy, but only a few countries possessed major oil fields. At the beginning of the century, the United States had been the chief source of petroleum; sixty years later its oil fields were running dry. By the early 1990s, over half of its needs in petroleum products had to be met by foreign imports. The Middle East (principally Iran, Iraq, and Saudi Arabia) became the leading producers in the 1960s. The major oil corporations were no longer able to control global production and prices. Nationalization, or state regulation, of oil production facilities took place in all petroleum-producing countries in the course of that decade. Rising demand, the power of the Organization of Oil Producing Countries (OPEC), and periodic wars in the Middle East sent prices soaring

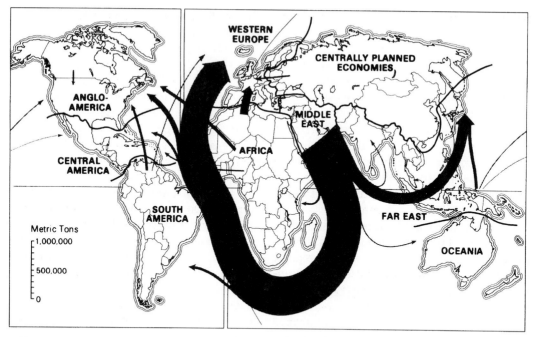

Major International Petroleum Movements, 1974

from their low level of $3 per barrel to $14 in the mid-1970s. The Iranian revolution and Iran-Iraq war forced prices for a time to $30. Rapid inflation in the developed countries and hardship in the poorer countries were the result. Oil-dependent countries recognized the urgent need to search for other means to power economic growth.

For a time, nuclear power appeared the most alluring alternative energy source. The program of "atoms for peace," funded by the U.S. government, promised technological marvels, among which the most hopeful was electricity generated by nuclear reactors. Nuclear power plants began to appear in large numbers in the 1960s; by the late 1990s, over 400 plants were in operation around the world. Their power output represented the energy equivalent to the total yearly production from the world's major oil country, Saudi Arabia. France implemented

the most comprehensive program, obtaining in the late 1980s over two-thirds of its total electricity from nuclear plants.

By then, however, many other countries had cut back or stopped nuclear power development. The new technology hid risks of grave accidents and its cost had become appreciably greater than other energy sources for electricity generation. Heightened concern over safety led to complex design changes and delays in plant construction that raised expenses. The nuclear accidents at Three-Mile Island in the United States in 1979 and at Chernobyl in the Soviet Union in 1986 raised public concern around the world about the very feasibility of safe nuclear power. A few countries, notably France and Japan, with well-run nuclear programs and a great need to reduce oil imports, continued their reliance on nuclear reactors. People and states throughout the world confronted painful economic choices touching their everyday lives as a result of their growing reliance on new sources of power to sustain satisfactory levels of production and consumption.

The rising demand for energy posed the crucial problem of the depletion of nonrenewable resources. Two directions were open to make better use of energy, one through conservation and the other through new technology for energy efficiency. The sudden rise of oil prices in the 1970s increased costs to a point where efficiency in energy use became a national priority in the industrial countries. The United States, having for a century expended its coal and petroleum at a prolific pace, began a major program of energy savings in industrial and home use and in transportation. In the decade between 1973 and 1983, it reduced energy consumption (measured in relation to gross national product) by one-fourth and curtailed its use of petroleum by one-fifth. This trend constituted a Conservation Revolution as important to future world development as the Green Revolution in food production.

New technology created opportunities for enlarging access to necessary resources and for the substitution of new resources still in abundant supply. The petroleum industry developed complex machinery to move their oil drilling into harsh environments, including offshore areas and sites in Arctic lands. The Alaska and the North Sea oil fields, both developed in the 1970s, became the last great Western oil discoveries. After the fall of the Soviet Union, the new governments of Central Asia invited Western companies to send geologists to search for oil in areas around the Caspian Sea, thought to hold vast reserves. When they had completed their analysis, the oil companies announced that they had discovered oil and natural gas fields with reserves as large as those of North America and Europe's North Sea area combined.

These discoveries promised adequate oil for the first decades of the twentieth-first century. Rising global production combined with conservation policies brought crude oil prices below $20 by the late 1980s. Oil prices remained stable through most of the 1990s and supplies abundant. In the mid-1990s, the international price of oil was nearly as low (when adjusted for two decades of inflation) as it had been in the early 1970s. Petroleum fueled the global economic boom of that decade. But that period of rapid growth sent oil demand rising. Once again, OPEC was able to use its power as a cartel to help push crude oil prices up, briefly reaching $35 in 2000.

The return of high oil prices forced countries to ask the question whether their plans for economic development had hit the barrier of limited resources. The answer in the late twentieth century was encouraging. As a result of technological discoveries, the prices of all basic resources needed for the global economy declined between the 1970s and 1990s. New plastics found many industrial applications in place of expensive metals. The risks posed by wasteful production and consumption were increasingly clear in environmental pollution and periodic shortages. Warnings from scientists of global warming led governments to explore the means of slowing or even reducing energy use from polluting sources, but the cost was high. These troubling conditions made the conservation programs of the 1970s a lesson to be relearned again at the end of the century. "Sustainable" economic growth, defined as growth limited by the need to protect natural resources and the human environment, set the sober but realistic limits on the global economy's capacity to offer the world's peoples a better life in the twenty-first century.

≋ HIGHLIGHT: The Global Environment ≋

Economic growth and the rapid expansion of the world's population came at a high price for the earth's environment. Before the twentieth century, the greatest environmental disruptions were caused by global natural forces such as volcanic eruptions and severe droughts; humanity acquired that dubious distinction in the last century. By the 1950s, the land, water, and air on all continents were showing the obvious, ugly signs of serious damage. In turn, this environmental decay contributed directly to loss of natural resources, the spread of infectious disease, and permanent changes in the earth's climate.

The origins of these problems differed substantially between developed countries, where environmental decline resulted primarily from high energy consumption and the wastefulness of consumer societies, and the Third World, where the principal causes lay in unregulated economic development and in the pressures generated by the population explosion, urban overcrowding, and impoverishment. Industrialists eager for profit had disregarded the deterioration caused by their enterprises. But state-run command economies of the Soviet Union and Eastern Europe proved equally destructive of the environment during their decades of intensive growth. Environmental problems intruded on people's lives in ways and to an extent never before experienced, disrupting the ordinary activities of billions of people and reaching into the least populated parts of the globe. Its global character was readily apparent in the pollution of the atmosphere.

The smokestack had been the symbol of the Industrial Revolution from the start. It re-leased the gases produced by coal-fueled steam engines powering factories and lighting streets and homes. The exhaust gases coming from the burning of refined petroleum by internal combustion and diesel engines marked in its smelly way the twentieth-century consumer societies. The consumption of these fossil fuels left its visible traces in the smog that was at the origin of London's nineteenth-century "pea-soup" fog, and that hung like a dirty haze over the major cities of the world a century later.

Even in the nineteenth century, a few scientists had pointed out that the accumulation of these gases, consisting primarily of carbon dioxide, would in the long run act like a blanket around the earth, altering the global climate and raising average temperatures. Until the late twentieth century, these forecasts were not substantiated by tangible evidence understandable to governments and to the public alike. Economic growth remained a key to public policy and private investments in the industrial countries. It was a vital goal for underdeveloped nations. Industrialization and rising levels of consumption were impossible without increased energy consumption from fossil fuels. In the global economy of the late century, its use was limited only by market prices and accessibility.

Awareness of the dangers of atmospheric pollution rose in the 1980s and 1990s as a result both of the work of scientists and of the concern of populations suffering the painful physical effects of a fouled atmosphere. The chemical process destroying the ozone layer was discernible only to the sophisticated equipment of researchers. By the mid-1980s, they were able to establish the direct link between the diffusion (through evaporation) of manufactured coolants, especially in air conditioning, and the decline of atmospheric ozone vital in protecting the earth from intensive solar radiation. Once understood, the problem became the subject of international conferences. Governments and manufacturers reached agreement in 1987 to end the production and use of these coolants by the end of the century. Their collaboration achieved an international treaty on a critical global environmental issue for the first time.

The increase in atmospheric pollution by carbon gases raised far more difficult questions. These touched on the very quality of life of both developed and developing countries. The level of carbon dioxide in the air in the 1990s was twenty-five times that of a century before. Western countries bore the major responsibility for this swift rise. Their prosperous economies depended increasingly on road transportation, which was a major cause of carbon dioxide pollution. The United States alone produced one-third of the total carbon emissions in the world. Third World countries produced ever more air pollution in the last third of the century. Their lack of modern technology and the pressure for economic growth at all cost prevented them from introducing serious pollution control measures. By the late century, their combined emissions were nearly equal to those of the Western countries.

In the mid-1990s, scientific findings uncovered clear signs of significant global warning. This evidence included melting of Antarctic and Arctic ice packs, severe summer heat waves, and greater storminess in northern and southern hemispheres. In 2000, the United Nations Panel on Climate Change published the definitive report on global warming, which it attributed to human deeds. Average air temperatures were rising everywhere, including the Antarctic and Arctic regions. Greenhouse gases, of which carbon dioxide was by far the most damaging, were the principal cause. And the consequences were already apparent in melting of the earth's ice caps, the increasing severity of storminess, and the rising level of the earth's oceans.

In this process, the destruction of the tropical forests played its own important part. The causes at work here included both the desperate search for resources on the part of impoverished populations in the Third World, and the appetite for forest products of the expanding global economy. The Brazilian settlers moving into the rainforest areas of Amazonia, and Indonesian farmers starting a new life in the forests of Sumatra, burned millions of acres of forest each year to begin farming. Their action helped to destroy a unique environment, and poured billions of tons of carbon dioxide into the air. Spurred on by the growing demand for wood, international lumber companies purchased enormous rainforest properties, first cutting the trees then burning the undergrowth to sell the land to agribusiness or small farmers. Their destructive burning of Indonesian forests produced smog so severe over a vast region inhabited by over 100 million people that in 1997 the government of Indonesia issued a public apology. But its own policies of support for big business and incentives for emigration from its overpopulated central islands to Sumatra and Borneo lay at the heart of this environmental crisis.

The rapid loss of forests around the world was harmful both because it devastated an invaluable resource and because it led to pollution of the air, the land, and the water.

In many parts of Africa and Asia, trees and bushes became the sole source of heating fuel as impoverishment and growing rural populations made other sources of heat inaccessible. The disappearance of forests brought decay of farmland, eroded by rains and overworked by struggling farmers. Tropical forests acted as powerful agents absorbing vast amounts of carbon dioxide. Their absence further accelerated the atmospheric accumulation of greenhouse gases. These forests were as well a treasure house of natural products useful to the health and well-being of populations. Once gone, the forests' treasures would be lost as well.

Water pollution and overuse were equally serious sources of environmental degradation. Growing shortages of water in areas such as the Ganges River basin and Tigris and Euphrates rivers in the Middle East became a serious political issue. Access to water in semidesert areas of rapid population growth and economic development became so critical that water was "more precious than oil." In the 1980s, the government of Turkey began the most ambitious water control project yet attempted in any non-Western country. It started construction of 20 dams, hydroelectric generators, and irrigation canals along the headwaters of the Tigris and Euphrates rivers, whose sources lay in Turkey's eastern mountains. By the end of the century, this Southeast Anatolia Project had completed half of its major projects. It was already bringing tangible economic benefits to a vast semidesert region, long stripped of its trees and topsoil by overfarming and deforestation. Land was again becoming fertile through irrigation, cheap electric power was fueling industrialization, and the region's peoples (including millions of Kurds) saw an escape

to their age-old impoverishment. The Project directors even began selling water (by the boatload) to thirsty Mediterranean lands such as Israel.

The price of their success was the limitation of water supplies to downstream regions of Syria and Iraq. Turkey's great dams promised a better life for some peoples, at the expense of those peoples living on the lower reaches of the rivers. Collaborative water agreements with Syria and Iraq might protect the well-being of these peoples; war for water was a real possibility too.

The need for international compromise on water use brought India and Bangladesh to just such an agreement. When India built a major dam on the lower Ganges River, Bangladesh faced severe water shortages for its people and crops. A 1996 treaty between the two states guaranteed that the water would be shared fairly. The problem of sharing would reemerge if their growing populations' needs exceeded the available water. By the end of the century, about one-half of the world's population faced a serious deficit of usable water.

Epidemic diseases in the Third World were inextricably bound up with water, air, and land pollution. Rivers filled with silt from deforested lands and from the pollutants of new factories and untreated human waste. Water drawn from these sources became a source of infectious disease and physical deformities for the population living along polluted rivers such as the Yangtze in China and the Ganges in India. Infectious diseases flourished from the untreated sewage and polluted air in enormous cities such as Cairo and Bombay, to which many millions of rural inhabitants migrated to escape the misery of village life. Countries such as India confronted the recurrence of diseases, such as the bubonic plague, that medical experts had thought forever eliminated by public health and modern medicine. In these terms, the most critical environmental needs at the close of the twentieth century were found in the Third World.

Economic development was a global dilemma as well as a promise. Progress had for a century been defined in large measure as the improvement of economic well-being. The newly independent countries of the Third World subscribed as fervently to that creed as did the West. Their leaders argued in fact that their needs for economic growth were a matter of survival as much as well-being because of the widespread poverty of their populations. They argued that the West had to make the greatest adjustments to low growth. Its total contribution to global pollution was largest by far and its skills were more readily applicable to energy conservation and pollution control. Yet the scale of the problem was so great that no international solution could succeed without the cooperation of all sides.

Two centuries before, an English physician, Thomas Malthus, had warned of an environmental crisis in his country. He calculated that the population was multiplying faster than food supplies necessary to meet their basic needs. The Industrial Revolution and the demographic transition in the West to low birthrates had proven him wrong. At the close of the twentieth century, however, the Malthusian trap was closing again. To address the global environmental crisis, effective solutions could come only on a global scale. These had to include both severe population limits and sweeping technological adjustments to restrain energy consumption and to protect the global environment.

Awareness of the seriousness of the crisis brought together representatives from around the world at the first United Nations Conference on Environment and Development in 1992. This so-called "Earth Summit," attended by the heads of over 100 countries, heard conflicting arguments. Environmentalists demanded immediate measures to protect nature, while Third World leaders insisted that only economic growth could overcome the distress of their peoples and create the financial means to halt pollution. Representatives from developed countries defended the high standard of living of their populations. The conference was unable to agree on measures to halt the degradation of land and water. It did finally put together a Global Warming Convention that called for a halt to the global rise of carbon dioxide emissions by the end of the century.

Measures to achieve this objective had to come from both developing and developed countries. Another conference in 1997 in Kyoto, Japan, produced an agreement by the industrialized states to initiate the painful steps to curb global warning. Their promise was to reduce by 2010 fossil fuel emissions in their countries to levels below those of 1990. Third World governments agreed to join the effort afterwards. They put off until 2000 a specific agreement on how this drastic and painful transformation was to occur. At the conference in 2000 in The Hague, Netherlands, negotiations on measures curtailing greenhouse gases fell apart over disagreements on how each developed country should actually meet the ambitious goal set at Kyoto. Demonstrators there from the world's environmental defense organizations warned that "the earth is in danger!" Negotiators from the United States, which remained the principal source of greenhouse gases, came to the conference knowing that the U.S. Congress was opposed to any treaty curtailing energy so severely as to threaten the country's economic growth. The global environment remained hostage to national interests.

Success in saving the earth's environment demanded the voluntary cooperation of states to introduce new energy policies. It also called for the collaboration of peoples around the world to practice conservation in their daily lives. It needed technological solutions for alternative energy sources. The environmental crisis required international collaboration on a scale never seen since the Second World War. The stakes in this crisis were as high as the outcome of the war had been. The consequences of defeat were ominous for the future of humanity.

The Move toward Global Free Trade

The global economy of the late twentieth century differed in important ways from the international economy of the early century. For the first time, businesses could disperse their economic activities throughout the world. Corporate headquarters clustered in a small number of cities. Financial operations and factory production gradually moved far from these centers into countries where labor was least expensive and governments granted special benefits to investors. The laboring population of towns in Mexico where factories manufactured car parts were from this perspective next to the Detroit headquarters of the major U.S. automobile corporations.

Because the most inexpensive labor was found in Third World countries, the operations of international corporations—notably those in textiles, automobiles, and electronics—split between executive and research offices in home countries and production in distant lands. These interregional operations were known as "global factories." U.S. corporations tended to look to Latin America for sites for factories. Japan increasingly occupied the leading trade, financial, and industrial role in southeast Asia. German companies began to move into eastern Europe in the late 1980s. Regional economic formations slowly emerged around one dominant country. These corporate giants operated in a world market but remained rooted in their country of origin.

A second characteristic of the global economy was the scope and ease of trading and exchanges in goods and services from country to country. The barriers that had divided national economies in the 1930s had crumbled by the late century. All the major developed countries, except for the communist lands, moved toward the reduction or elimination of tariffs on imported goods. The Global Agreement on Trade and Tariffs (GATT), formed by the western countries in the late 1940s to fight a return to 1930s protectionism, played an important role in this process. It sponsored a general reduction in tariffs in the early 1960s. This was followed by an even more substantial international tariff reduction in 1994. By then, the Agreement included over 100 countries from around the world.

The goal was to let trading and production be decided not by state regulations but by market forces. Factories would open and close according to profit and productivity. Price increases on goods would be kept in check by foreign imports, helping to reduce inflation and, ideally, the cost of living. World trade doubled in volume in the prosperous last decade of the century. Benefits were unevenly distributed, though. Half of the total world exports originated during that decade from the European Union and the United States. Global free trade was a formula weighted in favor of the industrialized countries.

Opposition to the end of protectionist and restrictive trade policies remained strong. Labor unions in developed countries objected to competition from lands where wages were low. Environmental groups protested the weakness, or nonexistence, in GATT of provisions for environmental protection and pollution control. In Europe, decades of special government subsidies and other protective measures for producers stood in the way of freer trade. These privileges slowly diminished as European unification proceeded and barriers fell to competition of imported goods from Asia and the United States. Still, many European countries remained afflicted by what critics called "Eurosclerosis."

Regional groupings were another arena of free trade. The expansion of the European Economic Community (European Union) showed the way. Its success, and the dismal economic results of protectionism led other areas to repeat this formula. Latin America ceased being a continent of hostile states after they moved in the 1980s to free market economies and democratic governments. Economic cooperation was built on these shared values and institutions. Brazil, Argentina, Paraguay, and Uruguay created their own common market in 1995. To the north, the 1994 North American Free Trade Agreement (NAFTA) set in motion the elimination of trade barriers among Mexico, the United States, and Canada.

Regional economic collaboration was weak where economies were underdeveloped and a large portion of the population was impoverished. These dangers emerged within NAFTA shortly after the treaty was signed. Life among the Mexican population of 100 million resembled in many ways conditions in Third World lands. Its government had grand visions of economic benefits from regional trade and investments from American and Canadian companies. But in 1995, these investors (as well as wealthy Mexicans) withdrew billions of dollars from Mexico when they began to doubt the glowing promises of quick profits made by the government. The Mexican currency lost half its value, undermining the government's economic plans and threatening the value of other Latin American currencies.

This "run" on the Mexican peso created a major international financial crisis. It was so serious that President Clinton decided to offer a 12-billion-dollar loan from U.S. government funds to protect the Mexican economy. Nothing like this had ever happened before. The backing of the United States and severe Mexican austerity measures ended the crisis, and the Mexican government repaid the loan within two years. The price was a painful two-year recession in Mexico.

The global economy brought with it the threat of unexpected financial crises caused by the rapid movement of speculative and investment funds around the world. In the 1990s, bankers and financiers from developed regions sought high profits for their investment funds in rapidly developing countries. They had strong encouragement from Western governments, which anticipated the diplomatic benefits of close financial ties with countries baptized "emerging markets." Under pressure from the U.S. government, the governments of Thailand, Indonesia, and South Korea opened their economies to foreign financial interests ready to make short-term loans at high interest rates. Investors made similar reckless loans to the Russian Republic. Risks were high, even among the productive Asian economies. At the time, Western investors preferred to turn a blind eye to signs that the debt burden in these countries was too great for the economies to sustain.

The "Asian way" of capitalism in states such as Japan, South Korea, and Thailand hid grave defects. The most serious were corporate secrecy and collusion between government leaders and favored business interest to extort high profits from protected industries. This "crony capitalism" revealed its flaws in country after country in the late 1990s. The Japanese economy was the first to suffer from reckless investments and government protection. The weakness of the Japanese economy made foreign investors worry about loans elsewhere in Asia. By 1997, they decided to pull out their funds, especially their short-term loans, fearing that their investments had become too risky. Panic selling by foreign investors spread to countries throughout the region. Within the space of a few months they had withdrawn $20 billion in investments. The result was a major financial crisis, in which stock markets lost half their value, banks went bankrupt, and the value of local currencies collapsed. The crisis spread to Russia, where the ruble lost half its exchange value in a few days and the government defaulted (that is, stopped payment) on its foreign debt.

The consequences of the crisis were everywhere similar: Imports shrank, companies went bankrupt, and millions of workers lost their jobs. Prosperity turned into a recession. Recovery required international cooperation, which was slow in coming. The Japanese government refused to provide rescue funds in the form of low-cost loans, for its own economy was stagnant and its budget in deficit. The International Monetary Fund, with financial backing from the U.S. government, did offer loans, but at such strict conditions that the recession worsened. Substantial recovery began only in 2000. The events of 1997 and 1998 revealed that the success of the global economy rested on fragile foundations. They also made clear that, in developing countries, the free market economy's promise of a "pot of gold at the end of the rainbow" was an illusion.

The third new trait of international economic relations in the late twentieth century was the ongoing coordination by the major industrial states of their policies in the areas of trade, finance, and economic aid. The well-being of all developed countries depended on the stability of global economic relations. Complex international economic operations in finance and investment were beyond the control of any individual government. Memories of the chaos of trade and finance in the 1930s haunted political leaders and industrialists alike. Regional conflicts and revolutionary movements in the newly decolonized world aroused fears of new obstacles to economic development. To give some order to global economic relations, the leaders of the seven major industrial states (the Western powers and Japan) began in the 1970s to meet regularly to discuss common industrial, financial, and trade problems.

Their basic goal was to keep intact the foundations of the global economy. These included the relatively free movement of goods and capital, the stability of the most important currencies, and the opening of economies around the world to private investors and industrialists. Their cooperation did facilitate ongoing economic operations. It was based upon a recognition of common economic interests and a shared commitment to liberal capitalism.

Their concerns included economic problems in the Third World. In the global economy, their countries' economic fortunes did feel the impact of prosperity or depression in underdeveloped lands. The unpaid debts owed their banks by Third World states (particularly in Africa) totaled nearly $100 billion by the late 1980s, with no chance of full repayment. In 1996, the "Group of Seven" offered to cancel $25 billion of their debts, on condition the governments adopt free market reforms. Economic aid to impoverished peoples did not drive their efforts. Private investment was the Group of Seven's preferred method of assistance to developing countries. Their financial advisers had become increasingly discouraged by the large amounts of aid wasted in many Third World countries by corrupt regimes. Their choice revealed to what extent the commitment to foreign aid had been replaced by concern over global finances and market economies.

The Third World itself altered dramatically as some areas, such as East Asia, began rapid economic growth. Other countries where poverty remained widespread, such as Brazil and India, fostered the new industrial revolution. It took hold in Indian cities such as Bombay and Bangalore, where an entire computer programming industry grew up in large measure to collaborate with computer companies such as Microsoft. These trends were the work of private investors, large and small, seeking profitable ventures and a cheap labor force. Economists foresaw a time in the early twenty-first century when India and Brazil, as well as Indonesia and Russia, would become among the most productive emerging economies in the world.

The Third World became those impoverished regions where modern industry was missing and where jobs were either unavailable or insufficient to meet the needs of the growing population. Legally or illegally, people from these poor regions set out for more prosperous lands in search of well-paying jobs. Gradually the global economy acquired what in essence was a global, or regional, labor force. The total number of these international migrants was estimated to have reached 100 million by the mid-1990s. In the previous two decades, over 20 million people arrived in the United States, most from Third World regions. This sudden influx produced a greater number of immigrants than in any comparable period in U.S. history. Similar trends were apparent in other developed lands.

Cities such as Paris, Berlin, New York, London, and Los Angeles were centers for this migration. It put in their midst a Third World laboring population. But these migrants appeared everywhere jobs were available. In the North African country of Libya, rich in petroleum, migrants from sub-Saharan Africa came in the 1980s and 1990s to fill the menial jobs that Libyans no longer accepted. They stayed until large-scale anti-immigrant riots forced them to flee in 2000. Similar violence against Third World migrants erupted in Europe as well in the 1990s. Social tensions rooted in hostility toward these alien intruders exposed the ethnic antagonisms hidden beneath the surface of prosperous countries.

In the expansion of the global economy lay also one hope for finding the means to restrain the expansion of the world's population. Where a better life appears a reality and a family has access to the means to ensure that life, fewer children become a desirable choice. This simple formula was proving its potent effect throughout the world. It depended upon the coincidence of many conditions, including medical care, civil order, literacy, women's rights, as well as a growing economy.

It was an important theme of the 1994 International Conference on Population and Development. Included in its final program was the injunction to include women in all development programs. Without their full participation, no effective population limits could come voluntarily. The proposal had the great advantage of relying on the free choice of people given the incentive as well as the encouragement to take control of their personal fate. In doing so, they would contribute to the well-being of their country, and ultimately of the globe. It was a great distance from the global economy to this level of individual choice, but the linkage was already taking shape.

LOCAL WARS AND PEACEKEEPING

The collapse of the Soviet Union left only the United States with the economic resources and the military might of a superpower. The global competition between the two states had sustained fears of nuclear war and had led them to take opposite sides in brief local wars in the Third World. Their influence among small states had for a time held conflicts in check by strengthening the regime in power with economic aid and military supplies. Within multiethnic communist lands, especially the Soviet Union and Yugoslavia, the one-party dictatorship had repressed the hostility dividing their diverse ethnic populations. When these states collapsed, that hostility quickly exploded in civil war. Among new Asian and African nation–states, similar conditions of ethnic conflict, violence, and political decay threatened the complete collapse of state authority and order. Their disintegration was at times halted by the intervention of strong neighboring states. The 1990s was a time of new wars as well as global economic expansion.

Failed States and Regional Peacekeeping

Local and ethnic conflicts erupted in countries around the world in the 1990s. By one count, they numbered nearly fifty, in-cluding civil war in the former state of Yugoslavia, the ongoing conflict in Afghanistan for a successor government to the communist regime, and the ethnic massacre in the African republic of Rwanda. These wars originated in the demand by one people to separate political recognition, even to the right to a separate state. In places, they were the result of brutal efforts by the regime in power to repress minority peoples. In Afghanistan, an Islamic movement called the Taliban conquered the entire country and instituted the rigorous laws of an Islamic Republic. In some African states, Islamic movements attempted also to replace civil law by Muslim law, producing civil disorder when Christian communities objected. Woodrow Wilson's call for national self-determination proved in these conditions incapable of ensuring elementary conditions of peace and security for the population.

In some cases, former imperial states sent troops into lands, once their colonial territories, to attempt to end ethnic and civil strife. Their interest in their areas emerged out of diplomatic and political ambitions and was strongly influenced as well by economic interests. The fall of empire left behind economic enterprises in mining and trading activities still owned by the former colonial people. In places large populations from the former colonial state had not left, and looked to their homeland for protection in times of crisis. Diplomatic ties between the former empire and the liberated colonies encouraged both sides to expect (or fear) continued political and military intervention. Former imperial states kept a sort of paternalistic interest in areas that they hoped to keep within their sphere of influence.

In the multiethnic borderlands of the former Soviet Union, political and ethnic violence flared up sporadically after 1991. The Russian Federation, heir to the Soviet Union's great power standing, intervened in civil disorders in regions of the Caucasus mountains and Central Asia in the 1990s. The borders that divided the new states of the area were the product of the Soviet state's policy (one applied by the Yugoslav communist government) of dividing its peoples into ethnoterritorial republics (see Chapter 2). These lands had boundaries that, despite all the efforts of Soviet mapmakers, could not form territories with ethnically uniform populations. Given the diversity of peoples living there, the task was an impossible one. The fall of the Soviet Union left these new states with ethnically diverse populations, often with large numbers of Russians or Ukrainian who had moved there in search of jobs. Minority peoples raised demands for special rights. In a few cases, governments of the new nation-states attempted to seize border areas from neighboring states where large groups of their own people lived.

Ethnic nationalism was the foundation of these successor states. In the region of the Caucasus mountains, Armenia and Azerbaijan fought a small-scale war between 1991 and 1994 over a remote area within Azerbaijan inhabited largely by Armenians. Armenian forces were victorious, forcing Azerbaijan troops to abandon the region. In the course of the war hundreds of thousands of Armenians and Azeris, who had lived at peace in the neighboring state during the Soviet period, had to flee to their homeland to escape persecution by the majority people. A war between two ethnically different communities forced populations to undergo what came to be known as "ethnic cleansing," dispossessing ethnic minorities of their homes and forcing them to live as refugees in the state belonging to their people. No peace treaty ended the hostilities, but the fighting stopped. The Azerbaijan government turned its attention to encouraging foreign petroleum companies to exploit its rich oil fields, and abandoned the war. The flow of oil through pipelines across the Caucasus region to Western markets was more important than disputed land to governments in the area. Western governments and international oil corporations spoke a language of peace and profits. In that region, the development of the oil industry was the best guarantee that the fighting was over.

At times, the Russians came at the invitation of the new leaders. At other times, they manipulated the local conflicts to impose their presence on the warring parties. In the Central Asian state of Tajikistan, powerful clans and former communists struggled to take power of the new nation-state. Long before the Russian conquest of the region in the nineteenth century, the Muslim faith had spread among the population. When the Soviet Union collapsed, a Muslim movement emerged there seeking to use the state to strengthen the Islamic bonds among the population. It, too, joined in the fighting. The war dragged on for years and left hundreds of thousands of refugees scattered throughout the region.

The Russian Federation, the only peacekeeper, encouraged negotiations and allowed arms to reach its favored militia force. It allied itself to the forces of former communists, with whom it had strong bonds. In 1997, an agreement among the warring Tajik clans to share power reduced the level of violence to a point where the country could begin to rebuild. Banditry and kidnapping remained the livelihood of some of the former warlords. Russian troops had permanent garrisons there to hold down the violence, and keep this failed state intact. There, as in other failed states, political leadership depended on conciliating and appeasing competing clans and tribes. The nation existed only in the imagination of those who dreamed of a community capable of healing the wounds and overcoming the flaws of unsuccessful state-building.

Across the border from Tajikistan, Islamic forces seized control of Afghanistan in the late 1990s. The Taliban ("students") movement had emerged out of the religious schools in Pakistan. They were drawn from the Afghan refugees who had fled the civil war against the Communist forces and Soviet troops in the 1980s. Within a few years, the Afghan refugee population numbered 1.5 million, some in Iran but most in Pakistan. The Soviet army's departure in 1989 left the country as prey to competing armed groups, united earlier only by opposition to the Communists. Civil war spread, increasing the suffering of the population.

Fervent Muslims made up the bulk of the Taliban forces. Their militant faith had inspired them in the war against the "godless" Communists. After the fall of the Communists, this same faith swelled to envisage the religious renewal of all Afghanistan under their leadership. They were Muslim fundamentalists and patriotic Afghans. The Pakistan government gave them sanctuary and secret military support when their army invaded Afghanistan in 1995. They obtained military and financial aid of Muslim fundamentalists in the Middle East.

By 1997, they had defeated the rival armies. Though the country was in ruins, they immediately set about creating the foundations for an Afghan Islamic Republic. They enforced strict Islamic law on the population. Women were confined to home and the family, forced to leave behind schooling or work. Criminal law followed traditional Muslim rules, with mutilation and stoning for serious offenses.

The Taliban's militant opposition to the West attracted self-proclaimed warriors against modernity. The wealthy Saudi Arabian, Osama bin Laden, established there the headquarters for his terrorist organization, which was implicated in attacks on targets as far away as U.S. embassies in Africa and the World Trade Center in New York City. Islamic fighters from Tajikistan and the Caucasus found refuge there as well.

Refugees from Afghan-Soviet War: Refugee Camps, Iran, 1985 (*UNHCR/16045/11.1986/A. Hollmann*)

The Taliban had no plans for economic development. In that war-torn country, the peasant farmers in desperate need of income reverted to their traditional crop of opium. Taliban leaders were opposed to the effects of drug trading and addiction in their part of the world. Despite their concern about their desperate need of taxes from the Afghan population, they acted to end opium growing in their country, once the principal source of the world's supply of heroin. The Russian and Central Asian states found common cause in attempting to close the borders with Afghanistan. They feared the spread of Islamic revolution, and fought to contain the secret drug smuggling out of Afghanistan to Russia and the West. The Soviet empire had vanished, but the diplomatic and military influence of Russia along its borderlands continued to hold in place some pieces of the old imperial realm.

Maintaining peace among the successor states of the Soviet Union under these conditions depended above all on keeping in place the existing political boundaries. The stability of these borders was the sole assurance that an entire region would not erupt in war. Millions of Russians lived as new minorities within the neighboring states of Ukraine and Kazakhstan. Some Russians there demanded that their area be annexed by Russia. The Russian government refused, content with the promise from these governments that they would respect the rights of this minority people. The decision proved correct. Except for the Armenian-Azerbaijan conflict, no wars among the former Soviet republics disrupted the difficult transition to independence. National liberation of minorities in neighboring nation-states was less important than maintaining civil order in the midst of the economic ruins of the fallen Soviet empire.

The Warring Peoples of the Balkans

The conflicts among peoples in the former Yugoslavia proved the tragic consequences of redrawing state borders to appease nationalist passions. The bloody civil wars that erupted after the fall in 1991 of the Yugoslav federation were the result of rivalries among nationalist leaders seeking new borders to unite the separate peoples each in their own nation-state. The communist rulers of Yugoslavia, heirs to the South Slav (Yugoslav) state formed in 1919, had managed to hold together various Slavic-speaking peoples of the Balkan area in one federal state (see Chapter 6). Tito, the founder of the communist movement and head of postwar Yugoslavia, enjoyed enormous personal authority among the peoples there.

After his death in 1980, his communist successors proved weak, turning each to their particular national republic to hold onto power. When the Soviet Union fell apart, disagreements among them grew so acute that they could not preserve the federal structure that held together the various republics. They allowed the people of each national republic in 1990 to vote on membership in Yugoslavia. Two (Slovenia and Croatia) immediately chose to leave. In 1991, their leaders formed independent nation–states, and the other republics soon followed (see map of Europe, 1992, p. 374). Each contained substantial minority populations from neighboring republics. The nationalist vision of ethnically pure territory went counter to the realities of ethnic intermarriage, migrations, and the generations-old persistence of ethnically mixed communities in the Balkan region.

Slobodan Milosovic, one of the survivors of the collapse of the Yugoslav state, made the defense of "Greater Serbia" his political rallying cry. He changed political persuasion from Yugoslav Communist to Serbian nationalist. Serbian history had been marked for centuries by foreign conquest, followed by popular revolts. In the First World War Serbs had fought against the Austrian-Hungarian Empire for national freedom for South Slavs. That history inspired Milosovic and his nationalist followers in 1992 to demand that all Serbian people live in one "greater" (i.e., enlarged) Serbian state. The weakness of the neighboring successor states convinced Milosovic that the plan could succeed. His nationalist ambitions destroyed the last hope for the preservation of peaceful relations among the peoples there. War had begun in 1914 when a Serbian terrorist had assassinated the Austrian-Hungarian Grand Duke in the Bosnian capital of Sarajevo. War began again in 1991 in the same region over Serbian efforts to expand their rule into the areas where large numbers of Serbians lived.

The small neighboring republic of Bosnia became the place where Serbian nationalism produced the worst fighting and bloodshed. It was a multiethnic land, divided among a Muslim population (labeled Muslim because they belonged to a distinct community, not because they all were practicing Muslims) in small majority, and large numbers of Serbs and Croatians. In 1992, the Serbian republic and Bosnian Serbs joined forces to take large areas of Bosnia under their control. Arms and military forces from the old Yugoslav army (largely Serbian) went into Serbian-inhabited areas of Bosnia. Armed groups of Serbs began a systematic effort to expel Muslims. Their "ethnic cleansing" included killing, rape, and intimidation on a massive scale. Its purpose was to force the bulk of the Muslims to flee into a small territory of their own and leave the Serbs in sole possession of most of Bosnia. The Serb forces put under siege the capital city, Sarajevo (site of the 1984 Winter Olympics). The Croatian government launched its own ethnic cleansing campaign, expelling Serbs from its territory and seizing parts of Bosnia where many Croatians lived. The Muslim government of Bosnia organized an army and fought desperately to defeat Serbs and Croats. Its forces employed at times methods as brutal as their opponents. Respect for innocent civilians and simple pity vanished in a ruthless civil war.

Reckless, ambitious political leaders started the process leading to civil war in former Yugoslavia. Antagonism among ethnic groups had remained alive despite three generations of peaceful life in the federation. Neighbors began to fear one another in a process fueled by demagogic calls for violence. Only small groups of soldiers carried on the battle. The civilian majority was unwilling to participate for fear of suffering for a cause that was less important than their own safety and well-being. At times, private armies took over large sections of the country. Their warlord leaders justified combat in nationalist terms, but seemed moved by the sheer love of battle.

Their message of ethnic hatred denied human dignity to other peoples, whose women became objects for sexual abuse and whose men became victims of brutalization. By 1994, 100,000 people had died as a result of the fighting throughout Yugoslavia. A million or more had become refugees, forced to flee their homes to escape the violence of war. The Balkan civil war, on the territory of the former Yugoslavia, embodied the ugliest, most inhuman features of the ethnic conflicts in other parts of the world.

Losing the war, the Bosnian government appealed in 1993 to the European Union and the United Nations for help. Both attempted to find a compromise solution to the conflict, but failed. The Serbian forces in Bosnia fought for victory. They continued their expulsion and execution of Bosnians, even

The Ruins of Civil War: St. Mary's Catholic Church, Sarajevo, December 1992 (*Novosti/Corbis-Bettmann*)

those living in U.N.-protected areas. The city of Sarajevo was under constant bombardment by Serbian guns. Only military intervention could halt the bloodshed. That action came in 1995 from the armed forces of the Western military alliance, NATO. Its leaders finally concluded that the war, which might spread to surrounding states, threatened the interests and well-being of all Europe. Led by the United States, the NATO air force began the bombing of Serbian positions in Bosnia. The NATO high command warned the Serbian Republic leaders that they risked seeing the war spread to their own territory unless the Bosnian Serbs

stopped fighting and agreed to a compromise peace treaty.

NATO's intervention ended hostilities in the region for a short time. The treaty signed that year included an agreement among all warring groups to reunite Bosnia. It left in place the armed militias of Serbs and Croatians, each stationed in the areas they had conquered. A united Bosnia remained a paper promise, and Milosovic remained leader of Serbia (which kept the formal name of Yugoslavia).

Four years later, his nationalist ambitions inspired him to begin yet another campaign of ethnic cleansing. This time the region to be purged of non-Serbs was the province of Kosovo. A majority of the population there spoke Albanian and practiced the Muslim religion. His forces destroyed villages and executed Kosovar men on suspicion of supporting anti-Serbian rebels, but the real objective was ethnic cleansing. Hundreds of thousands of Kosovar Muslims fled outside the borders of the state. Once again NATO finally intervened, bombing strategic sites in Serbia until Milosovic agreed to pull Serbian troops out of Kosovo in late 1999. After ten years, the Balkan civil wars ended. In that area, nationalism had become the tool of unscrupulous political leaders. For a time they had persuaded their peoples that their new nation-states required an ethnically "pure" land. It was a false message and a human tragedy.

Failed States and Local Wars in Africa

In Third World countries, the hostility dividing peoples of differing ethnic identity was worsened by conditions of misrule, poverty, and environmental decay. When resources were scarce and populations forced to move about, often to urban slums, in search of a livelihood, the occasions for violence multiplied. Social hardship led to rising crime rates. The failure of political leadership greatly increased the likelihood of failure of political compromise and respect for minority rights.

The manipulation of ethnic fears of their own people was one effective and vicious method of winning election or mobilizing backing. The conflict between majority Muslims and minority Christians in northern Nigeria began in early 2000 when ambitious provincial leaders there tried to strengthen their powers by imposing Islamic law on their entire provinces. The newly restored federal democratic leadership, in power in Nigeria after two decades of despotic military rule, hoped to establish its authority while still preserving the ethnic balance among its many peoples. Playing the "Muslim card" in the northern areas was the reply from local politicians opposed to the federal government. It was a formula for anarchy. When Christians protested by rioting and burning mosques, Muslims in turn attacked Christians in a spiraling process of violence leaving thousands of dead, refugees fleeing to the south, and embittered ethnic relations.

The worst ethnic violence of the 1990s occurred in central Africa. The small country known as Rwanda united all the forces capable of igniting ethnic conflict, including colonial favoritism for one people, economic hardship, and ethnic hatred. The Tutsi people had lost power at the time of the Belgian withdrawal in 1962. The majority Hutu peoples (90 percent of the inhabitants) forcibly ejected them from all positions of authority, from the central government to local administration. The economic rewards for political dominance was an important factor in this ethnic clash in Rwanda, as it was in other ethnically diverse Third World lands. Political power provided an important source of wealth in that mountainous land, which had one of the highest population densities (800 per square mile) in Africa. It was smaller than Switzerland, yet with a population substantially larger in size.

The new rulers found Western help. The Belgian and French governments supplied foreign aid to the Hutu leadership, just as they did to Mobutu's government in Zaire. Their goal was to protect their economic and political influence in a region where Franco-Belgian interests from the colonial period remained strong and which were rich in natural resources. Their concerns did not extend to ethnic relations and minority rights.

Hutu leaders retained the colonial system of identifying the population by ethnic group. In this way they could manipulate antagonism toward the Tutsi, whose living conditions were usually better than the Hutu. A secret extremist Hutu group devised plans to eliminate the Tutsi entirely. "Back to Ethiopia" was their slogan. Their propaganda portrayed the Tutsi as outsiders in their own country and placed Tutsi lives and property at risk. Ethnic cleansing was the extremists' goal. Periodic attacks on the Tutsi people occurred in the following decades. As a result, many Tutsi fled to neighboring states, some to organize for war against the Hutu.

The trigger for that war, and for the subsequent war in Zaire, came in 1994 when Hutu militia undertook the wholesale massacre of Tutsi. The suspicious death of the Hutu head of government in a plane crash gave the Hutu extremists the excuse to claim that the Tutsi were preparing to kill the Hutu. The accusation was absurd, intended only to mobilize the armed Hutu militia and the army. Extremist Hutu leaders had already laid plans for the mass execution of the Tutsi. They could rely on the loyalty of their followers and the deep distrust among the Hutu of their Tutsi neighbors.

They mobilized their militia forces and broadcast to their followers the message that "the Tutsi need to be killed." Their action was as close as any political fanatics had come to the policy of genocide since the Nazi Final Solution. When moderate Hutus attempted to halt the bloodshed and to protect Tutsi people, they also fell victims to the killing. A small United Nations peacekeeping force was powerless even to protect its own troops from the mobs, and fled the country. In the massacre that followed, one-half (500,000) of the Tutsi population in Rwanda were killed.

To stop the killings, Tutsi armed forces in exile in neighboring Uganda invaded Rwanda. They had the backing of the leader of Uganda. Ten years before, he brought his country out of civil war by what he called "no-party democracy" and effective protection of ethnic minorities. Repelled by the bloodshed and fearing that the violence would spread, he gave vital aid in arms and finances to the Tutsi army. His action raised the conflict in Rwanda to an African affair. The Tutsi invaders proved much better fighters than the Hutu, who fled the country. They were accompanied by an estimated 2 million Hutu refugees who feared death at the hands of their former prey. The massacres ended, and a new Tutsi government set out to restore order and to bring those they called the "agents of genocide" to justice.

That conflict exploded into an international crisis when Zaire became the center of the war. The bulk of the Hutu refugees had gathered in vast camps in Zaire bordering on Rwanda. Among them were most of the Hutu warlords and their militia. In the refugee camps, their survival was ensured by supplies provided for international aid organizations. They turned the camps into their base of guerrilla operations against the new Rwandan regime. The Zaire government had little control in that eastern region. It used what powers it did have to support the Hutu guerrillas in an effort to find allies and build its regional influence. It was a fatal move, for that action turned the conflict into a regional war.

By that time, Zaire had collapsed into disorder and decay. The former Belgian Congo, renamed Zaire in 1970, experienced three decades of such misrule by Mobutu that it had become one of the worst cases in the post-colonial regions of a failed state (see Chapter 9). Its internal disorder threatened to spread beyond its borders. Its abundant natural resources, including diamonds, attracted predatory militias and armies. For many reasons, an informal regional alliance of Mobutu's enemies came together in 1995. It included the Rwandan government, desperate to end the constant border war with Hutu guerrillas operating from sanctuaries in Zaire. It brought in political enemies of Mobutu, among whom the most capable was an opponent of thirty years named Laurent Kabila. It extended to the neighboring states of Angola, Zambia, and Uganda. Their leaders had an urgent need to bring some political stability to the region and they anticipated substantial benefits to their own economies when their armed forces occupied mineral-rich areas of Zaire.

Working together, these forces succeeded in a remarkably short time in organizing and supplying an army headed by Kabila and trained and led by Tutsi officers from Rwanda. In the summer of 1996, this army swept through Zaire to the capital. Mobutu's army collapsed and he fled the country. Kabila took control of the state, renaming it (as it had been at independence in 1960) the Democratic Republic of Congo. The government of the largest country in sub-Saharan Africa had changed hands in a war supported by what some observers called a "pan-African alliance."

The violence did not end. The Rwandan government promised protection for Hutu and Tutsi. But the hatred between the two groups flared up repeatedly in sporadic fighting. The United Nations war-crimes trials of Hutu assassins (similar to the trial it set up to try Serbian criminals in Bosnia) could not stop the pursuit of Hutu. The Democratic Republic of Congo remained a vast underpoliced land where Hutu militia could mount raids on Rwanda. Tutsi forces continued their hunt for Hutus responsible for the 1994 massacre, arresting some but killing many more. Troops of Uganda, Angola, Zambia moved into border areas, and soon

were fighting not only Congolese troops but also each other. The government of Zimbabwe sent 12,000 troops to prop up Kabila's fragile state. Civil and foreign war in central Africa continued for years.

The fighting degenerated into a struggle for the spoils of war. The diamond-rich regions of Zaire lured armed groups and foreign armed forces, all seeking to control the diamond trade. Civil wars among ethnic groups had in other African countries led to pillaging by self-styled armies whose warriors knew no other way of life. Precious raw materials were a prime target of these armed groups. The rich diamond mines of Angola sustained a rebel army that had been fighting to seize the central government ever since independence in 1976. Its military backing from foreign sources had dried up at the end of the Cold War, when Soviet and U.S. agents ceased competing for influence there. Control of the diamond trade kept the rebel army fighting through most of the 1990s, as long as it could find buyers for this war booty. One observer concluded that in those areas "diamonds are warfare's best friend."

A very fragile peace emerged by the end of the decade in central Africa. There, the colonial borders remained as the vestiges of imperial rule. New political leadership continued to talk of civic nationalism and the need for an end to ethnic and tribal hostility. The leaders of the new Rwandan government, like those in neighboring Tanzania and Uganda, recognized that human rights were a desirable goal. They insisted, though, that their regimes not be measured by Western political ideals. As one said, "the African and the Western worlds are many worlds apart." The term Third World continued to identify profound political differences among regions of the world in the new era of nations.

♨ SPOTLIGHT: Flora Mukampore ♨

Flora Mukampore would never have met international news correspondents or appeared on Western television had she not survived one of the worst ethnic massacres in the twentieth century. Her personal story is largely unknown. Her life was so ordinary until 1994 that we can infer what her life was like by the experiences of those around her, as well as by her own story.

She carried with her, as required by her government, an identity card that identified her as a Tutsi. The highland country of Rwanda was her native land. She lived in one of the villages in the lush countryside where most of Rwandans spent their lives. The land was fertile and the climate mild. Farming provided a meager livelihood for the families in her village, as elsewhere. Her Tutsi ancestors had ruled over and enjoyed greater well-being than the Hutu. When she was growing up, her family was better off than her Hutu neighbors, but not by much since the differences consisted of just a little more land and a few more cattle. They lived as neighbors, and she knew Tutsi men and women who had married Hutu. For the most part, Hutu and Tutsi families got along and minded their own business.

Relations with her Hutu neighbors and with the authorities did not change much after the Belgians left. Politics did not interest the villagers. They had heard of the attacks on Tutsi that had occurred at the time when Belgian troops and administrators left. They knew that Hutu leaders had taken control of their country. They heard too that some Tutsi had fled over the border to Uganda and had formed their own guerrilla force to take back power. But they were not involved. Their village leader, who used still the Belgian title of bourgmestre, was a Hutu. Flora and the other Tutsi villagers thought that they could count on him to run affairs fairly. On Sundays, they all went up the hill to the big Catholic church for services, and all their children were baptized by the priest.

Then they heard the news, in April 1994, that the Hutu president's plane had been shot down and he had died. They were aware that some of the young Hutu village men had in the months before joined militia forces, armed with spears and big knives called machetes, and had been training like other Hutu groups elsewhere. Rumors began to reach them that in other parts of the country these gangs had started killing Tutsi. Her husband joined a delegation to the village bourgmestre to ask for his protection. He refused, telling them that they should go to the church for shelter.

They all went there. They had no choice, since even Hutu friends who wanted to protect them said that just helping Tutsi was enough to get themselves and their families killed. She remembered later that in the end there must have been 3,000 Tutsi from the area all gathered together around the church in the hope of sanctuary. Still, some of the men came armed with bows and arrows and spears just in case. But it was no use.

When the Hutu militia attacked the church, the village bourgmestre was at their head. After the militia's first assault failed, he ordered government soldiers and police to use their guns and grenades against the

Genocide in Rwanda: Bodies of Massacred Tutsi inside Nyamata Catholic Church, 1994 (*Reuters/Corinne Dufka/Archive Photos*)

crowd of Tutsi. The Tutsi panicked and started to run, but the militia came after them with their machetes. The machetes were the preferred weapon for killing. All around her, people were hacked to pieces, falling in piles of dead and wounded. A Hutu militiaman, who she recognized to be a neighbor, came at her a machete and struck her over the head. She fell among the bodies. The militia continued to hunt down all the remaining Tutsi, and then returned to kill those who had fallen but were not yet dead.

She was lucky. Despite her head wound, she was able to lie absolutely still while the massacre went on all around her. In the next several days, she never left the church land. It was filled with bodies. Among all the dead, she found alive only five children, all badly wounded, and took care of them. She had no idea what had happened to her own family. Militia were still roaming the area looking for survivors. So she stayed there with the children among the thousands of decaying bodies until, a week later, soldiers from the Tutsi rebel army reached the church and took them to a hospital.

When she talked with the BBC correspondents several days later, what troubled her most of all was the betrayal by the village bourgmestre. Instead of trying to keep the peace, he turned out to be one of the Hutu extremists who wanted her and all the other Tutsi of his village dead. She simply could not understand why. A Belgian Catholic missionary, wounded in a vain effort to give shelter to a group of Tutsi children, explained to the correspondents "we were overwhelmed by this great evil. There is a madness at work." Faced with such inhumanity, he could find no other answer.

Internationalism and the United Nations

The brutality of these post–Cold War conflicts aroused calls for international peacekeeping efforts from humanitarian organizations, from governments, and from the United Nations. President Woodrow Wilson's vision of a new world order grounded in democratic government, national self-determination, and collective defense against aggression reemerged in the 1990s (see Highlight, pp. 156–158). The successful defeat of Iraq by a United Nations coalition of states demonstrated that the U.N. was freed at last from the constraints on its action produced by the Cold War stalemate. Peacekeeping missions had been a part of its operations since its founding, though at no point had its members agreed to allow it command of its own armed forces.

Support for U.N. intervention in local wars came from the European Union in the 1980s and 1990s. Once the Soviet threat had disappeared, its member governments, especially Germany and France, turned to the defense of human rights within Europe, and beyond. They made internationalism an important objective in the E.U.'s foreign relations. They were prepared to use armed forces to halt abuse by Serbs of human rights

in Bosnia, supporting first the use of U.N. peacekeeping forces there, and then the dispatch of NATO forces to the Balkans in 1995.

Private groups in the West were instrumental in promoting, and acting upon this liberal ideology on a global scale. Nongovernmental organizations (NGO) had existed since the nineteenth century. The Red Cross was the first NGO, making medical aid to war-torn lands its primary goal. To avoid taking sides, it had excluded all political judgments from its wartime operations. In the 1970s, this international humanitarianism became the inspiration for an increasing number of organizations. New groups such as the French "Doctors without Borders" and the British "Oxfam" sent their members into areas of violence to bring help to innocent civilians. They did not hesitate to take sides when they judged governments or armed groups responsible for crimes against humanity.

Their political involvement, based on humanitarian principles, was the grounds on which they could appeal for outside intervention. Bernard Kouchner, one of the founders of Doctors without Borders, had worked with the Red Cross in Biafra during the Nigeria civil war (see Chapter 9). His outrage at the crimes committed by Nigerian armed forces induced him to found the new organization in 1971. He openly broke with the apolitical position of the Red Cross. The charter of Doctors without Borders required that they "bear witness" publicly to atrocities and "care for" the sick and the wounded. Their efforts, and those of non-governmental organizations like theirs, were of enormous assistance to the civilian populations caught in the midst of the violence. In 1990, the U.N. Assembly formally recognized the desirability of their international humanitarian action.

The local wars of the 1990s drew the aid of the NGOs to the most distant parts of the globe. It also placed them in the middle of complex conflicts where their very presence became a political issue. Kouchner believed deeply in what he called a "right of intervention" by foreign powers, including the United Nations, in wars that inflicted brutal punishment on innocent civilian populations. In 1994, the Doctors without Borders went to Central Africa to assist the millions of Hutu refugees from Rwanda. They soon discovered that Hutu militia controlled the refugee camps of Zaire, seizing medical and food assistance and monopolizing aid services. The new Rwanda government protested that the NGO aid groups supplying the camps were supporting assassins of their people, not serving a humanitarian aim. In disgust at the Hutu warlords' use of their assistance, the Doctors without Borders stopped their lifesaving work there. They were trapped between their hopes of peace and the ugly reality of ruthless power-hungry warlords bent on violence.

The United Nations appeared the ideal choice to all those who believed a "new world order" should rely on the international community, not power politics, to resolve the local wars of the late century. Its charter called for peacekeeping action to produce fair settlements in the best interests of the war-torn countries. This peacekeeping mission fell under the direct responsibility of the Secretary General. The Security Council approved recommendations for intervention and voted the funds to pay for civilian personnel and, if necessary, troops to take charge of the operation. At times, the Security Council authorized member countries to dispatch their own troops to intervene against aggressive states in defense of the victim. The Korean War of 1950–1953, and the Gulf War of 1990–1991, were fought successfully in this manner. But for local wars, armed forces usually operated directly under the peacekeeping branch of the U.N. Secretariat. The Secretary General provide overall supervision the conduct of the operations.

The United Nations' troops wore a special military helmet with its distinctive emblem of a white dove over a blue background. The units themselves came from those member countries whose governments were willing to participate. They made up an unusual military force. They usually were composed of contingents, including commanding officers, from various U.N. nations. Their charge in conducting their operations was, until the early 1990s, to use their arms solely for self-defense. How was this militarily amateurish and toothless armed force to prevent the militias of warlords or regular armies from wrecking havoc and death if they were determined to kill anyone who got in their way? The U.N. was a military force of symbolic, not real, might.

For the first forty years of its existence, the U.N.'s peacekeeping role was exclusively to help enforce peace agreements that the combatants had already put into effect. When the Suez War of 1956 ended in the withdrawal of Israeli troops back within their borders, the U.N. sent peacekeepers to patrol that border. They were there to reassure the Israeli government that Egypt would no longer send Muslim terrorists into their land, and to help the Egyptian government respect a peace agreement very unpopular with the Muslim Brotherhood. These operations were useful, though they did not occur very frequently. Between 1945 and 1990, the United Nations sent troops to only thirteen peacekeeping operations. Operating at the invitation (more or less voluntary) of combatants and in conditions of relative order, the U.N.'s military interventions proved useful and (almost) bloodless.

Its activities accelerated dramatically in the 1990s. Suddenly local wars flared up throughout the world. The Security Council moved to prevent mass killing and atrocities in the spirit of the humanitarian defense of human rights. In 1991, it unanimously approved a policy of U.N. military intervention for the sake of "human security" when threatened by civil and ethnic conflict. In the next years, the United Nations found itself engaged in twenty wars requiring the participation of 70,000 U.N. troops. These actions involved peacemaking, not just peacekeeping, when the warring parties continued fighting and killing. The U.N. flag flew over military camps in very dangerous parts of the world.

That danger first became terribly apparent in the African country of Somalia. The nomadic peoples there had proven unable to create a stable government after receiving their independence in 1960. It became a failed state, like other Third World lands where poverty and clan loyalties fatally weakened vital functions of public life. Its precarious economic conditions worsened seriously

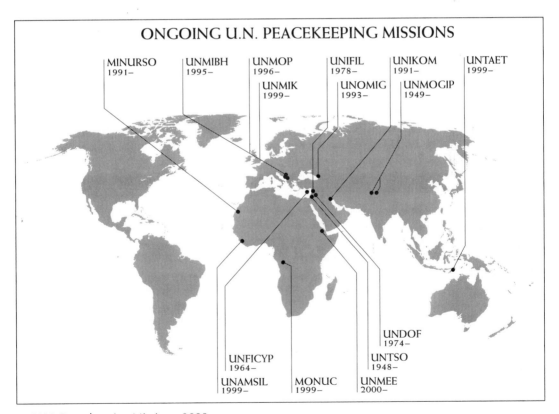

ONGOING U.N. PEACEKEEPING MISSIONS

U.N. Peacekeeping Missions, 2000

when serious drought hit the country in the 1980s. Nongovernmental organizations attempted to help the starving peoples. They denounced the brutality of warlord-led militia who stole their supplies and fought each other in an on-going civil war.

In 1991, the United Nations responded to the international outcry by approving military intervention to protect the aid activities. In 1992, it even agreed to the proposal of President George Bush to send U.S. forces, operating on their own, into Somalia. The Muslim warlords united against the "infidel" Americans, killing eighteen U.S. soldiers in a highly publicized military operation in Somalia's capital. The American military and the U.S. Congress raised serious questions why American military should die for a cause of no national interest to their country. Shortly after, the U.S. government ended its "armed humanitarianism," and the United Nations stopped as well its efforts at peacemaking in Somalia. The warlords had won; the United Nations (and the people of Somalia) had lost.

International peacemaking failed repeatedly to end ethnic atrocities inflicted on minority peoples in the next years. U.N. troops went to war-torn areas of the former Yugoslavia in 1993 to stop the brutal ethnic cleansing, directed primarily at the Muslim population in Bosnia and the Serbian people in Croatia. And in that same year, the Security Council authorized U.N. peacekeepers to go to Rwanda to help enforce a cease fire between the Hutu government and Tutsi rebel forces. In both cases, the Secretary General had at his disposal very few troops, armed only with light weapons, to contain heavily armed forces engaged in civil wars against hated minority peoples. The U.S. government under President Clinton refused to participate in the Bosnian and Rwandan operations, fearing public hostility to military intervention that might well end

in more bloodshed among U.S. troops. It claimed that the "disorders" there were an internal affair to be resolved by the states themselves. Without U.S. backing, the Security Council and the U.N. Secretariat preferred not to risk major military intervention in these lands.

The result was that the U.N. troops were helpless witnesses to the massacre of Bosnian Muslims and to the Rwandan genocide of 1994. Only the NATO intervention in 1995 stopped the Bosnian civil war. In Rwanda, the Tutsi guerrilla forces defeated the Hutu army only after the genocide had ended. "Bloodless" peacemaking in these areas was an absurdity, and the U.N. peacekeepers lacked the military might and the authorization from the Security Council to engage in real warfare. The 1949 U.N. Agreement on War Crimes had obligated the United Nations to take all steps necessary to prevent genocide, but the United Nations failed the test in Rwanda in 1994.

This tragic failure strengthened the resolve of the new Secretary General, Kofi Annan, to ensure that the United Nations acted promptly and decisively in areas where violence erupted. He became the U.N.'s highest officer in 1996. His election marked the first time a diplomat from sub-Saharan Africa had served as General Secretary. He made the troubles of Africa his prime concern. He explained that the U.N.'s task had to include intervening even in conflicts (including civil wars) where "the main aim is the destruction not of armies but of civilians and entire ethnic groups." It was a goal that went beyond the aims of Woodrow Wilson and other founders of the first collective peacekeeping organization, the League of Nations. But times had changed. Nation-states had replaced empires and had found their collective voice within the new United Nations. Annan believed deeply that it, better than any outside power, was suited to the task.

At least once in the last years of the century, his resolve led to successful military intervention. The people of the eastern half of the island of Timor had received their freedom from the Portugese Empire in 1975, only to be conquered the next year by the Indonesian army. For the next two decades Timorese nationalists fought an obscure, sporadic war for liberation from Indonesia. In the late 1990s, the new Indonesian civilian government decided to allow the East Timorese to vote on independence, but Indonesian militia continued the fight there, killing Timorese civilians to force their nationalist leaders to abandon the struggle. It was another local war coupled with ethnic massacres. The United Nations acted to end the fighting after the Indonesian government reluctantly accepted the presence of United Nations forces there. Australian troops were the first to intervene, capturing and disarming the Indonesian militia. After their combat ended, other U.N. civilian and military personnel supervised the elections. The Timorese people voted for independence. Nationalists began, with U.N. and NGO assistance, the slow, tortuous work of rebuilding their devastated land and constructing the new nation-state of East Timor.

The United Nations proved very capable in helping peoples recover from war, rebuild their lives, and put in place new political leadership. This task did not demand military intervention, and offered peoples an escape from seemingly endless conflict. In the 1990s, the United Nations sent negotiators to over one hundred areas of conflict to resolve the wars by peaceful negotiation. Often its help proved indispensable. In Cambodia, it helped negotiate the end to the country's twenty-year civil war. Permanent settlement required elections for national leaders. The U.N. officials set high standards for democracy. They insisted on conformity with the procedures for free elections and respect for

human rights on the part of the Cambodians. In their view, peace in that war-torn land depended upon the creation of a coalition government and economic recovery. It was a slow, painful process. Finally in 1998, the last of the Khmer Rouge guerrillas laid down their arms, in exchange for immunity from persecution for war crimes. That year democratic elections produced a stable coalition government. The war in Indochina, begun in 1946, had at last come to an end. The U.N. officials could take pride in their work there.

After the defeat of Iraq in the Gulf War, the U.S. president, George Bush, had proudly announced the emergence of a new "world order" replacing the Cold War. But the 1990s proved a time of instability and war, and the United Nations was incapable of controlling large-scale violence. Leaders of the new nation-states had the power to decide war and peace, after the fall of the last empires. Their readiness to promote civic nationalism could restrain ethnic hatreds and foreign war. But nationalism was still a potential force for war, as Saddam Hussein had proven. Ethnic rivalries became particularly violent in conditions of poverty and overpopulation in Third World lands. The emergence of regional alliances and the intervention by powerful states in the affairs of smaller countries continued the old policy of spheres of influence practiced by European powers in the nineteenth century. Even the United States, whose empire had never rivaled that of other Western powers, continued to treat lands once subject to "gunboat diplomacy" such as Haiti and Panama to a similar kind of protective oversight. It was an imperfect and inherently aggressive method of settling conflicts. At the end of the century internationalism enjoyed greater worldwide support as the way to bring peace to humanity than it ever had received since Wilson's appeal for an end to power politics and for a "world made safe for democracy."

SUMMARY

The closing years of the twentieth century bore little resemblance to earlier decades. Communism had disappeared from Europe, and remade itself in China into a free-market political dictatorship. Empires had vanished, and so too had the Cold War. The newly elected leaders of the former communist states began to restore free market economies and liberal democracy. It proved to be an extraordinarily difficult transition. In Russia it entailed a return to a culture and economic system that had disappeared three generations before. A market economy, Russian national leadership, and liberal democratic institutions had barely come into existence at the beginning of the century before being destroyed after the 1917 revolution. Western societies had moved in the half-century since the Second World War into a new industrial revolution and new global economy. Their living conditions were far different from those relics of outdated industrial life left behind by the communists.

The collapse of the communist order left people in these countries bitterly resentful at the turmoil. Some looked back wistfully at the "good times" of Stalinism. The North Atlantic Treaty Organization lost its principal enemy, and instead turned its efforts to keeping peace in areas of ethnic conflict such as the Balkans. Peoples in central European states continued to fear Russian might, and looked to NATO in search of military protection. Global war no longer threatened humanity, but memories of old wars did not disappear.

The 1990s were also a time of ethnic conflicts so severe that they threatened the very survival of new nation-states. The responsibility for these tragic events lay in large measure on ambitious leaders determined to seize and hold power regardless of the human consequence. Fearful people, often suffering hardship with little hope for the future, turned in desperation to political movements that offered easy solutions to complex social and economic problems. Extremist nationalist leaders appeared most often at the end of the century to hold that key. Their appeals to nationalist passions fanned the flames of ethnic hatred and at times heightened the risk of war with neighboring states. The work of the United Nations offered some hope that these conflicts could be contained, yet the poisonous effects of hatred and intolerance among peoples did not disappear.

In the last decade of the century, the living standards for large parts of the world's population rose to higher levels than ever before. New technology and the foresight and ingenuity of peoples promised substantial benefits to humanity. Bleak aspects of global trends continued to cast dark shadows on the hopes for the years ahead. Environmental degradation had extended to many areas of the globe. Overpopulation and poverty brought crowding in "mega-cities" that became places of refuge for many millions. Bloody conflicts obliterated in some lands the hopes of prosperity that economic development had promised.

Nationalist violence remained as much a part of the history of humanity at the end of the century as at the beginning. In 1914, a Serbian terrorist in the quiet, remote city of Sarajevo had set in motion the events that produced the first great war of the century. In the decades of wars and revolutions that followed, empires fell and new nations emerged throughout the world. But eighty years later, the ruins of that same city, destroyed by a bitter civil war, revealed the terrible power of ethnic hatred to unleash death and destruction over an entire country.

DATES WORTH REMEMBERING

1964   Integrated-circuit computers
1965   First communications satellite
1971   United States abandons gold standard
1973   Oil crisis and global recession
1978   Beginning of market reforms in China
1986   Chernobyl nuclear accident in Soviet Union
1980–1997   Asian economic boom
1991–1995   Civil war in Yugoslavia
1991   United Nations war against Iraq
1992   Global Conference on the Environment
1994   North American Free Trade Agreement
1994   Massacre of Tutsi people in Rwanda
1995   Brazil-Argentina-Chile Free Trade Agreement
1995   Mexican financial crisis
1995   Peace treaty ending war in Bosnia
1996–1997   War in Zaire (Republic of Congo)
1998   World population approximately 6 billion
1997   Asian financial crisis
1998   Russian financial crisis
1998   Taliban rebels conquer Afghanistan
2000   Global warming confirmed by U.N. Conference on Climate Change

RECOMMENDED READING

Global Economy, Global Environment

John McNeill, *Something New under the Sun: An Environmental History of the Twentieth-Century World* (2000). A carefully balanced study of what humanity did to its environment in the twentieth century.

Anthony Sampson, *The People and Politics of the World Banking Crisis* (1983). The best account of the fragile global financial network in the recession of the late 1970s to early 1980s.

Peacekeeping, Local War, and Ethnic Conflict

Christopher Bennett, *Yugoslavia's Bloody Collapse: Causes, Courses, Consequences* (1995). A brief account of the complex political and ethnic origins of Yugoslavia's civil war and the agony of ethnic cleansing.

William Shawcross, *Deliver Us from Evil: Peacekeepers, Warlords and a World of Endless Conflict* (2000). Despite the title, an optimistic view of the achievements of the United Nations in the 1990s in dealing with the mass mayhem of civil wars and local conflict.

Travelers' Tales and Visual Aids

*Michael Ignatieff, *Blood and Belonging: Journeys into the New Nationalism* (1993). Firsthand account, by a thoughtful observer of nationalist passions, of the human side to nationalism of the 1990s in Europe and the Middle East; also, *The Warrior's Honor: Ethnic War and the Modern Conscience* (1997). A perceptive inquiry into the forces that have created ethnic violence in places such as Yugoslavia and Rwanda.

*Fergal Keane, *Season of Blood: A Rwandan Journey* (1995). A BBC correspondent's vivid story of the 1994 Tutsi massacre, viewed at the very moment of the tragedy.

*Robert Kaplan, *The Ends of the Earth: A Journey to the Frontiers of Anarchy* (1996). An account of the writer's travels into some of the Third World lands where poverty is great and violence is a part of everyday life.

The Economist (British weekly news magazine). The editors and correspondents of this magazine bring to their accounts of weekly events around the world a sense of historical importance that makes it excellent reading for history-in-the-making; also very useful is the journal's web page (*www.economist.com*), which offers a complete, indexed library of articles from back issues.

www.un.org. A Web site, compiled by the United Nations, containing a rich array of information on its current and past activities.

INDEX